Rethinking the Age of Reform

This book takes a fresh look at the 'age of reform' from 1780, when reform became a common object of aspiration, to the 1830s – the era of the 'Reform Ministry' and of the Great Reform Act of 1832 – and beyond, when such aspirations were realized more frequently. It pays close attention to what contemporaries termed 'reform', identifying two strands, institutional and moral, which interacted in complex ways.

Particular reforming initiatives singled out for attention include those targeting parliament, government, the law, the church, medicine, slavery, regimens of self-care, opera, theatre and art institutions, while later chapters situate British reform in its imperial and European contexts. An extended introduction provides a point of entry to the history and historiography of the period. The book therefore makes available to both students and established scholars the fruits of research in various sub-disciplines and, by the manner in which it brings them together, aims to stimulate fresh thinking about this formative period of British history.

ARTHUR BURNS is Senior Lecturer in History, King's College London.

JOANNA INNES is Fellow and Tutor in Modern History, Somerville College, Oxford, and Lecturer in Modern History, University of Oxford.

Past and Present Publications

General Editors: LYNDAL ROPER, *Balliol College, Oxford*
CHRIS WICKHAM, *University of Birmingham*

Past and Present Publications comprise books similar in character to the articles in the journal *Past and Present*. Whether the volumes in the series are collections of essays – some previously published, others new studies – or monographs, they encompass a wide variety of scholarly and original works primarily concerned with social, economic and cultural changes, and their causes and consequences. They will appeal to both specialists and non-specialists and will endeavour to communicate the results of historical and allied research in the most readable and lively form.

For a list of the titles in Past and Present Publications, see end of book.

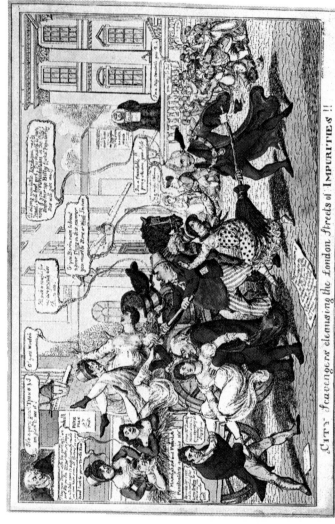

'City scavengers cleansing the London streets of impurities': Radical Londoners Matthew Wood and Robert Waithman display another face of reform when they promote a campaign against prostitutes, 1816. Reproduced by permission of the Guildhall Library, London.

Rethinking the Age of Reform

Britain 1780–1850

edited by

ARTHUR BURNS
and
JOANNA INNES

CAMBRIDGE
UNIVERSITY PRESS

CAMBRIDGE UNIVERSITY PRESS
Cambridge, New York, Melbourne, Madrid, Cape Town, Singapore, São Paulo

Cambridge University Press
The Edinburgh Building, Cambridge CB2 8RU, UK

Published in the United States of America by Cambridge University Press, New York

www.cambridge.org
Information on this title: www.cambridge.org/9780521823944

First published 2003
Reprinted 2004
This digitally printed version 2007

A catalogue record for this publication is available from the British Library

Library of Congress Cataloguing in Publication data

Rethinking the Age of Reform: Britain 1780–1850 / edited by
Arthur Burns and Joanna Innes.
   p.   cm. – (Past and Present Publications)
Includes bibliographical references and index.
ISBN 0 521 82394 3
1. Great Britain – Politics and government – 19th century.   2. Great Britain – Politics
and government – 1760–1820.   3. Great Britain Parliament – reform.   I. Burns,
Arthur (R. Arthur).   II. Innes, Joanna.   III. Series.

DA530.R45   2003
303.48′4′094109034 – dc21   2003043931

ISBN 978-0-521-82394-4 hardback
ISBN 978-0-521-03949-9 paperback

Contents

Notes on contributors

Ian A. Burney is Wellcome Research Lecturer at the University of Manchester's Centre for the History of Science, Technology, and Medicine. He is the author of *Bodies of Evidence: Medicine and the Politics of the English Inquest, 1830–1926* (2000), and is currently working on a study of criminal poisoning trials in nineteenth-century England.

Arthur Burns is Senior Lecturer in Modern British History at King's College London. He is the author of *The Diocesan Revival in the Church of England, c. 1800–1870* (1999), and has published articles and editions of texts on church reform and party in the nineteenth century. His edition of Richard Church's *The Oxford Movement: Twelve Years, 1833–1845* will shortly be published as an ebook. He is currently one of three directors of the *Clergy of the Church of England Database, 1540–1835* project.

Kathryn Gleadle is Tutorial Fellow in History at University College, Oxford. She has published widely on middle-class women and politics and is currently working on a monograph on British women and political culture, 1780–1860. Her publications include *The Early Feminists* (1995), *British Women in the Nineteenth Century* (2001), *Radical Writing on Women* (2002), and (edited with Sarah Richardson) *Women in British Politics, 1760–1860: The Power of the Petticoat* (2000).

Jennifer Hall-Witt is an independent scholar living in Hadley, Mass. She earned her Ph.D. at Yale and has taught at Smith College, Denison University, and the University of Tennessee at Chattanooga. She is currently completing a monograph on opera and elite culture in London, 1780–1880.

Philip Harling is Professor of History at the University of Kentucky. His books include *The Modern British State: An Historical Introduction* (2001) and *The Waning of 'Old Corruption': The Politics of Economical Reform in Britain, 1779–1846* (1996).

Holger Hoock is a British Academy Postdoctoral Fellow in the Faculty of History and at Selwyn College, Cambridge. His forthcoming publications include *The King's Artists: The Royal Academy of Arts and the Politics of British Culture, 1760–1840* (2003), and essays on artists' dinner culture and on the British pantheon in St Paul's Cathedral.

Joanna Innes is Fellow and Tutor in Modern History at Somerville College, Oxford, and a member of the *Past and Present* editorial board. Her interest in 'reform' dates back to her initial research on John Wilkes and the Wilkites. She has published extensively on the making of social policy in eighteenth- and early nineteenth-century Britain, and in that connection has sought to show that there was much reforming activity, as we might term it, before the 'age of reform'.

Michael Lobban is Reader in Law at Queen Mary, University of London. He is the author of *The Common Law and English Jurisprudence, 1760–1850* (1991), and articles on law reform in the early to mid-nineteenth century.

Katherine Newey is Senior Lecturer in Theatre Studies at Lancaster University. She has published widely in journals and essay collections on nineteenth-century popular theatre and women's writing.

Jennifer Ridden lectures in modern British and Irish history at the Australian National University. Her book, *'Making Good Citizens': National Identity, Empire and the Irish Elite* (forthcoming 2005), considers the roles played by the Irish elite in the development of distinctively 'British' institutions, ideologies, and identities, both within the United Kingdom and in the British Empire, and discusses ways in which British, Irish, and imperial historiographies interact.

Jonathan Sperber is Professor of Modern European History at the University of Missouri, Columbia. His publications on political, social, and religious conflicts, especially in nineteenth-century Germany, include *Popular Catholicism in Nineteenth Century Germany* (1984); *Rhineland Radicals: The Democratic Movement and the Revolution of 1848–1849* (1991); and *The Kaiser's Voters: Electors and Elections in Imperial Germany* (1997). He is currently working on a study of family, property, and the state in south-western Germany between 1820 and 1914.

Miles Taylor is Professor of Modern British History at the University of Southampton. He is the author of *Ernest Jones, Chartism and the Romance of Politics, 1819–69* (2003), and co-editor (with Michael Wolff) of *The Victorians since 1901: Histories, Representations and Revisions* (2003). He is currently completing a history of parliamentary representation and reform in Britain, 1828–1928.

David Turley is Professor of Cultural and Social History at the University of Kent, and Head of the School of History. His publications on both British and American history include *The Culture of British Antislavery, 1780–1860.*

Preface

This book began life as a *Past and Present* conference of the same title, held at St Anne's College, Oxford, in July 2000. We are grateful to the editorial board of *Past and Present* for their generous subsidy, and to Charles Philpin for his practical assistance. The conference was a memorably lively collaborative experience, and we would like to thank all the participants very warmly. We selected from the papers given those that we thought would make a coherent volume; we also owe much to those speakers whose papers are not included here: John Belchem, David Eastwood, James Epstein, Peter King, Tim Larsen, Rohan McWilliam, and Gareth Stedman Jones. Unfortunately, the death of Robbie Gray deprived us of the chance to include a reworked version of his paper. We owe a particular debt to Paul Langford and Peter Mandler, who helped to launch an extremely wide-ranging and stimulating final discussion.

Arthur Burns acknowledges with gratitude the 'long eighteenth-century' seminars at the Institute of Historical Research, which have provided him with regular opportunities to consider the interrelations between reform projects in the late eighteenth and early nineteenth centuries. For him the 2000 conference realized a long-standing ambition to explore connections and discontinuities between his own work on church reform and that of scholars working on other contemporary reform projects. Friends and colleagues have sustained this ambition through encouragement and stimulating discussion: he would like to thank David Eastwood, Boyd Hilton, Peter Mandler, the late Colin Matthew, Jon Parry, Mark Smith, Miles Taylor, Stephen Taylor, Dror Wahrman, and above all his co-editor. It was a happy circumstance that 'Rethinking the Age of Reform' was convened under the auspices of *Past and Present*, for it was while working on the articles published in that journal as sub-editor at the end of the 1980s that he came to see the potential value of a conference.

Joanna Innes was fortunate to be able to work on this volume during a sabbatical year, 2001–2. She worked on her own chapter and the introduction in the Humanities Research Centre, Australian National University, Canberra, and expresses her gratitude to the staff and her fellow visitors at that institution for their support and interest, and in particular to Paul Pickering for his comments on successive drafts of the introduction. She would also like to acknowledge an important intellectual debt to those of her graduate students who have worked on aspects of the 'age of reform': Chris Brown, Sue Brown, Josh Civin, Holger Hoock (who has an essay in this volume), Austin Gee, Marius Kwint, and Chikashi Sakashita. She believes that when more of their work is in print, the flow of influence, from supervisees to supervisor, may become more evident.

R. A. B.
J. M. I.

Abbreviations

Those abbreviations recurring most commonly throughout the essays which follow are listed below.

Brit. Lib.	British Library, London
Econ. Hist. Rev.	*Economic History Review*
Eng. Hist. Rev.	*English Historical Review*
Hist. Jl	*Historical Journal*
Jl Brit. Studies	*Journal of British Studies*
Jl Eccl. Hist.	*Journal of Ecclesiastical History*
Parl. Debs.	*Parliamentary Debates*
Parl. Hist.	*Parliamentary History*
P.P.	Parliamentary Papers (references give year, volume number, command number, and pagination in bound volume)
PRO	Public Record Office, Kew
Trans. Royal Hist. Soc.	*Transactions of the Royal Historical Society*

1. *Introduction*

JOANNA INNES AND ARTHUR BURNS

Historians have variously employed the notion of an 'age of reform': sometimes including within its scope the build-up of pressure for 'reform' from the late eighteenth or early nineteenth century, sometimes limiting their attention to the years following the 'Great Reform Act' of 1832.[1] A timescale weighted towards the later period is appropriate if the chief object is to assess reforming *achievement*: the effects of the restructuring of the representative system, or the fates of the diverse legislative projects laid before the 'reformed parliament' in its three and a half decades of life.

In this volume our primary concern lies elsewhere: with reform as *aspiration*. We survey the kinds of reform aspiration formulated from the 1780s – the decade when 'reform' first became a key political slogan – down to the 1830s and 1840s, when the enactment of parliamentary and other reforms began to bring about major changes in the political and cultural landscape. 'Reform' remained a key concept in political life for several decades thereafter, but its meaning and significance shifted. These later changes also warrant attention, but that attention is not provided here.[2]

A distinguishing feature of this volume is that we pay closer heed than historians of this period have usually done to contemporary uses of the terminology of 'reform'.[3] We do not suggest that it is possible to unravel reform projects in all their diversity – to understand all that contemporaries hoped and feared,

---

[1] Cf. Michael J. Turner, *British Politics in an Age of Reform* [1760–1832] (Manchester, 1999); A. S. Turberville, *The House of Lords in the Age of Reform, 1784–1837; with an Epilogue on Aristocracy and the Advent of Democracy, 1837–67* (London, 1958); E. W. Woodward, *The Age of Reform, 1815–70*, 2nd edn (Oxford, 1962); Peter Mandler, *Aristocratic Government in the Age of Reform: Whigs and Liberals, 1830–1852* (Oxford, 1990). For the 'Great Reform Act', Michael Brock, *The Great Reform Act* (Aldershot, 1973), though dated, remains the most comprehensive account.

[2] See section VII below for a brief discussion of continuity and change in thinking about reform in the mid-century decades, and references to the historiography of that period.

[3] Though for mid-nineteenth-century decades, see now Derek Beales, 'The Idea of Reform in British Politics, 1829–50', in T. C. W. Blanning and Peter Wende (eds.), *Reform in Great Britain and Germany, 1750–1850* (Oxford, 1999).

and how they argued and manoeuvred – simply by focusing on the uses made of one key term. We do, however, suggest that since 'reform' *was* a key term, and moreover a mutable, contested term, both embodying aspirations and conjuring up fears, there is something to be gained from observing closely what contemporaries did with the word and what it meant to them.

As Joanna Innes shows in her essay, when an extra-parliamentary movement first adopted as its goal the redress of abuses within parliament as a means to 'public reformation', the word already had a long and complex history behind it. Two enduringly common uses were, however, to denote the recasting of abuse-ridden laws and institutions and the correction of moral failings. Those two visions of reform shared some common ground: institutions were thought to become corrupt in part because of the moral failings of those within them; faulty institutions were thought to be important sources of corruption in society. Yet they were also distinguishable: some reform strategies targeted more the one, some more the other.

During the next few decades, the context for reforming effort changed radically, as first the French Revolution helped to bring institutional reform projects into disrepute, then – as the nature of the French regime changed, and ultimately the Allies achieved military mastery – the political climate lightened and reformers' prospects improved. Reforming effort diversified. Evangelicals and other 'practical' reforming activists pushed a broad agenda of 'reforms'; the success of the campaign to abolish the slave-trade, in 1807, showed that it was possible to secure some such reforms even from an 'unreformed' parliament. In the late 1810s, the rise of mass popular support for parliamentary reform, against a background of heated debate about the extent to which parliament should or should not regulate employment and commerce, supplied a new context for older hopes and fears. In the 1820s, the rise of rationalist and proto-socialist movements and of new cultures of the self (notably in the form of the temperance movement) further complicated the scene by giving new life and a variety of new twists to the project of moral reform. Yet it continued to be the case that much of what reform meant to contemporaries was informed by, on the one hand, institutional and, on the other hand, moral understandings of what 'reform' entailed.

Thus conceived, the reform agenda was not all-encompassing: not all schemes of improvement were 'reform' projects. But, conversely, that agenda did encompass many issues which – though they may have their own specialist literatures – have not featured much (if at all) in general accounts. Parliamentary reform was, undoubtedly, *the* reform par excellence: that was what people meant when they talked about 'reform' *tout court*. But alongside calls for parliamentary reform there were calls for the reform of a host of other (as it was claimed) exclusive, corrupt, and oppressive institutions: the church, the criminal law, and prisons; the high courts, and their modes of dealing with civil suits; municipal corporations; the universities; the medical colleges; the theatrical patent system; the Bank of England; the East India Company. Those who criticized some of these institutions did not necessarily criticize all others: many attracted specialized groups of critics, featuring especially those whose lives were most affected by them: lawyers, medical practitioners, merchants, and so forth, as the case might be. Criticisms were often particular: one might defend one institution and attack another. But there were overlaps in the membership of critical groups, and similarities of rhetoric. We narrow our view of what was at stake in the 'age of reform' unnecessarily if we do not allow this wide range of institutional targets to figure.[4]

Nor should the 'moral reform' strand in the story be overlooked. Quite how institutional and moral reform related, and should relate, was always a matter of debate. Could institutional reform be counted upon to bring moral reform in its train? Or was it a distraction from what needed to be a prior moral-reform project? Were institutional reform efforts even quite misconceived – diverting energy away from the only things truly in need of radical amendment: hearts, minds, and lives? Institutional and moral reformers sometimes saw eye to eye, sometimes they did not. The two projects sometimes interacted, as they did for William Wilberforce and the 'Saints', for example. Even when they were opposed, there might yet be significant critical exchange between them.

Our exploration of this terrain commences with an essay by Joanna Innes, charting the history of the words 'reformation', 'reform', 'reformer', and related terms. Four essays exploring reform efforts targeted on particular institutions follow: Philip Harling writes about demands for the reform of government; Michael Lobban about interest in reforming law; Arthur Burns about the reform of the Church of England; and Ian Burney about the reform of medicine. The next two essays explore reform efforts more 'moral' in character: David Turley writes about the antislavery movement; Kathryn Gleadle about some new cultures of the self.

The following three essays by Jennifer Hall-Witt, Katherine Newey, and Holger Hoock discuss 'reform and the arts'. Several of the themes explored in earlier essays recur here. Efforts to reform the arts sometimes focused on art institutions – the theatrical patent system, the Royal Academy – sometimes on the *content* of artistic production (of course, it was often thought that the institutional context influenced the content of art). Running through much debate on the arts was also a set of social themes: how could the arts be made

---

[4] Note thus that John Wade's *Extraordinary Black Book* (London, 1831 edn), often cited by historians for its observations on parliamentary representation, devotes chs. 1–2 to the church; 3–4 to the crown establishment and civil list; 5 to diplomats, and 6 to the peerage. Parliamentary representation features in ch. 7, following which eight further chapters deal with law, debt, taxation, the East India Company, the Bank of England, and sinecures.

accessible to a broader public? Was the current art scene in some way tainted by its privileged and restricted audience? Or would it be tainted if it were opened up to an undiscriminating public?

Three final essays set British reform in a wider context. Jennifer Ridden explores the salience of 'reform' in early nineteenth-century Ireland. Miles Taylor considers a broader set of interrelations: between Britain and her empire. British parliamentary reform had implications for the representation of extra-British interests. Imperial issues helped to create a climate in which reform could be represented as necessary; subsequently – partly in consequence – they presented a major challenge to policy-makers in the reformed polity. Jonathan Sperber sets British reform movements in a wider European context, and emphasizes their numerous distinctive features.

We regard it as a virtue of this collection that it brings into consideration topics that have not figured much in previous overarching accounts, including calls for reform in medicine and in the theatre, the place of reform in early nineteenth-century Irish politics, and the implications of parliamentary reform for the empire. We hope to have demonstrated that reform agendas in this period were more diverse than has sometimes been appreciated. We also demonstrate, incidentally, that reformers employed a wide range of strategies. Attempts to influence parliament through mobilizing public opinion were a feature of the age, but this approach was not appropriate for all varieties of 'reform'.

Our account is none the less selective and limited: selective, in that we have not included essays on by any means all of the topics suggested by our approach – thus on the Bank of England, on universities, or on temperance;[5] limited, in so far as there is much that our approach tends to marginalize or under-represent. In the remainder of this introduction, we make a small effort to remedy these deficiencies by outlining the larger historiographical and historical context in which this volume must be set. That it provides context for, not a summary of what follows perhaps needs emphasis. In a concluding section, however, we return to say a little more about the essays which follow against the background of the introduction.

I

Historians of eighteenth-century Britain working over the past half-century and more have fundamentally challenged ideas about the period embodying what

[5] For some insight into these topics see, however, Timothy L. Alborn, *Conceiving Companies: Joint-Stock Politics in Victorian England* (London, 1998); Anthony C. Howe, 'From "Old Corruption" to "New Probity": The Bank of England and its Directors in the Age of Reform', in Alan O'Day (ed.), *Government and Institutions in the Post-1832 United Kingdom* (Lewiston, N.Y., 1995); Richard Brent, *Liberal Anglican Politics: Whiggery, Religion and Reform, 1830–41* (Oxford, 1987), ch. 5; Brian Harrison, *Drink and the Victorians: The Temperance Question in England, 1815–72*, 2nd edn (Keele, 1994).

has been termed a 'reform perspective'.[6] As that term suggests, this view of the period had its origins in the writings of reformers trying to position their own efforts in time. Often lacking any very rich understanding of earlier generations, and inclined to denigrate the past in order to magnify their own aspirations and achievements, nineteenth-century writers sympathetic to the reform endeavours of their own day often portrayed the eighteenth century as an *essentially* 'unreformed' era. Eighteenth-century government was depicted as oligarchic and corrupt; parliaments as tools in the hands of 'the aristocracy' and 'the landed interest'; the church as self-satisfied and out of touch with the laity; criminal justice as bloody and barbaric; prisons as sites of oppression and moral degradation. Eighteenth-century manners and modes of conduct, correspondingly, were portrayed as coarse and lax, marred by gluttony, drunkenness, and tolerance for the sexual peccadilloes of lords and gentlemen. Some aspects of eighteenth-century life were equally often idealized, notably the paternalism of the squirearchy, the old poor law, and traditional master–apprentice relationships – but here again it is evident that nineteenth-century preoccupations strongly coloured the picture. The reports of royal commissions – a favourite tool of government from the 1830s – provide many classic formulations of such views, and have undoubtedly done much to shape the ways in which subsequent generations have cast their accounts.

One does not have to be an apologist for the eighteenth century to recognize that these are skewed perspectives. Several generations of historians have now striven to shift the balance, and to complicate our understandings of eighteenth-century practices and attitudes. The eighteenth century stands revealed by such research as having been less different from the nineteenth century than reformers liked to suppose. Both practices and aspirations anticipated much of what later generations took to be distinctive features of their own era. Thus, the late seventeenth and early eighteenth centuries saw important efforts to improve efficiency in government: nineteenth-century critics of 'Old Corruption' were in some respects trying to *complete* an earlier programme of reform, while simultaneously grappling with the dislocating consequences of the enormous increase in government business which followed from the French Wars and economic growth.[7] Eighteenth-century political power was

---

[6] For this phrase, see Joanna Innes and John Styles, 'The Crime Wave: Recent Writing on Crime and Criminal Justice in Eighteenth-Century England', *Jl Brit. Studies*, 25 (1986), 410. See also Paul Langford, 'Introduction: Time and Space', in Langford (ed.), *The Eighteenth Century* (Oxford, 2002), 1–8, for an overview of historiographical trends stressing recent reassessment of 'the nineteenth century's deep contempt for the eighteenth'. Recent examples of accounts adopting this perspective include Peter Virgin, *The Church in an Age of Negligence: Ecclesiastical Structure and Problems of Church Reform, 1700–1840* (Cambridge, 1989); Herbert Schlossberg, *The Silent Revolution and the Making of Victorian England* (Columbus, Ohio, 2000).

[7] These earlier developments are surveyed by John Brewer, *The Sinews of Power: War, Money, and the English State, 1688–1783* (London, 1989), esp. ch. 3. For the French Wars' exacerbation of earlier problems, see Philip Harling, *The Waning of 'Old Corruption': The Politics of Economical Reform in Britain, 1779–1846* (Oxford, 1996), 63–88.

not monopolized by the aristocracy and gentry: the business classes were experienced and demanding lobbyists, and the views of the electorate mattered. Though most eighteenth-century constituencies were small, most *voters* lived in large constituencies, characterized by an active political life. There were many political and quasi-political clubs, and much long-distance political networking. Eighteenth-century ministers and MPs were therefore exposed to a variety of more and less visible forms of 'pressure from without'.[8] Institutions and governmental practices were often criticized, and efforts made to improve them; John Beattie, for example, has uncovered a history of experimentation with criminal law, policing, trial, and punishment that dates back at least to the late seventeenth century.[9] From the 1750s, sentimental and philanthropic writings developed a specific form of social criticism.[10] Efforts to further the 'progress of politeness' among upper and middling social groups had as their counterpoint recurrent campaigns to 'reform the manners' of the lower orders – efforts which had some success, inasmuch as, for example, the once popular practice of 'throwing at cocks' seems to have been largely abandoned by the end of the century.[11] All this bears emphasizing because it is not our intention,

---

[8] For lobbying, see Brewer, *Sinews of Power*, ch. 8; Perry Gauci, *The Politics of Trade: The Overseas Merchant in State and Society, 1660–1720* (Oxford, 2001), ch. 5. For the vitality of the eighteenth-century electorate, see *inter alia* Geoffrey Holmes, *The Electorate and the National Will in the First Age of Party* (Lancaster, 1976); Nicholas Rogers, *Whigs and Cities: Popular Politics in the Age of Walpole and Pitt* (Oxford, 1989); Kathleen Wilson, *The Sense of the People: Politics, Culture and Imperialism in England, 1715–85* (Cambridge, 1995); Frank O'Gorman, *Voters, Patrons, and Parties: The Unreformed Electoral System of Hanoverian England, 1742–1832* (Oxford, 1989). For the developing concept of 'public opinion', see J. A. W. Gunn, *Beyond Liberty and Property: The Process of Self-Recognition in Eighteenth-Century Political Thought* (Kingston, Ont., 1983). Eighteenth-century 'public opinion' manifested itself most dramatically in the occasional storm of protest: see thus Geoffrey Holmes, *The Trial of Dr Sacheverell* (London, 1973); Paul Langford, *The Excise Crisis: Society and Politics in the Age of Walpole* (Oxford, 1973); T. W. Perry, *Public Opinion, Propaganda and Politics in Eighteenth-Century England: A Study of the Jew Bill of 1753* (Cambridge, Mass., 1962). Wilkite excitement in the 1760s and 1770s (surveyed by George Rudé, *Wilkes and Liberty* (London, 1962) and John Brewer, *Party Ideology and Popular Politics at the Accession of George III* (Cambridge, 1972), ch. 9) and the Association Movement of the 1780s (for which see n. 13 below) can be seen as successors to such earlier storms. But at a less dramatic level there was constant interaction between the propertied classes, very broadly defined, and parliament, for which see Paul Langford, *Public Life and the Propertied Englishman, 1689–1789* (Oxford, 1991), esp. chs. 3, 5; Joanna Innes, 'Parliament and the Shaping of Eighteenth-Century English Social Policy', *Trans. Royal Hist. Soc.*, 5th ser., 60 (1990).

[9] John Beattie, *Crime and the Courts in England, 1660–1800* (Oxford, 1986); John Beattie, *Policing and Punishment in London, 1660–1750: Urban Crime and the Limits of Terror* (Oxford, 2001). See also Lee Davison *et al.* (eds.), *Stilling the Grumbling Hive: The Response to Social and Economic Problems in England, 1689–1750* (Stroud, 1992).

[10] See, e.g., Tony Henderson, *Disorderly Women in Eighteenth-Century London: Prostitution and Control in the Metropolis, 1730–1830* (London, 1999), ch. 7.

[11] For the progress of politeness and the reformation of manners – a booming topic in modern scholarship – see *inter alia* Paul Langford, *A Polite and Commercial People: England, 1727–83* (Oxford, 1989); G. J. Barker-Benfield, *The Culture of Sensibility: Sex and Society in Eighteenth-Century Britain* (Chicago, 1992). For changes in popular manners, see R. W. Malcolmson,

(cont. on p. 7)

in directing attention to an 'age of reform' which we have dated from 1780, to add weight to the notion that preceding decades were 'unreformed'. On the contrary, if anything, we wish to reorient understandings of the reform era so as to achieve a better fit with the new historiography of the preceding period.

In what sense, then, can the year 1780 be said to have inaugurated an 'age of reform'?

What is at issue is in part a shift in vocabulary. This played a part in conditioning the ways in which subsequent generations understood their relationship to their own forebears, and thus in due course in shaping a distorting 'reform perspective' on the past. Attitudes and practices changed less than the ways in which those attitudes and practices were expressed and recorded. But the change in vocabulary itself reflected, and gained significance from, certain wider events, and certain slowly unfolding, but ultimately significant, changes in the forms of public life.

The War of American Independence (1776–83) marked a crisis for the British polity.[12] This was the only major war of the period to end in clear defeat for Britain. In the course of the war, indeed, the threat of losses on more than just the American continent loomed, as the Irish too protested at British misrule and demanded more independence, questions were raised about the justice and effectiveness of British rule in India, and the French, Spanish, and Dutch tried to strip away parts of Britain's global empire. Christopher Wyvill's Association movement – a movement of protest against an expensive and arguably misdirected war – helped to launch the career of the word 'reform' as a key term in British political life by turning the call for a restructuring of the relationship between parliament and public (a traditional enough demand) into a slogan that would resound many times through the next century: 'parliamentary reform'.[13] This period of crisis brought to the centre of British politics – uniquely in the

---

(cont.)
Popular Recreations in English Society, 1700–1850 (Cambridge, 1973); Peter Clark, *The English Alehouse: A Social History, 1200–1830* (Harlow, 1983), chs. 8–11; R. B. Shoemaker, 'The Decline of Public Insult in London, 1660–1800', *Past and Present*, no. 169 (Nov. 2000).

[12] Since Herbert Butterfield, *George III, Lord North and the People, 1779–80* (London, 1949) there has been a tendency to play this down, but the significance of the moment has been re-emphasized by recent scholarship. See, e.g., Linda Colley, *Britons: Forging the Nation, 1707–1837* (London, 1994), 132–45; Stephen Conway, *The British Isles and the War of American Independence* (Oxford, 2000). Note also Mark Philp, 'The Role of America in the "Debate on France" 1791–5: Thomas Paine's Insertion', *Utilitas*, 5 (1993).

[13] Wyvill's Association is assigned a prominent place in older studies of the rise of extra-parliamentary reforming politics: see, e.g., E. C. Black, *The Association: British Extraparliamentary Political Organization, 1769–1793* (Cambridge, Mass., 1963); John Cannon, *Parliamentary Reform, 1640–1832* (Cambridge, 1972). Though it clearly had various novel features, it has not been fully reassessed in the light of recent work on earlier popular politics (for which see n. 8 above) – though see Linda Colley, 'Eighteenth-Century English Radicalism before Wilkes', *Trans. Royal Hist. Soc.*, 5th ser., 31 (1981), for an attempt to provoke debate. For a recent study of Wyvillite agitation in the press, see Hannah Barker, *Newspapers, Politics and Public Opinion in Late Eighteenth-Century England* (Oxford, 1998). For the slogan 'reform', see Joanna Innes' essay below.

eighteenth century – two political leaders, William Pitt the Younger and Charles James Fox, *both* of whom at least ostensibly favoured 'reform', both in the form of 'parliamentary reform' and in terms of being prepared to countenance other significant reshaping of government.[14] It was symptomatic of the time that the two should have competed, in 1783–4, to find effective ways of reforming the East India Company, on whose faulty structure certain problematic features of British rule in India were blamed. The massively detailed reports of the parliamentary select committee set up to enquire into the Company's proceedings were unprecedented, in scale and ambition, as parliamentary publications.[15]

Among its many and varied effects, the American war helped to destabilize Britain's late-seventeenth-century religious settlement, arousing both hopes for change and determined opposition to change.[16] The desire to align England and Scotland's Catholic minorities and Ireland's Catholic majority behind the war effort prompted symbolically important modifications of anti-Catholic laws in 1778, but when Lord George Gordon's protestant crusade precipitated anti-Catholic rioting in London in June 1780, tensions within elite opinion were revealed. Much more significant concessions would follow in the 1790s, but full 'Catholic Emancipation' – the opening up of parliament and the highest offices in the state to Catholics – was to remain a contentious issue up to and beyond its passage into law in 1829.[17] The immediate response of protestant dissenters was to argue that concessions to Catholics should be matched by concessions to them, and these followed in 1779, but, because some among their number showed sympathy for the American cause, the war added weight to the view that dissenters were subversives.[18] In the late 1780s, dissenters

---

[14] Michael Duffy, *The Younger Pitt* (Harlow, 2000); for much more detail on this early period in Pitt's career, see John Ehrman, *The Younger Pitt*, 3 vols. (London, 1969–96), i; L. G. Mitchell, *Charles James Fox and the Disintegration of the Whig Party, 1782–94* (London, 1971).

[15] Detailed accounts are supplied in Lucy Sutherland, *The East India Company in Eighteenth-Century English Politics* (Oxford, 1962); Vincent Harlow, *The Founding of the Second British Empire*, 2 vols. (London, 1952–64), ii, chs. 2–3; for the political struggle, see also John Cannon, *The Fox–North Coalition: Crisis of the Constitution, 1782–4* (Cambridge, 1969). The reports occupy three volumes in the first series of *Reports from Committees of the House of Commons*, 15 vols. (London, 1806).

[16] Religious ramifications of the impact of the American War are now helpfully surveyed in Conway, *British Isles and the War of American Independence*, ch. 7.

[17] The British political context of important concessions to Catholics in 1791 (31 Geo. III, c. xxxii) has not been much studied, though see Ehrman, *Younger Pitt*, ii, 81–4, for a brief account. For an overview of Irish developments, see Thomas Bartlett, *The Fall and Rise of the Irish Nation: The Catholic Question, 1690–1830* (Dublin, 1992). For the politics of emancipation in the 1820s, see below, n. 135.

[18] For the argument that they *were* subversives, and that religious heterodoxy lay at the root of all political radicalism, see J. C. D. Clark, *English Society, 1660–1832*, 2nd edn (Cambridge, 2000), ch. 4; J. C. D. Clark, *The Language of Liberty, 1660–1832: Political Discourse and Social Dynamics in the Anglo-American World* (Cambridge, 1994), esp. ch. 3. Cf. James Bradley, *Religion, Revolution and English Radicalism: Nonconformity in Eighteenth-Century Politics and Society* (Cambridge, 1990); for a review and assessment, John Seed, "'A Set of Men

(cont. on p. 9)

campaigned for the repeal of the Test and Corporation Acts, full of hope that, in the new political climate, their efforts would meet with success. Not only were they disappointed, but concurrent theological controversy drew forth new champions of Anglican orthodoxy and contributed to the reinvigoration of the high-church tradition within the Church of England.[19]

This era of political crisis and change was marked also by heightened moral anxiety. The 1770s and 1780s saw a series of high-profile scandals among the social elite, publicized by the press both as objects of reprobation, and for titillating effect. The duchess of Kingston's trial for bigamy, and the murder of the earl of Sandwich's mistress by a disappointed lover, cast disturbing light on aristocratic mores. Concern about elite morals seems in 1779 to have prompted the first of a series of legislative attempts to discourage adultery. In the 1780s, it was argued that Fox's notorious penchant for gambling called his suitability for leadership into question.[20] The war played its part in shaping the new moral climate. Anxiety lest losses in war indicate withdrawal of God's approval helped to spur the diffusion of evangelicalism among both churchmen and dissenters. Local authorities undertook a concerted drive against 'vice' in common life: at the war's end, magistrates throughout England circulated plans to combat 'vice and immorality' and 'better' society by such means as building new model prisons and encouraging the establishment of contributory 'friendly societies'. William Wilberforce, newly emerged from a religious conversion experience, tried to coordinate local activity into a 'reformation of manners' campaign – echoing a late-seventeenth/early eighteenth-century effort.[21]

Also infused with moral energy, and also endorsed by Wilberforce, was another campaign that was at once more popular in its appeal, more innovative in its

---

(*cont.*)
Powerful Enough in Many Things": Rational Dissent and Political Opposition in England, 1770–1790', in Knud Haakonssen (ed.), *Enlightenment and Religion: Rational Dissent in Eighteenth-Century Britain* (Cambridge, 1996).

[19] For dissenting campaigns, see R. B. Barlow, *Citizenship and Conscience: A Study of the Theory and Practice of Religious Toleration during the Eighteenth Century* (Philadelphia, 1962); G. M. Ditchfield, 'The Parliamentary Struggle over the Repeal of the Test and Corporation Acts, 1787–1790', *Eng. Hist. Rev.*, 89 (1974). See also G. M. Ditchfield, '"How Narrow Will the Limits of This Toleration Appear?" Dissenting Petitions to Parliament, 1772–1773', and James Bradley, 'The Public, Parliament and the Protestant Dissenting Deputies', in Stephen Taylor and David Wykes (eds.), *Parliament and Dissent* (forthcoming, Edinburgh, 2005). For the high-church revival, see Peter Nockles, *The Oxford Movement in Context: Anglican High Churchmanship, 1760–1857* (Cambridge, 1994); F. C. Mather, *High Church Prophet: Bishop Samuel Horsley and the Caroline Tradition in the later Georgian Church* (Oxford, 1992).

[20] Phyllis Deutsch, 'Moral Trespass in Georgian London: Gaming, Gender and Electoral Politics in the Age of George III', *Hist. Jl*, 39 (1996); Donna Andrew, '"Adultery à la Mode": Privilege, the Law and Attitudes to Adultery 1770–1809', *Hist.*, 82 (1997); see also Donna Andrew and Randall McGowen, *The Perreaus and Mrs Rudd: Forgery and Betrayal in Eighteenth-Century London* (Berkeley, 2001), ch. 5.

[21] Joanna Innes, 'Politics and Morals: The Reformation of Manners Movement in Later Eighteenth-Century England', in E. Hellmuth (ed.), *The Transformation of Political Culture: England and Germany in the Late-Eighteenth Century* (Oxford, 1990).

methods, and more striking in its impact: the campaign against the slave-trade. The institution of slavery had long attracted diffuse criticism from 'freeborn Englishmen'. In the climate of imperial rethinking and moral self-criticism that followed the American War, some Quakers strove to give the issue a higher public profile. As its support base broadened in the late 1780s, the campaign developed in novel ways, combining the petitioning tactics of Wyvill's Association movement with publicity and fund-raising efforts more reminiscent of subscription charities. The rise in importance of the midlands and the north of England as commercial and manufacturing districts was reflected in the significant role urban centres and business leaders in these regions played in the campaign. Operating outside traditional political frameworks, and drawing upon religious and humanitarian among other forms of support, the antislavery campaign succeeded in 1791 in mobilizing petitions on an unprecedented scale: in contrast to the few dozen petitions previously evoked by major political and economic campaigns, this one elicited over five hundred. After the campaign achieved its goal, in 1807, the activist Thomas Clarkson published a history that detailed the way in which it had evolved and the tactics employed. This was the first developed history of a reform campaign. The campaign was subsequently cited as a model from which other would-be reformers might learn.[22]

The 1780s were a unique decade in eighteenth-century history: a decade in which not only were many forms of 'abuse' and 'vice' denigrated, but also a wide variety of 'reform' and 'improvement' campaigns commanded support across a broad front – though the decade also saw the crystallization of some anti-reform sentiment. Supporters of a variety of later reform efforts looked back to this as the period in which their cause first took clear shape: including parliamentary reformers, prison reformers, and antislavery activists. Such perceptions encouraged some caricaturing of previous decades, but also reflected real shifts in the character of political culture. All periodizations have an element of arbitrariness, and threaten to distort as much as they reveal – but these are the considerations that have led us to choose this decade as the starting-point for our enquiries. It must none the less be borne in mind – as some of the essays that follow will stress – that many varieties of 'reforming' thought and practice had important antecedents, even if, in the earlier period, these concerns were not expressed or pursued in quite the same way.

---

[22] Roger Anstey, *The Atlantic Slave Trade and British Abolition, 1760–1810* (London, 1975), remains a helpful survey. Recent studies include Seymour Drescher, *Capitalism and Anti-Slavery: British Anti-Slavery Mobilisation in Comparative Perspective* (New York, 1987); Judi Jennings, *The Business of Abolishing the British Slave Trade, 1783–1807* (London, 1997); J. E. Oldfield, *Popular Politics and British Anti-Slavery: The Mobilisation of Public Opinion Against the Slave Trade, 1787–1807* (London, 1998). See also Clare Midgley, *Women against Slavery: The British Campaigns, 1780–1870* (London, 1992). For Thomas Clarkson's pioneering history, see his *The History of the Rise, Progress and Accomplishment of the Abolishment of the African Slave-Trade by the British Parliament* (London, 1808).

II

Jonathan Sperber in his chapter emphasizes the distinctiveness of British reform projects in this period. But this is not to say that British developments can or should be studied in isolation from wider European and American currents. We turn now to provide an account of that broader context from the late eighteenth century through to the 1830s before examining in more detail British developments over the same period.

Historians have termed the late eighteenth century the era of the 'late Enlightenment'. In these decades, the possibility of improving the human condition through governmental or other forms of public action provided a focus for much discussion and indeed practical effort. The resolution of religious conflicts (sometimes by compromise, more often by force), and development of more powerful military and fiscal apparatuses in the course of a series of European wars from the 1660s down to the 1760s, had left many rulers and their advisers better equipped than before to pursue schemes of domestic improvement. What scope there was for such action, and in what forms it might best be undertaken, were increasingly debated by intellectuals. 'Reform' was a term that flitted through these continental discussions.[23]

English newspapers and magazines carried reports of some of these European efforts: the king of Prussia's 1730s scheme of law reform, for example, and Empress Catherine of Russia's establishment of a 'Legislative Commission'.[24] Continental essays and treatises were sometimes read in their original languages, sometimes in translation: Cesare Beccaria's treatise on crimes and punishments, thus, was translated into English in 1767, and repeatedly cited by English authors thereafter.[25] Englishmen interested in promoting reforms sometimes corresponded with fellow workers abroad: Jeremy Bentham developed an extensive network of European contacts, while English antislavery activists corresponded with their American counterparts. Some travelled to make contacts and see for themselves: Bentham visited Russia; the prison reformer John Howard toured the continent, and indeed died of a fever contracted while visiting Russian prisons.[26] The period saw an upsurge in what Jeroen Dekker has called 'philanthropic tourism'. This brought foreigners to Britain, as well as the reverse: the French physicians Jacques Tenon and Charles Auguste de Coulomb

---

[23] For an overview, see Hamish Scott (ed.), *Enlightened Absolutism: Reform and Reformers in Later Eighteenth-Century Europe* (Basingstoke, 1990).

[24] Both were also the subject of independent publications: *The King of Prussia's Plan for Reforming the Administration of Justice* (London, 1750); *The Grand Instructions to the Commissioners appointed to frame a New Code of Laws for the Russian Empire . . .* (London, 1768).

[25] A. J. Draper, 'Cesare Beccaria's Influence on English Discussions of Punishment, 1764–1789', *Hist. European Ideas*, 26 (2000).

[26] Ian R. Christie, *The Benthams in Russia, 1780–1791* (Oxford, 1993). John Aikin, *A View of the Character and Public Services of the late John Howard* (London, 1796), for Howard's travels and death.

were sent by the French Academy of Sciences to visit English hospitals; Baron von Voght, one of the promoters of a Hamburg poor-relief experiment, came to Edinburgh.[27] Britons became increasingly self-conscious about how their legal and social institutions stood up to comparison with the 'most improved' European and American laws and practices.

The French Revolution at first seemed to set the scene for more such fruitful interactions. As Frenchmen set about drafting and implementing unprecedentedly ambitious schemes for reform and regeneration, English reformers watched with interest. Samuel Romilly, a young barrister who had recently written against the excessive number of penal hangings in England, suggested in his *Thoughts on the Probable Influence of the French Revolution on Great Britain* (1790) that the time had come for the English to consider, in the light of their own reason and not that of their ancestors, the merits of not just the standing army (a long-standing concern), an unrepresentative parliament (an issue of the day), and cruel criminal statutes (his own chosen cause), but also the hardships of sailors; privateering; expensive law proceedings; the requirement that Church of England clergy subscribe to the Thirty-Nine Articles; the 'settlement' laws as they affected entitlement to poor relief; monopoly in commerce and the Navigation Laws more generally; municipal corporations; and classical education.[28] This is an interesting list, suggestive of the way in which a 'reform agenda' was taking shape; it is hard to imagine anyone compiling quite such an agenda twenty years before.

French assertion of the 'Rights of Man', attacks on feudal privilege, and moves to establish a representative assembly on a broad franchise encouraged those in Britain who would have liked to see more respect for individual rights and a shift towards democracy. The French Revolution breathed life and enthusiasm into the popular end of the parliamentary-reform movement; French-style caps of liberty and 'liberty trees' supplied popular radicalism with new icons. Thomas Paine's writings encouraged the view that the French Revolution carried forward the themes of the American Revolution, and that the two together marked the dawn of a new age, in which tyranny and superstition would wither or be crushed.[29]

---

[27] Jeroen Dekker, 'Transforming the Nation and the Child: Philanthropy in the Netherlands, Belgium, France and England, c. 1780–1850', in H. Cunningham and J. Innes (eds.), *Charity, Philanthropy and Reform from the 1690s to 1850* (Basingstoke, 1998), 137–9. For Anglo-European exchanges on welfare issues, see Joanna Innes, 'The State and the Poor: Eighteenth-Century England in European Perspective', in John Brewer and Eckhart Hellmuth (eds.), *Rethinking Leviathan: The Eighteenth-Century State in Britain and Germany* (Oxford, 1999).

[28] [Samuel Romilly], *Thoughts on the Probable Influence of the French Revolution on Great Britain* (London, 1790).

[29] Early enthusiasm for the French Revolution is chronicled in E. P. Thompson, *The Making of the English Working Class*, revd edn (Harmondsworth, 1968); Albert Goodwin, *The Friends of Liberty: The English Democratic Movement in the Age of the French Revolution* (London, 1979). For further discussion of English responses to the Revolution, see below pp. 16–20.

Yet, as the constitutional monarchy collapsed and the Terror took shape, what the French Revolution in fact precipitated in England was the reverse: a reaction against reform and reformers of all kinds.[30] The very word fell into disrepute. Pitt avowed that the time was no longer ripe for constitutional reform, and suggested that those who continued to urge it harboured sinister intentions. The 'Two Acts' of 1795 aimed to restrict popular political activity. Belief that the British constitution was perfect as it stood, and that established laws and institutions embodied the accumulated wisdom of generations, such that any innovation was likely to be for the worse, antedated the French Revolution: the early parliamentary-reform movement had broken on this recalcitrance. But the French Revolution buttressed and entrenched fear of change even among those who regarded the constitution as imperfect. For the next few decades, would-be reformers would have a harder time making their case. People's political identities came to be defined, in important part, by their attitudes to change – not previously a key divisive issue. Change remained possible: the slave-trade was, after all, abolished in 1807.[31] We shall say more about the continuing scope for improving activity shortly. But opponents of change, in general or in particular, gained an important new ideological resource.

The Revolution, and subsequent extension of French rule over much of Europe, also sundered lines of communication. Though Napoleon continued the work of reforming French laws and institutions, and imposed his reforms on many other parts of Europe, there was much less in the way of exchange of ideas between Britain and the continent between 1793 and 1815 – between the outbreak of war and the fall of Napoleon – than there had been before. The Peace of Amiens (1802) sparked a brief flurry of Anglo-French interaction: British tourists rushed over to inspect the new face of post-revolutionary Paris; Jeremy Bentham's writings on law reform were first published in French translation at this time. But this interlude proved brief.[32]

The changing geography of conflict shaped the patterns of interchange that were sustained. There was some enlivening of interest in Scandinavian and German societies and cultures. German drama, literature, and philosophy had been growing in popularity and prestige on the eve of revolution; this interest continued to grow.[33] The evangelical revival encouraged communication

---

[30] See the works cited in n. 29 above and, for the additional complications introduced by the outbreak of war, Clive Emsley, *British Society and the French Wars, 1793–1815* (London, 1979).

[31] Under the hybrid 'Ministry of All the Talents'. See also the works cited in n. 22.

[32] Constantia Maxwell, *The English Traveller in France, 1698–1815* (London, 1932). For Bentham, see J. R. Dinwiddy, 'Bentham and the Early Nineteenth Century', in Dinwiddy, *Radicalism and Reform in Britain, 1780–1850* (London, 1992), 293.

[33] Thus Thomas Malthus visited Denmark, Norway, and Sweden in 1799, when 'Englishmen were excluded from almost every part of the continent by the distracted state of public affairs': *The Travel Diaries of T. R. Malthus*, ed. P. James (Cambridge, 1966), 14–16, 24–220.

(cont. on p. 14)

between protestants in diverse states. Some protestant Germans were inspired by new English associational forms and endeavours.[34]

Though the French Revolution would long cast a shadow over British debate,[35] later changes in European politics somewhat eased British reformers' lot. At the start of the nineteenth century, especially in 1803, when Britain faced the most serious threat yet of French invasion, British political opinion muddled together into a patriotic middle ground. Thereafter left and right wings re-emerged – if not always on the same lines as before. The Spanish revolt against Napoleon, which took its rise from 1808, played a part, by relegitimating 'reform', even revolution, in the eyes of some. The recently founded *Edinburgh Review* first gained its role as an organ of liberal opinion when it came out in favour of Spanish opposition; its more conservative contributors and readers promptly deserted it to launch the rival *Quarterly Review*. Solidarity with Spanish rebels subsequently formed one of the first planks of radical internationalism.[36]

The Restoration era on the continent – post-1815 – brought with it divisions over how far *anciens régimes* should be restored, and how far the need to guard against further revolutionary outbursts legitimated the restriction of civil liberties – debates seen as critical to the future of Europe, and echoed within Britain.[37] Many Britons were not inclined to support the forces of 'reaction' or the efforts of European 'ultras' (new terms, both of French origin, which acquired currency in Britain at this time).[38] What was needed instead, many supposed, was some middle way between reaction and revolution. Within that middle way, there might be scope for reform. The argument that reform *did*

(cont.)

There exists no convenient general account of German cultural influence, but some insights are provided in F. W. Stokoe, *German Influence in the British Romantic Period, 1788–1818: With Special Reference to Scott, Coleridge, Shelley and Byron* (Cambridge, 1926); René Wellek, *Immanuel Kant in England, 1793–1838* (Princeton, 1931); H. C. G. Matthew, 'Edward Bouverie Pusey: From Scholar to Tractarian', *Jl Theol. Studies*, 22 (1981); Bertrand Evans, *Gothic Drama from Walpole to Shelley* (Berkeley, 1947), ch. 7; W. Vaughan, *German Romanticism and English Art* (New Haven, 1979), 15, 17–20, 23–6, 44, 83–5.

[34] There is unfortunately no early nineteenth-century equivalent of W. R. Ward's study of the early eighteenth century: W. R. Ward, *The Protestant Evangelical Awakening* (Cambridge, 1992), but some insights emerge from Christopher Clark, *The Politics of Conversion: Missionary Protestantism and the Jews in Prussia, 1728–1941* (Oxford, 1995), esp. ch. 3.

[35] See John Dinwiddy, 'English Radicals and the French Revolution, 1800–50', in Dinwiddy, *Radicalism and Reform*. Patrick Brantlinger, *The Spirit of Reform: British Literature and Politics, 1833–67* (Cambridge, Mass., 1971), 63–4, notes the effect of the appearance of a wave of histories of the Revolution in 1830.

[36] Peter Spence, *The Birth of Romantic Radicalism: War, Popular Politics and English Radical Reformism, 1800–15* (Aldershot, 1996), 62–98; John Clive, *Scotch Reviewers: The 'Edinburgh Review', 1802–15* (London, 1957), 110–13, for the split among reviewers; H. Weisser, *British Working-Class Movements and Europe, 1815–48* (Manchester, 1975), 7.

[37] For a recent survey, see David Laven and Lucy Riall (eds.), *Napoleon's Legacy: Problems of Government in Restoration Europe* (Oxford, 2000).

[38] For the emergence of these terms, see the *Oxford English Dictionary*. For 'reaction', see also Raymond Williams, *Keywords: A Vocabulary of Culture and Society* (London, 1976), 214–15.

represent a middle way – that, properly conceived, it was a preservative *against* revolution, not a precipitant of it – had been made by Edmund Burke as early as 1790. Those who tried to stem the flood tide of counter-revolution had made some use of it in the remainder of that decade. But not until the 1820s and 1830s did that contrast become formulaic, both in Britain and in Europe. Initially employed chiefly by representatives of new, inchoate 'liberalism', the formula gradually won a degree of acceptance even among conservatives; by the 1830s, even the notoriously conservative Austrian foreign minister Klemens von Metternich was prepared to countenance 'reform'.[39]

The conclusion of the Napoleonic episode opened the way once more for the pan-European circulation of ideas. One area of lively exchange was the relatively novel discipline of political economy. Britain's position particularly fascinated continental observers: they saw her burdened with an enormous war debt and rocked by industrial and agrarian protest, and wondered what might ensue, and what lessons might be drawn from her experience for continental states.[40] Some sceptical European observers found the forebodings of British radicals congenial. In this context the French economist J. B. Say became friendly with the 'utilitarian' James Mill. Much British public policy debate was mired in the particularities of British law and practice, which restricted its appeal; Bentham's highly abstract and programmatic writings on law re-form, however, constituted an exception, and acquired a global reputation: they were translated into not only French, but also Russian, Spanish, Italian, and German, and made an especial impact on Spanish liberals and in the newly independent states of Latin America.[41] In public policy, the form of European practice attracting most interest in Britain at this time was probably education. Pestalozzi's Swiss educational experiments attracted particular comment; they helped to spark the post-war foundation of British 'infant schools'.[42] Meanwhile British medical students, seizing opportunities presented by the ending of conflict to travel and study in France, acquainted themselves with new French medical and scientific ideas and practices.[43]

The outbreak of a wave of revolutions in 1820 – in Spain, Portugal, Naples, Sicily, Piedmont, and Greece – evoked shows of support among British re-formers of all classes. In line with notions of social progress prevailing at the time, these uprisings were celebrated as evidence of 'the progress of reason' or

---

[39] O. Brunner *et al.* (eds.), *Geschichtliche Grundbegriffe*, 8 vols. (1972–97), v, 341–55. For Burke, see below p. 88.

[40] Gareth Stedman Jones, 'National Bankruptcy and Social Revolution: European Observers on Britain, 1813–44', in Donald Winch and Patrick K. O'Brien (eds.), *The Political Economy of British Historical Experience* (Oxford, 2002).

[41] Dinwiddy, 'Bentham and the Early Nineteenth Century'.

[42] Philip McCann and Francis A. Young, *Samuel Wilderspin and the Infant School Movement* (Beckenham, 1982), esp. 61–6.

[43] L. S. Jacyna, *Philosophic Whigs: Medicine, Science and Citizenship in Edinburgh, 1789–1818* (London, 1964), 124.

'march of mind'.[44] Concern about the effect of British policy on the balance between the forces of liberalism and reaction elsewhere helped to make foreign policy a significant issue in the politics of the early 1820s. Perhaps inappropriately, Viscount Castlereagh's reputation was blackened, and George Canning's enhanced – even though the latter's success in fostering new republics in Latin America was paralleled on the European continent only in the peripheral case of Greece.[45]

A further wave of revolutionary outbreaks in 1830 – notably in France, Belgium, and Poland – coincided with the onset of Britain's own Reform crisis, encouraging debate as to how far British and European circumstances were analogous. The peaceful resolution of the British crisis reinforced notions of British exceptionalism: British institutions and social structures seemed peculiarly adept at containing change within constitutional and civil constraints. Yet it was widely supposed – perhaps more than it should have been supposed – that some of the same forces were in play in different states. Some disenchanted radicals framed their analysis in 'class' terms. As they saw it, in Britain as in France, liberal rather than reactionary outcomes – the triumph of 'moderate reform' – in truth represented the betrayal by the rising middle classes of the working classes, whose day was yet to come.[46]

III

In 1790, the penal reformer Samuel Romilly had expressed the hope that changes in France might 'diminish some of that horror at innovation, which seems so generally to prevail among us'. By 1808, he was certain that it had had the reverse effect:

> If any person be desirous of having an adequate idea of the mischievous effects which have been produced in this country by the French Revolution and all its attendant horrors, he should attempt some legislative reform, on humane and liberal principles. He will then find, not only what a stupid dread of innovation, but what a savage spirit it has infused in the minds of many of his countrymen.[47]

---

[44] Weisser, *British Working-Class Movements*, 17.

[45] Paul M. Hayes, *The Nineteenth Century, 1814–80* (London, 1975), 76–90.

[46] Clive H. Church, *Europe in 1830: Revolutions and Political Change* (London, 1983). Roland Quinault, 'The French Revolution of 1830 and Parliamentary Reform', *Hist.*, 79 (1994), argues that events in France played a crucial part in enlivening the English parliamentary-reform movement. For developing ideas about the nature of British exceptionalism, see J. W. Burrow, *A Liberal Descent: Victorian Historians and the English Past* (Cambridge, 1981), 11–93; Richard Brent, *Liberal Anglican Politics: Whiggery, Religion and Reform, 1830–41* (Oxford, 1987), 40–63; also Paul Langford, 'The English as Reformers: Foreign Visitors' Impressions, 1750–1850', in Blanning and Wende (eds.), *Reform in Great Britain and Germany*. For disenchanted radicals, see Weisser, *British Working-Class Movements*, 34–41.

[47] *Memoirs of the Life of Sir Samuel Romilly*, 3 vols. (London, 1840), ii, 253–4.

The claim was not without grounds. Yet it can be exaggerated, even if we restrict our attention to the years before Waterloo. Romilly's own initial comment makes it plain that 'innovation' had met with resistance previously. 'Reform' projects, moreover, came in many shapes and sizes, had their roots in a variety of preoccupations, and could be justified in diverse ways. In what follows, we partly endorse but also qualify characterizations of the war years as years of reaction.[48]

The years 1792–3, which saw the toppling of the French monarchy, the execution of the king, the institution of the Terror, and the outbreak of war between Britain and France, were years in which reform was particularly likely to be anathematized. These years saw a royal proclamation against seditious publication, moves to suppress popular political societies, and the formation of John Reeves' Association for the Protection of Liberty and Property against Republicans and Levellers to carry forward that effort.[49] A significant group of Whigs swung behind Pitt's government – a situation formalized by the coalition of 1794.[50] Even in this period, however, there were moderate voices contesting the counter-revolutionary hard line. Thus the Essex clergyman John Howlett wrote to the Reevesite executive to protest against their assertion that the British system of government was perfect in all respects. He entirely agreed, he said, with the need to repel the revolutionary threat from without and within – but, at a time when rising prices and changes in rural society were rendering the

---

[48] Among older assessments of the impact of the French Revolution and ensuing war, see once more Thompson, *Making of the English Working Class*; Goodwin, *Friends of Liberty*; Emsley, *Britain and the French Wars*. The bicentennial of the Revolution in 1989 prompted a number of collective efforts at reassessment: thus H. T. Dickinson (ed.), *Britain and the French Revolution, 1789–1815* (Basingstoke, 1989); M. Philp (ed.), *The French Revolution and British Popular Politics* (Cambridge, 1991). A notable feature of writing in the late 1980s and 1990s was the development of interest in conservative responses to revolution, for which see n. 49 below. Jenny Graham's extended account, *The Nation, the Law and the King: Reform Politics in England, 1789–99*, 2 vols. (Lanham, Md., 1999), provides a rare recent instance of a study focusing squarely on radicalism. Most recently, interest in ideas and representations has come to the fore. See thus David Bindman's bicentennial exhibition catalogue, *The Shadow of the Guillotine: Britain and the French Revolution* (London, 1989); Gillian Russell, *The Theatres of War: Performance, Politics and Society, 1793–1815* (Oxford, 1995); Emma Vincent, *A War of Ideas: British Attitudes to the Wars against Revolutionary France, 1792–1802* (Aldershot, 1998); Stuart Andrews, *The British Periodical Press and the French Revolution* (London, 2000); John Barrell, *Imagining the King's Death: Figurative Treason, Fantasies of Regicide, 1793–6* (Oxford, 2000).

[49] Accounts of conservative responses to revolution include Black, *Association*, ch. 7; Ian Christie, *Stress and Stability in Late Eighteenth-Century Britain: Reflections on Britain's Avoidance of Revolution* (Oxford, 1984); R. R. Dozier, *For King, Constitution and Country: The English Loyalists and the French Revolution* (Lexington, Ky., 1983); Philip Schofield, 'Conservative Political Thought in Britain in Response to the French Revolution', *Hist. Jl*, 39 (1986); Robert Hole, *Pulpits, Politics and Public Order in England, 1760–1832* (Cambridge, 1989); Matthew Grenby, *The Anti-Jacobin Novel: British Conservatism and the French Revolution* (Cambridge, 2001). Mark Philp responds critically in 'Vulgar Conservatism, 1792–3', *Eng. Hist. Rev.*, 110 (1995).

[50] For the Whig split, see Mitchell, *Charles James Fox and the Disintegration of the Whig Party*, ch. 6.

condition of the poor increasingly miserable, it was foolish to assert that the British polity was beyond improvement; nor was this the best way to win hearts and minds. Instead, efforts should be made to improve the lot of the poor, so that they had solid reasons for being loyal. (Magistrates who drew up generous tables of allowances in the bad-harvest, high-price year of 1795 were implicitly acting on the same diagnosis; in 1796, a largely evangelical group of senior clergy and well-placed laymen founded the Society for Bettering the Condition of the Poor with similar aims.)[51]

It may have served the needs of political polemic to suggest that the country was divided into foes and friends of revolution – but in practice the political scene was more complicated, and this became more evident once the first panic had passed. Among leading members of the governing coalition there was a range of views, Pitt's own being by no means the most reactionary.[52] Wilberforce and the 'Saints' (other religiously 'serious' MPs), though generally government supporters, could not always be counted upon: for them, the cause of religion and morality came first. In 1795, Wilberforce made life difficult for Pitt by criticizing his failure to take advantage of the fall of Robespierre and the appearance of a more moderate regime in France to seek peace.[53] Whigs who swung to support Pitt did not necessarily wish to support the status quo; in relation to Ireland especially it could be argued that significant further concessions to Catholics were needed if that island were to be kept on side. In 1793, in fact, restrictions on Irish Catholic worship were removed, and qualified Catholics given the vote. When the Whig Earl Fitzwilliam, as Irish lord lieutenant, seemed to be rushing towards total 'Emancipation' faster than Pitt thought prudent, and was dismissed, he left the government camp and rejoined the opposition.[54] Country squires by and large supported Pitt: probably at no time in the century had the landed classes been so much of one mind. But not all of them supported everything as it was, nor even accepted Pitt's argument that the time was not ripe for constitutional reform. The few dozen supporters of the young Whig Charles Grey's parliamentary reform motion of 1797 were not all Whigs: they included the evangelicals Sir Richard Hill and Henry Thornton, and a few 'country party' independents, such as Northamptonshire's

---

[51] Brit. Lib., Add. MS. 16,920, fos. 7 ff. For new initiatives in the treatment of the poor, see J. R. Poynter, *Society and Pauperism: English Ideas on Poor Relief, 1795–1834* (London, 1969), ch. 3; more generally, Roger Wells, *Wretched Faces: Famine in Wartime England, 1793–1801* (Gloucester, 1988).

[52] For a recent account that brings this out, see Jennifer Mori, *William Pitt and the French Revolution, 1785–95* (Edinburgh, 1997); also Jennifer Mori, 'Languages of Loyalism: Patriotism, Nationhood and the State in the 1790s', *Eng. Hist. Rev.*, 118 (2003). See also Harling, *Waning of 'Old Corruption'*, 42–5.

[53] Mori, *William Pitt*, 214–15.

[54] E. A. Smith, *Whig Principles and Party Politics: Earl Fitzwilliam and the Whig Party, 1748–1833* (Manchester, 1975), chs. 7–8.

Sir William Dolben (opponent of concessions to dissenters; but promoter of an act to regulate conditions on slave ships).[55]

The royal proclamation against seditious publications of 1792, ensuing prosecutions and 'Treason Trials', and the 'Two Acts' (the Treason and Seditious Meetings Acts) of 1795 were all designed to constrain popular political activity – and probably did have that effect, proving particularly damaging to the democratic political societies which had multiplied in the early 1790s.[56] None the less, the ordinary structures of political life still provided venues in which oppositional voices could be heard – as for example in the 1796 election when key seats were contested by the government's radical critics.[57] There was moreover some form of underground movement (though its exact scale and nature are contested) – manifest in naval mutinies at Spithead and the Nore in 1797, and in the various mainland 'United' groups identifying themselves with the United Irishmen, who helped to fan Irish discontent into rebellion in 1798.[58]

Once peace talks which had been convened in 1796 collapsed, and the French revolutionary regime lost its reforming edge and directed its military ambitions towards Italy and the eastern Mediterranean, Britons in general rallied behind the war effort. Numbers joining home-defence 'Volunteer' forces were considerably higher in 1797–8, in the face of a threatened French invasion, than they had been in 1792–4, when the Volunteers' chief function had been to repress sedition at home. As several historians have recently argued, however, we should not equate the home-defence nationalism that infused this mobilization with conservatism, in any very strong sense of that term. Given that more or less the whole of the adult male population was enrolled in one or another armed body by the century's end indeed, it is implausible that this rallying should have reflected more than important but limited forms of consensus. The volunteer and military association movements were, moreover, in their own way expressions of popular self-assertion. From the point of view of government,

---

[55] W. Cobbett (ed.), *Parliamentary History*, 36 vols. (London, 1806–20), xxxiii, cols. 734–5 for a list of the minority.

[56] Though note Clive Emsley's sceptical comments on this score: Clive Emsley, 'Repression, Terror and the Rule of Law in England during the French Revolution', *Eng. Hist. Rev.*, 100 (1985).

[57] E.g., J. Ann Hone, 'Radicalism in London, 1796–1802: Convergences and Continuities', in John Stevenson (ed.), *London in the Age of Reform* (Oxford, 1977), 83–5; Timothy Jenks, 'Language and Politics in the Westminster Election of 1796', *Hist. Jl*, 44 (2001); C. B. Jewson, *Jacobin City* (Glasgow, 1975), 71–2, and esp. 108–110.

[58] John Dinwiddy raised doubts about E. P. Thompson's account: 'The "Black Lamp" in Yorkshire 1801–2', *Past and Present*, no. 64 (Aug. 1974); Roger Wells, *Insurrection: The British Experience, 1795–1803* (Gloucester, 1983), argues that there was an insurrectionary fringe. The Irish case, which looms large in Wells' account, was explored in Marianne Elliott, *Partners in Revolution: The United Irishmen and France* (New Haven, 1982); David Dickson, Dáire Keogh, and Kevin Whelan (eds.), *The United Irishmen: Republicanism, Radicalism and Rebellion* (Dublin, 1993). The bicentennial of the Irish insurrection has stimulated a flood of publications: for an overview, see Ian McBride, 'Review Article: Reclaiming the Rebellion: 1798 in 1998', *Irish Hist. Studies*, 31 (1999).

though the movement had its uses, it also had disconcertingly democratic aspects. As the threat of invasion receded, the government therefore moved to discourage 1790s-style volunteering, promoting instead semi-professional 'local militias'.[59]

The changing religious climate of the war years had similarly ambiguous political and cultural implications. Outbreaks of revivalism embodied in some part a reaction against revolutionary excess and anarchy. But they also represented an excited, if anxious response to the opening up of new opportunities.[60] The growth of enthusiasm for domestic and foreign missions itself represented a kind of reform movement – one compatible with a variety of more explicitly political views. Domestic missionaries excited some alarm, being seen as bearers of irrational millenarian and democratic ideas. In 1800 and again a decade later there were moves in parliament to impose constraints upon them, though both efforts were repelled, Wilberforce arguing that itinerant preachers were misrepresented, and that they did more good than harm.[61]

In the new century, the political and cultural scene opened up further. Pitt's fall from power in 1801, when the king refused to countenance Catholic Emancipation, released Whig coalitionists to return to the party fold. Pitt's death in 1806 then opened the way for an experiment in power-sharing on terms more generally acceptable among Whigs, in the form of the 'Ministry of All the Talents' of 1806–7.[62] This was the ministry which abolished the slave-trade. The same ministers tried, in a somewhat underconsidered way, to reform the Scottish law courts, and raised hopes of a variety of reforms in Ireland. (Though the Act of Union of 1800 had yoked Ireland more closely to Britain, in the first few years after union this troubled country had received little more than

[59] Whereas Dozier, *For King and Country*, and H. T. Dickinson, 'Popular Conservatism and Militant Loyalism', in Dickinson (ed.), *Britain and the French Revolution*, stressed the conservatism of volunteers, this account has been nuanced by Colley, *Britons*, ch. 7, and still more by J. E. Cookson, *The British Armed Nation, 1793–1815* (London, 1997).

[60] W. R. Ward, *Religion and Society in England, 1790–1850* (London, 1972) stressed the polymorphous promiscuity of religious enthusiasms in this era. For unorthodox popular religion, see also J. F. C. Harrison, *The Second Coming: Popular Millenarianism, 1780–1850* (London, 1979); Deborah Valenze, *Prophetic Sons and Daughters: Female Preaching and Popular Religion in Industrial England* (Princeton, 1985); Iain McCalman, 'New Jerusalems: Prophecy, Dissent and Radical Culture in England, 1786–1830', in Haakonssen (ed.), *Enlightenment and Religion*.

[61] For the take-off of interest in foreign missions, see Roger H. Martin, *Evangelicals United: Ecumenical Stirrings in Pre-Victorian Britain, 1795–1830* (Metuchen, N.J., 1983), chs. 3–4; Elizabeth Elbourne, 'The Foundation of the Church Missionary Society: The Anglican Missionary Impulse', in J. Walsh, C. Haydon, and S. Taylor (eds.), *The Church of England, c. 1689–c. 1833: From Toleration to Tractarianism* (Cambridge, 1993). For domestic evangelism, see Deryck Lovegrove, *Established Church, Sectarian People: Itinerancy and the Transformation of English Dissent, 1780–1830* (Cambridge, 1988), including 124, 133–7 for proposed legislation; Deryck Lovegrove, '"A Set of Men whose Proceedings Threaten no Small Disorder": The Society for Propagating the Gospel at Home, 1798–1808', *Scottish Hist. Rev.*, 79 (2000).

[62] For a recent overview of party-political manoeuvrings in this period, see Turner, *British Politics*, 74–80.

repressive attention.)[63] When the king again refused to countenance Catholic Emancipation, the Talents fell apart, but the 1807 election laid that issue, among others, before the public, pitting 'protestants' against advocates of greater religious toleration. The long-discarded name of 'Tory' gained new currency at this juncture to denote supporters of the status quo in church and state. The complexities of the political scene, however, determined that those who were content to term themselves Tory because of certain of their beliefs did not always fit the profile in all respects; the scene was set for the emergence of those hybrid figures termed 'liberal Tories'.[64]

One underemphasized effect of the reaction that followed the French Revolution was the marginalization of some academics, artists, and professional men thought to be tainted by radical views. In the church and in English universities, some splits appeared even before the Revolution, in response to a liberal campaign to release students and Anglican clerics from the obligation to profess their adherence to (what some saw as) the narrow and illiberal Thirty-Nine Articles traditionally defining the Anglican faith.[65] In the aftermath of the Revolution, political tensions within many corporate institutions affected patterns of patronage, thus defining 'in' and 'out' groups. Partisan strife provided part of the background to the expulsion of the eminent painter James Barry from the Royal Academy. In Edinburgh, young lawyers with Whig sympathies found few clients, and Whig medical men were also marginalized. The effect of such splits and exclusions was often to reinforce the outs' dissident views, and to promote the development of Whig, radical, or reforming 'parties' within these various institutional contexts. In the more open political environment of the early nineteenth century, such out-groups were more easily able to make their presence felt. Young Scots Whig lawyers did so to great effect when they launched the *Edinburgh Review*.[66]

---

[63] For the abolition of the slave-trade, see n. 22 above. For Scottish law reform, see Nicholas Phillipson, *The Scottish Whigs and the Reform of the Court of Session* (Edinburgh, 1990), 21–2; for Ireland, R. B. McDowell, *Public Opinion and Government Policy in Ireland, 1801–46* (London, 1952), 69. Service under this ministry inspired both Samuel Romilly and Henry Parnell to play more active political roles. For their parliamentary careers, see Roland Thorne (ed.), *The History of Parliament, 1790–1820*, 5 vols. (London, 1986), iv, 723–6, v, 36–42.

[64] The fate of the name 'Tory' in the late eighteenth century is surveyed in James J. Sack, *From Jacobite to Conservative: Reaction and Orthodoxy in Britain, c. 1760–1832* (Cambridge, 1993). See also David Wilkinson, 'The Pitt–Portland Coalition of 1794 and the Origins of the Tory Party', *Hist.*, 83 (1998).

[65] John Gascoigne, *Cambridge in the Enlightenment: Science, Religion and Politics from the Restoration to the French Revolution* (Cambridge, 1989), ch. 7, for this campaign and the subsequent 'eclipse of Whig Cambridge'; A. M. C. Waterman, 'A Cambridge "Via Media" in Late Georgian Anglicanism', *Jl Eccl. Hist.*, 42 (1991), 419–36.

[66] For Barry, see Holger Hoock, *'The King's Artists: The Royal Academy of Arts and the Politics of British Culture, 1760–1840* (Oxford, 2003), 189–90 – in the context of a larger discussion of political tensions in the Royal Academy. For Scotland, see Henry Cockburn, *Memorials of his Time* (Edinburgh, 1856), 147–8; Phillipson, *Scottish Whigs*, 21–2; Jacyna, *Philosophic Whigs*.

Around the turn of the century, popular radicalism acquired a series of new leaders, two of whom – William Cobbett and Henry Hunt – had been government supporters in the 1790s. Concern about the impact of continuing war and the condition of the people helped to turn these men into advocates of parliamentary reform. The veteran reformer Major John Cartwright helped them to change the image of the parliamentary-reform cause by criticizing the inadequacy of the government's home-defence preparations. Criticisms of the government's Spanish campaign subsequently provided them with new ammunition. In the 1790s, aspirant reformers of the state had been branded disloyal. This would be harder in the new century, as radicals developed a more widely acceptable case against the conduct and impact of the war.[67]

Calls for reform of government, if not immediately of parliament, were boosted from 1805 by a series of scandals casting doubt on the probity of senior officeholders and the royal family.[68] Pitt's erstwhile Scots lieutenant Henry Dundas, latterly Lord Melville, was impeached for abuses committed at the Admiralty during his time as first lord – the first impeachment of a senior member of government since the 1720s. In 1807, the mistress of the king's brother, the duke of York, was plausibly charged with dabbling in the sale of army commissions. The parliamentary assault on such abuses was conducted by an alliance of evangelicals, radical Whigs, and independent radicals. In the public sphere, indignation raged more widely: the new Tory popular press was loud in its denunciations of royal and aristocratic vice.[69] Coordinating these diverse voices into any kind of effective political force inevitably posed a problem in its own right. Tensions between different camps among reformers were evident in the 1807 Westminster election; in the following years the nature of differences between, and possibility of union among, reformers became a major concern for reforming publicists and strategists.[70]

The British political scene was notably more open – and political debate more lively and contentious – at the end than it had been at the start of the nineteenth century's first decade. Meanwhile, the structures of 'public life', in the

---

[67] The 1980s and 1990s saw some illuminating new work on developments in this period: see esp. Spence, *Birth of Romantic Radicalism*; John Belchem, *'Orator' Hunt: Henry Hunt and English Working-Class Radicalism* (Oxford, 1985); John Belchem and James Epstein, 'The Nineteenth-Century Gentleman Leader Revisited', *Social Hist.*, 22 (1997). See Iain McCalman, *Radical Underworld: Prophets, Revolutionaries and Pornographers in London, 1795–1840* (Oxford, 1993) for radicalism's less respectable face. John Belchem, *Popular Radicalism in Nineteenth-Century Britain* (Basingstoke, 1996), ch. 2, provides an overview.

[68] Spence, *Birth of Romantic Radicalism*, chs. 6–8; Harling, *Waning of 'Old Corruption'*, ch. 4.

[69] Sack, *Jacobite to Conservative*, 131–45.

[70] J. Ann Hone, *For the Cause of Truth: Radicalism in London, 1796–1821* (Oxford, 1982), 159–61; Spence, *Birth of Romantic Radicalism*, ch. 3 for the Westminster election, chs. 4–6; for tensions between different strands of radicalism, Thompson, *Making of the English Working Class*, 665–90. There remains scope for much more work on how 'reforming' groups more broadly defined coped with the twin tasks of developing a common language and maintaining their distinct identities.

broadest sense of that term, were also developing. During the eighteenth century, voluntary initiatives of various kinds, especially in the charitable sphere, had proliferated, and clubs, societies, and associations had become standard features of both the social and the political scene – *inter alia*, providing opportunities for women to engage in a form of public life.[71] Against this background, the late eighteenth and early nineteenth centuries none the less saw important developments. Voluntary initiatives multiplied: the Sunday School movement of the early 1780s saw an unprecedentedly large number of school foundations in a startlingly short space of time.[72] Societies were increasingly commonly welded together into supra-local networks. In the 1790s, political societies' experiments in this vein had been hindered by legislation and persecution. In the next century, however, their philanthropic counterparts enjoyed more lasting success. It became common for London-based parent bodies to be linked with 'auxiliaries' or 'branches', which might channel funds towards the centre. Royal jubilee celebrations of 1809 apparently helped to catalyse these developments. In many localities, it was argued that the occasion should be marked not by military and nationalistic display only, but by new charitable initiatives. The interdenominational Bible Society (founded in 1804) began to spawn provincial auxiliaries in that year, setting an example that others would soon follow.[73]

In the larger cities and towns, much of this welter of activism was initially interdenominational: orthodox Anglican, evangelical, and rational dissenting activists were all involved, sometimes working in collaboration. Yet the trend seems to have been for philanthropy to become more sectarian through time.[74]

---

71 Peter Clark, *British Clubs and Societies, 1580–1800: The Origins of an Associational World* (Oxford, 2000); Donna Andrew, *Philanthropy and Police: London Charity in the Eighteenth Century* (Princeton, 1989).

72 Thomas Laqueur, *Religion and Respectability: Sunday Schools and Working-Class Structure, 1750–1850* (New Haven, 1976); for a contrasting view of the schools' origins and character, see P. B. Cliff, *The Rise and Development of the Sunday School Movement in England, 1780–1980* (Redhill, 1986), chs. 4–5. The diffusion of old and new associational forms in the early nineteenth century has not been systematically studied, but see R. J. Morris, 'Voluntary Societies and British Urban Elites 1780–1850: An Analysis', *Hist. Jl*, 26 (1983); Ford K. Brown, *Fathers of the Victorians: The Age of Wilberforce* (Cambridge, 1961), chs. 7, 9; Frank Prochaska, *Women and Philanthropy in Nineteenth-Century Britain* (Oxford, 1980); for a local case study, John Pickstone, *A History of Hospital Development in Manchester and its Region, 1732–1946* (Manchester, 1985), chs. 1–4.

73 We are indebted to Joshua Civin's research in progress on voluntary association in late eighteenth- and early nineteenth-century Liverpool and Baltimore for some of these insights. For the Bible Society, see Martin, *Evangelicals United*, chs. 5–7, 191 on auxiliaries. See also Arthur Burns, *The Diocesan Revival in the Church of England, c. 1800–1870* (Oxford, 1999), 114–19.

74 Cliff, *Rise and Development of the Sunday School Movement*, 42–3; for a local study of interdenominationalism comprehending even Catholics, see Gerard Conolly, 'The Transubstantiation of Myth: Towards a New Popular History of Nineteenth-Century Catholicism in England', *Jl Eccl. Hist.*, 35 (1984), 78–104. Martin, *Evangelicals United*, chronicles struggles to maintain a pan-evangelical front in the face of sectarian fissiparousness.

This partly reflected long-standing tensions between church and dissent, further exacerbated by the French Revolution, and developments in the theological traditions of the various denominations.[75] But it was also a result of the success of Methodist and evangelical old dissenters' efforts to recruit new converts and solidify existing support. All the figures that can be used to measure denominational growth are problematic, but, for what it is worth, the number of registered dissenting meeting houses more than tripled between 1800 and 1820; growth in numbers of Methodists (the best-documented denomination) was heavily concentrated in the same decades.[76] These developments helped to put churchmen on their mettle. As Arthur Burns shows below, they helped to stimulate various sorts of 'church reform' effort. At the same time, churchmen impressed by the revealed power of associationalism tried to turn this tool to their own ends: in 1810, the century-old Society for Promoting Christian Knowledge (SPCK) was remodelled and endowed with provincial auxiliaries; in 1811, the National Education Society was founded to coordinate nationwide educational effort. The Church Missionary Society (CMS), founded without fanfare in 1799, simultaneously began to throw up provincial offshoots. These efforts provided an important context for certain parliamentary petitioning campaigns of the 1810s which outstripped all previous efforts in terms of the numbers of petitions they elicited: notably the campaign to send Christian missionaries to India of 1813.[77]

Though philanthropy was increasingly coloured by sectarianism, associational life none the less continued to foster complex alliances: bringing together people who were prepared to make common cause, though aware that in other ways they differed. Evangelical–radical alliances especially were a striking recurrent feature of the very late eighteenth and early nineteenth centuries ('radicals' here implying both radical Whigs and more democratic radicals). Common interests in ending corruption and slavery, promoting education, and improving conditions in prisons and lunatic asylums formed bonds – though differences in outlook and style sometimes soured or obstructed

---

[75] General treatments are lacking, but see W. R. Ward, 'The Religion of the People and the Problem of Control, 1790–1830', in G. J. Cuming and D. Baker (eds.), *Popular Belief and Practice* (Cambridge, 1972), 237–57; P. B. Nockles, 'Church Parties in the Pre-Tractarian Church of England, 1750–1833', in Walsh, Haydon, and Taylor (eds.), *Church of England*.

[76] A. D. Gilbert, *Religion and Society in Industrial England: Church, Chapel, and Social Change, 1740–1914* (London, 1976), 23–42. For more extended discussions see Michael R. Watts, *The Dissenters*, vol. ii: *The Expansion of Evangelical Nonconformity, 1791–1859* (Oxford, 1995), ch. 1.

[77] Both the remodelling of the SPCK and National Education Society were the work of the high-church 'Hackney Phalanx': A. B. Webster, *Joshua Watson: The Story of a Layman, 1771–1855* (London, 1954), 34–6, 115. The CMS, by contrast, was primarily (but certainly not exclusively) evangelical: Elbourne, 'Foundation of the Church Missionary Society', 262–3. Note, however, the much more negative assessment of the Anglican contribution to petitioning in Penny Carson, 'The British Raj and the Awakening of the Evangelical Conscience', in Brian Stanley (ed.), *Christian Missions and the Enlightenment* (Grand Rapids, Mich., 2001), 65–7.

cooperation.[78] Among popular reform leaders, Cobbett and Hunt – who were prone to regard parliamentary reform as the prerequisite for all other meaningful reform – were inclined to regard evangelicals with suspicion – at worst, as abettors of oppression, at best, as sponsors of diversionary effort. Yet their antipathy has too often coloured our understanding of a considerably more complex relationship.[79]

Within parliament, evangelical and radical – including Whig-radical – MPs were probably more likely than the average MP to have links with vigorous extra-parliamentary associations, or, more loosely, the activist milieux within which much associational activity was generated. Thus changes in the broader context of public life worked through to reshape the nature of parliamentary politics. As out-of-doors opinion and organization developed and became more active and demanding across a variety of fronts, increasingly such MPs found themselves cast as mediators between public opinion and parliament. In this context there developed within parliament a loose-knit reforming phalanx, concerned to show up the government's deficiencies in morals and principles, but also having a rich and complex constructive agenda.[80] It is possible to cite antecedents for this development, perhaps most notably among the 'country party' MPs of the late seventeenth and early eighteenth centuries; to a lesser extent, among the 'patriots' of the mid-eighteenth century. These earlier reformers had made some use of devices favoured by their early nineteenth-century counterparts: petitioning campaigns and parliamentary inquiries. But early nineteenth-century campaigners employed petitioning campaigns for a wider range of purposes than their predecessors, and learnt to employ select-committee inquiries not only to publicize their concerns, but also to give extra-parliamentary activists a platform.[81]

---

[78] For cooperation, see Richard R. Follett, *Evangelicalism, Penal Theory and the Politics of Penal Law Reform in England, 1808–30* (Basingstoke, 2001), 76–80; Hone, *For the Cause of Truth*, 241–2. Some tensions are noted by M. J. D. Roberts, 'Reshaping the Gift Relationship: The London Mendicity Society and the Repression of Begging in England, 1818–69', *Internat. Rev. Social Hist.*, 36 (1991), 212.

[79] William H. Wickwar, *The Struggle for the Freedom of the Press, 1819–1832* (London, 1928), 78–84. The Saints' willingness to support many forms of repressive effort undoubtedly contributed to this hostility. Betty Fladeland, *Abolitionists and Working-Class Problems in the Age of Industrialization* (London, 1984), for an attempt to put the best face on the relationship.

[80] There is no study for this period comparable to Miles Taylor, *The Decline of British Radicalism, 1847–60* (Oxford, 1995), though some light is shed by Dean Rapp, 'The Left-Wing Whigs: Whitbread, the Mountain and Reform, 1809–15', *Jl Brit. Studies*, 21 (1982).

[81] David Hayton, 'Moral Reform and Country Politics in the Late Seventeenth-Century House of Commons', *Past and Present*, no. 128 (Aug. 1990); Andrew Hanham, 'Whig Opposition to Sir Robert Walpole in the House of Commons, 1722–34' (University of Leicester Ph.D. thesis, 1992); Bob Harris, *Politics and the Nation: Britain in the Mid-Eighteenth-Century* (Oxford, 2002). Peter Jupp surveys various aspects of the workings of parliament and its relation to government and public in *British Politics on the Eve of Reform: The Duke of Wellington's Administration, 1828–30* (Basingstoke, 1998), chs. 5–9. Peter Fraser, 'Public Petitioning and Parliament before 1832', *Hist.*, 46 (1961) and Colin Leys, 'Petitioning in the Nineteenth and Twentieth Centuries', *Political Studies*, 3 (1955), survey trends.

The state of the economy, and the character of economic development, were frequently topics of discussion in these years. Increasingly, proponents of reform found themselves forced to engage with them: to form some understanding of the relationship between Britain's institutions and laws and her socio-economic state. Debate partly revolved around the economic impact of war: thus, what were the implications of high taxation, the abandonment of the gold standard in 1797, the shifting of commerce into new channels, and new patterns of wartime demand?[82] There had for some decades been concern about the apparent growth of poverty, as evidenced by the upwards trend of poor-relief expenditure. Bad harvests and exceptionally high prices in 1795 and 1800–1 emphasized the need for vigorous and imaginative approaches to relief. Samuel Whitbread's Poor Bill of 1807 helped to focus discussion, attracting critical responses from, among others, Jeremy Bentham and Thomas Malthus. Malthus' argument that poor relief in practice made matters worse by encouraging the poor to reproduce gained in notoriety in consequence.[83]

There were also believed to be various structural economic changes in process. Smaller farms were thought to be giving way to larger, while the conditions of agricultural labourers and their families deteriorated.[84] The spread – from the 1760s – of new kinds of machinery, especially spinning machinery, attracted much attention. Attacks on machines became a common feature of labour protest – though the machines attacked were not in all cases new or threatening in themselves; the object might rather be to dramatize protest and exert pressure. Thus, when Nottinghamshire 'Luddites' attacked stocking-knitting frames in 1811–12, they did so essentially as a device in a campaign over working conditions.[85] Workers' organizations spread beyond their early strongholds in some metropolitan trades and in relatively proletarianized west country industry, becoming probably more common, certainly more visible in the midlands and north too. In both new and traditional sectors, workers protested against

---

[82] J. E. Cookson, *The Friends of Peace: Anti-War Liberalism in England, 1793–1815* (Cambridge, 1982), ch. 3.

[83] Poynter, *Society and Pauperism*, 207–22.

[84] For contemporary views, see, e.g., Edward Wilson, *Observations on the Present State of the Poor* (Reading, 1795); *Address and Report on the Enquiry into the General State of the Poor, Instituted by Order of . . . the County of Hampshire*, 2nd edn (Winchester, 1795). K. D. M. Snell, *Annals of the Labouring Poor: Social Change and Agrarian England, 1660–1900* (Cambridge, 1985), attempts to document change. See Ian Dyck, *William Cobbett and Rural Popular Culture* (Cambridge, 1992), for Cobbett's perceptions of this, esp. 29–33 for his first formative encounter with these issues.

[85] A. Charlesworth *et al.*, *An Atlas of Industrial Protest in Britain, 1750–1990* (Basingstoke, 1996), 7–46; Adrian Randall, *Before the Luddites: Custom, Community and Machinery in the English Woollen Industry, 1776–1809* (Cambridge, 1991), provides a detailed case study. For varying assessments of the Luddites, see Thompson, *Making of the English Working Class*, ch. 14; M. I. Thomis, *The Luddites: Machine-Breaking in Regency England* (Newton Abbot, 1970); J. Dinwiddy, 'Luddism and Politics in Northern Counties', in Dinwiddy (ed.), *Radicalism and Reform*.

the destructive effects of 'competition', including notably the reorganization of production to facilitate the employment of large numbers of cheap and relatively unskilled child or adolescent workers.[86] The early nineteenth century saw industrialists, workers, and philanthropists locked in debate about the best way forwards: whether by the maintenance and extension of increasingly idealized Elizabethan labour codes, or by freeing trade and industry from legal constraint. The first Factory Act, to protect the 'health and morals' of apprentices in cotton and other factories, passed in 1802, but a campaign by Yorkshire shearmen to bolster their position with protective legislation in the same decade failed to convince MPs, and in 1812–13, despite the best efforts of workers' representatives, the apprenticeship clauses of the Elizabethan Statute of Artificers were repealed.[87]

Debates over these matters stood in a complex relation to other kinds of reform debate. Distressed workers, small masters, and farmers and their sympathizers did not necessarily see parliamentary reform as a solution or part of a solution to their problems – but might do so. Conversely, some who opposed parliamentary regulation supported, or were prepared to consider supporting, parliamentary and other varieties of institutional reform. Critics of the status quo often agreed in denouncing an idle and greedy class of sinecurists, fundholders, war profiteers, and others, arguing that they must be cut down to size in some way if the nation as a whole was to flourish. But there was no consensus as to precisely what laws and policies should frame the new order.[88]

The years 1811–12 saw a worrying combination of high food prices and economic recession – blameable in part on a loss of markets associated with a broadening of the war. In these years Major Cartwright toured the midlands and north, raising popular support for the parliamentary-reform cause in industrial regions. At the same time, industrialists and men of commerce corresponded, held meetings, lobbied, and petitioned about the various adverse effects of

[86] John Rule, *The Experience of Labour in Eighteenth-Century Industry* (London, 1981), chs. 6–7; John Rule, *The Labouring Classes in Early Industrial England, 1750–1850* (Harlow, 1986), ch. 11; John Rule (ed.), *British Trade Unionism, 1750–1850: The Formative Years* (Harlow, 1988).

[87] Joanna Innes, 'Origins of the Factory Acts: The Health and Morals of Apprentices Act 1802', in N. Landau (ed.), *Law, Crime and English Society, 1660–1830* (Cambridge, 2002); John Smail, 'New Languages for Capital and Labour: The Transformation of Discourse in the Early Years of the Industrial Revolution', *Social Hist.*, 12 (1987); see subsequent exchange between Randall and Smail in *Social Hist.*, 15–16 (1991–2); Rule, *Experience of Labour*, 114–19; T. K. Derry, 'The Repeal of the Apprenticeship Clauses of the Statute of Artificers', *Econ. Hist. Rev.*, 3 (1931–2); I. J. Prothero, *Artisans and Politics in Early Nineteenth-Century London: John Gast and his Times* (Folkestone, 1979), ch. 3; Marc W. Steinberg, *Fighting Words: Working-Class Formation, Collective Action and Discourse in Early Nineteenth-Century England* (Ithaca, 1999).

[88] The fight over the repeal of the Statute of Artificers thus saw Henry Brougham, Samuel Romilly, and Francis Place advising the repealers; John Doherty and other working-class reformers opposing repeal: Prothero, *Artisans and Politics*, 60.

policy on the economy, as they saw them. The continuation and expansion of the war, the proposal to return to the gold standard at a rate likely to promote economic contraction, and the continuation of the East India Company's monopoly (its charter came up for renewal in 1813) were all targets of criticism.[89] Critics' stress on the adverse impact of the institutional order and public policy on economy and society set the scene for some central elements of post-war debate.

IV

The major wars of the eighteenth century had all been followed by periods of social and economic strain and readjustment, associated with the demobilization of armed forces and the shift from a war- to a peacetime economy. Taxation always mounted during the course of a war, and was not rapidly reduced at the war's end. Resulting problems fuelled domestic policy debate, which was facilitated by the fall-off in war-related business, leaving ministers and parliamentarians more time and energy for domestic affairs.[90]

The post-Waterloo years in many ways conformed to this pattern. But they also had distinctive features. Agricultural prices and profits had soared during the war, as British agriculture strove to meet the demands of an exceptionally rapidly growing population. When the ending of the war opened up new sources of supply, this artificial prosperity ended. Protective tariffs were meant to blunt the impact of this shift, but ministers did not suppose that they could, and did not intend that they should, cancel it out. A somewhat analogous crisis hit Britain's industrial economy, caught up as it was in a process of technological change that was sometimes painful. Exposed to more foreign competition, less competitive industrial regions went into decline. The nascent Irish cotton industry was among the casualties. Debate about the role government might appropriately play in promoting economic growth and alleviating poverty sharpened.[91]

High post-war crime and vagrancy rates prompted a characteristic wave of concern about moral values and social institutions. But debate about these issues now took place against the backdrop of the dense mesh of philanthropic initiative and association that we have described. A variety of extra-parliamentary

---

[89] Dinwiddy, 'Luddism and Politics'; Cookson, *Friends of Peace*, chs. 8–9.

[90] See Innes, 'Politics and Morals', 62–3, for the impact of the end of the American War. There has been some debate about exactly why crime prosecutions fell off in wartime and rose with peace. For the latest assessment, see Peter King, *Crime, Justice and Discretion in England, 1740–1820* (Oxford, 2000), 153–68.

[91] Boyd Hilton, *Corn, Cash, Commerce: The Economic Policies of the Tory Governments, 1815–30* (Oxford, 1977), chs. 1–3. For selective deindustrialization, see Sidney Pollard, *Peaceful Conquest: The Industrialization of Europe, 1760–1970* (Oxford, 1981), 21–3.

reforming lobbies had nostrums to peddle: a reduction in the number of death sentences; improvements in prison discipline; more welfare casework; greater discrimination in the payment of poor relief; education, education, education! Such publicly peddled strategies were, moreover, only the tip of the iceberg: much other local and judicial experimentation went on unheralded and unremembered.[92]

Against this background of economic and social anxiety, a variety of intellectual and cultural struggles were played out. A new high-cultural front, nascent in the later years of the war, came to flower in the post-war years. A younger generation of critics – notably Leigh Hunt and William Hazlitt – who were broadly sympathetic to political reform also undertook to question various pretenders to cultural authority. Themselves prepared to acknowledge literary genius even when (as they saw it) errant in its politics (as in the case of the turncoats William Wordsworth and Samuel Taylor Coleridge), they charged conservative critics with being unwilling similarly to recognize talent outside their own camp. They championed the operas of Mozart, whose librettos were seen by some as tendentiously anti-aristocratic, and turned a critical eye on the effects of privilege upon the patent theatres and the Royal Academy. More or less tightly linked to their circle were poets such as Lord Byron, Tom Moore, and Percy Bysshe Shelley: all open to projects of institutional reform, but more immediately engaged in promoting cultural regeneration. Contemporary accounts of the audiences at the various lecture series on English literature that Hazlitt delivered in the pubs and 'Institutions' on the burgeoning extra-mural educational circuit suggest that he was especially popular among those who shared his political and policy commitments: among dissenters and evangelical

---

[92] See, thus, M. J. D. Roberts, 'Public and Private in Early Nineteenth-Century London: The Vagrant Act of 1822 and its Enforcement', *Social Hist.*, 13 (1988); Roberts, 'Reshaping the Gift Relationship'; Ivy Pinchbeck and Margaret Hewitt, *Children in English Society*, 2 vols. (London, 1973), ii, ch. 16; Follett, *Evangelicalism, Penal Theory*, chs. 7–8; Robin Evans, *The Fabrication of Virtue: English Prison Architecture, 1750–1840* (Cambridge, 1982), ch. 6; H. J. Burgess, *Enterprise in Education: The Story of the Work of the Established Church in the Education of the People prior to 1830* (London, 1958); Henry Binns, *A Century of Education: Being the Centenary History of the British and Foreign Schools Society, 1808–1908* (London, 1908). Efforts to build more churches, sanctioned by legislation in 1818, also had an important voluntarist component: a combination of evangelicals and high churchmen had pressed the cause on the prime minister, and themselves founded an Incorporated Church Building Society; legislation provided for funding by a mixture of central grants, local rates, and subscription: Webster, *Joshua Watson*, ch. 5; T. V. Parry, 'The Incorporated Church Building Society, 1818–51', (University of Oxford M.Litt. thesis, 1984). Alongside such relatively high-profile reform initiatives there was much unheralded local experimentation: see for this, e.g., David Eastwood, *Governing Rural England: Tradition and Transformation in Local Government, 1780–1840* (Oxford, 1994); Peter King, *Crime and the Law in the Age of Reform, 1750–1850: Remaking Justice from the Margins* (Cambridge, forthcoming); Burns, *Diocesan Revival*, esp. chs. 1–6.

Anglicans. But his audience also contained self-improving businessmen and tradesmen, some of whom resented his stream of political asides.[93]

By comparison with the pre-war scene, the post-war landscape appears heavily ideological. People did not simply hold different views; they subscribed to widely differing philosophies, theologies, even cosmologies. Late Enlightenment social and political theorizing had not come to an end with the Revolution, even if the 'age of Enlightenment' has conventionally been held to terminate at that point. Theories both developed and diversified. Eighteenth-century social theorizing had often been loosely set within a framework of natural religion, but the late eighteenth century saw, initially in France, the development of some provocatively materialistic and mechanistic social theories. This tradition was carried forward in Britain by the 'utilitarians'. By contrast, many other nineteenth-century theorists strove to meld their theories with more orthodox religion.[94] A series of gurus emerged, each with their own view of man and society: thus William Godwin, Jeremy Bentham, Thomas Chalmers, Robert Owen, Samuel Taylor Coleridge, Edward Irving, and later Thomas Carlyle. Young men venturing out beyond the ambit of schoolmaster and don felt the pull of these competing world-views, and might feel themselves forced to take sides in the struggle for cultural authority.[95]

---

[93] For a recent account of the circle, see Jeffrey N. Cox, *Poetry and Politics in the Cockney School: Keats, Shelley, Hunt, and their Circle* (Cambridge, 1998). See also Kevin Gilmartin, *Print Politics: The Press and Radical Opposition in Early Nineteenth-Century England* (Cambridge, 1996), esp. chs. 5–6; Philip Harling, 'Leigh Hunt's "Examiner" and the Language of Patriotism', *Eng. Hist. Rev.*, 111 (1996); Philip Harling, 'William Hazlitt and Radical Journalism', *Romanticism*, 3 (1997); Peter Funnell, 'William Hazlitt, Prince Hoare and the Institutionalization of the British Art World', in Brian Allen (ed.), *Towards a Modern Art World: Art in Britain, c. 1715–80* (New Haven, 1995); Jane Moody, *Illegitimate Theatre in London, 1770–1840* (Cambridge, 2001), 33–4, 41, but see also 173–7. For Hazlitt's lecture audience, see Catherine Macdonald Maclean, *Born under Saturn: A Biography of William Hazlitt* (London, 1943), 371–3.

[94] Elie Halévy, *The Growth of Philosophic Radicalism*, 2nd edn with corrections (London, 1972), remains the classic account. W. E. S. Thomas, *The Philosophic Radicals: Nine Studies in Theory and Practice, 1817–1841* (Oxford, 1979), places affiliates in context and stresses the diversity of their concerns. Boyd Hilton, *The Age of Atonement: The Influence of Evangelicalism on Social and Economic Thought, 1795–1865* (Oxford, 1988), for the theological colouring of much thought. See A. M. C. Waterman, 'The Ideological Alliance of Political Economy and Christian Theology, 1798–1833', *Jl Eccl. Hist.*, 34 (1983); A. M. C. Waterman, *Revolution, Economics and Religion: Christian Political Economy, 1798–1833* (Cambridge, 1991), esp. ch. 4, for concern for theological orthodoxy in this context. The rise of the heavyweight periodical press undoubtedly helped to make both public life more intellectual and intellectual life more contentious: thus not merely the major review journals – *Edinburgh, Quarterly, Westminster* – but also the more self-consciously religious press: the *British Critic, Christian Observer*, and *Record*, etc.

[95] All these men have attracted biographers, some many biographers. Accounts by historians include Thomas, *Philosophic Radicals*, ch. 1: 'Bentham and his Circle'; Stewart J. Brown, *Thomas Chalmers and the Godly Commonwealth in Scotland* (Oxford, 1992); J. F. C. Harrison, *Robert Owen and the Owenites in England and America* (London, 1969); Sheridan Gilley, 'Edward Irving: Prophet of the Millennium', in Jane Garnett and H. C. G. Matthew (eds.),

(cont. on p. 31)

Political economy, promulgated in a variety of forms, first really made its mark as a form of intellectual discourse in these years, shaping the agendas of tracts and pamphlets, and supplying content for extra-mural lectures.[96] It was possible to subscribe to some of the doctrines of political economy and yet to retain faith in certain institutional reforms as ways of improving man's lot on earth: Bentham and his utilitarian disciples were among those who did this. But the belief that society and economy had their own laws, which human beings ignored at their peril, at least as often promoted scepticism about the potential of political action to achieve beneficial and enduring change. Reform of the institutional order so as to permit the free operation of natural laws might of course be advocated – though fear of the unsettling effect of unwelcome change encouraged caution in proceeding even down this path. Thus even those such as Malthus who believed that the poor laws did more harm than good often shied away from recommending their immediate abolition.[97]

(cont.)

Revival and Religion since 1700: Essays for John Walsh (London, 1993). For John Stuart Mill's perceptions of this scene, see his *Autobiography* (London, 1873), 98–114, 123–9; John Stuart Mill, 'The Spirit of the Age' (originally pubd. in *The Examiner*, 1831), repr. in John Stuart Mill, *Essays on Politics and Culture*, ed. G. Himmelfarb (Garden City, N.Y., 1963), esp. 3–4.

[96] This is not, of course, to suggest that it had earlier had no influence: see R. C. Teichgraber III, '"Less Abused than I had Reason to Expect": The Reception of *The Wealth of Nations* in Britain, 1776–90', *Hist. Jl*, 30 (1987). Notable publications of these years included T. R. Malthus, *An Essay on the Principle of Population*, 5th edn with additions (London, 1817); T. R. Malthus, *Principles of Political Economy Considered with a View to their Practical Application* (London, 1820); David Ricardo, *On the Principles of Political Economy and Taxation* (London, 1817); and, at a more popular level, [Jane] 'Mrs' Marcet, *Conversations on Political Economy* (London, 1817). For the take-up of political economy by ministers and MPs, see Hilton, *Corn, Cash, Commerce*; Barry Gordon, *Political Economy in Parliament, 1819–23* (London, 1976). Anna Gambles, *Protection and Politics: Conservative Economic Discourse, 1815–52* (Woodbridge, 1999) draws on parliamentary debates, pamphlets, and the press. Hilton, *Age of Atonement*, argues that as popularized, political economy was often embedded in a theological matrix, and derived its compelling power primarily from that. For its presentation and reworking in mechanics' institutes, see A. Tyrrell, 'Political Economy, Whiggism and the Education of Working Class Adults in Scotland, 1817–40', *Scottish Hist. Rev.*, 48 (1969); Gregory Claeys, 'Political Economy and Popular Education: Thomas Hodgskin and the London Mechanics Institute, 1823–8', in Michael T. Davis (ed.), *Radicalism and Revolution in Britain, 1775–1848* (Basingstoke, 2000). Maxine Berg, *The Machinery Question and the Making of Political Economy, 1815–48* (Cambridge, 1982), charts debate carried out in diverse arenas.

[97] For 'free-trade radicalism', see Ronald K. Huch and Paul R. Ziegler, *Joseph Hume, the People's MP* (Philadelphia, 1985), chs. 3–4. Historians of government growth in the 1960s and 1970s struggled with what could be portrayed as a paradox: that proponents of laissez-faire economics none the less also promoted certain forms of 'state intervention': see A. J. Taylor, *Laissez-Faire and State Intervention in Nineteenth-Century Britain* (London, 1972); Gillian Sutherland (ed.), *Studies in the Growth of Nineteenth-Century Government* (London, 1972). Boyd Hilton for his part hypothesizes that among evangelicals anti-interventionist post-millennialists co-existed with interventionist pre-millennialists (*Age of Atonement*, esp. 7–16), though his attempt to link theology with social theory in this way has not convinced all his readers: see, e.g., Schlossberg, *Silent Revolution*, 360 n. 38; Waterman, *Christian Political Economy*, 243–6. For Malthus, see Poynter, *Society and Pauperism*, chs. 6–8.

Some of the most notable post-war developments took place in the arena of popular politics. There were changes in the vigour and scale of popular political publishing. In 1816, William Cobbett had pioneered the single-sheet political weekly. Escaping newspaper tax, such weeklies could sell for as little as twopence, even a penny. Cheap radical publications proliferated. The melding of socio-economic with political discontent that had been a feature of the later war years continued apace, providing a source of energy in difficult post-war circumstances. Yet the popular reform movement was not merely a vehicle for these discontents. It was equally a movement for civil and political rights, including freedom of the press and freedom of thought. Ideas about the nature of these rights changed and developed. A few called for votes for women: John Wade's *Gorgon* thus claimed political rights 'for the whole biped race', in so far as they were accountable before law for their actions. Though few women pushed this claim, they did assume a higher public profile, as associations of 'Female Reformers' appeared at public gatherings. There was a revival of interest in Paine and his writings, including his freethinking *Age of Reason*.[98]

The popular arena was also increasingly peopled with rival gurus, and complicated by the pull of competing ideologies. Cobbett and Hunt each had a national following, but their appeal was not identical. The burgeoning of cheap political publications allowed plebeian radicals to refine their sense of their political identities in terms of their reading preferences: thus Richard Carlile later recorded that when T. J. Wooler's *Black Dwarf* appeared in 1817 he found it 'much more to my taste than Mr Cobbett's *Registers*'. Carlile promoted the revival of interest in Paine because he found Paine's writings an aid to systematic and constructive thought. Monarchist and republican, Christian and free-thinking, rights-based and utilitarian, interventionist, laissez-faire, and proto-socialist ideas competed and co-existed. This ferment of ideas helped to fuel the

---

[98] Jonathan Fulcher, 'The English People and their Constitution after Waterloo: Parliamentary Reform, 1815–17', in James Vernon (ed.), *Rereading the Constitution: New Narratives in the Political History of England's Long Nineteenth Century* (Cambridge, 1996), stresses the post-war political context. See also Gilmartin, *Print Politics*. Wickwar, *Struggle for the Freedom of the Press*, is concerned both with actual patterns of publishing and with arguments about the freedom of the press. For the quotation from Wade, see *ibid.*, 61. For women, see Anna Clark, *The Struggle for the Breeches: Gender and the Making of the English Working Class* (London, 1995). E. P. Thompson, in his classic *Making of the English Working Class*, strove to relate popular political culture to its social and economic context. Though some subsequent studies have developed that vein – thus Clive Behagg, *Politics and Production in the Early Nineteenth Century* (London, 1990); Prothero, *Artisans and Politics*; Dyck, *William Cobbett* – others have diverged: political historiography increasingly stresses the constitutionalist and 'rights' content of popular political discourse (equally acknowledged by Thompson); labour history (in so far as it is still written) is rooted in the careful reconstruction of working environments, with politics playing at most a marginal role. (Thus the various contributors to Vernon, *Rereading the Constitution*, on the one hand, Rule, *British Trade Unionism*, on the other.)

popular hunger for 'knowledge', which would become increasingly insistent over the next decade.[99]

The term 'radical reform' and 'radical reformer' were increasingly bandied about in these years, sometimes abbreviated to 'radical'. The term connoted a plebeian reformer, *or* a proponent of ambitious democratizing schemes, *or* a materialist utilitarian rationalist: someone who aligned themselves with the intellectual legacy of the radical Enlightenment.[100] Popular radicalism had its gentry and middle-class sponsors: Cartwright, Cobbett, Hunt, Bentham. But it also threw up leaders from the ranks: men like Francis Place, the radical tailor, or John Gast, the shipwrights' leader. Such men also operated on the margins of the formal political scene; helping to organize elections, and making appearances before parliamentary committees. (Place helped amass evidence for a committee on lunatic asylums, and gave evidence to – among others – committees on the tailoring trade, mendicity, education, and the Combination Acts.)[101]

The growing scale and visibility of the popular reform movement, the increased vigour of radical rhetoric (whether in rationalist, revolutionary, or scoffing mode), and the association of radical reformism with worker protest, were, in combination, an energizing force. They stimulated many to think harder about the pros and cons of parliamentary reform – not least, for its possible use as prophylactic, as alternative to revolution.[102] The variety of popular concerns also helped to broaden conceptions of what was or might be entailed by 'reform'. To the young Shelley, 'Right government being an institution for the purpose of securing such a moderate degree of happiness to men as being experimentally practicable', and the miserable state of the labouring poor showing that that government was not currently right, the object of reform had

---

[99] For Carlile, see Wickwar, *Struggle for the Freedom of the Press*, and more fully Joel Wiener, *Radicalism and Freethought in Nineteenth-Century Britain: The Life of Richard Carlile* (Westport, Conn., 1983). For insight into the diversity of radical popular culture in these years, see Thompson, *Making of the English Working Class*, ch. 16; McCalman, *Radical Underworld*, chs. 5–8. James Epstein, *Radical Expression: Political Language, Ritual and Symbol in England, 1790–1850* (New York, 1994), 10, argues that we should not assume differences among leaders were straightforwardly mirrored among their followings: admiration for a bold leader did not always imply admiration for, or even detailed knowledge of, the intricacies of his views. For hunger for knowledge, see J. F. C. Harrison, *Learning and Living 1790–1960: A Study in the History of the Adult Education Movement* (London, 1961), ch. 2; see also the literature on mechanics' institutes, below n. 121.

[100] J. C. D. Clark, 'Religion and the Origins of Radicalism in Nineteenth-Century Britain', in Glenn Burgess and Matthew Festenstein (eds.), *English Radicalism, 1550–1850* (forthcoming) – following the lead of John Galt's novel *The Radical* (1832) – equates 'radicalism' with utilitarianism, materialism, and atheism. But contemporaries used the term more variously.

[101] For Place, see Dudley Miles, *Francis Place, 1771–1834: The Life of a Remarkable Radical* (Brighton, 1988). For Gast, see Prothero, *Artisans and Politics*.

[102] E. A. Wasson, 'The Great Whigs and Parliamentary Reform, 1809–30', *Jl Brit. Studies*, 24 (1985), 44–6.

to be to deliver more happiness, for example by abridging working hours (he thought this might be achieved indirectly through such relatively conventional radical nostrums as paying off the national debt; disbanding the standing army; abolishing sinecures; abolishing tithes; making all religions equal; and making justice cheap, certain, and speedy).[103]

Of course, these developments also caused much alarm.[104] Liverpool's government was prepared, under pressure, to countenance certain parts of the reform programme. Indeed, in the aftermath of war, some slimming down of government and cutting back of expenditure was not only possible, but prudent: a matter of good husbandry. Some common ground could moreover be found in reprobating other nations' persistence in slave-trading, and in trying to promote education. Yet this certainly did not entail – indeed, moral-reform sentiment strongly militated against – condoning threatening, arguably seditious, language and conduct. Accordingly, ministers ushered repressive legislation through parliament, collected reports on popular political activity, launched libel prosecutions, and encouraged the deployment of troops or non-professional armed forces to contain trouble.[105] There may, as some of their opponents suggested, have been an element of tactical calculation in all this: by playing up the extent of the threat, they may have hoped to rally unconnected MPs around them, even to split more conservative from more radical Whigs, as Pitt had succeeded in doing in the early 1790s.[106]

In practice, repression sometimes backfired. The exposure of an agent provocateur, 'Oliver the Spy', in 1817 raised doubts about the plausibility of some of the government's fears; some libel trials ended with embarrassing acquittals.[107] The government's endorsement of Manchester magistrates' brutal handling of the pro-reform crowd who assembled at St Peter's Fields in the summer of 1819, and the dismissal of the Whig Earl Fitzwilliam from his lord lieutenancy when he offered criticism, gave the Whigs a stick to beat them with – indeed,

---

[103] Percy Bysshe Shelley, *A Philosophical View of Reform*, ed. T. W. Rolleson (London, 1920), 38–66.

[104] Sack, *Jacobite to Conservative*, 150–2, suggests that they also stimulated the emergence of resolute opposition to reform in a Tory popular press that had not previously closed the door on all such schemes.

[105] For a general overview of the policies of Liverpool's post-war administration, see J. E. Cookson, *Lord Liverpool's Administration: The Crucial Years, 1815–22* (Edinburgh, 1975). Particular policies are explored by Harling, *Waning of 'Old Corruption'*, ch. 5; Hilton, *Corn, Cash, Commerce*, chs. 1–5; Wickwar, *Struggle for the Freedom of the Press.*

[106] *Thomas Creevey's Papers, 1793–1838*, ed. John Gore (Harmondsworth, 1985), 157–9.

[107] For Oliver, see Thompson, *Making of the English Working Class*, 711–36; Wickwar, *Struggle for the Freedom of the Press*, 58–9. Michael Lobban, 'From Seditious Libel to Unlawful Assembly: Peterloo and the Changing Face of Political Crime, c. 1770–1820', *Oxford Jl Legal Studies*, 10 (1990), notes that given the demonstrated limits of libel law, the courts began developing an alternative offence of unlawful assembly – a particularly useful tool in the age of the 'mass platform'.

more than that, offended their sense of how governments needed to operate in order to maintain popular support. Some up-and-coming young Whigs, heirs to the great Whig titles, were particularly dismayed: for them, this was a formative experience.[108] 'Peterloo' aroused widespread concern and reinforced other anxieties, too: thus, the willingness of some prominent clergy to countenance the slaughter of innocents fuelled anger against a clerical establishment apparently more concerned to protect the political status quo than to uphold basic Christian values.[109]

In 1820 diverse anti-government forces, from Whig to popular radical, rather improbably came together to protest against the king's high-handed treatment of his estranged and putatively adulterous queen.[110] In the next few years, continuing depression in agriculture at a time of industrial and commercial recovery led the rural propertied to protest that government was also failing them; some in consequence became more sympathetic to the case for constitutional change. Whig grandees addressed county meetings called to petition for parliamentary reform. The diehard Tory J. W. Croker wrote that 'at tables where ten years ago you would no more have heard reform advocated than treason, you will now find half the company reformers'. In 1822, Lord John Russell introduced into the Commons a relatively modest reform motion, which would have deprived the smallest hundred boroughs of seats, and redistributed these among counties and larger towns. Though this was defeated, it was the first such measure to be proposed by a leading political figure in over twenty years, and as such was a straw in the wind.[111]

V

A sense of incipient crisis had overhung the immediate post-war years. In the 1820s, this diminished, although it never disappeared. In Europe, it looked as if the post-war settlement might hold. In Britain, the high tide of industrial and political working-class protest ebbed.

Political dividing lines blurred. The notion that, in 1822, Liverpool's administration abruptly entered a 'liberal Tory' phase, thanks especially to a series of new ministerial appointments, has been criticized. It has been argued that this administration had from its early years a constructive and not just a repressive programme: Wilberforce noted a change in the tone of debate, a lessening

---

[108] Wasson, 'Great Whigs', 49.

[109] G. F. A. Best, *Temporal Pillars: Queen Anne's Bounty, the Ecclesiastical Commissioners and the Church of England* (Cambridge, 1964), 245–50; Paul Pickering, *Chartism and the Chartists in Manchester and Salford* (Basingstoke, 1995), 112–13.

[110] The episode has recently attracted much attention. See Nicholas Rogers, *Crowds, Culture and Politics in Georgian Britain* (Oxford, 1998), ch. 8, and references to other accounts there.

[111] Hilton, *Corn, Cash, Commerce*, chs. 4–5; Cannon, *Parliamentary Reform*, ch. 8, esp. 183–4.

of blanket resistance to 'innovation', as early as 1819; in the case of trade, important early liberalizing measures were implemented between 1820 and 1823. Liverpool's aim in making the new appointments, moreover, was not to change policy, but simply to strengthen government debating talent in the lower house.[112]

An impression was made in 1823, none the less, when the programme of fiscal rationalization came to fruition: British tariffs were streamlined and consolidated (the number of finance bills introduced each session dropped precipitately thereafter); British and Irish duties were largely brought into line. Thereafter excise duties were reduced; treaties providing for bilateral tariff reductions encouraged, and the Navigation Laws liberalized. The recovery of industry and commerce had wider causes, but the government gained some credit for it.[113] With this recovery, moreover, came some diminution of popular protest; giving the government less reason to constrain civil liberties.

As for the two highest-profile new appointees: George Canning as foreign secretary may not have had very different intentions from his predecessor Castlereagh, but he operated in a different climate. As the European revolutionary wave of 1820 sputtered out, there was less reason for the powers of the 'Holy Alliance' to exert themselves to uphold the cause of monarchy and religion. Canning also gained reflected glory from an indirect consequence of the Spanish troubles of 1820: the emergence of independent Latin American states – increasingly valued as trading partners. Interventions to defend the independence of Portugal on the death of its king in 1826, and to keep the Ottoman fleet away from Greece in 1827, sealed his reputation. Canning genuinely differed from Castlereagh in his willingness to publicize his policies, both inside and outside parliament. He also had a relatively liberal record on other issues, being a long-term supporter of antislavery endeavour, a shift from capital to reformative punishment, and Catholic Emancipation. He had, however, been marked for life by his youthful experience of counter-revolutionary rallying in the 1790s, and had no time for the slogan 'reform'.[114] Peel for his part was somewhat readier to use the language of reform: perhaps because he had served important apprentice years as Irish secretary. British officials tended to diagnose Irish government as needing reform. As home secretary, Peel laboured to bring to fruition several long-mooted reform projects, in courts, penal laws, penal institutions, and police – if only to

---

[112] Cookson, *Lord Liverpool's Administration*, 395–8; Boyd Hilton, 'The Political Arts of Lord Liverpool', *Trans. Royal Hist. Soc.*, 5th ser., 38 (1988), suggests that there was a changing balance between competing attitudes. For Wilberforce, see Follett, *Evangelicalism, Penal Theory*, 159.

[113] Hilton, *Corn, Cash, Commerce*, ch. 6.

[114] Jonathan Parry, *The Rise and Fall of Liberal Government in Victorian Britain* (New Haven, 1993), 39–45, provides an interesting sketch.

ensure that calls for action on these fronts were met in considered and effective fashion.[115]

Some of the young Whigs who had taken umbrage at the government's heavy-handedness in the era of Peterloo were mollified, even impressed by these 'liberal' moves.[116] In this context it became harder to see what might constitute a distinctively 'Whig' stance. Some 'liberal Tories' received cross-party support in their home constituencies: thus, Canning and William Huskisson in Liverpool. In fact even at the highest level the distinction between government and opposition had never been hard and fast; Grenvillites in particular had drifted in and out of office. Against this background, Liverpool's stroke in 1826 seemed briefly to open up the possibility of new forms of coalition. However, Canning's untimely death aborted his short-lived ministry, to which he had succeeded in attracting a number of Whigs. Though the same group agreed to serve under Viscount Goderich, he lasted only till the meeting of parliament in 1828.[117]

One slogan that petrified into cliché in the 1820s was that of the 'march of mind'. That phrase had its own partisan connotations: it derived ultimately from the marquis de Condorcet and the French materialist tradition. Some objected to what they took to be the slogan's implication: that progress could take place through an increase in knowledge alone, regardless of a society's spiritual state. But, more loosely interpreted, the phrase does evoke central themes of this decade, a decade in which many sought to further the dissemination of knowledge.[118]

The notion that it was to an increase in knowledge and understanding that one must look to drive forwards a process of improvement and reform across a broad front had been an important strand in seventeenth-century thought, its most prominent English proponent at that date being Francis Bacon, lord chancellor, law reformer, and enquirer into natural phenomena.[119] Bacon was a

[115] Norman Gash's biography, *Sir Robert Peel*, 2 vols., revd edn (London, 1985–6), of which vol. i covers this period, endlessly praises its subject's good sense. For recent accounts of Peel's deft handling of police and penal reform, see Elaine Reynolds, *Before the Bobbies: The Night Watch and Police Reform in Metropolitan London, 1720–1830* (Basingstoke, 1998), ch. 8; Follett, *Evangelicalism, Penal Theory*, ch. 9.

[116] Mandler, *Aristocratic Government*, 29–31 (Wasson, 'Great Whigs', 62, however, notes that they held aloof from the Lansdowne coalition).

[117] Austin Mitchell, *The Whigs in Opposition, 1815–30* (Oxford, 1967), provides an overview; see also Mandler, *Aristocratic Government*, 13–33.

[118] A. M. Caritat, marquis de Condorcet, *Outlines of the Progress of the Human Mind* (London, 1795); Duncan Forbes, *The Liberal Anglican Idea of History* (Cambridge, 1952), esp. 5–7. For the young Newman's hostility to the notion of the 'march of mind', see Nockles, *Oxford Movement in Context*, 69–70. For visual satire, see Dorothy George, *English Political Caricature*, 2 vols. (Oxford, 1959), ii, 212–13.

[119] Bacon's importance and influence in seventeenth-century England are stressed in Charles Webster, *The Great Instauration: Science, Medicine and Reform, 1626–60* (London, 1975). Bacon scholarship has boomed in recent years: for a recent study which explores the

(cont. on p. 38)

helpfully *national* tutelary spirit for those who wished to advance such notions in the early nineteenth century. He was the avowed hero of Edinburgh lecturer Dugald Stewart, whose lectures many young Whigs and liberals attended in the generation when it was fashionable for men of these leanings to attend Scottish universities. Other Bacon fans included the Whig lawyers and law reformers Sir James Mackintosh and Basil Montagu (Montagu produced an edition of Bacon's *Works*), the liberal Anglican academic Richard Whately (who edited Bacon's *Essays*), and the natural and moral philosopher William Whewell, for whom Bacon was in a specific sense an intellectual hero: a man who had broken the chains of authority to seek a proper understanding of the relationship between facts and ideas. 'Knowledge is power', a Baconian slogan, was the watchword of the mechanics' institutes; the slogan was open to a variety of readings.[120]

The late eighteenth and early nineteenth centuries had seen the spread, in both London and the provinces, of an older habit of instructive public lecturing. Because they often provided a vehicle for political comment, lectures 'relating to the Laws, Constitution, Government, or Policy of these Kingdoms' had been restricted to premises licensed by magistrates in 1795; from 1819, all lecture halls other than those sited in certain recognized educational institutions were required to seek such licences. In practice, lectures spanned an enormous variety of topics. Natural philosophy – or 'science' as it was now coming to be called – was a long-established staple. Glasgow's Andersonian Institution, initially conceived as a site for the delivery of lectures to gentlemen and ladies, was as such by no means remarkable. More notable was George Birkbeck's decision to offer a set of lectures there specifically for an audience of 'mechanics'. The Glasgow Mechanics' Institution, which broke away from its parent body in 1823, was the model for many others, founded in London (with encouragement from Francis Place) and in provincial towns from 1825. Over seventy were apparently founded in 1825 alone, as enthusiasm for their improving and incorporating potential briefly peaked.[121]

(*cont.*)

interconnections between his political and scientific interests, see Julian Martin, *Francis Bacon, the State and the Reform of Natural Philosophy* (Cambridge, 1992).

[120] The upsurge of interest in Bacon in the nineteenth century has not been synoptically surveyed. For Stewart's enthusiasm for Bacon, and his influence, see Stefan Collini, John Burrow, and Donald Winch (eds.), *That Noble Science of Politics: A Study in Nineteenth-Century Intellectual History* (Cambridge, 1983), ch. 1. Nineteenth-century editions included *The Works of Francis Bacon*, ed. Basil Montagu, 16 vols. (London, 1825–36); *Bacon's Essays, with Annotations by R. Whately* (London, 1856). For Whewell, see Menachem Fisch and Simon Schaffer (eds.), *William Whewell: A Composite Portrait* (Oxford, 1991), esp. 135–6. Coleridge was among the less predictable of Bacon's admirers: Douglas Hedley, *Coleridge, Philosophy and Religion: 'Aids to Reflection' and the Mirror of the Spirit* (Cambridge, 2000), 203–15. For a radical appropriation of Bacon, see Wickwar, *Struggle for the Freedom of the Press*, 164–5.

[121] For the early public lecturing, see Nicholas Hans, *New Trends in Education in the Eighteenth Century* (London, 1950), chs. 7–8; Jan Golinski, *Science and Public Culture: Chemistry and*

(cont. on p. 39)

As Holger Hoock shows in this volume, there was concern to diffuse not only knowledge, but also taste: an important theme in discussions that eventuated in the decision to found a National Gallery in 1826. Debates in the same period about the 'decline of the theatre' – a perennial theme – acquired special resonance in the context of these other hopes and fears.[122]

The most ambitious product of this age of educational projects was London University, founded in the form of a joint-stock company in 1826. The Whig Henry Brougham coordinated a group – among whom utilitarians and dissenters figured prominently – to bring this about; Whig magnates, such as the dukes of Bedford and Devonshire, were among the major financial backers. Unlike Oxford and Cambridge, it imposed no form of religious test, and set out to promote especially the study of the sciences and social sciences. In 1828, a group made anxious by its lack of firm religious, especially protestant commitment, began planning a rival: King's College London. Durham University was launched soon after (1831) by a bishop and chapter who hoped in this way to defend their revenues from anticipated church reform.[123]

Though the relative social and political calm of the early and mid-1820s suggested that the immediate crisis of the late war and post-war years was over, the sense that British society was in the grip of – if not an acute, none the less a profound – moral and cultural crisis remained. The French Revolution was seen to have posed a series of challenges to which no entirely satisfactory solution had been found. The sense that mere 'useful knowledge' would not do the trick helps to explain the mockery that came to be directed against what Thomas Love Peacock catchily termed 'steam intellect'.[124] The crucial question presented itself somewhat differently to those on the political left and the political right:

(cont.)
Enlightenment in Britain, 1760–1820 (Cambridge, 1999). For later developments see Morris Berman, *Science and Social Organization: The Royal Institution, 1799–1844* (London, 1978), 20–6, 124–6; David Hadley, 'Public Lectures and Private Societies: Expounding Literature and the Arts in Romantic London', in Donald Schoonmaker and John A. Alford (eds.), *English Romanticism: Preludes and Postludes* (East Lancing, Mich., 1993). For staged public debates between protestant and Catholic lecturers, see Stewart J. Brown, *The National Churches of England, Ireland and Scotland, 1801–46* (Oxford, 2001), 113–16; John Wolffe, *The Protestant Crusade in Great Britain, 1829–60* (Oxford, 1991), ch. 2. For Birkbeck and mechanics institutes, see Thomas Kelly, *George Birkbeck: Pioneer of Adult Education* (Liverpool, 1957); Ian Inkster (ed.), *The Steam Intellect Societies: Essays on Culture, Education and Industry, c. 1820–1914* (Nottingham, 1985). See H. Smith, *The Society for the Diffusion of Useful Knowledge, 1826–46* (London, 1974), for a publishing venture aimed at such institutions and their members.

[122] See chapters by Hoock and Newey in this volume.

[123] N. B. Harte, *The University of London, 1836–1986: An Illustrated History* (London, 1986), 61–76. For more detail on UCL, see H. Hale Bellot, *University College London, 1826–1926* (London, 1929); on King's, F. J. C. Hearnshaw, *The Centenary History of King's College London, 1828–1928* (London, 1929). On Durham, see E. A. Varley, *The Last of the Prince Bishops: William van Mildert and the High Church Movement of the Early Nineteenth Century* (Cambridge, 1992), 149–79.

[124] In Thomas Love Peacock's satire *Crotchet Castle* (London, 1831), ch. 2.

to the former, it was how to achieve change without cataclysm; to the latter, how best to defend traditional institutions and attitudes in the face of changes in both society and belief. Regardless of precisely how the question was framed, however, the answer, it seemed, had to lie in the forging of some form of new moral order: society had either to be remoralized, or moralized in new ways, to survive the challenges of the age.

This perceived need was addressed in many different ways. In the old universities, evangelicals and high churchmen combined a commitment to the 'Protestant Constitution' with a concern to promote authentic spirituality; Oxford 'Noetics' or 'liberal Anglicans', though suspicious of theological and ecclesiological innovation, none the less responded to changing times by developing a more inclusive, progressive vision of the national religion and its future. Young male members of the ruling classes were exposed in late adolescence to more challenging and more creative forms of piety than had been the case for several generations.[125] At the level of practical policy, MPs and philanthropists continued to try to develop and extend new approaches to punishment and poor relief. Childhood education was looked to to perform a wide range of purposes, but probably most commonly to impart piety and morals.[126]

At a more popular level, the cotton-factory owner Robert Owen and his more and less plebeian followers preached their own cooperative vision of the new moral world. The temperance movement – imported from America via Scotland – harnessed the power of association to the cause of self-improvement.[127]

The 1820s was not an era of stormy political conflict. Yet it is possible to overstate its quiescence. As in other apparently quiescent eras – such as the decade and more following 1792, and the post-Chartist years – activists often continued to be active, and to maintain their sense of identity, outside the

[125] For the growth of evangelicalism at Cambridge, see Brown, *Fathers of the Victorians*, ch. 8; at Oxford, J. S. Reynolds, *Evangelicals at Oxford, 1755–1871: A Record of an Unchronicled Movement* (repr., extended, Appleford, 1975); for high churchmen, see Peter Nockles, '"Lost Causes and . . . Impossible Loyalties": The Oxford Movement and the University', in M. Brock and M. Curthoys (eds.), *The History of the University of Oxford*, vol. vi: *The Early Nineteenth Century* (Oxford, 2000), 199–206; for Noetics, see Richard Brent, 'The Oriel Noetics', in Brock and Curthoys (eds.), *History of the University of Oxford*, 72–6; Pietro Corsi, *Science and Religion: Baden Powell and the Anglican Debate, 1800–60* (Cambridge, 1988); Forbes, *Liberal Anglican Idea of History*. For the impact of this on younger members of the ruling classes, see Mandler, *Aristocratic Government*, 51, 64–5.

[126] See works cited in n. 92 above. Peter Mandler, 'Tories and Paupers: Christian Political Economy and the Making of the New Poor Law', *Hist. Jl*, 33 (1990), for the argument that new currents of thought in the universities influenced attitudes to the poor. For the continued development of 'visiting' as a vehicle for disseminating both religion and charity, see D. M. Lewis, *Lighten their Darkness: The Evangelical Mission to Working-Class London, 1828–60* (New York, 1986).

[127] Harrison, *Robert Owen*; Greg Claeys, *Citizens and Saints: Politics and Anti-Politics in Early British Socialism* (Cambridge, 1989); Harrison, *Drink and the Victorians*. Iain McCalman surveys, but sounds a cautionary note about, the nature of the 'ultra-radical march of mind' in his *Radical Underworld*, ch. 9.

main national political arena: within informal networks; in societies; within the structures of particular institutions; or in the arena of local politics. The arena of urban politics in this era remains remarkably under-explored; yet, throughout England and Scotland, groups of 'independents' and 'radicals' harried away at municipal corporations' secretive, arbitrary, and monopolistic habits. James Acland, later an Anti-Corn-Law League lecturer, in the 1820s was an anti-corporation journalist in Bristol and Hull; in 1830, he promoted the Hull Political Union with the aim of freeing the country 'from the domination of our National and Local Aristocracy'.[128]

The repeal of the Combination Acts in 1824 brought trade unions – many of which had previously presented themselves as friendly societies – out into the light of day. The relatively prosperous conditions of the 1820s made this a good time for workers to put pressure on masters; John Gast had campaigned for the wronged Queen Caroline in 1820; in 1825 he helped to organize a shipwrights' strike.[129] The decade was also marked by a series of attempts to create federations in particular trades. As the economy moved into depression in the late 1820s, conflict became more bitter. John Doherty's Grand General Union of Operative Cotton Spinners of Great Britain and Ireland was one of the more ambitious federative ventures: it held its inaugural conference on the Isle of Man in 1829. But Doherty had a greater vision, reflected in the inauguration in the same year of the National Association for the Protection of Labour (in practice, drawing its strength chiefly from the Lancashire region). By 1831, Doherty was using the mouthpiece of this organization, *The Voice of the People*, to support the cause of parliamentary reform.[130]

The 1820s saw the eruption of a number of remarkably vigorous single-issue campaigns. One such was the campaign for the abolition of slavery in Britain's West Indian colonies, jolted into life from 1823 by the efforts of James Cropper and other Liverpool merchants, and of the Leicester Quaker Elizabeth Heyrick. Their calls for speedy and radical action were echoed in other provincial centres, and effectively forced upon the more dilatory or prudent London committee. They also pushed for the adoption of more energetic methods for arousing

---

[128] Rosemary Sweet, *The English Town, 1680–1840: Government, Society and Culture* (Harlow, 1999), ch. 6, sets such conflicts in the context of urban reform effort more broadly conceived. Beatrice and Sidney Webb, *The Manor and the Borough*, 2 vols. (London, 1924), contains much relevant material: see esp. ii, 699–705. Local studies include P. Cadogan, *Early Radical Newcastle* (Durham, 1975); G. Bush, *Bristol and its Municipal Government, 1820–51* (Bristol, 1976); and for reformism in an unincorporated town, Michael J. Turner, *Reform and Respectability: The Making of Middle-Class Liberalism in Early Nineteenth-Century Manchester* (Preston, 1995). For Acland, see Patricia Hollis, 'Introduction', to Hollis (ed.), *Pressure from Without in Early Victorian Britain* (London, 1974), 13–14; Nancy D. LoPatin, *Political Unions, Popular Politics and the Great Reform Act of 1832* (Basingstoke, 1999), 113.

[129] Prothero, *Artisans and Politics*, ch. 8.

[130] R. G. Kirby and A. E. Musson, *The Voice of the People: John Doherty, 1798–1854: Trade Unionist, Radical and Factory Reformer* (Manchester, 1975), chs. 4–7.

public opinion, including the holding of mass meetings and employment of travelling lecturers. James Stephen at the Colonial Office found himself exposed to invigorating pressure from without.[131]

'Free trade' was at one level a technical administrative matter, achieved by the dedicated labours of civil servants. Businessmen did not campaign for free trade as such, we are told.[132] Some of them did, however, campaign vigorously for the freeing or protection of *particular* trades. Import duties, protecting the price of English corn – the 'Corn Laws' – had attracted some critical attention from large urban centres in 1791 and 1815, but it was only after the passage of a modifying law in 1822 that certain merchants, industrialists, and other town-dwellers combined to mount a concerted attack. Newspapers supportive of their efforts were scathing in their repeated denunciations of the greed of landlords and farmers – who for their part submitted several hundred counter-petitions supportive of protection. Further modifications introduced in 1828 did not meet critics' wishes, and left them hungry for more.[133]

The East India Company was an old shibboleth: provincial merchants had protested against its monopoly recurrently since the 1730s. In 1813, when its charter was renewed, it lost its monopoly of British–Indian trade, though the Company retained its privileged access to China. Its critics and would-be rivals would have liked to see it lose that, too. Not only as a trading company, but also as the effective government for much of India, the Company found itself under attack in the 1820s. 'Suttee' – *sati* or widow-burning – was the focus of a campaign by those who felt that the Company was not doing enough to Christianize or civilize the peoples in its care. Like the campaign against slavery, this was a campaign in which middle-class women assumed an unwontedly prominent role.[134]

The most remarkable of all single-issue campaigns of the 1820s, however, was undoubtedly Daniel O'Connell's Irish campaign for Catholic Emancipation: the removal of remaining restrictions on Catholic officeholding, most notably on the right to seek election as an MP. From 1823, O'Connell sought to give this campaign a mass popular base; his success, in a largely rural, peasant economy, was startling. Hundreds of thousands of poor families contributed

[131] E. F. Hurwitz, *Politics and the Public Conscience: Slave Emancipation and the Abolitionist Movement in Britain* (London, 1973); David Brion Davis, *Slavery and Human Progress* (New York, 1984), chs. 5–6; A. Tyrrell, *Joseph Sturge and the Moral Radical Party in Early Victorian Britain* (London, 1987), ch. 5; Midgley, *Women Against Slavery*, 103–18.

[132] Hilton, *Corn, Cash, Commerce*, ch. 6.

[133] D. G. Barnes, *A History of the English Corn Laws, 1660–1846* (London, 1930), ch. 9.

[134] A. Webster, 'The Political Economy of Trade Liberalization: The East India Company Charter Act of 1813', *Econ. Hist. Rev.*, 43 (1990); Clare Midgley, 'From Supporting Missions to Petitioning Parliament: Women and the Evangelical Campaign Against Sati', in Kathryn Gleadle and Sarah Richardson (eds.), *Women in British Politics, 1760–1860: The Power of the Petticoat* (Basingstoke, 2000).

their penny-a-week 'Catholic Rent' to sustain the movement, and give it moral force. Given Ireland's recent history of episodic rural disturbance – which had taken its most challengingly political form in the 'rebellion of 1798' – the latent (and ultimately manifest) threat of physical force was also very evident, and vital to the final wresting of agreement from the Wellington administration in 1829.[135]

In England, attitudes to this cause varied sharply. 'Popery' was traditionally associated with arbitrary power and superstition, as well as with England's enemies. Many English and Scottish evangelicals maintained friendly links with Irish 'Protestant Crusaders' who, since the early nineteenth century, had been striving to promote their own solution to Ireland's troubles: the doctrines of the Reformation. From England accordingly came hundreds of petitions against as well as for concessions.[136] Awareness of the issue as an *Irish* issue was sharpened by the rising tide of Irish immigration from 1823 – encouraged by English prosperity at a time of Irish depression, and facilitated by new steamboats, which offered cheap and speedy passage between the two countries. Irish immigrants sometimes aroused antipathy, but some were moved to lament with them the shortcomings of the regime prevailing in their native land. Some towns in the industrial north called not only for Catholics to enjoy full political and civil rights, but also for a poor law for Ireland.[137]

One group who found it particularly difficult to formulate a common position on the Catholic Question were English dissenters, some of whom favoured equal treatment for all, regardless of religious affiliation, while others maintained their traditional hostility to what they saw as a tyrannical church and unreasonable faith. For much of the 1820s, this difference of views inhibited the dissenters' traditional campaigning body, the 'Protestant Dissenting Deputies', from renewing their efforts to secure the repeal of the Test and Corporation Acts, last vigorously prosecuted in the 1780s – for simple repeal would equally have benefited all non-Anglicans. Reputedly, it was in part because the Catholic campaign appeared to have reached a dead end that the Deputies did decide to pursue the issue in 1827. In line with the increase in the scale of petitioning evident across a wide range of causes in the post-war years, they elicited many

---

[135] O'Connell's efforts have been much studied. See *inter alia* Oliver MacDonagh, *O'Connell: The Life of Daniel O'Connell, 1775–1847* (London, 1991); F. O'Ferrall, *Catholic Emancipation: Daniel O'Connell and the Birth of Irish Democracy* (Dublin, 1985). For the politics of repeal, see G. I. T. Machin, *The Catholic Question in English Politics, 1820–30* (Oxford, 1964); Wendy Hinde, *Catholic Emancipation: A Shake to Men's Minds* (Oxford, 1992).

[136] Desmond Bowen, *The Protestant Crusade in Ireland, 1800–70: A Study in Protestant–Catholic Relations between the Act of Union and Disestablishment* (Dublin, 1978); Wolffe, *Protestant Crusade*; Brown, *National Churches*, ch. 2.

[137] Donald M. McRaild, *Irish Migrants in Modern Britain, 1750–1922* (Basingstoke, 1999), 42–57; Belchem, *'Orator' Hunt*, 185; Kim Lawes, *Paternalism and Politics: The Revival of Paternalism in Early Nineteenth-Century Britain* (Basingstoke, 2000), 128–40.

more separate petitions than they ever had in the past: 1,114 in 1827, 1,362 in the following year.[138]

Historians of this campaign have stressed its leaders' cautious and pragmatic approach. Barely held in check by such cautious pragmatism, however, was much strong feeling at the grass roots. One source of discontent was the issue of church rates. This would surge into prominence in the 1830s, but was already becoming a bone of contention in some communities. Dissenters were normally expected to contribute not only to poor rates, which parish vestries administered, but also to rates for the maintenance of church buildings and furnishings. Since the passage in 1818 of an act to encourage the building of new churches in populous towns, church rates had increased notably in some places. Some dissenters began to try to block their imposition, on grounds of conscience.[139]

There was thus increased criticism of the Church of England as established. Nor was this sentiment unique to dissenters; it was shared by many rank-and-file Anglicans, to say nothing of deists and freethinkers. Interest, so characteristic of this decade, in the need to remoralize society, itself encouraged critical attention to the church and the character of its contribution to this effort. The church hierarchy came under attack as one element of the predatory apparatus of 'Old Corruption'. Tithes were an object of criticism in England, and of widespread popular agitation in Ireland (also reported in the English press). As Arthur Burns indicates, there were serious and loyal voices within the church establishment calling for 'church reform'. Among the disaffected laity, criticism was sometimes more crudely and abrasively expressed.[140]

It is necessary to note this build-up of feeling around a range of particular issues to understand the energy and character of the agitation which took shape when the third and most successful attempt to construct a successor to Liverpool's long-lived administration fell apart: that is, when the Wellington ministry

---

[138] Watts, *Dissenters*, ch. 8; Bernard Manning, *The Protestant Dissenting Deputies* (Cambridge, 1952), 217–53; R. W. Davis, *Dissent in Politics, 1780–1830: The Political Life of William Smith, MP* (London, 1971), ch. 12.

[139] Watts, *Dissenters*, 477–9; Jacob P. Ellens, *Religious Routes to Gladstonian Liberalism: The Church Rate Controversy in England and Wales, 1832–1868* (University Park, Pa., 1994), intro., ch. 1. For early admonitory noises from the Dissenting Deputies, see Manning, *Protestant Dissenting Deputies*, 176–7.

[140] For critical scrutiny of the church's role in promoting morality, see Eileen Groth Lyon, *Politicians in the Pulpit: Christian Radicalism in Britain from the Fall of the Bastille to the Disintegration of Chartism* (Aldershot, 1999), 64–75. For the church as an arm of 'Old Corruption', see its inclusion in Wade's *Black Book* (n. 4 above), and Burns' chapter below. See also Eric Evans, 'Some Reasons for the Growth of English Anti-Clericalism, c. 1750–1830', *Past and Present*, no. 66 (Feb. 1975); Eric Evans, *The Contentious Tithe: The Tithe Problem and English Agriculture, 1750–1850* (London, 1976); McCalman, *Radical Underworld*, ch. 7. In Marylebone, initial civil dissent gave way to scabrous assault: F. W. H. Sheppard, *Local Government in St Marylebone, 1688–1835: A Study of the Vestry and the Turnpike Trust* (London, 1958), chs. 16–17. See also John Miller (ed.), *Religion in the Popular Prints, 1600–1832* (Cambridge, 1986).

resigned in November 1830. The immediate occasion for the ministry's fall was its failure to maintain the confidence of the Commons, given its unyielding opposition to all but the most trivial measures of parliamentary reform. In this context, it was inevitable that the Whig-dominated ministry appointed in its place would have to address the reform issue in a more broadly conceived and systematic way.[141] Nor is it surprising that, once the reform issue was on the cards, reform agitation in the country should have revived: proponents of reform could now push on an at least partly open door. The fact that all this took place against a background of an economic downturn, moreover, goes some way to explain the breadth and urgency of support for parliamentary reform, and some of the other issues canvassed alongside it, such as retrenchment, improved management of the currency, and repeal of the Corn Laws.

Yet what bears emphasis is the range of further issues canvassed, including the abolition of slavery, abolition of all commercial monopolies (but especially that of the East India Company), dissolution of the union between church and state, and restructuring of the system of rating for the poor. The slogan 'reform' had many resonances for people, and much was expected from a 'reformed parliament'.[142]

The difficulties the government encountered in getting its Reform Bill, first through the Commons, then through the Lords, added higher colouring and more elements to the picture. There were calls for a change in the constitutional position of the Lords; episcopal opposition to reform stoked the fires of anti-church rhetoric, and not rhetoric alone: the bishop's palace in Bristol was burnt down.[143] The rhetoric of 'union' was widespread, and this often seems to have connoted cross-class cooperation. But the rhetoric of 'class' was also increasingly deployed. In London in 1831, a variety of radical groups – members of the Radical Reform Association and the Metropolitan Trades Union, parish radicals, deists, Rotundaists (followers of Richard Carlile), British Cooperators (Owenites), and Irish radicals – came together to form the grandly titled 'National Union of the Working Classes'. In the course of the 1820s, 'march of mind' theories of social change had begun to give way to social-conflict-driven models. As the political crisis deepened, there were fears that British society might disintegrate into cataclysmic class war.[144]

---

[141] Brock, *Great Reform Act*, chs. 3–4.

[142] Parry, *Rise and Fall*, 58–71, for an effective evocation of the combination of practical frustration and moral anxiety that characterized public opinion in 1829–30. See LoPatin, *Political Unions*, 38–81, for an overview of the range of issues canvassed; Brock, *Great Reform Act*, 193–203, for the extraordinary breadth of support for the Reform ministry revealed in the 1831 election, called to counter the House of Lords' resistance to sweeping reform.

[143] Lo Patin, *Political Unions*, ch. 4, for riots at Bristol and elsewhere.

[144] *Ibid.*, for many illustrations of the rhetoric of union. For the NUWC, see Kirby and Musson, *Voice of the People*, 243–6; Belchem, *'Orator' Hunt*, ch. 8. See Thompson, *Making of the*

(cont. on p. 46)

VI

It has often been observed that the Reform Act, as passed in 1832, made relatively modest changes to the size and character of the electorate (at least in England; in Scotland it had a more dramatic impact). It has recently been noted that the size of the pre-reform electorate has, moreover, habitually been underestimated: figures commonly cited relate to totals known to have voted, not (as fair comparison would require) to numbers eligible to vote. When the figures are corrected, 'reform' as enacted is further cut down to size. The social composition of the House of Commons was also little changed – indeed, it changed in what can be portrayed as a retrograde direction, with an increase in the number of MPs who were country gentlemen.[145]

These are important conclusions. Such things helped at the time to fuel the belief that the Reform Act represented a betrayal by the 'middle classes' of the 'working classes'. Subsequently they have been used to support the argument that the Reform Act was a triumph for Whig paternalists, who leagued with Tory ultras to maintain the social status quo.[146]

However, extending the vote to new classes of voter was not the reformers' only object. Many attached as much if not more importance to increasing parliament's responsiveness to the sorts of people who were *already* voters. Parliamentary reform was expected to help achieve this in so far as it eliminated small

(*cont.*)

English Working Class, for a classic account of the rise of class conflict; Dror Wahrman, *Imagining the Middle Class: The Political Representation of Class in Britain, c. 1780–1840* (Cambridge, 1995), for a very different approach, focusing on rhetorical shifts. Some recent accounts stress the prevalence of a less conflictual populist rhetoric – notably Patrick Joyce, *Visions of the People: Industrial England and the Question of Class, 1848–1914* (Cambridge, 1991); class rhetoric was none the less indubitably more prominent than it had been in the eighteenth century. See Forbes, *Liberal Anglican Idea of History*, 15–29, for German influence on the development of an academic model of history as driven by conflict.

[145] Cannon, *Parliamentary Reform*, ch. 11; for problems with estimates of the size of the electorate see O'Gorman, *Voters, Patrons, and Parties*, 178–80. For those returned, see W. O Aydelotte, 'The House of Commons in the 1840's', *Hist.*, 39 (1954); W. O. Aydelotte, 'A Statistical Analysis of the Parliament of 1841: Some Problems of Method', *Bull. Inst. Hist. Research*, 27 (1954). Studies of the 'reformed' system in operation include Norman Gash, *Politics in the Age of Peel: A Study in the Technique of Parliamentary Representation, 1830–50* (London, 1953); T. J. Nossiter, *Influence, Opinion and Political Idioms in Reformed England: Case Studies from the North-East, 1832–74* (Brighton, 1975); John A. Phillips, *The Great Reform Bill in the Boroughs: English Electoral Behaviour, 1818–41* (Oxford, 1992). For Scotland, William Ferguson, 'The Reform Act (Scotland) of 1832: Intention and Effect', *Scottish Hist. Rev.*, 45 (1966); M. Dyer, '"Mere Detail and Machinery": The Great Reform Act and the Effect of Redistribution on Scottish Representation, 1832–65', *Scottish Hist. Rev.*, 62 (1983).

[146] For early claims that the working classes were betrayed by the Whigs, see Belchem, '*Orator*' *Hunt*, ch. 8. Perhaps the most influential statement of the social interpretation is D. C. Moore, *The Politics of Deference: A Study of the Mid-Nineteenth Century English Political System* (Hassocks, 1976). Moore's analysis has been much questioned, especially by R. W. Davis, e.g. in his *Political Change and Continuity, 1760–1885: A Buckinghamshire Study* (Newton Abbot, 1972). For a different perspective on the Whig agenda, see L. G. Mitchell, 'Foxite Politics and the Great Reform Bill', *Eng. Hist. Rev.*, 107 (1983).

constituencies, and increased the size of the electorate in larger constituencies. According to this model, reform would function by filling parliament with independent men of property, whose object as MPs would be, not to please government, but to advance the interest of the people by criticizing errant ministers and promoting good laws. A wide range of people came to see the reformed parliament's performance as in some manner disappointing. But disappointment focused not just on the fact that the social profile of the political nation had changed only marginally, but just as much or more on the fact that parliament's achievements had failed to fulfil specific hopes.[147]

Though it certainly did not fulfil all hopes placed in it, the 'reformed parliament' did in fact address in some fashion many reform agendas. Thus, 1833 brought the abolition of slavery, the opening up of the China trade to all comers, a redefinition of the powers and a modification of the monopoly of the Bank of England, a reduction in duties on newspaper advertisements (intended to lower the price of newspapers), parliamentary sanction for a grant to aid school-building, the establishment of a system of elective government for Scottish burghs, and Irish church reform. The year 1834 brought the new poor law; 1835, municipal corporation reform; 1836, civil registration, the Established Church Act and the Tithe Commutation Act; 1838, the Pluralities Act and the first Irish poor law; 1840, the establishment of county courts to hear lesser civil suits, the Dean and Chapter Act, and Irish municipal reform. Other issues canvassed in parliament, but not resolved, included the abolition of church rates (proposed in unsuccessful government bills of 1834 and 1837); abolition of the patent theatres' monopoly (recommended by a Commons select committee, but not implemented until 1843); and total abolition of capital punishment (unsuccessfully proposed by the evangelical William Ewart in 1840; the number of crimes liable to capital punishment was, however, reduced by a series of measures through the 1830s).[148]

---

[147] For recent studies emphasizing such aspects of contemporary thinking see Parry, *Rise and Fall*, 78–89; Taylor, *Decline of British Radicalism*. David Nicholls, 'Friends of the People: Parliamentary Supporters of Popular Radicalism, 1832–49', *Labour Hist. Rev.*, 112 (1997), identifies among MPs a group of heterogeneous personal background whose voting record none the less marks them out as supporters of radical and working-class causes.

[148] For a contemporary survey of the ministry's achievements in its first post-Reform Act session, see Sir Denis Le Marchant, *The Reform Ministry and the Reformed Parliament*, 4th edn (London, 1833). Recent surveys include Ian Newbould, *Whiggery and Reform: The Politics of Government* (London, 1990); Mandler, *Aristocratic Government*; Brent, *Liberal Anglican Politics*. Many of these topics have substantial historiographies of their own, esp. the New Poor Law, for which see the recent survey by Alan Kidd, *State, Society and the Poor in Nineteenth-Century England* (Basingstoke, 1999), and references there. For antislavery, see Izhak Gross, 'The Abolition of Negro Slavery and British Parliamentary Politics, 1832–3', *Hist. Jl*, 23 (1980); Seymour Drescher, *The Mighty Experiment: Free Labour versus Slavery in British Emancipation* (Oxford, 2002). For church reform, see Best, *Temporal Pillars*, esp. ch. 7. For the reform of capital punishment, see Sir Leon Radzinowicz, *A History of English Criminal Law and its Administration*, 5 vols. (London and Oxford, 1948–86), i, *Grappling for Control*; V. A. C. Gatrell, *The Hanging Tree: Execution and the English People, 1770–1868* (Oxford, 1994).

Ministers were not of one mind in their attitude to particular reforms; thus, it has been suggested that Whigs, keen to reshape society through reformed institutions, differed from liberals, chiefly concerned to lighten the hand of government. None the less, the Grey ministry of 1830, its successor, the Melbourne ministry of 1834, and their supporters, did all explicitly espouse the cause of 'reform'.[149] Supporters were termed 'reformers' in parliamentary handbooks and often presented themselves to the electorate as such. Defenders of the new regime celebrated the progress that had been made in 'the work of general reform'.[150] The effect was to shift the contours of public debate. Both well-wishers and critics of reform aspirations now had to engage with actually existing reforms.

Some criticisms came from among those who also termed themselves 'reformers', though sometimes distinguishing themselves as 'radical reformers'. They had vocal representatives in parliament, a presence in the press, and a not insignificant following outside parliament, though the nature of that following varied from one issue to another. Radical reformers argued that the work of reform had not been carried far enough. Parliament had not established manhood suffrage (and had explicitly denied the vote to women); it had not established equal electoral districts, or a secret ballot. It had not reformed county government. It had not reformed Canadian government enough or quickly enough – precipitating rebellion in 1837. It had not abolished penal transportation to Australia – and thus, as critics claimed, had failed to serve the best interests either of Australian colonists or of convicts. It had not done enough to reform the Church of England or to reduce its privileges, and had not abolished 'taxes on knowledge': newspaper stamp duties.[151]

Other charges levelled against the record of 'reforms' achieved stood in a more ambiguous relationship to the reform tradition. First, it was said that too little had been done to redress Irish grievances. Church reform, the establishment of a non-denominational education system, and the creation of an Irish poor law were not enough: the country remained disturbed, and government and parliament's response to disturbance continued to be coercion. From Ireland, and Irish and other supporters elsewhere, calls for the 'Repeal' of the 1801 Union

---

[149] For the differences indicated, see Mandler, *Aristocratic Government*. For other analyses, see Brent, *Liberal Anglican Politics*; Boyd Hilton, 'Whiggery, Liberalism and Social Reform: The Case of Lord Morpeth', *Hist. Jl*, 37 (1994); Peter Gray, *Famine, Land and Politics: British Government and Irish Society, 1843–50* (Dublin, 1999), 17–26.

[150] Parry, *Rise and Fall*, 167. The phrase is from Le Marchant, *Reform Ministry*, 3.

[151] For radical critics of reform policy, see Thomas, *Philosophic Radicals*, chs. 4–9; see also W. E. S. Thomas, 'The Philosophic Radicals', in Hollis (ed.), *Pressure from Without*. For particular issues mentioned, see also John Gascoigne, *The Enlightenment and the Origins of European Australia* (Cambridge, 2002), ch. 7; Joel H. Wiener, *The War of the Unstamped: The Movement to Repeal the British Newspaper Tax, 1830–36* (Ithaca, N.Y., 1969). For church reform, see Best, *Temporal Pillars*, 312–13. Such criticism of course came not only from radical reformers, but also from dissenters: see thus Ellens, *Religious Routes*, 9, 48–95.

began to be heard – though exactly what it was that an Irish parliament would do differently remained unclear. Melbourne's wobbly alliance with O'Connell from 1835 kept the nascent Repeal movement in check, but did not sap it at the root.[152]

Ministers and parliament were also charged with having shown peculiar insensitivity to the needs of the English common people – notably by amending the poor law in such a way as to limit the poor's traditional 'rights', though also by refusing to reduce the cotton-factory working day below twelve hours. There was protest from sections of propertied opinion as well as from working people: *The Times* newspaper was a swingeing critic of the New Poor Law. Those who emerged as opinion-leaders in these matters varied in their politics: they included Whigs, radicals, Owenites, evangelicals, and paternalist Tories.[153]

In 1838–9, Chartism took shape as an umbrella movement, articulating these domestic discontents and at the same time endorsing Irish grievances. It championed the six points of the People's Charter as a necessary first step towards remedying both. Inasmuch as the six points provided a recipe for further, radical, parliamentary reform, Chartists were indubitably 'reformers', and termed themselves such. But it is surely no accident that they presented themselves to the world first and foremost as 'Chartists'. Events of the 1830s had lessened the attraction of 'reform' as a slogan for a movement such as theirs.[154]

From the moderate right, meanwhile – from among those beginning to term themselves 'conservatives' – came other forms of criticism. Reform ministries were admitted to have grappled with many important issues. Their pompous self-presentation as 'reformers' was, however, argued not to conduce to clarity of thought. It led them to overstate the novelty of some of what they attempted. It encouraged, moreover, a certain impatience with the lessons of experience. The world was a complicated sort of place, and the serious problems it presented

---

[152] See Ridden in this volume; also Angus D. Macintyre, *The Liberator: Daniel O'Connell and the Irish Party, 1830–47* (London, 1965).

[153] For protests against the New Poor Law, see Nicholas C. Edsall, *The Anti-Poor Law Movement, 1834–44* (London, 1971); John Knott, *Popular Opposition to the 1834 Poor Law* (London, 1986); for a recent study of the factory issue, Robert Q. Gray, *The Factory Question and Industrial England, 1830–1860* (Cambridge, 1996). For biographies of some of those who emerged in such contexts as advocates of popular rights, see Cecil Driver, *Tory Radical: The Life of Richard Oastler* (New York, 1946); Stewart Angas Weaver, *John Fielden and the Politics of Popular Radicalism, 1832–1847* (Oxford, 1987); Michael Stone Edwards, *Purge this Realm: A Biography of Joseph Rayner Stephens* (London, 1994); Lawes, *Paternalism and Politics* (on Michael Sadler).

[154] The best survey remains Dorothy Thompson, *The Chartists* (Hounslow, 1984); for an influential collection, see James Epstein and Dorothy Thompson (eds.), *The Chartist Experience: Studies in Working-Class Radicalism and Culture, 1830–60* (London, 1982). A more recent collection is Owen R. Ashton, Robert Fyson, and Stephen Roberts (eds.), *The Chartist Legacy* (Rendlesham, 1999). See the same editors' *The Chartist Movement: A New Annotated Bibliography*, (London, 1995), for a survey of recent work. For Chartists and the term 'reform', see comments in the chapter by Innes below, pp. 95–6.

were not susceptible to quick fixes. Government policies had to be carefully assessed on their merits, which were not always compelling.[155]

Finally, there were those who thought that 'reform' was radically changing the face of the country – but for the worse. For some such critics, the most painful blow had been Catholic Emancipation, which, as they saw it, radically altered the relationship between state and church. The Reform Act threatened to make matters worse by inflaming the hopes and enhancing the power of enemies of the church: dissenters, Catholics, and atheists. John Keble's Oxford Assize Sermon of 1833 expressed and crystallized these anxieties. Meanwhile, in parishes up and down the land, battles over church rates impressed upon ordinary churchmen how challenging were the forces that had been unleashed.[156]

One form of alienated response to the new order took the form of developing an alternative political rhetoric: a rhetoric that eschewed what were thought to be the materialistic and mechanistic assumptions of the reforming frame of mind. Combining certain traditional strands of Tory and church imagery with a folksiness first cultivated by counter-revolutionary propagandists in the 1790s, and subsequently developed by Cobbett as an instrument of social and political criticism, this alternative rhetoric had at its centre the trinity Throne, Altar, and Cottage. Elements of this rhetoric could be deployed, as Cobbett had once deployed them, in combination with arguments for radical reform. But in some of its forms – as, for example, in the writings of the Young England movement – 'reform' had no place. The process by which harmony might be restored to a damaged society (if it might) was not imagined as a process of 'reform'.[157]

A striking feature of the reform legislation of the 1830s is the extent to which it was ministerially initiated. This represented a development within an established trend – but at the same time a notable shift in gear. In the eighteenth century, ministers had mainly concerned themselves with war, finance, some elements of trade, and church–state relations. Other matters – including, for example, most crime, poor relief, and highway legislation, as well as narrowly local legislation – had been left to the initiative of backbench enthusiasts. From the start of the nineteenth century, both the number and the ambition of amateur

---

[155] See thus Nahum Whistlecraft, *The Reform Ministry and the Reformed Parliament, Done into Verse*, 10th edn (London, 1834); Gash, *Sir Robert Peel*, ii, ch. 2.

[156] For the context and influence of Keble's sermon, see Nockles, *Oxford Movement in Context*, ch. 1; Peter Nockles, 'Church and King: Tractarian Politics Reappraised', in P. Vaiss (ed.), *From Oxford to the People: Reconsidering Newman and the Oxford Movement* (Leominster, 1996), 99–123; for the sermon itself and commentary, J. Keble, *National Apostasy*, ed. Arthur Burns (British Heritage Database ebooks, forthcoming). For church rates, see n. 139 above.

[157] John Morrow (ed.), *Young England: The New Generation: A Selection of Primary Texts* (London, 1999); Simon A. Skinner, 'Liberalism and Mammon: Tractarian Reaction in the Age of Reform', *Jl Victorian Culture*, 4 (1999).

legislators had grown – in part, as we have noted, because they were increasingly pushed from outside by associational networks and other forms of mobilized public opinion. In response, ministers had increasingly judged it prudent to take responsibility for steering what might otherwise have proved protracted and inconclusive discussions towards an acceptable outcome. Peel's decision to take responsibility for penal and metropolitan police reform in the 1820s exemplifies the trend.[158]

Even against that background, the ministries of the 1830s none the less stand out as remarkably activist. This was in part because they were anxious to distinguish themselves from their immediate predecessors – who had signally failed to deal decisively with most of the issues an aroused public were pressing upon their attention at the end of the previous decade. It was also because reform-era ministers were inclined to assume that decisive solutions to most issues canvassed entailed as a necessary first step major institutional reconstruction. Rarely would it be enough simply to tinker with *what* was done; the *means by which* things were done, institutions themselves, had also to be reformed. But fundamental institutional reconstruction could not properly be left to back-benchers.[159]

In truth, even ministers were not obviously well equipped to tackle major exercises in institutional reconstruction. Outside traditional areas of central-government competence, both expertise and administrative capacity were limited. One resource to which ministers therefore increasingly turned was the royal commission. Ideally, royal commissions drew together men with some relevant expertise, from a variety of backgrounds, and with varying political views. Aided by salaried assistants to do the legwork for them, and untrammelled by the confines of the parliamentary session, they could take the full measure of a problem, sound out a range of opinion, and set out reasoned recommendations. A number of such commissions had been established earlier in the century – to look at Irish education, for example, Scottish law reform, and English charitable trusts. Now commissions were charged with clearing the way for the reform of the church and its courts, poor laws, and municipal corporations. Their reports varied in tone. Enquiries into the church, instigated in part by prudent churchmen for defensive purposes, were conducted in a relatively sympathetic spirit. But generally they served to reinforce the view

---

[158] David Eastwood, 'Men, Morals and the Machinery of Social Legislation, 1790–1840', *Parl. Hist.*, 13 (1994). See n. 115 above for Peel. For trends, see Peter Fraser, 'The Growth of Ministerial Control in the Nineteenth-Century House of Commons', *Eng. Hist. Rev.*, 75 (1960); Valerie Cromwell, 'The Losing of the Initiative by the House of Commons, 1780–1914', *Trans. Royal Hist. Soc.*, 5th ser., 18 (1968); Gary W. Cox, *The Efficient Secret: The Cabinet and the Development of Political Parties in Victorian England* (Cambridge, 1987).

[159] Parry, *Rise and Fall*, pt II, especially emphasizes their distinctive activism.

that intolerable levels of abuse and bad practice prevailed, and that 'reform' of some kind was urgently needed.[160]

The implications of the reform process for the pattern of interaction between ministers and parliament had not been clearly foreseen. As these consequences unfolded, they proved a source of some discontent in their own right. Commissionerships and assistant commissionerships could be seen as so many jobs for the boys, to say nothing of the permanent administrative posts created to supervise the implementation of some policies: poor-law commissioners and factory inspectors – so much for the reformers' commitment to reducing government patronage and 'influence'! Some royal commission reports – for example, the report on the poor laws – played a part in creating a broad parliamentary consensus, but did less to rally those at the sharp end of change. It was apparent to critics, if not to sympathizers, that for all their parade of dispassionate enquiry, such reports were highly ideologically charged: profoundly shaped by disputable assumptions. Ministers' ways of getting things done involved soliciting some forms of public participation – notably in filling in questionnaires or giving evidence – but marginalized others: petitions were side-lined, so that their presentation would no longer take up valuable parliamentary time; government laid claim to a greater share of the parliamentary timetable; and independent members found their chances of promoting their own bills reduced.

We must, however, not overstate ministerial dominance of the reconfigured political scene. In the longer term, the trend towards ministerial dominance of parliament would continue – but not until the century's final decades would it be substantially complete. For the moment, and for several decades yet, MPs were a relatively undisciplined force, only occasionally manifesting party loyalty. Contemporaries were less struck by reform ministers' activism than by their frequent failure to carry their proposals. Moreover, there remained some scope for backbench initiative, and thus for extra-parliamentary activists to float their own schemes: 1835 legislation against cruelty to animals, proposed by the Quaker MP Joseph Pease, provides an instance from this period; a private member's bill to abolish religious tests at the old universities passed the Commons, but was lost in the Lords.[161]

---

[160] H. McD. Clokie and J. W. Robinson, *Royal Commissions of Enquiry: The Significance of Investigations in British Politics* (Stanford, Ca., 1937); Best, *Temporal Pillars*, ch. 7; for ways in which the commissions served to overemphasize the deficiencies of the unreformed establishment, see Burns, *Diocesan Revival*, 143–5, 156–61, 266–9.

[161] As well as studies listed in n. 158 above, see Angus Hawkins, '"Parliamentary Government" and Victorian Political Parties, c. 1830–c. 1880', *Eng. Hist. Rev.*, 104 (1989); Parry, *Rise and Fall*, pt II. See Taylor, *Decline of British Radicalism*, for the continuing but increasingly constricted activities of backbenchers at mid-century. For difficulties experienced in reconciling various pressures on the parliamentary timetable in the early Gladstonian era, see Agatha Ramm, 'The Parliamentary Context of Cabinet Government, 1868–74', *Eng. Hist. Rev.*, 99 (1984).

In this setting, extra-parliamentary activity aimed at influencing not so much ministers directly as parliament itself continued to grow in scale and develop in technique. Numbers of petitions multiplied; countless public meetings were held; more and less transient societies, associations, and leagues proliferated. The verb 'agitate' and the nouns 'agitator' and 'agitation' entered the political lexicon.[162] The 'reformer' was reconceptualized as a certain kind of quasi-professional political broker. Basil Montagu – himself a veteran campaigner for penal-law reform – sketched a profile of the type. He was envisaged to be not a minister, but an independent operator, possibly an MP, whose task it was to educate and arouse, but also to lead, public opinion, and to bring it to bear on the political process. He needed a wide array of qualities of mind and character as well as practical political skills. The domestication of reform had advanced to the point where the reformer had a job description![163]

In the sphere of what was coming to be termed 'local government' reform legislation wrought major change. There had been local experimentation in this sphere for a century and more: poor-law administrative arrangements had been variously reconstructed; municipal corporations had – sometimes reluctantly – changed some of their ways, and had often been partially bypassed by local acts of parliament establishing elective 'street' or 'improvement' commissions.[164] After 1832, however, for the first time the institutional matrix was comprehensively reconfigured. Parishes lost the power to allocate poor relief, and were reduced to mere rating bodies, responsibility for overseeing the distribution of relief being vested instead in elected Boards of Guardians, sitting together with local magistrates. Old-style municipal corporations lost both their property and their governmental powers, again being replaced by elective bodies.[165]

---

[162] Hollis (ed.), *Pressure from Without*, goes so far as to suggest that it was only in these years that this form of activity was normalized. For petitions see n. 81 above; also P. A. Pickering, '"And-your-petitioners-etc": Chartist Petitioning in Popular Politics, 1838–48', *Eng. Hist. Rev.*, 116 (2001). For a recent case study emphasizing the ways and means of agitation, see Paul A. Pickering and Alex Tyrrell, *The People's Bread: A History of the Anti-Corn Law League* (London, 2000). The Oxford English Dictionary suggests that the term 'agitate' had come into this sort of use by *circa* 1828, citing the marquess of Anglesey to an Irish deputation: 'If you really expect success, *agitate, agitate, agitate.*' Alex Tyrrell, *A Sphere of Benevolence: The Life of Joseph Orton, Wesleyan Methodist Missionary, 1795–1842* (Melbourne, 1993), cites an 1830 instance: a Wesleyan preacher told an antislavery meeting that the Wesleyans were ready 'as a body to *agitate* – yes, he would not recal [sic] the word, – agitate the subject by petitions and every other lawful means'.

[163] Basil Montagu, *Essays and Selections* (London, 1837), 75–99.

[164] For a recent survey, see Sweet, *English Town*, chs. 2, 3, 5; the most thorough accounts remain the studies of Beatrice and Sidney Webb, *Manor and Borough*, and *Statutory Authorities for Special Purposes* (London, 1922). For the continued interest in local legislation, see J. Prest, *Liberty and Locality: Parliament, Permissive Legislation and Ratepayers' Democracies in the Nineteenth Century* (Oxford, 1990).

[165] Josef Redlich and Francis W. Hirst, *The History of Local Government in England*, 2nd edn, ed. Bryan Keith-Lucas (London, 1970); T. W. Freeman, *Geography and Regional Administration*

(cont. on p. 54)

The consequence was again that terms of debate changed, as calls for 'reform' gave way to arguments about the merits of actually existing reform. Were new structures manifestations of 'centralization'? Were they petty oligarchies in their own right? Or were they over-politicized, or perhaps too democratic?[166]

New electoral arrangements placed power squarely in the hands of ratepayers, large among whose concerns usually loomed concern for economy. As at the centre, so in the localities, reformed bodies were expected to demonstrate their virtue by their determination to retrench. This was not conducive to the development of new governmental capacities. Indeed, the workhouse-building programme mandated by the New Poor Law proved difficult to implement partly on these grounds – for all that its ostensible objective was to cut costs by deterring applications; some critics felt that the same end could be achieved more cheaply by just saying no.[167] There was none the less some growth of interest in the provision of new kinds of public amenity, to further the progress of civilization by improving the bodies and minds of the people: by the provision of public parks, and, in the next decade, public bathhouses and public libraries. Empowering legislation gave local authorities the power to provide all these amenities, and implicitly encouraged them to consider it. Public health legislation moreover gave any of a range of local authorities – whichever local people judged best for the purpose – substantial powers to deal with epidemics. These were small straws in the wind, but arguably they suggest that reform was operating to rehabilitate the notion that *government* – rather than charity or voluntary effort – should be the source of public benefits.[168]

Voluntary effort none the less remained a major fount of energy in local as in national life. Successive waves of voluntary initiative had endowed

---

(*cont.*)

in *England and Wales, 1830–1968* (London, 1968). Among recent surveys, David Eastwood, *Government and Community in the English Provinces, 1700–1870* (Basingstoke, 1997), is more interpretative, and tends to celebrate the 'unreformed' system; Bryan Keith-Lucas, *The Unreformed Local Government System* (London, 1980), has the opposite bias.

[166] See thus for London, Sheppard, *Local Government*, chs. 6, 17; John Davis, *Reforming London: The London Government Problem, 1855–1900* (Oxford, 1988); more generally, Derek Fraser, *Urban Politics in Victorian England: The Structure of Politics in Victorian Cities* (London, 1979).

[167] Edsall, *Anti-Poor Law Movement*, 65, ch. 10.

[168] Hazel Conway, *People's Parks: Development and Design of Victorian Parks in Britain* (Cambridge, 1991); Sally Sheard, 'Profit is a Dirty Word: The Development of Public Baths and Wash-houses in Britain, 1847–1915', *Social Hist. Medicine*, 13 (2000); T. Kelly, *A History of Public Libraries in Great Britain, 1845–1975* (London, 1973); Christopher Hamlin, 'Muddling in Bumbledon: Local Government and Large Sanitary Improvements: The Cases of Four British Towns, 1855–85', *Victorian Studies*, 32 (1988). For the powers and activities of local government more generally, see Redlich and Hirst, *History of Local Government*; Martin Daunton (ed.), *The Cambridge Urban History of Britain*, vol. iii: *1840–1950* (Cambridge, 2000), pt II; E. P. Hennock, *Fit and Proper Persons: Ideal and Reality in Nineteenth-Century Urban Government* (London, 1973).

communities up and down the country with a wide array of improving institutions: hospitals, dispensaries, Sunday Schools, denominational day schools, mechanics' institutes, and visiting societies being only a few of the more standard items on a long and varied list. These were maintained only at the cost of much routine fund-raising, administrative, supervisory, and hands-on voluntary effort.[169] The number of institutions run not merely for, but by – or at least with substantial input from – ordinary working people was also expanding. Benefit societies were increasingly associated with nationwide organizations, such as the Oddfellows and the Foresters, and their administration and proceedings standardized. Temperance societies multiplied from the 1830s. Frustration with what was often perceived to be the paternalistic ethos of mechanics' institutes encouraged efforts to provide reading rooms and opportunities for study and learning better geared to people's own perceptions of their needs.[170]

Though there remained plenty of scope for dispute about the merits and limitations of 'reformed' structures of government, the heterogeneous public sphere constituted by this mix of official and voluntary bodies plainly offered a wealth of opportunities for the pursuit of projects of moral and social reform. The 'reform communities' constituted by this means might, when the larger political conjuncture favoured it, provide a basis for political mobilization. But more commonly moral and social reform were the targets upon which self-proclaimed 'reform' effort focused.

The explosive growth of Chartism in the late 1830s illustrated early Victorian British society's self-mobilizing capacity, even at a relatively humble social level. It also illustrated, in more than one way, the powerful and potentially competing pull of alternative conceptions of reform.

Though Chartist sympathizers, even Chartist leaders, included some relatively prosperous businessmen and professionals, Chartism was overwhelmingly – as continental observers were surprised to find – a movement by and for the working classes.[171] This was possible because associational networks,

169 There is much of general interest in R. J. Morris, *Class, Sect and Party: The Making of the British Middle Class: Leeds, 1820–50* (Manchester, 1990); F. K. Prochaska, *Women and Philanthropy in Nineteenth-Century England* (Oxford, 1980). See also the work of M. J. D. Roberts, esp. his *Making Victorian Morals* (Cambridge, forthcoming).

170 Relevant studies include P. H. J. H. Gosden, *Self-Help: Voluntary Association in the Nineteenth Century* (London, 1973); Harrison, *Drink and the Victorians*; Eileen Yeo, 'Robert Owen and Radical Culture', in Sidney Pollard and John Salt (eds.), *Robert Owen: Prophet of the Poor* (London, 1971).

171 The extent to which Chartism was 'a working-class movement' has recently been debated: see esp. Gareth Stedman Jones, 'Rethinking Chartism', in his *Languages of Class: Studies in English Working-Class History, 1832–1982* (Cambridge, 1983), 90–178; and for a critique focusing esp. upon his account of Chartism, P. A. Pickering, 'Class without Words: Symbolic Communication in the Chartist Movement', *Past and Present*, no. 112 (1986). We are inclined to favour the irenic approach outlined by Miles Taylor, 'Rethinking the Chartists: Searching for Synthesis in the Historiography of Chartism', *Hist. Jl*, 39 (1996), esp. at 487. For broader debate about class, see also n. 144 above.

institutions, and practices so thoroughly permeated society. Chartists drew on experience not only in previous political agitations, but also in friendly societies, trade unions, religious congregations, and temperance societies. They held speaker meetings, meetings for group song and prayer, and invaded other people's meetings. They made extensive use of the press, but also of 'missionaries' to link together scattered organizations and itinerant lecturers to spread the word and cater to popular hunger for information and ideas. They lobbied, propagandized, petitioned, armed and drilled, and attempted a general strike. The enormous repertoire of forms and practices which they had to draw upon, and the flexibility they showed in adapting this repertoire to their own ends, were conditions for Chartism's impressive flowering among people whose material resources were often meagre.

Yet in a sense these same characteristics set the scene for its dissolution. For, as hopes of persuading parliament to implement the six points of the Charter waned, it was easy for members to reallocate their energies between projects, and thus in effect to turn their backs on Chartism, in so far as they increasingly pursued the Charter's ultimate object – an improvement in the condition of ordinary people – not by politico-constitutional, but by moral, social, and economic endeavours.[172]

Among some members of the parliamentary and governing classes, meanwhile, there took place a different kind of shift to the social. Some observers, not persuaded by Chartists' constitutional diagnosis of their situation, and alarmed by their militancy, were yet ready to believe that there must be some real ground for their grievances. As they came to see it, government at all levels and the public-spirited could best respond by striving to improve material and social conditions in Britain's workplaces, cities, towns, and largely proletarianized countryside. In this diagnosis, Chartists confused the issue by invoking the 'rights of Englishmen', when what was really in question was 'the condition of England'.[173]

---

[172] Eileen Yeo, 'Christianity in Chartist Struggle, 1838–1842', *Past and Present*, no. 91 (May 1981); Eileen Yeo, 'Some Practices and Problems of Chartist Democracy', in Epstein and Thompson (eds.), *Chartist Experience*. Lyon, *Politicians in the Pulpit*, ch. 6, extends Yeo's account. There is also much of interest on this theme in Pickering, *Chartism and the Chartists*. Of course some Chartists continued to be active in reformist politics. For Chartist destinations, see Christopher Godfrey, *Chartist Lives: The Anatomy of a Working-Class Movement* (New York, 1987), pt III.

[173] Thus Robert Slaney, on whom see Paul Richards, 'R. A. Slaney, the Industrial Town, and Early Victorian Social Policy', *Social Hist.*, 4 (1979). Thomas Carlyle is commonly credited with coining the catchphrase 'condition of England' in his 1839 essay, 'Chartism'. These concerns of course had older roots, and the particular form they took at this time was shaped by wider trends – see Andrew Lees, *Cities Perceived: Urban Society in European and American Thought, 1820–1940* (Manchester, 1985). But political disturbances in these years helped to focus British attention upon them, as illustrated by the proliferation of 'social problem' novels: Kathleen Tillotson, *Novels of the 1840s* (Oxford, 1956).

VII

If this volume has a centre of gravity, it lies in the 1820s and 1830s. Many of the chapters cover longer spans of time, but all cover these decades, and some focus primarily upon them. These were the years when reform enthusiasms were, by earlier standards, most diverse and widespread, by later standards most intense.

The choice of 1850 as the terminal date for this collection does not imply that we think that that year marked a great watershed – indeed, we attach less significance to this than to our starting date. We chose the year to mark the approximate point at which one important reform project – the Chartist project – dissolved into a myriad parts. There were changes thereafter in what 'reform' meant to people; in the kinds of reforms that were pursued, and in the environment in which and the means by which they were pursued. Yet so had there been throughout the decades we have been surveying. Moreover, some important continuities stretch through from the years on which we have focused into the decades that lie beyond this volume's reach.

Until the 1860s – in most respects, for longer than that – mid-Victorian generations lived in an institutional landscape that, in its main features, was the landscape the reformers had made. This was so, first, because there was no 'restoration': no part of the work of reform was ever reversed. Second, because following the dramatic innovations in the structures of government enacted in the early 1830s, the pace of institutional reform slackened. The system of parliamentary representation was not further 'reformed' until 1867. Local government arrangements changed little until elective 'school boards' were established in 1870; elective county councils were not introduced until 1888. The church–state relationship was not significantly altered until William Gladstone took the symbolically significant step of abolishing church rates in 1868 (in practice, collection had in many places already become impossible to enforce), and then, in 1869, proceeded to sanction the disestablishment of the Irish portion of the 'Established Church of England and Ireland'.[174]

Throughout these mid-century decades, none the less, 'reform' remained a persistent theme. This was so firstly because, if usually in less dramatic ways than in the 1830s, the work of implementing 'reform' continued, both at national and at local levels. Some institutional issues, left – as it were – on the table at the end of the 1830s, were pursued.[175] Peel, the first post-Reform Tory

---

[174] A recent survey of these years is K. Theodore Hoppen, *The Mid-Victorian Generation, 1846–86* (Oxford, 1998). For specific 'reforms' noted here see John Garrard, *Democratisation in Britain* (Basingstoke, 2001) for the progress of franchise reform; for local government see n. 165. For Gladstone, see Ellens, *Religious Routes*, ch. 5; H. C. G. Matthew, *Gladstone, 1809–1898* (Oxford 1996), 141; O. Anderson, 'Gladstone's Abolition of Compulsory Church Rates', *Jl Eccl. Hist.*, 25 (1974).

[175] Parry, *Rise and Fall*, pt III, offers a survey unsympathetic to Tory efforts; Gash, *Robert Peel*, leans the other way. E. D. Steele, *Palmerston and Liberalism, 1855–65* (Cambridge, 1991), makes a case for Palmerston as reformer.

prime minister, though content to work within reformed structures, showed little appetite for further such change, but he did attempt to resolve outstanding questions about the role of the Bank of England, presided over continuing programmes of law and church reform, and endorsed attempts to grapple with the inherently controversial issue of how to enhance educational provision in a religiously divided society. Subsequent ministries – Whig (or Liberal) and Tory (or Conservative) – occasionally flirted with the idea of further parliamentary reform, and considered options for civil service and army reform. Faced with Indian 'Mutiny' in 1857, government and parliament removed from the East India Company responsibility for the government of India. They launched inquiries into the ancient universities and into endowed schools. 'Pressure from without' upon government through parliament continued to run high through the 1840s – when, to use only one indicator, as Colin Leys has shown, total numbers of signatures on petitions presented to parliament peaked; numbers of petitions would indeed not fall off much until the end of the century. In this setting, many issues confronting ministers and parliaments were highly charged, in ways often inflected by ideas about what should or could be expected from a reformed parliament.[176] Several of the initiatives listed above were embarked upon in the context of this kind of pressure, as was Peel's 1846 decision to repeal the Corn Laws. Agitations against 'taxes on knowledge' elicited a series of concessions, while anti-tithe agitation prompted the establishment of commutation procedures. Despite initially vigorous anti-poor-law protest, especially in the north of England, ministers refused to reconsider more than the central administrative apparatus of the New Poor Law. They did, however, concede a ten-hour factory working day, and developed new procedures for dealing with epidemics and promoting sanitary reform, thus going some way to meet the expectation that a reformed parliament would grapple vigorously with social problems and promote improvement in the condition of the people.[177] There was similarly at the local level a continuing trickle of both institutional and social-reform activity. Some free-standing institutions, moreover – hospitals,

---

[176] Hollis (ed.), *Pressure from Without*, is a classic collection on this theme; see also Leys, 'Petitioning'. Recent accounts of various aspects of pressure-group politics include G. R. Searle, *Entrepreneurial Politics in Mid-Victorian Britain* (Oxford, 1993); Timothy Larsen, *Friends of Religious Equality: Nonconformist Politics in Mid-Victorian England* (Woodbridge, 1999); Lawrence Goldman, *Science, Reform and Politics in Victorian Britain* (Cambridge, 2002).

[177] Though there has been much stimulating work on all these topics in recent decades, among general surveys surprisingly, U. Q. R. Henriques, *Before the Welfare State: Social Administration in Early Industrial Britain* (London, 1979) has not been effectively superseded. More specialized surveys include Geoffrey Finlayson, *Citizen, State and Social Welfare in Britain, 1830–1990* (Oxford, 1994); Lynn Hollen Lees, *The Solidarities of Strangers: The English Poor Laws and the People, 1700–1948* (Cambridge, 1998); Gray, *Factory Question*; Christopher Hamlin, *Public Health and Social Justice in the Age of Chadwick* (Cambridge, 1998). Mary Poovey, *Making a Social Body: British Cultural Formation, 1830–64* (Chicago, 1995), offers a cultural perspective.

endowed schools, universities – made more or less voluntary efforts to put their own house in order.[178]

Implicit in the above account is the persistence of interest in 'reform' on the part of those not in a position to enact reforms themselves. Reform agitators came in more and less passionate varieties. The drama and excitement of the early 1830s helped to shape the expectations of a generation for whom 'reform' tended to summon up the image of a crusade: a mighty moral struggle, likely to entail clashes with titans. In this climate were formed the uncompromising 'philosophical radicals' of the 1830s and 1840s; the Chartists; and what Alex Tyrrell has termed the 'moral radicals', men such as the Quaker Joseph Sturge: long-term antislavery activist, Corn-Law repealer, promoter of 'complete suffrage', and luminary of the peace movement. (Sturge also sponsored a juvenile reformatory, favoured spelling reform, and patronized alternative medical therapies.)[179]

A younger, post-Reform generation matured in an environment in which reform was less instinctively conceived as entailing confrontation; rather, as a normal feature of public life, a process at which one had simply to plug away. A younger generation of reform activists did none the less emerge, formed by attending university in an era of university-reform debates; by exposure to metropolitan intellectual radicalism or nascent bohemianism; by the experience of growing up within a still distinctive dissenting culture – within which traditions of resistance were revered – or by adult experience in trying to oversee reform in the public service, local government, or the voluntary sector; in the temperance movement; in trade unions; or any of the many other forums in which reform projects of one or another kind were pursued in mid-Victorian Britain.[180]

For – and this is our final general point about the persistence of interest in 'reform' through the middle years of the nineteenth century – though reforming activists in a strong sense – initiators, leaders – were inevitably a minority, the range of opportunities to engage in some kind of reforming activity in this

---

[178] Matters given classic fictional treatment in Anthony Trollope, *The Warden* (1855) and George Eliot, *Middlemarch* (1871–2). See also G. F. A. Best, 'The Road to Hiram's Hospital', *Victorian Studies*, 5 (1961–2); Ralph Arnold, *The Whiston Matter* (London, 1961).

[179] Thomas, *Philosophic Radicals*; Tyrrell, *Joseph Sturge*.

[180] Christopher Harvie, *The Lights of Liberalism: University Liberals and the Challenge of Democracy, 1860–86* (London, 1976); C. A. Kent, 'The Idea of Bohemia in Mid-Victorian England', *Queen's Quarterly*, 80 (1973); C. A. Kent, 'The Whittington Club: A Bohemian Experiment in Middle Class Social Reform', *Victorian Studies*, 18 (1974); Larsen, *Friends of Religious Equality*; Goldman, *Science, Reform*. See also Kathryn Gleadle, *The Early Feminists: Radical Unitarians and the Emergence of the Women's Rights Movement, 1831–51* (Basingstoke, 1995). General overviews of continuity and change in reforming causes and personnel are provided in Brian Harrison, 'A Genealogy of Reform in Modern Britain', in C. Bolt and S. Drescher (eds.), *Anti-Slavery, Religion, and Reform: Essays in Memory of Roger Anstey* (Folkestone, 1980); Roberts, *Making Victorian Morals*.

society were very many, and the numbers of those who were in some more dilute sense of the term 'reformers' multitudinous indeed. Of course within this culture there was endless scope for disagreement as to what reforms were desirable and what reforms were practicable. Yet certain values, aspirations, and preoccupations were widely shared.[181]

There existed counter-discourses. There were those outraged or at least unconvinced by particular reforms; those suspicious of hunger for change; those who thought reform utopian, or mechanistic, or puritanical. Many who supported some versions of reform criticized other versions in these terms. In due course Conservatives, without setting their faces against all reform, would nevertheless exploit this array of counter-reform impulses to fashion a new – vote-winning – identity for themselves. At mid-century, however, this counter-reform ethos remained as yet underdeveloped. Reform values, though by no means unchallenged, were more hegemonic.[182]

Among sub-types of reform, 'social reform' was a relatively new formulation. By attending more closely to some of the things that were discussed under this rubric we can further illuminate aspects of continuity and change at mid-century.[183]

'Social reform' meant broadly 'changing society for the better'. One tradition of thought about how to do this emphasized the need to change governmental and quasi-governmental (charitable or voluntary) institutions and practices in such a way as to improve in turn individuals' material and moral states. This might entail reforming civil or criminal law; improving penal regimes – probably with the aim of making them more reformative; reforming welfare institutions – so as to encourage independence, while at the same time not failing to alleviate inescapable hardship; promoting both formal education and all kinds of opportunities for learning; and improving living and working environments to make them more conducive to health of body and purity of mind. It is evident that much 'social reform' endeavour of this kind, though not previously described as such, had a long pedigree. Without tracing these various causes back to their most distant origins, we might yet observe that Samuel Romilly, Samuel Whitbread, and the young William Wilberforce would not have felt entirely out of place at the meetings of that great mid-century social-reform think tank, the Social Science Association.[184]

---

[181] For stress on shared values, Eugenio Biagini, *Liberty, Retrenchment and Reform: Popular Liberalism in the Age of Gladstone, 1860–1880* (Cambridge, 1992).

[182] For conservative ideology in the making, see Jon Lawrence, *Speaking for the People: Party, Language, and Popular Politics in England, 1867–1914* (Cambridge, 1998); Allen Warren, 'Disraeli, the Conservatives and the National Church, 1837–81', in S. J. C. Taylor and J. P. Parry (eds.), *Parliament and the Church, 1529–1960* (Edinburgh, 2000); Heera Chung, 'The Church Defence Problem in Conservative Politics, 1841–7' (University of Cambridge Ph.D. thesis, 2002).

[183] For the novelty of the term, and early examples of its use, see Innes, below, p. 96 and n. 91.

[184] Goldman, *Science, Reform*.

Three things about that body would probably nevertheless have surprised them. First, that the Association was as well patronized by MPs and even ministers as it was: it would have been evident that the tone and ethos of government had changed since their day (even granted that the SSA was formed in part out of frustration at the difficulties of getting complex but considered legislation through mid-Victorian parliaments). Second, they would probably have been surprised at just how elaborate – how empirically dense, how ramified in argument, how systematic in presentation – discussion of such matters had become. This was in no way peculiarly a British development. 'Social questions' were the subject of similarly dense and sophisticated argumentation on the continent, and information and ideas were increasingly exchanged at international congresses.

Third, they would probably have been surprised at the presence of women alongside men in many (though not all) of the Association's proceedings, and at the relatively prominent place given to questions about women's role in society. The agenda of women's issues would probably have surprised them too: women's rights within marriage; procedures for ending marriages; women's needs for higher and professional education and employment. Women had been coming into view as charitable and reforming activists in the late eighteenth and early nineteenth centuries, but women's place in the charitable, campaigning, literary, and political world was one of the things that changed most rapidly from the 1830s, and these newly prominent women had helped to develop this largely new agenda of women's issues.[185]

---

[185] There has been much illuminating writing on women and public life in recent years. Some relevant works have been cited above (nn. 72, 98, 131, 134). See also Jane Rendall (ed.), *Equal or Different: Women's Politics, 1800–1914* (Oxford, 1987); Amanda Vickery (ed.), *Women, Privilege and Power: British Politics 1750 to the Present* (Stanford, Calif., 2001); Leonore Davidoff and Catherine Hall, *Family Fortunes: Men and Women of the English Middle Class, 1780–1850* (London, 1987); Barbara Taylor, *Eve and the New Jerusalem: Socialism and Feminism in the Nineteenth Century* (London, 1983); Jutta Schwarzkopf, *Women in the Chartist Movement* (Basingstoke, 1991); Alex Tyrrell, '"Woman's Mission" and Pressure Group Politics in Britain (1825–60)', *Bull. John Rylands Lib.*, 113 (1980); Pickering and Tyrrell, *People's Bread*, ch. 6. Biographies of prominent, publicly active women include R. K. Webb, *Harriet Martineau: A Radical Victorian* (London, 1960); F. B. Smith, *Florence Nightingale: Reputation and Power* (London, 1982); Sheila R. Herstein, *A Mid-Victorian Feminist: Barbara Leigh Smith Bodichon* (New Haven, 1985). Gleadle, *Early Feminists*, focuses on the emergence of a set of 'women's issues'; most studies with this focus, however, concentrate on the years after 1860. For some insights into the 1850s, see Martha Vicinus, *Independent Women: Work and Community for Single Women, 1850–1920* (London, 1985); Lee Holcombe, *Wives and Property: Reform of the Married Women's Property Law in Nineteenth-Century England* (Toronto, 1983); Mary Lyndon Shanley, *Feminism, Marriage and the Law in Victorian England, 1850–95* (Princeton, 1989) – though see also Olive Anderson, 'Hansard's Hazards: An Illustration from Recent Interpretations of Married Women's Property Law and the 1857 Divorce Act', *Eng. Hist. Rev.*, 112 (1997); Jane Rendall, 'A Moral Engine? Feminism, Liberalism and the English Woman's Journal', in Rendall (ed.), *Equal or Different*; Philippa Levine, *Feminist Lives in Victorian England: Private Roles and Public Commitment* (Oxford, 1990). See also E. K. Helsinger, R. L. Sheets, and W. Veeder, *The Woman Question: Society and Literature in Britain and America, 1837–83*, 3 vols. (Chicago, 1983).

The social reform enterprise, so conceived, thus had certain features traceable back to the earliest years of our period, or even earlier, alongside others that were more novel.

But 'social reform' was also sometimes understood at this time to mean something more profound, harder to achieve, more dangerous to attempt, more likely to meet overt and powerful resistance. When Owen and the Owenites, probably the first regular users of the term, employed it in the 1820s, they meant by it radical change in the way society was structured: in family and household, in the workplace, in the relation of people to land. Doubting the power of legislation to effect such change – or the likelihood that any legislature would attempt it – they had urged rather the need for direct change in social practice: people had to take it upon themselves to live differently. Aspirations for 'social reform' thus conceived played an important part in the background to Chartism. The European revolutions of 1848 saw for the first time the emergence of demands for 'social revolution', thus understood. In Britain, some ex-Chartists, when they lost hope in political solutions, aligned themselves with the international social revolutionary movement.[186]

This did not immediately reshape British politics. On the contrary, those who argue that British politics was played out in terms of *broadly* similar ideas and preoccupations from, say, the second to the final quarter of the nineteenth century, seem to be right. Yet changes within that time-span must not be overlooked either. One effect of the prominence that this vision of 'social reform' briefly achieved around 1848 was the reorientation of ideas about political options along a new continuum: from 'individualism' to 'socialism'. In the late eighteenth and early nineteenth centuries, 'reform' had been a bogey word, against which many had chosen to define themselves, leaving those who thought reform a valid cause struggling to legitimize their efforts. By mid-century, 'reform' had been largely naturalized and tamed. In its place, a new bogey was beginning to take shape.

VIII

As we stated at the outset, our object in writing this introduction has been not to summarize what follows, but to set the scene for it. In conclusion we would, however, like to say a little more about the essays that follow, chiefly in relation to this initial overview. We emphasize in this volume that 'reform' was a multi-stranded project, and that the language of 'reform' was used by diverse people to diverse ends. It follows that numerous difficulties attend the task that we

---

[186] For Owen and Owenites, see Harrison, *Robert Owen*; Claeys, *Citizens and Saints*; Pollard and Salt, *Robert Owen*. For radical internationalism, see Margot Finn, *After Chartism: Class and Nation in English Radical Politics, 1848–74* (Cambridge, 1993), 82–92.

have just attempted: that of setting the scene for something so polymorphous. By exploring some of the ways in which the following chapters complicate the picture we have provided, and indeed raise questions about it, or suggest further questions deserving of enquiry, we hope to launch readers into the main body of the volume in an appropriately questioning frame of mind.

Joanna Innes' chapter focuses upon the word 'reform': upon the heritage of associations it had at the start of our period, and upon ways in which its use changed during our period. Students of language distinguish between the 'lexical field' of words – the array of uses and meanings associated with specified words – and their 'semantic field' – the array of words used to denote similar things.[187] In her chapter, Joanna Innes is primarily concerned with the lexical field of 'reform': with the range of ways in which the word 'reform' was employed. She suggests that its use was coloured by its diverse associations, making it at once ambiguous and flexible. But the chapter is also concerned with the word's semantic field. Thus, it focuses especially upon certain uses of the word, and considers these in relation to other words denoting similar things: words such as 'innovation' and 'improvement'.

Reflection upon such issues of language points up a difficulty which inevitably attends the construction of any survey of 'reform' activity, in this or any other period: a difficulty which we cannot wish away, but which we think it beneficial to highlight. In this collection, we direct attention to projects that contemporaries talked about as projects of 'reform'. We think that this is useful because connections between these projects were not merely contingent. They embodied common, or at least overlapping, preoccupations and concerns: by considering them together, we gain (we suggest) an enhanced understanding of contemporary outlooks. In practice, there were important overlaps between the supporters of different 'reform' projects, lending credibility to the notion that they reflected related concerns. Of course, supporters of one reform project did not usually – probably did not ever – support all other reform projects. But their common description *as* reform projects encouraged at the very least reflection on their interrelations – prompting, among other things, repeated attempts to distinguish between different kinds of reform.

There is none the less certainly something arbitrary about allowing the use of a common term to determine the scope of an enquiry. In practice, those who supported 'reforms' commonly also supported other projects *not* routinely termed reforms, which might be every bit as significantly interlinked in their minds with their prime concerns as any so-called 'reform' projects were. In this introduction, we have not restricted ourselves to a discussion of developments and projects termed 'reforms' only, but have also sketched other aspects of the

---

[187] Iain Hampsher-Monk, Karin Tilmans, and Frank van Vree (eds.), *The History of Concepts: Comparative Perspectives* (Amsterdam, 1998), introduction, 2.

contemporary scene in so far as we have judged them relevant. Yet this approach – a more common approach in the historiography – also has its problems. If we cease to employ contemporary uses of the term 'reform' as a guide to what does and what does not merit inclusion, what *is* our guide? Do we not run the risk of imposing an arbitrary, perhaps anachronistic framework of interpretation upon the period: charting it in terms of subsequent understandings of what was, and what was not, a 'reform' effort? Both approaches thus have their problems. By adopting an approach not commonly taken we hope to provide some new perspectives.

In most accounts of the age of reform, parliamentary reform holds pride of place. In this collection, despite the fact that we acknowledge it as the most common referent of the term 'reform', we have marginalized it: we have not given it direct or extended treatment. This may seem perverse. However, we do not mean thereby to denigrate its importance. Debates over parliamentary reform have played a large part in this introduction. (Perhaps even too large? Perhaps in this respect we have veered too far back into the grooves worn by a traditional historiography?) Though not the main focus of any of the chapters that follow, parliamentary reform moreover finds a place in most of them. Joanna Innes' essay suggests that it was the campaign for parliamentary reform that popularized 'reform' as a slogan – and helped to shift uses of the term away from the moral towards the institutional. In an age that attached great importance to constitutionalism, it is perhaps unsurprising that the constitutional associations 'reform' acquired should have loomed so large in the contemporary imagination. Attitudes to parliamentary reform coloured people's willingness to use the term for other purposes. Parliamentary reform moreover had important implications – both practical and symbolic – for the achievement of other 'reform' projects. The fact that those who were wary of parliamentary reform also tended to be wary of other projects called 'reforms' helped to convince many supporters of particular reform projects that parliamentary reform was a necessary means to their end. The 'reform ministry' and the 'reformed parliament' were commonly expected to implement other 'reforms'.

Parliament was, however – as we have emphasized, and as the following chapters demonstrate at greater length – by no means the only institution thought to have become corrupt, or to have failed to adapt to changing times, and in consequence to stand in need of 'reform' or 'reformation'. Within other institutional contexts, moreover, the word 'reform' had its own distinctive connotations and histories. Contemporaries *might* in institutionally distinct contexts be prepared to avow themselves 'reformers' even though unsympathetic to parliamentary reform. Though parliamentary action was seen as a possible means of achieving all manner of 'reforms' it was rarely the only possible means and by no means always the preferred one.

Chapters on government, the law, the church, and medicine bring these points out. They introduce us to a variety of institutional settings, each with its own reforming sub-culture. Within the fields of law and the church especially, the language of 'reform' had a local history. Some 'reformers' in these institutional settings had a broader identity as reformers: thus, for example, Joseph Hume, dogged administrative and fiscal reformer; Henry Brougham, law reformer; Jonathan Shipley would-be church reformer, and Thomas Wakley, medical reformer. But there were others still more deeply enmeshed with particular institutions, whose concern to improve them was not matched by reforming commitments, or even reforming sympathies, elsewhere. Within each institutional setting there were also debates about what was, and what was not, a 'reform' or a desirable reform. Self-proclaimed 'reformers' did not invariably figure on the 'reform' side in all such debates, as Ian Burney shows in the case of Wakley.

In this introduction, we have attempted to provide a general account of the development of reforming opinion and activity over seven and more decades. But of course there were variations from one strand of reforming thought and practice to another. In practice, the accounts given in the several institutional reform chapters seem broadly to fit the introduction's outline chronology. In the cases of government, law, and church, though there were longer histories of reforming effort, there were new initiatives – in the case of government, major new initiatives – in the 1780s. Thereafter, demands for 'reform' seem to have fallen off, reviving in the 1820s, when the pace and ambition of reforming activity also quickened. The medical-reform debate, though again drawing on older ideas and concerns, took shape *as* a 'reform' debate only at that time.

In their chapters on anti-slavery and 'physiological reform', David Turley and Kathryn Gleadle explore projects also described by contemporaries in terms of 'reform' – but drawing at least as much on moral as on institutional understandings of that term. In these versions of 'reform', we encounter a broader and more diverse array of 'reformers': including, notably, women, who played little if any part in the reform sub-cultures described in the preceding, institutional chapters. Proponents of this latter set of reforms did not need to have established places in formal institutional settings in order to operate as reformers. Part of the creative genius of the first generation of antislavery campaigners, the generation of the 1780s, had indeed lain in their ability to find ways of making ordinary people, men and women, feel that they should and *could* do something about the evils of slavery and the slave-trade. The reforms of the self with which Kathryn Gleadle is concerned were largely addressed within the home, and as such relatively easily engaged with by women responsible for managing households and families – or at least by those who had time, energy, and means to consider novel ways of discharging those responsibilities. But, as this chapter emphasizes, this version of reform was in important respects also dependent on support networks beyond the domestic setting: upon example, information, and facilities for alternative therapy; it had a public as well as a private dimension.

Given that different conceptions of 'reform' underpinned these projects, we might expect that their link with institutional reforming projects would have been loose. In fact, there were important interconnections, though these were not constant over time. The antislavery movement, though in part a moral-reform project, and as such able to draw in supporters whose other commitments were moral and religious, also embodied a call for radical legislative and governmental action: for the prohibition of a profitable trade; the criminalization of previously legitimate activity; the exercise of armed might to uphold prohibition; and, ultimately – as attention moved on from the slave-trade to slavery itself – for the abolition of a species of property. We should not be surprised to find important overlaps between those who supported these initiatives and those prepared to countenance other kinds of radical institutional overhaul – or between those who opposed the one and the other. Initially, in the optimistic ambience of the 1780s, opposition to slavery was not a *very* partisan stance – except in towns such as Bristol and Liverpool where some were deeply implicated in the trade. When the French Revolution made projects of radical change look perilous, attitudes became more polarized – though the antislavery cause continued to attract some wary of other institutional reforms. In the rather different atmosphere of the 1820s, antislavery mobilization seems, by contrast, to have helped arouse interest in broader reform projects – especially in the late 1820s, when it began to be argued that no unreformed parliament would ever address this mighty task. It has been suggested that the antislavery cause played an important part in politicizing a new generation of dissenters.

Why 'physiological reform' should have been associated with sympathy for institutional reform causes is harder to see – and it is of the nature of Kathryn Gleadle's evidence that she cannot precisely evaluate the strength of these interconnections. It none the less seems plain that in important instances the two did go hand in hand. Perhaps more than any of the other chapters, this chapter raises intriguing – if not immediately resolvable – questions about the existence and character of a broad 'reform culture'.

The next three chapters explore aspects of reform and the arts: in the opera, in the theatre, and in 'art institutions' – that is, in institutions devoted to the encouragement or display of the visual arts, such as the Royal Academy, British Institution, and National Gallery. These topics do not figure in most mainstream accounts of the 'age of reform'. In our view, interconnections of language, thought, and personnel entitle them to consideration. In these contexts, institutional and moral aspects of reform – never entirely separable – were closely intertwined. Opera, theatre, and the visual arts all operated within a

formal institutional context – which in the case of the theatre was closely regulated by statute. All these institutions were vulnerable to critical scrutiny in
the light of general reforming tenets. Were they excessively oligarchic or 'aristocratic'? Did they enjoy indefensible privileges? Often they could be argued
to be wanting on one or the other ground. The substance of what they offered
was also open to moral scrutiny – in a broad understanding of that term. Was
what they offered likely to promote social and cultural improvement? Was this
fare reaching the right audiences to work to optimal effect? Our understanding
of how wide-ranging and how multivalent reform critiques of contemporary
society were is enhanced when we bring the arts into our purview.

Once again, we find some significant and suggestive overlaps of personnel.
Though he does not figure in Katherine Newey's essay, the 'radical tailor of
Charing Cross', Francis Place, provides a link between the world of popular
radicalism and the theatre. Active in the 'Old Price' riots of 1809, Place thereafter retained an interest in problems associated both with the patent theatres'
privileged status and with the influence the theatre had and might have on the
moral tone of society.[188] In the 1830s, as Katherine Newey does tell us, it was
expected that the reformed parliament would among its many other enterprises
set about 'reforming' the theatre – though in the event no significant legislation
emerged.

The moral and cultural dimension of arts-reform projects, however, helped to
ensure that they had the potential to command interest across a broad spectrum.
In fact, both the founding of the National Gallery – with a broadly conceived
cultural mission in view – and the rescinding of the patent theatres' monopoly
took place under Tory administrations: in 1826 and 1843 respectively.

As in other contexts, so in the sphere of the arts reforming strategies proceeded along diverse lines: recourse to parliament being only one option. For
contemporaries the enterprise of reforming the arts in fact sharply posed important and difficult questions about the extent to which cultural and moral
change *could* be brought about by institutional means.

Whereas in this introduction we have attempted to construct a form of overall
narrative – though a loosely articulated one – the individual chapters thus display
much diversity. We suggest that there *are* general patterns discernible across the
various fields that the individual chapters survey: commonalities of language,
thought, and personnel. We suggest furthermore that it is possible to discern
an underlying chronology, in which certain periods were more conducive to
'reform', or to particular versions of 'reform', than others. In the end, however,
we want to present a picture that combines unity and diversity. There were
common themes and preoccupations, but they were played out across a range of

---

[188] Marc Baer, *Theatre and Disorder in Late Georgian London* (Oxford, 1992); Moody, *Illegitimate Theatre*, 45–6.

differing fields in differing circumstances. The reform critique was multivalent: not infinitely adaptable, but adaptable for many different ends. We have fulfilled one of our objectives if we have effectively illustrated that.

One issue, which we think an important issue, is not engaged with at length either in the introduction or in the individual chapters of this book. We have in mind the distinction traditionally made between 'middle-class' and 'working-class' reformism or radicalism. Many (though not all) proponents of the reform causes explored in detail here were middle-class, in some intelligible sense of that fuzzy term. We did not set out to marginalize working-class reform projects – and in this introduction, we have attempted to ensure that they have a place within our larger narrative. It remains the case that working-class protagonists have a low profile within the main body of this book. We do not wholly regret this. In the past few decades, a succession of hard-working and imaginative historians have done sterling work uncovering the world of working-class thought and action in relation to parliamentary and other forms of reform. In that context, the study of 'middle-class reform' has rather languished.[189] It would be pleasing if this volume helped to revive interest in the wide range of 'middle-class' reform projects.

But this way of defining the task also needs refinement. As our use of quotation marks is intended to indicate, though we are prepared to use the labels 'middle-class' and 'working-class' as convenient shorthand, we do not think that such ascriptions should pass unexamined. We think there is a need for the constituencies supportive of different versions of 'reform' to be carefully mapped, and for varying patterns of support to be explored and accounted for. The terms 'middle-class' and 'working-class' will probably prove blunt tools for use in that context. Some of the issues we are concerned with here appear to have had wide appeal: thus not only parliamentary reform, but also antislavery. The same could be said for some other causes only touched upon in passing here, such as the campaign for a free press.[190] Mediating figures such as Francis Place – a journeyman tailor in his youth, who retained links with working-class activists through into his profitable retirement – were certainly interested in reform causes beyond the narrowly political and economic: in the case of Place,

---

[189] This is less true for the years after 1840: see, e.g., Pickering and Tyrrell, *People's Bread*; Searle, *Entrepreneurial Politics*.

[190] The place of the slavery issue in late eighteenth- and early nineteenth-century popular politics remains unclear. Thompson, *Making of the English Working Class*, strikingly ignores it altogether; Drescher, *Capitalism and Anti-Slavery*, hypothesizes, but does not demonstrate, significant working-class support. Fladeland, *Abolitionists*, critically examines the charge that abolitionists were indifferent to – even wished to distract attention from – working-class problems at home, but her study focuses on elite, not popular attitudes. Among studies of reforms other than parliamentary reform, Wiener, *War of the Unstamped*, is unusual in being substantially constructed around an exploration of differing forms of middle- and working-class engagement with an issue.

including theatre reform, as noted above. MPs who struck radical stances and hoped to garner broad popular support (such as Thomas Wakley), publicists and writers who favoured radical democracy (such as Jeremy Bentham and James Mill), editors of popular newspapers, and lecturers in relatively open forums (such as Richard Carlile) certainly had interests and agendas which included items covered here. We have much to learn about the range of concerns represented to and espoused by members of different social milieux, including the milieu of petty shopkeepers and clerks, who sustained a good deal of radical activity at the local level, alongside that of the trades and other 'mechanical' employments – or (to employ a different kind of typology) in the varying milieux of public meetings and societies, lecture halls and debating clubs, major and minor theatres and other cheap entertainment venues, and in the pages of pamphlets and newspapers composed and sold with varying audiences in mind.[191]

To the extent that we find differences between concerns canvassed and endorsed in these different settings, how should these differences be explained? In terms of fundamental differences of sympathy or ideology separating one social class from another? Or in terms of differences of sympathy or ideology that cut *across* classes? Or, alternatively, perhaps, in terms of differences in what people felt to be their sphere of competence, or in what they thought they had the power to affect? Or, again, might differences have resulted from different strategies pursued by different opinion-formers (and then, how should these be explained)? We might also expect to find some regional or local variation – the repertoire of causes that attracted interest in London, for example, being different from those that attracted attention in Birmingham, or Exeter, or in the Welsh valleys. (Only David Turley among our contributors directs attention to this last form of difference.)[192]

The introduction to this volume has been largely English in focus, with only the occasional glance at other parts of the British Isles and empire. Among our concluding chapters, those by Jennifer Ridden and Miles Taylor go some way to redress this deficiency. Jennifer Ridden argues interestingly that we would be wrong to suppose that reform politics had little salience in an Irish setting in the aftermath of Catholic Emancipation. Irish historians have most commonly written either about peasant rebels and O'Connellite proto-nationalist protest or

---

[191] McCalman, *Radical Underworld*, provides a sophisticated account of diverse reform milieux in London, 1795–1840.

[192] Both the social relationships of politics and regional variation in political culture have received more attention in the historiography of the 1840s. See for the former, e.g., Thompson, *Chartists*, ch. 10; for the latter, classically, Asa Briggs (ed.), *Chartist Studies* (London, 1959); and for both approaches, Pickering and Tyrrell, *People's Bread*. Some light is shed on social relations in early nineteenth-century politics in L. G. Mitchell, 'The Whigs, the People and Reform', in Blanning and Wende, *Reform in Britain and Germany*; Belchem and Epstein, 'Nineteenth-Century Gentleman Leader'.

about Irish Toryism; yet in fact, there was also an important but under-explored strand of Irish liberalism. Jennifer Ridden's essay compares the ways, means, and appeal of O'Connellite and Liberal reform movements in an Irish setting. Miles Taylor offers an introduction to a very large subject: that of reform and the empire. He is chiefly concerned with the impact of imperial issues on British reforming thought and practice – but much has also been written and much more might be written about the ways in which reform concerns were echoed and adapted in different imperial settings.[193]

Finally, Jonathan Sperber compares British with European reforming thought and practice. In this introduction we have stressed European influence upon Britain and the interchange of ideas between Britain and the continent. Jonathan Sperber stresses differences in the goals of British and continental reformers, in the means they employed to achieve change, and in their understandings of the possibilities for change. Though he identifies some trend towards convergence around the middle years of the nineteenth century, he is chiefly concerned to stress difference throughout. If we adopted a different emphasis in this intro-duction, this is not because we wish to take issue with his analysis; rather, we have simply been concerned to ensure that other aspects of the total picture find a place somewhere in this account.

As we have underlined in this final section, we do not suggest that this volume represents the only way of approaching the study of 'the age of reform'. Nor do we think that it resolves all the questions that its contents pose. If, however, it provides interesting insights into recent and current research, suggests some new perspectives, and poses some worthwhile questions, then the labours of its contributors will have been rewarded.

---

[193] Historiographies of other parts of the empire do not always employ 'reform' as an organizing category, but for some relevant studies, see Eric Stokes, *The English Utilitarians and India* (Ox-ford, 1959); Bruce Robertson, *Raja Rammohan Roy, the Father of Modern India* (Delhi, 1995); Lynn Zastoupil, 'Defining Christians, Making Britons: Rammohan Roy and the Unitarians', *Victorian Studies*, 44 (2002); Gascoigne, *Enlightenment and the Origins of European Australia*; Jeffrey McNairn, *The Capacity to Judge: Public Opinion and Deliberative Democracy in Upper Canada, 1791–1854* (Toronto, 2000); Stanley Trapido, 'From Paternalism to Liberalism: The Cape Colony, 1800–1834', *Internat. Hist. Rev.*, 12 (1990); Catherine Hall, *Civilising Subjects: Metropole and Colony in the English Imagination, 1830–1867* (Cambridge, 2002); Jennifer Ridden, *'Making Good Citizens': National Identity, Religion and Liberalism among the Irish Elite, c. 1800–1850* (Cambridge, forthcoming). In an American context, political 'reform' was not sought by means of any national movement after the ratification of the Federal Constitution of 1787: the making of that constitution was America's 'reform' process. In the early nineteenth century, the term had primarily moral and social connotations. See thus Ralph Waldo Emerson's essays 'Man the Reformer', 'New England Reformers', and 'English Reformers', and Steven Mintz, *Moralists and Modernizers: America's Pre-Civil War Reformers* (Baltimore, 1995).

2. 'Reform' in English public life: the fortunes of a word*

JOANNA INNES

Between 1780 and 1782, Christopher Wyvill's Association movement, formed to mobilize the political classes against the government and its disastrous American War, came to identify as its chief aim 'parliamentary reform'. This choice of slogan helped to give the word 'reform' a centrality in English public life which it had not had before, but which it would retain for more than half a century.

The very noun-form 'reform' was novel. This is not to say that it had never previously been used; yet it had been uncommon. The standard noun-form of the verb 'reform' had been 'reformation'. The Wyvillite slogan probably helped to popularize the shortened form of the noun.

The verb 'reform' and the nouns 'reformer' and 'reformation' had all had some role in English political discussion for several centuries previously. Over time, their associations and connotations had shifted, and they had risen and fallen in favour. My impression is that they increased in use from the mid-eighteenth century: shifts in 1780 did not mark an unheralded break with the past. Yet it seems clear that the Wyvillite campaign both significantly promoted their use, and helped to change the ways in which they were used.

In this chapter, I survey patterns in the use and further shifts in the associations and connotations of this cluster of words down to the 1830s and beyond. I begin with a sketch of their previous history. Though these words took on new associations and were given new applications from 1780, their use and reception continued to be coloured by older patterns. Thereafter, their use developed through a series of stages. Interest in 'reforms' of various kinds flourished in the 1780s, but the French Revolution brought this vocabulary into some

* I have incurred many debts in preparing this chapter, and am especially grateful to the following for their exemplary scholarly generosity: Miriam Griffin, John Watts, John Morrill, Jonathan Scott, David Hayton, Colin Brooks, Julian Hoppit, Christine Gerrard, Jeremy Osborn, Eliga Gould, Robert Poole, Mark Philp, Iain McCalman, Greg Claeys, Derek Beales, and Iain McLean. This list falls far short of the full tally of those who have lent a sympathetic ear to my concerns, and supplied references to me. I have also benefited from the comments of those who heard versions of the paper at St John's College Cambridge, the Institute of Historical Research, London, and the Humanities Research Centre, Canberra.

discredit; thereafter, down at least to 1820, those who wished to use these terms either had to live with their negative connotations, or to struggle to legitimate them. In the more liberal 1820s, the words were somewhat more widely used, though not everyone was equally happy to employ them. The appointment of a 'Reform ministry' in 1830, and advent of a 'Reformed parliament' in 1832, briefly linked the terms to a particular regime and its policies, which in turn played some part in shaping subsequent patterns of use.[1]

I should stress that it is not my intention, in focusing attention on words here, to conflate words and ideas. It is not suggested that the idea that institutions or practices or people can be recast or made better *need* be expressed in the terminology of 'reform': of course that idea could be, had been, and continued to be expressed in many other ways. But neither were these terms merely functional descriptors. They had associations, which changed in consequence of changes in use and changes in the broader context of use. Those who employed them were commonly, as part of their ordinary competence as language-users, alive to those associations; they made more or less conscious and elaborate tactical choices when they decided to use them or not. If we want to understand what contemporaries were doing in using these words, we need among other things to be sensitive to their history as words: to the baggage they carried with them, and how that baggage changed. In so far as the words' changing freight was itself a consequence of wider changes in the way people thought and acted, studying the forces that shaped change in use should also provide insight into the thought and life of the time.[2]

The word 'reform' and its variants stood in an especially important relationship to two broader groups of words. One was the set of words that embodied variations on the theme of re-forming or re-newing: words such as 'renovation', 'regeneration', 'renaissance', and 'revival'. Purely formally, these were very similar words, and they were sometimes used interchangeably. Each also had its own historically specific connotations, however. Historic patterns of

---

[1] The history of 'reform' and allied words in English has been surveyed only by Raymond Williams, *Keywords: A Vocabulary of Culture and Society* (London, 1976), 221–2. Paul Slack sheds light on early modern usage in *From Reformation to Improvement: Public Welfare in Early Modern England* (Oxford, 1999). See also, on mid-nineteenth-century use, Derek Beales, 'The Idea of Reform in British Politics, 1829–50', in T. C. W. Blanning and Peter Wende (eds.), *Reform in Great Britain and Germany, 1750–1850* (Oxford, 1999), although it will be apparent from what follows that I think he has overstated his case at some points. Much light on the early history of the word, in a variety of languages, is shed by G. B. Ladner, *The Idea of Reform: Its Impact on Christian Thought and Action in the Age of the Fathers* (Cambridge, Mass., 1959).

[2] The methodological issues raised by this exercise are many and contentious; it is not my intention here to engage with them in any ambitious way. For an introduction, see Annabel Brett, 'What is Intellectual History Now?', in David Cannadine (ed.), *What is History Now?* (Basingstoke, 2002); for discussions, James Tully (ed.), *Meaning and Context: Quentin Skinner and his Critics* (Cambridge, 1988); Terence Ball, James Farr, and Russell L. Hanson, *Political Innovation and Conceptual Change* (Cambridge, 1989); Iain Hampsher-Monk, Karin Tilmans, and Frank van Vree (eds.), *History of Concepts: Comparative Perspectives* (Amsterdam, 1998).

use helped to determine that one or other was seized upon and used to name certain periods or developments: thus 'the Renaissance' (or – the standard eighteenth-century phrase – 'the revival of learning'), and 'the Reformation'. William Cobbett suggested in 1831 that, when parliamentary reform was finally achieved, it would come to be known, by a similar process, as 'the Reform'.[3]

The word 'reform' had a lot of baggage attached to it by the late eighteenth century. Yet what that baggage did *not* do was to determine whether the word and its cognates had positive or negative evaluative force. By contrast, certain other words, denoting similar things, had rather clearer connotations. Two such terms in common use were 'innovation' and 'improvement'. At this time (for reasons I shall consider shortly) 'innovation' was almost always a negative term; 'improvement' almost always a positive one. One way of trying to shape the connotations of 'reform' was, therefore, to associate it or contrast it with these other terms.

The especially indeterminate force of 'reform' is nicely illustrated by newspaper reports of debate on the first Factory Act: the Health and Morals of Apprentices Act of 1802. At this period, reports of speeches were not verbatim; rather, they offered paraphrases or summaries of what MPs said. According to one report, Sir Robert Peel the elder, the promoter of the bill, defended his measure as no 'theoretical reformation', but instead a 'gradual improvement'. Yet according to another account of the same debate, he defended it as no 'speculative innovation', but instead a 'reform'.[4]

I

The verb 'reform' and the noun 'reformation' came into English from Latin (*reformare*, *reformatio*). Patterns of use continued to be coloured in certain ways by the classical and Christian history of these terms. English forms of these words were clearly in common use in public life by the later middle ages, and they were key terms in the religious and political disruptions of the sixteenth and seventeenth centuries.

Surviving classical texts suggest that the noun *reformatio* was not in common use in the pre-Christian world (although the first-century philosopher and statesman Seneca did employ it in the phrase 'reformatio morum', 'reformation of manners', a phrase with a long Latin and English future ahead of it). In much more common classical use was the related term *renovatio*.[5] In classical

---

[3] Cited in John Belchem, *'Orator' Hunt: Henry Hunt and Working-Class Radicalism* (Oxford, 1985), 222.

[4] *Parliamentary Register*, ed. J. Debrett, 45 vols. (London, 1781–96), xviii (1802), 1457; *The Senator: Debates of the Imperial Parliament*, 5 vols. (London (1801–2)), v, col. 1556.

[5] Seneca, Letter 56 §. 28. I am grateful to Miriam Griffin for searching 'The Packard Humanities Institute (PHI) CD-ROM #5.3 Latin Texts'.

Latin, *renovatio* connoted a good change, the renewal of something that had been lost or become corrupted. By contrast, *innovatio* connoted a bad change: wanton disregard for established standards. Of course, these terms were used tactically, and it was not the case that all changes described as constituting *renovatio* involved no more than the reinstatement of older ways! The English word 'innovation' retained a negative connotation down to the twentieth century – although there were occasional attempts to rehabilitate it: thus the early seventeenth-century lord chancellor and natural philosopher Francis Bacon (an important figure in our story, to whom we shall return) argued that all medicine was innovation; the Whig politician Charles James Fox argued in 1785 that innovation really meant no more than amendment, and as such should be desired.[6] In English usage, innovation came commonly to be contrasted not with 'renovation', but with 'reformation'.

Greek analogues of 'reform' appeared here and there in the Epistles of St Paul, and Latin forms in Latin versions of the Epistles. But it was not until the fourth century that 'reformation' and 'reform' became common terms in the Christian vocabulary. That century saw a revival of interest in projects of 'renovation' associated with the desire to defend and exalt Rome. As an alternative to this vision, St Augustine and others developed a less Rome-centred version, based on a specifically Christian theory of the nature and limits of human capacities. *Reformatio* in their hands meant fallen men's necessarily limited attempts to improve themselves and their world. It did not necessarily entail harking back to the past: one might 'reform for the better' (*reformare in melius*).[7]

Under the influence of these writers, *reformatio* became a key term in penitential thought and practice: Christians were henceforth frequently exhorted to reform their lives. Reform acquired an important association with correction, and with chastisement as an instrument of correction, as well as with amendment. 'Reformation of abuse' became a standard phrase. From the fifth century, the idea that canon law might become corrupt and stand in need of renovation was admitted; later, this would be termed reform. From the time of Pope Gregory VII (that is, from the eleventh century) the notion that the church might be susceptible to reform also made its appearance. By the time of the fifth Lateran council (1512–17), talk of the need to 'reform' the church and its laws was commonplace.[8]

Writers of the Renaissance drew on classical, pre-Christian notions of the cyclical renewal of states and societies in seeking to understand developments

---

[6] For 'innovation' in early English usage, see Caroline Robbins, 'Selden's Pills: State Oaths in England, 1558–1714', *Huntingdon Lib. Quart.*, 35 (1971–2), 317. *The Works of Francis Bacon*, ed. James Spedding, Robert Leslie Ellis, and Douglas Denon Heath, 14 vols. (London, 1857–74), iii, 433. For Fox, see W. Cobbett (ed.), *Parliamentary History*, 36 vols. (London, 1806–20), xxv, col. 466.

[7] Ladner, *Idea of Reform*, 41–5, 47–8, 133–283.   [8] *Ibid.*, 298–315, 423–4.

of their own time. Often they echoed classical usage, employing variants of such words as renewal and rebirth. When Machiavelli, in the first chapter of the third book of his *Discourses* – in a passage much cited in subsequent centuries – remarked that states commonly fell periodically into decay, from which they could be revived only by a return to first principles, the verb he used was *renascere*, 'to be reborn'. In eighteenth-century England, this passage was often cited in connection with discussions of reform.[9]

The word 'reformation' was clearly well established in English usage by the later middle ages. As one might expect, given its already complex history, the uses made of it were diverse. It was employed in a moral/religious context: thus we find individuals called upon to reform, and church courts enforcing morals by actions *pro reformatione morum* (Seneca's phrase). It was also employed in connection with official – especially civic – projects of social regulation. In this context, the subject to be reformed might be not the errant individual, but the 'commonweal', a term that encompassed both the notion of a collectivity of individuals, and that of a social and political order. Civic leaders, thus, lamenting decay in the morals of citizens, the fabric of buildings, and in the energies and commitment of those who should have maintained both, often described all these things as in need of 'reformation'.[10] From here, it was an easy and natural step to the term's emergence in political discussion. In the fifteenth century, it can be found in manifestos of the Wars of the Roses, and again in a chronicle description of the intentions of Cade's rebels, who are said to have risen up 'to Reffourm the comon wele of this land . . . which . . . hath been long mysorderid'.[11]

In the sixteenth century, the term was influentially employed by religious 'reformers' – if not quite in the ways that it would retrospectively be used of this era.[12] In early uses – as in John Knox's manuscript account, 'The History of the Reformation of Religion within the Realm of Scotland' – 'reformation' was a process, not an event: not *the* capital 'R' Reformation. But the notion that the key period of religious change had been a finite one, that could be dated, emerged quickly, and from there it was not a long step to the notion of reformation as event. The Reformation was certainly reified (in this context)

---

[9] *Ibid.*, 22. See, e.g., *Works of the Famous Nicolas Machiavel* (London, 1695), i, 379. For invocations of Machiavelli in the context of reform, see, e.g., Thomas Carte, *A General History of England*, 5 vols. (London, 1747–55), iv, 5; Cobbett (ed.), *Parliamentary History*, xxviii, col. 462; James Mackintosh, *Vindiciae Gallicae: Defence of the French Revolution against the Accusations of E. Burke* (London, 1791), 107.

[10] Slack, *Reformation to Improvement*, 6–8.

[11] M. L. Kekewich *et al.*, *The Politics of Fifteenth-Century England* (Stroud, 1995), 187, 220, 223; see also 191; A. H. Thomas and I. D. Thornley, *The Great Chronicle of London* (London, 1938), 183.

[12] Euan Cameron, *The European Reformation* (Oxford, 1991), 38–9. A. G. Dickens and John Tonkin, *The Reformation in Historical Thought* (Oxford, 1985), does not focus on terminological issues.

in English usage by the 1650s, when more than one book title contained the phrase 'since the Reformation'.[13] This reification is also agreed to have taken place on the continent by the late seventeenth century.

More than just changes in usage were at issue here. The question of whether the Reformation *was* an event that had finished, or a process that should continue, provided a focus for religious controversy in England and elsewhere for the next few centuries. But even proponents of continuing change commonly acknowledged the reified usage. As a Latin slogan had it, *Ecclesia reformata semper reformanda*, or, as Milton put it, one might hope 'even for the reforming of Reformation itself'.[14]

In the same era, if not earlier, another enduring connection was forged: between the terms 'reformation' and 'law'. The early history of that association probably lies in the history of canon law. In early sixteenth-century England, when the Reformation (as we say) made necessary the revision of English ecclesiastical law, a commission drew up a proposed new code under the title *Reformatio legum ecclesiasticarum* – although this failed to obtain parliamentary sanction. By the 1590s at the latest, the notion that English law might need reform was also current. In 1597, for example, a parliamentary committee was appointed to consider abridging and reforming the excessive number of superfluous and burdensome laws.[15]

It is clear that by the early seventeenth century the term was in common, diverse use in English public life. But developments during that century would see the term brought into disrepute, such that it would enter the eighteenth century with something of a cloud hanging over it. The problem arose from its use by puritans, commonwealthmen, and the successor to a slaughtered king, the Lord Protector, Oliver Cromwell.

We can follow Cromwell's patterns of use in his speeches, which no doubt had distinctive features, but seem in this respect not unrepresentative. He employed the term quite narrowly and one might say conventionally. He spoke of the need for a reformation of manners; very occasionally he spoke of the need for reformation in the church; more commonly, he urged work on the reformation of laws. He was a more ardent advocate of reformation in all these spheres than the Stuarts had been – and to that extent the term became a slogan of the regime. Yet he notably did not term his overall project a project of 'reformation'; on the contrary, when he spoke in general terms of his political aspirations, he most

---

[13] E.g., Edward Boughen, *An Account of the Church Catholick: where it was before the Reformation* (London, 1653); Hamon L'Estrange, *The Alliance of Divine Offices, Exhibiting all the Liturgies of the Church of England since the Reformation* (London, 1659).

[14] In Areopagitica: *Complete Prose Works of John Milton*, 8 vols. (New Haven, 1953–82), ii, 553.

[15] Norman L. Jones, 'An Elizabethan Bill for the Reformation of Ecclesiastical Law', *Parl. Hist.*, iv (1985), tentatively dates to the 1560s a 'bill for the Reformacion of the Ecclesiasticall Lawes'. For the 1590s, see Simonds D'Ewes, *The Journals of All the Parliaments during the Reign of Queen Elizabeth both of the House of Lords and House of Commons* (London, 1682), 553.

commonly talked of the need for 'restoration' (a term only later hijacked by royalists).[16]

Not even Levellers seem to have used the term in the way that it would subsequently be employed: to call for a restructuring of the political order. Tellingly, the one call I have seen for a 'reformation of parliament' is explicitly a call to remove ungodly MPs from the chamber: it is a call for a 'reformed and purged' parliament. This was a moral reformation project extended into political institutions.[17]

Though the word 'reformation' seems often to have been on the lips of supporters of religious and political change, it is to their critics that we must look if we wish to find the centrality of 'reformation' to the whole project insisted upon. A royalist tract thus satirically invoked the whole experiment: *The Anarchie, or Blest Reformation*.[18] This suggests that, despite 'reformation' being ostensibly a positive word for change, it had garnered enough problematic connotations from its history, and probably most especially its very recent history, to be easily turned to denigratory effect.

One result of the term's shifting connotations can be seen in the new terminology developed by the followers of Sir Francis Bacon. Lord chancellor, law reformer, and would-be proponent of a wider 'reformation of learning', Bacon, together with like-minded contemporaries, had made much use of the terminology of 'reformation'.[19] Mid- and late seventeenth-century heirs of his project did not abandon the term altogether, but they did pioneer what was to prove a very successful alternative: the word 'improvement'. Until this date, to improve something (such as – very commonly – a piece of land) had meant to increase its yield. But at mid-century, initially especially by this circle, the term began to be more extensively and metaphorically employed. It became possible thus to urge 'England's improvement by foreign trade'. Lacking both the religious and the corrective – even punitive – associations of 'reform', 'improvement' won wide acceptance in the eighteenth century as the ultimately unthreatening word for ameliorative change.[20]

---

[16] *Cromwell's Letters and Speeches*, ed. T. Carlyle (London, 1888). I am grateful to John Morrill and Jonathan Scott for discussing seventeenth-century patterns of use with me.

[17] A. S. P. Woodhouse (ed.), *Puritanism and Liberty*, 2nd edn (London, 1974), 414. The phrase was Cromwell's, but Captain Francis Allen, speaking for the Agitators, seems to have agreed that parliament should be so 'reformed', and questioned only if it had been.

[18] Royalist ballad of 1648, cited by John Cannon, *Parliamentary Reform, 1640–1832* (Cambridge, 1975), 1. See also, e.g., H. J., *The Antipodes, or Reformation with Heeles Upward, being a Compendious Narrative of the Great Hypocrisy of our Pretended Reformers* (Oxford, 1647).

[19] Charles Webster, *The Great Instauration: Science, Medicine and Reform, 1626–60* (London, 1975); Mark Greengrass *et al.* (eds.), *Samuel Hartlib and Universal Reformation* (Cambridge, 1994). Note, however, that Bacon himself contrasted wholly beneficial discovery in the natural world with 'the reformation of a state in civil matters', which, he said, was 'seldom brought in without violence and confusion': Bacon, *Works*, iv, 113. Note that the Latin text does not employ the word *reformatio*: *ibid.*, i, 221.

[20] Slack, *Reformation to Improvement*, 80–1.

Mid-century events rendered the term 'reformation' problematic as a political slogan for a generation and more. Under the Restoration monarchy, it remained more likely to be applied to someone's aspirations by their enemies than by their friends. Anthony Ashley Cooper, earl of Shaftesbury and 'first Whig', did not advertise himself as a reformer; his opponents by contrast were happy to attach that term to him and his fellow Exclusionists.[21] The 1688 Revolution gave the reformation project a small fillip, but no more. Gilbert Burnet, historian of the capital 'R' Reformation, helped persuade the new monarchs to sponsor a new reformation of manners campaign – but this was targeted as much as possible on abuses amongst the populace: sabbath-breaking, prostitution, and the like. It was not allowed to develop into an assault on the rulers of the commonweal.[22] It is striking that even country MPs of this period, whom we might expect to have employed the language of reformation in their battles against the accumulation of power in the hands of ministers, official corruption, and the manipulation of parliament, do not appear to have done so – despite the fact that these same people might well have been proponents of a reformation of popular manners.[23] Apparently it had simply become too explosive for such use. Those who did use it used it in mid-seventeenth-century fashion, to imply an extension of a moral and religious project into the political sphere. Thus the London nonconformist Elias Pledger wrote that his hopes for 'a reformation in Church and State' had been thwarted by the king's failure to purge enough of the 'ministers and tools of the last raigne that helped to enslave and debauch us'.[24]

In the early eighteenth century, even the popular reformation of manners project was increasingly discredited. The term ran at a very low ebb. The Reformation capital 'R' was still held to be a good thing; errant individuals could be implored to embark on a course of reformation. Otherwise the term had the ring of utopian cant – as discredited as the term 'communist' at the end of the twentieth century.[25] The discrediting of an older reform project did, however, clear the way for the term to take on new functions.

---

[21] E.g., *Ignoramus: An Excellent New Song* (1686 ballad in Bodleian Lib., Oxford, printed books Aston 16 [162]) or at Bodleian Ballads on-line: *www.bodley.ox.ac.uk/ballads/*.

[22] For the latest of numerous discussions of this episode, see Tony Claydon, *William III and the Godly Revolution* (Cambridge, 1996); 110–21, for its most studied aspect, the campaign to enforce a reformation of manners by law.

[23] I advance this claim after discussion with David Hayton – though of course it is always hard to establish a negative, and it may be that future research will prove me wrong on this point.

[24] Craig Rose, *England in the 1690s: Revolution, Religion and War* (Oxford, 1999), 200–1.

[25] Interestingly, the term also seems to have had some aesthetic afterlife: Whigs continued to strive for the reformation of drama and poetry, for instance on lines adumbrated by John Dennis, *Advancement and Reformation of Poetry* (London, 1701). See, more generally, Abigail Williams, 'Whig Literary Culture: Poetry, Politics and Patronage, 1678–1714' (University of Oxford D.Phil. thesis, 2000), esp. 160–72.

II

From the 1720s to the 1770s, 'reform' and related terms underwent a slow, but cumulative, revival.

In order to understand how such terms functioned within political discourse in the Walpolean and post-Walpolean eras, we need first to consider the forms of criticism levelled against these regimes. Relevant forms of criticism operated at several interrelated levels. First, the regimes were often denounced as corrupt in themselves: staffed by corrupt men, who were motivated primarily by the desire for personal wealth and power, and who corrupted all those who in one way or another served under them. Second, they were charged with failing to use the power of government for the public benefit. Third, they were charged, at best, with leaving unchecked, at worst, with positively encouraging, popular vice and immorality – by, for example, failure to take sufficiently tough action against gin-drinking.

Various parts of the heritage of the vocabulary of 'reform' made reform terminology applicable at all three levels. Thus, first, the corruption of the regime itself could be condemned, in broadly Machiavellian terms, and represented as necessitating some form of renewal.[26] Second, the want of public-spirited government could be said to suggest that others must take it upon themselves to promote public projects – among which projects the reform of legal institutions was, in the 1720s and 1730s, a special favourite.[27] Third, the morals of the people evidently required the attention of moral reformers.[28] Walpole – who cheerfully said of himself that he was 'No saint, no Spartan, no reformer' – was, for those attracted to this line of attack, an especially vulnerable target. Talk of 'reformation' accordingly fluttered through the utterances of his opponents. As the MP and courtier Lord Hervey observed in his *Conduct of the Opposition*, the 'spirit of reformation' was abroad.[29] 'Reformation' did not become a leading slogan; Walpole's opponents were commonly termed Patriots, not Reformers. But the terminology was sufficiently clearly associated with opposition for the

---

[26] A strictly Machiavellian analysis would have had it that corruption was likely to bring about collapse, unless averted by reform – but in practice critics of Walpole usually stopped short of suggesting that. For this reformulation, see Shelley Burtt, *Virtue Transformed: Political Argument in England, 1688–1740* (Cambridge, 1992), ch. 5.

[27] Wilfrid Prest, 'Law Reform in Eighteenth-Century England', in Peter Birks (ed.), *The Life of the Law* (London, 1993); Andrew Hanham, 'Whig Opposition to Sir Robert Walpole in the House of Commons, 1722–34' (University of Leicester Ph.D. thesis, 1992), ch. 7.

[28] Lee Davison, 'Experiments in the Social Regulation of Industry: Gin Legislation, 1729–51', in L. Davison *et al.* (eds.), *Stilling the Grumbling Hive: The Response to Social and Economic Problems in England, 1689–1750* (Stroud, 1992). The *Diaries of Thomas Wilson DD, 1731–7 and 1750*, ed. C. S. L. Linnell (London, 1964), shed more general light on the milieu of Walpole's moral critics.

[29] For Walpole's self-description, see Philip Dormer Stanhope, *Characters* (first pubd 1778, Augustan Reprint Soc., Los Angeles, 1990), 32. John, baron Hervey, *The Conduct of the Opposition and Character of Modern Patriotism* (London, 1734), 59.

anti-patriot *Free Briton* to carry in 1732 an ostensibly abstract meditation 'Of Reformation', about what kinds of reformers should and should not be trusted, which was in fact clearly partisan political comment.[30]

One problem with the call for reformation at this time was that this diagnosis of what was needed did not come handily wrapped up with any very promising set of ideas about *agencies* of reform. Traditionally, in both Christian and Machiavellian traditions, if people were too corrupt to reform themselves, the most likely agent of reform was a reforming magistrate – in the case of a state, the prince. Lower-level figures could – and in this era did – do what they could to reform laws and public morals. But it was not clear how they could reform the state: the image of the secular 'reformer' was underdeveloped.

One possible way forwards lay in the accession of a 'patriot king'. In the 1730s, the patriot opposition did indeed pin high hopes on Frederick prince of Wales, and the poets and writers who hung around his court talked a great deal about the renewal, renovation, and regeneration that would come with his accession. It was above all Henry St John, viscount Bolingbroke, in his pamphlet *The Idea of a Patriot King* (written in the 1730s, though not published until 1749), who attached the terminology of 'reform' to these aspirations. 'A PATRIOT KING', wrote Bolingbroke, 'is the most powerful of all reformers.'[31]

The mid-eighteenth century also saw some interesting developments in religious employment of the term. The evangelical awakening – from the 1730s – was sometimes presented by its supporters as continuing the work of the capital 'R' Reformation, sometimes as a second reformation.[32] Since attitudes to Methodism and the like were mixed, this surely had a mixed impact on people's attitudes to 'reformation'. Yet at the same time, many who were not supporters none the less accepted that this movement did represent something other than old-style puritanism. The project of national religious renewal was to some extent rehabilitated from the disrepute into which the events of the previous century had cast it.

Others prepared, from a somewhat different perspective, to give currency to talk of the need for further reformation were those dissenters and Anglicans who saw a need for change in the country's religious constitution. This was emphatically not old-style puritanism, inasmuch as their desire to change ecclesiastical arrangements was clearly disjoined from any ambitious and immediate moral project, morals being seen primarily as a matter for the individual

---

[30] Reproduced in the *Gentleman's Mag.*, 2 (1732), 1105–6.

[31] Christine Gerrard, *The Patriot Opposition to Walpole: Politics, Poetry and National Myth, 1725–42* (Oxford, 1994), ch. 7, esp. 225. Interestingly, Bolingbroke appears to have made relatively little use of the term in his earlier writings, if anything seeming to associate it with the cause of Whig or 'fake' opposition.

[32] Some light on patterns of use is shed by Frank Lambert, *Inventing the 'Great Awakening'* (Princeton, 1999).

and his or her conscience. These were latitudinarian voices, proponents of reasonable Christianity. Among them was the Anglican cleric John Jones – who at mid-century called for reformation in the calendar and the Prayer Book, as part of a larger project of reformation in the church – and, more famously, the Yorkshire cleric Francis Blackburne, who in his influential work *The Confessional* admitted himself to be 'seized with that epidemical malady of idle and visionary men, THE PROJECTING TO REFORM THE PUBLIC'. The radical dissenting campaigner Thomas Hollis prefigured a long line of radical apologetic when he conscripted Christ to his cause. In the 1760s, he was in the habit of showing his friends an image of Christ on the cross, labelled 'Behold the fate of a reformer.'[33]

In the 1730s and 40s, reformation had chiefly been an oppositional project. In the 1750s, however, prime ministers stepped to the fore. Henry Pelham's policy of administration-led improvement and the elder William Pitt's patriot ministry opened the way – unusually, in terms not so much of the practice as of the rhetoric of this century – for government to emerge as a sponsor of reformation. The Pelhamite era thus saw the reformation of the calendar (bringing England into line with continental Europe). Pitt's ministry saw what most commonly seems to have been described as the new 'regulation' of the militia, but was also sometimes talked about as its 'reformation'.[34]

When the young George III came to the throne in 1760, some – like the future parliamentary reformer James Burgh – hoped that he would play the part of 'patriot king'.[35] But George's early blundering rapidly disposed of any

---

[33] [John Jones], *Free and Candid Disquisitions relating to the Church of England* (London, 1746), esp. 181–222; Francis Blackburne, *The Confessional* (London, 1766), esp. 283–336. For these men, see R. B. Barlow, *Citizenship and Conscience: A Study of the Theory and Practice of Religious Toleration during the Eighteenth Century* (Philadelphia, 1962), ch. 4; John Gascoigne, 'Anglican Latitudinarianism, Rational Dissent and Political Radicalism in the Late Eighteenth Century', in Knud Haakonssen (ed.), *Enlightenment and Religion: Rational Dissent in Eighteenth-Century Britain* (Cambridge, 1996). Peter Miller stresses their commitment to extending the Reformation project in *Defining the Common Good: Empire, Religion and Philosophy in Eighteenth-Century Britain* (Cambridge, 1994), 322; among other things, they were doggedly anti-Catholic. For their support for calendar reform, see Robert Poole, *Time's Alteration: Calendar Reform in Early Modern England* (London, 1998), 161. For Hollis, see Franco Venturi, *The End of the Old Regime in Europe, 1768–76* (Princeton, 1989), 393.

[34] Calendar revision had for many centuries been termed 'reformation'. For mid-eighteenth-century British calendar reform, see Poole, *Time's Alteration*; for militia reform, Eliga Gould, 'To Strengthen the King's Hands: Dynastic Legitimacy, Militia Reform and Ideas of National Unity in England, 1745–60', *Hist. Jl*, 34 (1991). I am grateful to both these historians for answering my queries. The term 'regulation' was quite commonly employed in the late seventeenth and early eighteenth centuries for administrative improvements that would later very probably have been termed reforms. I owe this suggestion to Colin Brooks, but my own research supports it: see thus Christopher Tancred, *An Essay for General Regulation of the Law* (London, 1727).

[35] Carla Hay, 'The Making of a Radical: The Case of James Burgh', *Jl Brit. Studies*, 2 (1979), shows interestingly that Burgh came to parliamentary reform out of an earlier enthusiasm for the moral reform and regeneration of society and polity.

such hopes, and helped to ensure that this terminology would remain primarily opposition property. As the tide of opposition rose, reform terminology gained all the more currency, even as people despaired of the ability of opposition politicians – many of them recently ejected members of the venal old guard – to deliver the goods. The young Henry Grattan, newly arrived in England to read for the bar, wrote later that 'It was as if the moral sense was dead in England . . . No scheme of real action, no pertinacious opposition, no reformation could be adopted or enforced in an age so luxurious, so venal, so unproductive.'[36]

Some of the anxieties released found vent in the early 1770s in a campaign against venality, corruption, and abuse in the East India Company, seen to be embodied especially in the person of Robert Clive, who, under threat of retribution, committed suicide in 1774. This campaign was explicitly conducted as a campaign to 'reform' the East India Company – and as such it played a part in keeping alive belief in the urgency of change as Wilkite excitement died away.[37]

The stage was set for the efflorescence of reform rhetoric in the 1780s. Yet 1780 would mark a turning-point. Though, as we have seen, through the middle decades of the eighteenth century, numerous people found use for the terminology of 'reform' in characterizing their aspirations, still the term was not yet a key political slogan. It was not, for instance, a watchword of the Wilkite movement of the 1760s; indeed, calls for 'reformation' as then understood might have sounded incongruous in the mouth of the libertine John Wilkes. Even during the 1770s it remained relatively unusual for people to formulate their aspirations for political change in terms of a desire to see the 'reformation of parliament'. That project not only had less importance than it would soon acquire, but when it was talked about, it was often discussed in different terms. If we can trust the parliamentary reports in this respect, when in 1776 Wilkes brought in a motion for amending the representation, it was of amendment that he spoke; it was left to his opponent Lord North to deride 'ideal schemes of reformation'.[38] Major Cartwright, who, from 1776, identified reforming parliament as a precondition for all other desirable changes, did favour the language of 'reform' to characterize his proposed schemes of constitutional reconstruction, but this was not yet standard practice.[39]

Before 1780, moreover, it is notable how easily people slid between institutional and moral uses of the term. The project of an institutional reform that was not necessarily at the same time, or first and foremost, a moral reform

---

[36] Cited in S. L. Gwynn, *Henry Grattan and his Times* (Dublin, 1939), 26.

[37] For the most recent account of this crisis, see H. V. Bowen, *Revenue and Reform: The Indian Problem in British Politics, 1757–73* (Cambridge, 1991). The politics of the episode differed from those of the Wilkite agitation. One would-be defender of Clive in the *Public Advertiser*, 27 June 1772, indeed denigrated the campaign against him as a 'Scotch Reformation': in effect, as the work of just such men as Wilkes had attacked.

[38] Cobbett (ed.), *Parliamentary History*, xviii, cols. 1287–93.

[39] Thus *Legislative Rights of the Commonalty Vindicated, or Take Your Choice* (London, 1776).

seems to have had an insecure grip on people's imaginations. Thus, when the Whig MP William Hay commented on a place bill (to exclude officeholders from parliament) in 1740, he argued in debate that 'This is not the right way to reform parliament . . . Let the Gentlemen propose but to restrain luxury or improve education and I will readily concur in it as the best way to reform parliaments.' Again, at a time of widespread popular rioting against the conscriptive element in Pitt's 1757 militia reforms, one MP's wife wrote to a friend that the scheme was impractical 'since our people must be reformed before anyone would choose to put arms into their hands – and *that* reformation is the difficulty'.[40]

The extent to which demands for reform of the East India Company were demands for moral purging, rather than for structural change, is nicely brought out in the usage of Warren Hastings. Hastings was appointed first governor-general of British India in 1773 with 'full powers to make a reformation', meaning to punish or dispense with corrupt company servants. Hastings did not think chastising every petty misdeed by men upon whom he inevitably relied to carry on both the governmental and the commercial work of the Company the best way forward. He preferred to proceed by restructuring both governmental and judicial arrangements in Company territory, giving more power and responsibilities to Indians. Historians have described this as a process of reform, but Hastings, evidently understanding the word differently, repeatedly denied 'reforming' proclivities. 'I never called myself a Reformer', he said in his own defence – oddly, as it might seem to us, though his meaning becomes clearer as he continued: 'nor lamented that all men were not so virtuous and disinterested as myself'.[41]

III

On the continent, as in Britain, the later eighteenth century saw the term 're-form' increasingly bandied about, and put to new uses. The hope that society might be improved by benevolent legislation was widely cherished in the era of Enlightenment. This implied the need to 'reform' law.[42] In France from the

---

[40] *Tory and Whig: The Parliamentary Papers of Edward Harley, Third Earl of Oxford, and William Hay, MP for Seaford, 1716–53*, ed. Clyve Jones and Stephen Taylor (Woodbridge, 1998), 158; Eric Stockdale, *Law and Order in Georgian Bedfordshire* (Bedford, 1982), 23. As will become clear, it remained relatively easy to 'slide' in this way for many decades to come; still it seems to me that it became more possible, after 1780, to envision schemes of institutional change that might produce good effects even if those operating within the institutional framework were not themselves virtuous. This was no doubt as much a result of changes in thinking about institutions and their operations – further noted below – as in habits of deploying words.

[41] Keith Feiling, *Warren Hastings* (London, 1954), esp. 84, 101, 161. Feiling's main chapter on this theme is called 'Reform of the State'.

[42] *The King of Prussia's Plan for Reforming the Administration of Justice* (London, 1750).

1760s, this vocabulary was also pressed into the service of a variety of other re-constructive projects. In the wake of the expensive Seven Years War (1756–63) there was much talk of the need for a *réforme des finances* – so much that in 1764 the king banned further publication on this theme. Voltaire, affronted by the *parlement* of Toulouse's condemnation of the Huguenot Jean Calas, and by the obstructive posture that *parlements* in general struck in public affairs, urged a 'réforme des parlements'. The idea that the Enlightenment built on intellectual foundations laid by the religious Reformation also gained some currency.[43]

Habits of thought characteristic of the 'Enlightened' era also helped to shape patterns in the use of the term from this time. It was increasingly commonly supposed that men were made good or bad by the socio-political framework in which they operated. If this were the case, then moral reform need not precede institutional reform, as had previously been supposed; on the contrary, institutional reform might represent the necessary first step towards a reform of morals.

In Germany, the noun-form of the verb employed until this era had been *Reformation*. It has been suggested that it was under the influence of French usage that Germans began, at about this time, to speak instead of *Reform*.[44] It is tempting to suppose that French usage may also have encouraged the adoption of a parallel shortened form of the noun in England at this time. Certainly the French example loomed large in the thinking of some English 'reformers'. Edmund Burke made a careful study of French fiscal plans, and cited the work of the reforming minister Jacques Necker when he introduced his own proposal for retrenchment into the House of Commons – although that was published as a proposal for 'economical reformation'.[45]

Burke came out as a 'reformer' – protesting against the system of misgovern-ment laid bare, as he saw it, by the outbreak and conduct of the war on America – in 1779. But his thunder was to some extent stolen by the extra-parliamentary

---

[43] For German usage, see O. Brunner *et al.* (eds.), *Geschichtliche Grundbegriffe*, 8 vols. (1972–97), v, 313–60; for French, Christof Dipper, 'Réforme', in Rolf Reichardt *et al.* (eds.), *Handbuch politisch-sozialer Grundbegriffe in Frankreich, 1680–1820* (Munich, 1985–), xix–xx, 117–39. My understanding of European patterns of use is also informed by a search in electronic library catalogues. For *réforme des finances*, see James Riley, *The Seven Years War and the Old Regime in France* (Princeton, 1986), ch. 7; André Morellet, *Réflexions sur les avantages de la liberté d'écrire et d'imprimer sur les matières de l'administration: écrites en 1764 à l'occasion de la Declaration du roi du 28 mars de la même année, qui fait défenses d'imprimer, debiter aucuns écrits, ouvrages, ou projets concernant la réforme ou administration des finances, &c.* (London, 1775). I have used the CD-ROM *Voltaire electronique* to check Voltaire's patterns of use. For 'réforme des parlements', see his *Histoire de parlement de Paris* (1768), and his *Questions sur l'Encyclopédie* (1752–70). For Enlightened ideas about 'the Reformation', see Brunner *et al.* (eds.), *Geschichtliche Grundbegriffe*, v, 332 f.; also Dickens and Tonkin, *Reformation*, 121–46.

[44] Brunner *et al.* (eds.), *Geschichtliche Grundbegriffe*, v, 339.

[45] *The Writings and Speeches of Edmund Burke*, gen. ed. Paul Langford, 9 vols. (Oxford, 1981–97), iii: *Party, Parliament, and the American War, 1774–1780*, ed. W. M. Elofson, John A. Woode, and William B. Todd, 481–551; 488 for 'reform' in a French context.

initiative launched a few weeks later: the Yorkshire squire Christopher Wyvill's campaign for 'public reformation'. Wyvill's Yorkshire ginger-group echoed Burke in condemning abuses in the management of public monies. Already by May 1780, however, the allied Westminster sub-committee was urging the case for *parliamentary* reformation, and by August the York committee too affirmed that abuses in parliament must be the principal object of public reformation.[46]

By 1782, the slogan 'parliamentary reform' had general currency.[47] Thereafter, down to the 1830s and indeed beyond, 'reform' in English public life connoted 'parliamentary reform' first and foremost; similarly, 'reformer' was – unless the context suggested otherwise – first and foremost a supporter of parliamentary reform.[48] Other 'reform movements', as we might term them, came to be denoted by other one-word slogans: thus, 'retrenchment' – meaning cuts in public spending; 'repeal' – the repeal of the Test and Corporation Acts; 'emancipation' – Catholic Emancipation; and 'abolition' – the abolition of the slave trade.

As the term became more prominent, then, in a sense its usage narrowed. But the use of 'reform' to mean parliamentary reform never entirely crowded out other uses. Less obvious than the rise of the slogan 'parliamentary reform' is an associated shift in other ways in which the word was used.

There was a shift, first, towards giving the word institutional application: towards using it to mean legal change, or institutional restructuring. This was not to break new ground. As we have seen, the idea that one might 'reform' law had a very long heritage behind it, and there had been other institutional uses over the years. But these usages seem to me to have become more common – probably partly, as I have suggested, because of a larger 'enlightened' shift in mentality. The new noun-form 'reform' also lent itself to snappy coinages: 'poor-law reform', 'prison reform', 'police reform', 'army reform'. As a series of historians have exerted themselves to show, in recent decades, there had been earlier projects of institutional amendment in all these fields; yet it was in the

---

[46] For references to the need for 'a reform in the expenditure of public money', see, e.g., *Political Papers*, ed. Christopher Wyvill, 6 vols., (London, 1794–1802), i, 58, 67, 144; references to Burke's plan for 'economical reform', *ibid.*, 105; to a meeting to formulate plans for public and constitutional reform, 111; to plans for 'Public Reformation', 146. For the Westminster sub-committee commending 'parliamentary reformation', see *ibid.*, 232; for the echo at York, 263.

[47] This can be traced in Hannah Barker, *Newspapers, Politics and Public Opinion in Late Eighteenth-Century England* (Oxford, 1998).

[48] Cf. Edward Ward, *The Reformer: Exposing the Vices of the Age in Several Characters* (London, [n.d., early eighteenth century]); *The Parallel Reformers* (London, 1748), suggesting John Wycliff and George Whitfield were parallel in zeal and Christian fortitude; 'Walter Wagbucket', *The Reformer* (London, 1756), a periodical dedicated to William Pitt the elder as a virtuous politician: promised to revive the art of satire, but ran for three numbers only; *The Reformer* (London, 1780) was critical of the 'patriots' and their projects of extending religious toleration and reforming the constitution.

1780s that they came to be sloganized as 'reforms'. Similarly, earlier talk of the need for change in the national church metamorphosed into calls for 'church reform'.[49]

More than just a renaming of individual projects was in question here. Also beginning to come into shape under the umbrella of this terminology was the notion of a reforming *programme*: of an interconnected series of 'reforms' a 'reformer' might be expected to support.[50]

This is not to suggest that reformers were, in practice, all of a mind. Wyvill's movement split over whether parliamentary reform was indeed a precondition for other reforms, and over the kind of parliamentary reform that should be sought.[51] Evangelicals construed defeat in war as evidence of sin, implying a need to repent and reform – reform the self, society, and its institutions. But not everyone was happy with this religious reading. When, in 1787, William Wilberforce tried to drum up elite support for a campaign against vice and immorality, he was coldly received by most Whigs; sabbatarian efforts in the same decade were denounced in parliament as neo-puritan.[52]

Nor is it suggested that the shift in emphasis towards institutional reform, and the rise of the role of 'reformer', so domesticated these concepts as to remove their sting. Even in this decade, we can find examples of these terms being used as if they had inherent negative force. Thus the Quaker David Barclay wrote in anger of American Quakers who proselytized against slavery: '[They] are come here among us as *Reformers*.' Connotations of chastisement, and of readiness to turn the world upside down, continued to colour some uses of these terms.[53]

Potentially important in distinguishing between more and less threatening varieties of reform were the qualifying adjectives 'radical' and 'moderate'.

---

[49] G. O. Paul, *A State of Proceedings on the Subject of a Reform of Prisons* (Gloucester, 1783); Edward Sayer, *Observations on the Police or Civil Government of Westminster, with a Proposal for a Reform* (London, 1784); [anon], *Some Observations on the Militia; with the Sketch of a Plan for the Reform of It* (London, 1785); 'A Country Gentleman', *A Letter to Thomas Gilbert, Esq; on his Intended Reform of the Poor Laws* (London, 1787); 'Mr Warburton', *A Letter to the Chancellor of the Exchequer, shewing the Necessity of a Clerical Reform* (London, 1788). Note also *The Medical Reform, containing a Plan for the Establishment of a Medical Court of Judicature* (London, 1788).

[50] Thus Hannah More on a discussion with William Wilberforce and others on 'all the great objects of reform which they have in view', cited in Ford K. Brown, *Fathers of the Victorians* (London, 1961), 106. Mackintosh, in *Vindiciae Gallicae*, 343, wrote of 'subaltern reform' that might be expected to flow from parliamentary reform. William Belsham suggested in 1800 that repeal of the Test and Corporation Acts 'would have led the way to other liberal and rational reforms in their proper gradation': cited by John Cookson, *The Friends of Peace: Anti-War Liberalism in England, 1793–1815* (Cambridge, 1982), 16.

[51] Cannon, *Parliamentary Reform*, 78–97.

[52] Joanna Innes, 'Politics and Morals: The Reformation of Manners Movement in Later Eighteenth-Century England', in E. Hellmuth (ed.), *The Transformation of Political Culture: England and Germany in the Late Eighteenth Century* (Oxford, 1990), 75, 79–84, 101–2, 109.

[53] For Barclay, see Historical Soc. of Pennsylvania, Philadelphia, Pemberton papers, vol. 39, fos. 51–2 (I owe this reference to Chris Brown).

These came into use from the inception of the Wyvillite movement.[54] Since historians have often used these terms to distinguish different fractions within the parliamentary reforming camp – country gentlemen from metropolitan radicals, for example – it bears emphasizing that, at this time, most proponents of parliamentary reform seem to have considered themselves to be 'radical reformers'. When matters of principle were at stake, they urged, it was disreputable to be 'moderate' – or, in Cartwright's analogy, 'Can we trust a man who is moderately honest, or esteem a woman who is moderately virtuous?'[55] The adjective 'moderate' probably did have some currency, but it is noticeable that reformers commonly described themselves as 'temperate' when they wished to mollify. Thus Wyvill in 1802 commended the dissenting MP William Smith as 'an advocate for a radical reform of parliament on temperate principles' – by these two adjectives neatly distinguishing views about ends from views about means.[56]

IV

Though the outbreak of the French Revolution originally encouraged reformers of all kinds to suppose that history was on their side, as revolution degenerated into terror, its effect was to discourage both the pursuit of many of the reforming projects that had been canvassed in the 1780s and use of the language of 'reform'. It cannot have helped matters that *réforme* and *régénération* were words initially much on the lips of makers and shakers in France.[57]

Opponents of reform in Britain employed a variety of rhetorical tactics to render illegitimate the language of reform. They of course equated reform with 'innovation'. To counteract the potentially positive connotations of the term, they spoke of 'pretended reform' and of 'modern reformers'. They portrayed reformers as propounding 'speculative reforms' (the speculative and theoretical generally had a bad name in the eighteenth century, that age of empiricism – and were particularly associated with foreign thought). Following Burke's lead,

[54] For early references to 'radical reformation', see *Parliamentary Papers*, ed. Wyvill, i, 341, 361, 374, 379; iv, 247; for Wyvill commending 'radical reformation' to Shelburne, see Shelburne MSS (microfilm in Bodl. Lib., RCat 106X and MS Films 1988–2032), letter in Box 74, fo. 113. For an early reference to 'Radicalls', see E. Milner, *Records of the Lumleys of Lumley Castle* (London, 1904), 259.

[55] F. D. Cartwright, *Life and Correspondence of Major Cartwright*, 2 vols. (London, 1826), i, 194 n. For much later restatement of the argument that all reformers worth their salt must be radical reformers, see Basil Montagu, *Essays and Selections* (London, 1837), 94–5.

[56] R. W. Davis, *Dissent in Politics, 1780–1830: The Political Life of William Smith MP* (London, 1971), 66.

[57] Dipper, 'Réforme', 126–9. For regeneration, see Mona Ozouf, 'Régénération', in F. Furet and M. Ozouf (eds.), *Dictionnaire critique de la Révolution française* (Paris, 1988), 821–31; Antoine de Baecque, *The Body Politic: Corporeal Metaphor in Revolutionary France, 1770–1800*, trans. Charlotte Mandell (Stanford, 1993), ch. 3.

some also linked reform with religious 'enthusiasm', forging the link in such phrases as 'new-light reformers'.[58]

These denigratory efforts were sufficiently successful to scare off some potential users for two decades, perhaps particularly advocates of miscellaneous benevolent projects that were sometimes classed as 'reforms', but that could equally well be described in other terms. As late as 1812, a contributor to *The Philanthropist*, a journal of improving social endeavour backed by Quakers, evangelicals, and utilitarians, noted approvingly that the African Association had 'not been afraid' to use the word 'reform' in their annual report; few contributors to *The Philanthropist* itself had that temerity.[59]

Not everyone was scared away from using the word, however – and those who continued to favour parliamentary reform had little alternative but to use it: the word had become too closely associated with the thing to be discarded. Those who continued to use the term developed a variety of strategies to defend it.

Two of the most common and powerful defensive strategies were also employed by Burke. Unusually among counter-revolutionaries, Burke did not distance himself from all forms of 'reform' when he set his face against the French Revolution. He had nailed his flag to the reform cause in the past, and did not see himself as having changed his position. Burke's understanding of 'reform' had always been a relatively narrow one; most notably, he had never endorsed the cause of parliamentary reform. He had primarily been concerned with the curbing of royal influence, and, latterly, with the extirpation of corruption, greed, and ambition in the East India Company. He did not think that the French Revolution revealed that there had been anything wrong with those commitments. Accordingly, he strove to distinguish reform from the sort of thing he reprobated in France, and among France's British sympathizers. He did this first by suggesting that 'reform' denoted pragmatic, limited improvement: the correction, by minor adjustment, of faults that stood clearly revealed. 'Reform', so understood, was inherently empirical and not 'speculative'. Second, he argued that reform so conceived, far from being tantamount to revolution, or likely to bring revolution in its train, represented the chief *alternative* to revolution. It was by timely reform that revolution was best averted: 'A state without the means of some change is without the means of its own preservation.'[60]

---

[58] Thus *Proceedings of the Association for Preserving Liberty and Property against Republicans and Levellers* (London, [1793]), nos. 1, 2, 4. Burke wrote wryly of 'our new light and knowledge': Burke, *Writings and Speeches*, viii, 125. For a jibe at 'new light reformers' in a more popular medium, see *The Sturdy Reformer* (Bodleian Lib., shelfmark 11648 g. 29 [2]).

[59] *The Philanthropist, or Repository for Hints and Suggestions Calculated to Promote the Happiness and Comfort of Man*, ii (1812), 186.

[60] Burke, *Writings and Speeches*, viii, 72, 81–5, 111–13, 213–20. Some later Whig reformers were happy to acknowledge Burke as a forebear: see thus Brougham in *Edinburgh Rev.*, 68 (1838), 205–11.

Both ways of defending reform were widely echoed by other reformers. We need not see Burke as their source. Both represented fairly obvious moves within the intellectual framework of the day; the idea that reform might stave off catastrophic collapse was indeed a standard Machiavellian notion. But Burke may have helped to give them currency and authority.

In the 1790s, reformers were most keen to urge that reform was not tantamount to revolution. Reformers were 'no rioters'.[61] That reform might indeed stave off revolution was urged by the Whig MP Sir James Mackintosh, as he reconsidered the enthusiasm for French developments he had expressed in his 1791 *Vindiciae Gallicae*.[62] In the mid- and later 1790s, the case for reform as prophylactic of revolution was especially commonly argued in an Irish context. Proving the point in reformers' eyes, insufficiently reformed Ireland did indeed experience an abortive revolution in 1798.[63]

In the early nineteenth century, when it became easier to think of advancing a reforming agenda, the argument that reform was, or could be, a practical, empirical project gained in importance. Piecemeal parliamentary reform could be legitimated in these terms. Lord Grenville, leader of the most conservative – or perhaps office-hungry – Whig faction was prepared to back piecemeal reform in 1804 on the grounds that this did not presuppose 'any theoretical views'.[64] The would-be penal reformer Samuel Romilly strove hard to devise proposals that would not be vulnerable to the charge of being merely speculative, but could be shown to be grounded in practical experience, and to entail only strictly necessary, limited change.[65]

These were not the only ways of legitimating 'reform'. It could also be linked, not with dreaded 'innovation', but instead 'a progression of improvement'.[66] Analogies could be drawn between political and religious reformation: after all, how could staunch protestants, in good conscience, set their faces against 'reformation'? This analogy seems sometimes to have been a source of comfort to reformers worried about how they – characteristically rather marginal people – could hope to transform a polity. Thus James Mill wrote to David Ricardo: 'All great changes . . . are easily affected . . . when the time is come.

[61] London Corresponding Society, *Reformers no Rioters* (London, 1795). For a sturdy protest against 'a wicked and deliberate attempt to impose on the public' by casting indiscriminate odium on all reformers, see Liverpool Record Office, 900 MD 18, William Rathbone to the mayor of Liverpool, 1 Dec. 1792. I owe this reference to Josh Civin.

[62] Mackintosh, *Vindiciae Gallicae*. For another early example, see Cobbett (ed.), *Parliamentary History*, xxviii, col. 455.

[63] Thus Fox, in Cobbett (ed.), *Parliamentary History*, xxxiii, cols. 703–6; M. E. Sandford, *Thomas Poole and his Friends* (Somerset, 1996, first pubd 1888, retains original two-volume pagination), i, 124.

[64] *Parl. Debs.*, 1st ser., ii, col. 516.

[65] Richard R. Follett, *Evangelicalism, Penal Theory and the Politics of Criminal Law Reform in England, 1808–30* (London, 2001), ch. 2.

[66] Davis, *Dissent in Politics*, 146.

Was it not an individual, without fortune, without name, and in fact without talents, who produced the reformation?'[67]

Yet another strategy, quite widely employed, was especially favoured by those early radical leaders of the century's opening decades who have been termed 'restorationist radicals'. This involved insisting that reform was not innovation, but restoration: the reinstatement of a previous order of things. Calls to return the constitution to a putative original state had been a common feature of eighteenth-century oppositional (or, as we might say, reformist or radical) politics. The idea that annual parliaments and manhood suffrage had been components of the original, Anglo-Saxon constitution continued to surface in 'Jacobin' rhetoric in the 1790s (implicitly also countering suggestions that reforming ideas were all imported from France). In the early nineteenth century William Cobbett, himself a recruit from 1790s Toryism, was particularly insistent on this theme, sloganizing: 'We want nothing new!'[68] As a strategy for defending radical reformism to sceptical members of the social elite, this was pretty unpromising stuff: in the eyes of many, radicals compounded their faults by demonstrating that they were not merely enthusiasts, but also historically illiterate. Yet it may have done its work in helping to convince a popular audience that radicalism was compatible with patriotism. It also represented an attractively abrasive way of debunking the pretensions of defenders of the status quo, who were (fairly

---

[67] W. E. S. Thomas, *The Philosophic Radicals: Nine Studies in Theory and Practice, 1817–41* (Oxford, 1979), 124. Francis Horner drew the parallel in his journal for 1801: 'The transactions as well as the characters by which the period of the Reformation was distinguished suggest a very obvious application to the recent events by which the public mind has been agitated': Francis Horner, *Memoirs and Correspondence* (London, 1843), 167. See also *Philanthropist*, 2 (1812), 205, 279, urging philanthropic reformers not to quail in the face of hostility to 'reform': 'had it not been for a glorious Reformation, the enlightened sons of Albion might have remained even to this day involved in darkness and superstition'. Or, in rather different vein, Byron enthusing about the Luddites: 'How go on the weavers – the breakers of frames – the Lutherans of politics – the reformers?' From a letter to Thomas Moore, Dec. 1816, quoted in Jeffrey N. Cox, *Poetry and Politics in the Cockney School: Keats, Shelley, Hunt and their Circle* (Cambridge, 1998), 56. Cf. William Cobbett, *A History of the Protestant 'Reformation' in England and Ireland* (London, 1824–6). Also of interest is B. J. Elliott, 'The Scottish Reformation and English Reform: David Wilkie's "Preaching of Knox" at the Royal Academy Exhibition of 1832', *Art Hist.*, 17 (1994).

[68] For restorative radicals, see Philip Harling, *The Waning of 'Old Corruption': The Politics of Economical Reform in Britain, 1779–1846* (Oxford, 1996), 96–104. See also Peter Spence's overlapping category, 'romantic radicals': Peter Spence, *The Birth of Romantic Radicalism: War, Popular Politics and English Radical Reformism, 1800–15* (Aldershot, 1996). James Epstein, *Radical Expression: Political Language, Ritual and Symbol in England, 1790–1850* (New York, 1994), ch. 1, argues that defensive constitutionalism was compatible with radical aspirations and militant tactics. For Jacobin restorationist rhetoric, see, e.g., [Joseph] Pearson, *Pearson's Political Dictionary* (London, [1792]), 16, 30 (where 'Innovation' is defined as 'Restoring the British Constitution to its original purity'); *The Address of the British Convention assembled at Edinburgh* (London, [1793]), 14. Note also Thomas Spence, *The Restorer of Society to its Natural State* (London, 1801) – which earned him a prosecution for seditious libel. For Cobbett claiming radicals wanted nothing new, see, e.g., Epstein, *Radical Expression*, 10.

enough) thus exposed as defenders not of timeless truths and age-old ways, but of modern and historically contingent arrangements.[69]

Willingness to entertain schemes of reform, called by that name, became *somewhat* more widespread in the 1810s. The variety of types of reformist discourse around, however, ensured that no 'reform' consensus would emerge. On the contrary, something of a gulf opened up between those who favoured pragmatic tinkering with the laws and philanthropic endeavour – who might, in the right circumstances, also be prepared to consider some limited form of parliamentary reform – and those who saw no merit in anything less than manhood suffrage, and whose policy agendas might also be rather different: being concerned less with prisons, asylums, and education, and more with ready credit, fair wages, or cheap bread. There were common causes – such as reducing the burden of taxation, promoting freedom of enquiry and improving the condition of the people (although, on this last point, agreement diminished rapidly when one turned from ends to means). Moreover the 'gulf' was not unpeopled: during the 1810s, Benthamite utilitarians emerged within it, as supporters of law reform and practical improvement, including better prisons, *and* of manhood suffrage. Furthermore there were others, like the Whigs of the 'Mountain', interested in trying to build collaborative relationships across the gap.[70]

Yet consciousness of such a gap was general, and was reflected in increasing use of the adjectives 'radical' and 'moderate' to distinguish reformers from one another. I have suggested that the distinction had some currency earlier: it was mocked by a propagandist for John Reeves' 1792 Association for the Protection of Liberty and Property, who instructed his audience that there were two sorts of reformers: the 'Demolishers' and the 'Bodgers'. But, from the 1810s, the distinction became more salient: an issue reformers had to engage with not only in presenting themselves to the public, but in negotiating relationships with one another; a problem and challenge for entrepreneurs of reform. In the wake of Thomas Brand's 'moderate' parliamentary reform proposal of 1810, which was unusually well supported in parliament, Cartwright commented, as if upon a new phenomenon, that people seemed to be arranging themselves into two groups: the real and rational reformists and the moderate reformists (it was clear where his preferences lay).[71] A would-be bridger of gaps, John

---

[69] For yet another strategy, see Philip Harling, 'Leigh Hunt's *Examiner* and the Language of Patriotism', *Eng. Hist. Rev.*, 111 (1996), esp. 1116–18. Hunt focused attention on critics' rhetorical strategies, observing that they found it necessary to pervert language and descend to ridicule to counter a case for change not easy to counter rationally.

[70] We lack studies that effectively survey the whole of this scene, and the pattern of connections within it. Some references to relevant secondary literature are supplied in the Introduction to this volume, esp. at nn. 18, 22, 36, 78, 79, 94. For the Mountain, see Dean Rapp, 'The Left-Wing Whigs: Whitbread, the Mountain and Reform, 1809–15', *Jl Brit. Studies*, 21 (1982).

[71] *Proceedings of the Association for Preserving Liberty and Property*, nos. 2, 9; Cartwright, *Life and Correspondence of Cartwright*, ii, 12–14, and note also J. Cartwright, *The Comparison;*
(cont. on p. 92)

Cam Hobhouse, got into hot water at the Westminster election of 1818, when he claimed to be not a moderate, but an enthusiastic reformer – while leaving his precise creed so vague that both Whigs and radicals demanded clarification.[72]

'Radical reformer' increasingly came to connote a supporter of popular reform movements – and was increasingly commonly abbreviated to 'radical'. In this context 'reformer' *tout court* was sometimes used to denote a moderate. The first instance of this usage I have found comes from 1817, in the wake of the Spa Fields disorders, when Orator Hunt charged 'reformers' with hypocrisy and betrayal of the cause.[73] In effect, the growth of the vocabulary of 'radicalism' began to free 'reform' for other uses just at the time when moderate reformism as a positive stance in its own right was beginning to take shape.

V

In the 1810s, I have argued, it became common to attempt to distinguish 'moderate' from 'radical' reform. In the 1820s, the picture became considerably more complex. There was much more general willingness to use the vocabulary of 'reform' – though some continued to avoid it, like the Liberal Tory George Canning, who in this respect contrasted with Robert Peel, in many ways more traditionally inclined.[74] In this context, discussion more often focused on the sorts of 'reform' that were and were not desirable or acceptable. The term itself was applied to a widening range of projects. There was also a proliferation of what might be termed 'hyphenated' reforms: variants of reforming ideology distinguished by their prefatory adjectives, such as 'rational reform' and 'social reform'.

Some 'reforms' touted in the 1780s received government sanction, such as prison reform and police reform. As home secretary Peel, invoking the blessing

---

(*cont.*)

in which are considered Mock Reform, Half Reform and Constitutional Reform (London, 1810). For insistence on the difference, and identification of moderate reformers as the enemy, see also Jeremy Bentham, *Plan for Parliamentary Reform . . . Shewing the Necessity of a Radical and the Inadequacy of Moderate Reform* (London, 1817).

[72] Thomas, *Philosophic Radicals*, 76, 79–82.

[73] J. Ann Hone, *For the Cause of Truth: Radicalism in London, 1796–1821* (Oxford, 1982), 269. However, Hone provides no footnote so the usage is not securely documented. Certainly 'radical reformers' often continued to refer to themselves as 'reformers' or 'reformists' at this time. See n. 84 below for a later instance.

[74] This appears from *The Speeches of George Canning, with a Memoir of his Life*, ed. George Therry, 6 vols. (London, 1828). See also the *Edinburgh Rev.*, 37 (1822), 379–407, for the review of the earlier *Speeches of George Canning . . . at Liverpool*, under the title 'Mr Canning and Reform'. After becoming prime minister in 1827 Canning did, however, claim credit for having made in recent years 'such temperate and gradual reforms as I thought were consistent with . . . general and permanent good': *Speeches of Canning*, vi, 193.

of Bacon, the patron saint of pragmatic reform, was prepared to contemplate simplification and amendment of the law.[75] The early 1820s saw the development of interest in what was termed 'colonial reform', meaning an amelioration in the condition of the workforce in the West Indies, with a view to preparing the ground for the day when slaves might be transmogrified into free workers. The end of the decade saw an upsurge of interest in 'church reform' and a call for 'financial reform'.[76]

The 1820s saw differences among supporters of 'radical reform' become more manifest. This is not to say that they became incapable of joining together to advance radical extension of the suffrage. That they would unite to promote that cause was demonstrated in the reform agitation that took off from the end of the decade. Yet among radicals, it became clear, there was a variety of overlapping sub-cultures, distinguished by concerns that were as much religious, moral, or social as political. Thus, for Richard Carlile and the Rotundaists, free speech and enquiry, especially in religious matters, and the right to submit religious doctrine and ceremony to radical scrutiny and parody, were key concerns: reform in thought was, in their view, at least as important as institutional reform. Disciples of Robert Owen were still more inclined to downgrade politics as an arena of struggle: to them, the key to change lay in a programme of 'social reform', in a radical reordering of social relationships, above all in family, workplace, and neighbourhood.[77]

I have suggested that an effect of the high-profile 'parliamentary reform' gained from 1780 was that the word 'reform' was increasingly commonly associated with projects of structural, institutional change. Yet it never ceased to be used in a moral context too. Indeed if we considered general usage, and not public discourse only, I am sure that we would find that at all times through this period the word was chiefly used with reference to personal conduct. This pattern of use encouraged reflection on the relationship between reform of the state and reform of the self. This was a talking-point in the 1790s, when even some radicals questioned whether political reform would have much effect

[75] Robert Peel, *The Speeches of Sir Robert Peel Delivered in the House of Commons*, 4 vols. (London, 1853), i, 397 ff. In this speech, however, Peel eschewed talk of reform/ation, except when quoting Bacon.

[76] British and Foreign Anti-Slavery Society, *The Progress of Colonial Reform, a Brief View of the Real Advance Made since May 15 1823* (London, 1826). Arthur Burns discusses the history of the phrase 'church reform' in his chapter in this volume; a series of publications in 1829 prompted *The Times* and some of the review journals to attend to the subject. H. B. Parnell, *On Financial Reform* (London, 1830); historians talk of calls for currency reform in this decade, but I have not found contemporaries using that label.

[77] For an overview of the moral turn in popular politics, see John Belchem, *Popular Radicalism in Nineteenth-Century England* (Basingstoke, 1996), 51–6. Carlile in the *Moralist*, 1 [1823], 2, asserted 'the first principle of all reform must be to reform ourselves'; Robert Owen propounded his distinctive vision in *A New Theory of Moral and Social Reform* (London, 1823).

unless accompanied, or perhaps preceded, by moral reform. Wilberforce and his cronies – 'the Saints' – always strove to run moral and socio-institutional projects in harness.[78] The aggressive tone of plebeian radicalism in the 1810s, and the increasing prominence within it of an anti-religious strain, exacerbated tension between the two projects. The *true* route to reform, some argued, was the way of moral reform.[79]

The coming to power in 1830 of a government universally expected to introduce some measure of parliamentary reform realigned diffuse opinion into warring camps: those for and against reform, and, among reformers, moderate and radical reformers. Various parts of the heritage of ideas that had built up around the project of 'reform' over the centuries were deployed, and took on new life and meaning. Anti-reformers denounced 'innovation'. Whigs emphasized that they served a patriot king, and thus had the highest of all political endorsements for reforming endeavour (Bolingbroke's mid-eighteenth-century paean to this ideal figure was reprinted).[80] Popular excitement, and recurrent disorders, held by anti-reformers to show that what was afoot represented, of all dread things, democracy in action, were argued by apologists for reform to demonstrate instead that reform was the only alternative to revolution.[81] 'Reform' generically was in any case (it was argued) the inevitable concomitant of social progress.[82] Moderates sometimes arrogated to themselves the title of reformers, disparaging those who wanted thoroughgoing change as radicals: according to Joseph Parkes in 1830, a meeting of the Birmingham Political Union was best likened to a volcanic eruption, sending forth 'a burning lava of red hot radicalism devastating the fair appearance of the field of reform'.[83]

---

[78] See thus [London Corresponding Society], *Moral and Political Mag.* (London, 1796), 124–5, 156–8. That moral and religious concerns were always just below the surface of the Saints' reforming projects is stressed by Brown, *Fathers of the Victorians.* John Bowdler's prominent propagandist tract, *Reform or Ruin: Take Your Choice!* (London, 1797), stressed the need to give priority to moral reform, as did several other publications of that decade. See R. P. Soloway, 'Reform or Ruin: English Moral Thought during the First French Republic', *Rev. of Politics*, 25 (1963).

[79] Thus *An Address to the Ministerial Radicals* (London, 1820). I owe this reference to J. C. D. Clark. Wilberforce's support for attempts to repress blasphemous publications encouraged radicals to denounce him and the Saints generally as no true reformers: William H. Wickwar, *The Struggle for the Freedom of the Press, 1819–1832* (London, 1928), 189, 224; see also Hazlitt's stress on the ambiguities of Wilberforce's image in William Hazlitt, *The Spirit of the Age* (London, 1825), 211–15.

[80] David Armitage, 'A Patriot for Whom? The Afterlives of Bolingbroke's Patriot King', *Jl Brit. Studies*, 36 (1997), 415–17.

[81] Thus 'S. W.', *A Word in Season . . . Proving the Projected Reform not only not Revolutionary, but the Only Means of Preventing Revolution* (London, [1832?]); for a general discussion, see Joseph Hamburger, *James Mill and the Art of Revolution* (New Haven, 1963).

[82] See, e.g., John Stuart Mill, 'The Spirit of the Age', *Examiner* (Jan.–May 1831), repr. in John Stuart Mill, *Essays on Politics and Culture*, ed. G. Himmelfarb (Garden City, N.Y., 1963).

[83] Quoted Thomas, *Philosophic Radicals*, 252.

Radicals, conversely, argued that 'effectual reform' *was* radical reform, and denounced mere 'pseudo Reformers'.[84]

VI

The Representation of the People Act (1832) was universally known as 'the Reform Act'. The ministry that brought it in was dubbed the 'Reform ministry', and the parliament elected according to its prescription was 'the Reformed parliament'.[85] The act had in fact been brought in by a hybrid ministry, consisting mainly of Whigs, but also of some Canningites and one Tory ultra. In this context 'Reformer' was a convenient umbrella title for a supporter of the government, and accordingly a title under which many MPs presented themselves to the electorate (it also provided a way of cashing in on the popularity of the scheme). As reconstituted in mid-decade, the ministry rested upon the support of a Whig–radical–Irish alliance; the title 'Reformer' remained current for those of this group who chose so to label themselves through into the next decade.[86]

Co-option of 'reform' as the slogan of a political faction – and an elite, moderate faction at that – did not persuade everyone else to surrender claims to the term. The radical wing of the governing coalition liked to think of themselves as the true reformers; it was they who founded the Reform Club, from which base they planned to press for further, thoroughgoing systemic reforms – which they now began to distinguish as 'organic reforms'. But, symptomatically, the club was embraced by the Whigs.[87] In the era of liberal hegemony after 1846, advanced liberals sought to distinguish themselves as 'the reform party', and united in pressing for further financial and constitutional 'reform'; yet 'radical' proved the more enduring name for the parliamentary left.[88] Meanwhile Chartists, in so far as they remained wedded to the cause of parliamentary reform, continued to term themselves 'reformers': the term was employed

---

[84] Belchem, *'Orator' Hunt*, 199, 236. Among other ringing of changes on established themes, note Thomas Arnold's *Englishman's Register* (London, 1831), esp. i, 1–2, prioritizing moral and intellectual reform, the key object, in his view, being the Christianization of men's feelings on political matters.

[85] My impression is that Cobbett helped to popularize these uses. But note that Brougham, for example, spoke of income tax being defeated in 'an unreformed parliament': *Speeches of Henry Lord Brougham upon Questions relating to Public Rights, Duties and Interests*, 4 vols. (Edinburgh, 1838), i, 499.

[86] Jonathan Parry, *The Rise and Fall of Liberal Government in Victorian Britain* (New Haven, 1993), 167.

[87] For the Reform Club, see Thomas, *Philosophic Radicals*, 234. Thomas cites various references to 'organic reform' (201, 288, 299). Richard Cobden in 1846 argued that 'questions of organic reform . . . have no vitality in this country': quoted in Harling, *Waning of 'Old Corruption'*, 253.

[88] For nomenclature, see Miles Taylor, *The Decline of British Radicalism, 1847–60* (Oxford, 1995), 23–4. Taylor's larger argument is that the middle decades of the nineteenth century saw first the rise, then the fall, of a significant *parliamentary* party committed to promoting further reform.

in several Chartist publications, including Bronterre O'Brien's proto-Chartist *National Reformer* of 1837. But it is notable that it was not as 'reformers', but as 'Chartists', that they primarily sought to present themselves.[89]

Preference for an alternative vocabulary may have guided the naming of the 'Factory Regeneration Society', founded by an alliance of radical Tories, sympathetic Whigs, and working-class activists in 1831, to promote the 'short-time' movement across the north of England. Certainly Richard Oastler's 'throne, altar, and cottage' rhetoric avoided the standard tropes of reform discourse, though it did overlap with some elements of 'restorationist radical' rhetoric (both Sir Francis Burdett and Cobbett's son John in fact aligned themselves with the Tories in the post-Reform era).[90]

Though still a politically loaded term in the 1830s, 'reform' passed into more general currency thereafter. The rise of Peel – who even in the 1820s had been prepared to espouse suitably pragmatic reforms – to leadership of the Conservative party, must have helped (it was of course as much against Peelite conservatism as against reformist Whiggery that radical Tories sought to define themselves). Burke's defence of reform as a device by which societies might preserve themselves helped to supply the word with an acceptable lineage. From the 1830s, moreover, it became more common to term all sorts of efforts to improve social conditions – especially the conditions of life of the 'lower orders' – 'social reforms'. The cause of 'social reform' thus conceived was not the cause of any one party, indeed was often not the stuff of party politics at all.[91]

---

[89] J. Bronterre O'Brien (ed.), *Bronterre's National Reformer* (London, 1837). See also the *Halifax Reformer*: a pro-Chartist, radical, dissenting newspaper. 'Regeneration' was another term which retained power among Chartists. Thomas Paine Carlile (son of Richard Carlile) thus produced the *Regenerator and Chartist Circular*, cited in Paul Pickering, *Chartism and Chartists in Manchester and Salford* (Basingstoke, 1995), 42. Note the absence of the word 'reform' from the slogans on Chartist banners listed in *ibid.*, 214–16.

[90] J. T. Ward, 'Richard Oastler on Politics and Factory Reform, 1832–33', *Northern Hist.*, 24 (1988), 124–45, 135 n. for Cobbett's son; M. W. Patterson, *Sir Francis Burdett and his Times*, 2 vols. (London, 1931).

[91] The first references I have found to social reform/ation date from the 1790s; the usage probably reflects not only willingness to employ the term 'reform/ation' in new ways but also increased use of the adjective 'social' to mean (in the terms of Dr Johnson's definitions) 'Relating to a general or publick interest; relating to society' rather than the previously common 'Easy to mix in friendly gaiety; companionable'. See *Political and Philosophical Writings of William Godwin*, ed. Mark Philp, 7 vols. (London, 1993), iii, 124 (1793 edition of Godwin's *Political Justice*); Janet Semple, *Bentham's Prison: A Study of the Panopticon Penitentiary* (Oxford, 1993), 210 (an instance from 1803). However, it remained rare for some decades. As Beales, 'Idea of Reform', 170–1, has noted, Robert Owen used the term in the 1820s. Its increased use from 1830 probably in large part reflects a desire to distinguish 'political reform', as just achieved, from other varieties of reform, although the contrast was variously constructed. Thus Henry Brougham implied that social reform could be expected to be less controversial than political reform (Brougham, *Speeches*, iii, 171–2), whereas Daniel O'Connell stated that 'social' change

(cont. on p. 97)

'Reform' and cognate terms continued to provide ground for debate. Did a particular policy deserve the name of 'reform'? What did genuine reform consist in? What commitments did being a 'reformer' entail? But the age when the term was so heavily freighted as to be bandied about as a badge of identity, struggled over, assailed, avoided, affirmed in testimony to courage and true belief, or acclaimed as a cause fit to live and die for, had largely passed.

(*cont.*)
would be the more fundamentally disruptive (cited by Jennifer Ridden below, p. 276). Patrick Brantlinger, *The Spirit of Reform: British Literature and Politics, 1832–67* (Cambridge, Mass., 1971), provides an interesting account of later changes in the discourse of reform. He argues that the belief that political change might change society and morals steadily dwindled; it was increasingly supposed that the causal flow must be from the moral and social to the political.

3. Parliament, the state, and 'Old Corruption': conceptualizing reform, c. 1790–1832

PHILIP HARLING

During and after the Napoleonic Wars, popular radicals such as William Cobbett routinely drew attention to what they called 'Old Corruption', or simply 'Corruption', or 'the System', or 'the Thing'. They used such words interchangeably to describe a parasitic political system that took an unprecedented amount of tax money out of the pockets of Britons and transferred it to those of a narrow band of well-connected insiders through a wide variety of nefarious means. The latter included the grant of sinecures, reversions, church patronage, lucrative government contracts, an indirect-tax regime that obliged the common people to pay a disproportionate share of the state's fiscal burden, and a series of commercial and financial policies that served the interests of large landowners and City financiers at the expense of the unenfranchised.[1]

   This critique of systematic rapacity obviously owed much to the traditional 'country' suspicion of placemen, stockjobbers, and the like, and just as much to Thomas Paine's *Rights of Man*, which devoted so much attention to the maldistributive effects of a 'government of loaves and fishes' that thrived on chronic warfare. But the critique of 'Old Corruption' in the early nineteenth century was in many respects a critique of something quite new, for it was chiefly propelled by the enormous scale of the British war effort against revolutionary and Napoleonic France. Net public spending nearly quadrupled in real terms over the course of the wars, and at the peak of the conflict with Napoleon the government was engorging over 30 per cent of national income.[2] Popular radicals assumed that the scope of elite corruption grew in more or less direct proportion with the growth of the fiscal-military state. They also cited as proof

---

[1] Philip Harling, *The Waning of 'Old Corruption': The Politics of Economical Reform in Britain, 1779–1846* (Oxford, 1996), 1; W. D. Rubinstein, 'The End of "Old Corruption" in Britain, 1780–1860', *Past and Present*, no. 101 (Nov. 1983), 55–86; Martin Daunton, *Trusting Leviathan: The Politics of Taxation in Britain, 1799–1914* (Cambridge, 2001), 55–7.

[2] Harling, *Waning of 'Old Corruption'*, 136; Michael Mann, *The Sources of Social Power*, vol. ii: *The Rise of Classes and Nation-States, 1760–1914* (Cambridge, 1986), 115–16.

of elite misgovernment a number of other wartime and immediate post-war developments that had little or nothing to do with higher taxes, such as the legal assault on combinations and apprenticeship statutes, the accelerated pace of parliamentary enclosure, repressive legislation, and the turning of the industrial north into a veritable armed camp. Thus, in the very broad sense in which popular radicals tended to use it, 'Old Corruption' was a metaphor for systematic political oppression; and, since the opportunities for oppression within what they perceived to be a thoroughly rotten system were virtually limitless, 'Old Corruption' was itself virtually without limit.[3] More than anything else, it was 'Old Corruption' that prompted popular radicals to demand 'reform' in this era, and by 'reform' they almost invariably meant *parliamentary* reform. For they perceived that the sole antidote to 'Old Corruption' was universal or at least near-universal male suffrage, which would ostensibly force MPs to govern frugally and disinterestedly for fear of being voted out of office at the next election.

'Old Corruption', however, provided the vocabulary for only one of the competing languages of reform, offered only one diagnosis of the political problems facing Britons in the wartime and immediate post-war years, and proposed only one cure for them. Until at least after Peterloo, 'respectable' opinion – i.e., Tory, Whig, and independent MPs and the propertied gentlemen who sent most of them to Westminster – almost unanimously dismissed that diagnosis as wildly exaggerated, and the cure as worse than the putative disease. There were nevertheless widespread calls for retrenchment and administrative improvement within the political elite in this era, and like the radical critique of 'Old Corruption' they were chiefly inspired by the perceived excesses of the fiscal-military state. Until the late 1820s, however, most elite prescriptions for curbing those excesses fell well short of comprehensive parliamentary reform, and a good many of them were at least partly designed to demonstrate that substantive parliamentary reform was unnecessary. Indeed, much of the language of elite 'reform' was a language of 'anti-Reform', in the sense that, like their popular radical adversaries, what most elite commentators meant by 'reform' was parliamentary reform, almost invariably with a capital 'R'. Other prescriptions for political change, many of them offered up as less dangerous alternatives to parliamentary reform, were commonly called by some other name, such as 'improvement' or 'amendment', or (in connection with the tax structure) 'retrenchment'.[4]

---

[3] Kevin Gilmartin, *Print Politics: The Press and Radical Opposition in Early Nineteenth-Century England* (Cambridge, 1996), 170.

[4] I owe my thoughts on this subject to D. Beales, 'The Idea of Reform in British Politics, 1829–1850', in T. Blanning and P. Wende (eds.), *Reform in Great Britain and Germany, 1750–1850* (Oxford, 1999), esp. 162–6.

The task here is to explain why most of the elite felt that what might be called 'practical improvement'[5] was necessary, why most of them thought it preferable to parliamentary reform, and why that preference had narrowed into a Tory obsession by the end of 1830. There are two points that I wish to make as a means of furnishing this explanation. The first is that the mounting cost and seeming ineffectuality of the war against Napoleon inspired demands for institutional change from within parliament itself, but that independent and opposition MPs generally pressed for (and often achieved) 'practical improvement' rather than parliamentary reform in their effort to legitimate elite authority to themselves and to their propertied observers. In the turbulent years after Waterloo, most elite politicians continued to advocate 'practical improvement' rather than parliamentary reform as the proper means of ensuring political and social stability, and independent and Whig MPs foisted retrenchment on a generally reluctant series of Tory governments as the chief means of legitimating elite political authority to hard-pressed taxpayers. The second point is that the post-war Tories themselves facilitated 'practical improvements' such as tariff liberalization as a means of disengaging the state and its elite stewards from the clash of sectional interests. Most of them also insisted that substantive parliamentary reform, far from doing away with 'Old Corruption', would establish a system of 'New Corruption' that would turn MPs into pandering delegates and drive all disinterestedness from the House of Commons.

Before 1830, a great deal of 'practical improvement' was generated from within the political elite, in response to the internal pressures brought to bear on a series of mostly Pittite and Tory governments by independent and Whig MPs. The main point was to reduce the size and cost of the fiscal-military state, which had grown to colossal dimensions over a quarter-century of almost non-stop warfare on an unprecedented scale. There were two main varieties of 'practical improvement': administrative restructuring and retrenchment. The former was intended to reduce the expense and enhance the efficiency of government office-holders whilst imposing upon them a more lofty standard of public service and accountability, while the latter was intended to reduce a bloated state whilst providing relief to hard-pressed taxpayers. Both were designed to reduce the 'influence of the crown' and its ministers over the House of Commons by curbing their patronage powers.

A brief summary of the more pertinent statistics suggests that 'practical improvement' was broad-ranging indeed. The number of MPs who held places, pensions, and/or sinecures fell from some two hundred in 1780, to eighty-nine in 1822, and to sixty in 1833, by which time virtually all placemen held efficient offices. The number of unregulated sinecures in the central establishment

---

[5] 'Practical improvement' is admittedly my term rather than theirs; I use it here simply as a shorthand for a broad range of ameliorative measures that had nothing to do with the franchise.

was cut from around six hundred in 1780, to some two hundred and fifty in 1810, to ten in 1835. While there were about a hundred claims to reversions to civil offices in 1809, no new reversions were granted after 1814. The annual cost of pensions on the various civil lists fell from almost £200,000 in 1809 to £75,000 in 1830. As sinecures and reversions were gradually abolished or reformed from the late 1790s onwards, fees in many of the major departments of state were pooled together into central funds from which officers were paid strict salaries.[6] While internal pressure for administrative reform was reducing parliamentary patronage and bureaucratic waste, internal pressure for retrenchment was leading to the gradual reduction of the fiscal-military state. At constant prices, net public spending had risen some 400 per cent between the Peace of Utrecht (1713) and the Congress of Vienna (1815); it fell 25 per cent over the next twenty years, reaching its nineteenth-century low in 1834. Per-capita public spending was cut by 40 per cent between 1811 and 1821, and fell another 30 per cent over the next two decades. By 1851 it remained well under half its wartime height.

It is nevertheless important to stress that retrenchment was a long, drawn-out affair. As Julian Hoppit has recently noted, between 1815 and 1832 absolute levels of public expenditure at constant prices were still roughly twice what they had been immediately after the American War of Independence, and about four times what they had been at the end of the Seven Years War.[7] By the mid-Victorian years there was, however, no doubt that the burdens of state were much lighter on the backs of Britons than they had been on their late-Georgian ancestors and still were on many of their continental counterparts. This owed something to success in reining back spending and something to the *pax Britannica*, but more to growing national wealth. The British central government had absorbed some 30 per cent of gross national product at the height of the Napoleonic War; it was absorbing only 8 per cent of it by the 1870s, compared with 13 per cent in France and 12 per cent in the German states.[8]

It is worth briefly stressing here, as I have done at much greater length elsewhere, that administrative restructuring and retrenchment were not simply commonsensical exercises in bureaucratic rationality, good housekeeping, or Tory 'pragmatism'. Rather, they were the products of political struggle, chiefly the results of sporadic but often intense pressure that was exerted on a series

---

[6] Harling, *Waning of 'Old Corruption'*, 16, 20–1, 109–10.
[7] J. Hoppit, 'Checking the Leviathan, 1688–1832', in P. O'Brien and D. Winch (eds.), *The Political Economy of British Historical Experience, 1688–1914* (Oxford, 2002), 12.
[8] Harling, *Waning of 'Old Corruption'*, 11–13; P. Harling and P. Mandler, 'From "Fiscal-Military" State to *Laissez-faire* State', *Jl Brit. Studies*, 32 (1993), 56–60; Mann, *Sources of Social Power*, ii, ch. 11. As a proportion of GNP, even on the eve of the First World War, British state expenditure remained lower than it had been in 1820, in marked contrast to France and Prussia–Germany: Daunton, *Trusting Leviathan*, 65.

of mostly hesitant Pittite and Tory ministries by opposition and independent MPs and occasionally by 'respectable' outdoor critics, most notably the country gentlemen and tenant farmers who turned out at county meetings to petition for retrenchment during the post-war agricultural depression. Let us simply highlight a few of the more compelling examples. A good many of the wartime bureaucratic reforms, most notably compulsory superannuation, owed less to treasury initiative than they did to the work of the Select Committee on Public Expenditure. That committee was appointed by the Ministry of All the Talents in 1807 only because Sir Robert Myddleton Biddulph and other independent-minded MPs insisted that the government take steps to reduce waste and potentially corrupt practices throughout the expanding wartime bureaucracy. It was only after waging a running battle with ministers that Henry Bankes, an independent Dorset grandee, secured the appointment of an influential select committee on sinecures in 1810 and forced the suspension of grants of reversion a few years later. Similarly, it was independent and opposition MPs who were uneasy with the widespread perception of wartime corruption in high places that forced Henry Dundas to resign as first lord of the Admiralty in 1805 and the duke of York to resign as commander-in-chief of the army in 1809. The former was forced out of public life when it was rumoured that his subordinate at the Admiralty had with his knowledge contrived to divert public money into private bank accounts, while the latter was compelled to step down after it was revealed that his former mistress was trafficking in army commissions.

Finally, it was parliamentary pressure augmented by well-orchestrated county meetings that forced the pace of post-war retrenchment. Country gentlemen within the Commons and without who were suffering from the economic transition to peace joined with the Whigs to force the Liverpool government abruptly to abandon the wartime property tax and malt duties in 1816. Sporadic pressure thereafter guaranteed that the pace of retrenchment would remain brisk, most notably in the early 1820s, when the Liverpool ministry found itself under sustained assault from the Whig opposition, from the indefatigable independent MP Joseph Hume, and from hard-pressed agriculturists who organized dozens of county meetings to protest at their plight and to insist on political solutions to it.[9]

Having briefly traced the lineaments of wartime and post-war retrenchment and administrative reform, let us now discuss the motives for them. One of the most obvious and potent of them was the widespread sense that war with Napoleon, while widely acknowledged to be an unavoidable necessity, had grown intolerably expensive, and that the post-war establishment thus needed to be dramatically cut back. Indeed, in the immediate post-war years Whig and radical MPs alike expressed a fervent desire to shrink the civil and military

---

[9] See also Daunton, *Trusting Leviathan*, ch. 3; Hoppit, 'Checking the Leviathan', 8–11.

establishments all the way back to their pre-war levels.[10] The Liverpool ministry was itself deeply enough committed to post-war retrenchment to try to meet that very same standard, albeit at a considerably more gradual pace than its critics demanded.[11] Of course this was a totally unrealistic goal, and the government never came close to achieving it. But that ministers themselves could seriously contemplate attempting a return to pre-war 'normalcy' in the scope of the central government is a vivid testament to the intensity of post-war retrenchment pressure.

A second motive for 'practical improvement' was the need to demonstrate the patriotism of the political elite at a time when it was encouraging an un-precedented number of Britons to take up arms on behalf of the political status quo. While the British state was fighting for survival, 'patriotism' could be broadly construed to include any measure that expedited the war effort, includ-ing fiscal improvements such as the streamlining of property-tax collection that wartime governments adopted without any prompting at all. But ministerial critics in the Commons insisted that true patriotism also meant demonstrating to 'respectable' opinion that, unlike its French counterpart, the British elite still deserved to lead the nation because it remained virtuous. Thus the Whig grandee J. C. Curwen sought to force the government to curb the number of sinecures not because doing so would save much money, but because sinecures 'tend to impeach all public character', and because above all else it had been 'the want of character, and consequent want of confidence in their successive leaders', that had led the French people to undertake a revolution that quickly 'led to the total extinction of that liberty which at one moment there was a fair prospect of their obtaining'.[12] Administrative reformers in the Commons persistently sought to make the example of France a patriotic warning to Britain's leaders that they had better take what steps they could to discourage the perception of elite cupidity.

A third and related catalyst for 'practical improvement' was evangelicalism. Most noteworthy here were the exploits of William Wilberforce and the compact squad of thirty or so of his fellow 'Saints'.[13] They provided crucial support to the Whig opposition on a number of issues because at a time of revolutionary tumult they feared the wrath of God if Britain's political leaders did not live up to a lofty standard of disinterested comportment. Thus in playing a pivotal role in the chastisement of Dundas and York, Wilberforce felt himself an instrument

---

[10] Brit. Lib., Grenville papers, Add. MS 58,949, fos. 149–50, Grey to Grenville, 25 Jan. 1815; *Parl. Debs.*, 2nd ser., vi, cols. 64–6 (5 Feb. 1822, Joseph Hume).

[11] Brit. Lib., Liverpool papers, Add. MS 38,264, fos. 72–3, Liverpool to Palmerston, 30 Dec. 1816.

[12] *Parl. Debs.*, 1st ser., xiv, cols. 365–6 (4 May 1809).

[13] For the Saints' disproportionate influence, see esp. Ian Bradley, 'The Politics of Godliness: Evangelicals in Parliament, 1784–1832' (University of Oxford D.Phil. thesis, 1974), ch. 2.

of divine justice. 'If we believe the Bible', he affirmed, 'we must believe that the vices of the great, both directly and consequently, call down the judgments of the Almighty.' Hence he was 'strongly influenced by the persuasion, that by marking such shameful debauchery, thus publicly disclosed, with the stigma of the House of Commons, we should be acting in a manner that would be pleasing to God, and directly beneficial to the morals of the community'.[14] It is only fair to assume, moreover, albeit difficult to prove, that the religious convictions of Liverpool and his colleagues encouraged many of them to cultivate the image of high-minded, hard-working professionalism for which the second-generation Pittites were notorious. In any case, they were obliged to function within a religious environment in which the pursuit of private gain at public expense was widely perceived to be a sin.

The fourth factor driving 'practical improvement' was the abiding Whig pre-occupation with the influence of the crown, i.e., the patronage that the king and his appointed ministers had at their disposal to help ensure for themselves a safe parliamentary majority. This preoccupation of course stemmed from the young George III's effort to break the Whigs' monopoly of office, and it turned into an obsession during their fifty years in the political wilderness. Hence the Whigs took every opportunity to insist that the wartime growth of public offices had given the king's ministers an enormous windfall of patronage that they used to preserve their monopoly of office. As late as 1820 Lord John Russell could insist that, in spite of post-war retrenchment and the reduction of the civil es-tablishment, the 'produce of the taxes' still 'descend[ed] upon the proprietors, the agents, and the members of boroughs', and that there remained sufficient patronage 'to create and support an independent, unpopular, incapable admin-istration'.[15] The wartime growth of patronage probably did add to the floating strength of a sitting government,[16] but there is little question that the Whigs would have taken advantage of it had George III or George IV given them a proper opportunity to do so. But of course they did not, and as Michael Roberts noted long ago, the Whigs' 'grievance was not so much the existing spoils system, as the fact that they were increasingly excluded from it'.[17] There is no doubt that the Whigs pursued 'practical improvement' chiefly for the party-political dividends that it was expected to yield. As it happened, these efforts bore little fruit in the 1818 and 1820 general elections. 'Respectable' opinion, particularly in the agricultural districts, could welcome the Whig retrenchment campaign whilst resisting the notion of a Whig government. But while constant

---

[14] Robert and Samuel Wilberforce (eds.), *The Life of William Wilberforce*, 3 vols. (London, 1839), iii, 405, Wilberforce to Lord Muncaster [1809?].
[15] [Lord John Russell], *Essays and Sketches of Life and Character* (London, 1820), 148, 146.
[16] J. Dinwiddy, 'The "Influence of the Crown" in the Early Nineteenth Century: A Note on the Opposition Case', *Parl. Hist.*, 4 (1985), 189–200.
[17] Michael Roberts, *The Whig Party, 1807–1812* (London, 1939), 221–4.

parliamentary pressure did not immediately pay off for the Whigs at the hustings, it gave them hope that they had finally found an issue that might one day loosen the Tory stranglehold on office.[18]

The fifth major source of 'practical improvement' was the desire of post-war Tory ministers to foster policies that would return society to its 'natural' pre-war condition and disentangle the elite stewards of the state from the clash of sectional interests. As Boyd Hilton has argued, specie resumption and gradual tariff liberalization can be seen as parts of a systematic effort to return to 'pre-war normalcy'. The point of such exercises was to promote a static and essentially self-regulating economy that reflected the Tory commitment to fostering a sort of mechanical harmony 'by stripping away anomalous powers, monopolies, preferences, special favours, and backstairs influences', such that 'society would run itself so as to create, if not a Paleyan context of beauty and happiness, at least a Butlerian framework of moral harmony, truth, and justice'.[19] But of course an equally important and complementary point behind the Tory promotion of 'natural' harmony was to shield the state from clamorous special interests by convincing Britons that there was precious little that political institutions could do to ameliorate perceived social injustices or sectional disadvantages. No interest group, according to Liverpool, had any business expecting the government to step in on their behalf, not only because intervention would force ministers into the dangerous game of playing favourites, but because 'on enquiry, it would be found that by far the greater part of the miseries of which human nature complained were in all times and in all countries beyond the control of human legislation. "How small, of all the ills that men endure,/ The part which kings or states can cause or cure!"'[20]

Historians often quote this declaration of government passivity that Liverpool borrowed from Samuel Johnson, but without noting that he quoted it only a few days before his government proceeded to introduce the bills that would soon become the Six Acts. Liverpool's broader point was that the popular radical agitation for parliamentary reform was not only reckless, but also pointless, because the prevailing economic distress had nothing to do with the forms of the constitution and everything to do with the inevitably difficult transition from war to peace. The sub-text of his remarks was that Britons should rest content with a representative system that put continuous 'respectable' pressure on ministers to govern as frugally, disinterestedly, and judiciously as possible,

---

[18] See, classically, Austin Mitchell, *The Whigs in Opposition, 1815–1830* (Oxford, 1967), chs. 4–6.

[19] Boyd Hilton, *The Age of Atonement: The Influence of Evangelicalism on Social and Economic Thought, 1795–1865* (Oxford, 1988), 220–1. See also Boyd Hilton, *Corn, Cash, Commerce: The Economic Policies of the Tory Governments, 1815–1830* (Oxford, 1977); Maxine Berg, *The Machinery Question and the Making of Political Economy, 1815–1848* (Cambridge, 1980), ch. 4.

[20] *Parl. Debs.*, 1st ser., xli, col. 497 (30 Nov. 1819).

and with ministers who responded to that pressure whilst shielding themselves and the state over which they presided from the charge that they were privileging any one set of propertied interests over others. Indeed, this defence of the efficacy of the representative system was one that ministers shared with most of their parliamentary critics, who routinely advertised 'practical improvement' as a means of demonstrating that the MPs returned to Westminster under the existing constitutional arrangements were vigilant and public-minded enough to safeguard the nation's political virtue. The chief reason, for instance, why Wilberforce and the Saints were such vigilant watchdogs of elite comportment was that they were concerned to shore up the existing constitutional order. Like them, Henry Bankes was as dedicated to the suppression of radicalism as he was to retrenchment, and he thought of public economy as an effective way of stifling the popular radicals.[21] In short, most elite proponents of 'practical improvement' saw it as a defence against, rather than an antecedent to, radical parliamentary reform.

If MPs in general and Tory ministers in particular rejected substantive parliamentary reform as a cure for 'Old Corruption', this was of course largely because they rejected the assumption on which 'Old Corruption' was predicated: that elite public men were too greedy and selfish to be entrusted with a monopoly of political power. The implicit point behind 'practical improvement' was to prove that this was not so, but the proof was offered only to 'respectable' critics of the government within doors and without. Rather than stooping to engage with the critique of 'Old Corruption' that was limned in the radical press, Tories either ignored it[22] or sought to suppress it through fitful rounds of libel prosecution and, when that failed, through the Six Acts, which greatly reduced the circulation of radical publications by forcing up their prices. Tories often did bestir themselves to argue against parliamentary reform as a means of curbing the perceived excesses of the fiscal-military state, however. It is worth highlighting these anti-reform arguments here not simply because historians of the 'age of reform' have paid too little attention to what the losers had to say, but because, whether intentionally or not, the anti-reformers turned the argument against 'Old Corruption' on its head. Popular radicals insisted that the chief political problem facing Britain was the insatiable greed of elite public men, and that the only feasible cure for this greed was root-and-branch parliamentary reform. But the elite defenders of the established constitution argued that parliamentary reform would destroy the ideal of disinterested public service that 'practical improvement' had helped to enshrine in the existing political structure, and would turn MPs into the puppets of their greedy constituents.

---

[21] *The Diary of Lord Colchester*, ed. Charles, Lord Colchester, 3 vols. (London, 1861), iii, 253, Henry Bankes to Lord Colchester, 6 May 1822.

[22] See, e.g., Stanley Jones, *William Hazlitt: A Life, from Winterslow to Frith Street* (Oxford, 1989), 240–1.

Anti-reformers routinely gave voice to the same series of propositions in their efforts to stymie parliamentary reform. The first was that the decline in the number of placemen meant that the House of Commons as presently constituted provided a potent check to executive power. Hence Sir Robert Peel argued in debate on the Reform Bill that the revolving-door cabinets of the last several years provided indisputable evidence that patronage had been trimmed back so decisively that it was now by no means sufficient to keep a government in power. 'The influence of the Crown, indeed!', he scoffed, '. . . and this is gravely said at a time when you had five different Administrations in four years; five Prime Ministers in rapid succession.'[23] According to this argument, sitting governments now scarcely possessed sufficient patronage to ensure their longevity, let alone enough systematically to corrupt the erstwhile representatives of the people.

A second and rather more plausible argument of the anti-reformers was that while the growth of the wartime civil and military establishments had obviously enhanced the government's opportunities to influence electors and MPs, the countervailing influence of other forces had more than offset it. Growing affluence, a burgeoning population, the increase of popular knowledge, the 'tenets which the French Revolution and other circumstances had diffused over the face of the community – the vast increase in the power and influence of the public press', Viscount Castlereagh noted in 1822: 'let all these be considered for a moment, and then let any member stand up and state that the influence of the Crown had been increased beyond, or even equal to its due proportion'.[24] Government supporters were especially forceful in their insistence that the power of the press trumped any additional influence that wartime patronage had procured for ministers. '[A]gainst the increase of patronage must be set off this mighty increase of public opinion', George Canning argued, and the strength of the latter had been most notably magnified by the publication of the parliamentary debates. This was 'a power, under the influence of which I, Sir, now address you, knowing that tomorrow, whatever I now say, will be submitted to a thousand eyes, and criticized by a thousand tongues'.[25] Thanks to the journalists in the gallery, Sir Robert Inglis noted, 'everything which passes in this House, appears on our tables the next morning, and is thence carried over the whole world'.[26] While it was true that 'ministers were not made accountable as regarded their lives or their fortunes', Frederick Robinson argued, the press ensured that 'they could not walk through the public streets without meeting men who knew all that they had said, and all that they had done'.[27] Politicians who

---

[23] *Parl. Debs.*, 3rd ser., ii, col. 1353 (3 Mar. 1831).
[24] *Ibid.*, 2nd ser., vii, col. 1300 (24 June 1822).
[25] *Ibid.*, 1st ser., xxxv, col. 683 (25 Feb. 1817).
[26] *Ibid.*, 3rd ser., ii, col. 1121 (1 Mar. 1831).
[27] *Ibid.*, 2nd ser., vi, col. 1089 (13 Mar. 1822).

were subjected to such probing scrutiny, anti-reformers argued, were hardly in a position to indulge in systematic corruption even if they had been tempted to do so.

A third implicit retort of anti-reformers to the critique of 'Old Corruption' was that a reformed government was likely to accumulate even more patronage, because its inevitable bellicosity would broaden the scope of the fiscal-military state rather than narrowing it. 'History does not teach us that democratic states, if great or powerful, are less irritable, or less inclined to war than other states', Sir John Nicholl insisted in 1817. 'It was not so with the ancient republics. It was not so with the French republic', nor was it likely to be so with a reformed House of Commons that was even more susceptible than the present one to popular war-mongering.[28] 'The accusations of the reformers against that House were exactly those which could be made justly against themselves', Canning argued in 1810, 'for there never yet was a state democratic and powerful which had not a tendency to war.'[29] A recurring theme of Peel's speeches during the reform crisis was that each and every British war of the eighteenth century had been popular at the outset; that it thus stood to reason that a reformed House of Commons was likely to be even more belligerent than its predecessors; and that under its tutelage taxes, patronage, and opportunities for official corruption were consequently bound to rise.[30]

A fourth argument of anti-reformers was that the wartime experience showed that it was not so much the government as the people who were corrupt, and that an extension of the franchise would only multiply the number of greedy patronage-seekers within the electorate. After all, J. W. Ward noted in 1812, in their heart of hearts most voters were hoping:

> not for an able independent representative, but for an active useful agent, some person that may represent them not merely within the walls of this House, but at the door of the Treasury; a channel through which some rivulet of the great stream of patronage may be drawn to fertilize their own native spot . . . An elector looks much less to the vote of his representative, than to the good things he has obtained, or is likely to obtain for himself or his neighbours, and for the purposes of a sure re-election, a morning well employed in Downing-street, is worth many an evening in this House.[31]

In short, it was not elite public men who were insatiably greedy, but the voters who relentlessly badgered them for some small crumb of patronage.

It thus stood to reason, anti-reformers suggested, that the public men who were in gravest danger of compromising their own virtue were those who had to vie for the votes of a large electorate, and the larger it was, the more corrupt it

---

[28] *Ibid.*, 1st ser., xxxvi, col. 742 (20 May 1817).   [29] *Ibid.*, xvii, col. 161 (21 May 1810).
[30] See, e.g., *ibid.*, 2nd ser., xxii, cols. 899–900 (23 Feb. 1830); xxiv, 1243 (28 May 1830); 3rd ser., vii, cols. 449–51 (21 Sept. 1831).
[31] *Ibid.*, 1st ser., xxiii, cols.128–9 (8 May 1812).

would be. 'The plain truth is, that nothing is more corrupt than popular election', Ward affirmed in 1812. 'It has any merit you please besides purity. One well fought county gives occasion to more bribery than half the boroughs in Cornwall put together.'[32] Twenty years later, Horace Twiss was willing to concede in debate on the Reform Bill that borough-mongering could be just as expensive as running in a large county or an open borough, but he nevertheless insisted that purchasing a seat was far less ethically compromising than competing for the votes of a drunken mob. 'The expense then being equal . . . he asked any one who had witnessed the scene of a contested election, the state of the public-houses, and the state of the electors, stimulated to outrage by every idle watch-word, which was the preferable system?'[33] In any case, Canning argued in 1822, corruption was only one of many charges that the 'successful candidate of a popular election' had to contend with. For he was certain to arrive in the House of Commons 'loaded with the imputation of every vice and crime that could unfit a man, not only for representing any class of persons, but for mixing with them as a member of society'. That being the case, 'the first effect of a reform which should convert all elections into popular ones, would probably be, to ensure a congregation of individuals, against every one of whom a respectable minority of his constituents would have pronounced sentence of condemnation'.[34]

Ultimately, then, anti-reformers concluded, it was not government patronage, but the threat of excessive 'democratical influence' that was most likely to compromise the disinterestedness of public men. If such influence prevailed at election time, Ward insisted, then candidates could only hope to win:

> by teaching every man that the first, and the last, and in fact the only ma-
> terial step towards political reputation and power, was popularity, and, con-
> sequently, by raising the art of flattering and bribing the people, above all
> other arts. Sir, I hope I may be pardoned for saying that I do not see why
> the practice of this art ought to be made a necessary step in the education of
> every English statesman.[35]

Similarly, one of the most common refrains of the Tory opponents of the Reform Bill was that it would deny liberty of conscience to MPs, who would be forced to pander to the whims of their constituents if they hoped to keep their seats at the next election. As Sir Edward Sugden put it, 'if the Bill should pass, the voice of the people would be predominant in that House – there would no longer be deliberation, but a voting by delegation'.[36] The voice of the people, moreover, was likely to be loud and obnoxious. Sugden cited the 'barbarous mirth' that had accompanied the reading in the Commons of Schedule A as a sign of ungentlemanly things to come, 'indicating, that when the reformed

---

[32] *Ibid.*, col. 136. [33] *Ibid.*, 2nd ser., vii, cols. 88–9 (25 Apr. 1822).
[34] *Ibid.*, col. 123. [35] *Ibid.*, 1st ser., xxiii, col. 134 (8 May 1812).
[36] *Ibid.*, 3rd ser., iv, col. 1218 (13 July 1831).

Parliament came, measures would be carried rather by acclamation than calm investigation'.[37]

Of course, this Tory prediction of a post-reform system of 'New Corruption' proved to be no more accurate than the most exaggerated popular radical variations on the theme of 'Old Corruption'. Indeed, one of the points most frequently made about the Reform Act has been how little it changed the political system. Norman Gash and others have stressed the similarities between pre- and post-1832 politics, emphasizing the continued importance of patronage as a means of winning votes, the continuities within the party-political apparatus, and the preservation of landed influence within the reformed parliament.[38] More recently, Frank O'Gorman and James Vernon have drawn attention to the conservatism of the Act, stressing that it increased the electorate from a mere 14 to a mere 18 per cent of adult men; that it actually decreased the number of voters in some of England's more open boroughs; and that it spelled the extinction of the Georgian conception of the election as an event in which the entire community – enfranchised and unenfranchised alike – could participate in meaningful ways.[39] There is certainly much truth in this assessment. But it misses an important point about the Reform Act: that it was an unprecedented acknowledgement on the part of the parliamentary majority that the 'borough-mongering system' was indeed damaging to the reputation of public men, and that to help restore this reputation it was necessary to divest 143 MPs of their seats. A good many patrons had paid immense sums to gain control of their rotten boroughs, and now these were confiscated outright by the Grey ministry from the belief that at least in perception and sometimes in reality they compromised the integrity of the MPs who sat for them by making them beholden to the will of the highest bidder.[40] A remarkable fact about the Whig coalition that has received precious little comment is the alacrity with which it meddled with propertied interests that its Tory predecessors had not dreamt of touching: West Indian planters and clergymen of the Irish church as well as borough patrons. While the first two groups were handsomely compensated for their losses, the 'borough-mongering interest' most emphatically was not.

The Reform Act's assault on the proprietary boroughs was of course only one way in which it marked a noteworthy break from the political past. It was the product of an administration that took a much more expansive view of its legislative powers than had any of its predecessors, which goes far to explain

---

[37] *Ibid.*, v, col. 445 (27 July 1831).

[38] Norman Gash, *Politics in the Age of Peel* (London, 1953); Frank O'Gorman, *Voters, Patrons, and Parties: The Unreformed Electoral System of Hanoverian England, 1734–1832* (Oxford, 1989), 392–3.

[39] O'Gorman, *Voters, Patrons, and Parties*; James Vernon, *Politics and the People: A Study in English Political Culture, c. 1815–1867* (Cambridge, 1993).

[40] See, e.g., *Parl. Debs.*, 3rd ser., v, col. 117 (20 July 1831, Sir Thomas Denham).

why the number of divisions related to bills sponsored by the government rose from 20 per cent of the total in 1832, to over 50 per cent by 1840, to over 60 per cent a decade later.[41] If the government was significantly more active after 1832, so too were voters. As Derek Beales has shown, there were many more contested elections in the partisan climate fostered by the Reform Act; as late as 1859 the percentage of the UK electorate that actually voted was well over twice what it had been in 1826.[42]

According to a number of different measurements, then, the Reform Act was indeed a pivotal event. What had prompted the Whigs thus to acknowledge that 'practical improvement' had proved insufficient to legitimate elite authority to the mass of Britons? Above all, perhaps, it was the sheer force of the outdoor reform agitation of the late 1810s, as well as the force with which the Liverpool government had sought to suppress it. Before Peterloo it had been only the radical wing of Whiggery that had committed itself to the principle of parliamentary reform. In its wake, the Whig leadership gave its support to the notion that seats from boroughs that had been disfranchised for corruption should be transferred elsewhere. By April 1822 Russell was able to garner a minority of 164 for his motion to deprive the hundred smallest boroughs of one member each and to distribute the seats to the counties and to unrepresented towns, the largest minority on a reform vote since Pitt's proposal of 1785.[43]

Whig enthusiasm for parliamentary reform waned along with the waning of outdoor agitation in the relative prosperity of the mid-1820s, however. It took an extraordinary combination of events to revive it and to give the Whigs an opportunity to carry it through. Historians are divided as to the relative weight to assign to the pressures that brought parliamentary reform to the top of the political agenda towards the end of 1830. But few of them would now quarrel with the assertion that 'it took a dramatic and unrepeatable conjunction of circumstances actually to transform the electoral system'.[44] Catholic Emancipation provoked a Tory schism, and some disaffected ultras looked to parliamentary reform as a means of revenge and a means of securing a measure of tax relief that did not seem obtainable within the existing system.[45] The onset of depression in the winter of 1829–30 prompted a search for political nostrums. Wellington's aloofness in response to the far-flung distress provoked

---

[41] T. A. Jenkins, *Parliament, Party and Politics in Victorian Britain* (Manchester, 1996), 37–8.

[42] D. Beales, 'The Electorate Before and After 1832: The Right to Vote, and the Opportunity', *Parl. Hist.*, 11 (1992), 148–9.

[43] Mitchell, *Whigs in Opposition*, 133–5; John Cannon, *Parliamentary Reform, 1640–1832* (Cambridge, 1973), 184.

[44] O'Gorman, *Voters, Patrons, and Parties*, 390–1. For other recent accounts that stress the suddenness of the reform crisis, see esp. Jonathan Parry, *The Rise and Fall of Liberal Government in Victorian Britain* (New Haven, 1993), ch. 2; J. C. D. Clark, *English Society 1660–1832*, 2nd edn (Cambridge, 2000), ch. 6.

[45] D. C. Moore, 'The Other Face of Reform', *Victorian Studies*, 5 (1961–2), 19–22.

widespread anger even within 'respectable' circles, and the seeming failure of the government's retrenchment efforts to allay that distress focused attention on parliamentary reform as a more potent antidote to it.[46] George IV's death prompted a general election that brought in a House of Commons that was far more sympathetic than its predecessor to the principle of parliamentary reform. Extra-parliamentary goings-on – the Swing riots, the collapse of the Bourbon regime in France, the sudden re-emergence of a formidable outdoor reform movement in the shape of the political unions[47] – convinced a growing number of MPs that they faced a crisis of governance that would result either in reform or in revolution. Wellington's bald assertion that he would not preside over the former lost him the support of MPs who feared the latter. It was this exceptional series of events that brought the Whigs into office in November 1830 and prompted them to commit themselves to a much more sweeping version of parliamentary reform than they had hitherto contemplated.

The 'practical improvements' by which the political elite had generally sought to curb the perceived excesses of the fiscal-military state before 1830 had no discernible impact on the popular radical critique of 'Old Corruption',[48] chiefly because these 'improvements' were largely intended to stave off the wholesale parliamentary reform that popular radicals insisted was the only effective antidote to it. Did the Reform Act make any difference here? The verdict is mixed. On the one hand, it is clear that the Whig assault on the 'borough-mongering system' convinced some of the staunchest critics of 'Old Corruption' that elite statesmen – the leaders of an elite *faction*, no less – might after all be trusted to serve the national interest and not merely their own. Thus John Wade could praise the Whigs for equating the government's interests 'with those of the people', for 'divest[ing] it of every thing like a corporate and exclusive interest separate from that of the community'.[49] After thirty years of struggle as a radical independent, Sir Francis Burdett could tell his Westminster constituents in the wake of 1832 that 'reform having been granted, our occupation is at an end'.[50] The rejectionist politics at the heart of radical Westminster had been grounded in the assumption that the elite factions were both rotten to the core, and that the only way to achieve substantive parliamentary reform was through the persistent efforts of stout-hearted independents. But when the Whigs carried out their assault on borough patrons, Burdett happily admitted that he had

[46] Harling, *Waning of 'Old Corruption'*, 191–5.

[47] Nancy LoPatin, *Political Unions, Popular Politics, and the Great Reform Act of 1832* (Basingstoke, 1999).

[48] Contrary to some of the bolder assertions in my own past work. See esp. Harling, *Waning of 'Old Corruption'*, 2, 255–66; Philip Harling, 'Rethinking "Old Corruption"', *Past and Present*, no. 147 (May 1995), 131, 157–8.

[49] John Wade, *The History of the Middle and Working Classes* (London, 1833), 477.

[50] Quoted in M. W. Patterson, *Sir Francis Burdett and his Times (1770–1844)*, 2 vols. (London, 1931), ii, 612.

been done out of a job. Of course, the elite's propensity for extravagance and greed remained a persistent radical theme after 1832, but, as Miles Taylor has shown, the influx of economy-minded radicals into the House of Commons in the wake of the Reform Act meant that this propensity could now be guarded against within doors, and not only railed against without.[51]

On the other hand, it was perhaps more than anything else the limits of the Reform Act and the perceived abuses of Whig activism that spawned in Chartism the most formidable plebeian political agitation of the nineteenth century. The Chartists were obviously no less mistrustful of elite political authority than Cobbett or Henry Hunt had been, and they were just as strongly convinced of the elite's insatiable greed. But Chartist indignation was inspired far less by the putative abuses of the fiscal-military state than it was by the putative sins of Whiggery, most notably the disappointing limits of the Reform Act itself, the New Poor Law, the extension of police forces, coercion in Ireland, and the hostility directed at trade unions and the short-time movement.[52] It certainly seems accurate to suggest along with Gareth Stedman Jones[53] that the political elite partly relied on a new series of 'practical improvements' to try to defuse Chartism: the 1842 Mines Act, the revival of income tax, the repeal of the Corn Laws, and the 1847 Factory Act. But the final point to make here is that the political context in which these measures were deployed had been fundamentally reshaped by the very instalment of parliamentary reform that the 'practical improvements' of the post-war era had sought, but failed, to avoid.

---

[51] Miles Taylor, *The Decline of British Radicalism, 1847–1860* (Oxford, 1995).

[52] See esp. Dorothy Thompson, *The Chartists: Popular Politics in the Industrial Revolution* (New York, 1984), ch. 1; Stewart Weaver, *John Fielden and the Politics of Popular Radicalism, 1832–1847* (Oxford, 1987), 11–12.

[53] Gareth Stedman Jones, 'Rethinking Chartism', in Stedman Jones, *Languages of Class: Studies in English Working-Class History, 1832–1982* (Cambridge, 1983), 174–8.

4. 'Old wine in new bottles': the concept and practice of law reform, c. 1780–1830

MICHAEL LOBBAN

In 1652, after a decade which had seen widespread calls for law reform, a commission under Sir Matthew Hale was appointed to consider the problem of delay and costs in the courts, and to investigate 'the speediest way to reform' general inconveniences in the law.[1] Its proposals were far-reaching. The commission recommended rationalizing the superior courts by simplifying pleadings, abolishing the sale of offices, and regulating fees. It proposed the transfer of marriage and probate jurisdiction from the civilian courts to the common law, and recommended the creation of small-claims courts, county courts, and registries of deeds. It favoured ending imprisonment for debt and making freehold land chargeable for debts. However, neither the proposals of the Hale Commission, nor the ambitious projects of William Sheppard, 'Cromwell's law reformer', resulted in legislation,[2] and it was only in the Victorian period that the reforms set out by Hale's commission began to be implemented. In this sphere, the 'age of reform' provided an impetus to implement ideas that had been in circulation for much longer.

Law reform was not entirely dormant in the interim. Firstly, the eighteenth century saw continuing 'internal' development of the substantive law. Two notable King's Bench judges, Sir John Holt (chief justice between 1689 and 1710) and Lord Mansfield (chief justice between 1756 and 1788), developed a body of commercial law without resort to legislation.[3] At the same time, equity jurisprudence was developed, notably by Lord Hardwicke, lord chancellor between 1737 and 1756. These changes did not respond to particular political pressures for reform, but reacted to demands from a developing

---

[1] Mary Cotterell, 'Interregnum Law Reform: The Hale Commission of 1652', *Eng. Hist. Rev.*, 83 (1968), 689. For the wider debate, see Donald Veall, *The Popular Movement for Law Reform, 1640–1660* (Oxford, 1970).

[2] See N. L. Matthews, *William Sheppard: Cromwell's Law Reformer* (Cambridge, 1984).

[3] David Lieberman, *The Province of Legislation Determined: Legal Theory in Eighteenth-Century Britain* (Cambridge, 1989), ch. 5; James Oldham, *The Mansfield Manuscripts and the Growth of English Law in the Eighteenth Century*, 2 vols. (Chapel Hill, N.C., and London, 1992).

commercial society, through the cases that arrived in court on novel questions. Legal developments also influenced legal literature and thought.[4] Sir William Blackstone's *Commentaries on the Laws of England* (1765–9), which provided a comprehensive survey of English law, organized in a systematic manner, and which was aimed at an audience wider than the legal profession, was itself a reformist exercise.[5] It was both a reaction to a decline in legal education at the Inns and part of the wider European intellectual movement of writing institutional treatises of national law.[6]

Secondly, there were continuing attacks on the cost and delays in the law, which echoed seventeenth-century comment. The chaotic state of the statute book was criticized, and there were calls both for a reduction in the number of laws[7] and for a digest of the existing law into a code, in the manner of Justinian's. This would both allow the law to be known by all, and would show 'how far we have deviated from the fair Paths of our wise Ancestry'.[8] There were similar attacks on legal procedure[9] and the officers of the courts.[10] Christopher Tancred expressed a common view in 1727 when he stated that the frame of the constitution was excellent, but that its lustre was tarnished by the 'corrupt, dilatory and expensive Proceedings of the Courts'.[11] He was writing at a time when concern about fees and offices had grown significantly, partly in reaction to the impeachment of Lord Macclesfield in 1725.

The late 1720s and the 1730s saw a brief flurry of law reform activity in parliament.[12] Interest in the issue at this time may be related to the activities of the opposition to Robert Walpole. By focusing attention on corruption in the

---

[4] Michael Lobban, 'The English Legal Treatise and English Law in the Eighteenth Century', in Serge Dauchy, Jos Monballyu, and Alain Wijffels (eds.), *Auctoritates: Law Making and its Authors* (Iuris Scripta Historica, xiii, Brussels, 1997), 69–88.

[5] David Lemmings, 'Blackstone and Law Reform by Education: Preparation for the Bar and Lawyerly Culture in Eighteenth-Century England', *Law and Hist. Rev.*, 16 (1998), 211–56.

[6] J. W. Cairns, 'Blackstone, an English Institutist: Legal Literature and the Rise of the Nation-State', *Oxford Jl Legal Studies*, 4 (1984), 318–60.

[7] See, e.g., *Law Quibbles* (London, 1724), 32–3.

[8] J. A. Purves, *The Law and Lawyers Laid Open* (London, 1737), xxiii. See also Richard Hemsworth, *A Key to the Law: or, an Introduction to Legal Knowledge* (London, 1765), prefatory discourse, v–vi; *Considerations on Various Grievances in the Practick Part of Our Laws: With Some Observations on the Code Frederick, the Roman Law and Our Own Courts of Equity* (Dublin, 1756).

[9] [Anon.], *Animadversions upon the Present Laws of England* (London, 1750), 8.

[10] *Proposals, Humbly Offered to the Parliament, for Remedying the Great Charge and Delay of Suits at Law and in Equity*, 3rd edn (London, 1724).

[11] Christopher Tancred, *An Essay for a General Regulation of the Law and the More Easy and Speedy Advancement of Justice*, 2nd edn (London, 1727). For a later restatement of the same view, see *A Free Enquiry into the Enormous Increase of Attornies, with Some Serious Reflections on the Abuse of our Excellent Laws: By an Unfeigned Admirer of Genuine British Jurisprudence* (Chelmsford, 1785), 4.

[12] See Wilfrid Prest, 'Law Reform in Eighteenth-Century England', in Peter Birks (ed.), *The Life of the Law* (London, 1993), 113–23; A. A. Hanham, 'Whig Opposition to Sir Robert Walpole in the House of Commons, 1727–1734' (University of Leicester Ph.D. thesis, 1992), 226–85.

legal process, Tories and patriot Whigs hoped to broaden the base of opposition to the Robinocracy. For its part, the government was not keen to embrace the issue of law reform, since it neither wished to encourage investigations that would reveal abuses implicating the ministry, nor to reduce its own network of patronage. None the less, even in the 1730s, law reform was not simply a tool of opposition: proposals could attract support from friends of the ministry as well as its opponents.[13] In the event, law reform proved a difficult subject on which to focus opposition, since disagreement tended to centre less on the need for reform than on the details of the kinds of reform to pursue. As a result, the initiatives of this decade bore limited fruit. A petition of justices from the West Riding of Yorkshire, presented in February 1729, complaining of the activities of unqualified practitioners, led to the passing of the Attorney Act of that year.[14] Another petition resulted in legislation in 1731, requiring all law proceedings to be in English, though in the face of opposition from lawyers who felt that it would make the law less certain, and the public more litigious. In other areas, however, reform initiatives failed. For instance, Yorkshire petitioners had called for the abolition of special pleading, and for an improvement in the recovery of small debts.[15] Although the Commons passed a resolution against special pleadings, they continued to be used.[16] Equally, there was little headway made in reforming the fees and offices in the superior courts. Several investigations were made into this matter, first by parliamentary committee, and then by royal commission. However, no final report was issued for the common-law side; and while Lord Hardwicke did issue a set of orders in 1743 following the 1740 report on Chancery, they were ignored by Chancery practitioners in important respects.[17] As a result, criticism of the high level of fees and the nature of officeholding continued throughout the century, even from conservative lawyers.[18]

Finally, attempts to reform the court structure stalled. Bills introduced in 1733 and 1734 to reform the ecclesiastical courts failed, largely owing to a lack of consensus on how to proceed with reform.[19] Reform of these courts therefore did not begin in earnest until after the appointment of the Ecclesiastical Courts

---

[13] See Stephen Taylor, 'Whigs, Tories and Anticlericalism: Ecclesiastical Courts Legislation in 1733', *Parl. Hist.*, 19 (2000), 329–55.

[14] Robert Robson, *The Attorney in Eighteenth-Century England* (Cambridge, 1959), 9–12; Christopher W. Brooks, *Lawyers, Litigation and English Society since 1450* (London and Rio Grande, 1998), 155.

[15] *Commons Jls*, xxi, 622–3.   [16] *Animadversions upon the Present Laws of England*, 22.

[17] Thus, the orders forbade the payment of expedition money, yet this continued to be charged: John Beames, *The General Orders of the High Court of Chancery from the Year 1600 to the Present Period* (London, 1815), 448 n.

[18] See *Reflections or Hints founded upon Experience and Facts, Touching the Law, Lawyers, Officers, Attorneys and Others Associated in the Administration of Justice, Humbly Submitted to the Consideration of the Legislature* (London, 1759), 72.

[19] Taylor, 'Whigs, Tories and Anticlericalism', 352.

Commission in 1830.[20] Small-debts bills were brought in 1730, 1734, and 1741 to empower the judges at *nisi prius* to dispose summarily of small cases brought by petition or bill.[21] They were opposed by officers in the superior courts, who feared a loss of income, and failed to pass.[22] These were the last major projects for reviving a small-debts jurisdiction integrated into the common-law system until the 1820s. In their place, the second half of the eighteenth century saw a steady growth in local small-debts acts, creating (non-professional) courts of requests. Similarly unsuccessful were the bills brought to establish deed registries in 1739, 1740, and 1758, though an act in 1735 did pass creating a registry in Yorkshire. Once more, this was a law reform much discussed in the 1650s, which had to await the nineteenth century to be taken up again. Each of these areas, left dormant for over half a century, attracted the attention of law reformers from the 1820s. Nineteenth-century law reform was hesitant and halting, and often imperfect. In what follows, we will seek to examine why law reform revived at the time and in the manner in which it did, and who and what were the driving forces behind it. It will be seen that the process was largely managed by lawyers, who sought piecemeal, pragmatic reform. In so doing, they took up positions which had been discussed in earlier periods, rather than seeking radical new departures. It will be seen that the most important driving force behind the need for reform was the early nineteenth-century surge in civil litigation. While the early nineteenth century did not see a popular movement for law reform as seen in the seventeenth century, the insistent demand of litigants forced the issue back onto the agenda.

I

The late eighteenth and early nineteenth centuries were throughout Europe an age of new law codes, most notably in Prussia, France, and Austria. In this context, the question is begged whether the revival of interest in law reform in England was part of an Enlightenment project, linked to new thinking about the nature of law and the state. England of course had her own unauthorized

---

[20] There had been a number of minor initiatives in between. In 1787, J. P. Bastard's Act (27 Geo. III, c. xliv) passed, which forbade the bringing of a prosecution for immorality in the church courts after a lapse of six months. More importantly, in 1812, Viscount Folkestone sought an inquiry into the jurisdiction of the inferior ecclesiastical courts, with a view to reforming them, but his initiative only resulted in a modest act piloted in 1813 by Lord Stowell (53 Geo. III, c. cxxvii). This act abolished excommunication in most cases, but did little to address the question of the structure of the courts. See G. F. A. Best, *Temporal Pillars: Queen Anne's Bounty, the Ecclesiastical Commissioners and the Church of England* (Cambridge, 1964), 191–2; G. M. Ditchfield, 'Ecclesiastical Legislation during the Ministry of the Younger Pitt, 1783–1801', *Parl. Hist.*, 19 (2000), 67.

[21] *House of Commons Sessional Papers of the Eighteenth Century*, ed. Sheila Lambert, 145 vols. (Wilmington, 1975), vii, 13, 159, 459.

[22] See, e.g., *Commons Jls*, xxi, 512, 524, 531, 534, 537, 554.

codifier, Jeremy Bentham. If the vocabulary of 'law reform' had been in circulation ever since the seventeenth century,[23] Bentham even coined a new term: 'codification'.[24]

In the 1770s and 1780s Bentham wrote extensively on the nature of law in general, and the inadequacies of the common law,[25] though it was not until the publication of Etienne Dumont's editions of his work after the turn of the century that his ideas reached a wide audience.[26] Bentham argued that the common law was essentially unknowable, since it was all *ex post facto*, and that it needed replacement by a new legislated code. However, while Bentham's command theory of law gained widespread acceptance, his proposals for a new substantive code of law did not. He never completed the code he projected, since by the 1820s he had decided to await a request from a ruling government before undertaking the task. By then, it was hardly likely that he would receive any invitation from a British government. For after the collapse of his Panopticon project, Bentham had turned to political radicalism,[27] and had begun to work more extensively on constitutional writings, which rooted sovereignty in the people and sought a system of universal suffrage. For Bentham, the *Constitutional Code* became an inseparable component of his *Pannomion*.

Besides seeking to construct his ideal code, Bentham also sought to engage in current debates about law reform. After the turn of the century, his attention turned increasingly to matters of procedure, and he began to write extensively on evidence and judicial organization. His remained an insistent voice of criticism, and his writings a fund of ideas and argument for those attacking the mechanisms of the law. In 1804–6, at a time when reforms of the Scottish Court of Session were being proposed, he wrote on *Scotch Reform*. In 1825, he published a pamphlet severely attacking the lord chancellor, Lord Eldon, and the system of fee-gathering in the Chancery.[28] He made comments and suggestions to the royal commission appointed in 1828 to inquire into the state of the law of real property, and to propose reforms in that area. When the state of the Court of Chancery was being widely debated in 1830, he published his *Equity Dispatch Court Proposal*. Bentham also kept in touch privately with politicians and reformers. Nevertheless, his own direct influence on the reform process may be doubted. Those lawyers who were close to Bentham, and who were keen to

---

[23] According to John Cook, soldiers in the Civil War had fought for 'law reform' (quoted by Veall, *Popular Movement*, 73).

[24] J. R. Dinwiddy, 'Early-Nineteenth-Century Reactions to Benthamism', *Trans. Royal Hist. Soc.*, 5th ser., 34 (1984), 47–69.

[25] Lieberman, *Province of Legislation Determined*, chs. 11–13; Michael Lobban, *The Common Law and English Jurisprudence, 1760–1850* (Oxford, 1991), chs. 5–6.

[26] J. Bentham, *Traités de législation civile et pénale*, trans. E. Dumont, 3 vols. (Paris, 1802).

[27] J. R. Dinwiddy, 'Bentham's Transition to Political Radicalism', *Jl Hist. Ideas*, 36 (1975), 683–700.

[28] Jeremy Bentham, *Indications Respecting Lord Eldon, including History of the Pending Judges' Salary-Raising Measure* (London, 1825); see also Jeremy Bentham, *Official Aptitude Maximized; Expense Minimized*, ed. P. Schofield (Oxford, 1993), 205–341.

promote law reform – such as Samuel Romilly, Henry Bickersteth, and Henry Brougham – tended to follow their own agendas, rather than his.[29] Moreover, by the time his work was widely debated, the issues of reform were already on the agenda.

The wider question of the desirability of codification continued to be debated throughout the early nineteenth century. Many lawyers associated it with the creation of brand new rules, developed from a priori principles, and rejected it for that reason. It was argued that the Napoleonic codes were made with a particular political objective, in a context where the old political order had collapsed; whereas in England the only need was to improve the administration of the laws.[30] Lawyers worried especially that the common law (and with it the judges' role) would be abolished. They argued that a code could only give broad outlines and would never be complete.[31] In addition, it was argued that abolishing the common law would create huge uncertainty, unsettling property and requiring the development of a new jurisprudence to settle the meaning of various provisions. Those who attempted to write particular codes tended to receive a hostile reaction, even when some of their detailed ideas were well regarded.[32] Anti-codifiers found ready ammunition in the work of Friedrich von Savigny's attack on A. F. J. Thibaut's proposal for a code,[33] which argued that a people's law was bound up in its *Volksgeist* and could not be reduced to the propositions of a code. It was argued that Bentham's key principle – utility – was too mechanical and took no account of actual experience.[34] Anti-codifiers also urged that to codify the law would ossify it, and lock it in to one political moment.[35] By contrast, the common law's incremental method was praised. Thus, J. J. Park argued that there were infinite conclusions which could be drawn from the judicial premises already given: '[e]very proposition once decided', he said, 'becomes a datum from which to reason to the conclusion upon a new combination'.[36]

Nevertheless, by the early nineteenth century, there was some criticism of the common law and an acknowledgement of the need for authoritative rules

---

[29] See Michael Lobban, 'Henry Brougham and Law Reform', *Eng. Hist. Rev.*, 115 (2000), 1184–215.

[30] Charles Purton Cooper, *Lettres sur la cour de la chancellerie et quelques points de la jurisprudence angloise* (London, 1827), 178.

[31] *Ibid.*, 184–6. See also J. J. Park, *A Contre-Projet to the Humphresian Code* (London, 1828).

[32] See B. Rudden, 'A Code Too Soon: The 1826 Property Code of James Humphreys: English Rejection, American Reception, English Acceptance', in P. Wallington and R. M. Merkin (eds.), *Essays in Memory of Professor F. H. Lawson* (London, 1986), 101–16; K. J. M. Smith, 'Anthony Hammond: "Mr. Surface" Peel's Persistent Codifier', *Jl Legal Hist.*, 20 (1999), 24–44.

[33] Cooper introduced English audiences to Savigny in his *Lettres*, 172–3, which led the Tory lawyer Abraham Hayward to translate the work into English in 1832.

[34] John Reddie, *A Letter to the Lord High Chancellor of Great Britain on the Expediency of the Proposal to Form a New Civil Code for England* (London, 1828), 45–6.

[35] Cooper, *Lettres*, 179.   [36] Park, *Contre-Projet*, 21.

to be articulated. It was argued that in an era of rapid legal developments it was impossible for individuals to know the law.[37] The common law was also attacked for being out of date, with judges being bound by imperfect precedents. As Romilly put it, for a judge to operate in this world was like asking an artist to supply what was imperfect in a statue. In similar vein, James Mill roundly attacked William Paley's argument that when novel cases came before the courts, they could be settled by the common lawyers' method of drawing analogies between the case at hand and existing precedents.[38] Nevertheless, Mill said that '[w]hen we speak of expressing the law better, we mean nothing else. We mean not to alter the law in a tittle.' He admitted that to abolish the existing law 'would be tantamount to a scheme of universal confiscation'.[39] In this context, debate over codification could become muddled. Those who urged it often only meant an authoritative restatement of the rules of the common law, leaving the judges the same flexibility they already enjoyed in applying them.[40] It was an approach not unlike that of those eighteenth-century writers who sought a reduction or restatement of the laws.

In fact, law reformers did not need the Benthamic impulse to encourage them into reform in the early nineteenth century. They could look back to the example of Francis Bacon. While wishing to preserve ancient rules of law, Bacon had recognized that the law could never be static. He sought to digest both statute law and common law, in order to reduce the bulk, and remove those laws that were merely snares for the unwary. 'The work which I propound', he wrote (in a phrase often quoted by nineteenth-century writers), 'tendeth to pruning and grafting the law and not to ploughing up and planting it again; for such a remove I should hold indeed for a perilous innovation.'[41] This reformist tradition had been taken up by Hale, whose *Considerations Touching the Amendment or Alteration of Laws*, written after the Restoration, were first published in 1787. Hale agreed that the law needed 'due husbandry'.[42] For him, legal change occurred in two ways. Firstly, alterations could be made 'by the power and authority of the court and judges, without troubling parliament'. However, this should 'not so much constitute a new law, as amend the old', so that nothing

---

[37] John George Phillimore, *Letter to the Lord Chancellor on the Reform of the Law* (London, 1846), 60.

[38] James Mill, *The Principles of Law Reform* (London, 1835), 5. For Paley's argument about the 'competition of opposite analogies', see William Paley, *The Principles of Moral and Political Philosophy* (London, 1785), 520–2.

[39] Mill, *Principles of Law Reform*, 14.

[40] Michael Lobban, 'How Benthamic was the Criminal Law Commission?', *Law and Hist. Rev.*, 18 (2000), 427–32.

[41] *The Works of Francis Bacon*, ed. James Spedding, Robert Leslie Ellis, and Douglas Denon Heath, 14 vols. (London, 1857–74), xiii, 63, 67.

[42] Francis Hargrave (ed.), *A Collection of Tracts Relative to the Law of England, from Manuscripts* (Dublin, 1787), 266.

should be 'altered that is a foundation or principal integral of the law'.[43] At the same time, Hale saw that some laws 'in their very constitution and fabrick . . . are rotten and faulty', necessitating parliamentary intervention, albeit under the guidance of judges.[44] In Hale's view, it was the development of the substantive law which should be left largely to the 'internal' development of the judges, while parliament reformed the procedural excrescences, which had so long dogged the courts. This was an attitude widely shared by nineteenth-century lawyers. Many reforming lawyers were thus happy to appropriate Bentham's suggestions, and fit them into their own more modest notions of reform, without accepting the full implications of his complete code. Their ambiguous approach to Bentham is well summed up in the enthusiastic comment of Charles Sinclair Cullen, 'What Bacon desired, Bentham has accomplished.'[45]

II

Law reform in many ways appears to be the work of the 'Reform Ministry' of a 'Reformed Parliament'.[46] As Philip Harling has pointed out, although an increasing concern to retrench and to root out corruption in government can be traced back to 1780, abuses in the law were not systematically attacked until the 1830s.[47] For many mid-nineteenth-century commentators, the movement to reform the law was initiated by Henry Brougham's six-hour speech on the subject in the Commons in February 1828, which was followed by numerous royal commissions: on real property, the common-law courts, the ecclesiastical courts, and the criminal law. These commissions set the terms of the debate on reform in their respective areas for decades, although in the event, in each area, their more ambitious proposals encountered such strong opposition that they were seriously delayed or even (as in the case of the proposal to enact a code of criminal law) frustrated.[48] However, it should be noted that these commissions were themselves the product of a pressure for reform which had built up for a longer period of time. Historians have long been aware of the concerns of

---

[43] *Ibid.*, 258.   [44] *Ibid.*, 269, 272.

[45] C. S. Cullen, *Reform of the Bankrupt Court*, 2nd edn (London, 1830), xxi.

[46] The phrase is taken from Denis Le Merchant (ed.), *The Reform Ministry and the Reformed Parliament* (London, 1833).

[47] Philip Harling, *The Waning of 'Old Corruption': The Politics of Economical Reform in Britain, 1779–1846* (Oxford, 1996), 198.

[48] For attempts to reform the land law, see J. Stuart Anderson, *Lawyers and the Making of English Land Law, 1832–1940* (Oxford, 1992). For the movement to codify the criminal law, see A. H. Manchester, 'Simplifying the Sources of the Law: An Essay in Law Reform', *Anglo-American Law Rev.*, 2 (1973), 395–413, 527–50; Lobban, *Common Law*, 202–7; Lindsay Farmer, 'Reconstructing the English Codification Debate', *Law and Hist. Rev.*, 18 (2000), 397–425. For the reform of the testamentary jurisdiction of the ecclesiastical courts, see Brian G. Hutton, 'The Reform of the Testamentary Jurisdiction of the Ecclesiastical Courts, 1830–1857' (Brunel University Ph.D. thesis, 2002).

evangelical reformers to reduce the number of capital statutes that made up the Bloody Code, and of Robert Peel's work at the Home Office in consolidating and reforming the statutes. In what follows, it will be seen that there were also numerous initiatives to reform areas of civil law and procedure before 1828, but that the slow pace of reform in this area may be explained in part by the nature of the problems to be solved.[49]

Law was clearly a prime target for the critics of 'Old Corruption'. Eldon's Chancery seemed the very model of old-world inefficiency, and one that through its fees enriched the lord chancellor to the tune of almost £20,000 a year. It is not surprising, therefore, that law was embraced in the retrenchment movement of the 1790s, with the courts being examined by the Finance Committee in its twenty-seventh report in 1798.[50] In practice, retrenchment in the law stalled, not because of a lack of interest, but because it was difficult to effect. To understand why, we must note the unusual position of the law in the world of 'Old Corruption'. To begin with, the law fitted uneasily into the world of 'public expenditure' and 'public service'. Although the senior judges received some payment from the civil list, much of their income came from fees, as did that of other court officials. While remuneration by fee was to be found throughout the late eighteenth-century public service, the high charges faced by the litigant were not imposed by the crown to swell its own power. Instead, legal officers became richer as a consequence of increased activity by litigants in the courts. From the government's point of view, the legal establishment was largely self-financing, paid for by litigants who chose to go to court.[51] Indeed, from the point of view of the litigant, it was generally the attorney who delivered the bill who was the first target of blame.[52] The reduction of fees for litigants was thus not a high priority for government; and indeed in 1807, in an era of retrenchment, the Whig lord chancellor Lord Erskine issued an order increasing fees in Chancery.[53]

---

[49] For the movement to reform the penal code in the early nineteenth century, see Leon Radzinowicz, *A History of the English Criminal Law and its Administration from 1750: The Movement for Reform, 1750–1833* (London, 1948); Randall McGowen, 'The Image of Justice and the Reform of the Criminal Law in Early Nineteenth-Century England', *Buffalo Law Rev.*, 32 (1983), 89–125; Richard R. Follett, *Evangelicalism, Penal Theory and the Politics of Criminal Law Reform in England, 1808–30* (Basingstoke, 2001). Peel's motives remain controversial and debated. See Norman Gash, *Mr. Secretary Peel: The Life of Sir Robert Peel to 1830* (London, 1961); V. A. C. Gatrell, *The Hanging Tree: Execution and the English People, 1770–1868* (Oxford 1994), 566–85; Boyd Hilton, 'The Gallows and Peel', in T. C. W. Blanning and David Cannadine (eds.), *History and Biography: Essays in Honour of Derek Beales* (Cambridge, 1996), 88–112.

[50] *Commons Sessional Papers*, ed. Lambert, cxi, *passim*.

[51] In some respects, it was cost-free: in 1739, the act 12 Geo. II, c. xxiv had empowered the Chancery to invest suitors' money, using the proceeds to pay for charges in the accountant-general's office. This paved the way for many more acts allowing the Suitors' Fund to be used to pay for the Chancery establishment.

[52] See, e.g., A. Grant, *The Progress and Practice of a Modern Attorney* (London, n.d. [1794]), 14.

[53] Beames, *General Orders*, 465, 471. For a discussion, see [James Lowe], *Observations on Fees in Courts of Justice* (London, 1822), 246.

Furthermore, the savings to litigants from retrenchment in the law were minimal. Reform of the courts in an era of growing litigation did not mean a reduction in the establishment, but a reorganization of offices, which, given the cost of new offices and compensations, did not translate into a lowering of fees. When there was a surplus (as in the late 1830s, as a product of reforming legislation), this was paid to the Treasury, which thus became a beneficiary of unpopular law taxes.[54] In response, commentators from Bentham to Lord Langdale argued that the machinery of justice (and compensation to the holders of abolished offices) should be paid for entirely by the state, with suitors only paying for the advice of their lawyers.[55] However, two counter-arguments were consistently advanced: first, that those going to law were asking for a service for which they should pay; and second, that the imposition of costs through fees provided a check to litigiousness.[56]

Retrenchment in the law presented other practical problems. The legal system was full of offices which involved minimal labour, but which were not strictly speaking sinecures, since they had a function in the legal process. They could not easily be abolished. When, in June 1832, Eldon's son died, holding two Chancery offices worth £2,600, the reformist chancellor Brougham had to fill them by appointing his own brother, pending their planned abolition.[57] Similarly, though there was much criticism of the Six Clerks' Office in Chancery, 'the very pet of the place-men', worth £2,000 a year, according to *The Times*,[58] the Chancery Commission in 1826 favoured retaining the clerks, since it was necessary to keep a body of practitioners familiar with the practice of the court.

Even the reform of saleable offices – the most obvious location of abuse – created problems. One of the most lucrative sinecures in law was the chief clerkship in King's Bench, a saleable office worth over £6,000 a year, conferred by the chief justice, Lord Ellenborough, on his son.[59] Rather than being seen as corruption, however, it was regarded by many in the legal profession as part of

---

[54] E. W. Field commented in 1842 that the Treasury received up to £60,000 a year surplus from common-law fees: *Legal Observer*, 25 (1842), 5–6.

[55] Jeremy Bentham, *A Protest against Law Taxes*, 2nd edn (London, 1852; 1st edn London, 1793); Thomas Duffus Hardy, *Memoirs of the Right Honourable Henry, Lord Langdale*, 2 vols. (London, 1852), ii, 9–15.

[56] Thus it was often argued that cheap county courts would stir up excessive litigation: e.g., *Parl. Debs.*, 3rd ser., lvii, col. 172 (12 March 1841, Sir Frederick Pollock).

[57] *Parl. Debs.*, 3rd ser., xiv, cols. 741–5 (26 July 1832).

[58] 27 Dec. 1826, quoted by Joseph Parkes, *A History of the Court of Chancery* (London, 1828), 576.

[59] The chief justice of the King's Bench had from 1733 been granted a salary of £4,000 (reduced by various taxes to £2,900). In addition, he received more than £6,000 of emoluments from the office of chief clerk, and £2,600 from the office of clerk of the errors (P.P. 1817, xvii (105), 'Return of Offices in Courts of Law and Equity in England Held in Trust for Judges', 1), as well as thirty-three other fees. Ellenborough was said to have been offered £80,000 for the chief clerkship, which he turned down: *Parl. Debs.*, 2nd ser., x, col. 1426 (26 Mar. 1824, speech of the attorney-general, Sir John Copley).

the legitimate remuneration of the judge.[60] It was therefore exempted from the Sale of Offices Prevention Bill in 1809 (along with other saleable legal offices), pending consideration of an 'adequate equivalent' for the judges.[61] Legislation was finally introduced in 1825 to abolish the offices and to raise judicial salaries, a politically controversial subject.[62] Reforming the chancellor's emoluments should have been a matter of equal priority, given the controversy over Eldon's income. However, this issue was complicated by the fact that much of the chancellor's income derived from bankruptcy fees. Alterations in his remuneration therefore depended upon a reform of bankruptcy procedure. Since a commission had been appointed the previous year to look at Chancery reforms (which had not yet reported), it was considered premature in 1825 to address this question.[63] The decision to pay that officer by salary (and in consequence to abolish a number of Chancery sinecures)[64] was only taken in 1831, after the new lord chancellor, Brougham, had decided on a wide-ranging reform in the bankruptcy system.[65]

Reform of what appeared to be corrupt offices in the law courts was thus highly problematic. First, the reform of any single office had implications for a large number of other offices, which could only be resolved by rethinking the whole structure of the court. This was particularly evident in Chancery, and helps explain why the reform of the Six Clerks and Masters' Offices took so long. Second, there was a political price to be paid for retrenchment, given that the patronage removed when one set of offices was abolished was replaced by the patronage of newly created offices. When Brougham lost the power to appoint seventy-two London commissioners of bankruptcy, he acquired the power to appoint judges to the new court of bankruptcy. As a result, he was portrayed as the 'Harlequin Chancellor', who 'fill[s] his own pockets, which he renders highly amusing, by loudly declaring that he is in fact emptying them'.[66]

---

[60] The right of the chief justice to dispose of this saleable office was defended not only by the main beneficiary, Ellenborough's son (*Parl. Debs.*, 3rd ser., ii, col. 1058, 1 Mar. 1831), but also by the attorney-general, who defended it as part of the just and legal emoluments of the chief justice: *ibid.*, 2nd ser., x, col. 1426 (26 Mar. 1824).

[61] *Ibid.*, 1st ser., xiv, col. 270 (27 Apr. 1809, speech of Spencer Perceval). The question of saleable offices was referred to a royal commission of lawyers. It recommended the abolition of the saleable offices, coupled with an increase in the salaries of judges, and the performance of offices in person, by those learned in law: P.P. 1810, ix (358), 'Royal Commission on Saleable Offices in Courts of Law', 125.

[62] For the controversial question of how much was proper for a judge to be paid, see, e.g., Thomas Denman's speech on 16 May 1825: 'At present', he said, judges 'might be said to be at the head of people of middling fortune, which was better than being at the foot of the higher order': *Parl. Debs.*, 2nd ser., xiii, col. 620.

[63] *Ibid.*, cols. 932 (27 May 1825, speech of Frederick Robinson), 1379–80 (27 June 1825, speech of Lord Eldon).

[64] 2 and 3 Will. IV, cc. cxi, cxxii.

[65] *Legal Observer*, 1 (1831), 254.   [66] *Ibid.*, 2 (1831), 373.

III

Under the long chancellorship of Eldon, the Tories acquired a reputation for legal conservatism and resistance to reform. Their Whig opponents, notably Brougham, M. A. Taylor, and John Williams, frequently raised the state of the courts (and especially the Chancery) in the 1820s as a means of attacking the government, provoking very defensive reactions. When Sir John Newport brought a motion in 1814 to inquire into fees charged in the courts, ministers responded that his motion put the integrity of the courts in doubt without foundation.[67] His motion was seen as politically and personally motivated, for as Castlereagh put it, 'only some general plan of reform appeared to be in contemplation'.[68] A similar reaction can be seen to the criticisms of the lord chancellor in the 1820s. As Eldon saw it, the Whigs were seeking to bring 'into hatred and contempt the Tribunals of the Country' simply 'because John Williams hates John Scott [Lord Eldon]'.[69] When, in February 1824, Williams moved for a select committee of the Commons to look into the Chancery, Peel sought to deflect criticism from Eldon, and to ensure that the inquiry would be by a royal commission, which would not consider the question of whether to separate the political and legal roles of the chancellor.[70] Peel was in general keen to have inquiries staffed by legal experts, rather than to have them dominated by politicians.

Nevertheless, Tory governments did respond to the need for reform in the civil law before 1830, in part because the question was practically unavoidable. Perhaps the biggest factor in compelling law reform was the increase in litigation in the early nineteenth century and the problems that this caused for the courts. To understand the timing of law-reform movements, it helps to map them against trends in litigation, and the consequent pressure on the courts. The era before the Restoration, which saw vocal calls for law reform at all levels of society, saw the most litigious society in English history. By contrast, the eighteenth century (when proposals for reform were relatively few) saw a profound slump in litigation, which did not recover until after 1790, when the revival of litigation was matched by renewed pressure for law reform.[71]

There is a late eighteenth-century exception that proves the rule. While there was relatively little agitation to reform the procedure in the superior courts in the 1780s and 1790s, there were constant demands for the reform of bankruptcy and imprisonment for debt, which appeared to its victims and critics alike

---

[67] *Parl. Debs.*, 1st ser., xxvii, col. 399 (31 Mar. 1814); *ibid.*, xxviii, col. 379 (28 June 1814, speech of the attorney-general, Sir William Garrow).

[68] *Ibid.*, xxviii, 377 (28 June 1814).

[69] Brit. Lib., Add. MS 40,315, Peel papers, fo. 183, Lord Eldon to Robert Peel, Feb. 1825.

[70] *Parl. Debs.*, 2nd ser., x, col. 410 (24 Feb. 1824).

[71] See Brooks, *Lawyers, Litigation and English Society*, chs. 3–4.

to violate Magna Carta and the liberties of the Englishman.[72] Arresting and imprisoning debtors in effect bypassed the courts altogether, for where the law was used as a means of coercion to enforce the payment of debts, litigants never got as far as the pleading stage, or the payment of high fees. If relatively few went to the advanced stages of litigation, arrest for debt was much more widely used.[73] The traditional solution to the problem of debtors' gaols was found in periodic Insolvent Debtor Relief Acts (to release those imprisoned), and through private relief, such as that afforded by the Society of the Thatched-House Tavern. However, by the 1790s, there was increasing pressure for a more permanent solution.[74]

This issue revealed how even the most apparently conservative politician could contemplate institutional reform. Discussing an insolvent debtors' bill of 1806, Eldon agreed that there needed to be a permanent measure, with a 'certain and permanent system of procedure'.[75] After a decade of debate, in 1813 a new Insolvent Debtors' Court was set up, on the principle that the insolvent who gave up all his property could obtain a release. The act was piloted by Lord Redesdale, with the support of Eldon and the law officers, who wanted to obviate the need for temporary acts, while sparing the common-law courts from having to deal with a large number of applications from insolvents.[76] The Insolvent Debtors' Court turned out to be an imperfect machine, and required much amendment,[77] but its conservative provenance should be noted.

The pressure of business helped generate reform elsewhere. By the early nineteenth century, it was evident that the House of Lords was unable to deal with

---

[72] See, e.g., James Stephen, *Considerations on Imprisonment for Debt* (London, 1780); Edward Farley, *Imprisonment for Debt, Unconstitutional and Oppressive Proved from the Fundamental Principles of the British Constitution and the Rights of Nature* (London, 1788); Basil Montagu, *Enquiries Respecting the Insolvent Debtors' Bill, with the Opinions of Dr. Paley, Mr. Burke and Dr. Johnson, upon Imprisonment for Debt*, 2nd edn (London, 1816).

[73] According to Brooks, *Lawyers, Litigation and English Society*, 35, 'there is little reason to doubt that there was an overall increase in the use of arrest on *mesne* process during the period from 1670 to the end of the eighteenth century'.

[74] *Parliamentary History*, xxx, col. 648 (27 Mar. 1793, speech of Lord Rawdon, praising the work of the society of the Thatched-House Tavern); *ibid.*, xxxiii, col. 180 (debate of 27 Mar. 1797).

[75] *Parl. Debs.*, 1st ser., vii, col. 151 (14 May 1806). For Eldon, commercial credit was sapped by the fact that the legislature appeared to treat debtors harshly, but then released them. His view contrasts sharply with that of Lord Kenyon, who in 1797 resisted the appointment of a committee to look into the law, 'as it would bring the whole code of our laws into discussion, and give rise to the projection of new schemes without end, which would do no good, but might be productive of infinite confusion and mischief': *Parliamentary History*, xxxiii, col. 182 (27 Mar. 1797).

[76] The court was set up by 53 Geo. III, c. cii. The provision allowing an appeal to a superior court was repealed by 54 Geo. III, c. xxiii.

[77] For the later history, see V. M. Lester, *Victorian Insolvency: Bankruptcy, Imprisonment for Debt and Company Winding Up in Nineteenth-Century England* (Oxford, 1995).

its increasing case-load.[78] One response was to attempt reforms of the Court of Session in Edinburgh, which accounted for more than four in five cases heard in the Lords. Between 1807 and 1810, parliament enacted important reforms in the Court, the first time it had reorganized a central Scottish institution since the Act of Union.[79] A key component of the reform was the introduction into Scotland of the civil jury, both in order to speed up trials, but also to perfect the Union by adopting an essentially English model. Much of the initiative for this reform – an essentially political project – came from north of the border, notably from Scottish Whigs. A sweeping reform was proposed by William Grenville in 1807. His bill aroused a good deal of lawyerly opposition,[80] and ultimately failed, not least thanks to practical problems pointed out by Eldon. However, major reforms did follow the fall of the Ministry of All the Talents, which satisfied both the political aims of the Scottish Whigs and the practical aims of the Tory lord chancellor, Eldon. The latter's approach in managing these reforms was to secure measures approved by the body of the Scottish profession. A Judicature Act was passed in 1808, which reorganized the Court of Session, and which authorized the establishment of a royal commission to consider (among other matters) the introduction of civil juries (which occurred in 1815). The work of this commission was done primarily by Scots lawyers, with English members only being consulted in an advisory capacity.[81] In contrast to the Scots, the English Whigs lacked a clear political programme of law reform. Instead, their demands often centred on demands for inquiries into the English courts following the Scottish example.

In England, the problem of the House of Lords was intimately connected with the reform of the Chancery, given that the lord chancellor presided in both. As the business of the Lords had increased, so too had that in Chancery.[82] By

---

78 According to Charles Purton Cooper, 290 appeals were brought between 1791 and 1800, and 492 between 1801 and 1810: Charles Purton Cooper, *A Brief Account of Some of the Most Important Proceedings in Parliament Relative to the Defects in the Administration of Justice in the Court of Chancery* (London, 1828), 116.

79 Nicholas Phillipson, *The Scottish Whigs and the Reform of the Court of Session, 1785–1830* (Stair Soc., xxxvii, Edinburgh, 1990), chs. 4–5. See also John W. Cairns, 'Historical Introduction', in Kenneth Reid and Reinhard Zimmermann (eds.), *A History of Private Law in Scotland*, 2 vols. (Oxford, 2000), i, 142–55.

80 Phillipson writes, the bill 'can only be regarded as the work of men infatuated with English forms and an augustan *Zeitgeist* on the one hand and possessed by a deep ignorance of the true nature of the system they were anxious to introduce on the other': Phillipson, *Scottish Whigs*, 98.

81 *Ibid.*, 117.

82 Where in 1784/5 there were 1,544 bills of complaint exhibited in Chancery and 3,612 active cases, in 1818/19 the respective figures were 2,335 and 6,014: Henry Horwitz, *Chancery Equity Records and Proceedings, 1600–1800* (London, 1995), 29. See also H. Horwitz and P. Polden, 'Continuity or Change in the Court of Chancery in the Seventeenth and Eighteenth Centuries?', *Jl Brit. Studies*, 35 (1996), 24–57.

1810, it was evident to both government and opposition that something needed to be done on the English side as well as the Scottish. For the government, the main problem was finding time for the lord chancellor to dispose of cases in the Lords. To increase the number of days that could be devoted to its judicial business, a select committee of the Lords in 1811 proposed appointing an additional Chancery judge.[83] The opposition took a different approach, blaming the problem on Eldon's notorious indecisiveness. M. A. Taylor sought a select committee to consider the causes of Chancery arrears, which would also investigate the lord chancellor's emoluments.[84] To protect the chancellor, the ministry placed a number of obstacles in Taylor's way, packing the select committee with its supporters, and ensuring that it did not interview barristers or inquire into the causes of delay.[85] Taylor's political initiative was duly frustrated, and the government's preferred option – of appointing an extra Chancery judge – was implemented in 1813. The episode is significant because of the contrasting political and legal impulses. The Whig position, though politically combative, was legally conservative. The Whigs saw the problem of arrears as temporary, caused in large part by an increase in the lucrative bankruptcy petitions rather than in equity bills.[86] They sought to maintain the lord chancellor's position as the sole equity judge, and instead put forward a range of alternative solutions.[87] The government, by contrast, was politically defensive, shielding Eldon, while introducing a legal innovation, based on a recognition that the problems of litigation were not temporary. As with the Insolvent Debtors' Court, the creation of the vice-chancellor of England did not solve the problems of Chancery, but was the first in a series of reforms that continued throughout the century to increase the personnel of the Chancery.

This area of reform was revived in 1824, with the appointment of the Chancery Commission. Though prompted by John Williams' motion that had elicited Peel's defence of Eldon, the commission was in part the government's reaction to the report of a select committee of the Lords in 1823 on continuing arrears there.[88] In spite of being dismissed by Williams as 'nothing but a parliamentary manoeuvre' of Peel's,[89] the commission proved highly important, making a number of proposals on how to speed up the proceedings before the hearing stage, and setting the agenda for a decade of reform. It suggested reforms in the Masters' Offices, to give them greater control over the

---

[83] *The Times*, 31 May 1811, 3b.   [84] *Ibid.*, 12 July 1811, 3c.

[85] See Taylor's version in *Parl. Debs.*, 2nd ser., xvi, col. 708 ff. (27 Feb. 1827).

[86] This was Romilly's view: *ibid.*, 1st ser., xxiv, col. 491 (11 Feb. 1813).

[87] These ranged from removing bankruptcy from the chancellor's jurisdiction through to various expedients that would render him assistance in the Lords, both in his capacity as speaker and as judge. See *ibid.*, xxiv, cols. 480, 483, 491, 519 (debates of 11, 15 Feb. 1813).

[88] *Ibid.*, 2nd ser., x, col. 431 (24 Feb. 1824, speech of George Canning).

[89] *Ibid.*, xiii, col. 960 (31 May 1825). It may be noted that Williams (not a Chancery barrister) had few concrete ideas on how to reform the Chancery.

proceedings and to replace the payment by fees for office copies with payment by salary. Significantly, it also recommended that the law of real property should be looked at, which paved the way for the Real Property Commission of 1828.

A second initiative spurred on by the needs of litigants was the attempt to reform local courts, which began in 1820. There was by now a significant demand for cheap justice, which had been partially satisfied by the periodic creation of courts of requests in particular towns. Although they worked well, it was doubted both whether the system could be extended geographically throughout the whole kingdom and whether the jurisdiction of these juryless, lawyerless courts could be extended.[90] Once again, the first major bill came from the conservative Redesdale, who sought to give a jurisdiction up to £10 to county courts presided over by judges sitting with juries.[91] The principle was then taken up in turn by the Whig Viscount Althorp, the Tory Peel, and the maverick Brougham: it was clearly a measure with cross-party support. As in other areas, the reform process continued over a long period; and the creation of new county courts had to await legislation in mid-century.[92] However, one reason for the delay derived from the difficulty of resolving the relationship of local courts with the superior courts.

It was only in the wake of attempts to reform the local courts that attention was turned to the reform of the superior common-law courts. There had of course been consistent criticism of these since before the turn of the century, particularly focusing on the increasing levels of fees.[93] Newport's motion on this question in 1814 – which he won by a single vote – had been followed by the appointment of a royal commission. It proved a disappointment.[94] Rather than looking a priori at what fees should be charged, it reported on the existing offices with very conservative results. Where a fee had existed in 1731 (the date of the previous inquiry), the commission generally recommended allowing it 'without any note or comment', even though it was acknowledged that in many cases the fee depended on usage rather than any authority.[95] The commission only sought to question such fees as had developed since 1730. In consequence,

---

[90] See P.P. 1823, iv (386), 'Report from the Select Committee on the Recovery of Small Debts', 186. See also *Parl. Debs.*, 2nd ser., ix, col. 542 (27 May 1823, speech of Lord Althorp).

[91] *Parl. Debs.*, 2nd ser., i, col. 743 (1 June 1820).

[92] Patrick Polden, *A History of the County Court, 1846–1971* (Cambridge, 1999).

[93] According to one practitioner, 'like a leprosy, [they] are rapidly spreading over the body of the law, and . . . if not cured, will soon destroy its constitution'. [Lowe], *Observations on Fees in Courts of Justice*, 7. For earlier criticism, see John Frederick Schiefer, *An Explanation of the Practice of the Law: Containing the Elements of Special Pleading . . . also Elements for a Plan for a Reform* (London, 1792), 329.

[94] *Parl. Debs.*, 1st ser., xxxviii, col. 992 (27 May 1818, speech of Sir John Newport).

[95] P.P. 1818, vii (292), 'Royal Commission on Duties, Salaries, and Emoluments of Officers and Courts of Justice in England and Wales: Report on King's Bench', 250 (King's Bench).

a statute was passed to empower the judges to set new ones,[96] but this did little to solve the problem.

The first sustained political assault on the superior courts came from Brougham in his speech of 1828.[97] However, there was sufficient interest in law reform already existing for the proposal to be well received, and the speech was followed by the appointment of the Common Law Commission to look into reforms in pleading and practice in the superior courts. This commission, staffed by experts, recommended a raft of reforms that were implemented by Grey's government in the early 1830s. Notably, it recommended an equalization of the business of the three superior courts and a rationalization of their procedures.[98] With Brougham's appointment as lord chancellor, the political language of reform changed, for the new chancellor was clearly driven by a broad commitment to law reform, which was linked to his wider reform agenda. None the less, it is clear that despite the apparent reluctance of Tory governments to reform, a reform process had already begun in all the legal institutions before 1832; while (for all the rhetoric) even after the Whigs came to power the implementation of reform was slow and difficult.

IV

It was the realization of the need to reform the courts that in turn provided the crucial impetus to the reform of corrupt offices. In the mid-1820s, it became apparent that the demand for cheap local courts could not be satisfied without first resolving the problem of offices in the superior courts. As in the 1730s, strong opposition emerged from officers in the superior courts who stood to lose from a diversion of litigation elsewhere. In 1824, the attorney-general therefore proposed that compensation be given to those who held patent offices in the Common Pleas, for which large sums had been paid.[99] If the principle of compensation was well established,[100] however, it was hard to apply in cases such as this one, where legislation would only incidentally reduce the income of other officers.[101] Having initially accepted the principle of compensation,[102] Peel abandoned the local-courts bill in 1828, considering it to be unwise to

---

[96] 3 Geo. IV, c. lxix.   [97] See Lobban, 'Henry Brougham', 1188–90.

[98] P.P. 1829, ix (46), 'First Report of the Royal Commission on the Practice and Procedure of the Common Law Courts', 23.

[99] *Parl. Debs.*, 2nd ser., x, col. 728 (4 Mar. 1824).

[100] It had been recognized by the Finance Committee of 1798. Moreover, when legislation was passed in 1826 to prevent the bringing of frivolous writs of error – a reform long demanded to prevent vexatious litigation – generous compensation was awarded to the holders of patent offices: 6 Geo. IV, c. xcvi. By 1830, over £39,000 had been paid in compensation to eleven officers: P.P. 1830, xxix (409), 237.

[101] *Parl. Debs.*, 2nd ser., x, cols. 1425–31 (26 Mar. 1824).

[102] *Ibid.*, xix, col. 877 (22 May 1828).

proceed until the whole question of compensation in the superior common-law courts had been settled once and for all by the recently appointed commission. For, in his view, a partial reform that diminished some incomes ran the risk of raising others in a way that might generate compensation claims in any future reorganization, thus creating a vicious circle.[103] Peel argued that 'officers should in future hold all legal situations of a subordinate nature in dependence upon those by whom they were appointed, so as to enable Parliament to proceed to legal reforms and alterations, without giving to individuals who might be affected by them a claim to compensation'.[104] This step was taken in 1830, when an act created a body of four commissioners, who were to examine fees and certify the value of each office. Officials were to be paid according to that certified value, and compensated accordingly if the office was abolished. No one appointed in the future was to receive compensation.[105] The act also included the crucial principle that surplus fees were to be paid into the Consolidated Fund. This act opened the way for the reform of many offices. At the same time, the recommendations of the Common Law Commission led to reforms in the restrictive court of Exchequer,[106] as well as the abolition of useless offices connected with obsolete forms.[107] When in 1833 the fee commissioners were asked to draw up a new table of fees, they urged the need for uniformity in the structure of offices in the courts, and proposed the abolition of nineteen offices in King's Bench and twenty-five in Common Pleas.[108] Four years later the offices were duly abolished, and a new table of fees was directed to be drawn up.[109]

A similar pattern of reform is found in Chancery, where the abolition of offices went hand in hand with cautious attempts to restructure the court at no cost to the state. Again 1830 proved a key date. In that year, Sir Edward Sugden brought a bill to reform the Six Clerks' Office, abolish the sworn clerks, and reform the Registrars' Office and Report Office, as well as introducing salaries for masters.[110] He claimed that this would have been a government bill had Wellington not fallen. Meanwhile, the new chancellor, Brougham, had taken

---

[103] *Ibid.*, col. 1475 (23 June 1828). Peel was influenced both by the experience of generous compensations in Ireland and by the problems with the 1826 statute altering the law on writs of error.

[104] *Ibid.*, xxii, 654–5 (18 Feb. 1830); see also *ibid.*, xxiv, 1202 (28 May 1830).

[105] 1 Will. IV, c. lviii.   [106] 2 and 3 Will. IV, c. cx.

[107] See *Legal Observer*, 10 (1835), 307, for bills brought in consequent upon the Uniformity of Process Act (2 Will. IV, c. xxxix) and the Act for the Abolition of Fines and Recoveries (3 and 4 Will. IV, c. lxxiv).

[108] P.P. 1835, xlvi (314), 'Report on Consolidation of Offices in Courts of King's Bench and Common Pleas', 105.

[109] The Common Law Offices Act, 1 Vict., c. xxx, discussed in *Legal Observer*, 14 (1837), 284. For the motivations behind this act, see *Parl. Debs.*, 3rd ser., xxxv, col. 1277 ff. (18 Aug. 1836, speech of Lord Langdale).

[110] See *Parl. Debs.*, 3rd ser., i, col. 1279 ff. (16 Dec. 1830).

up the issue of Chancery reform, proposing a wide-ranging set of reforms.[111] Brougham's plan was ambitious, but not all were convinced of its workability, and it ran into opposition at the committee stage. Where he had initially proposed abolition of the Six Clerks, the bill was amended so that vacancies would not be filled until the number had fallen to two.[112] The resulting Chancery Regulation Act of 1833 restructured many offices in the court, providing compensation for those who lost their places.[113] The act also provided that a new table of fees was to be settled, which was done in December. It should be noted that this act was the product of a wider reform project initiated by Brougham, which failed in part because of the practical difficulty of reforming the court. There was clearly resistance to reforms from some officers – who were paid dearly for their offices once abolished – but at the same time, there were difficulties in reforming the structure of the courts themselves.

As with the common law, the problem of Chancery reform continued to drag on into the mid-nineteenth century. Brougham's reforms were only partial, and in 1840 renewed attacks were made on the Chancery by Thomas Pemberton in parliament,[114] and by the solicitor Edwin Field in print.[115] It was as a consequence of this pressure that the reforms looked to in 1833 – the abolition of the Six Clerks' and Sworn Clerks' Offices – were finally effected,[116] though at an enormously high cost in terms of the sums paid out in compensation. It is ironic that 'Old Corruption' seemed to reach it apogee in the courts in 1843, when the orders for compensating the sworn clerks was issued. The legal press was outraged that a sworn clerk like George Gatty could receive £5,232 in compensation (half of which was to be paid for seven posthumous years to his heirs) in addition to a new salary of £2,000 a year as a taxing master.[117] This

---

[111] Brougham's initial aim was to create a new kind of record office in Chancery, which involved abolishing the existing Report Office, the six clerks, and the sworn clerks. He also proposed changes in the Masters' Offices, to give the masters some judicial functions: *Legal Observer*, 5 (1833), 424, 501; *ibid.*, 6 (1833), 81.

[112] *Ibid.*, 6 (1833), 212, 257.

[113] 3 and 4 Will. IV., c. cxiv. The compensation given is shown in *Legal Observer*, 7 (supplement for Mar. 1834), 459.

[114] *Parl. Debs.*, 3rd ser., lv, col. 1305 (5 Aug. 1840). Pemberton (1793–1867) was a successful Chancery barrister and Tory MP, who declined the offer of various legal promotions to remain at the bar. In 1842 he inherited a fortune from a distant relative (and took on the name Pemberton-Leigh), and retired from active life, though he was later appointed to the judicial committee of the privy council. In 1858, he obtained a peerage and took the title of Lord Kingsdown.

[115] Edwin W. Field, *Observations of a Solicitor on Defects in the Offices, Practice, and System of Costs of the Equity Courts* (London, 1840). A prominent Unitarian, Field (1804–71) continued to represent the views of the lower branch of the legal profession on questions of law reform, both as a senior member of the Metropolitan and Provincial Law Association, and as a witness before official inquiries. See Thomas Sadler, *Edwin Wilkins Field: A Memorial Sketch* (London, 1872).

[116] 5 and 6 Vict., c. ciii.   [117] *Law Times*, 2 (1844), 445.

was at a time when the chief justice was only drawing a salary of £8,000 a year. The 'Chancery Compensation Job' was all the more outrageous for lawyers, given that it was the suitors who were to pay. It was anger over this measure that impelled W. H. Watson, the MP for the Irish constituency of Kinsale, to continue to agitate for a select committee into fees, and in 1847 the government agreed to appoint one.[118] Just as in 1814, it was practitioners and their clients who were more agitated by 'Old Corruption' in the courts than politicians, for they were the ones to pay.

The question remains why the reform of the structure of the courts was so halting. After all, in 1830, when Grey's ministry took office, the conditions seemed ripe for a major overhaul of the legal system: royal commissions were examining various aspects of the law; the principle of removing patent offices had been established; and there was a growing public debate on the need for law reform. One answer to this question can be found in the fact that there was little central coordination in law reform. Governments remained happy throughout the middle years of the century to allow different aspects of law reform to be handled by different individuals, and indeed to be investigated by distinct royal commissions, which might (and did) come up with contradictory recommendations. This partly reflected the fact that law reform was often a reaction to particular pressures in different courts; but it equally reflects a deeper conservatism, both legal and political. The obvious way in which to coordinate policy would have been to create a ministry of justice, something that was called for by Langdale in 1836 and much debated thereafter. Yet creating such an office would have involved reforming the office of the lord chancellor, and even the most apparently progressive reformers, such as Brougham, were hesitant to alter an office so central in the constitution, and so much the prize of lawyers.

The corollary to this is to note that control of law reform remained in the hands of lawyers, who remained institutionally conservative in a way that chimed well with the financially cautious desires of government. This can be seen in the fate of the local courts in the 1820s and 1830s. As early as 1824, the Whig reformer John Williams opposed the creation of local courts since it would increase the influence of the crown and undermine the independence of the bar.[119] These were objections repeatedly rehearsed throughout the 1830s in the legal periodical press, which feared that the quality of law would suffer from a decentralized system. Moreover, if a desire to revive local justice had preceded the move to reform the superior courts (and, with Peel's act of 1830, paved the

---

[118] See *Legal Observer*, 32 (1846), 41; *Parl. Debs.*, 3rd ser., lxxxvi, col. 176 (7 May 1846); *ibid.*, xcii, col. 381 (4 May 1847).

[119] *Parl. Debs.*, 2nd ser., xi, col. 854 (24 May 1824).

way for it), many lawyers came to the conclusion that local judicatures would be unnecessary if Westminster Hall were improved.[120] Numerous attempts were hence made to forestall the need for these courts. Lord Wynford, for instance, brought in a bill in 1831 to speed up suits in the common-law courts, seeking to reform procedure in highly Benthamic ways,[121] while the Law Amendment Act of 1833 allowed cases under £20 to be referred to sheriffs on writs of inquiry or to any other judge of record.[122] Throughout the 1830s, bills on local courts stalled, as governments remained unclear over whether to extend the powers under the 1833 act, or to reorganize the courts of Quarter Sessions, or to establish wholly new courts. In the end, the court structure was slowly reformed. Legislation establishing local courts came in 1846; while in 1841 two new vice-chancellors were instituted at the same time that the equity side of the Exchequer was abolished. None the less, these reforms remained reluctant, and resulted from the ever-present pressure of litigation.

V

Law reform remained a process dominated by lawyers, responding to the demands of their clients or potential clients. Reform was thus driven by interested parties. The great demands placed by the growth in litigation increased the strain on the courts, and increased pressure for means to cheapen and expedite justice. At the same time, litigants also had their own voices demanding changes. Petitions were regularly presented to parliament by individuals, including debtors complaining of the hardships of their imprisonment, or those gaoled for contempt of court when they were unable to pay high fees. Equally, there were petitions from communities, such as traders in country towns seeking better small-debts courts.[123] Finally, there were petitions from more organized groups, such as the London merchants who sought reforms in the late 1820s of the law of bankruptcy.[124] Such groups became more important as the century

---

[120] One solicitor commented in 1831 that it was 'utterly inconsistent with the avowed purposes of the common law commission' to withdraw two-thirds of their business and to give it 'to a new and experimental tribunal': *Legal Observer*, 1 (1831), 170.

[121] This is a good example of Bentham's influence on detail. Wynford and Bentham corresponded over the bill, the former telling the latter that 'we differ but little (if we differ at all) as to the examination of the parties': Brit. Lib., Add. MS 33,546, fo. 480, Wynford to Bentham, 9 Jan. 1831.

[122] 3 and 4 Will. IV, c. xlii, §. 17.

[123] *Parl. Debs.*, 2nd ser., xxiv, col. 1258 (30 June 1830: petition from a gaoled debtor); *ibid.*, xxii, col. 1305 (5 Mar. 1830: petitioner gaoled for contempt of court after being unable to pay ecclesiastical court fees); *ibid.*, 3rd ser., vi, col. 158 (17 Aug. 1831: petition of traders for small-debts courts).

[124] See Williams' comments *ibid.*, 3rd ser., viii, col. 16 (5 Dec. 1831). Lord Lyndhurst presented a petition in 1845 from the Society for the Protection of Trade for better remedies to recover small debts. *Legal Observer*, 30 (1845), 269.

progressed. A metropolitan committee of merchants and traders was created in the 1830s to urge reform, and to propose and comment on legislation, notably on insolvency and bankruptcy, and later on the workings of the county courts.[125] However, they tended to work very closely with the professional law reformers.[126] The link between law reformers and commercial interests from mid-century was a very close one, in which law reformers sought to use their commercial contacts to promote reform as much as commercial men sought to influence the lawyers. For example, reformers in the Law Amendment Society in mid-century, who were keen to codify and assimilate the commercial law of the whole kingdom, sought the cooperation of chambers of commerce in this enterprise. A Mercantile Law Conference was organized in 1852 to promote this end by forcing the government to appoint a commission.[127] The close participation of the mercantile community in law reform continued after the formation of the Social Science Association.[128] These groups did not put forward a rival vision of the nature of reform, one driven by 'outsiders' to the system: rather, they spoke the same language of reform as the progressive lawyers. By mid-century, there were indeed hostile voices, in the press and among the public, which sought to demonstrate the hardships and evils of the unreformed legal system, and to urge change. The most famous attack on the old system came from Dickens' picture of the Chancery in *Bleak House* in 1853. Yet the era of its publication saw the implementation of reforms that had been debated and considered by specialists for more than two decades.

[125] See Lester, *Victorian Insolvency*, 64–7. For its activities, see, e.g., *Legal Observer*, 31 (1846), 467; *Law Times*, 15 (1850), 167.

[126] Bodies such as the Law Amendment Society actively recruited non-lawyers to their membership: *Law Times*, 7 (1846), 309.

[127] See, e.g., letters from James Stewart to Henry Brougham: University College London, Brougham MSS, 12,691 (13 Aug. 1851), 15,140 (30 Sept. 1852), 15,147 (10 Dec. 1852).

[128] Thus, Russell's Bankruptcy Bill of 1858 was the product of close collaboration with the mercantile committee of the Social Science Association: *Law Times*, 33 (1859), 14; Lester, *Victorian Insolvency*, 126–9.

5. English 'church reform' revisited, 1780–1840*

ARTHUR BURNS

'Church reform' is one of the most widely deployed concepts in ecclesiastical historiography. In the modern English context, it moved seamlessly during the late nineteenth and early twentieth centuries from being of central importance in the discussions of ecclesiastical policy-makers to assume a place as a key category in the conceptual apparatus of historical inquiry into the shaping of the Victorian Church of England.[1] From the late 1950s to the early 1970s, the heroic age of ecclesiastical and institutional historiography of the nineteenth-century church, it was ubiquitous.[2] The ecclesiastical reforms of the first half of the nineteenth century were indeed unprecedented in extent, including as they did the redrawing of the diocesan map of England and Wales, a systematic reallocation of church revenues both geographically and between different levels of the church hierarchy, and significant new statutory regulation of clerical practice. While other projects of the 'age of reform' attracted a resurgence of interest during the 1990s, however, this did not extend to its ecclesiastical

* I am grateful not only to participants in the 'Rethinking the Age of Reform' conference for their comments, but also members of seminars in London, Cambridge, and Reading. In particular Nigel Aston, Pene Corfield, Tim Hitchcock, Robert Ingram, Jonathan Parry, Mark Smith, and Stephen Taylor offered perceptive commentaries from which the present chapter has benefited.

[1] For landmarks in this process, see Charles Gore (ed.), *Essays in Aid of the Reform of the Church* (London, 1898), a collection of reform proposals whose spine carried the short title *Church Reform*; William Law Mathieson, *English Church Reform, 1815–1840* (London, 1923), a pioneering study.

[2] This period saw the publication of, among others, Olive J. Brose, *Church and Parliament: The Reshaping of the Church of England 1828–1860* (Stanford and London, 1959); G. F. A. Best, *Temporal Pillars: Queen Anne's Bounty, the Ecclesiastical Commissioners and the Church of England* (Cambridge, 1964); W. O. Chadwick, *The Victorian Church*, 2 vols. (London, 1966–71); Desmond Bowen, *The Idea of the Victorian Church* (Montreal, 1968); K. A. Thompson, *Bureaucracy and Church Reform: The Organizational Response of the Church of England to Social Change, 1800–1965* (Oxford, 1970).

dimension, even though 'religious' dimensions of modern British history were also attracting renewed attention.[3]

Why? The answer lies partly in intellectual fashion. Many Hanoverian historians still unconsciously marginalize the theological or religious dimensions of their subjects.[4] But historians of modern British religion are as much to blame. They escaped their professional marginalization of the 1960s and 1970s through significant advances in the social history of religion, studies focusing on popular belief and culture, and considerations of the religious dimension of the 'history of ideas', all of which had important implications for 'secular' histories. Much of this scholarship asserted its claims through an explicit renunciation of a supposedly outmoded and introspective 'ecclesiastical', institutionally focused history, of which 'church reform' was an identifying theme.[5] The irony that this happened when other historians of Hanoverian and Victorian Britain were rediscovering institutions went unremarked.

The neglect of 'church reform' also had more mundane origins. There seemed nothing left to say. Outstanding studies published in the mid-twentieth century, above all Geoffrey Best's magisterial *Temporal Pillars*, reaped such a rich harvest as apparently to leave room only for antiquarian gleaning. Moreover, the enduring historiographical construction of the nineteenth-century church through narratives of reform cast the eighteenth-century church in the role of the 'unreformed' object of that reform. Yet eighteenth-century studies adopting this 'reform perspective',[6] notably Peter Virgin's *The Church in an Age of Negligence*, have in turn been accused of adopting inappropriate and anachronistic Victorian categories that are unhelpful in understanding the Hanoverian

---

[3] Most controversially, J. C. D. Clark, *English Society 1688–1832* (Cambridge, 1985); see also Boyd Hilton, *The Age of Atonement: The Influence of Evangelicalism on Social and Economic Thought, 1785–1865* (Oxford, 1988); Robert Hole, *Pulpits, Politics and Public Order, 1760–1832* (Cambridge, 1989); P. B. Nockles, *The Oxford Movement in Context: Anglican High Churchmanship, 1760–1857* (Cambridge, 1994). For significant exceptions to the prevailing neglect of late Hanoverian church reform see the recent work of Richard Brent, Grayson Ditchfield, Frances Knight, Mark Smith, and the present author, in works footnoted below.

[4] E.g., the ecclesiastical dimension is the least satisfactory aspect of Philip Harling's account of *The Waning of 'Old Corruption': The Politics of Economical Reform in Britain, 1779–1846* (Oxford, 1996); see also Derek Beales' stimulating essay on usage of the word 'reform', 'The Idea of Reform in British Politics, 1829–1850', in T. C. W. Blanning and P. Wende (eds.), *Reform in Great Britain and Germany, 1750–1850* (Oxford, 1999), 159–74, which fails to do justice to the variety and ubiquity of the use of the term in an ecclesiastical context.

[5] See, e.g., Sarah Williams, 'The Language of Belief: An Alternative Agenda for the Study of Victorian Working Class Religion', *Jl Victorian Culture*, 1 (1996), 310. For a good account of contemporary trends see J. R. Wolffe, 'Anglicanism', in D. G. Paz (ed.), *Nineteenth-Century English Religious Traditions: Retrospect and Prospect* (Westport, Conn., 1995), 1–31.

[6] For this concept, see J. Innes and J. Styles, 'The Crime Wave: Recent Writing on Crime and Criminal Justice in Eighteenth-Century England', *Jl Brit. Studies*, 25 (1986), 383.

church 'on its own terms'.[7] Partly in response recent so-called 'revisionist' scholarship has preferred to investigate the Hanoverian church's functionality as a structure.[8] Finally, the concerted attempt to 'rehabilitate' the Hanoverian church has served to fix 1828–33 as a watershed that few studies cross. Hanoverian church historians have shown little interest in integrating the major reforms of the mid-1830s into their accounts. Yet there are good reasons for tracing continuities in reform projects across the reform crisis. In short, the subject of Hanoverian church reform needs to have a few cobwebs dusted off, and deserves a reappraisal.

This chapter does not attempt to offer a new and comprehensive narrative of church reform from 1780 to 1840. Instead, it aims to subject our existing understandings to an overdue re-examination in the light of new perspectives afforded both by developments in religious history and in the historiography of reform beyond the church. Above all, it singles out the 'language' of church reform for particular attention.

The first section of the chapter examines the contexts in which the term 'church reform' was used, and offers a summary of the development of this discourse considered in tandem with the enactment of concrete measures of 're-form' at both the national and the local level. The second section then considers how best to account for the contours of this narrative, in particular comparing the histories of church and state reform in parallel, identifying similarities and dissimilarities in the reform debates and rhetorics of the two traditions. One theme that emerges is the particular role of historical legitimation in the discussion of church reform, and an examination of this leads into the third section of the chapter, which discusses the obvious – but rarely remarked – fact that the terms 'reform' and 'reformation' had specific religious resonances, and how this affected the ways in which 'church reform' rhetoric could be deployed, and who could deploy it. The chapter concludes by offering some more speculative suggestions as to how such closer attention to language might assist in

---

[7] See Peter Virgin, *The Church in an Age of Negligence: Ecclesiastical Structure and Problems of Church Reform, 1700–1840* (Cambridge, 1989). For an example of the critique, see Mark Smith, 'The Reception of Richard Podmore: Anglicanism in Saddleworth, 1700–1830', in J. Walsh, C. Haydon, and S. Taylor (eds.), *The Church of England c. 1689–1833: From Toleration to Tractarianism* (Cambridge, 1993), 110–23.

[8] This observation applies, e.g., to William Gibson, *The Church of England 1688–1832: Unity and Accord* (London, 2001); William Gibson, *The Achievement of the Anglican Church 1689–1800: The Confessional State in Eighteenth Century England* (Lewiston, 1995); to a lesser extent to Jeremy Gregory, 'The Making of a Protestant Nation: "Success" and "Failure" in England's Long Reformation', in N. Tyacke (ed.), *England's Long Reformation, 1500–1800* (London, 1998). For a good measure of current tendencies of scholarship, see J. Gregory and J. Chamberlain (eds.), *The National Church in Local Perspective: the Church of England and the Regions, 1660–1800* (Woodbridge, 2002). For the contrary argument that the apparent 'non-subject' of eighteenth-century church reform merits further investigation, see Stephen Taylor, 'Introduction' to 'Bishop Edmund Gibson's Proposals for Church Reform', in Taylor (ed.), *From Cranmer to Davidson: A Church of England Miscellany* (Woodbridge, 1999), 171–86, esp. 171–2, 186. The forthcoming study of Thomas Secker by Robert Ingram will also be important in this regard.

explaining how the national church-reform debate so rapidly calmed in the later 1830s from the fever pitch observable at the outset of the decade.

I

A good place to start this re-examination is by asking a simple question: when the phrase 'church reform' was employed in this period, to what did it refer? A crude classification of the contents of pamphlets and speeches employing the term between 1780 and 1840 yields the following list:[9]

A: Proposals for institutional/structural adjustment
  i. The ending of prominent 'abuses', in particular sinecures, non-residence, and pluralism.
  ii. The mobilization of resources either from within the church or without for church extension, church building, and to provide additional clergy.
  iii. The improvement of conditions for the poorest or 'working' clergy, both beneficed and unbeneficed (curates), through raising incomes and providing fit residences.
  iv. The creation of mechanisms both to enable the implementation of such projects (such as the Ecclesiastical Commission) and to monitor their effectiveness (e.g., statistical measures, or improved episcopal oversight and discipline, with the assistance of archdeacons and rural deans).
  v. The removal of sites of ostentatious luxury within the church, above all cathedral offices and the richest livings, to allow their resources to be redeployed or simply to eliminate a focus of criticism.
  vi. The redistribution of episcopal revenues, both as allocated among the episcopate and with reference to the disproportion existing between these incomes and those of the lower clergy; the limitation of episcopal translations, commendams, and pluralism; and the adjustment of the balance between bishops' parliamentary and diocesan duties.
  vii. Adjustments to ecclesiastical geography and jurisdictions at both diocesan and parochial level to respond to new pastoral challenges.
  viii. Adjustments to the operation of church patronage at all levels of the church.
  ix. Reform of the ecclesiastical courts.
B: Proposals for doctrinal reform
  Chiefly adjustments to the doctrinal formularies, liturgy, or articles of the Church of England, with a view to making it more inclusive.

---

[9] Relevant pamphlets and speeches were identified by searching the British Library catalogue for publications employing the word 'church' and related terms in combination with 'reformation' and 'reform' in their titles; an investigation of pamphlets and speeches intervening in debates in which these combinations or variant forms were regularly being deployed, and other more serendipitous discoveries.

C: Proposals for alterations to collection or sourcing of church revenues
Focusing in particular on the replacement or commutation of tithe, but with church rates becoming more significant towards the end of the period.

In considering this list, it is worth noting absences as well as presences. 'Church reform' rarely encompassed readjustments of the denominational definition of citizenship or the state, such as the repeal of the Test and Corporation Acts or Catholic Emancipation (although it could accommodate changes to the church to permit those currently excluded to be incorporated once more). Nor was it generally employed to refer to developments in the church's educational work, or novel forms of domestic or overseas missionary endeavour, all topics sometimes discussed in terms of church reform by modern scholarship.[10]

Among the list, proposals for institutional/structural adjustment were the most common, and could be advocated or resisted for pastoral, political, or occasionally explicitly theological reasons. Proposals for alterations to church finances at times rivalled them in popularity. Reform of the tithe system was the most significant theme of this type in 'church reform' publications. However, this was often discussed in the context of a consideration of agricultural improvement or distress rather than ecclesiastical reform. This gave the topic distinct dynamics, and consequently tithe reform will not be considered at length here.[11]

We now turn to the chronological development of both the discussion and implementation of these church-reform projects from the mid-eighteenth to the mid-nineteenth century, outlined in summary manner in table 5.1. There is no reason to dissent from the now prevailing 'gradualist' narrative of the enactment of modern English church reform, locating its origins in the late eighteenth century. For present purposes, however, it is important to distinguish between two strands of initiatives, contrasting both in approach and the extent of controversy they excited.

First, largely invisible in the chronology in the table, as it was until recently in current historiography, there was a strand of local (and/or regional) and largely clerically directed reform initiatives aimed at overhauling the church's pastoral, disciplinary, and consultative structures. Sporadic and erratic in the eighteenth century, this variety of reform gathered pace from the 1790s into what became a nationwide movement of 'diocesan revival'.[12] These initiatives, often

---

[10] Cf. Best, *Temporal Pillars*, 186: 'Church reform up to 1831 may be summarily viewed under these heads: *education*, tithes, patronage, ecclesiastical courts, church rates, church building and the division of parishes, episcopal revenues and diocesan boundaries, the collection of information, and poor livings (comprising the inseparable sub-heads non-residence and pluralism, residence houses, and relief for poor clergy)' (my italics).

[11] For the agricultural context, see in particular Eric J. Evans, *The Contentious Tithe: The Tithe Problem and English Agriculture, 1750–1850* (London, 1976); Eric J. Evans, 'Some Reasons for the Growth of Anti-Clericalism in England', *Past and Present*, no. 66 (Feb. 1975), 84–109.

[12] For a detailed discussion of this strand of reform, see A. Burns, *The Diocesan Revival in the Church of England, c. 1800–1870* (Oxford, 1999).

Table 5.1 *A chronology of English church reform, 1780–1840*

Date	Legislation (italics = abortive)	Some publications
1770s		
1777	Gilbert's Residence Act	
1780s		
1781	Gilbert's Residence Act (amended)	
1783		R. Watson, *Letter to the Archbishop of Canterbury*
1790s		
1791	*Pitt proposes tithe commutation*	R. Watson, *Charge to . . . Llandaff*
1795		M. Cove, *An Essay on the Revenues of the Church of England*
1796	Curates Act (36 Geo. III, c. lxxxiii) raises upper limit of curates' salaries to £75	
1800s		
1800	*Pitt 'Ecclesiastical Plan'*	
1801	*Clergy Non-Residence Bill*; 41 Geo. III c. xl provides partial relief from Horse Tax for poor clergy	
1802	*Clergy Non-Residence Bill*	
1803	Spiritual Persons' Relief Act (43 Geo. III, c. lxxxiv: revises regulations for non-residence, demanding annual returns to privy council from bishops, who also license; *Stipendiary Curates Bill*	
1805	*Curates Bill* (Perceval)	
1806	*Curates Bill* (Perceval)	
1808	*Curates Bill* (Perceval)	
1809	First annual parliamentary grant to Queen Anne's Bounty of £100,000, continued to 1816, then 1818–20	
1810s		
1812	Publication of tabulated statistics of church accommodation and stipendiary curates' salaries; *Curates Bill* (Harrowby)	
1813	Clergy Penalties Suspension Act; Stipendiary Curates Act (Harrowby)	
1814	Clergy Penalties Suspension Act	
1815		R. Yates, *The Church in Danger*
1816		*Pamphleteer* republishes Watson's *Letter*
1817	Non-Residence Act	
1818	'Million Pound Grant', Church-Building Commission established	J. Bentham, *Church of Englandism Examined*

Table 5.1 (*cont.*)

Date	Legislation (italics = abortive)	Some publications
1820s		
1820		J. Wade, *Black Book*
1822		*Remarks on the Consumption of Public Wealth by the Clergy of Every Christian Nation*; 'Durham Case: Clerical Abuses', *Edin. Rev.*
1823		'Church Establishments', *Edin. Rev.*
1824	'Half Million Grant'	
1828		*Church Reform: By a Churchman* (E. Berens)
1830s		
1830	Ecclesiastical Courts Commission established	
1831	Augmentations Act (Howley) makes augmentation of livings by ecclesiastical bodies easier; *Pluralities Bill* (Howley); *Tithe Composition Bill* (Howley)	*Extraordinary Black Book*; *Church Reform without Legislation* (F. Massingberd); R. M. Beverley, *A Letter to the Archbishop of York*; E. Burton, *Thoughts upon the Demand for Church Reform*
1832	Appointment of Ecclesiastical Revenues Commission; *Pluralities Bill* (Howley)	R. Henley, *A Plan of Church Reform*
1833	Irish Church Temporalities Act	T. Arnold, *Principles of Church Reform*; J. Keble, *Assize Sermon*
1835	Ecclesiastical Revenues Report published; Ecclesiastical Commission appointed (Peel)	J. H. Newman, *On the Restoration of Suffragans*; W. Dansey, *Horae decanicae rurales*
1836	Established Church Act (plans for jurisdictional reorganization for sees and redistribution of episcopal incomes authorized as life interests expired); Ecclesiastical Commission made permanent; Tithe Commutation Act	
1838	Pluralities Act (imposes much stricter limits on pluralism and non-residence)	
1840	Ecclesiastical Duties and Revenues Act (reduction of cathedral establishments, monies redeployed by Commission to parochial purposes; all bishops added to Commission); Church Discipline Act (new procedures for clerical discipline)	

explicitly described as 'reforms' by the 1830s, made a decisive contribution to the elimination of non-residence and clerical poverty as a vital auxiliary to the more familiar tradition of legislative reform. For the latter would have been difficult to enforce without a reinvigoration of the church's local disciplinary machinery, which had to varying degrees decayed since the Restoration. Among the most significant reforms enacted in this tradition were the revival of the system of rural deans (both as investigative officers under the command of bishop and archdeacons, and as representatives of the lower clergy in consultative bodies), the reinvigoration of the archdeacons, and the reform of the episcopal visitation (generally triennial assemblies at which the condition of the diocesan clergy, churches, and parochial life could be systematically investigated). These reforms often involved little or no additional expenditure of money as opposed to effort – the rural deans, for example, were not remunerated for their labours. Moreover, unlike most significant adjustments to the polity or 'plant' of the Church of England, they did not require legislation and could be enacted solely on episcopal authority, or by personal initiatives from even more junior officers. These characteristics also explain why this strand of reform proceeded without exciting much public discussion beyond the clerical forum.

Instead the national and parliamentary initiatives charted in the chronology provided the focus for public debate. These had fewer Georgian antecedents. Much of the eighteenth century can be regarded as an extended interlude both in the implementation of legislation addressing the main themes of what would later be called 'church reform' and in their widespread public discussion. As Stephen Taylor has noted, 'no significant measure of [church] reform reached the statute book between the accession of George I and the end of the eighteenth century'.[13] What Geoffrey Best dubbed 'the second church reform movement' left as its most enduring legacy Queen Anne's Bounty, founded in 1704 to receive the first-fruits and tenths diverted to the state at the Reformation and to employ them to augment the capital endowment of poorly endowed livings.[14] This 'movement', however, was already running out of steam before the prorogation of convocation in 1717. Conscientious prelates such as Edmund Gibson and Thomas Secker[15] conceived extensive programmes of what was variously described as 'regulation' or 'alteration' and only occasionally as

---

[13] Taylor, 'Gibson's Proposals for Church Reform', 171.

[14] Best, *Temporal Pillars*, 5: 'The second [church reform movement] faded out with the coming of the Hanoverians, leaving only a few institutions of which the least inadequate was Queen Anne's Bounty.' The 'first church reform movement' was identified by Best with Archbishop John Whitgift's primacy (1583–1604). For Queen Anne's Bounty, see *ibid., passim*; for its impact, among others see Eric J. Evans, 'The Anglican Clergy of the North of England', in Clyve Jones (ed.), *Britain in the First Age of Party, 1680–1750* (London, 1987), 221–40.

[15] Edmund Gibson (1669–1748), bishop of Lincoln 1716–20, bishop of London 1720–47, author of the *Codex juris ecclesiastici Anglicani* (1713); Thomas Secker (1693–1768), bishop of Bristol 1735–7, bishop of Oxford 1737–58, archbishop of Canterbury 1758–67.

'reformation',[16] but they generally refrained from launching them in what they regarded as a politically unsympathetic environment.[17]

None the less a 'discourse' of church reform had achieved wider public currency some time before the first important legislative measures reached the statute book. This took the form of the increasing ubiquity of the usage in relevant contexts of the terms 'reform' (especially as a verb or as a noun designating institutional adaptation) and 'reformation'. The latter now loosened its former association with projects of moral improvement and came to be more commonly adopted in the contexts in which it had previously competed with 'regulation' and 'alteration'. Both 'reform' and 'reformation' achieved novel ecclesiastical currency from the mid-century in the unsuccessful campaign for a relaxation of the terms of subscription to the national church through which theologically liberal Anglicans sought to extract themselves from the need to commit perjury in formally assenting to doctrinal articles before admission to a living.[18]

Yet even five years after the Feathers Tavern petition it was still the case that institutional and legislative adjustments to the church's structures were not readily described as 'reforms'. A small and isolated instalment of what to a later age would appear 'church reform' occurred in 1777 and 1781, when Thomas Gilbert first sponsored and then amended an act 'to promote the residence of the clergy' by facilitating the building or repair of parsonage houses.[19] But neither of the words 'reform' and 'reformation' occurred in Gilbert's measures. It was only during the course of the 1780s that the next significant stage in defining the *topos* of 'church reform' occurred, as the term 'reform' began to be employed in initiatives addressing church institutions, finance, and patronage.

This development was heralded by Bishop Richard Watson's *Letter to the Archbishop of Canterbury* of 1783, which could almost be called the founding document of the modern church-reform tradition: a significance acknowledged in the fact that it was republished a number of times during the following forty

---

[16] Taylor, 'Gibson's Proposals for Church Reform', 186. For further examples of the use of 'reformation' or the verb 'to reform' with reference to ecclesiastical matters in this period, see [T. Sherlock], *Some Considerations upon Pluralities, Non-Residence and Salaries of Curates* (London, 1737), complaining of 'the indulging a *Need* to be Reforming', ii.

[17] See Stephen Taylor, 'Whigs, Bishops and America: The Politics of Church Reform in Mid-Eighteenth-Century England', *Hist. Jl*, 36 (1993), 331–56.

[18] For the campaign, see G. M. Ditchfield, 'The Subscription Issue in British Parliamentary Politics, 1772–9', *Parl. Hist.*, 7 (1988), 45–80. For an example of the usage, see *A Letter to the Members of the Honourable House of Commons: Respecting the Petition for Relief in the Matter of Subscription: By a Christian Whig*, 2nd edn (London, 1772), 33, calling for a 'Reformation in our Religious Establishment'; see Joanna Innes, chapter 2, p. 81, for further examples of such usage from latitudinarian Anglicans such as John Jones and Francis Blackburne.

[19] 17 Geo. III, c. liii and 21 Geo. III, c. lxvi. Strikingly, the act seems to have been little taken advantage of before the early nineteenth century: see Virgin, *Church in an Age of Negligence*, 66.

years, still remaining a point of reference in 1840.[20] Watson's letter advocated the equalization of episcopal incomes and the appropriation of cathedral chapter monies for the relief of impoverished clergy. The letter also provides the first instance of a prominent churchman publicly if tentatively adopting the vocabulary of 'reform' in this context. The novelty of such usage from a man in his position was acknowledged at the outset. Watson insisted that his letter was not prompted by 'a silly vanity of being considered a Reformer; a character which in all ages has met with as much detraction as praise', and at its conclusion he resigned himself to bear any censure resulting from becoming, 'as some will scoffingly phrase it, a Reformer'.[21]

A flurry of pamphleteering followed. As might have been expected, there were replies from clergy who feared that 'compatriots, taking their cue from your Lordship, will go on to level, and pretending to reform will really destroy. A rebellion can hardly be named that did not set out with the pretence of reformation.' But there were also interventions from clergy and churchmen both welcoming Watson's appearance as 'a leader in the business of *Ecclesiastical Reformation*' and offering further recommendations for action, insisting that the 'enemies of the Church are those who know these things [abuses] and have it in their power to reform them, and yet neglect to do it – It is not the man who pleads earnestly for Reformation . . . that injures the Church.'[22]

Further such publications continued to appear sporadically into the 1790s, but during this decade the stakes attached to explicit advocacy of reform were raised. The spectacle of ecclesiastical reform of a different tenor in revolutionary France served – along with more visible and aggressive radical anticlericalism, and tithe agitation – to recommend caution. Yet Watson, for example, continued to call for church reform, and his episcopal charge of 1791 (initially published without his permission) looked sympathetically on some aspects of the new ecclesiastical dispensation across the Channel while pleading for 'temperate Reform'.[23] Few clerical authors were prepared to associate reform proposals with the projects of the National Assembly.[24] It should nevertheless be emphasized that even in the 1790s the vocabulary of church reform was not surrendered completely to dissenting and radical critics, although the latter's voices emerged

---

[20] Richard Watson, *A Letter to His Grace the Archbishop of Canterbury* (Dublin, 1783). Richard Watson (1737–1816), bishop of Llandaff 1782–1816. See T. J. Brain, 'Some Aspects of the Life and Work of Richard Watson, Bishop of Llandaff, 1737 to 1816' (University of Wales Ph.D. thesis, 1982). Edward Baines cited Watson in the debates on the Ecclesiastical Duties and Revenues Bill in 1840: see *Parl. Debs.*, 3rd ser., liii, col. 609 (6 Apr. 1840).

[21] Watson, *Letter*, 2, 76.

[22] *A Letter to the Lord Bishop of Landaff . . . By a Country Curate* (London, 1783), 7; *A Letter to . . . Richard Lord Bishop of Landaff on the Projected Reformation of the Church* (London, 1783), v, 40; *A Letter from a Clergyman to the Bishop of Landaff* (London, 1783); R. Cumberland, *A Letter to Richard Lord Bishop of Landaff* (London, 1783).

[23] R. Watson, *A Charge to the Clergy of the Diocese of Landaff, June 1791* (London, 1792), 5.

[24] A Country Curate, *A Letter to the . . . Lord Bishop of Landaff* (London, 1792); see also *Vindiciae Landavenses* (Oxford, 1792).

in the debates more directly than before, some now proclaiming 'radical' church reform as a cause supported by the 'public'.[25]

In terms of concrete initiatives, the late 1780s and 1790s also saw the first in a series of parliamentary church-reform initiatives that extended into the early 1820s.[26] These were mostly constructive in their aims of making the church more effective in pastoral terms and less vulnerable to hostile criticism. They were also generally sponsored by lay statesmen. The high churchman William Scott's efforts to combine an effective if unambitious assault on clerical non-residence with increased protection for clergy under threat of lay prosecution for the same offence were certainly welcome to the church authorities. Other initiatives, however, met at best a lukewarm response from the higher clergy. This was the case, for example, with the bold pragmatic initiatives developed by Pitt's administration in the abortive 'Ecclesiastical Plan' of 1800, which envisaged augmentation of clerical incomes to a minimum value of £70 for curates, charged where necessary on the consolidated fund, and an overhaul of the system for monitoring and disciplining the residence of clergy. There was much suspicion among beneficed clergy when it came to attempts to improve conditions for curates, above all their remuneration. Bills to this end, sponsored by the evangelicals Spencer Perceval and the earl of Harrowby, could be suspected of being exercises in church party warfare, and did in fact reflect a belief that 'godly' clergy suffered from a glass ceiling in the profession. Consequently they were opposed not only by those resenting the direct financial implications of the measures for incumbents (especially those of poorer benefices), but also by others who claimed to have uncovered a cunning ploy to provoke depreciation in the market value of livings charged with these new burdens and so render them easy targets for purchase by evangelical trusts.[27] Such initiatives were nevertheless welcomed by a growing constituency calling

---

[25] See, e.g., *Thoughts on the Necessity and Means of a Reform in the Church of England* (London, 1792). The whole relationship of anticlericalism to the theme investigated here is a complex one meriting further investigation, as radical anticlerical voices appear to have been far less prominent in *church-reform* debates than commonly supposed. It is important to remember that interventions in the church-reform debate required more than simply a *protest* at the current condition of the church or the burdens it imposed on the poor, but proposals for change. The subject of anticlericalism in this period has been surprisingly little studied since Eric Evans' pioneering work in the 1970s, esp. 'Reasons for the Growth of Anti-Clericalism in England'; Eric Evans, 'The Church in Danger? Anti-Clericalism in Nineteenth-Century England', *European Studies Rev.*, 13 (1983), 201–23. For a starting place for a reassessment, see the essays in Nigel Aston and Matthew Cragoe (eds.), *Anticlericalism in Britain, c. 1500–1914* (Stroud, 2000), esp. G. M. Ditchfield, 'The Changing Nature of English Anticlericalism, c. 1750–c. 1800'; Frances Knight, 'Did Anticlericalism Exist in the English Countryside in the Early Nineteenth Century?'

[26] For the reform initiatives of the 1790s and 1800s, see G. M. Ditchfield, 'Ecclesiastical Legislation during the Ministry of the Younger Pitt', in J. P. Parry and S. Taylor (eds.), *Parliament and the Church, 1529–1960* (Edinburgh, 2000), 64–80.

[27] For this critique, see Lord Ellenborough's speech on the Curate Bill of 1813 in *Parl. Debs.*, 1st ser., xxvi, col. 300 (21 May 1813).

for the elevation of the condition of those who would come to be dubbed 'the working clergy'.[28] And all churchmen welcomed the most spectacular demonstrations of state support for the church in this period: the annual parliamentary subsidies for augmentation of livings initiated in 1809, and the two substantial one-off grants of 1818 and 1824 for the construction of new churches.[29]

Most of these early measures attracted strikingly little opposition in parliament from critics of the church. The mood in both Commons and Lords became less receptive to such initiatives after the upsurge in popular and elite anticlericalism (the latter articulated most effectively in the *Edinburgh Review*) sparked by the role of clergy at Peterloo and the subsequent high-profile stand-off between the cathedral clergy in Durham and local Whigs and radicals following the former's spirited response to local demonstrations against the Manchester magistrates' actions. The half-million grant of 1824 consequently generated more heated debate than the million of 1818.[30]

In the mid- and late 1820s, church reform receded in importance in public ecclesiastical policy-making with the campaigns for Catholic Emancipation and the repeal of the Test and Corporation Acts taking centre stage. These developments certainly created a sense of impending crisis among more conservative churchmen. It was the political turmoil generated by parliamentary reform, however, that had most immediate impact in stimulating intensified debate on church reform and the far-reaching legislation of the 1830s.[31] Tithe agitation provoked by agricultural distress combined with the prominent role of the episcopate in the Lords' rejection of the Reform Bill to render out-of-doors anticlericalism both more bitter and pervasive, and its demands for root-and-branch reform more strident. Churchmen viewed this in the context of a Reform Act that promised a significant accession of strength to the forces of

---

[28] For an early usage, see [Rowland Hill], *Spiritual Characteristics, Represented in an Account of a Most Curious Sale of Curates . . . by an Old Observer* (London, 180[?]), 88. At the end of the eighteenth century Morgan Cove spoke of 'real labourers' and 'drones' in a similar context: Morgan Cove, *An Essay on the Revenues of the Church of England* (London, 1795), 200. This was a marked and telling development from the military terminology adopted by Addison in the *Spectator*, no. 21 (24 Mar. 1711), where the clergy were divided into 'generals, field officers, and subalterns': quoted in Donald A. Spaeth, *The Church in an Age of Danger: Parsons and Parishioners, 1660–1740* (Cambridge, 2000), 31.

[29] For these reforms, see Best, *Temporal Pillars*, 213; M. H. Port, *Six Hundred New Churches: A Study of the Church Building Commission, 1818–56, and its Church Building Activities* (London, 1961).

[30] See *Parl. Debs.*, 1st ser., xxxvii, cols. 1116 ff. (16 Mar.), xxxviii, cols. 426 ff. (30 Apr.), 709 ff. (15 May), 830 ff. (20 May 1818); *ibid.*, 2nd ser., xi, cols. 173 ff. (6 Apr.), 328 ff. (9 Apr.), 384 ff. (12 Apr.), 1080 (3 June), 1093 (4 June), 1431 (17 June 1824). For the Durham stand-off, see Best, *Temporal Pillars*, 245–50; G. C. B. Davies, *Henry Phillpotts, Bishop of Exeter, 1778–1869* (London, 1954), 27–33.

[31] For this phase, see the standard accounts in Brose, *Church and Parliament*; Best, *Temporal Pillars*; Chadwick, *Victorian Church*, supplemented by R. Brent, *Liberal Anglican Politics: Whiggery, Religion, and Reform, 1830–1841* (Oxford, 1987), for the view from the Whig side, and Burns, *Diocesan Revival*, for the view from the dioceses.

dissent and radicalism in a state apparatus already rendered more threatening by the accession of a Whig administration. Concern grew when that administration revealed its appetite for dramatic church reform with the Irish Church Temporalities Bill of 1833, with its provisions for abolishing Irish bishoprics and a clause for appropriation of their revenues for non-denominational education (excised before the bill became law). The early 1830s consequently saw the episcopate itself sponsoring significant if limited reform initiatives, while lower clergy bombarded policy-makers with pamphlets promoting self-styled reform programmes conservative and radical. Both Conservative and Whig administrations then found the church hierarchy willing to cooperate in the most significant church-reform initiative of the nineteenth century, the creation of the Ecclesiastical Commission. This permanent body would oversee the rationalization of the jurisdictional geography of the church, redistribute cathedral revenues to augment the incomes of the parochial clergy and promote a more rational system of episcopal remuneration, sponsor disciplinary reform acts, and assume responsibility for the management of church estates. Although the Erastian overtones of the body implementing this agenda generated serious concern (most famously among the leading figures of the Oxford Movement), many conservatives and churchmen came to collaborate, however reluctantly, in its extensive programme of constructive reform. They saw only too clearly the potential benefits of the removal of the detail of ecclesiastical reform from the parliamentary arena through the agency of the Orders in Council by which the regular business of the commission would be conducted, and also welcomed the demonstration of continued if muted support of the state for church extension and establishment it represented.

II

Having established a framework for the discussion of late Hanoverian church reform, we now turn to the issue of how best to understand the ebbs and flows in debate and action we have just considered.

It is clearly the case that critiques of 'abuses' in the Hanoverian church were central to the discussion of church reform throughout this period. Perhaps in consequence there has been a tendency for ecclesiastical historians to seek to explain its dynamics in terms of the willingness or reluctance of the clergy and leading laymen to confront the painful and sometimes self-denying challenge of tackling such problems, as determined by changes in the theological climate and the consequent concern or disdain of churchmen for pastoral effectiveness. Yet surely the most striking aspect of the chronology of church reform outlined above is its close relationship with that posited in Philip Harling's recent work on the movement for 'economical reform' of the Hanoverian state and 'Old

Corruption'.[32] Here too the 1780s are a key decade, while Pitt again takes credit for a promising initiative in reform that foundered in the difficult waters of the 1790s and on resistance from less reform-minded members of the elite. As in the critique of 'Old Corruption', discussions of church reform in the first decades of the nineteenth century saw increased reference to the demands of a 'public' conjured by politicians and periodicals, while radical critiques had only a limited impact in shaping the reforms then attempted. In both instances the 1830s witnessed spectacular reforms that masked the extent of what had already been achieved.

If we focus more specifically on rhetoric, similar parallels emerge. As in the case of state reform, so in the church the vocabulary of reform was deployed both by those seeking to reduce the power of the institution and those seeking to render it more effective and efficient. In both cases before 1830 most accomplished reforms were enacted in the latter cause, if nevertheless encouraged by increasing pressure to be seen to be responding to 'public opinion'.

There are further similarities if we turn to more critical articulations of 'church reform'. Bishop Watson's letter of 1783, earlier identified as effectively establishing the vocabulary of 'church reform' as the prevailing mode of addressing deficiencies in the ecclesiastical system, is strikingly proximate to a key juncture in the wider history of the rhetoric of 'reform' which Joanna Innes has identified in her own contribution to this volume: the adoption of the term in the Association movement.[33] This is no coincidence. Watson himself had a track record as an outspoken latitudinarian frequently suspected of unitarian tendencies, a correspondent of Rockingham, and a preacher who in 1780 had denounced the American War and endorsed the economical reform campaign, for which he acted as an agent in Cambridge.[34] His letter had originated in 1782 as part of a plan forwarded to the second earl of Shelburne, who wished Watson to be his ecclesiastical Dunning (the Shelburnite lawyer responsible for the eponymous motion of 1780 that 'the influence of the crown has increased, is increasing, and ought to be diminished'). Shelburne lacking both the nerve and the parliamentary strength to pursue the scheme, Watson had thrown caution to the wind and presented it to the public. While Watson expounded the pastoral benefits to be expected from episcopal equalization, his main interest was in securing the financial means for all bishops to cease to be instruments of crown influence in the House of Lords.[35] His fiercest critics, consequently, were not

---

[32] See Harling, *Waning of 'Old Corruption'*.   [33] See pp. 71, 85.

[34] For this and what follows, see Brain, 'Richard Watson', *passim*, esp. ch. entitled 'Church Reform'. See also Watson's own remarkable memoir, R. Watson, *Anecdotes of the Life of Richard Watson, Bishop of Landaff: Written by Himself at Different Intervals, and Revised in 1814* (London, 1817), esp. 95 for the analogy with Dunning.

[35] As Brain notes, his plan was thus 'the ecclesiastical equivalent of the political movement for "economical reform"': Brain, 'Richard Watson', 161.

clergy nervous for their prebends, but those who wished 'to God it was as truly, as your Lordship says it is frequently, urged against your order that you support the influence of the crown'.[36]

It should be noted in this regard that church historians have undoubtedly neglected the extent to which many church reforms promising pastoral advantages were simultaneously open to advocacy as attacks on illegitimate political influence or corruption. The church's place in the nexus of 'Old Corruption' was always the most effective stimulus to extra-parliamentary support for church reform, as the importance of Peterloo and the Reform Bill in the chronology above indicates. All discussion of reform of the episcopate was coloured by this concern: not just proposals for the exclusion of bishops from the Lords, but equally the response to initiatives intended to assist bishops in raising clerical standards. One might anticipate that the radical Francis Burdett would have welcomed new restrictions on the abuse of clerical non-residence proposed in 1803, for example: but in fact he worried that as this involved giving bishops more power to regulate it, the measure had the potential merely to make it easier for these ministerial creatures to mobilize their clergy as an electoral interest.[37] Twenty years later, John Wade saw the statistical anatomy of 'Old Corruption' in the church he presented in the *Black Book* as exposing the deployment of church patronage for sinister purposes – as in the preferment bestowed on one of the clerical magistrates involved in Peterloo, proof that 'the Revenues of the Church reward the tools of the Borough System'.[38] Cartoonists, too, frequently portrayed church reforms as a direct equivalent of the assault on the state aspect of 'Old Corruption' (see plate 1).

Wade's often highly misleading analysis of the distribution of church wealth was only the most famous of numerous audits to which the church was subjected by both friend and foe from the 1790s onwards, and leads to another point of similarity with the discourse of state reform.[39] For many beside Wade such statistical accounts served the purpose of identifying waste and extravagance at the public expense, and the church of the 1820s joined the state in finding its most persistent parliamentary auditor in the independent radical Joseph Hume.[40]

---

[36] *Letter to . . . the Lord Bishop of Landaff . . . by a Country Curate*, 15.

[37] W. Cobbett (ed.), *Parliamentary History*, 36 vols. (London, 1806–20), xxxvi, col. 1516 (26 May 1803).

[38] John Wade, *The Extraordinary Black Book* (London, 1831; repr. Shannon, 1971); [John Wade], *Manchester Massacre!! An Authentic Narrative of the Magisterial and Yeomanry Massacre at Manchester . . . by the Editor of 'the Black Book'* (London, 182[?]), 48, referring to the preferment of W. R. Hay – whom Wade dubbed a 'clerical ruffian' (33) – to the vicarage of Rochdale by Archbishop Manners Sutton of Canterbury in 1820.

[39] For the most important 'friendly' analyses, see Cove, *Essay on the Revenues of the Church of England*; R. Yates, *The Church in Danger: A Statement of the Cause, and of the Probable Means of Averting that Danger* (London, 1815).

[40] See, e.g., his contribution to the debate on the church-building grant of 1824, *Parl. Debs.*, 2nd ser., xi, cols. 384–5 (12 Apr. 1824).

Plate 1. 'No Reform. No Reform'. Cartoon by I. Cruikshank, April 1795. (British Museum, Collection of Personal and Political Satires, Cat. no. BMC 8635. Reproduced by permission of the trustees of the British Museum.)

With church endowments treated as a state trust for the delivery of a moral population, the call for economy in times of economic hardship became a central feature of the church-reform debate. Hume and others demanded the redistribution of church resources in preference to further public expenditure on the established church. As with the state, the increased flow of official and unofficial statistical information necessary as a precondition of much effective constructive reform added fuel to the critique, not least when placed in juxtaposition to figures ostensibly revealing the cost of maintaining morality through public support for religion in other European states. Thus *Remarks on the Consumption of Public Wealth by the Clergy of every Christian Nation* (1822) calculated that whereas post-revolutionary France got its religion for £35,000 per million inhabitants, securing clergy for its population at a ratio of 1:1,150, the Church of England cost £3.25 million per million, providing clergy at the ludicrously lavish rate of 1:333, the contrast being underlined by the fact that the French received a better ratio of church accommodation. Even priest-ridden Italy spent only £40,000 per million, while closer to home Scotland was a model of economy.[41] In fact the church's internal economy could also be treated as a microcosm of the contemporary relation of state and society, with the 'working clergy' standing proxy for the middle classes in terms of their imputed virtue and exploitation.[42]

Finally, just as parliamentary reforms of the church enacted in the 1830s mirrored other contemporary legislative reforms, involving royal commissions and bureaucratic structures created at a national level to overcome localist obstruction of effective reform, so they shared the prevailing 'utilitarian' rhetoric in their justification. The utility of the established church as a guarantor of social hierarchy and a prophylactic against unrest was a prominent theme of both lay and clerical proposals for church reform from the 1790s, just as similar considerations were advanced in calls for penal and poor-law reform. In the debates of the 1830s the leading clerical champion of the Ecclesiastical Commission, Charles James Blomfield (significantly also a prominent member of the poor-law commission), went so far as to celebrate the 'true beauty of the Church' as lying in 'the beauty of its holy usefulness'.[43]

While acknowledging the importance of utilitarian language, however, we should also note a very different but equally important rhetoric, and here we can begin to establish some distinctive aspects of the discourse of church reform. In the locally implemented diocesan revival, reform was primarily legitimated in terms of ecclesiology and an explicitly antiquarian appeal to history.[44] Thus the restoration of the office of rural dean, perhaps the single most effective and efficient diocesan reform, was most effectively publicized in a floridly gothic volume hailed by one reviewer as 'redolent of good old times' entitled *Horae decanicae rurales*, and justified in the following terms:

> in proportion as we search out the practices of our forefathers . . . as we stand in the old ways marked out for our guidance, and submit to those ecclesiastical

---

[41] *Remarks on the Consumption of Public Wealth by the Clergy of Every Christian Nation, and Particularly by the Established Church in England, Wales and Ireland: With a Plan for Altering its Revenues Subject to Existing Interests* (London, 1822), *passim*. A manuscript note on the British Library copy of this volume identifies it as the work of 'Mr Moon of Liverpool . . . a Catholic and a Bentham'.

[42] See, e.g., *A Letter to the King on the Unjust Distribution of Church Property: By a Country Curate* (London, 1831); *Safe and Easy Steps towards an Efficient Church Reform: One More Efficient than that of Lord Henley: By a Clergyman of the Church of England* (London, 1832), 23–33.

[43] Charles James Blomfield (1786–1857), bishop of Chester 1824–8, bishop of London 1828–57. For the quotation, see C. J. Blomfield, *A Charge delivered to the Clergy of the Diocese of London* (London, 1834), 17.

[44] For a fuller discussion of what follows, see R. A. Burns, '"Standing in the Old Ways": Historical Legitimation of Church Reform in the Church of England, *c.* 1825–65', in R. N. Swanson (ed.), *The Church Retrospective* (Studies in Church Hist., xxxiii, Woodbridge, 1997), 407–22; Burns, *Diocesan Revival*, 271–5.

rules of government from which our reformers never meant we should depart, we shall find ourselves, under God, compact and strengthened.[45]

The ecclesiastical history to which diocesan reform appealed for legitimacy exhibited a respect for the heritage of the Church of England, before, during, and after the Henrician Reformation, and a discriminating interest in the early church; it also emphasized the value of establishment without exhibiting the Erastian tendencies of utilitarianism. This version of the church's past was sufficiently irenic and inclusive to resonate with churchmen of all Anglican traditions as members of a historic belief community at either the local or national level. Moreover reference to the past though ubiquitous was never slavish, diocesan reformers not fighting shy of the word 'reform' and regularly deploying utilitarian arguments alongside their historical references, explicitly setting 'efficiency' as a central objective of their schemes.

Historical legitimation here underpinned church reforms that for all their apparently archaic rhetoric could be judged effective in utilitarian terms, and this rhetoric was integral to its success. This deserves further comment in the context of nineteenth-century institutional reform projects considered more generally. Perhaps the best-known secular reform initiative legitimated in similar antiquarian terms was the much less successful project of the eccentric radical champion of secular parochial self-government in the 1840s and 1850s, Joshua Toulmin Smith.[46] So why was such rhetoric effective in efficient church reform, but not apparently elsewhere?

One consideration is the audience for the rhetoric. 'Utilitarian' rhetoric spoke eloquently to parliamentary or public audiences including many at best indifferent to the church. It was less suited to rallying the voluntary cooperation of the clergy on whom diocesan reforms depended. In contrast, antiquarian and localist rhetoric mobilized in support of reform sentiments and allegiances which when viewed from a national perspective usually appeared as *obstacles* to effective reform.

Although historical legitimation was not as prominent in national church-reform debates, it was still more commonplace than in contemporary elite discussion of state reform. To explain this one might note that the legitimatory authority of history received additional reinforcement in the case of church reform from the centrality of the historic church to both theology and ecclesiology. In the English church in particular the absence of significant jurisdictional or economic reform since the Reformation gave history resonance in that its

---

[45] W. Dansey, *A Letter to the Archdeacon of Sarum, on Ruridecanal Chapters* (London, 1840), 44. For the review of W. Dansey, *Horae decanicae rurales*, 2 vols. (London, 1835), see *Brit. Critic*, 19 (1836), 274.

[46] For Toulmin Smith, see W. H. Greenleaf, 'Toulmin Smith and the British Political Tradition', *Public Administration*, 55 (1975), 25–44.

institutional structure exhibited remarkable continuity.[47] Moreover, this was equally true of many 'abuses' – most obviously clerical poverty, pluralism, and non-residence – and of the pastoral objectives of the clergy, which Jeremy Gregory has explored as the 'long Reformation' project.[48] As a direct consequence there was therefore a storehouse of unrealized schemes addressing precisely the issues which church reformers now wished to tackle, from the *Reformatio legum ecclesiasticarum* of 1553 through to the proposals of Francis Bacon, Gilbert Burnet, Edmund Gibson, and Thomas Secker, many of which were being contemporaneously recovered and edited by antiquarian scholars.[49] The arguments of church reformers were liberally laced with references to these historic precedents, perhaps most notably the *Reformatio*. The extent to which even quite major alterations – given the Dissolution of the Monasteries, even appropriation – could be related to both achieved reforms and unfulfilled agendas such as the *Reformatio* helped maintain a defensible distinction between 'reform' and 'innovation' useful in mobilizing the middle ground of church opinion. Indeed one reason why certain aspects of church activity that might have been anticipated to have formed part of the subject matter of church reform, such as the development of voluntary agencies for promoting mission or schooling, did so only occasionally, may have been the absence of direct historical precedent. Finally, we also need to note the particular resonance of the terms 'reformation' and 'reform' in the English ecclesiastical context, which needs to be examined in more detail.

III

Within the ecclesiastical sphere the terms 'reform' and 'reformation' had intense historical resonances. This may help explain why many ostensibly 'conservative' churchmen appear to have felt reasonably comfortable with the term in the ecclesiastical sphere when so many like-minded contemporaries refused to adopt it for their secular projects.

Even when clearly and immediately imported from the economical reform tradition, for example, the terms possessed a rich ambiguity. Those assuming the character of reformers, or so characterized by opponents, could exploit this by identifying themselves with the protestant reformers of the sixteenth century rather than contemporary radicals. Thus in his 1783 letter, while acknowledging that he would now be labelled a 'reformer', even Richard Watson observed that:

---

[47] A point also made by R. J. Smith, *The Gothic Bequest: Medieval Institutions in British Thought, 1688–1863* (Cambridge, 1987), 173.

[48] Gregory, 'Making of a Protestant Nation'.

[49] Dansey's *Horae decanicae rurales*, with its comprehensive appendices of reform proposals and precedents, both national and local, is a good example of this. For the *Reformatio*, see the modern edition edited by G. Bray in *Tudor Church Reform: The Henrician Canons of 1535 and the Reformatio legum ecclesiasticarum*, ed. Gerald Bray (Church of England Record Soc., viii, Woodbridge, 2000).

I know it is commonly said that wise and good men look upon every attempt to reform what is amiss, either in Church or State, as a matter of dangerous tendency; but it may be justly doubted, whether there is not as much timidity as wisdom, as much indolence as goodness in this caution; certain I am, that if *Luther* and the Reformers had been men of such dispositions, the Church of Christ would never have been purged in any degree, by them at least, of its Antichristian corruptions.[50]

Before 1833 the Reformation was not a contentious issue among English churchmen, and this almost certainly allowed them to feel more comfortable in adopting the rhetoric of 'reform' on church issues. If this was so, one would predict that as doubts set in about the Reformation, they would be accompanied by greater misgivings about the term 'reform'. After 1830, this was indeed the case with the Tractarians, who disowned the lexicon of reform on account of its association with liberalism and protestantism. Thus John Henry Newman's 1835 pamphlet on *The Restoration of Suffragan Bishops Recommended*, a pragmatic response to urban pastoral challenges, painstakingly eschewed the term 'reform'. Newman lamented the 'misfortune of the Established Church during the last several years, when, in common with our other institutions, its framework and actual operations have been freely discussed, that the plans recommended for the increase of its efficiency have taken the shape of reforms, and not of restorations of its ancient system'.[51]

The ecclesiastical resonances of 'reform' obviously buttressed the historical legitimations already considered. But its theological/ecclesiological aspect gave it added value, for where historical precedent was not available, it was in consequence still possible to present certain innovations in the legitimizing context of the 'unfinished' Reformation, or a 'Second Reformation', a tactic most characteristic of those making more ambitious proposals.[52]

This theological dimension also ensured that 'reform' projects almost unavoidably acquired a 'protestant' resonance, perhaps one particularly acute in the 1820s, when the inauguration of the 'New Reformation' crusade in Ireland, which at least until the later 1820s appeared to its most optimistic adherents to offer real hope of a mass conversion of the Roman Catholic masses, offered a forceful reinforcement of this association.[53] This did not at any point make the church-reform project an evangelical or dissenting preserve. But it did make it more difficult for committed high churchmen to establish a public

[50] Watson, *Letter to the Archbishop of Canterbury*, 7.
[51] J. H. Newman, *The Restoration of Suffragan Bishops Recommended, as a Means of Effecting a More Equal Distribution of Episcopal Duties* (London, 1835), 1.
[52] For the 'second' Reformation, see, e.g., T. Sims, *A Model of Non-Secular Episcopacy: Including Reasons for the Establishment of Ninety-Four Bishopricks in England and Wales* (London, 1832), 5.
[53] For the 'New Reformation', see the excellent summary account in Stewart J. Brown, *The National Churches of England, Ireland, and Scotland, 1801–1846* (Oxford, 2001), ch. 2, which also sets it in a broader United Kingdom context.

reputation as a 'reformer' even if they actively pursued constructive reform objectives and employed the vocabulary of reform in writings and speeches.[54] It was almost impossible if 'secular' political commitments aligned them against other 'reform' projects. Thus the orthodox high-church bishop of Exeter, Henry Phillpotts, whom Jonathan Clark singled out as the ultra boy on the burning deck of the 'ancien régime', was unquestionably an opponent of 'reform' in his 'secular' politics.[55] He nevertheless merited though never acquired a reputation as a '*church* reformer' as a committed advocate of the stricter regulation of clerical activity who favoured Sir Robert Peel with an extended wish-list of desirable reforms on the latter's appointment as prime minister in 1835.[56] Ironically perhaps the most important example of resistance to constitutional reforms fixing the reputation of high-church opponents as 'reactionaries', regardless of their ecclesiastical policy, was their fierce opposition to an important religious reform falling outside the customary usage of 'church reform': Catholic Emancipation. It was thus paradoxically when at their most 'protestant' that some high churchmen effectively excluded themselves from public recognition as reformers.[57]

The protestant resonances of 'reform' had a further consequence. The persistence both within the established church and in the traditions of 'rational' dissent of 'liberal' versions of protestantism alongside more evangelical varieties helped ensure that, however much 'economical reform' or utilitarian understandings of the term 'reform' came to predominate, it was always possible for those seeking to liberalize the Church of England to try to reappropriate 'church reform' rhetoric – and through this exploit the gathering momentum of a quite different project – for this purpose. A small but steady trickle of interventions in the public discussion of church reform attempted this from the 1780s onwards. Nor was this theological appropriation confined to the liberalizer. We noted earlier that by the early 1830s some high-church Anglicans – especially the future leaders of the Oxford Movement – rejected the lexicon of 'reform' as indelibly associated with the political threat posed by theological liberalizing epitomized for Keble and Newman by the liberal Anglican tradition in Whiggery. For some, moreover, it appeared that the distinction between 'liberal' (or as they would sometimes denote it 'Germanizing') and 'protestant/evangelical'

---

[54] Particularly if they also turned to historical or ecclesiological precedents other than the Reformation to legitimate their initiatives.

[55] Phillpotts signed more protests against successful bills in the House of Lords than all but two of its other nineteenth-century members: R. A. Soloway, *Prelates and People: Ecclesiastical Social Thought in England, 1783–1852* (London, 1969), 253.

[56] For Phillpotts (1778–1869), bishop of Exeter (1831–69), see Burns, *Diocesan Revival*, 138–43, 168–73, 223–33; J. R. Wolffe, 'Bishop Henry Phillpotts and the Administration of the Diocese of Exeter', *Report and Trans. Devonshire Assoc.*, 94 (1982), 99–113; Davies, *Henry Phillpotts*. For the proposed reforms, see Brit. Lib., Add. MS 40,410, fos. 75–80.

[57] I owe the full refinement of this point to a discussion with Mark Smith.

theology was being exposed as more apparent than real.[58] The positive initial response to the Oxford agitation of many among those the Tractarians despised as 'low' churchmen demonstrated that 'protestant' Anglicans were actually often as suspicious as the high churchmen of the latitudinarian tendencies of the political elite, and a key ingredient in the Conservative revival from the later 1830s would be evangelical 'protestant' agitation.[59] The conspiracy theorizing apparent in Newman's circles may nevertheless have been encouraged by the fact that whereas formerly 'theological' church-reform proposals had emanated from those seeking a more latitudinarian church, as evangelical Anglicans gained in confidence by the 1830s they too came forward with 'reform' proposals intended to shift their church's centre of gravity in a differently understood protestant direction by adaptations to its polity, liturgy, and articles, which, like some liberals, they thought tainted with popery.[60]

Those fearing such developments might have taken some consolation from the fact that the ecclesiastical resonances of 'reform/reformation' at the same time encouraged the development of a distinction between 'church reform' and more radical assaults on the church by limiting the range of possible meanings available for church 'reform'. In a profoundly protestant culture, they also presented problems for prospective reformers such as William Cobbett who came to disapprove of the Reformation itself. John Wade offered an obvious play on words in his *Extraordinary Black Book* in noting that 'though the Church of England is ostentatiously styled the *Reformed* Church, it is, in truth, the most *unreformed* of all the churches'. But for all its deficiencies, Wade went on to insist that the inadequate English Reformation had nevertheless been 'a great blessing', without which the English people would have been left in as miserable a condition as those of Spain. He consequently explicitly distanced himself from Cobbett's 'moon-struck' adoration of cathedrals and monastic wealth, which in Wade's eyes disqualified him from serious consideration as a reformer.[61]

---

[58] See Nockles, *Oxford Movement in Context*, esp. ch. 1; S. Thomas, *Newman and Heresy: The Anglican Years* (Cambridge, 1991); for a new and controversial reading of the relationship, see Frank M. Turner, *John Henry Newman: The Challenge to Evangelical Religion* (New Haven and London, 2002); Brent, *Liberal Anglican Politics.*

[59] See Nockles, *Oxford Movement in Context*, 321; J. R. Wolffe, *The Protestant Crusade in Great Britain, 1829–1860* (Oxford, 1991).

[60] See, e.g., from the earlier period, Richard Watson, *Considerations on the Expediency of Revising the Liturgy and the Articles of the Church of England* (London, 1790); William Knox, *Observations upon the Liturgy: With a Proposal for its Reform, upon the Principles of Christianity* (London, 1789); from the 1830s, *Church Reform by a Church Radical, Comprising a Review of the Thirty-Nine Articles* (London, 1835); *A Letter on Church Reform, with Reference to the Policy of Our Times* (London, 1836).

[61] See Wade, *Extraordinary Black Book*, 5, 13–14.

IV

By way of conclusion, this last point about the constraints associated with the adoption of the language of reform in an ecclesiastical context will be examined a little further in some necessarily brief and exploratory reflections on the state of the debate on church reform around 1840. These are also intended to suggest the explanatory potential of a closer attention to issues of linguistic practice along the lines advocated in the preceding sections.

The parliamentary debates over the appropriation of cathedral revenues and the creation of a church bureaucracy proposed in the Ecclesiastical Duties and Revenues Bill of 1840 reveal a perception that the 'pressure from without' for extensive church reform was waning. As Henry Galley Knight, Conservative MP, ecclesiological writer, and friend of the church argued in urging the measure: 'The cry which had been raised against the church, a short time ago, had only the effect of shewing the number of her friends . . . She was now in a situation to reflect with composure and concede with dignity.'[62] No doubt, as Peel observed at the time, this development reflected the fact that the church had visibly cooperated in reform in a manner not hitherto witnessed in parliament, and that the boil of the tithe issue had been at least partially lanced in the Tithe Commutation Act of 1836.[63] By the end of 1840, significant legislative, diocesan, and voluntary initiatives had at least made a start on addressing several of the key issues identified as demanding action in the reform debates: pluralities, non-residence, sinecures, disparities in clerical incomes. None the less, far-reaching though they were, the impact of these reforms scarcely answered the demands characteristic of the peak of vociferous and hostile calls for church reform from radicals and dissenters in particular a decade before.[64] Can the themes pursued in this essay throw any further light on the explanation for the fact that the demand for 'reform' nevertheless ebbed?

Here it is obviously particularly important to consider the linguistic practices of the church's radical and dissenting critics, but one might begin by examining comments from advocates of reform from within the Anglican fold. In the febrile atmosphere of the early 1830s, reacting to criticism that they represented a dissenting fifth column, radical Anglican church reformers began forcefully to insist that their project should not be confused with a full-frontal assault on the establishment principle. One might cite the instance of Thomas Arnold, whose liberal Anglican vision of a more comprehensive national church, the buildings of which would be shared by a series of congregations committed to

---

[62] *Parl. Debs.*, 3rd ser., liii, col. 602 (6 Apr. 1840).

[63] *Ibid.*, 3rd ser., liii, col. 603 (6 Apr. 1840).

[64] One might in passing note here something of a contrast with Philip Harling's account of the contours of the discussion of 'Old Corruption', in which the 1830s witnessed a failure to acknowledge the extent to which its destruction had already been initiated. See Harling, *Waning of 'Old Corruption'*, 138–9.

different varieties of orthodox Christianity, scandalized fellow Anglicans when presented in his *Principles of Church Reform* of 1833. In this work, Arnold took great pains to define his terms:

> Church Reform being a very vague term, it is of great consequence to know what they, who use it, mean by it. It is impossible that a man can care, properly speaking, about the reform of any institution, if the objects of the institution are of no interest to him . . . If then a man, without being a Dissenter, is one who seldom or never goes to Church and appears to have very little value for Christianity personally . . . [and] who neither value[s] the social nor the religious benefits conferred by an establishment, [he] cannot rightly be said to desire its reform; [he] merely wish[es] to see it destroyed; and destruction is so very different from reform, that it is a gross fraud to call ourselves friends of the one, when what we really desire is the other . . . The avowed Dissenters join also in the call for Church Reform; and they again use the term with singular impropriety. They can hardly care about the reform of an institution from which they have altogether separated themselves. They belong, in fact, either to the class of Church Destroyers or of Self-seekers: to the former, if being convinced that an establishment is an evil, they wish to see it altogether put down: to the latter, if their object be simply to be relieved from Church rates, Easter dues and tithes, because they support a ministry of their own. But I have heard as yet no language from the Dissenters which could entitle them justly to the name of Church Reformers.[65]

A similar point was made in the doggerel of the 'poor curate' responsible for *Modern Church Reform* in 1834:

> . . . 'may not I,
> Dissenter though I be, still fairly try
> To mend what in your Church to me seems wrong
> Though to that Church I wish not to belong?'
> 'Good friend, your proffer'd interference kind
> Recalls another like event to mind;
> When godless France across the Channel sent
> To Albion's shore agents of discontent.'[66]

If we turn to the rhetoric of radical and in particular dissenting critics of the church during the later 1830s and 1840s, it does in fact appear that they became less inclined to construct their attacks using the lexicon of church reform. Of

---

[65] T. Arnold, *Principles of Church Reform*, ed. M. J. Jackson and J. Rogan (London, 1962), 89, 90–1. For other attempts to draw this distinction, see the evangelical C. Cator's *'The Writings of a Man's Hand' to the Reformed British Parliament* (London, 1833), 4; E. Burton, *Thoughts upon the Demand for Church Reform* (London, 1831).

[66] *Modern Church Reform: A Poem* (London, 1834), 9.

course this was not because Arnold's strictures had hit home. But the development none the less may have reflected the increasing salience of the distinction Arnold was insisting upon. His claim that dissenters could not call for reform of an institution that they wished to see destroyed was more apposite for some sections of the dissenting community than others. It was perhaps least effective with reference to at least some representatives of the Unitarian tradition which had provided the political leadership of the dissenting cause in the late eighteenth and early nineteenth centuries. Such dissenters had observed with interest the progress of the Feathers Tavern petition in the 1770s, hoping for the doctrinal and ecclesiological redefinition of the state church in ways that would allow reunion. Even in the 1830s Unitarians like the anticlerical radical Wade, however hostile in his *Extraordinary Black Book* to the establishment as it was, still voiced a lingering aspiration for it to be remodelled following their own prescriptions. In other cases this may simply have been a rhetorical device to gain admittance to the church-reform debate for those whose normal mode of expression might have denied them such access. Certainly, this seems the most likely explanation for the fact that in 1835 the radical Richard Carlile, writing from his prison cell, presented church-reform proposals to Peel and 'his diocesan' Blomfield designed to rid the nation of 'the Theatre of the drama of the Books of Common Prayer, The Thirty-Nine Articles and the Old and New Testament', Carlile solemnly but unconvincingly informing Peel that 'my lamp has been constantly trimmed for your advent as a Reformer in the Church'.[67] In Wade's case, however, his positive valuation of the Reformation and the space devoted to the liturgy in the *Extraordinary Black Book* were elements in an overall approach founded on the belief that 'Sensible men of all ages have treated with respect the established worship of the people.' As he later insisted: 'We have no dislike to the Church, but we hate its oppressiveness on the honest and industrious . . . Will government timely interfere and afford the Church a chance of prolonged duration [?].'[68]

By the late 1830s, in contrast, despite Thomas Chalmers' influential restatement of the pastoral case for establishment,[69] the apparent success of the voluntarist strategy in outperforming the state church in evangelization and church growth encouraged many evangelical dissenters to see the institutional apparatus of the state church as at best an irrelevance and at worst an obstacle to evangelical mission. For such individuals the apparent superiority of the voluntary model made them less interested than their predecessors in adapting

---

[67] R. Carlile, *Church Reform: The Only Means to that End* (London, 1835), 8, 26. Carlile, however, undermined his rhetorical pose by stating that as things stood it was better to be a 'destructive' than a conservative or reformer: *ibid.*, 53.

[68] Wade, *Extraordinary Black Book*, 2, 80.

[69] T. Chalmers, *Lectures on the Establishment and Extension of National Churches* (Glasgow, 1838).

an establishment to make it more congenial, more interested in challenging it directly. In the later 1830s, as the political leadership of dissent was assumed by a new generation headed by Baptists and Congregationalists, religious liberty and equality within a pluralist state thus became much more central to dissenting political activity.[70] During the mid-nineteenth century, the focus of dissenting politics oscillated.[71] At times the priority was an all-out assault on the existence of a state church epitomized in the Anti-State Church Association which became the Liberation Society; at others a pragmatic focus on those aspects of church privilege or financing which had direct impacts on the lives of dissenters was preferred, the most enduring such demand being the abolition of church rates. Despite Arnold's designation of the latter as essentially 'self-seeking', even to other Anglicans it could be construed as a church-reform project. The former, however, could not. The conflict of 'church and chapel' was consequently *not* conceptualized as a church-reform project, and generated a separate debate with its own dynamics and protocols. We might note in passing that this in one respect marked a further distinction between the dynamics of the church-reform debate and those of the discussion of the other elements of 'Old Corruption' to add to those already noted above. Whereas critics of the state or law could not evade the need to alter the existing institutions and so were restricted to a 'reform project', this was not the case with the church's critics.

Meanwhile, within the church, discussion increasingly concerned *means* to reform rather than the *principle* of reform itself, and the conclusions reached led to a diminishing interest in the consideration of the kind of institutional reforms which had predominated in the debate before 1840. This development was fostered by increased sensitivity to ecclesiological concerns in commission-led reforms after this date, and what was in some respects the transformation of the church itself into a reform movement at least at the diocesan level.[72] The creation of an accurate statistical account of the church by the mid-1830s not only drew the sting from the exaggerated tabulated critiques of the 1820s but also provided a measure against which Victorian churchmen could measure progress. It is striking, however, that while these provided the benchmark, the institutional reforms for which they had been assembled, and the structural reorganization which they had assisted, did not form the focus of most contemporary assessments of the changing fortunes of the church.

It was not that there was no sense of change: indeed it is striking just how quickly a sense of discontinuity from the Hanoverian church arose. But this

---

[70] See T. Larsen, *Friends of Religious Equality: Nonconformist Politics in Mid-Victorian England* (Woodbridge, 1999).

[71] See J. P. Ellens, *Religious Routes to Gladstonian Liberalism: The Church Rate Conflict in England and Wales, 1832–1868* (University Park, Pa., 1994).

[72] For these developments, see Burns, *Diocesan Revival*, 62–5, ch. 6, 192–215.

discontinuity was not characterized by contemporaries in terms of institutional differentiation. Rather it was attributed by men of all parties to an internal and theologically driven accession of zeal that found expression in the transformation of clerical performance. Much of this is today discussed in historical terms as a process of professionalization and occupational differentiation.[73] But contemporaries saw it, even if ironically, in more moralistic terms. A poignant and bitter assessment was delivered in the sexagenarian (and in his own way still reformist) Sydney Smith's lament to William Gladstone in 1835 that 'whenever you meet a clergyman of my age you may be quite sure that he is a bad clergyman'.[74]

And here perhaps lie the origins of a final irony. A transformation from the (bad) Hanoverian to the (good) Victorian church driven by the impact of an internalized moral reorientation as denoted in the concept of an access of 'zeal' recalls the use of the term 'reformation' in contexts such as the 'reformation of manners' before the Association movement on the one hand, and Richard Watson in his *Letter to the Archbishop* of 1783 on the other, took it in the direction which came to dominate in the early nineteenth-century tradition of institutional reform. These new usages of 'reform' and 'reformation' which had developed not least in the ecclesiastical context during the late eighteenth and early nineteenth centuries had by 1840 made it difficult to articulate such moral transformation as clergy believed their generation to have experienced in the language of reform. Instead, as they tried to explain how the church had moved from Hanoverian horror to Victorian virtue, 'zeal' rather than 'reforming' inclination was their focus. In this context one favoured illustration of the eighteenth-century laxity that Victorian churchmen believed themselves to have left behind became the example of a superannuated and heterodox prelate, who had held no fewer than sixteen livings in plurality with his see. Recent studies have qualified Victorian verdicts on the bishop's diocesan administration, but as recently as the 1960s it was possible for a historian to congratulate the Victorians for having put an end to 'the bad old days' of Richard Watson,[75] despite the fact that, as we have seen, he was the first dignitary of the Church of England ever to voice a demand for a significant overhaul of the apparatus of the establishment employing the language of 'church reform'.

---

[73] From a large literature, see, e.g., B. Heeney, *A Different Kind of Gentleman: Parish Clergy as Professional Men in Early and Mid-Victorian England* (Hamden, Conn., 1976); A. Haig, *The Victorian Clergy* (London, 1984); A. Russell, *The Clerical Profession* (London, 1980); P. Corfield, *Power and the Professions in Britain, 1700–1850* (London, 1995).

[74] W. E. Gladstone, *Gleanings*, 7 vols. (London, 1879), vii, 220.

[75] Bowen, *Idea of the Victorian Church*, 28.

6. *Medicine in the age of reform**

IAN A. BURNEY

One week following the royal assent to the 1832 Reform Act, an editorial in the medical journal the *Lancet* remarked: 'The abuses under which we groan in all the departments of our profession have but *one* source, and that is, *misgovernment*. Hence to this one point, and to this one point only, should the whole of our remedial exertions be directed.'[1] The *Lancet*'s identification of 'misgovernance' as its prime target is indicative of a fundamental assumption shared by reformers in medicine and politics – that is, their diagnosis of the ills of society as essentially political in nature. Given the characteristics of this particular crusading journal, its focus on governance should come as no surprise. Founded in 1823 by the surgeon Thomas Wakley, the *Lancet* stood at the centre of a sustained and vitriolic campaign for wholesale medical reform, a campaign in which medicine and politics blended insensibly into one another. Wakley's own activities and associations embodied this very conflation: a regular participant and chair of National Political Union meetings in the 1820s and 1830s, an intimate of William Cobbett, Henry Hunt, and Joseph Hume, editor of the short-lived *Ballot* newspaper (1830) dedicated to the cause of radical political reform, and from 1834 MP for the newly created borough of Finsbury, Wakley was deeply engaged in metropolitan radicalism.[2]

This political engagement is fully evident in both the tone and substance of Wakley's medical journalism. In the pages of the *Lancet*, medical bodies like the Royal Colleges and the great metropolitan voluntary hospitals were castigated as 'rotten corporations' teeming with 'boroughmongers', 'placemen', and

---

* For helpful comments on earlier drafts of this chapter, I thank Phil Harling, Chris Lawrence, John Pickstone, and James Vernon.
[1] 'Address to the Medical Profession on the Influence They Will Possess in the New Parliament', *Lancet*, 1 (1831–2), 339.
[2] S. Squire Sprigge, *The Life and Times of Thomas Wakley* (London, 1889), is a comprehensive though anecdotal biography. For thematic discussions relevant to this essay, see Adrian Desmond, *The Politics of Evolution: Morphology, Medicine, and Reform in Radical London* (Chicago and London, 1989); Ian A. Burney, *Bodies of Evidence: Medicine and the Politics of the English Inquest, 1830–1926* (Baltimore, 2000).

'self-electing corruptionists' intent on sacrificing to a perverse status quo the legitimate interests of an emergent, useful, but as yet disenfranchised group – surgeon-apothecaries, or, as they were coming to be called, general practitioners. These were only the most obvious instances of an extended and often obscured network of corruption. Exposing this network entailed instruction in a totalizing critique of the British medical world, one that required the broadest of canvasses to represent adequately: 'In our discursive wanderings through the wilds of medical politics', Wakley advised his readership, 'we are often compelled to associate our observations on the abuses which arise on every side, with topics which, at first sight, may appear to have little or no connection with the subjects of our remarks, and seem foreign to the duties of medical journalists.'[3] Thus, like the journalism exemplified in its political mirror, Cobbett's *Political Register*, the *Lancet* unfolded a world of interlocking and self-reinforcing 'misgovernance' which stood as the principal impediment to a wholesome reconstitution of British society.[4]

Casting medical reform within explicitly political terms was by no means peculiar to Wakley and his journal. It also informed the responses of orthodox 'ultras' who regarded with apocalyptic foreboding the threat of medical 'destructives' and 'levellers', and that of reforming 'moderates' who sought to eliminate the worst features of corruption in order to preserve the system as a whole. In its content and form, then, there is much in the 'wilds of medical politics' that should be immediately recognizable to the student of politics in the 'age of reform'. Medical historians, too, have been alive to the political nature of medicine in this period, which has been traditionally viewed as a peculiarly vitriolic episode in the making of the British medical profession.[5] In these analyses the politicized rhetoric adopted by a wide range of medical commentators is often noted as an outgrowth of the professionalizing debates. This is to be expected, of course, since professionalizing reform is in important respects an explicitly political project: defining the boundaries of 'legitimate' knowledge and practice entails the exercise of power, and results in institutional and intellectual frameworks of governance that validate some and marginalize others.

---

[3] 'Representation of Medical Men in Parliament', *Lancet*, 1 (1829–30), 748.

[4] On Wakley's journalistic links to Cobbett, see, in addition to Sprigge, *Life and Times*, Betty Bostetter, 'Thomas Wakley: Radical Journalist', in Joel Wiener (ed.), *Innovators and Preachers: The Role of the Editor in Victorian England* (Westport, Conn., 1985).

[5] There is a formidable literature on the history of medical professionalization in this period. The best overview for non-specialists is Christopher Lawrence, *Medicine in the Making of Modern Britain, 1700–1920* (London, 1994). See also Irvine Loudon, 'Medical Practitioners 1750–1850 and the Period of Medical Reform in Britain', in Andrew Wear (ed.), *Medicine in Society* (Cambridge, 1992), 219–47; M. J. Peterson, *The Medical Profession in Mid-Victorian London* (Berkeley, 1978); Ivan Waddington, *The Medical Profession in the Industrial Revolution* (Dublin, 1984).

A number of scholars, however, have sought to press the connection further, setting the process of professional reform firmly within the context of the politics of the period more closely defined. Adrian Desmond's magisterial account of medicine and morphology in the reform era, for instance, shows how seemingly internal medico-scientific debates about comparative anatomy resonated with, and gained impetus from, the fundamental political issues of the day: hierarchy and equality, status and merit, representation and the rights of individuals and interests. In analyses like Desmond's, visions of the past, present, and future shape of the English medical world are seen as articulated within an intensely politicized framing discourse that fundamentally structured the terms of debate.[6]

The present chapter seeks to develop this line of inquiry by focusing on one important strand of political debate in the reform period – the standing of 'traditional' English representative institutions in the wake of the French revolutionary upheavals.[7] The revolution in France fundamentally reshaped the reformist terrain in medicine and politics. The political side of this story is well known: long-standing dissatisfaction with the failings of the political status quo took an urgent and threatening turn, especially after 1792. Reformist discourse also polarized, and the range of options seemingly narrowed into a stark set of alternatives: accommodation of change within the particularistic, individualistic, and historic institutions of 'established' society, on the one hand; on the other, change based upon universalistic, abstracted, rationalistic principles.

The distinction between historical particularism and universalizing abstraction, most famously articulated by Edmund Burke, serves as a productive analytical matrix within which to read the rhetorical and cognitive aspects of the politics of medical reform. To demonstrate this in the limited space available, my intention is to align the opposing elements of Burke's schema with two exemplary voices from the field of medical politics. The first, already introduced, is that of Wakley and his allies. The second voice on offer here is that of conservative reform, represented principally by the editors of, and contributors to, the *London Medical Gazette* (*LMG*). Founded in 1827 as an antidote to Wakley's attacks on establishment medicine, the *LMG* served as the mouthpiece for members of a medical elite anxious to reform in order to preserve. The *Lancet* and

---

[6] Desmond, *Politics of Evolution*. Other important accounts focusing on the interplay between medicine and (especially radical) politics include Roger Cooter, *The Cultural Meaning of Popular Science: Phrenology and the Organisation of Consent in Nineteenth-Century Britain* (Cambridge, 1984); Steven Shapin, 'The Politics of Observation: Cerebral Anatomy and Social Interests in the Edinburgh Phrenology Disputes', *Sociol. Rev. Monograph*, 27 (1979), 139–78; Alison Winter, *Mesmerized: Powers of Mind in Victorian Britain* (Chicago, 1998).

[7] To clarify my use of the terms 'British' and 'English', I will use the former to denote the broad national context within which reform debates took place, which included Scotland; I use the latter term where English exceptionalism constituted an explicit feature of the discussion or debate.

the *LMG*, then, ostensibly represented two distinct and irreconcilable voices of medical reform: on the one hand, unblinking adherents of a French-inspired enthusiasm for root-and-branch reform of historically entrenched medical corruption; on the other, apologists for the peculiarities of English medicine. There is much to be said for this view, as the opening sections of this chapter make clear. The first section will sketch the main features of the cognitive dimensions of medicine forged in the crucible of revolution, paying special attention to their connections with the principles of universalism and abstraction. Next, the appropriation of this medical model by British radical reformers will be briefly outlined. The second section turns to the terms of the conservative response, showing how this radical universalism was countered by the supposed virtues of embedded and embodied English practice. Having thus sketched out how medical debates worked within Burke's framework, however, the concluding section argues that the terms of opposition were more fluid than might be expected. Here, by re-examining the terms of Wakley's medical radicalism, I will suggest that – like its political counterpart – it was not immune to the lure of a more 'native' approach to reform.

I

French medicine, like its politics, cast a long shadow across the British reform landscape. Historians of medicine are in general agreement on the broad features of the French medical system (described variously as 'hospital medicine', the 'anatomico-clinical method', and most recently as 'analytical medicine') that emerged from the revolutionary period.[8] For the purposes of my analysis, the following points are crucial: first, increased medical control of large, publicly financed hospitals which drew together vast numbers of (poor) patients, and which enabled their systematic arrangement into 'cases' according to the class of disease suffered; second the elaboration of diagnostic and (secondarily) therapeutic intervention aimed at uncovering commonalities between ostensibly different symptom complexes, using (often instrumentally assisted) physical diagnosis which elicited information that could be used for comparative purposes, and which could be embodied in statistical representations of 'cases'; third, a shift in the unit of anatomical analysis (under the rubric of 'general anatomy') from a large number of discrete and discontinuous organs to a more

---

[8] The classic accounts of medicine in revolutionary France are Michel Foucault, *The Birth of the Clinic: An Archeology of Medical Perception*, trans. A. M. Sheridan Smith (New York, 1973); Erwin Ackerknecht, *Medicine at the Paris Hospital, 1794–1848* (Baltimore, 1967). See also N. D. Jewson, 'The Disappearance of the Sick-Man from Medical Cosmology', *Sociology*, 10 (1976), 225–44; John Pickstone, 'The Biographical and the Analytical: Towards a Historical Model of Science and Practice in Modern Medicine', in I. Löwy *et al.* (eds.), *Medicine and Change: Historical and Sociological Studies of Medical Innovation* (Paris, 1993), 23–47.

limited set of interconnecting elemental tissues; fourth, diagnosis oriented towards the localization of disease as a distinct, tangible entity, the presence of which was signalled by a lesion on a specific (internal) bodily structure; and, finally, routinized autopsy to confirm the suspected correlation of disease symptom and bodily lesion.

French medicine, in its ideal form, thus privileged a 'universalist' approach to the diseased body: at the cognitive level, it emphasized commonality over uniqueness, smoothing over the diagnostic and therapeutic consequences of individual (constitutional, historical, social) difference; at the level of practice, it merged the two main division of medicine by integrating symptomology with localization (respectively the traditional domains of physic and surgery). In this it displaced a prior form of medicine, broadly similar to the classical medicine of 'humours', for which the primary concern was individuation. In this framework, each patient was supposed to be treated as a unique 'constitution'. Health and disease resulted from the cumulative interaction between individual constitutional endowment and its particular, and broadly construed, environmental circumstances. Disease was not a specific entity (in either its causes, its course, or its physical signs), but was instead a disequilibrium of generalized elements, either solid, fluid, or both, which implicated the whole person. Diagnostics and therapeutics followed from this focus on the unique aspects of any given case: the privileged diagnostic technique was dialogue with the patient, in which the doctor sought to elicit complex (and deeply historical) narratives about patient habits, actions, and circumstances in order to determine the patient's own 'natural' state, and to discern how the patient had deviated from (and might be brought back to) his or her proper nature.[9] As the peculiarities of an active and largely self-informing patient structured diagnosis, so too therapeutics, with its deep suspicion of 'standardized' treatment, followed a highly individuated cognitive model.

It is not difficult to see how a hierarchical medical structure might map onto this 'traditional' model of conceptualizing disease. Classically trained physicians were perched at the top of the system. Steeped in logic and languages, they could decode the most complex symptoms and draw upon past experience or first principles to construct an appropriate regimen. Shunning manual work, their acutely trained and uncoarsened senses were able to recognize fine qualitative characteristics in a patient's bodily expressions – for example the tone of his or her pulse, or the subtle mix of elements that composed a unique, literally 'idiosyncratic' constitution. Surgeons' remit, by contrast, was supposed to be

---

[9] This medicine of natural balance contrasts with the rising interest in statistically represented bodily 'norms' derived from analyses of patient populations. For a discussion of this trend in the American context, see John Harley Warner, *The Therapeutic Perspective: Medical Practice, Knowledge and Identity in America* (Cambridge, Mass., 1986), ch. 4, esp. 85–91. For England see Lawrence, *Medicine in the Making*, 44–5.

restricted to the superficial and the specific. Until the mid-eighteenth century yoked with barbers (as tradesmen who worked with instruments to remove unwanted growth from the surface of the body), surgeons were regarded as doers rather than thinkers, charged with excising simple excrescences rather than reasoning upon subtle imponderables. To be sure, the rise in standing of localization and disease specificity associated with the French school, and represented in native guise by John Hunter (1728–93) and Matthew Baillie (1761–1823), had brought surgery to a more complex and elevated stage by the end of the eighteenth century (surgeons gained their independence from the barbers in 1745 and in 1800 won their own royal charter of incorporation). But, as Stephen Jacyna has observed, this rise in standing paradoxically intensified status differentiation within surgery – the Royal College of Surgeons insisted on a distinction between minority 'pures', who practised only surgery, and surgeon-apothecaries (general practitioners in all but name) who, by dispensing medicines and attending midwifery cases, compromised themselves by association with trade and manual labour.[10] These distinctions had real consequences: only 'pures', for example, could vote in College matters, be appointed to consultant posts at voluntary hospitals, or teach courses that were recognized by the College for the purposes of licensing medical students.

It was these types of invidious distinction that most rankled with reformers like Wakley, who, as one of the ranks of the 'impure', inveighed against the anachronistic and corrupt basis of the established medical hierarchy. For such critics, as John Harley Warner has shown, 'science' played the pivotal role in assessing the influence that continental – and particularly French – medicine should have on reconstituting the conceptual and institutional foundations of English medicine.[11] In his important analysis Warner stresses the rhetorical dimension of the call made by many medical reformers for more science in English medicine. For these critics of established medicine, science was first and foremost a way of invoking an alternative model of training and classification that obviated traditional distinctions (distinctions, for example, between medicine and surgery, manual and intellectual work, theoretical and practical knowledge), promising a new framework for medicine based on a shared, systematically transmissible, and meritocratically accessible body of knowledge. In the view of enthusiasts for French medicine like Wakley, in short, science was co-extensive with the broader vision of a modern, democratic medical

[10] Stephen Jacyna, 'Images of John Hunter in the Nineteenth Century', *Hist. Science*, 21 (1983), 85–108. For a useful overview of the contemporary status conflicts within British medicine, see Paul Underhill, 'Alternative Views of Science in Intra-Professional Conflict: General Practitioners and the Medical and Surgical Elite, 1815–58', *Jl Historical Sociol.*, 5 (1992), 322–50.

[11] John Harley Warner, 'The Idea of Science in English Medicine: The "Decline of Science" and the Rhetoric of Reform, 1815–45', in R. French and A. Wear (eds.), *Medicine in an Age of Reform* (London, 1991), 136–63. For a more detailed exploration of these themes as they relate to the rise of pathology, see Russell Maulitz, *Morbid Appearances: The Anatomy of Pathology in the Early Nineteenth Century* (Cambridge, 1987).

administration, and served simultaneously as a way to account for contemporary professional disorder and to define a path of resolution.

As others have demonstrated, however, this reformist discourse also had more direct, political resonances. Desmond's analysis, for example, details the complex dynamic through which a Tory and Anglican anatomy, informed by the natural theological tradition, was challenged by a French-inspired comparative anatomy whose reading of the natural world mapped on to the egalitarian agenda of contemporary radicalism. This connection between the content of radical science and radical politics is also evident within the terms of the universalist/particularist opposition that structures the present discussion. As I will suggest at the end of this chapter, radical medical reform was in important respects framed within a discourse of English particularism. But here I want briefly to indicate that the converse was also true – that conceiving of medicine as unified in theory and practice could easily fit with the ahistorical rationality demanded by revolutionary enthusiasts. For an explicit and programmatic embrace of revolutionary principles, we need look no further than the oft-quoted declaration made at a gathering of the Liverpool Medical Society in 1835, that 'the laws of medical science ... were universal and republican'.[12] But for a more fully fleshed-out version of this medico-political conflation, Robert Grant's inaugural address on medical reform delivered to the British Medical Association (BMA) in October 1841 serves as a useful text.

Both orator and venue are noteworthy. Grant was one of the leading exponents of the French radical morphology, and was celebrated in Wakley's *Lancet* as a paragon of progressive medical science. The BMA, founded in 1836 as a militant forum for articulating general-practitioner demands for a unified system of education and governance, provided an ideal platform for Grant's assault on the medical establishment.[13] The overarching theme of Grant's remarks was a criticism of hierarchical distinctions in medicine and in society resting not on reason, but on 'compacts founded on convention'. Convention derived from historical contingency, agreed upon by consenting parties not on the grounds of nature or reason but to effect 'a limited and determinate object'. Given the historically determined (and interested) nature of any such 'object', its tendency was to be superseded by the progress of knowledge, and thus to 'degenerate'. This was especially the case for interests purporting to represent science, which, experiencing most acutely the tension between 'the rapid advancement of knowledge around them, and the defined nature of their trust', inevitably become 'conservatories of bigotry and ignorance'.[14]

---

[12] 'Medical Reform: Meeting of the Members of the Liverpool Medical Society', *Lancet*, 1 (1833–4), 634.

[13] Desmond, *Politics of Evolution*, ch. 3, gives a full account of Grant's reform programme.

[14] Robert Grant, *On the Present State of the Medical Profession in England: Being the Annual Oration Delivered before the Members of the British Medical Association, on the 21st October, 1841* (London, 1841), 5, 6.

Nature and reason rather than history and convention were thus the proper foundations of a healthy society. The cornerstone of Grant's argument rested on a vision of medicine promoted by the modern universalism attributable to (French) science. At its core lay a physical body understood as a trans-historical object. 'Human structure and its derangements', Grant declared, 'do not vary perceptibly with time or place.' From this simple statement – itself a repudiation of the differentiated medicine of the bedside – flowed a critique of the hierarchical and stratified world of corporate medicine. Education 'must be one and uniform', reflecting the core truth that, as with the unvarying physical body, 'there are no natural grades in the Healing Art'. This principle, Grant argued, also extended to the social side of medical practice, and entailed the sweeping away of the system of differently qualified practitioners for the poor and for the rich that was, in his estimation, 'revolting to humanity'.[15]

This medical universalism, in Grant's analysis, was part and parcel of the broader reforming spirit of the age. 'The busy hand of reform', he had declared in an earlier address, was 'everywhere aiding reason against custom and power in establishing the rights of man'.[16] Guided by reason and science, he assured his BMA audience, 'the universal race of man is up and stirring. The antiquated qualities which command admiration in the Institutions of ancient times, are no longer suited to the condition of mankind, and fail to procure even respect for their antiquity.'[17] Against the dead hand of history, Grant embraced the political icons of his fellow radicals: the popular constitution, popular election, repre-sentative government; each predicated on the premise that 'the only legitimate source of [governmental] power, is in the intelligence and will of the entire community'.[18] In keeping with this analysis, Grant concluded his address with a list of distinctly political remedies for the state of the medical profession, demanding, among other things, 'the census and registration of the profession, Vote by Ballot, Annual Elections . . . [and] uniformity of education, rank, title, and privilege'.[19]

Grant's insistence on the unity of physical bodies in 'time and place', and his extension of this principle into the social realm, was grounded in the les-son of modern (French) medicine which, like French politics, demonstrated the error of viewing bodies (physical and political) as highly stratified and his-torically differentiated entities. Medical statistics, associated with the work of Pierre Louis, won praise amongst English radical reformers for its capacity to liberate the medical view from an artificial stress on a case's unique as-pects. General anatomy posited a simplified, continuous body at a still deeper level: Xavier Bichat's displacement of an organ-centred mapping of the body

---

[15] *Ibid.*, 40.

[16] Robert Grant, *On the Study of Medicine: Being an Introductory Address Delivered at the Opening of the Medical School of the University of London* (London, 1833), 17.

[17] Grant, *On the Present State*, 7, 8.   [18] *Ibid.*, 89, 24.   [19] *Ibid.*, 92–3.

(which stressed the structural and functional singularity of the body's component parts) by a tissue-centred vision presented the body as a network of more fundamental, homologous matter.[20] On a properly scientific analysis of bodies, the surgical firebrand Thomas King declared, the hierarchically differentiated body beloved by the traditional physician was revealed as an illusion: 'what appears complex and difficult when presented in an insulated and immethodical manner, becomes simple and easy in the extreme when viewed scientifically'.[21] With this insight, the University of London's prominent and controversial professor of surgery William Lawrence informed his students, the task of medicine shifted from the understanding of unique quality to the analysis of distributive equality: 'The entire structure and functions are universally and intimately connected . . . [A]lthough individual organs are numerous, the elements of organic structure are few. The various proportions in which they are combined make the difference, as the various combinations of a few letters produce the infinite variety of words.'[22] In the hands of medical radicals, then, the ahistorical and abstract truths of reason and science promoted a vision of the physical body as a template not merely for reorganizing the structure of English medicine, but for reconceptualizing the social relations within which it was suspended.

II

It was precisely these characteristics of medical radicalism that the *London Medical Gazette*, as the voice of conservative medical reform, found most disturbing. In opposing Grant, Wakley, and their allies, the *LMG* embraced a similarly political set of arguments, one grounded in the value of 'native' sensibilities. At an institutional level, opponents of radical medical reform mixed a Burkeian defence of English institutions with a plea for the recognition of English social realities. It was clear to the *LMG*, for example, what were the underlying motives of, and inspiration for, those urging a 'republic of medicine': like their political fellow travellers, medical 'destructives', in seeking to 'annihilate all existing colleges and corporations – all institutions – all grades – all educational regulations', were following the example of French revolutionary excesses.[23] There, medical revolutionaries had erected a 'gaudy' new system upon the 'ruins' of the old, a system which, like all those built on ahistorical and

---

[20] For Louis's 'numerical method', see J. Rosser Matthews, *Quantification and the Quest for Medical Certainty* (Princeton, 1995); for theories of pathology and general anatomy, see Maulitz, *Morbid Appearances*.

[21] Thomas King, *The Substance of a Lecture, Designed as an Introduction to the Study of Anatomy Considered as the Science of Organization* (London, 1834), 25.

[22] 'Mr Lawrence's Lecture Introductory to Surgery', *Lancet*, 1 (1829–30), 36.

[23] 'Reform – College of Physicians', *London Medical Gazette*, 11 (1832–3), 485.

abstract foundations, carried within it 'the seeds of anarchy and instability'.[24] For levellers, reform, 'in medicine as in politics, means not reformation – not the regeneration and improvement of exiting institutions, but their destruction'.[25]

Happily, in the *LMG*'s view, this wantonness ran counter to the pronounced national inclination to protect 'the spirit of its ancient and congenial freedoms', and to resist the 'true revolutionary principle of "levelling down" all the old establishments bequeathed by the wisdom of their ancestors, and erecting a wholly new and immaculate system'.[26] Abstract propositions ('immaculate systems') obscured more fundamental truths grounded in custom and usage, and this in itself could legitimate a defence of professional distinctions. The ultimate correctness of the divisions in medicine, for instance, was of secondary importance to its practical involvement in English life: 'these are so firmly established by usage, by courtesy, by chartered rights, and all the provisions of law, that they have become interwoven with the very constitution of society. No enactment, even if characterized by all the fervour which accompanies revolution, could annihilate the existence and practical operation of these divisions in our profession.'[27]

Usage, of course, was grounded in an analysis of the composition and nature of the users who, like practitioners, were embedded in historically sanctioned social relations legitimating the medical system that had developed within them. Stratified and hierarchical medicine in this sense simply reflected a society based on essential hierarchies. Criticizing the social and medical egalitarianism espoused by Grant and his fellow 'ultras', the *LMG* observed that:

> It is all very fine to tell us that science knows no gradations – that the diseases of the poor require the same skill as those of the rich – which may be true in the abstract, but which practically is mere talk. When the Deity ordains that ranks, gradations, and distinctions in society, shall cease – that there shall be no rich man and no poor – that is to say, when the millennium comes – the 'One Faculty' scheme may be broached.

In the meantime, defenders of differentiated medical estates sought to maintain or improve the educational and practical conditions within which practitioners could operate according to the distinctive social characteristics of their clients.[28]

Resistance to 'immaculate systems' operated not merely at the level of institutional and sociological realities, but also with respect to theories of medicine.

---

[24] 'Medical Reform in Germany', *ibid.*, 13 (1833–4), 723. Despite the editorial title, the comments cited referred to French medicine, 'the child of the first revolution . . . raised upon the ruins of all the institutions overturned by the *National Convention*'.

[25] 'Reform – College of Physicians', 485.   [26] 'Medical Reform in Germany', 725.

[27] 'Medical Education and Professional Grades', *London Medical Gazette*, 13 (1833–4), 132.

[28] 'Effect of General Practitioners becoming Faculty Doctors', *ibid.*, 598. Desmond cites the example of the conservative reformer J. H. Green, who in 1834 sketched out plans for an educational system aimed at preparing distinct 'grades' of practitioner to care for the needs of an equally differentiated client base: Desmond, *Politics of Evolution*, 269–70.

This is certainly true in terms of the type of intellectual engagement in medical theory expected of a properly 'conventionalized' English practitioner. Warner has shown that the typical response of those resisting the superiority of continental science was to defend the English system on the basis of its practical results.[29] In its very first editorial, the *LMG* conceded that continental students, compared with their English counterparts, received 'a more elaborate scientific education . . . and have a more minute knowledge of morbid anatomy, that is, of disease, as an object of natural history'. Yet it was not on these abstract grounds that the relative merits of the systems should be judged. Instead, when evaluated on their practical results, it was the continental scientists who were found wanting. English physicians and surgeons were 'infinitely superior to their Continental brethren in a knowledge of the treatment of disease, of the power of remedies, and of the best modes of employing them', a result that could easily be explained with reference to national character – that is, 'by dint of plain practical sense . . . for which the English are remarkable'.[30] The supposed inadequacies of the English medical system – its lack of system, its individualist orientation – were in fact the source of its strength, 'partak[ing] of the free character of all the institutions of the country'.[31]

This recourse to custom and usage clearly sought to displace 'republican' reformers' emphasis on a universalizing science as the foundation for a reformed medical world. English practitioners' engagement with medical theory, and the application of this knowledge in a therapeutic context, was properly informed by their 'Englishness'. But perhaps we can go further, and ask whether, like their 'levelling' antagonists, conservative reformers connected their defence of medicine (as a historically sanctioned system responding to the needs of historically situated individuals) with a view of the human body that similarly resisted the universalistic pull proposed by Grant and his allies. Was there, in other words, a 'particularist' physical body that served as a referent for a particularist medical practice?

It would seem as though, at a programmatic level, defenders of the English way of medicine ceded critical epistemological ground on this question to their 'French' counterparts. *LMG* editorials acknowledged the 'theoretical truth' that medicine is 'one and indivisible', and granted the conclusion in principle that this implied that no fundamental distinction existed between physic and surgery, between approaches to disease and therapeutics, and ultimately between the fundamental make-up of individual bodies. But at another level, in writing about bodies and their subjection to universalizing epistemologies (such as statistics and general anatomy) traditionalists tended to emphasize limits rather

---

29 Warner, 'Idea of Science', 141–3. Warner also shows that science-minded reformers by and large shared this view of the superiority of English practice (147).
30 'Medical Education in England', *London Medical Gazette*, 1 (1827–8), 11.
31 'Medical Education', *ibid.*, 182.

than possibilities. Their view of the body, and the diagnostic and therapeutic interventions appropriate to it, retained a strong element of 'particularism' resistant to what they regarded as the foreign-inspired collapsing of the distinct physical realities of individual bodies into a composite entity.

Once again, their dissent was grounded in a preference for embodied practice over theoretical perfection. The obsession of foreign anatomists with locating and minutely describing morbid lesions, the Barts consultant physician Peter Mere Latham informed his students, was threatening to turn clinical instruction into 'a discussion of abstract pathology and therapeutics'.[32] This, Latham argued, was a fundamental error, as it led students to imagine that the peculiarities of the individual sufferer were tangential, if not irrelevant. But, like Englishmen generally, the English practitioner ignored the products of an embodied constitution at his peril: 'Diseases are not abstractions; they are modes of acting . . . modes of disorganizing, modes of suffering, and modes of dying; and there must be a living, moving, sentient body, for all this.'[33] The same could be said for other signal techniques of French medicine. Diagnostic signs that yielded to statistical representation, for example, were of lesser value than those that indicated something unique about the case at hand. Thus Latham urged in time-honoured fashion that his students attend to qualitative diagnostic features (the tonality of a pulse rather than beat per minute, for instance) since 'these qualities, much more than its mere number, serve to guide us'.[34]

General anatomy came under similar criticism. Its tendency to break bodies down into underlying, unifying elementary tissue bypassed attention to the body as a collection of discrete organic units, and artificially reduced the body to an assemblage of homologous matter. The tendency to carry this kind of analysis 'too far', the metropolitan physician Leonard Stewart informed a meeting of the establishment Medical Society of London, produced an overly schematized conception of the body that obscured (or even destroyed) its qualitative realities:

In systems of general anatomy, we see it trace all the tissues to one or two primary elements; so simple, that they cease to represent the modified structure of the organs which are variously constructed from these fundamental materials . . . Their proper organic character is destroyed, and in their new shape we cannot recognize them. So also there are results obtained by analysing very closely the anatomical mechanism of some diseases, which may be called scientific, but which have no similitude with the tumult and activity of living pathological phenomena.[35]

In its systematizing and abstracting zeal, then, continental science had lost sight of the qualitative aspects of life – its 'tumult and activity' – that were the proper remit of the practical, English, medical man.

---

[32] Peter Mere Latham, 'Observations on Clinical Medicine', *ibid.*, 11 (1832–3), 103.
[33] *Ibid.*, 105.   [34] *Ibid.*, 200.
[35] Leonard Stewart, 'Modern Medicine Influenced by Morbid Anatomy', *ibid.*, 6 (1830), 10–11.

III

It is clear that, as far as opponents of the brand of reform espoused by 'radicals' were concerned, the medical establishment faced a revolutionary-minded enemy. 'Destructives' and levellers were at the gates, and had to be resisted through an appreciation and wise adjustment of established institutions of medical society. But the neatness of this polarity can be overstated: when one examines the discourse of much that was castigated as 'ultra' radicalism, one can discern a significant strand of a more 'native' analysis that, in its embrace of the politics of popular constitutionalism, shares features of a Burkeian embrace of historic institutions. As I have argued at length elsewhere, this is certainly the case for Wakley in one of the causes close to his heart – the reform of the ancient inquest system. Against what one might expect of a French-inspired radical, Wakley framed his demand for a medical coronership resolutely within the discourse of English liberties. A restorative reform of inquest became part of the radical popular constitutionalist programme in the years following Peterloo, with Hunt, Cobbett, and Wakley insisting on a (dubious) historical lineage in which the inquest featured as a relic of a bygone age of participatory institutions that were the birthright of every freeborn Englishman.[36]

By enacting a salutary reign of transparency, popular participation of this sort was to serve as a check against abuse. Like its political counterparts, the *Lancet* harboured a deep abhorrence of secrecy, and placed great faith in exposure as a solvent for the corruption that was its inevitable result.[37] The most telling of Wakley's inventive epithets for his corporate antagonists, in this vein, was the one reserved for the council of the Royal College of Surgeons – 'BATS'. Wakley left his readers in no doubt as to why he considered this an appropriate epithet: bats, he explained in the preface to the 1831 *Lancet*, are 'haters of light' who 'are bred in dark dreary recesses'. It was the purpose of the *Lancet* to submit their secretive practices to the public eye: 'the bright glare of the day has, through the influence of the press, been made to penetrate into the inmost recesses of their unhallowed caverns'.[38]

These radical demands for 'light' are evident across the full spectrum of reformist causes – for instance in calls for the public examination of candidates

---

[36] For more detailed discussions on the relationship between inquest reform and political radicalism, see Burney, *Bodies of Evidence*; Ian A. Burney, 'Making Room at the Public Bar: Coroners' Inquests, Medical Knowledge, and the Politics of the Constitution in Early-Nineteenth-Century England', in James Vernon (ed.), *Re-Reading the Constitution: New Narratives in the Political History of England's Long Nineteenth Century* (Cambridge, 1996), 123–53.

[37] See J. W. Burrow's *Whigs and Liberals: Continuity and Change in English Political Thought* (Oxford, 1988), ch. 3, for a cogent analysis of the theme of transparency in English radical thought.

[38] 'Preface, Advertisement, Address and a Rare Whack at the Voracious Bats', *Lancet*, 1 (1831–2), 4.

for collegiate licences, and for public competition in appointing individuals to positions of medical power (notably to consultant and teaching posts at the major voluntary hospitals). On the one hand, these demands had impeccable revolutionary credentials, the French system of *concours* (or public contest) being favourably contrasted to the secretive practices of examination and appointment operating in the corrupt world of English medicine. But it is also significant that such secretive practices were denounced by Wakley from within the discourse of English popular liberties – as 'star chambers' redolent of the dark days of Tudor/Stuart despotism.[39] This more historically minded critique also provided a more general framework for conceptualizing medical reform. Urging rank-and-file practitioners to pressure the establishment for fundamental reform – to, in his words, obtain 'their Magna Charta', a *Lancet* correspondent observed: 'There cannot be a better pattern of liberty than is to be found in the constitution of England, which gradually attained its perfection by the people unanimously and repeatedly insisting on their rights.'[40] Radical medical reform, notwithstanding the charges of continental abstractionism levelled against it by its critics, could and often did embrace historical wisdom as a foundation for progressive renewal and repair.

A similar 'bilingualism' is apparent when one looks at Wakley's views on representation. In his explicitly political pronouncements, Wakley positioned himself as an exponent of the 'direct' or 'delegate' theory of democratic representation, in which representatives were chosen and bound by the majority view expressed by an expansive electorate divided into equal franchise districts. But through the *Lancet* Wakley also expressed a more traditional 'Whig' view of representation featuring qualitatively distinct electoral constituencies, based not on number, but on property and intelligence.[41] Here Wakley, accepting the moderate reformist argument that English representative institutions needed to be reformed in order to eliminate the worst aspects of corruption and to incorporate rising elements into the system, argued that the rank-and-file general practitioner constituted one such element that needed inclusion in a renewed constitutional dispensation. In an editorial promoting 'Representation of Medical Men in Parliament', the *Lancet* asked how 'that numerous and important class of the community, the medical profession, stands in relation to the representative system, justly the pride of our form of government'. According to constitutional theory, it continued, parliament 'not only takes in the entire state under its salutary protection, but . . . the individual interests of each, even of the

---

[39] *Ibid.*, 13.   [40] Letter from 'Scrutator', *ibid.*, 11 (1826–7), 684.
[41] The distinction between the 'delegate' and 'Whig' or 'virtual' theories of political representation is elaborated in Samuel Beer, 'The Representation of Interests in British Government: Historical Background', *American Political Science Rev.*, 51 (1957), 613–50. For a more recent analysis, see David Eastwood, 'Parliament and Locality: Representation and Responsibility in Late-Hanoverian England', *Parl. Hist.*, 7 (1998), 68–81.

smallest departments of the whole common weal'. But unlike other categories of recognized interest, the rising ranks of progressive medical scientists had no viable representation. True, the 'ancient wisdom' of the constitution provided for representation of science in the form of university seats, but these had fallen prey to corruption, representatives being chosen not for 'the advancement of the interests of science' but for patronage. In the face of this degenerate system, the *Lancet* demanded restitution:

> Let us, therefore, at least hope, as the original draft of our constitution pre-
> sumes a representation of the medical, as well as of every other great division
> of the state, that in any reform of the abuses, or addition made to its present
> powers, this salutary indication may not be slighted; but that, instead of being
> a mockery, as at present, it will be improved into a virtual advocacy of the
> interests of science and its practical cultivators.[42]

Wakley's embrace of 'virtual' interest, reminiscent of the theory of parliamentary representation famously espoused by Burke in his address to the Bristol electors, was further elaborated in response to on-going discussions about whether the University of London should be granted a parliamentary seat. Such a plan, as the former home secretary Sir James Graham explained in an 1852 speech, recognized interest and intelligence, rather than raw number, as the proper basis for adjusting parliamentary constituencies: 'In distributing the representative privilege, I should pay respect to numbers in some degree; but at the same time I do think, that, with great advantage, the representative power might be conferred on parties possessing intelligence and science to an eminent degree who do not now return representatives.' The *Lancet* agreed, arguing that a seat for advanced science on the basis of 'fitness and responsibility' would be universally accepted: those of wealth and station would embrace it as the surest guarantee of good order, while the middling and industrial classes would cheerfully recognize the rising ranks of medical-scientific interest as analogous to their own advancements:

> It is a claim which conciliates every interest, binding together, by the sacred
> fellowship of knowledge, the extremes of society, awakening in all, by the
> eloquent voice of science, the purest feeling of brotherhood and the deepest
> sense of mutual responsibility. Who would not hail with satisfaction the in-
> stallation of the University of London in that place in the constitution which
> has been defiled by the degraded borough of Sudbury? Who would not wel-
> come an electoral body dignified by their learning, secure against corruption,
> who might restore to the national councils a Macaulay or a Grote?[43]

The *Lancet*'s claim that a constitutional adjustment enabling parliamentary representation of its brand of medical science would be welcomed by the whole

---

[42] 'Representation of Medical Men in Parliament', *Lancet*, 1 (1829–30), 748–9, 751.
[43] 'Claims of the University of London to Parliamentary Representation', *ibid.*, 1 (1852), 451.

of society was, unsurprisingly, a contentious one. This is because the *Lancet*'s brand of science was, to recall Warner's analysis, an inextricably politicized intervention in the contested field of medical reform. As we have seen, the meritocratic overtones of the call for science in medicine was at one level directed against the patronage-bound world of the medical corporations. But, as historians of medicine have recognized, Wakley and his colleagues were not simply fighting a battle against the medical elite. Instead, their calls for progressive reform were aimed at establishing the scientifically trained general practitioner as the cornerstone of a medical world that defined itself against the retrograde forces both of the elite *and* of the great unwashed – the world of alternative (or 'quack') medicine.

The *Lancet* was founded as an instrument for exposing 'Old Corruption' in the medical elite. But, long before the official launch of its onslaught against the practices of 'untrained' practitioners (in the form of the 'Anti-Medical Quackery Society' announced in 1835), it had been doing battle against this demotic threat to the economic and professional standing of the licensed general practitioner. In its view, the two causes were linked. Announcing the society, the *Lancet* fulminated against the rising threat from below: 'never have quacks, quackish doctrines, and quack medicines, exercised a greater influence over the minds and bodies of the people of this country, than they exert at the present epoch'. The cause of this scourge was clear: it was the necessary consequence of 'the odious, the exclusive conduct of our rotten and contemptible medical corporations'.[44] By excluding the medical rank and file from full membership, the royal colleges were telling the public that those who served them were unfit, thereby 'disgracing' the majority of practitioners and implying that their qualifications were not sufficient to distinguish them from those practising without a licence.

The *Lancet*'s anti-quackery campaign was in this sense an integral component of its broad objective of eliminating medical corruption. But the campaign also exposed the limits of its 'democratic' credentials. As Logie Barrow has observed, Wakley deployed the full range of egalitarian imperatives with respect to those he recognized as constituting a worthy polity, but his democracy was grounded in a meritocratic vision of professional order that had its explicit limits: 'When meritocrats are democrats', Barrow aptly observes, 'they are so on one absolute precondition: that they define merit.' Meritocracy, he concludes, may also 'have its sectarian aspects'.[45]

---

[44] 'Means of Checking the Operations of Quacks', *ibid.*, 1 (1835–6), 948. Roy Porter wrote extensively and informatively on the history of quackery and anti-quackery. See, e.g., Roy Porter, *Health for Sale: Quackery in England, 1660–1850* (London, 1989); Roy Porter, *Quacks: Fakers and Charlatans in English Medicine* (London, 2000).

[45] Logie Barrow, 'Why Were Most Medical Heretics at their Most Confident around the 1840s? (The Other Side of Mid-Victorian Medicine)', in French and Wear (eds.), *British Medicine*, 175.

Thus, when faced with the full-scale 'levelling' that its opponents attributed to its campaign for reform, the *Lancet* insisted on moderation. In an editorial response to a 'heretical' suggestion from one of its correspondents that all corporations be eliminated in the interest of medical 'free trade', the *Lancet* recoiled:

> it is no argument, because corporate and other public medical bodies have behaved wrongfully, and created much injustice . . . that, as a consequence, all medical corporate bodies, present and future, are, and must be, radically bad and mischievous. The present evils are a very good reason for reform, but hardly, as we conceive, for destruction, except in the minds of very rash and sanguine persons.[46]

In its pursuit of meritocratically derived distinction, the *Lancet* also found itself a (professedly reluctant) supporter of exclusive privilege. In the case of inquest reform, for instance, the *Lancet*'s long-standing campaign for medically trained coroners exposed it to charges of monopolistic designs, charges that the *Lancet* rebutted with some unease. It declared itself, as a matter of principle, averse to legislative interference 'in any case where the people are capable of exercising important privileges which have been handed down to them by their forefathers' (in this case freeholder rights to elect coroners). Yet because medical qualification was necessary for the proper functioning of the system, it urged that 'a diploma, or licence, obtained from a medical corporation, shall be deemed an indispensable qualification for every coroner'.[47] In a further editorial in the same year, the *Lancet* sought to defend its apparent embrace of monopoly (this time with reference to the payment of licensed medical practitioners giving evidence at inquests) on broader ground, challenging the common presumption that special privileges conferred on a particular class of the community constituted a 'sacrifice of a portion of the rights and privileges of the multitude'. On the contrary, an advanced society required this dispensation of privilege; such a society needed

> a system of government compounded of many parts, all working in union, the generality of them having reference to the maintenance of national advantages, but giving to persons, and particular institutions, the possession of special rights . . . All the ancient charters were conferred on particular bodies of our ancestors with a similar object, and, in more modern times, we have witnessed the practical operation of the theory which sustained that principle.[48]

The *Lancet*'s campaign to elevate the general practitioner to a privileged role was thus framed as a necessary and benign extension of the ancient constitutional dispensation. But unsurprisingly, for those who fell outside the pale of its

---

[46] 'Medical Corporation Reform', *Lancet*, 2 (1849), 77.
[47] 'Medical Coroners', *ibid.*, 2 (1835–6), 186.
[48] 'Advantages of Conferring Exclusive Privileges on Particular Persons', *ibid.*, 1 (1836–7), 52, 53.

definition of merit, its arguments merely represented the manoeuvrings of the old enemy of progressive reform. As Barrow and others have shown, medical 'sectarians' – including homoeopathists, naturopathists, hydropathists, herbalists, and medical botanists – flourished during the period under discussion, their strength in no small part due to their insistence that patient choice in practitioner and therapeutic regime was a fundamental right threatened by medical professionalization. Resisting the trend towards an orthodoxy of knowledge insulated from popular understanding, they promoted a democratic, patient-centred epistemology of health and disease, best captured in the politically resonant slogan 'The People their Own Physicians'.[49]

These practitioners challenged Wakley's community of privileged equals, and impugned his reformist motives, casting him not as a beacon of healthful reform, but as representative of another species of medical monopolism endangering the rights and liberties of freeborn Englishmen. In so doing they built up an alternative reformist arsenal – complete with crusading journals, mass meetings, and national petitions. Take, for example, the case of Isaac Coffin, the leading English promoter of the American Thompsonian school of medical botany. His mouthpiece, the *Botanical Journal* (founded 1847), shared many characteristics of Wakley's *Lancet*: a polemical, crusading style, and a determination to expose monopoly in the name of the public good. Its inaugural number read like the pages of the *Lancet*, promising to 'expose, as far as in us lies, and to reform the abuses of the profession', and to provide information to the public 'at as low a rate as possible', 'divested of all technicalities and written as plainly and simply as possible'.[50] Among the objectives of such plain speaking was to expose medical reform, as conceived by 'that superannuated old mountebank Wakley',[51] as a subterfuge masking monopolistic designs: a 'monstrous attempt to infringe on the rights of British freedom'.[52] The science of medicine peddled by professed reformers was grounded in self-interest, its aggressive claims to exclusive truth a crude attempt to silence true reformist medical science by the tried and tested methods of corruptionists: 'men love darkness rather than light', Coffin observed in a passage worthy of his principal antagonist, 'because their deeds are evil'.[53]

This is no place to detail the grievances and remedies outlined by sectarians like Coffin. Two concluding observations must suffice. First, Coffin's

---

[49] On the politics of medical sectarianism, see, in addition to Barrow, J. F. C. Harrison, 'Early Victorian Radicals and the Medical Fringe', in W. F. Bynum and Roy Porter (eds.), *Medical Fringe and Medical Orthodoxy, 1750–1850* (London, 1987), 198–215; Ursula Miley and John Pickstone, 'Medical Botany around 1850: American Medicine in Industrial Britain', in Roger Cooter (ed.), *Studies in the History of Alternative Medicine* (London, 1988), 140–54.

[50] 'To Our Readers and the Public', *Coffin's Botanical Jl and Medical Reformer* (2 Jan. 1847), 1.

[51] 'Sign of the Times', *ibid.* (2 Oct. 1847), 78.

[52] 'To Our Friends, and the Friends of Humanity', *ibid.* (7 July 1849), 258.

[53] 'Meeting of Parliament: Medical Monopoly', *ibid.* (3 Feb. 1849), 210.

identification of Wakley as his opponent in the battle for popular liberties was by no means coincidental, for one of the *Botanical Journal*'s campaigns was a mirror image of Wakley's described above – that is, deciding the qualifications for coroners. For both, a medical coronership was a weapon in the struggle to consolidate a reformist orthodoxy. In Wakley's view, a medical coroner would be best suited to expose and legally punish 'quacks' like Coffin, thereby earning the 'special privilege' that he sought in legislation. For Coffin, medical coroners (and lay coroners indebted to 'the Medical Faculty') were representatives of repression, usurping their constitutional position as 'guardian of British freedom' to persecute Coffinite practitioners whenever a death happened to occur under their care.

Second, the democratic epistemology espoused by the likes of Coffin laid bare the limits of Wakley's embrace of popular participation as a basis for legitimizing medical reform. As noted above, public scrutiny was one of the key tools in waging war against the secretive practices of 'bats' and other corruptionists. But there were distinct restrictions on what the public could know, and what it could be expected to judge. These extended not merely to institutional arrangements wherein, for example, public interest in the management of hospitals needed to be mediated through competent (i.e. 'scientific') medical representatives, but also to the more fundamental question of the public's capacity to exercise power in a properly constituted medical order. However pleasing in theory, a reformed medical polity could not be based on simple egalitarian principles. '"Every man his own Esculapius", the *Lancet* declared,

> should be the motto of ALL the followers of popular medicine; and that it is a most mischievous one we need hardly attempt to prove . . . The public is so intimately indoctrinated with popular physic, that every third man is, in his own conceit, quite able to give an opinion upon an abstract point in scientific medicine or surgery. This is one great source of the little respect borne by the public towards the profession.[54]

As an organ of radical reform, then, the *Lancet*'s position was anything but straightforward. A resolute enthusiast of a French-inspired model of medical universalism, it also embraced a version of English particularism; a champion of participatory institutions as a check on monopolistic corruption, it equally argued the cause of professional prerogative; a proponent of direct democracy, it nevertheless embraced interest-based representation. As an exemplary voice from within the fractious world of medical politics, the *Lancet* shows that medicine shared fully in the complex of contradictory forces that marked the age of reform.

---

[54] 'Sketch of the *Lancet* Anti-Quackery Campaign', *Lancet*, 1 (1847), 391–2.

7. British antislavery reassessed

DAVID TURLEY

The most obvious and distinctive feature of the antislavery movement when compared with other examples of social activism in the age of reform is that the very nature of antislavery objectives gave the movement a dual character, domestic and imperial. Antislavery required within Britain the development of a sophisticated form of the politics of alliances that had to be reconstituted as new social forces emerged. Only by such means could sufficient leverage be developed to change state policy on the slave-trade and the reliance on slave labour in colonial economies. Abolitionists soon concluded, however, that changes in policy could only be effective if the conditions of the populations raided by the slave-traders and of the slaves in the colonies were remade in order that they would be able to live in civilized freedom. Thus antislavery also required imperial action to alter the character of societies in West Africa and in the West Indies. From the beginning of organized antislavery in the late 1780s this imperial aspect was envisaged as possessing linked institutional, moral, and commercial components.

Many abolitionists were also involved in other efforts at changing public institutions or practices. The Anglican evangelical Clapham Sect, evangelical dissenters, Quakers, rational dissenters, and Unitarians separately – and sometimes together – pursued a whole range of changes in personal behaviour, institutions, and social practices.[1] Modern historians have, therefore, not surprisingly, regarded abolitionists as reformers. But the language of successive generations of contemporaries indicates a more complicated history as to how antislavery was perceived. The language of 'improvement' was pervasive in the later eighteenth century and the first half of the nineteenth century, when antislavery was at its most influential. The term was understood to embrace not only cumulative material and mechanical advance, but also moral development and intellectual progress. This in turn often had as a corollary institutional restructuring that was frequently focused on particular communities. In the late eighteenth century

---

[1] David Turley, *The Culture of English Antislavery, 1780–1860* (London, 1991), 108–18.

abolitionists were heavily implicated in projects of 'improvement' in the sense of institutional renovation.[2] In friendly quarters antislavery activities themselves might also be understood as contributing to 'improvement' as moral advance. Opponents sometimes denied them this positive label, and charged them rather with being 'reformers'. For one thing, the campaign against the slave-trade was intended to end it completely rather than improve it. 'Reform' as distinct from 'improvement' could be seen as destructive. In the 1780s James Ramsay was denounced by a writer responding to his attack on the trade and the treatment of West Indian slaves as 'the head of those fanatics who set themselves for reformers'. His critic, however, was ready to find common ground with him if he were to propose a law for the British West Indies similar to the French *Code Noir* to set a framework for slavery, and if he recommended the passage of an act 'for the *better* regulation of the slave trade'.[3]

With growing anxiety in the early 1790s in Britain about the radical turn of the French Revolution, opponents began to characterize antislavery even more negatively. Hostile opinion represented the movement as alien and extreme, revolutionary rather than improving. Abolitionists were 'the JACOBINS of ENGLAND', who were either dupes or divorced from 'an honest and enlightened Public'.[4] Meanwhile the Claphamites were working to bring moral and social improvement abroad in Sierra Leone. They envisaged this in part in terms of carrying Christian enlightenment to the ignorant, and the consequent dispelling of 'the terrors of superstition . . . before the beams of knowledge': a form of religious improvement with social benefits.[5] The word 'reform' was not regularly and positively associated with antislavery before the 1820s, but by the 1830s the term linked it to a programme most fully expounded by the group around Joseph Sturge in Birmingham. In 1835 they started a weekly paper, the *Reformer* (its successor was called the *Philanthropist*), that placed the completion of emancipation alongside support for freer trade, the ballot, further franchise reform, temperance, and rational recreation for 'the people'. The language of 'improvement', 'reform', and 'philanthropy' was now thoroughly intermingled in regard to antislavery and increasingly employed within

---

[2] For comment by William Turner to the Manchester Literary Society on local improvement, see Derek Orange, 'Rational Dissent and Provincial Science: William Turner and the Newcastle Literary and Philosophical Society', in Ian Inkster and Jack Morrell (eds.), *Metropolis and Province: Science in British Culture, 1780–1850* (London, 1983), 211–12.

[3] George Turnbull, *An Apology for Negro Slavery: or the West India Planters Vindicated from the Charges of Inhumanity* (1786), quoted in Folarin Shyllon, *James Ramsay: The Unknown Abolitionist* (Edinburgh, 1977), 81–2.

[4] 'Truth', *A Very New Pamphlet Indeed!* (London, 1792), 3–4. Part of the problem for abolitionists was that it was easy to associate a few of their number with Jacobinism. See Turley, *Culture*, 167–8.

[5] Brit. Lib., Add. MS 41,262A, Clarkson family papers, Henry Thornton to John Clarkson, 30 Dec. 1791; also Thomas Clarkson to John Clarkson [Jan. 1792?].

a context of abolitionist support for nonconformist aspirations to a voluntaryist religious system.[6]

Part of the complexity of understanding the changing alliance politics of the movement and the shifting ways through which antislavery was articulated arises from the long period and changing contexts in which it flourished. Antislavery went through a number of distinct phases. The first was characterized by a network of local committees communicating with the London Abolition Committee founded in 1787, and through this with a parliamentary leadership that presented petitions and introduced parliamentary motions against the trade in the years up to 1796. The French threat and internal unrest then enforced a period of quietude. Amongst the political class some 'sagacious manoeuvring within', accompanied by limited petitioning, brought the first success in 1806 with legislation against British involvement in the foreign slave-trade and in 1807 prohibition of the slave-trade to the British colonies. The African Institution, taking over from the London Committee, entered a close, largely behind-the-scenes relationship with government to enforce British abolition, encourage international collaboration to suppress the transatlantic slave-trade, and monitor the impact of abolition on the conditions of West Indian slaves.[7] Dissatisfied with progress, the Anti-Slavery Society, established in 1823, pursued complete though gradual emancipation of the slaves. Abolitionists eventually organized massive mobilization primarily of religious nonconformists in the late 1820s and early 1830s at the same time that antislavery associations were closely allied to missionary and 'civilizing' efforts in Africa and the West Indies. Knowledge derived in part from this involvement convinced them that the official policy of 'amelioration', supposed to lead eventually to emancipation, was inadequate.[8] Abolitionists committed themselves to immediate emancipation and undertook, particularly through the breakaway Agency Committee, a national campaign of mass meetings addressed by touring speakers to accompany petitioning, a saturation distribution of literature, and quizzing of parliamentary candidates. The emancipation legislation of 1833, eased in its passage by parliamentary reform, provided for a period of apprenticeship for the ex-slaves. This provoked further agitation leading to complete emancipation in 1838. Thereafter local antislavery organizations withered as British abolitionists internationalized their cause, particularly in regard to American slavery, and divisions opened up in the 1840s over the character of post-emancipation societies in the colonies.[9]

---

[6] Turley, *Culture*, 189–90; Alex Tyrrell, *Joseph Sturge and the Moral Radical Party in Early Victorian Britain* (London, 1987), 71–2.

[7] Turley, *Culture*, 55.

[8] J. R. Ward, *British West Indian Slavery, 1750–1834: The Process of Amelioration* (Oxford, 1988).

[9] W. L. Burn, *Emancipation and Apprenticeship in the British West Indies* (London, 1937); William Green, *British Slave Emancipation: The Sugar Colonies and the Great Experiment, 1830–1865* (Oxford, 1976).

I

The historiography of antislavery in recent decades has led to striking advances in understanding and a rich scholarly debate. But it leaves room for further analysis of the movement defined in the terms suggested at the outset of this essay: as a dual phenomenon involving both mobilization at home and institutional and moral change in the colonies. Since the 1970s scholars have laboured mightily to transcend the alternative interpretations of antislavery either as a successful humanitarian crusade underpinned by philosophical and religious ideas[10] or as economically determined and an instrument for sweeping away obstacles to the interests of industrial capitalism.[11] Although many recent historians have concluded that Eric Williams' approach in *Capitalism and Slavery* (1944 and 1964) was too economically determinist, they have not denied the larger implication of his argument. They accept significant connections between the changes in British society in the late eighteenth and first half of the nineteenth centuries (Williams' 'industrial capitalism'), the development of an antislavery movement, and the turn in British state policy against the slave-trade and colonial slavery.[12]

To indicate the space the argument of this chapter occupies, a brief review of features of the analyses of David Brion Davis, Seymour Drescher, and Robert W. Fogel will help. Concluding that slavery posed 'a symbolic test of the efficacy of Christian faith', Davis has explained the successful growth and diffusion of antislavery in terms of a process of cultural hegemony, frequently expressed in the language of religion and ultimately favourable to industrial capitalism. During substantial social and industrial change antislavery constituted an element of stability in underlining the illegitimacy of labour derived from the ownership of another human being. Implicitly, however, it contributed to sanctioning forms of labour control convenient to both rural and urban employers. Antislavery acted as a '"projective screen" for testing ideas of liberation, paternalism and controlled social change that were prompted in part by domestic anxieties'. In promoting the notion of autonomy as well as legitimizing particular forms of control, antislavery shared ideological ground with other reform activities, thus helping make familiar assumptions that eased popular accommodation to change.[13]

[10] Sir Reginald Coupland, *Wilberforce: A Narrative* (Oxford, 1923); Frank J. Klingberg, *The Anti-Slavery Movement in England* (New Haven, 1926); Roger Anstey, *The Atlantic Slave Trade and British Abolition, 1760–1810* (London, 1975).

[11] Eric Williams, *Capitalism and Slavery* (London, 1964 edn).

[12] Barbara L. Solow and Stanley L. Engerman (eds.), *British Capitalism and Caribbean Slavery: The Legacy of Eric Williams* (Cambridge, 1987).

[13] David Brion Davis, *The Problem of Slavery in the Age of Revolution, 1770–1823* (Ithaca, N.Y., 1975), 346–85: David Brion Davis, 'Capitalism, Abolitionism and Hegemony', in Solow and Engerman (eds.), *British Capitalism*, 210–11, 217–19.

Drescher has also focused on the diffusion and particularly the processes of antislavery. He argues that slavery was increasingly perceived as diverging from the norms of the metropolis and that in striving to eliminate that divergence abolitionists constructed a cross-class movement embodying the 'popular' in its methods of mobilization. Antislavery was on the leading edge of a liberalizing and democratizing tendency that ran through even periods of elite manoeuvre and public passivity; a 'climate of opinion' had been entrenched and could be brought rapidly into operation again. This opinion and the mobilization that followed was crucial in Drescher's argument, since his earlier work had undermined the view that the West Indian slave system had declined after the American Revolution. Abolition could not be explained in terms of West Indian economic weakness. Popular mobilization was crucial, but did not draw significantly on the philosophical or religious concepts to which other historians had attributed importance. What counted was what seemed sense to antislavery petitioners. The religious dimension of popular antislavery consisted in drawing strength from social milieux also infused by forms of evangelicalism and particularly Methodism. It thus found support from industrializing and mining regions. Antislavery was a response to the changes of the industrial revolution, but in the particular sense that it expressed the release of new social forces in popular form. Antislavery petitioners were the 'artisanal expansion of the industrial revolution in the half century after 1780', emerging as a nonconformist middle class in the 1830s.[14]

For Fogel the key to understanding the struggle to achieve emancipation lay in the ways in which the antislavery campaign intersected with the struggle for power in an undemocratic political system under pressure and vulnerable to the threat or fear of disorder. This is the perspective, he argues, that led the parliamentary abolitionists to accommodate to gradualism in the 1820s and to try to ensure a peaceful transition to freedom through pressing colonial legislatures to make a reality of 'amelioration'.[15]

All these interpretations imply or articulate within a broad national framework a relationship between a national movement and leadership and support in the localities. But they do not directly deal with the meanings of antislavery in different communities or much with antislavery as an aspect of colonial reform. Davis suggests the operation of cultural hegemony and the link between a distant slavery and local concerns through the antislavery expression of prominent figures, leaving unclear the channels and the extent of impact in different places. Drescher acknowledges that antislavery cannot be projected directly

---

[14] Seymour Drescher, *Econocide: British Slavery in the Era of Abolition* (Pittsburgh, 1977); Seymour Drescher, *Capitalism and Antislavery: British Mobilization in Comparative Perspective* (Basingstoke, 1986).

[15] Robert William Fogel, *Without Consent or Contract: The Rise and Fall of American Slavery* (New York, 1989), 205–25.

from purely economic motives or pure moral consciousness, but does not recognize that there may be a parallel problem in his use of the idea of the 'popular'. Questions about the sources of initiative in communities and the meanings local activists gave to their efforts remain unasked. How local communities were tied to Fogel's posited political coalitions to overcome the entrenched power of pro-slavery governing forces has also been indicated only in general terms. Antislavery was, of course, a national movement organizationally and in the distribution of much of its propaganda. The national leadership's parliamentary interventions helped shape the pattern of the movement outside parliament. But to get at questions about connections between centre and locality within antislavery, and how ordinary abolitionists may have envisaged their activity, the issue of how *mediation* operated between the national leadership and local communities needs to be faced. This – one of the two lines of discussion pursued in the remainder of this chapter – will be approached via brief analyses of Manchester in the late 1780s and early 1790s and Sheffield a generation later. The other, in the light of the dual character of antislavery, will look at abolitionist involvement in colonial reform, whether through pressure to alter plantation practices, direct moral and educational means, or the manipulation of fiscal and commercial policy to have both material and, eventually, moral effects.

Moral reforming activity in the 1780s that drew in figures soon to be active in antislavery initially had a 'top down' character. Gentry and clerical magistrates became more active against forms of vice and immorality. Some associated with William Wilberforce as a central figure in the Proclamation Society. Giving effect to objectives at county level and securing moral improvement in particular localities had to engage prominent community figures.[16] Some of these notables had settled local influence radiating from established positions, others strove for influence in their localities. How the links were made, with whom, and with what effects, was crucial to the process of mediation in antislavery as well as in other efforts at moral improvement.

How are we to understand mediation in general terms? Economic change in the decades covered in this volume had substantial effects on the kinds of urban communities to be cited below. Improved information and its distribution through cheap reading material in press and pamphlet, the emergence of a consciousness of community and pride in it, activity through social and voluntary associations to advance both group and wider interests in the improvement of the locality all developed. The network of local associations and institutions helped both group and community identity and at the same time contributed to national integration in particular areas of activity. Community involvement,

---

[16] Joanna Innes, 'Politics and Morals: The Reformation of Manners Movement in Later Eighteenth-Century England', in E. Hellmuth (ed.), *The Transformation of Political Culture: England and Germany in the Late Eighteenth Century* (Oxford, 1990), 66–9, 72–3, 78–80.

through local institutions, was the most immediate way that individuals had of coming into contact with the wider social world. In doing so they were likely to be influenced by the outlook on the world adopted by community notables occupying interlocking leadership positions in local institutions. They became part of the dominant ethos within the community or shared in the struggle for contested community dominance. Yet each community had specific features that were registered in the variable social relations among different sections of the propertied classes and in their relations with other social groups. These relations were in part structured through religious affiliation and membership of a range of private and public bodies. There were, that is, both broad similarities and specific differences in the social and group structures through which translation of issues like the slave-trade and slavery occurred. The differences were bound to affect the meanings local activists gave to their antislavery activities at different times and in different places.[17]

The remarkable success of the anti-slave-trade petitions from Manchester in 1788 (10,000 signatures) and 1792 (20,000 signatures) is less surprising the more one appreciates the cohesiveness of the reform culture in the town, at least until the latter year. Thomas Walker, a latitudinarian Anglican manufacturer, chaired the anti-slave-trade committee, but drew some of his most active associates from rational dissent and particularly from the wealthy and educated congregation at the Cross Street Chapel. This group had an intellectual base in the Literary and Philosophical Society; the anti-slave-trade committee was one of several committees with overlapping membership through which they sought to press a programme of improvement. In addition to their liberal religion several shared a dissenting academy or Scottish higher education, some training in medicine or science, and involvement in manufacturing and commerce. Though successful, they still felt they had to make a mark on their community. As dissenters, most were politically excluded from the old manorial institutions of the unincorporated town dominated by Tories attached to the Anglican collegiate church. In consequence the group pursued their drive for influence through reshaping or establishing and running community institutions in a spirit of scientific improvement. The Infirmary (founded in 1752) became a point of conflict in 1789–90 when physician reformers and their supporters, members of the Lit. and Phil., attached to Cross Street and with a presence on the anti-slave-trade

---

[17] J. R. Oldfield, *Popular Politics and British Anti-Slavery: The Mobilisation of Public Opinion against the Slave Trade, 1787–1807* (Manchester, 1995), 7–40; Peter Clark, *British Clubs and Societies, 1580–1800: The Origins of an Associational World* (Oxford, 2000), 487–90; M. Billinge, 'Reconstructing Societies in the Past: The Collective Biography of Local Communities', in Alan R. H. Baker and Mark Billinge (eds.), *Period and Place: Research Methods in Historical Geography* (Cambridge, 1982), 19–32; John Seed, 'From "Middling Sort" to Middle Class in Late Eighteenth and Early Nineteenth Century England', in M. L. Bush (ed.), *Social Orders and Social Classes in Europe since 1500: Studies in Social Stratification* (London, 1992), 114–35.

committee, pressed to expand the institution, reorganize its activities, make new appointments, and develop home visiting, particularly in poorer districts of the town. Figures such as Thomas Percival, Thomas Butterworth Bayley, and Thomas Walker, as well as other Manchester abolitionists, were active in relation to the Infirmary and had previously supported repeal of the Test and Corporation Acts to gain civic equality for dissenters. Many of the same people were behind the establishment of the new Manchester College in 1786; Percival was its first president, Thomas Barnes its first principal, and James Touchet the treasurer. All three were on the 1787 anti-slave-trade committee, and ten other members of the college committee were on the abolitionist subscription list in January 1788. Dr John Ferriar, a member of the anti-slave-trade committee, developed more humane forms of treatment at the asylum, and both Bayley and Percival were active in getting a new penitentiary built and treatment of prisoners reformed. The minister Ralph Harrison expressed the self-definition of the Manchester group as having 'good natural powers, a vigorous application of their talents and the blessing of God on their endeavours', while operating under 'the holy light of truth, of reason, and of righteousness'. In this ethos of rational improvement the anti-slave-trade committee employed the Scots scholar James Anderson of Monkshill to write on the impolicy of slavery, an issue for 'serious and dispassionate enquiry', in a pamphlet suffused with the cool discourse of political economy.[18]

Manchester abolitionism contained a sub-group, especially Thomas Walker, Thomas Cooper, and George Philips, who, between 1787 and the end of 1792, were advocates of improvement and drastic *political* change to which they connected antislavery. Cooper saw opposition to the slave-trade as the duty of Englishmen, since it constituted 'the most diabolical exertion of political tyranny which the annals of oppression can exhibit'. Other abolitionists outside Cooper's tradition of militant rational dissent, including the Methodist Samuel Bradburn, were influenced by this politicized view of antislavery.[19] Equally significantly, local antislavery was able to hold together for some years despite

---

[18] V. A. C. Gatrell, 'Incorporation and the Pursuit of Liberal Hegemony in Manchester, 1790–1839', in Derek Fraser (ed.), *Municipal Reform and the Industrial City* (Leicester, 1982), 24–8; Mark Billinge, 'Hegemony, Class and Power in Georgian and Early Victorian England: Toward a Cultural Geography', in Alan R. H. Baker and Derek Gregory (eds.), *Explorations in Historical Geography: Interpretive Essays* (Cambridge, 1984), 49–57. Harrison is quoted in Arnold Thackray, 'Natural Knowledge in Cultural Context: The Manchester Model', *Amer. Hist. Rev.*, 79 (1974), 687; Turley, *Culture*, 118–20, 25–6; Grayson Ditchfield, 'Manchester College and Anti-Slavery', in Barbara Smith (ed.), *Truth, Liberty, Religion: Essays Celebrating Two Hundred Years of Manchester College* (Oxford, 1986), 187–224; James Anderson, *Observations on Slavery: Particularly with a View to its Effects on the British Colonies in the West Indies* (Manchester, 1789).

[19] Compare Thomas Cooper, *Letters on the Slave Trade* (Manchester, 1787) and Samuel Bradburn, *An Address to the People called Methodists: Concerning the Evil of Encouraging the Slave Trade* (Manchester, 1792).

the Paineite sentiments of Cooper and Walker because it was part of a culture of improvement under challenge from more traditionalist elements. The network of Tory families, with the mill-owning Peel family at its heart, was less closeknit than the Lit. and Phil. group, but had opposed them over several years on important issues. These included Walker's campaigns against the fustian tax in 1784 and in favour of lower tariffs under the 1786 treaty with France, dissenting support for the repeal of religious tests between 1787 and 1790, and the proposed changes at the Infirmary. A prominent member of the Peel family was the main organizer of anti-abolition petitioning from Manchester.[20] Only after the 1792 September massacres in France and loyalist violence in Manchester in December, however, did the antislavery alliance of radicals influenced by Paine with libertarian Whigs such as Percival and Barnes that gave local antislavery its particular character break up.[21]

Sheffield abolitionists a generation later in the late 1820s and 1830s were also involved with a multiplicity of associations for doing good. The reform culture of Sheffield, however, was very different. Evangelical protestantism assumed a central place in the town's religious life from the beginning of the nineteenth century. This influenced local Anglicanism, but at the height of the campaign for emancipation two-thirds of those attending religious services were members of nonconformist congregations. The most prominent figures in local abolitionism and their main popular support came from evangelical dissent, though flanked by Anglican and Unitarian elements. James Montgomery, popular poet and editor of the *Iris* until 1825, became a Moravian and worked closely with fellow evangelicals Samuel Roberts and Rowland Hodgson, as well as the Unitarian and moderate political reformer Thomas Asline Ward. Active at the organizational level of antislavery (including animating the Ladies' Anti-Slavery Society) were the family of the manufacturer Joseph Read, and the Rawson family into whom Read's daughter, Mary Anne, married. They were 'Calvinistic Independents' and Baptists. A local doctor and science lecturer, Charles Favell, formerly a Unitarian, turned into the most prominent Anglican abolitionist in the town.[22]

Montgomery and Roberts demonstrated a morally paternalist attitude to the less fortunate as well as concern about social stability. Montgomery promoted

[20] Turley, *Culture*, 120; Charles Webster and Jonathan Barry, 'The Manchester Medical Revolution', in Smith (ed.), *Truth, Liberty, Religion*, 167–83.

[21] Frida Knight, *The Strange Case of Thomas Walker: Ten Years in the Life of a Manchester Radical* (London, 1957), 74–5, 78–9. Note Percival's assertion of 'temperate and constitutional' Whiggism and distaste for innovation based on 'philosophic fancy': Thomas Percival, *The Works, Literary, Moral and Philosophical*, 2 vols. (London, 1807), i, pp. clxxv–vi, ccxxxvi–vii.

[22] Dennis Smith, *Conflict and Compromise: Class Formation in English Society, 1830–1914: A Comparative Study of Birmingham and Sheffield* (London, 1982), 81, 122–4, 127–8; Sheffield Central Lib., Wilson-Rawson papers (hereafter SCL, W-R), MD 5079, J. Graham Spencer to 'Mr Wilson' [H. J. Wilson], 18 Jan. 1907.

savings banks to encourage thrift among the poor and took over control of the Mechanics' Library in its early years, excluding morally suspect fiction and political literature. Montgomery, Ward, and Favell, all involved in the Mechanics' Institute, saw it as an instrument for encouraging the most sober and loyal of the working class to collaborate in producing industrial peace and social harmony. This was at a time when the local cutlery and edge tool trades were facing difficulty and some working people in the town were challenging the limited character of political change in the 1830s.[23]

Equally indicative of concern for the true moral order that Sheffield abolitionists assumed must underlie social harmony were the campaigns, led by Roberts, to improve the physical and moral conditions of climbing boys and gypsies, both suitable cases for evangelism. Language drawn from antislavery, particularly in defence of the family, informed his writing on these topics. Roberts also became nationally prominent for his opposition to the New Poor Law. He saw the law as contrary to 'the immutable laws of God', but also the result of a moral declension in public life and the break-up of the old social order of the countryside that had had 'all the advantage of constant residence of the Squire at the Hall'. The evangelical, and particularly nonconformist, ethos of Sheffield abolitionists was further expressed through support of overseas missions, Sunday schools, and temperance and bible societies. The Anti-Slavery Society on occasion met at the premises of the local bible society, and used Sunday schools to distribute antislavery literature.[24]

There was an evangelical flavour to the antislavery propaganda that local abolitionists put out. Roberts insisted that slavery was a sin and thus to be totally and immediately removed. He believed too that religious conviction harmonized with the most practical course of action since the policy of amelioration, supposedly leading gradually to emancipation, allowed planters to delay the process. Unless they were emancipated, slaves would act to free themselves. Emancipation was both prudential and a religious imperative; it would constitute not only admission of the former slaves to legal freedoms, but complete the conditions prepared already by white missionaries for them to be led 'forth

---

[23] Smith, *Conflict*, 139–40; Mabel Tylecote, *The Mechanics' Institutes of Lancashire and Yorkshire* (Manchester, 1957), 54–5, 58, 110–11; Billinge, 'Reconstructing Societies', 25; John Salt, 'The Creation of the Sheffield Mechanics' Institute: Social Pressures and Educational Advance in an Industrial Town', *Vocational Aspect*, 17 (1966), 143–50; Ian Inkster, 'Introduction: The Context of Steam Intellect in Britain (to 1851)', in Inkster (ed.), *The Steam Intellect Societies: Essays on Culture, Education and Industry circa 1820–1914* (Nottingham, 1985), 4–5.

[24] Samuel Roberts, *A Cry from the Chimneys or an Integral Part of the Abolition of Slavery throughout the World* (London, 1837); Colin Holmes, 'Samuel Roberts and the Gypsies', in Sidney Pollard and Colin Holmes (eds.), *Essays in the Economic History of South Yorkshire* (Barnsley, 1976), 233–46; Samuel Roberts, *The Rev. Dr Pye Smith and the New Poor Law* (London, 1839); SCL, W-R, MD 6041; John Rylands Lib., Manchester, Rawson family papers (hereafter JRL, RFP), MS 743 [R63635], Sheffield Anti-Slavery Society minute book, 26 May 1830.

to liberty indeed', that is, to true Christianity. The religious logic extended not only to opposing compensation for the sinful slave-owners, but to mass petitioning to free the country from 'the blackest stain she has upon her character'.[25] When it was achieved, the freeing of the slaves could therefore be celebrated as a British national triumph in Montgomery's 'The Negro is Free'. Even more appropriately he composed hymns for Emancipation Day on 1 August 1834 that were sung at a gathering of 'Protestant Dissenters of Sheffield united in public thanksgiving and congratulation':

> Tidings, tidings of salvation!
> Britons rose with one accord,
> Purged the plague-spot from our nation,
> Negroes to their rights restored;
> Slaves no longer,
> Free-men, – free-men of the Lord.[26]

Antislavery was also significant for the way that it drew women into community action and reflected their influence, though more markedly in the 1820s and 1830s than earlier. Initially decorum restricted public action by female supporters. Even so, in 1787–8, women comprised a respectable proportion of lists of subscribers in Manchester: 68 of 302. By 1791–2 wives were often taking the initiative in a consumer boycott of slave-grown sugar. Women debated the slave-trade in female gatherings and a few signed 'mixed' petitions in 1792; in 1814 separate women's petitions appeared against the resumption of the French trade. Only from the late 1820s did women play a full part as petitioners, culminating in the massive female petition of 1833 with 187,000 signatures.[27]

Women also wrote their way into antislavery. Women poets took up the topic as the campaign against the trade got under way. But it was in the 1820s that the Leicester Quaker Elizabeth Heyrick significantly influenced the discourse of antislavery in developing the case for immediate emancipation. Her argument placed reliance on divine power rather than human calculation. Immediatism avoided the danger of retributive justice on the nation, removed the planters from

---

[25] Samuel Roberts, *The Tocsin, or, Slavery the Curse of Christendom* (Sheffield, 1825); Samuel Roberts, *Tocsin the Second, or, the Total and Immediate Abolition of Slavery* (Sheffield, 1827); Samuel Roberts, *A Letter to the Rev. Thomas Smith, A. M., on the Subject of Slavery with some Remarks on His Conduct at the Late Meeting Held at the Cutler's Hall on the Ninth of June* (Sheffield, 1828); [Samuel Roberts], *The Second Trumpet: A Blast for the Pledged Colonial Secretary, by the Watchman* (Sheffield, 1833); 'Africanus' [handbill] (Sheffield, 1830).

[26] James Montgomery, 'The Negro is Free' [leaflet] (Nottingham, 1834); James Montgomery, *Hymns for the First of August 1834* (Sheffield, 1834).

[27] Clare Midgley, *Women against Slavery: The British Campaigns, 1780–1870* (London, 1992); see also Drescher, *Capitalism*, 78, 85, 215 nn. 44–5, 221–2 nn. 69–70; Oldfield, *Popular Politics*, 137–41.

moral bondage, and provided obvious advantages to the labourers. It would also maintain interest in the country.[28]

Heyrick's prediction of raised interest was soon fulfilled with the emergence of separate ladies' antislavery associations, beginning in 1825. Their role was understood primarily as speaking for slave women and children, and to 'keep up' the moral concern of their men. In 1828 the Claphamite Zachary Macaulay concluded that the ladies' associations 'seem to form the mainstay of our hopes'.[29] Some groups, as in Sheffield, adopted immediatism in the late 1820s and supported the agency system of travelling lecturers in the early 1830s. In the campaign against apprenticeship female abolitionists acted when their male colleagues held back. This militancy caused strains within antislavery coalitions in some places, both with male abolitionists and with more reticent female colleagues, but illustrates the capacity of antislavery in its most dynamic phase to expand the possibilities of women's public action.[30]

The analysis of Manchester and Sheffield abolitionism makes evident the different cultural and political meanings that could be attached to antislavery and emphasizes the need to complicate our ideas about the 'popular'. Potential supporters were likely to be aware of, and variously to respond to, the features of local reform in adopting an understanding of local antislavery and its leaders and assessing their own attitude to the national campaign. In both towns there was a shared sense of the cruelties of the slave-trade and slavery and recognition that they disrupted proper order in the world. This posed dangers, both moral and political, to the national community.[31] At the local level progress towards a true order could be achieved through understanding of the laws governing human society, such as those of political economy, and laws ruling the natural world, both ultimately compatible with religion. Equally men and women could submit themselves to the dictates of Providence and encourage others to do the same. Yet these local cultures also differed: Manchester antislavery in the late eighteenth century was part of an Enlightenment enterprise of 'reformation' including a wider recognition of rights. There was a clearly defined local leadership with an initiating role and a local opposition unconvinced

[28] Oldfield, *Popular Politics*, 133–6; Elizabeth Heyrick, *Immediate not Gradual Abolition* (London, 1824).

[29] Rhodes House Lib., Oxford (hereafter RH), Brit. Emp. MSS, S18, C1/28, Daniel Hack to Thomas Pringle, 2 Feb. 1831; JRL, RFP, MS 743 [R63635], Sheffield Ladies Anti-Slavery Society minute book, 12 July 1825; MS 742 (47) [R63635]; Univ. Coll. London, Brougham MSS, 10275, Z. Macaulay to ?, 16 Feb. 1828.

[30] Sheffield Ladies Anti-Slavery Society, *A Word for the Negro* (Sheffield, 1827), 10; Agency Committee of the Anti-Slavery Society, *Report* (London, 1832), 22; JRL, RFP, MS 741 (123) [R63635], Elizabeth Walker to Mrs M. A. Rawson, 23 Oct. [1837]; MS 742 (58) [R63635], Mrs M. A. Rawson to secretary of Men's Committee, 23 Feb. 1838.

[31] Turley, *Culture*, 36, 38.

that antislavery (or other projects for change) would be in the local interest. The cumulative effect of elite antagonisms and community conflict produced clear divisions that probably aided mobilization on both sides. Neither a united manufacturing interest pursuing a vigorous antislavery policy nor a popular upsurge expressing pure antislavery sentiment imposed itself upon the community. Sheffield a generation later shared in the wide mobilization on behalf of antislavery based predominantly on dissenting congregational and denominational petitioning and public meetings. Antislavery in the 1830s had become a mass movement, yet in Sheffield some antislavery leaders remained rather conservative moralists in uneasy alliance with more liberal elements. The popular features of Manchester antislavery were not the basis of its link to other forms of community improvement, as Drescher's interpretation of the movement would imply. In Sheffield antislavery was undoubtedly popular but it did not invariably foster support for other forms of social and political change, though it could do so.

II

Where antislavery was central to engineering change was in colonial reform. From the beginning abolitionists were convinced of the un-Christian character of the slave system, but also conscious of the economic value of the plantation colonies. They faced the formidable strength of the West India interest with its support in parliament and planter control of local assemblies in the colonies. Removing the moral stain of the slave system, maintaining the prosperity of the West Indies, and establishing a sustainable order in the colonies required the pursuit of separate strands of policy, often simultaneously.

Abolitionists promoted some policies that would reform economic organization and institutional practices on the sugar plantations. Recurrently they argued that plantation work should be reorganized to give slaves more time to spend on their garden plots or in other ways to gather resources for progressive self-purchase. Ending of discipline by the whip in the amelioration period was intended to alter daily conditions of work and mark a change in how authority was exercised. Alongside this institutional approach antislavery aimed to advance free black people in Sierra Leone and slaves and ex-slaves in the Caribbean in morality and Christian civilization. The aim of 'civilizing' Africans (through the agency of black settlers) and taking moral progress to West Indian slaves involved their education and religious instruction. The latter theme was central to the revitalized movement in the decade before emancipation and an evident feature of local antislavery cultures, such as that of Sheffield, in the amelioration period of the 1820s. It reflected the expansion of missionary activity after the Napoleonic Wars. Abolitionists also understood that trade between colonies and metropolis was a crucial feature of the empire, and they were convinced of the power of commerce to advance both material prosperity and their moral and political objectives.

Different strands of policy pursued at the same time, abolitionists supposed, would have a cumulative effect because they envisaged the strands as interwoven. Developing trade from Africa in more 'legitimate' products than human beings or altering the terms of the commerce on which the sugar plantations depended were measures intended to influence change towards free labour and more just social relations. Abolitionists believed these changes were being legitimated and transition potentially eased through a combination of legislative reform of the daily routine of slavery and the education of slaves in religion and the virtues needed to work in freedom. Until late on, therefore, the campaign for emancipation had a built-in gradualism. It was also evidently premissed on the interdependence of institutional, moral, and commercial reform.[32] The remainder of the chapter will illustrate this argument in more detail.

Individual proposals for basing the imperial system on free labour had been advanced in the 1760s and 1770s, but failed to gain effective backing at the time of the American crisis.[33] With the slave-trade under scrutiny in the 1780s Sierra Leone became a site of antislavery experiment. It had a double significance for abolitionists. Positively, the experiment was to demonstrate (especially under the guidance of the Claphamite Sierra Leone Company from 1791) that black settlers could prosper as free farmers and labourers with commercial links to the outside world and without resort to the slave-trade. There was hope that neighbouring chiefs could be persuaded that it was in their material and moral interests to follow suit. Governor Zachary Macaulay early manifested the antislavery commitment to spreading 'civilized' practices and values amongst the settlers when, in 1796, he tried to impose marriage regulations on them. The negative significance of Sierra Leone was that it revealed how difficult it could be to gain acceptance of these policies from the black subjects of antislavery benevolence as well as other interested parties. Some settlers protested at interference in their personal lives.[34] There was periodic disorder and eventually the Claphamites were accused of continuing the slave-trade by enlisting as apprentices in the settlement slaves rescued from ships on the Middle Passage.[35]

In antislavery terms Sierra Leone did not provide a persuasive model for creating a free-labour black society, but abolitionists could not concede their approach had received a fair trial. Thus Sierra Leone prefigured later efforts to

---

[32] *Ibid.*, 17–46.
[33] Christopher L. Brown, 'Empire without Slaves: British Concepts of Emancipation in the Age of the American Revolution', *William and Mary Quart.*, 3rd ser., 56 (1999), 273–306.
[34] Lamin Sanneh, *Abolitionists Abroad* (Cambridge, 1999), 121.
[35] Michael J. Turner, 'The Limits of Abolition: Government, Saints and the "African Question", 1780–1820', *Eng. Hist. Rev.*, 112 (1997), 319–57; David Eltis, *Economic Growth and the Ending of the Transatlantic Slave Trade* (New York, 1987), 22–3, 300 n. 20.

deal with the African slave-trade and introduced strands of policy also carried forward to abolitionists' involvement with colonial reform in the West Indies. Much was familiar about Thomas Fowell Buxton's efforts in the early 1840s to create settlements on the Niger based on protestant Christianity and free agricultural communities trading products with the outside world. What was primarily different about the later context was the growth in the intervening years in Britain of evangelical dissenting denominations involved in missionary work and the impact their zeal had on antislavery at home and in the colonies. Missionaries in the West Indies were instructed to avoid taking an explicit stand on slavery, but their work influenced slaves' outlook and frequently seemed dangerous to masters. Implicitly, mission religion offered a perspective on future, post-slave colonial development.[36]

Why and how this was so is exemplified in the figure of the Wesleyan Methodist Richard Watson.[37] He was a member of the London committee of the Anti-Slavery Society in the later 1820s and clearly articulated the religious grounds of this phase of antislavery. Worldly affairs were linked to the spiritual world through the notion of Providence; the providential duty of Christians was to preach the Gospel. The spread of Christianity, moreover, had great temporal significance; it was the most efficient way of fostering civilization since 'it is the parent of morality, industry and public spirit . . . the strength . . . of all well-ordered society'. God's design was to banish all evil and for the purpose He had 'given us wealth, commercial connexions, a mercantile navy, and colonies . . . and religious liberty'. By 1830 Watson was asserting that 'We cannot care for the salvation of the negro without caring for his emancipation from bondage.' Methodists and other mission-minded dissenters were mobilized by these sentiments and by the victimization of missionaries and their congregations that occurred in the colonies.[38]

Within the context of Christianizing and 'civilizing' the colonial black population, abolitionists could accommodate to the policy of amelioration introduced in 1823. It initially held out some hope of altering the behaviour of slave-owners and gave more time for moral improvement amongst the slaves. Abolitionists accepted this gradualist approach so long as the mechanisms for improvement appeared to be working. Yet, at least from late 1825 onwards, criticism of the policy as ineffectual emerged within the Anti-Slavery Society.[39] The assertion of a minority of abolitionists that immediate emancipation was necessary

---

[36] C. A. Bayly, *Imperial Meridian: The British Empire and the World, 1780–1830* (London, 1989), 139–41; Howard Temperley, *White Dreams, Black Africa: The Antislavery Expedition to the Niger, 1841–42* (New Haven, 1991); Mary Turner, *Slaves and Missionaries: The Disintegration of Jamaican Slave Society, 1787–1834* (Urbana, 1982).

[37] I owe appreciation of Watson's significance to conversations with the late Roger Anstey.

[38] Richard Watson, *Works*, 12 vols. (London, 1834), ii, 30–1, 10; iv, 138–9, 233; i, 502; *Anti-Slavery Reporter*, no. 65 (Aug. 1830).

[39] RH, Anti-Slavery MSS, E2/2, ASS minute book, 21 Dec. 1825.

because the planters were resisting improvements did not, however, signal abandonment of the project of Christianizing and civilizing the bondsmen. Ending slavery rapidly was to release slaves into a regime of 'strict laws', to pay wages 'but to let the idle starve', to maintain religious instruction, 'not to supply the Negroes with the power of committing acts of violence, but . . . to take away from them the inducement'.[40]

Even after the Anti-Slavery Society had espoused immediatism in 1830, government ministers thought immediate emancipation an impractical policy. They favoured an approach that maintained discipline and a sufficient labour supply. All the various emancipation proposals entertained by politicians in the early 1830s assumed the primacy of civilized order incorporating the value of work. The period of apprenticeship thus marked a continuation of the gradualist perspective. Some reformers were bound to resist the scheme, but none of them dissented from the need to ensure good order and an ethic of work amongst the former slaves.[41] Under apprenticeship, both abolitionists who accommodated to it, such as Buxton, and those opposed to it, like the Birmingham Quaker Joseph Sturge, stressed the importance of religious and practical education amongst the freed people. A similar emphasis continued into the 1840s after the end of apprenticeship, though in later years it was complicated by denominational rivalries between missionaries.[42] Some differences existed amongst abolitionists after 1834 about the most appropriate economic pattern to ensure that the former slaves worked within a framework that encouraged their growth in civilization. A minority envisaged the possibility of peasant proprietorship in villages (though normally involved in the discipline of supplying at least local markets). Others assumed that peasant plots would provide some autonomy, but act as a supplement to wage labour on the plantations. Yet others (Buxton among them) concluded that tough vagrancy laws should prevent 'squatting' on spare land and that otherwise the disciplines of an unregulated labour market should operate through 'the influence of want'.[43] These differences, however, operated within a broad area of agreement about the moral and material components of

---

[40] Sheffield Female Anti-Slavery Society, *Report* (Sheffield, 1827), 5–6.

[41] *The Holland House Diaries, 1831–1840*, ed. A. D. Kriegel (London, 1977), 55–6, 17 Sept. 1831; Brit. Lib., Add. MS 51,820, Henry Taylor memo. 7 Jan. 1833; Samuel Roberts, *The Safe, Satisfactory, Efficient, Immediate, and Total Abolition of Slavery: To J. S. Buckingham. Esq. M.P.* (Sheffield, 1833); David Brion Davis, *Slavery and Human Progress* (New York, 1984), 189–90.

[42] RH, Brit. Emp. MSS, S 444, iii, fos. 37–9, T. F. Buxton to secretaries of the missionary societies, 28 Nov. 1832; Jamaica Education Society, *Report* (Birmingham, 1838); *The Nineteenth Annual Report of the Ladies' Society for Promoting the Early Education and Improvement of the Children of the Negroes and People of Colour in the British West Indies* (London, 1844); Mary Anne Rawson, *The Thompson Normal School, Jamaica* (Sheffield, 1845); Carl Campbell, 'Denominationalism and the Mico Charity Schools in Jamaica, 1835–1842', *Caribbean Studies*, 10 (1971), 152–72.

[43] Eltis, *Economic Growth*, 21, 24–5, 298–9 n. 13; Davis, *Slavery and Human Progress*, 215–19.

progress that the freed people were to internalize. Both former slaves and abolitionists initially saw emancipation as a major break from the past, but it was also part of a longer-term process of change in the West Indies in which antislavery acted throughout as a channel of cultural imperialism.

Commercial reform as a recurring strand of antislavery also ran through from amelioration to the post-apprenticeship period with the supposed leverage it provided against the inefficiencies of slavery and indirect influence on the 'civilizing' project. This conviction that commercial and moral objectives could be fused was an extension of the view that free labour was more efficient than slavery because free labourers were energized by receiving the rewards of their efforts, whereas in slavery the masters appropriated them. Initially appearing in antislavery writings in the 1780s the idea became a commonplace in the 1820s as a result of the pamphlets of the Liverpool abolitionists James Cropper and Adam Hodgson. Cropper especially pressed for the removal of the tariff advantages of West Indian sugar producers in the British market, and argued that the consequent competition from East Indian free-labour producers would compel West Indians to become more efficient. They would conclude that efficiency required them to move towards free labour. Eventually the institutional character and ethos of slave societies would be altered.[44] Although there were only minor commercial adjustments on sugar in the 1820s the commercial reform policy re-emerged in the 1840s when the progressive equalization of sugar duties in the British market was enacted in 1846. A majority of abolitionists consistently supported the invigorating effects of what was to be a free market in sugar by 1854. But for some the different context of commercial reform posed a problem. The fact that free labour now grew West Indian produce provoked a minority to reverse Cropper's earlier confident yoking of the moral and economic arguments. With no Caribbean slavery to be subverted by the competition of other producers, they feared that the ex-slaves still settling into freedom would be the victims of a free market. Some abolitionists, and especially Joseph Sturge with his concern for the firm establishment of peasant village communities in the islands, found themselves allied with West Indians in favour of maintaining preferences.[45]

The strength of the 'civilizing' theme in antislavery was intended to ensure a smooth transition to freedom and to create societies closer in their values and practices to metropolitan Britain. Racial differences were deemed less important than the power of religion and education and the channelled impulses of

---

[44] Seymour Drescher, *From Slavery to Freedom: Studies in the Rise and Fall of Atlantic Slavery* (Basingstoke, 1999), 408–17; James Cropper, *Letters Addressed to William Wilberforce* (Liverpool, 1822); James Cropper, *A Letter Addressed to the Liverpool Society* (Liverpool, 1823); Adam Hodgson, *A Letter to M. Jean-Baptiste Say* (Liverpool, 1823).

[45] Rev. John Clark, *A Brief Account of the Settlements of the Emancipated Peasantry* (Birmingham, 1852).

man's economic nature. The peaceful achievement of emancipation, and the pushing to the margins of such a strong support of the pre-reform political order as the West Indians, were the chief marks of the success of antislavery as a reform endeavour. Later negative conclusions on the longer-term achievement were shaped by scepticism about the very possibility of 'civilizing' the racially different.

8. 'The age of physiological reformers': rethinking gender and domesticity in the age of reform

KATHRYN GLEADLE

In 1852 the *Westminster Review*, musing upon the widespread popularity of alternative medicine, declared it to be 'pre-eminently the age of physiological reformers'.[1] Certainly for many early Victorian radicals, the concept of reform extended far beyond demands for political, economic, and social changes; it encompassed a desire to democratize the very care and feeding of the body. As J. F. C. Harrison observed, a striking number of Owenites and Chartists rejected the heroic, interventionist medical practices of the day, and turned to alternative health therapies;[2] so too did the families of numerous middle-class reformers, including the Sturges, McLarens, Ashursts, and Stansfelds. This is not to say, of course, that there is a necessary causal link between radical politics and popular medicine. However, the frequency of these connections raises important questions, not least for assessments of women's political activism and the construction of the home within radical discourse.

By focusing upon the importance of the domestic site and female activism within five areas of health reform (namely, vegetarianism, homoeopathy, hydropathy, hygeism, and medical botany) this chapter seeks to problematize the assumption that women became alienated from reforming politics during the 1840s as its structures and organization became increasingly formalized and bureaucratized.[3] In so doing, it aims also to further debate concerning the nature of female political consciousness. The restricted nature of female political identities has been much discussed, such identities drawing so frequently upon

---

[1] [Samuel Brown], 'Physical Puritanism', *Westminster Rev.*, 1 (1852), 405–42.
[2] J. F. C. Harrison, 'Early Victorian Radicals and the Medical Fringe', in W. F. Bynum and Roy Porter (eds.), *Medical Fringe and Medical Orthodoxy, 1750–1850* (London, 1987), 198–215.
[3] Dorothy Thompson, 'Women and Nineteenth-Century Radical Politics: A Lost Dimension', in Juliet Mitchell and Ann Oakley (eds.), *The Rights and Wrongs of Women* (Harmondsworth, 1976), 112–38. Other historians have been similarly pessimistic regarding the potential for women's political agency during this period: Sally Alexander, 'Women, Class and Sexual Difference in the 1830s and 1840s: Some Reflections on the Writing of Feminist History' (1983), repr. in Sally Alexander, *Becoming a Woman and Other Essays in 19th and 20th Century Feminist History* (London, 1994), 97–125.

socially constructed norms of wife and motherhood.[4] However, it is argued here that domestic roles formed a far more significant and intricate facet of early Victorian radicalism than is often recognized. In these milieux, domestic activities were necessarily privileged over formal, public, procedural politics. Reform, that is, began at home. The place of women within radical sub-cultures was, therefore, far more complex, and potentially empowering, than is often conveyed. Health reform, however, also enabled women to utilize a variety of strategies to express ideological conviction in the 'public' world of reforming politics.

It is necessary first to provide a brief overview of the movements under consideration. Vegetarianism, with which we shall begin, has a long and intricate history.[5] Following the German mystic Jacob Böhme (1575–1624), British mystics such as William Law eschewed meat as part of a desire to triumph over bodily passions. From the late eighteenth century vegetarianism was also propounded in the small, discrete circles of advanced radicals such as Percy Bysshe Shelley and Richard Phillips. They dwelt upon the supposedly iniquitous effects of meat consumption upon the human character and related their vegetarianism to wider, humanitarian concerns. However, it was in Salford that the most significant advance was made towards the institutionalization of vegetarian ethics. Here, a congregation of Bible Christians, a Swedenborgian sect led by the Rev. William Cowherd, pledged themselves to abstain from meat and alcohol in 1809.[6] Cowherd's successor, the Revd James Scholefield, similarly followed Swedenborg in attaching considerable importance to the correlation between spiritual and physical phenomena. Accordingly, as a keen scientist, Scholefield perceived his role as pastor to involve his congregation's bodily as well as spiritual health. The Bible Christians, who probably numbered less than 2,000, were further known for their support for political radicalism. Characteristically,

---

[4] Jutta Schwarzkopf, *Women in the Chartist Movement* (Basingstoke, 1991); Catherine Hall, 'The Tale of Samuel and Jemima: Gender and Working-Class Culture in Early Nineteenth-Century England' (1986), repr. in Catherine Hall, *White, Male and Middle Class: Explorations in Feminism and History* (Cambridge, 1992), 124–50.

[5] John Belchem, '"Temperance in All Things": Vegetarianism, the Manx Press and the Alternative Agenda of Reform in the 1840s', in M. Chase and I. Dyck (eds.), *Living and Learning: Essays in Honour of J. F. C. Harrison* (Aldershot, 1996), 149–62; Colin Spencer, *The Heretic's Feast: A History of Vegetarianism* (London, 1994); Julia Twigg, 'The Vegetarian Movement in England 1847–1981, with Particular Reference to its Ideology' (London School of Economics, Ph.D. thesis, 1982). My thanks to James Gregory for helpful and informative discussions concerning his forthcoming University of Southampton Ph.D. thesis on vegetarianism.

[6] See Paul A. Pickering and Alex Tyrrell, '"In the Thickest of the Fight": The Reverend James Scholefield (1790–1855) and the Bible Christians of Manchester and Salford', *Albion*, 26 (1994), 461–82; Peter J. Lineham, 'Restoring Man's Creative Power: The Theosophy of the Bible Christians of Salford', in W. J. Sheils (ed.), *The Church and Healing* (Oxford, 1982), 207–23; W. R. Ward, 'Swedenborgianism: Heresy, Schism or Religious Protest?', in Derek Baker (ed.), *Schism, Heresy and Religious Protest* (Cambridge, 1972), 303–10.

Scholefield suggested that the Bible should be referred to as 'The Rights of Man',[7] and Chartist meetings were organized in their chapel.[8]

Bible Christians were closely involved in the Vegetarian Society (formed in 1847), but other influences were critical. Vegetarianism was in vogue among left-leaning networks of middle-class intellectuals, particularly in London[9] and also among Owenites and Owenite-influenced sub-cultures. (The ascetic First Concordium community at Ham Common, for example, stated their abhorrence of 'unnecessary cruelty' and evinced a desire to sublimate bodily wishes so as to liberate the self from the tyranny of physical desires.[10]) Indeed, while the Vegetarian Society itself never amounted to more than several hundred members, there was a broader (if always small) basis of support for the cause amongst an eclectic range of socialists, radicals, and rational dissenters.[11] The Vegetarian Society itself attracted interest and support not only in Manchester, Salford, and London, but also in other urban centres such as Liverpool, as well as in small, rural settings. Padstow in Cornwall, for example, often hosted vegetarian events.[12]

The early Victorian vegetarian movement articulated a holistic conception of radical politics that underlined an intimate relationship between the bodily and spiritual state. It was concerned to obey the dictates of natural, God-given laws of health and to create temperate, lean citizens whose very living functioned as a

---

[7] Twigg, 'Vegetarian Movement', 100.

[8] Joseph Brotherton MP, another key member of the church, although more moderate in his politics, also championed a whole gamut of radical causes.

[9] Adrian Desmond, *The Politics of Evolution: Morphology, Medicine and Reform in Radical London* (Chicago and London, 1989).

[10] *A Brief Account of the First Concordium, or Harmonious Industrial College* [n.d.], 3. For a full account of the personnel involved in the First Concordium, see J. E. M. Latham, *Search for a New Eden: James Pierrepont Greaves (1777–1842): The Sacred Socialist and his Followers* (London, 1999). For a consideration of the community's significance for female political expression, see Kathryn Gleadle, '"Our Several Spheres": Middle-Class Women and the Feminisms of Early Victorian Radical Politics', in Kathryn Gleadle and Sarah Richardson (eds.), *Women in British Politics, 1760–1860: The Power of the Petticoat* (Basingstoke, 2000), 135–40. For other vegetarian communities, see J. F. C. Harrison, *Robert Owen and the Owenites in Britain and America: The Quest for the New Moral World* (London, 1969), 130.

[11] Vegetarian Chartists, for example, included Charles and Elizabeth Neesom: Joyce M. Bellamy and John Saville (eds.), *Dictionary of Labour Biography*, 9 vols. (Basingstoke, 1972–93) viii, 179–80; *Vegetarian Advocate* (Aug. 1848), 16–17. Travers Madge and James Haughton are both examples of radical Unitarian vegetarians: Brooke Herford, *Travers Madge: A Memoir* (London, 1868); *Water-Cure Jl and Hygienic Mag.*, 1 (1848), 342–3. In Leicester, Mary Coltman, sister of the antislavery activist, Elizabeth Heyrick, formed part of a vegetarian network: Kathryn Gleadle, 'British Women and Radical Politics in the Late Nonconformist Enlightenment, c. 1780–1830', in Amanda Vickery (ed.), *Women, Privilege and Power: British Politics, 1750 to the Present* (Stanford, 2001), 147–8. The White Quakers also practised vegetarianism: *Herald of Co-operation and Organ of the Redemption Soc.* (Mar. 1848), 116.

[12] E.g., *Vegetarian Messenger*, no. 7 (May 1850), 74. The *Vegetarian Messenger* (later the *Dietetic Reformer and Vegetarian Messenger*) provided full accounts of the range of vegetarian meetings and soirées held across the country.

witness against the excesses and corruption of the established political system. Vegetarians insisted that political reforms would prove superficial unless they were accompanied by more fundamental transformations in citizens themselves. As the *Vegetarian Messenger* put it, 'Can we expect that war will cease whilst the love of dominion is cherished in the human heart? Can the tree of liberty flourish in the human soil, whilst man is the slave of intemperance, revenge, and all the "household tyrants" to which he has resigned the government of his will?'[13] The movement appears to have declined sharply in the 1860s (its fortunes were to be revived in the 1880s with the growth of the socialist movement), but in the 1840s many practitioners believed vegetarianism to have visionary promise. It was frequently perceived as a progressive force that would facilitate the accomplishment of other pivotal reforming goals. One prominent activist, Henry S. Clubb, declared at a vegetarian event in Worcester that 'Every Vegetarian with whom he was acquainted, was a zealous supporter of the Peace, Temperance, Education, Sanitary, Financial, and Parliamentary Reform Movements. The reason was, their system being deeper and wider than those, comprehended them all.'[14] As a model of individual reformation, it was, declared the *Vegetarian Advocate*, the 'beginning and end of all true reforms'.[15]

Homoeopathy (the treatment of illness through the administration of infinitesimal doses of medicine) was a movement that attracted far more support than vegetarianism. Homoeopathy being perceived as a holistic system of medicine that encouraged the natural healing of the body, radical homoeopaths in common with contemporary vegetarians were concerned to practise a therapy that functioned in accordance with God-given laws. Nevertheless, the widespread and eclectic support homoeopathy attracted warns against any simple equation between alternative medicine and radicalism. The therapy had begun to attract attention in Britain during the 1820s and 1830s when it was particularly associated with Frederick Quinn, who had extensive connections with the Whig nobility. Indeed, until the 1840s, it was predominantly practised in upper-class and fashionable circles. However, at this point, the movement underwent a period of rapid growth, becoming the site of considerable conflict. A radical element, led by political activists such as John Epps (physician to many of the metropolitan middle-class reforming network) and other prominent radicals including William Henry Ashurst, James Stansfeld, and William Case, came to champion homoeopathy as part of their political programme.[16] Under the aegis of the English Homoeopathic Association (the EHA, established

---

[13] *Vegetarian Messenger*, no. 2 (Dec. 1849), 17.
[14] *Ibid.*, no. 11 (Sept. 1850), 126; see also *ibid.*, no. 3 (Jan. 1850), 36; no. 10 (Aug. 1850), 112.
[15] *Vegetarian Advocate* (Mar. 1850), 73.
[16] For further details on this reforming network, see Kathryn Gleadle, *The Early Feminists: Radical Unitarians and the Emergence of the Women's Rights Movement. c. 1831–51* (Basingstoke, 1995).

in 1845) and the *Journal of Health and Disease* they infuriated their rivals, the British Homoeopathic Society (formed in 1844), by encouraging efforts to 'democratize' the practice of medicine. They supported the medical practice of non-professionals, and encouraged 'domestic homoeopathy'.[17] As Case made clear in an address to the EHA, homoeopathy could be implicated in a political project that championed the 'liberty of the subject'.[18] The movement, publicized by its various organizations, was flourishing by the 1850s (by which time it could boast of fifty-seven dispensaries and three hospitals). At the end of 1866, the London Homoeopathic Hospital alone had treated nearly sixty thousand patients. However, by the 1870s, recruitment to homoeopathy was on the wane and its distinctive philosophy had become blurred as increasing numbers of homoeopaths merged their practice with conventional medicine.[19]

A similar pattern may be detected in the water-cure movement. Hydropathy sought the restoration of health through the application of water.[20] This was to be achieved through a complex system of bathing techniques (including wet-sheets, the vapour bath, the douche, the sitz bath, the rain bath, and even finger baths), tailored to suit the requirements of particular ailments. Hydropathy, in common with many sectors of the homoeopathic movement, further insisted upon a reform of lifestyle, stipulating the importance of a frugal regime, abstention from alcohol and dietary stimulants, and vigorous exercise. It was, as one practitioner insisted, 'the art of living according to nature'.[21] While drawing upon an attenuated medical tradition that had long exhorted the use of cold-water bathing, it cohered as a movement from the early 1840s, inspired by the techniques of the Austrian Vincent Priessnitz. Priessnitz's theories were circulated in Britain by Captain R. T. Claridge, and popularized by practitioners such as James Manby Gully and William McLeod. In common with homoeopathy, it earned some popularity amongst fashionable, and particularly intellectual, circles and remained in vogue from the 1840s through to the 1870s, when it lost its proselytizing zeal. One of the best-known hydropathists, John Smedley, claimed to have treated 85,000 patients by 1872.[22] Like the other therapies under discussion, it frequently overlapped with other medical heresies, most notably

---

[17] Radical homoeopaths were influenced by the work of American practitioners, e.g. J. H. Pulte, *Homoeopathic Domestic Physician* (London, 1852); C. Hering, *The Homoeopathist; or Domestic Physician* (London, 1845). See also Glynis Rankin, 'Professional Organisation and the Development of Medical Knowledge: Two Interpretations of Homoeopathy', in Roger Cooter (ed.), *Studies in the History of Alternative Medicine* (London, 1988), 46–62.

[18] *Jl Health and Disease* (Apr. 1850), 293.

[19] Phillip A. Nicholls, *Homoeopathy and the Medical Profession* (London, 1988), 134, 103–5; Phillip Nicholls, 'Homoeopathy in Britain after the Mid-Nineteenth Century', in Mike Saks (ed.), *Alternative Medicine in Britain* (Oxford, 1992), 7.

[20] Robin Price, 'Hydropathy in England, 1840–70', *Medical Hist.*, 25 (1981), 269–80.

[21] A. Courtney, *Hydropathy Defended by Facts, or the Cold Water Cure* (London, 1844), 6.

[22] Kelvin Rees, 'Water as a Commodity: Hydropathy in Matlock', in Cooter (ed.), *Studies in the History of Alternative Medicine*, 34.

teetotalism,[23] homoeopathy,[24] and vegetarianism.[25] Moreover, the movement was particularly associated with a network of radical liberal Quakers and Unitarians (many of whom were also homoeopaths) such as the families of W. H. Ashurst, Duncan and Priscilla McLaren, Elizabeth Pease, Joseph Sturge, and James and Caroline Stansfeld.[26] For reformers such as these, hydropathy could be co-opted as part of a radical programme. Such an approach was particularly associated with William McLeod's hydropathic establishment at Ben Rhydding, near Ilkley in the West Riding of Yorkshire, which was used by many radicals for both recuperation and networking. It sponsored a democratic philosophy, its *Water-Cure Journal* arguing that all were equal as all operated according to fixed physical laws.[27]

Some activists worried that costly hydropathic establishments reinstated a hierarchy between the physician and the patient, the rich and the poor.[28] However, radical hydropaths made attempts to redress the balance. Both the Stansfeld and Sturge families established hydropathic institutions expressly for use by the working class,[29] and while such philanthropic gestures may not have appeased their critics, there was a discernible mood in these circles in favour of demystifying medical practice so as to encourage self-treatment. The *Water-Cure Journal* deliberately used journalists with no medical training: 'we make no apology, as this is especially a journal for the people'.[30] While home treatment may not have played as large a part in hydropathy as it did in the other treatments discussed in this chapter, manuals on domestic treatment were common.[31]

The final two movements to be considered were associated with a lower socio-economic stratum. The medical botanists were inspired by the work of the

---

[23] One practitioner declared hydropathy and teetotalism to be the 'twin sisters in the work of purifying and elevating the human race': *Water-Cure Jl and Hygienic Mag.*, 1 (1848), 368.

[24] E.g., William Macleod, *Directory of Ben-Rhydding, with a Chapter on the Water Cure and Homoeopathy* (London, 1852); Edwin Lee, *Homoeopathy and Hydropathy Impartially Appreciated* (London, 1859). For a contrasting position, see Andrew Henderson, *Hydropathy and Homoeopathy Compared* (London, 1860).

[25] The vegan First Concordium community of 'sacred socialists' at Ham Common were early practitioners of the system: Latham, *Search for a New Eden*, ch. 10. The foundation of the Vegetarian Society in 1847 took place at the Horsells' hydropathic hospital. Hydropathic publications, such as the *Water-Cure Jl*, published debates on the merits and pitfalls of vegetarianism: see *Water-Cure Jl and Hygienic Mag.*, 1 (1848), 342–3; 2 (1849), 115–16; 2 (1849), 378.

[26] Alex Tyrrell, *Joseph Sturge and the Moral Radical Party in Early Victorian Britain* (London, 1987); Anna M. Stodart, *Elizabeth Pease Nichol* (London, 1899); Nat. Lib. Scotland, Edinburgh, McLaren papers, MS 24823, *passim*.

[27] *Water-Cure Jl and Hygienic Mag.*, 1 (1848), 257–8.

[28] W. Horsell, *The Board of Health and Longevity: or Hydropathy for the People* (London, 1845), 138–9.

[29] Tyrrell, *Joseph Sturge*, 184. Hamer Stansfeld wished to establish a hydropathic centre, 'not in the way of speculation, but generously with a view to do good to the human family'. McLeod, *Directory*, 42 n.

[30] *Water-Cure Jl and Hygienic Mag.*, 1 (1847), 3.

[31] E.g., Joseph Constantine, *Hydropathy at Home* (London, 1868).

American practitioner, Samuel Thomson, who argued that disease was caused through a loss of internal heat. Through the judicious use of herbal remedies (in particular lobelia) it was believed that the body's natural balance could be restored. Thomson's ideas were circulated in England largely through the agency of Albert Isaiah Coffin, who was active in Manchester in the late 1840s. The movement spawned numerous societies, particularly in the industrial north, and also in the north-west where twenty-nine localities have been found to have been active in the movement.[32] By 1850, medical botanic societies might be found in the majority of Lancashire towns (there was also a strong presence in the south-west) and, indeed, it was during the 1850s that medical botany was at its zenith. While Coffin's claim that *Coffin's Botanical Journal and Medical Reformer* had a fortnightly circulation of some ten thousand must be treated with caution, none the less hostile medical professionals feared that there were several thousand actual practitioners.[33] The movement attracted a predominantly plebeian following (although its practitioners may have come from slightly higher socio-economic backgrounds) and drew closely upon networks of religious dissent and temperance activism. It was characterized by its uncompromising emphasis upon 'medicine for the people',[34] and an open hostility towards the medical establishment which readily distinguished it from traditional herbal therapy. By the 1860s this political edge was noticeably muted, and the distinctions between it and traditional herbalism became less readily apparent.[35]

The fifth therapy, hygeism, enjoyed a similar socio-economic makeup to that of medical botany, although it was probably numerically less significant. Hygeists believed in the need to purge impure blood through the agency of James Morison's vegetable pills, first introduced in 1821. Hygeists entertained fewer connections with other alternative medicines, Morison declaring hydropathy and homoeopathy to be quackery.[36] However, it shared with the medical botanists a political agenda to protect the 'inherent and inalienable rights of every human being' and combat the 'goading yoke of medical bondage' by dissolving a medical monopoly concerned only with the protection of its own 'exclusive privileges'.[37]

---

[32] See Ursula Miley and John V. Pickstone, 'Medical Botany around 1850: American Medicine in Industrial Britain', in Cooter (ed.), *Studies in the History of Alternative Medicine*, 140–54.

[33] *Ibid.*, 141; P. S. Brown, 'Herbalists and Medical Botanists in Mid-Nineteenth-Century Britain with Special Reference to Bristol', *Medical Hist.*, 26 (1982), 412.

[34] Brown, 'Herbalists and Medical Botanists', 410.

[35] John V. Pickstone, "Establishment and Dissent in Nineteenth-Century Medicine: An Exploration of Some Correspondence and Connections between Religious and Medical Belief Systems in Early Industrial England', in Sheils (ed.), *Church and Healing*, 176–81; Logie Barrow, *Independent Spirits: Spiritualism and English Plebeians, 1850–1910* (London, 1986), 162–7; F. B. Smith, *The People's Health, 1830–1910* (London, 1979), 339–41.

[36] *Hygeist* (July 1843), 89, (Sept. 1847), 297.

[37] John Stevens, *Medical Reform, or Physiology and Botanic Practice for the People* (London, 1847), vii; *Hygeist* (Oct. 1843), 105–7; Miley and Pickstone, 'Medical Botany', 140–54.

Intersecting the reforming community, then, from the working-class followers of James Morison, to wealthy influential figures in Victorian radical politics, lay a holistic application of the radical principles of individual rights, wherein lifestyle and bodily care were closely implicated in the reform project. Although it is impossible to construct precise figures as to the numbers involved, statistics for attendance at treatment centres, the existence of dedicated publications and journals for individual therapies, and the formation of societies to support each movement, together indicate that this was a vibrant and flourishing aspect of contemporary reform culture. Clearly not all those who followed such movements would have fully embraced the political agendas publicized by the leadership. Medical botany, for example, must have merged, at times almost imperceptibly, with traditional recourse to herbal remedies. Equally, highly successful and commercially orientated treatments, such as hydropathy, attracted followers of diverse political sensibilities. Thomas Carlyle, for example, sampled hydropathic medicine.[38] What is clear, however, is that each of the movements under consideration was either led by, or contained, a prominent constituency of radical political reformers for whom health reform was central to their wider ideological agenda. Indeed, a significant number of leading radical politicians and reformers and their families, including, for example, the Ashursts, Brothertons, McLarens, Stansfelds, and Sturges, were keen devotees of health reform. This adherence to alternative 'democratic epistemologies'[39] requires a recognition that, for a sizeable constituency of radicals, reform was conceived not merely in terms of constitutional measures, but involved a close scrutiny of the domestic site. Furthermore, whereas the 1840s have traditionally been viewed as the highpoint of radical activity, this model suggests an alternative, or at least more variegated, trajectory. Many of the medical heresies considered here began to flourish in the 1840s, but reached their peak in the 1850s and 1860s.[40] No doubt this was partly fuelled by such measures as the compulsory vaccination of infants (1853) and the Medical Registration Act (1858) that galvanized medical heretics.[41] However, the continuing success of these causes may also have derived from an internalization of radical sensibilities following the defeat of the Chartist programme.[42] This point is fundamental

---

[38] Price, 'Hydropathy in England', 277. One recent assessment of the movement, noting that many hydropathic practitioners were conventionally trained, assumes that they were therefore drawn to the therapy as much for its commercial potential as for its radical ideological premiss: James Bradley and Marguerite Dupree, 'Opportunity on the Edge of Orthodoxy: Medically Qualified Hydropathists in the Era of Reform, 1840–60', *Social Hist. Medicine*, 14 (2001), 417–37.

[39] Barrow, *Independent Spirits*, 174.

[40] Many of these activists, particularly those involved in the overlapping networks of vegetarianism, teetotalism, and Owenism, also gravitated into the plebeian spiritualist movement: *ibid.*, *passim*.

[41] A number of initiatives depended upon a coalition of followers and practitioners of these various therapies, e.g., the anti-vaccination movement, the National Medical Reform League, and the Medical Liberty Society: *ibid.*, 187.

[42] Pickstone, 'Establishment and Dissent', 180; Twigg, 'Vegetarian Movement', 106.

to considerations of women's political activism. For, if many reformers were concentrating upon domestic issues such as the practice of hygiene, diet, and nursing, then it follows that a significant number of women experienced not alienation from politics during this time, but closer involvement.

Indeed, adherence to an alternative medical agenda had major repercussions for women's household and affective labour, for it necessitated new family practices of consumption and hygiene. As a consequence, the customary domestic activities of women were immediately politicized. The daily demands of 'physical puritanism'[43] demanded continual vigilance over household management: the provision of appropriate food at strictly regular intervals, the correct bath temperature for children, early rising – all were seen as critical details in the successful reform of the body. Many vegetarian writers recommended that families should mill their own wholemeal flour, whilst the *Dietetic Reformer*, noting the prevalence of animal-based domestic products such as scrubbing brushes and spoons, argued that its readers should strive for a 'Vegetarian home in which there is nothing, in the attainment of which it has been necessary to hurt or to destroy'.[44] It was clearly essential that women were fully committed to these ideals, as well as zealous in their execution. Indeed, women were often urged that many domestic tasks should not be entrusted to hired help. Hence Mrs Asenath Nicholson explained in her *Kitchen Philosophy for Vegetarians* the 'importance of every mistress of a family being devoted to the superintendence of her own household and kitchen, without leaving the preparation of food to servants'.[45]

The intensification of household work has typically been interpreted as an additional burden that further alienated women from the possibilities of alternative fulfilment.[46] This may certainly have been true for some women. (Although, interestingly, the asceticism of contemporary vegetarianism enabled a small minority of campaigners to argue that a vegetarian diet would actually liberate women from their current position as 'little more than cooking-and-boiling machines'.[47]) However, it seems probable that, for most vegetarian women, infusing domestic acts with political significance would have made the fulfilment of domestic chores *more* satisfying. It may have provided a meaningful way

---

[43] For a discussion of this term, see Virginia Smith, 'Physical Puritanism and Sanitary Science: Material and Immaterial Beliefs in Popular Physiology, 1650–1840', in Bynum and Porter (eds.), *Medical Fringe*, 174–97.

[44] Job Caudwell, *Vegetarian Cookery for the Million* (London, 1864), 2; *Dietetic Reformer and Vegetarian Messenger*, 1, no. 3 (July 1861), 70–1.

[45] As quoted in the *Vegetarian Advocate* (Sept. 1849), 10.

[46] Leonore Davidoff, 'The Rationalization of Housework', in Davidoff, *Worlds Between: Historical Perspectives on Gender and Class* (Cambridge, 1995), 73–102.

[47] *Vegetarian Messenger*, no. 50 (Dec. 1853), 74. See also William Horsell, *The Science of Cooking Vegetarian Food* (London, 1847), 4; Charles Lane, *Dietetics: An Endeavour to Ascertain the Law of Human Nutriment* (London, 1849), 41; *Truth-Tester*, 2 (May 1848), 130; *Dietetic Reformer*, 2, no. 20 (Oct. 1865), 106–8.

to reconcile domesticity with politics, and formed a viable strategy whereby women were able to express their ideological views. The *Vegetarian Messenger* was particularly optimistic, arguing that under the vegetarian system women would find that domestic duties were 'replete with satisfaction and delight'.[48] Some vegetarian writers also hinted at possibilities for enhanced status within the household, arguing that women's role in preparing vegetarian food was so essential to family health that their function was comparable to that of a physician.[49] As the *Truth-Tester* explained, 'Other educators . . . seldom reach the *physical* man. This whole field, or nearly so, is left to the sole direction and disposal of the mother. How important, then . . . that mothers should understand this subject.'[50]

Practical considerations aside, it is not surprising that mothers were envisaged as critical to reform. As recent historians have noted, radical campaigners, in particular the Chartists, could politicize the ubiquitous cultural trope of motherhood by articulating a 'militant domesticity' which sanctioned maternal political activism in the public sphere.[51] Although Albert Coffin might pragmatically suggest the formation of 'Maternal Associations' to disseminate knowledge of juvenile health,[52] the discourses of health reform tended rather to recast the maternal role within the domestic site than to argue for mothers' public political engagement. The evocation of motherhood within the discourses of health reform could easily slide into the stereotypical and sentimental,[53] yet there was a recurring strain that stressed the intellectual role mothers might play within their families. William Horsell envisaged boys and girls assisting with the preparation of vegetarian meals, whilst their mothers instructed them in the 'geography, history, character, laws, and dietetic habits of the various nations' as well as discussing the chemistry of food, comparative anatomy, vegetable and animal physiology, and the laws of health.[54] Such a concern was also explicit in radical hydropathic circles. The *Water-Cure Journal*, for example, argued that women should be educated to be the 'prophylactic physician of the family', conversant with the technical details of digestion, and the mechanisms of the heart and lungs.[55]

The construction of women as well-informed domestic physicians is an image that may well have appealed to many radical women. As mothers and carers,

[48] *Vegetarian Messenger*, no. 2 (Dec. 1849), 24.   [49] *Ibid.*

[50] *Truth-Tester*, 1 (1847), 94.

[51] See Anna Clark, 'The Rhetoric of Chartist Domesticity: Gender, Language and Class in the 1830s and 1840s', *Jl Brit. Studies*, 31 (1992), 62–88.

[52] *Coffin's Botanical Jl and Medical Reformer* (12 Oct. 1850), 233.

[53] See, e.g., Lewis Gompertz, 'An Appeal to Mothers', in *Fragments in Defence of Animals, and Essays on Morals, Soul, and Future State* (London, 1852), 90–1; Mrs Asenath Nicholson, *Treatise on Vegetable Diet, with Practical Results* (London, 1848), 26–8.

[54] Horsell, *Science of Cooking Vegetarian Food*, 5.

[55] *Water-Cure Jl and Hygienic Mag.*, 1 (1847), 158–62.

women could fulfil ideological beliefs through the practice of democratic health, without transgressing conventional expectations of female behaviour. Indeed, without their agency it was possible that the whole project of domestic medicine was doomed. As one practitioner admitted, 'though you were Priessnitz himself, unless you have the co-operation of the ladies, or happen to live in some favoured neighbourhood, we defy you satisfactorily to carry out the prescriptions of a hydropathic physician'.[56] The vegetarian movement was similarly insistent as to women's importance, the *Vegetarian Advocate* noting that 'The ultimate success of our movement, no less than its gradual growth and adoption, depend most materially on the co-operation of wives, sisters, and servants. The influence of woman's voice and example will ever be one of the greatest means for the furtherance of social reform, and in no department of it more than in that which pertains to eating and drinking.'[57]

Numerous women did indeed function as the conduits through which knowledge of alternative methods of nursing, meal preparation, and hygiene could flow. As Mr Torrington, a medical botanist, explained, 'I was brought up by my mother in a knowledge of medical botany.'[58] Within the vegetarian movement, the upbringing of James Simpson (president of the Vegetarian Society) at the hands of a strictly vegetarian mother was frequently cited with approval.[59] Eulogies to deceased members of the Bible Christian church also captured the important, yet publicly invisible, contribution of mothers to the vegetarian cause who could foster and encourage particular sensibilities in their offspring.[60]

Indeed, while women's access to public political forums is certainly a vital issue (and one to which we will return later), the alternative lifestyles presaged in medical heresies had the potential to empower women at a more fundamental level, and on a more day-to-day basis, than did participation in those projects seeking purely constitutional reforms. Health-reform advocates could be ambivalent, or even hostile, to contemporary discussions on women's rights,[61] and yet most articulated a programme of female empowerment over their own bodies. Emergent feminist discourses concerning the need for female physicians[62] merged very closely with the demand for female midwives that issued from the

---

[56] *Hydropathic Record and Jl of the Water Cure*, 1 (1868), 17.
[57] *Vegetarian Advocate* (supplement, 1850), 15–16.
[58] *Coffin's Botanical Jl and Medical Reformer* (26 Oct. 1850), 240.
[59] E.g., *Truth-Tester*, 1 (1847), 141.
[60] Cordelia Clark, for example, was remembered as a quiet woman, but 'she was firm in her convictions, and had the pleasure to see her children grow up and do honour to the principles she valued': William E. A. Axon, *A History of the Bible Christian Church, Salford* (Manchester, 1909), 128 n.
[61] See, e.g., *Dietetic Reformer*, 2, no. 23 (July 1866), 91–2; *Hydropathic Record*, 1 (1868), 15–16.
[62] See Alison Bashford, *Purity and Pollution: Gender, Embodiment and Victorian Medicine* (London, 1998); Catriona Blake, *The Charge of the Parasols: Women's Entry to the Medical Profession* (London, 1990); Jean Donnison, *Midwives and Medical Men: A History of Inter-Professional Rivalries and Women's Rights* (London, 1977), ch. 4.

networks of alternative medicine. Both medical botanists and hygeists (some of whose works on female midwifery were published by prominent vegetarians) supported demands for female education and employment.[63] This frequently formed part of a broader aspiration to 'induce the females of this country to think and act for themselves' and to instruct women in midwifery.[64]

Although radical homoeopaths, such as John Epps, championed natural childbirth,[65] most homoeopathic women were said to have little choice but to use the services of conventional physicians during their confinements. Even in these circumstances, however, they could assert their control by refusing to take any medication prescribed by such a doctor.[66] Medical botanists were more fortunate. Practising female midwives in the movement, such as Mrs Lee in Leeds and Anna Naylor in Sheffield, were committed to natural childbirth, the latter claiming that she treated up to 170 women in one year.[67] Hydropathic establishments, like those set up in Matlock by Mr and Mrs Ralph Davis, Mr and Mrs Stevenson, Mr and Mrs Bartin, and Caroline and John Smedley, were run by married couples, as it was thought important that women should be treated by female physicians.[68] Caroline Smedley argued that labour was safer in the hands of female midwives. She lambasted the conventional management of births, criticizing, for example, the use of laxatives.[69] Given the repeated pregnancies faced by most women during this period, the opportunities to assert autonomy over their bodies in this way may have formed one of the most attractive and immediate facets of the political agendas of health-reform movements. This appears to have been equally true in other areas of political radicalism. The Owenite lecturer Emma Martin practised as a midwife and delivered popular, women-only lectures on female physiology. This formed an integral facet of her feminist agenda to facilitate women's control over their own bodies.[70]

[63] [John Browne], *The Accoucheur: A Letter to the Rev Mr. Tattershall, on the Evils of Man-midwifery* (London, 1857); John Stevens, *Extracts from Man-Midwifery Exposed* (London, 1862); *Hygeist* (June 1845), 185, (Mar. 1855), 20–1; *Coffin's Botanical Jl and Medical Reformer* (23 Nov. 1850), 265–6.

[64] A. I. Coffin, *Treatise on Midwifery* (1853), xi–xii.

[65] John Epps, *Domestic Homoeopathy: or Rules for the Domestic Treatment of the Maladies of Infants, Children and Adults* (London, 1844), 158.

[66] *Jl Health and Disease* (Jan. 1847), 206.

[67] *Coffin's Botanical Jl and Medical Reformer* (1 July 1848), 158–9; (5 Jan. 1850), 15; (30 Mar. 1850), 66.

[68] See the advertisements in Joseph Buckley, *Matlock Bank, as It Was and Is: Being an Account of the Origins and Development of the Matlock Bank Hydropathic Establishments* (London, 1867); Rees, 'Water as a Commodity', 28–44.

[69] Mrs Smedley, *Ladies' Manual of Practical Hydropathy for Female Diseases* (London, 1861). The relationship between hydropathy and feminism has only been fully explored in the American context: Susan E. Cayleff, *Wash and Be Healed: The Water-Cure Movement and Women's Health* (Philadelphia, 1987).

[70] Kathryn Gleadle (ed.), *Radical Writing on Women, 1800–1850: An Anthology* (Basingstoke, 2002), 150.

Despite the existence of feminist strands within the discourses of democratic medicine, and the importance of women in effecting reform, representations of women remained contested and variable.[71] Even given its pro-feminist sentiments and the important role it assigned to mothers, *Coffin's Botanical Journal and Medical Reformer* could still publish articles arguing that mothers could interfere in the cause of progress, being 'too apt to indulge' children.[72] Indeed, the very need to rely upon women to effect health and food reform could form a source of palpable tension. Vegetarian editors often published letters from disgruntled male members, captious at their wives' lack of support for the cause.[73] The figure of the conservative wife, reluctant to alter domestic arrangements, became a common trope in vegetarian circles. In vegetarian meetings up and down the country, James Simpson repeatedly blamed women for the perpetuation of meat consumption. His speech to the vegetarian soirée in Leeds in 1853 is exemplary: 'Ladies did not reason upon this question! they did not inquire into it; if they did, the custom would soon die out. It existed only because woman, with her gentle nature and sensitiveness, did not trace back the dishes on the table to the animals that lived and breathed but a few hours before.'[74]

Other activists repeated similar tales of female obstinacy. Although one sympathetic man observed that it required courage for women to break the customary boundaries of social etiquette and provide meat-less refreshment for guests and family,[75] others were less sensitive. One reported that mothers and wives feared that their menfolk would kill themselves by adhering to a vegetarian diet, but obligingly noted that such sentiments were 'natural, so long as the understanding of the fair sex is less operative in reason than in affection'.[76]

Complaints of female implacability were not universally accepted within the movement, however. Indeed, there are hints of frictions over the attitude of some members. At a soirée of the Liverpool Vegetarian Association in 1853, Simpson's customary swipe at women was followed by two speakers who pointedly emphasized their delight at the number of women present and reiterated women's importance to the movement.[77] Moreover, despite the comments of

---

[71] For a superb account of the fluidity of representations of gender in another context of alternative healing, see Alison Winter, *Mesmerized: Powers of Mind in Victorian Britain* (Chicago and London, 1998). Equally, it has been noted that the contemporary phrenological movement could play a restrictive role in reinstating hierarchies based on gender, race, and class: Roger Cooter, *The Cultural Meaning of Popular Science: Phrenology and the Organization of Consent in Nineteenth-Century Britain* (Cambridge, 1984).

[72] *Coffin's Botanical Jl and Medical Reformer* (1 May 1847), 34.

[73] See, e.g., 'Notices to Correspondents', *Vegetarian Messenger*, no. 7 (May 1850); *Dietetic Reformer*, 2, no. 19 (July 1865), 82.

[74] *Vegetarian Messenger*, no. 45 (July 1853), 28.

[75] *Dietetic Reformer*, 2, no. 10 (April 1863), 55–6.

[76] *Vegetarian Messenger*, no. 41 (Mar. 1853), 18.

[77] *Ibid.*, no. 42 (Apr. 1853), 9–12. Similar frictions were evident at annual meetings of the society. For example, at the seventeenth annual meeting, there were clear, if muted, tensions

(cont. on p. 213)

those such as Simpson, women were frequently observed to comprise up to 50 per cent of the audience at vegetarian events (often the figure was much higher); and public criticisms of women's lack of interest in vegetarianism were usually undercut by 'Votes of thanks to the ladies' for their active contribution to the evening's preparations.[78] An analysis of the society's membership in 1866 concluded that although men greatly outnumbered women in the organization (women forming but 22.5 per cent of the membership), female members were generally more persistent in their support.[79]

Beneath these tensions lay complex issues pertaining to marital dynamics and the domestic site. It would be simplistic to assume that those families who converted to vegetarianism automatically provide evidence of female involvement in reforming projects. In some cases, vegetarian practice might actually signal extreme male domination over both the public and private activities of the family. For example, William Lambe, a vegetarian of the early nineteenth century, was reported as being 'somewhat despotic in his family in exacting the strict observance of his laws'.[80] It would be equally misguided to construct a rigid paradigm of Victorian marriages, in which domesticity is conveyed as uniquely the realm of women. As recent discussions of Victorian masculinity have indicated, notions of domesticity were in fact central to the formulation of male identities. Men played integral domestic roles, not merely as parents, but in nursing the family sick or (especially amongst plebeian males) in perpetuating the use of particular medical treatments.[81] Significantly, many health reformers stressed not the maternal role, but rather joint parental responsibility to engage in rational enquiry to question conventional medicine or meat-based diets.[82] The vegetarian cause, moreover, in itself required a renegotiation of the meanings attached to domestic activities. The *Vegetarian Advocate*, for example, recognized a need to 'dwell among the pots and the pans, and to discourse on the modes of frying, stewing, and baking', in the cause of progress,[83] and a number of vegetarian cookery books were male-authored.[84]

(*cont.*)
between Mr Barker, Mr Gaskell, and Mr Holcroft regarding women's contribution to the movement: *Dietetic Reformer*, 2, no. 17 (Jan. 1865), 7–10, 16.

[78] See, for example, supplement, *Vegetarian Messenger*, no. 16 (Feb. 1851), 14.

[79] *Dietetic Reformer*, 2, no. 24 (Oct. 1866), 98–9; also argued in Nicholson, *Treatise on Vegetable Diet*, 93.

[80] E. Hare, *The Life of William Lambe* (London, 1807), 154.

[81] John Tosh, *A Man's Place: Masculinity and the Middle-Class Home in Victorian England* (New Haven and London, 1999); Leonore Davidoff and Catherine Hall, *Family Fortunes: Men and Women of the English Middle Classes, 1780–1850* (London, 1987), 329–31. I am grateful for discussions with Stuart Hogarth on this point, whose forthcoming Ph.D. thesis promises to elucidate many of these issues.

[82] *Jl Health and Disease* (Sept. 1848), 60; *Dietetic Reformer*, 1, no. 2 (Apr. 1861), 58; John Smith, *Fruits and Farinacea the Proper Food of Man* (London, 1845), 354.

[83] *Vegetarian Advocate* (Sept. 1849), 2.

[84] John Smith, *The Principles and Practice of Vegetarian Cookery* (London, 1860); Horsell, *Science of Cooking Vegetarian Food*.

None the less, as the many frustrated would-be vegetarian husbands indicated, there was a widespread cognizance of the weight of female domestic authority, and there is evidence to suggest that incidents of male usurpation of such authority were viewed as transgressive.[85] This, combined with the social courage required of those adopting heterodox lifestyles, enables us to postulate that most families who did participate in such movements probably did so with the conviction and support of the woman of the family; and that women would typically function as the primary practitioners and facilitators of family adherence to particular lifestyles.

Within the vegetarian movement, the importance of family engagement was made particularly evident by the recurring patterns of familial commitment. Tight networks of religious and political dissent were often cemented through kinship and marriage ties – as is evident from the Bible Christians in Salford in which the interrelated Brotherton, Clark, Collier, Gaskill, and Lomas families predominated.[86] Such models of family cohesion were not confined to those in the health-reform movements, but applied equally to the broader radical milieu. Many historians have noted the importance of family-based social activities to both Chartist and Owenite politics. This is indicative of a much wider, but less tangible manifestation of political activism that drew upon the vitality of a home-based culture of political discussion, commitment, and practice.[87]

Yet it would be misleading to imply that women's ideological commitment lay solely in the specific performance of domestic and child-rearing duties. Women's activities were extremely diverse, drawing upon their multi-faceted contribution to social, cultural, and economic life, and upon female traditions of public engagement. Philanthropy, for example, formed a central strategy for promoting radical ideological viewpoints. Elizabeth Pease, an active political campaigner (and assistant manager of the Ben Rhydding hydropathic establishment), was closely involved with the establishment of the Benevolent Hydropathic Institution; whilst a committee of ladies proved central to the foundation of a homoeopathic hospital for the working classes in 1850.[88] The phonographic movement, which promoted spelling reform as a means of bringing intellectual freedom to the people, was a cause in which vegetarians

---

[85] A. James Hammerton, *Cruelty and Companionship: Conflict in Nineteenth-Century Married Life* (London and New York, 1992), 114–15. Female domestic authority could also influence electoral decisions: see Matthew Cragoe, '"Jenny Rules the Roost": Women and Electoral Politics, 1832–1868', in Gleadle and Richardson (eds.), *Women in British Politics*, 153–68.

[86] Axon, *History of the Bible Christian Church*.

[87] Barbara Taylor, *Eve and the New Jerusalem: Socialism and Feminism in the Nineteenth Century* (London, 1983), ch. 7; Paul A. Pickering, *Chartism and the Chartists in Manchester and Salford* (Basingstoke, 1995). James Vernon, however, dismisses the possibility of female agency, initiative, and authority in assuming that even within this context 'the forms and terms of that participation were regulated by men': James Vernon, *Politics and the People: A Study in English Political Culture, c. 1815–67* (Cambridge, 1993), 229.

[88] *Water-Cure Jl and Hygienic Mag.*, 1 (1848), 264–5; *Jl Health and Disease* (Apr. 1850), 284.

and political radicals were closely involved. Here, women formed a Ladies Phonographic Corresponding Society providing free correspondence courses in phonographic techniques.[89]

One campaigner, Sarah Ann Clubb, neatly conflated these issues in her 1854 story, *Good Influence*. The central character, Mrs Mowbray, lectures her servant's family on the importance of vegetarianism in the maintenance of family health, and superintends allotments for the local poor (to enable them to embrace a meat-free diet). When Mrs Mowbray's daughter, Julia (a vegetarian, early-riser, and phonographer!), laments that the villagers did not appear grateful for this assistance, Mrs Mowbray explains that 'it must inspire us to do more for them, because ingratitude is a sign that people are not enlightened enough to perceive the benefit we would confer'.[90]

Despite the democratic sentiments underpinning radical health reform, middle-class women evidently utilized traditional relationships of philanthropic authority. This was clearly displayed by prominent middle-class vegetarian women, such as Mrs Simpson (the wife of James Simpson), who reiterated their superior status by presenting prizes to working-class allotment holders.[91]

Wealthy women could further promote vegetarianism through their role as patrons to contemporary activists.[92] For those of more moderate means, such as Emma Philbrick and Mrs Dornbusch, loyalty to the cause could be expressed through circulating and promoting progressive periodicals.[93] Such publications also benefited from women's willingness to engage in debate via correspondence pages. The importance which health-reform movements attached to the intimate daily routines of family life facilitated female interaction of this kind. Letters were published on such topics as the temperature of children's bath water; the propriety of cooking with baking soda; descriptions of breast-feeding problems; and details of home cures.[94]

Contributions to reforming periodicals were but the tip of a larger literary iceberg. Women's writing on health and food reform, and the related issue of animal welfare,[95] was a varied and eclectic phenomenon, and constituted

---

[89] *Phonotypic Jl*, 2 (1843), 36–9.

[90] S. A. Clubb, *Good Influence: A Tale for the Young who are Willing to Seek the Stepping Stone to Health, Intelligence and Happiness* (London, 1854), 26. Clubb came from a Colchester family of active phonographers, vegetarians, and Swedenborgians. In 1850 she was running a ladies' phonetic short-hand class from the Vegetarian Home Colony in Stratford St Mary, Suffolk: *Vegetarian Advocate* (supplement, Dec. 1850), 75. Her brother, Henry Stephen Clubb, edited the *Vegetarian Messenger*: Twigg, 'Vegetarian Movement', 85.

[91] 'Fox-Hill Bank Temperance Garden Allotments', supplement to the *Vegetarian Messenger* (1851).

[92] Gleadle, 'Our Several Spheres', 134–9.   [93] *Truth-Tester*, 2 (1848), 10, 20, 128.

[94] *Jl Health and Disease* (Mar. 1850), 270–1; *Hydropathic Record*, 1 (1869), 78; *Truth-Tester*, 2 (1848), 102.

[95] Moira Ferguson, *Animal Advocacy and Englishwomen, 1780–1900: Patriots, Nation and Empire* (Ann Arbor, 1998); Hilda Kean, *Animal Rights: Political and Social Change in Britain since 1800* (London, 1998).

a central arena in which women could commit themselves to reform. Martha Brotherton's *Vegetable Cookery* was enormously important to the movement, forming the basis of most subsequent works on vegetable cookery;[96] while homoeopathic women could also use recipe books to promote their (less abstemious) injunctions for a healthy lifestyle.[97]

In addition to cookery books and works on domestic management, such as Elizabeth Horsell's *Domestic Assistant: Being a Guide to Vegetarian Cookery*, vegetarian women also furthered their views through imaginative literature, as we saw in the case of S. A. Clubb. Fanny Lacy managed to publish one of her vegetarian tales in the *Metropolitan Magazine* and composed the poetical invitation to the Physiological Festival (a key event in the founding of the Vegetarian Society);[98] while Anna Blackwell provided an extended examination of the vegetarian philosophy in her novel *Ellen Braye*.[99]

Other women found that their foreign-language skills formed a viable route to support reform movements. Ellen Epps made a major contribution to the homoeopathic movement by translating the works of the founder of homoeopathic theory, Samuel Hahnemann.[100] She also published her own, cheerful work on health, *Practical Observations*, which Epps placed within the political context of wishing to encourage people to question established authority and to contribute to the 'good conferred on the brotherhood of man'.[101]

For others, commitment to alternative medicine or vegetarianism was indicated through economic ventures. As already noted, hydropathic establishments were often run jointly by wives and husbands. In Manchester, Mrs Hollinworth established a vegetarian restaurant in 1850, and W. H. Barnesley and his wife set up a Vegetarian and Temperance Hotel.[102] Susan Havill in Exeter ran a temperance hotel from which she also provided medical care and dispensed Morison's pills.[103] Lower down the social scale, hygeists worked, as we have seen, as

---

[96] Martha Brotherton was the wife of Joseph Brotherton MP. Her book, originally published in 1821, went through several editions and revisions.

[97] *A Manual of Homoeopathic Cookery, by the Wife of a Homoeopathic Physician* (London, 1866); Ellen Epps, *Practical Observations on Health and Long Life* (London, 1855).

[98] *Truth-Tester*, 2 (1848), 20, see also 30–1.

[99] *Ellen Braye, or, the Fortune-Teller*, 2 vols. (London, 1841), esp. i, 152–92. The work was favourably reviewed in the *Healthian*, 2 (1842), 13–14. Blackwell (the sister of the medical pioneer, Elizabeth Blackwell) was closely involved in Fourierist circles: Peggy Chambers, *A Doctor Alone: A Biography of Elizabeth Blackwell: The First Woman Doctor, 1821–1910* (London, 1956).

[100] *Jl Health and Disease* (Dec. 1848), 153–64; (May 1849), 333–44. See also the translation work of Sophia C. Chichester, the leading patron of the Ham Common Concordium: Gleadle, 'Our Several Spheres', 138.

[101] Epps, *Practical Observations*, 2, 15.

[102] *Vegetarian Advocate* (Feb. 1850), 62; advertisement in *Vegetarian Messenger*, no. 17 (Mar. 1851).

[103] *Hygeist* (May 1848), 332.

midwives or medical agents.[104] The medical-botany movement similarly relied upon female as well as male agents to sell Coffin's cures and to dispense advice and medication.[105] Following the death of her husband, the enterprising Elizabeth Horsell opening a boarding school for young ladies, particularly those of vegetarian families, and William Turley and his wife, leading figures in the metropolitan vegetarian movement, offered education to vegetarian children from their home in Hampstead.[106]

Women's participation in the formal affairs of health-reform societies was, as we have seen, more problematic. The Vegetarian Society did not embed gender-equal policies into its structure, and the officers of the society all appear to have been male.[107] In practice, women continued to assist in the running and organization of the society, none the less, attending business meetings and pledging significant financial contributions to ensure its continued survival.[108] Very occasionally, women managed to make their views heard during the movement's public events, sometimes through the agency of a sympathetic male who would read or describe their activities.[109] In reports of vegetarian discussion classes, there is sporadic mention of the large numbers of ladies present. Hannah Bond (formerly the matron of the Alcott House School at the Ham Common Concordium) spoke proudly of her membership of a Mutual Instruction Society that organized discussions on vegetarianism.[110]

Perhaps more typically, within the vegetarian movement it was women's primary responsibility for food provision that enabled them to contribute to the public face of reforming politics. In this capacity they were central to the social politics of the movement, hosting vegetarian soirées from their homes, as did Mrs Hurlestone.[111] Elsewhere, female members of the Vegetarian Society formed local committees to organize the catering arrangements for the movement's activities.[112] At a vegetarian banquet in Padstow, sitting next to the president of the Vegetarian Society, James Simpson, was Mrs Griffin, who had

---

[104] *Ibid.* (Nov. 1843), 111.

[105] See, e.g., *Coffin's Botanical Jl and Medical Reformer* (4 Sept. 1847), 71–2; (10 Nov. 1849), 339.

[106] *Vegetarian Advocate* (Aug. 1849), 143; *Dietetic Reformer*, 2, no. 16 (Oct. 1864), 128.

[107] This is in contrast to the earlier vegetarian society established at the First Concordium: Gleadle, 'Our Several Spheres', 139.

[108] Greater Manchester Rec. Office, G24/1/1/1, minutes of Vegetarian Soc., 29 July and 28 Oct. 1859.

[109] *Truth-Tester*, 2 (1848), 29; *Dietetic Reformer*, 2, no. 17 (Jan. 1865), 8.

[110] *Truth-Tester*, 1 (1847), 83; *Vegetarian Messenger*, no. 43 (May 1853), 4; *Dietetic Reformer*, 2, no. 18 (Apr. 1865), 63.

[111] *Vegetarian Messenger*, no. 20 (June 1851), 45; no. 48 (Oct. 1853), 22. For the use of the term 'social politics', see Elaine Chalus, '"That Epidemical Madness": Women and Electoral Politics in the Late Eighteenth Century', in Hannah Barker and Elaine Chalus (eds.), *Gender in Eighteenth-Century England: Roles, Representations and Responsibilities* (London and New York, 1997), 151–78.

[112] E.g., *Vegetarian Messenger*, no. 16 (Feb. 1851), 14; no. 49 (Nov. 1853), 64.

organized the event.[113] At public meetings of the Vegetarian Society individual women – typically women of considerable status in the movement, such as Martha Brotherton and Mrs Simpson – assumed responsibility for the catering of each table. Following the second annual meeting of the Vegetarian Society, the *Vegetarian Advocate* published a plan of the tables for the evening to show which woman had presided over each table, thus literally mapping out women's control of the public space.[114] At subsequent events, the image of women *presiding* over the tables at such functions was frequently reiterated.[115] Whilst reports of vegetarian meetings usually indicate male dominance over their oral proceedings, a more subtle and modified understanding of gendered roles within the movement may be constructed from embracing these visual signifiers. Women's contribution may have been heavily circumscribed by cultural convention, but activities such as cooking were, within this context, a means to establish authority and recognition.

Furthermore, it would also appear that the vegetarian movement, or at least one element within it, did attempt to institute innovative practices of mixed-sex public engagement. At vegetarian events held at the Talfourd Hotel in Farringdon Street, London, women were actively encouraged to deliver speeches. Elizabeth Horsell was elected lady president on one such occasion and frequently delivered impassioned (and lengthy) speeches on vegetarianism and teetotalism, exhorting her fellow activists to do all they could to bring others 'into the green and perfumed path of Vegetarianism'! Other speakers present expressed their approval of Horsell's speeches and their admiration of the way in which she conducted these meetings.[116] Indeed, it is possible that the reports, cited previously, of women *presiding* at vegetarian events signalled a greater role for women than merely that of social hostess. The *Vegetarian Messenger* used the same verb of 'presiding' to describe both this activity and Mrs Horsell's presidency of the Farringdon Street meetings.[117] Moreover, although Horsell's speeches attracted the greatest attention, she was evidently not exceptional. The *Vegetarian Advocate*, reporting on such occasions, declared itself to be 'delighted with the addresses of women, many of them mothers, on the broad and beautiful system of Fireside Reform, which they had been aiding in progression'.[118]

Among the wider health-reform movement, those movements which attracted greater lower-class support tended to be marked by even more overt female

---

[113] *Ibid.*, no. 7 (May 1850), 74.

[114] *Vegetarian Advocate* (Aug. 1849), 147; see also *ibid.* (Aug. 1848), 1.

[115] *Vegetarian Messenger*, no. 12 (Oct. 1850), 130; no. 16 (Feb. 1851), 14; no. 24 (Oct. 1851), 79; no. 47 (Sept. 1853), 43.

[116] *Vegetarian Advocate* (supplement, Nov. 1850), 66–8; (supplement, Dec. 1850), 74. See also *Vegetarian Messenger*, no. 20 (June 1851), 45.

[117] *Vegetarian Messenger*, no. 20 (June 1851), 45.

[118] *Vegetarian Advocate* (supplement, Feb. 1851), 94.

public involvement. In the medical-botany movement, women such as Mrs Kitson rose at meetings to explain their allegiance to the cause and their own contribution to administering herbal medicine.[119] Although it is not clear that women necessarily enjoyed membership of medical botanic societies in their own right, it is evident that they could still have influence at a managerial level. When the Liverpool branch issued a document complaining of the behaviour of the executive, the signature of Mrs Howell (a practitioner in the movement) appeared alongside that of the male committee members.[120] Moreover, at least one of the local 'botanic colleges' established by Coffin had a woman, Mrs Umpleby, at its head.[121]

An analysis of the workings of gender within dietary- and medical-reform movements serves to reorientate many perceptions as to the role of women, the household, and the family within early Victorian radicalism. For the followers of these movements, the family, rather than the workplace or radical society, was constructed as the unit and means of reform. It would be unwise to discount the patriarchal assumptions that could fuel domestic relationships in even the most radical of households, and equally tendentious to construct an alternative, unproblematic narrative of female domestic authority. Women's activism, moreover, remained rooted within clearly defined cultural roles. Nevertheless, the sustained attention paid by male reformers to the politicization of the domestic space is significant, as is the necessity of securing women's involvement to effect the success of alternative medicine. This in itself led to the formulation of highly active and engaged models of politically astute womanhood. Many women evidently embraced the opportunities to invest their family and household responsibilities with political meaning and to involve themselves in the reform project. At the same time, women's contribution to the economic, literary, and social dimensions of health reform highlights the subtle and varied strategies whereby women could engage in 'public' debate and practice. These perceptions necessitate a rejection of conventional chronologies of mid-century political 'closure' for women, as well as suggesting the importance of the home and family in perpetuating and sustaining radical ideologies.

[119] *Coffin's Botanical Jl and Medical Reformer* (6 Mar. 1847), 18.
[120] *Ibid.* (5 May 1849), 243–4.   [121] Smith, *People's Health*, 340.

9. *Reforming the aristocracy: opera and elite culture, 1780–1860* *

JENNIFER L. HALL-WITT

During the debates over the Reform Act in 1832, the concept of 'reform' was applied not only to parliament, but also to another bastion of elite influence: the King's Theatre, London's only Italian opera house.[1] In February 1832, the *Court Journal* expressed its regret that 'no "spirited individual"' had undertaken 'a radical reform in that most "corrupt" of houses – the Italian Opera house'.[2] That same month, Thomas McLean issued a print depicting the debates over the Reform Bill as 'A New Serio-Comic Opera' performed by leading figures from across the political spectrum[3] (Plate 2). Whether the language of politics was used to interpret operatic affairs, or whether opera became a means of expressing divergent political views, both sources linked the opera to the politics of electoral reform. Was there any substance to such a relationship, or were these merely effective rhetorical flourishes reminding the public that the fate of the Reform Act then rested in the hands of the House of Lords, whose members often whiled away their time at the opera and who showed little interest in passing the bill?

By examining the opera within its historical context, this chapter will attempt to tease out the elusive answers to this question. It will argue that calls for electoral reform are best understood as part of a broad, but diffuse, assault on the power of the aristocracy in politics, society, and culture. Attacks on the opera, along with the complaints about 'Old Corruption' and spoofs of fashionable society, contributed to a wide-ranging critique of patricians' power and

---

* An earlier version of this essay was presented in 2000 at 'Music in Britain: A Social History Seminar' at the Institute for Historical Research, London. I am grateful for the participants' questions and comments.

[1] For an overview of the theatre's history, see Daniel Nalbach, *The King's Theatre 1704–1867: London's First Italian Opera House* (London, 1972).

[2] *Court Jl*, 11 Feb. 1832, 90.

[3] Brit. Museum, Satire no. 16,939, 'King's Theatre, Persons Engaged to Bring out the New Opera of Reform', Feb. 1832. For a description, see M. Dorothy George, *Catalogue of Political and Personal Satires Preserved in the Department of Prints and Drawings in the British Museum,* 11 vols. (London, 1935–54), xi, 574–5.

legitimacy. Moreover, in the decades before the Reform Act, the political and operatic arenas were, indeed, linked by a common set of social networks and a shared patronage culture. While the transformation of opera-going during the reform era was only indirectly connected to the reform of parliament, viewing elite culture through the lens of opera-going none the less adds to our understanding of the long-term decline of the British aristocracy.

I

Although historians often refer to the 'aristocracy' neutrally as a social category, during the reform era this term was used relatively loosely and often held pejorative connotations. Although it literally meant 'the government of a state by its best citizens', the singular form was only invented during the French Revolution, when, as Albert Soboul has observed, 'The word "aristocrat"... was used to describe all the enemies of sans-culotterie – bourgeois as well as noble.'[4] Thus, the 'aristocrat' came into being as a rather nebulous social type characterized by his anti-democratic sentiments. During the ensuing decades, reform-minded writers in Britain followed suit, regularly blaming the aristocracy – by whom they generally meant the ruling oligarchy and/or the social elite, titled or not – for whatever they thought was wrong with the nation. For instance, John Wade, author of the infamous *Black Book* that provided a chronicle of the beneficiaries of various forms of patronage, argued that 'the aristocracy may be considered only one family, plundering, deluding, and fattening on the people; and by its connexions possessing more power and influence in society than the ancient barons, with all their feudal immunities'.[5] Many peers of the realm played little role in the distribution of official positions and rarely participated in London's high society, where such 'connexions' could be formed; conversely, a modicum of wealthy families without any claim to a noble heritage profited from the patronage system and were accepted into the beau monde. The lumping of the various sub-sets of the elite together under the socially imprecise rubric of the 'aristocracy' allowed the critique of operatic culture and London's fashionable society to dovetail with the political critique of the peerage, fuelling popular perceptions of an entire class in need of reform.

Calls for the moral reform of the aristocracy and for a more open elite regularly took on political dimensions. When literature characterizing Britain's upper crust as parasites on the nation began appearing in the late 1760s and 1770s, it was focused on the manners, morals, and attire of the macaronis and

---

[4] *Oxford English Dictionary*, s.v. 'Aristocracy', 'Aristocrat'; Albert Soboul, *Parisian Sans-Culottes and the French Revolution, 1793–4*, trans. Gwynne Lewis (Oxford, 1964), 22.
[5] John Wade, *The Black Book; or, Corruption Unmasked!* (London, 1820), 94.

the ladies of *bon ton* and, increasingly, of the aristocracy as a whole.[6] By the 1770s, as Donna Andrew has demonstrated, attacks on aristocratic morals were becoming much more systematic, and these mores were portrayed as part of a set of vices: duelling, suicide, gambling, and adultery were repeatedly linked together in writings of the day and were predominantly associated with the upper class.[7] During the political turmoil of the 1780s, depictions of such immorality took on political connotations: in the 1784 Westminster election, for instance, journalists pilloried the gambling habits of Charles James Fox as a means of raising fears about his credibility if entrusted with public funds.[8] By then, of course, various extra-parliamentary groups had been calling for economic reforms that would curb the role of patronage, imposing fiscal restraint and reducing undue influence.[9] Among those who competed to establish themselves as patrons of this cause were the aristocratic Whig party, led by the very Charles James Fox whose gambling, and other habits, were attracting censure. The attack on the 'aristocracy' therefore had an ambiguous relationship with reform politics. But – at least in the mouths of non-aristocratic reformers – they often went together. The French Revolutionary and Napoleonic Wars, which swelled the size of government and the opportunities for lucrative perquisites among officeholders, intensified the attack on the patronage system decried as 'Old Corruption'.[10] When satirical images of the aristocracy's social exclusivity proliferated in the

---

[6] Diana Donald, *The Age of Caricature: Satirical Prints in the Reign of George III* (New Haven, Conn., 1996), 75–108; Linda Colley, *Britons: Forging the Nation, 1707–1837* (New Haven, 1992), 152–5; Paul Langford, *Public Life and the Propertied Englishman 1689–1798* (Oxford, 1991), 540–58.

[7] Donna Andrew, '"Adultery à-la-Mode": Privilege, the Law and Attitudes to Adultery 1770–1809', *History*, 82 (1997), 5–23.

[8] Phyllis Deutsch, 'Moral Trespass in Georgian London: Gaming, Gender, and Electoral Politics in the Age of George III', *Hist. Jl*, 39 (1996), 637–56.

[9] For a general history, see John Cannon, *Parliamentary Reform, 1640–1832* (Cambridge, 1973).

[10] For recent studies of 'Old Corruption', see W. D. Rubinstein, 'The End of "Old Corruption" in Britain, 1780–1860', *Past and Present*, no. 101 (Nov. 1983), 55–86; Philip Harling, *The Waning of 'Old Corruption': The Politics of Economical Reform in Britain, 1779–1846* (Oxford, 1996).

Plate 2. 'King's Theatre, persons engaged to bring out the new opera of reform', published by Thomas McLean, 1 February 1832 (British Museum, Prints and Drawings, DG 16939) (Reproduced by permission of the trustees of the British Museum.) This print depicts six portraits of opera characters who, in reality, were important figures in the Reform crisis. William IV, the lessee (top left), and Queen Adelaide, the soprano (top middle), are both portrayed as supporting reform. Lord Grey, the stage manager (top right), worries about whether or not to create new peers in order to pass the bill: 'if I engage new forces the old ones will be sulky'. The primo basso (bottom left) sings 'Curse the piece I don't like it a bit' while dressed in a fool's costume. He is Sir Charles Wetherell, the ultra-Tory MP who was one of the most conspicuous opponents of the bill. Next to him in Roman armour stands Lord Brougham, the tenor, a 'spirited reformer' who has to 'attack the Hydra of corruption in his very den'. John Bull (bottom right) wears the Union flag as he bellows out the tunes of reform and threatens 'to rear you like any sucking Dove'.

press in the early nineteenth century, they probably reinforced doubts about the legitimacy of the ruling class aroused by such reform propaganda.

Depictions of the elite at the opera employed the standard tropes of anti-aristocratic satire. For instance, Tom and Jerry's spoof on *Life in London*, published in 1821, highlighted the haughtiness of a marchioness upon seeing a family of nouveaux riches at the opera: 'Good heavens! What can such people mean by showing themselves at the Opera; are there not theatres and other minor places of amusement for folks of that description?'[11] Dr Syntax's satirical tour through London, published the previous year, conveyed an even more damning picture of the beau monde: at the opera, the poet claimed,

> ... noble lords and titled dames,
> Indulge their taste, indulge their flames,
> With music brought from foreign climes,
> Ah, more immortal than my rhymes.
> To see this splendid gay resort,
> Of fools of fashion and of court.[12]

It described an elite fixated on the petty pastimes of fashionable life and on satisfying its myriad desires. George Cruickshank's 1818 poem, *Fashion: Dedicated to All the Town*, even suggested that such activities were diverting patricians from their responsibilities. Its introduction claimed that 'Fashion has become so arbitrary a tyrant, that, like despotic governments, it requires reform.'[13] The text of the poem associated opera-going, card-playing, and other fashionable amusements with the nobility's abandonment of its paternalist duties. In reference to Dame Fashion, it said that

> For one rout – for one year shuts her gate on the poor.
> Then the box at the Opera, shar'd with a few,
> Makes her give up, in church the old family pew.[14]

By the late 1820s, when opponents of electoral reform argued that the landed elite's paternalist responsibilities served as justification for its privileges, such images were doubly powerful.

The political implications of this critique of elite culture were highlighted in discussions of the wave of silver-fork novels that were so popular in the 1820s and 1830s. Such works included Lady Charlotte Bury's *The Exclusives*, which focused on the elite's snobbish pursuit of high status and selective social circles, and Catherine Gore's *The Opera*, which portrayed the King's Theatre as a place

---

[11] [Pierce Egan], *Life in London* (London, 1821), 331.
[12] [William Combe], *The Tour of Doctor Syntax through London* (London, 1820), 61.
[13] George Cruikshank, *Fashion: Dedicated to All the Town*, 4th edn (London, 1818), v.
[14] *Ibid.*, 40.

devoted to idle amusement and flirtation, and as a stage for intrigue and the discovery of deception. Such fiction generally caricatured life in the beau monde,
but since many of the authors were themselves titled, the public seems to have
regarded the novels as credible accounts of the rules governing the fashionable
world.[15] Journalists suggested that they were potentially dangerous politically
because they damaged the reputation of the aristocracy as a whole. As Richard
MacKenzie Bacon remarked in the *New Monthly Magazine*, the silver-fork novels gave the impression 'that the entire lives of the entire order are consumed in
vice, idleness, and frivolity'.[16] Andrew Bisset, writing for the philosophical radicals' *Westminster Review* in 1835, observed astutely that these novelists 'let out
something more than prudence would warrant' by 'exposing [the aristocracy's]
vices to the public gaze'. He even argued explicitly that the fashionable novels
helped convince the public of the need for parliamentary reform.[17] Likewise,
in October 1832, Henry Taylor remarked in the Tory *Quarterly Review* that 'on
political grounds', one might 'regret the exposure' of the more superficial and
ostentatious aspects of high life in the fashionable novels, since this made the
Tories' defence of the House of Lords more difficult.[18] Contemporary writers
from across the political spectrum, then, believed that the silver-fork novels
helped harden the public's antagonism toward the aristocracy by disseminating
negative visions of fashionable society, including its patronage of the opera.

The use of similar tropes to describe the elite linked the radical critique
of 'Old Corruption' to the broader assault on the aristocracy. The opera was
distinguished from 'Old Corruption' in the sense that it was not supported by
public funds, as were the sinecures, reversions, and pensions reviled by many
reformers. Yet whether one turns to political pamphlets, satirical cartoons, or
fashionable novels, one finds the elite described as morally bankrupt, overly exclusive, highly superficial, and exceedingly extravagant. Such imagery allowed
the opera – and fashionable society more broadly – to become potent symbols
of what radicals disliked most about the unreformed political system and its
wealthy participants.

II

The images of the upper class promulgated in satires and novels were exaggerated; yet they were persuasive precisely because they were drawing on certain
observable trends. However partisan Wade's assertion in 1820 that 'At no

---

[15] Alison Adburgham, *Silver Fork Society: Fashionable Life and Literature from 1814 to 1840*
(London, 1983), 1.

[16] [Richard MacKenzie Bacon], 'The Aristocracy of England', *New Monthly Mag.*, 41 (1834), 8.

[17] [Andrew Bisset], 'Aristocratic Revelations', *Westminster Rev.*, 22 (1835), 320.

[18] [Henry Taylor], 'Novels of Fashionable Life: *Arlington, The Contrast*', *Quart. Rev.*, 48 (1832),
189.

former period of history was the power of the Aristocracy so absolute', the facts support his general claim.[19] According to David Cannadine, the landed elite 'became more rich, more powerful, more status-conscious and more unified' between the 1780s and the 1820s. What he called the 'making of the British upper classes' in these decades culminated in groups of patricians more actively involved in politics, the civil service, the church, the armed forces, and local government.[20] Even the number of patronal peers, lords with control over the nomination of various seats in the House of Commons, reached a high point around 1807.[21]

References to the exclusiveness of the elite, repeated ad nauseam in the press, also had some basis in reality, particularly after the 1750s. Among the evidence for a growing gap between the landed elite and the business classes is the fact that in the second half of the eighteenth century younger sons of the nobility and gentry were less likely to go into trade than earlier, as Nicholas Rogers and Daniel Baugh have shown. Conversely, according to Rogers and Christopher Clay, it was somewhat more difficult for men of new wealth to purchase landed estates in the late eighteenth century.[22] We should not overemphasize this gap, of course. Aristocrats were increasingly involving themselves in business affairs such as mining and canals.[23] And nearly one-third of those men elevated into the peerage between 1802 and 1830 were from non-landed backgrounds, often without extensive wealth to their names.[24] Yet the public's sense of a growing gap that was setting the high aristocracy apart from everyone else must have been enhanced by the fact that peers began showcasing their wealth ever more ostentatiously. High-stakes gambling was on the rise from the 1770s into the

---

[19] Wade, *Black Book*, 389.

[20] David Cannadine, *Aspects of Aristocracy: Grandeur and Decline in Modern Britain* (New Haven, 1994), 1–36 quotation at 10. The degree to which aristocrats' greater involvement in public life was conscious is a matter of scholarly debate. Colley, *Britons*, 147–93, argues that the elite remade their image in this period as a means of sustaining their legitimacy in the eyes of the public. By contrast, Paul Langford, *A Polite and Commercial People: England, 1727–1783* (Oxford, 1989), 595–6, noted that some of the increased demand for offices among younger sons of aristocrats occurred because of a change in demographics: as mortality rates decreased among the landed elite over the course of the eighteenth century, the demands for offices naturally rose.

[21] James Sack, 'The House of Lords and Parliamentary Patronage in Great Britain, 1802–1832', *Hist. Jl*, 23 (1980), 919.

[22] Nicholas Rogers, 'Money, Land and Lineage: The Big Bourgeoisie of Hanoverian London', *Social Hist.*, 4 (1979), 444, 448–9; Daniel A. Baugh, 'Introduction: The Social Basis of Stability', in Daniel A. Baugh (ed.), *Aristocratic Government and Society in Eighteenth-Century England: The Foundations of Stability* (New York, 1975), 12–13; Christopher Clay, 'Marriage, Inheritance, and the Rise of Large Estates in England, 1660–1815', *Econ. Hist. Rev.*, 2nd ser., 21 (1988), 503–18.

[23] J. V. Beckett, *The Aristocracy in England, 1660–1914* (Oxford, 1986), 206–61.

[24] Michael W. McCahill, 'Peerage Creations and the Changing Character of the British Nobility, 1750–1830', *Eng. Hist. Rev.*, 96 (1981), 274–5.

Regency period, and aristocratic mansion-building seems to have peaked from the 1790s to about 1830.[25]

While historians will continue to debate the reality of such a gap at the sociological level, public perceptions of it were further backed by some very real changes in elite culture. Ellen Moers' description of Regency society captures the tone of this trend: 'In no other society has the mechanism of exclusion been so prominent, elaborate and efficient. It was the universal, often the only, interest. Regency Society called itself exclusive, its members the exclusives, and its ruling principle exclusiveness. A whole language, expressing the subtleties of the mechanism, grew up around the central words.'[26] Such qualities were particularly evident at the elite's public entertainment venues. Probably the earliest example was Carlisle House in Soho Square, where the former opera-singer Teresa Cornelys organized concerts and balls in the 1760s. Admission was controlled by several elite women who ushered in a spirit of exclusiveness. As Count Friedrich von Kielmansegge described the process, 'In order that only those people may be subscribers who are known to one of the ladies, the subscription books are kept by the ladies only, and the power to admit or exclude whom they like is confined to them.'[27] Almack's, a competitor that opened in 1765, had become the temple of elite social exclusiveness by the Regency period. Admission to its balls, which were held every Wednesday night during the Season, was controlled by a group of women of *haut ton* who were known for excluding anyone connected with commerce, although they did not always do so in practice.[28]

This model was applied to a number of other elite entertainments. When the Concert of Ancient Music began in 1776, its organizers developed a similar system whereby the noblemen who directed the series granted subscriptions on a socially exclusive basis.[29] By 1806, Colonel Henry Francis Greville was using his house in Little Argyll Street for dramatic performances; as at Almack's, a group of lady patronesses soon controlled access to the concerts, balls, and French plays performed there.[30] In the 1820s, committees of noblewomen similarly monitored the distribution of tickets to the balls at the King's Theatre, held one to four times per season.[31]

---

[25] E. Beresford Chancellor, *Life in Regency and Early Victorian Times: An Account of the Days of Brummell and D'Orsay, 1800 to 1850* (London, [1927]), 59–69; Beckett, *Aristocracy*, 326–8.

[26] Ellen Moers, *The Dandy: Brummel to Beerbohm* (New York, 1960), 41.

[27] Count Frederick von Kielmansegge, *Diary of a Journey to England in the Years 1761–1762*, ed. Countess Sophia Philippa Kielmansegg (London, 1902), 196.

[28] Chancellor, *Life in Regency and Early Victorian Times*, 50.

[29] William Weber, *The Rise of Musical Classics in Eighteenth-Century England: A Study in Canon, Ritual, and Ideology* (Oxford, 1992), 143, 158.

[30] *Survey of London*, ed. F. H. W. Sheppard, 45 vols. (London, 1963), xxxi, 302–3; on the patronesses, see the newspaper clippings at the Royal College of Music, London (hereafter RCM), volume on the Argyll Rooms, 1807–37.

[31] See, e.g., the *Morning Post*, 28 May 1822; *The Times*, 13 Apr. 1826.

The nobility had long been especially associated with opera. But between the 1780s and the 1820s noble influence at the opera increased markedly on that exercised in previous decades, whether in the form of financing the opera, organizing rival companies, or overseeing affairs at the King's Theatre. Such involvement peaked between 1821 and 1824, when two successive committees of noblemen actually ran the opera with the help of a hired manager. They applied for the annual licence, secured the king's patronage, hired a musical agent, recruited performers, negotiated contracts, and on occasion intervened in casting decisions and choice of repertoire.[32] Though this might be seen as a form of public engagement, it was more easily perceived as another aspect of this culture of exclusiveness. And in certain respects opera did become more exclusive. Newcomers interested in renting a box at the King's Theatre often found it difficult to obtain one between the 1780s and the early 1810s, particularly since the old subscribers were given first priority. Waiting lists were not uncommon, even as the price of the subscription doubled from 150 guineas in 1791 to 300 guineas in 1811.[33] Even the nobility might find themselves squeezed by competition. In 1811 the manager William Taylor apparently 'told the Marchioness of Downshire and some other ladies, if you do not like to comply to my terms, you may quit your box, [as] I have ladies in the city ready to give as much more'.[34] The suggestion was that the commercial elite was bidding for entry into the opera circle and willing to pay enormous sums.

Whether in boxes or not, the untitled elite did have a presence at the opera – helping, by their eagerness to attend, to drive up prices, but perhaps also precipitating a snobbish reaction. By the turn of the century, well-known nabobs like Paul Benfield and Sir Charles Rouse-Boughton, banking families like the Coutts and the Goslings, and the merchant and art collector, John J. Angerstein, were subscribing to the opera. While about 66 per cent of subscribers were styled Lord, Lady, Sir, or Hon. in 1783 (236 out of 358), that figure dropped to 56 per cent in 1804 (303 out of 538).[35] Thereafter, the lists of opera-goers printed in the newspapers after each performance suggest no more than a slight dip in noble attendance. During the 1822 season, the lists of opera-goers regularly printed in the *Morning Post* indicated that at least 28 per cent of all English

---

[32] Jennifer Lee Hall, 'The Re-Fashioning of Fashionable Society: Opera-going and Sociability in Britain, 1821–1861' (Yale University Ph.D. thesis, 1996), 175–88. Such commitment among titled gentlemen was common at the opera in the first half of the eighteenth century, but then declined until its resurgence in the 1780s. See William Weber, 'L'Institution et son public: l'Opéra à Paris et à Londres au XVIIIe siècle', *Annales: ESC*, 48 (1993), 1519–39.

[33] Veritas, *Opera House: A Review of this Theatre, from the Period Described by the Enterpriser* (London, 1820), 31, 33.

[34] *Ibid.*, 12.

[35] The number of boxes in the King's Theatre nearly quadrupled between 1777 and 1800: *A Descriptive Plan of the New Opera House, with the Names of the Subscribers to Each Box Taken from the Theatre Itself by a Lady of Fashion* (London, [1783]); William Lee, *The Plan of the Boxes at the King's Theatre, Haymarket* (London, [1804]).

peers appeared at the opera at least once.[36] This compares with a figure of approximately 25 per cent of all English peers who subscribed in 1783.[37] Although we do not know how many were actually subscribers in 1822, by then the peerage was about 60 per cent larger than in the 1780s. The opera clearly sustained a high-status audience, even as the growing number of wealthy, but untitled, subscribers must have created a more competitive social climate. Perhaps as a result of this, from the 1780s appearance in an opera box became an important mark of prestige. Subscription lists were regularly published for public consumption between 1783 and 1807, and the newspapers acknowledged the importance of being seen at the opera by regularly printing lists of audience members from the 1780s to the 1820s, reviving the practice briefly in the 1840s and 1850s.[38] Thus, in the half-century before 1832, the opera house offered a dual attraction for the socially ambitious: an aura of exclusivity combined with opportunities for access to the elite.

Popular spoofs of fashionable society and the opera not only emphasized the elite's selectivity, but also caricatured its propensity for frequent and large-scale socializing as a mark of its superficiality and excessive leisure time. Yet the rounds of calls, dinners, parties, balls, and operas served a vital purpose: the London Season, as it was called, coincided with both the parliamentary session and the opera season, and if we imagine the social ties cemented during the Season as roads on a map, we can envision them as the very passages through which patronage flowed. For young men interested in a political career, the advice offered in Bulwer-Lytton's novel *Pelham* (1826) was apt: 'Never talk too much to young men – remember that it is the women who make a reputation in society.'[39] Scholars such as Elaine Chalus, Leonore Davidoff, K. D. Reynolds, and Michael Curtin have recognized the social dimensions of political life and the important role that elite women played as social doorkeepers.[40] As hostesses, they exerted influence over who could enter elite social circles by virtue of whom they chose to recognize in public and invite to their private

---

[36] Calculation of the total number of English peers from *The Royal Kalendar, and Court and City Register for England, Scotland, Ireland, and the Colonies, for the Year 1822* (London, 1822).

[37] William Weber has kindly allowed me to cite this figure, which he discusses in an unpublished essay.

[38] For information on the location of the various subscription lists, see Curtis Price, Judith Milhous, and Robert D. Hume, *Italian Opera in Late Eighteenth-Century London*, 2 vols. (Oxford, 1995), i: *The King's Theatre, Haymarket, 1778–1791*, 11. After 1807, at least two more subscription lists were issued by the opera house, one in 1845 and the other in 1856 (see references below).

[39] Edward Bulwer-Lytton, *Pelham; Or, Adventures of a Gentleman* (London, 1952), 20.

[40] Elaine Chalus, 'Elite Women, Social Politics, and the Political World of Late Eighteenth-Century England', *Hist. Jl*, 43 (2000), 669–97; Leonore Davidoff, *The Best Circles: Society Etiquette and the Season* (London, 1973); K. D. Reynolds, *Aristocratic Women and Political Society in Victorian Britain* (Oxford, 1998). Michael Curtin, *Propriety and Position: A Study of Victorian Manners* (New York, 1987), 260–1, offers a nuanced analysis of the varied influence elite women had on men's careers, depending on whether the men were from aristocratic backgrounds or not.

gatherings. The success of the patronage system in politics thus relied on the social networks cultivated by such women.

The King's Theatre, the central public meeting place for fashionable society during the Season, was a key venue for displaying these webs of relationships. Women of *ton*, perched elegantly in their boxes and dressed in elaborate gowns and glittering jewels, approached the opera as a site for advertising themselves as leading socialites, and as those with the power to monitor access to the beau monde. By contrast, noblemen and dandies of the finer set wandered from box to box, paying tribute to the female leaders of fashionable society, and then descended to the pit to mingle with each other and ogle the panoramic display of feminine beauty in the boxes above. Visits to a particular woman's box not only highlighted her importance to other members of the audience, but could also be a first step towards entering her inner circle and tapping into her extensive social network.[41]

The King's Theatre readily served as a meeting place for the beau monde because box-holders could expect to find their friends in their places on most Tuesday and Saturday evenings during the Season. Subscription lists from the 1780s to the 1800s show 95 to 100 per cent subscription rates in the first three rows of boxes, which were the most fashionable tiers. They also document the consistency of seating from year to year: between 1804 and 1805, for instance, 88 per cent of boxes were held by the same primary subscriber or, on occasion, her spouse.[42] Such consistency in seating, combined with the fact that the lights remained on in the auditorium throughout the evening, meant that it was easy for people to use the opera to glean information about the elite's changing social networks. For example, in a letter from the 1790s, Lady Charlotte Campbell (who later became the society novelist Lady Charlotte Bury) wrote to Camilia M. Campbell that 'Saturday I went to the Opera . . . Lady Abercorn has got the D[uche]ss. of Gordon's Box, as the latter is obliged for lack of [money] to remain at Kimbolten [*sic*]'.[43] The duchess of Gordon's absence was a sign (or perhaps a confirmation) that financial problems kept her from living up to the expectations associated with her rank, including a subscription to the opera. Even in the 1820s, Harriet Arbuthnot, the confidante of the duke of Wellington, fretted about whether to obey the king's orders that she should not sit in the box of Lady Hertford, the king's former lover, because it upset his current

---

[41] I have elaborated on these points more fully in Hall, 'Re-Fashioning of Fashionable Society', 93–151.

[42] Women were generally the primary subscribers who headed the box from year to year, finding different sets of friends and relatives to join them as secondary subscribers. See Lee, *Plan of the Boxes* [1804]; William Lee, *The Plan of the Boxes at the King's Theatre, Haymarket* (London, [1805]).

[43] Although this letter is undated, it was written after Prince George broke off his affair with Mrs Fitzherbert, but while he was still clearly longing for her: *Intimate Society Letters of the Eighteenth Century*, ed. the duke of Argyll, 2 vols. (London, 1910), ii, 655.

mistress, Lady Conyngham.[44] The opera thus functioned almost like a private club among the subscribers, who generally knew enough about each other to attach meaning to who was sitting with whom.

Not only did opera-going support the patronage system in politics by helping advertise and consolidate elite social networks, but the opera's leading supporters were also among the nation's most powerful political patrons. The noblemen on the committee of management at the King's Theatre in the early 1820s were not particularly active in parliamentary politics as ministers or in debates, but they none the less epitomized the patronage system that radicals wanted abolished. Excluding an Italian nobleman, the four other members of the first committee of management – Lords Ailesbury, Fife, Mount Edgcumbe, and Lowther – were all Tories who were opposed to political reform. Other men closely involved in running the opera in the 1820s included the duke of Argyll, the marquis of Hertford, the earls of Cholmondeley and Glengall, and Lord Burghersh. Including the men on the first committee, over half of their names appeared in John Wade's *Black Book* as recipients of sinecures and other lucrative offices. Wade pointed out, for instance, that Mount Edgcumbe brought in £1,000 as captain of the Band of Gentlemen Pensioners, while Lowther earned £1,500 as commissioner for India Affairs and another £1,600 as lord of the Treasury.[45] Furthermore, while less than a third of all peers, most of them Tories, controlled the nomination to a parliamentary seat, nearly all of the noblemen (or their fathers) involved in operatic affairs in the 1820s were borough patrons named in Wade's *Black Book*. As James Sack's recent research has confirmed, Lowther's father could nominate MPs for nine constituencies between 1802 and 1831 and bestowed nearly as many church livings, a level of patronage second only to the duke of Norfolk. During the same period, Mount Edgcumbe controlled five seats, Hertford and Ailesbury four each, Argyll and Burghersh's father two each, and Cholmondeley one.[46] Among those targeted in the radical attack on 'Old Corruption' were the very men who were running the opera.

In a variety of ways, then, the opera could easily be regarded as a vivid symbol of the need for parliamentary reform in 1832. The Tory men who helped to run the opera in the early 1820s were among the leading participants in the patronage system. Likewise, members of fashionable society utilized the opera as a venue for consolidating the social networks that bound together patrons and

---

[44] *The Journal of Mrs Arbuthnot, 1820–1832*, ed. Francis Bamford and the duke of Wellington, 2 vols. (London, 1950), i, 297–8, 3 Apr. 1824.

[45] Wade, *Black Book*, 66, 60. On the others, see *ibid.*, 22, 27, 51.

[46] Sack, 'House of Lords', 931–7; Wade, *Black Book*, 60. Wade's estimate for Lowther (eight) was actually lower than Sack's more careful calculation. I did not include Fife in the list because his influence was not consistent throughout this period: he controlled one seat in 1806–7 and two in 1827–31.

clients within the elite. They also epitomized a patrician class that seemed to be gaining in power and influence and that was accused of increasingly excluding the commercial classes from its social circles. For a middle-class public reared on the silver-fork novels, the satirical cartoons of dandies and high-society dames, and the tales of Tom and Jerry reproduced in the dramatic theatres, the elite's penchant for amusement at places like the opera must have contributed to the public's sense of an entire class in need of reform.

III

Even as journalists in 1832 called for a reform of the opera, the elite's relationship with the King's Theatre was already in a process of transition. After the opera's subscription culture reached a pinnacle in the 1800s, it began to deteriorate gradually in the 1810s. Yet the aristocracy's formal influence over the management and finances of the opera ended only in 1825, when the property boxes that so many wealthy families owned from the 1790s onward expired.[47] By the 1830s and 1840s, audiences began to grow more attentive and quiet, focusing less on the spectators and more on the performance itself. The transformation of opera-going, therefore, was not caused by the Reform Act, but it *was* part of a more wide-ranging reform of elite culture.

The commercialization of ticket sales was one of the most important causes of the erosion of the opera's subscription culture. By the 1810s and 1820s, the emergence of outside ticket agents allowed subscribers to sell their tickets to the fashionable booksellers on the nights when they did not need them instead of giving them to friends, a tradition that had helped consolidate social ties. By mid-century, booksellers were purchasing about half of all subscriptions at the beginning of the season and renting boxes out by the night or for very short terms. Individuals typically subscribed to approximately 150 boxes out of about 200 in the first decade of the nineteenth century, but that number dropped to 117 in 1813 and to a dismal 87 in 1832. It rose to 125 in 1845, but then slumped to 72 in 1856.[48] Consequently, opera-goers were much less likely to sit in the same seats from season to season or even from night to night. Of the primary subscribers and their spouses in 1797, 34 per cent were still the primary subscriber to the same box in 1807, a decade later. By contrast, only 7 per cent of the subscribers in 1832 still held the same box in 1845, and only 9 per cent of

---

[47] The history of the origin and sale of the property boxes is complicated: Judith Milhous, Gabriella Dideriksen, and Robert D. Hume, *Italian Opera in Late Eighteenth-Century London*, 2 vols. (Oxford, 2001), ii: *The Pantheon Opera and its Aftermath, 1789–1795*, 123–34, 169–81.

[48] PRO, C108/215, handwritten book kept by the management, containing an alphabetical list of the subscribers for 1813, unfoliated; *Court Jl*, 26 May 1832; *Her Majesty's Theatre: A List of the Subscribers for the Season, 1845* (London, 1845); *Her Majesty's Theatre: A List of Subscribers for the Season, 1856* (London, 1856).

subscribers in 1845 still rented the same box in 1856.[49] The commercialization of ticket sales therefore led to more fluctuating audiences rather than groups of box-holders who all knew each other.[50]

Elite influence on operatic affairs continued, but it was more sporadic and informal than earlier. After 1824, a noblemen's committee of management did not reconvene, except for a few months during a financial crisis in 1852.[51] Nobles still scouted for singers and composers on a few occasions, but there is no evidence that they carried out the negotiations, as they had in the early 1820s. Subscribers continued to complain to the management when they were displeased with the singers or dancers; and when Benjamin Lumley, the lessee, purchased the opera house in 1845, he raised much of the necessary capital by selling a number of boxes to 'members of the aristocracy, and men of fashion and standing'[52] who were 'principally Members of both Houses of Parliament'.[53] Nevertheless, Lumley was among a group of managers who, beginning in the late 1820s, had adopted a more entrepreneurial set of practices that chipped away at the elite's power and influence.[54]

Particularly in the 1830s and 1840s, audience behaviour began to conform to these changes in operatic culture. Because spectators were less likely to know each other, they could attach little significance to the movements in and out of the boxes. Hence, after the 1820s one finds almost no evidence of the kind of intrigue at the opera that had been so common in the previous century. Gossip, if reported, tended to centre on the performers rather than the audience, a marked change from earlier decades. In 1839, for example, Lady Chatterton's descriptions of her visit to the opera to see *Norma* with Edward Bulwer Lytton included 'looking at some of the celebrated beauties in different boxes who were no longer young'. But the dialogue she reported focused on the prima donna: '*between* the acts we had some very pleasant talk. I was surprised to hear him say that he does not admire Grisi, except her voice, and that if she were an Englishwoman, nobody would think her beautiful.'[55] Indeed, by all appearances, titled opera-goers began to conduct themselves more decorously by the 1840s, perhaps even seeing themselves as models of behaviour for the middle classes and nouveaux riches in attendance. By the 1860s, when the

---

49 William Lee, *The Plan of the Boxes at the King's Theatre, Haymarket* (London, [1797]); William Lee, *The Plan of the Boxes at the King's Theatre, Haymarket* (London, [1807]); see also the subscription lists for 1845 and 1856 identified in n. 48 above.

50 For just such an observation from a Victorian music critic comparing the years 1834 to 1859, see Henry F. Chorley, *Thirty Years' Musical Recollections*, ed. Ernest Newman (New York, 1972), 56.

51 *Morning Post*, 17 June 1852.

52 Benjamin Lumley, *Reminiscences of the Opera* (London, 1864), 123–7, quotation at 130.

53 PRO, LC 1/27, letter from Lumley to the lord chamberlain, 27 Aug. 1846.

54 Hall, 'Re-Fashioning of Fashionable Society', 207–44.

55 My emphasis. Edward Heneage Dering, *Memoirs of Georgiana, Lady Chatterton: With Some Passages from her Diary* (London, 1878), 74.

newspapers' practice of printing audience lists ended, visiting and socializing during the performance had significantly diminished.[56] The opera was clearly still a place to see and to be seen, but it became less central to the elite's status-enhancing activities. While the audience was not yet completely silent during the performance, and the lights would not be turned out in the auditorium until the 1890s, the flamboyancy of Regency culture was giving way to the more refined etiquette of the Victorian period.[57]

The commercialization of the opera was probably the most important catalyst for these changes in opera-going, but it was not the only factor. The growing influence of music critics, who regularly attacked the listening habits of the fashionable classes; the explosion of concert life and musical periodicals in the 1830s and 1840s, which created a more competitive climate in the musical world and a more informed audience; and a new aesthetic orientation that promoted the concept of certain musical compositions as great works of art, worthy of the audience's undivided attention, also played a role in changing listening practices.[58] Musical life, however, did not exist in a vacuum. The transformation of operatic culture reinforced other types of reform among the elite, and was perhaps even affected by them.

The radical critique of 'Old Corruption', combined with the widespread lampooning of the aristocracy in the press and the passing of the Reform Act itself, rendered the elite's social exclusiveness much less viable. With the periodical literature of the 1820s and 1830s discussing the legitimacy of the House of Lords so relentlessly, members of the elite seem to have internalized the virtues of tempering their behaviour in public: from the late 1820s to the 1840s, one finds a general reaction against social exclusiveness. Almack's continued its tradition of lady patronesses, but by all accounts it was much easier to gain access as its popularity waned in the 1830s. Indeed in 1838 William Shee remarked that he considered 'the decline of "Almacks" as one of the most striking and not the least momentous changes worked in our system by that revolutionary inroad on the privileges of the aristocracy', the Reform Act.[59] Likewise, after

---

[56] This observation is based on my reading of numerous diaries, letters, and memoirs from the period. One piece of evidence is the fact that after 1858 Fops' Alley was removed. It was the wide aisle in the pit where the male subscribers socialized, thus allowing them to leave room in their boxes for other male visitors: see Lumley, *Reminiscences*, 62–3; Chorley, *Musical Recollections*, 87.

[57] On changes in audience behaviour in London, see William Weber, 'Did People Listen in the 18th Century?', *Early Music*, 25 (1997), 678–91; Jennifer L. Hall-Witt, 'Representing the Audience in the Age of Reform: Critics and the Elite at the Italian Opera in London', in Christina Bashford and Leanne Langley (eds.), *Music and British Culture, 1785–1914: Essays in Honour of Cyril Ehrlich* (Oxford, 2000), 131–7; Christina Bashford, 'Learning to Listen: Audiences for Chamber Music in Early-Victorian London', *Jl Victorian Culture*, 4 (1999), 25–51.

[58] See Hall-Witt, 'Representing the Audience'; William Weber, *Music and the Middle Class: The Social Structure of Concert Life in London, Paris and Vienna* (London, 1975), table 1, 159.

[59] William Archer Shee, *My Contemporaries, 1830–1870* (London, 1893), 65, a diary entry for 2 July 1838.

the Argyll Rooms were rebuilt as a result of a fire in 1830, they never again attracted such a high-ranking audience as in earlier decades.[60] The Concert of Ancient Music also deteriorated, with the number of subscribers in 1833 dropping to nearly half its prior level and eroding enough by 1848 that the series was forced to fold.[61] At the opera, lady patronesses no longer organized balls or controlled access to them after 1832. At the same time, the prestigious men's clubs like Brooks' were becoming more inclusive by expanding their membership, and the gambling craze was winding down, particularly after the demise of Crockford's Club in 1844.[62] The shift away from exclusiveness at the opera was clearly part of a broader movement away from selectivity and subscriptions, even if the specific causes for these developments differed.

The deterioration of the opera's subscription culture also coincided with the weakening of the patronage system in politics. As Harling has shown, with the onset of the French and Napoleonic Wars various ministries took care to portray an image of frugality and administrative efficiency. From the 1780s onward they slowly trimmed the number of sinecures, reversions, and pensions through various administrative reforms.[63] With the state components of 'Old Corruption' eroded by the 1810s, substantially removed by the early 1830s, and almost entirely dismantled by 1850, the traditional socio-political foundations for elite operatic attendance were rapidly disappearing just as commercialization was restructuring the nature of opera-going. If ministers and other patrons had significantly fewer offices and perquisites to offer, then social networking at the opera and at other high-society venues lost some of its political resonance.

The nature of reform within operatic culture differed from that of parliament in some important ways. Because the nobility's influence at the opera had never been enshrined in law, reform occurred not through new legislation, as in the case of electoral reform, but in a more informal, piecemeal way. And while the movement for parliamentary reform could be quite organized, and its literature relatively systematic in its analysis, attacks on the opera were instead part of a broader, more diffuse, critique of elite culture that mainly took the form of satire and fiction. Yet despite such differences, one finds some striking parallels when comparing the reform of parliament and the opera. What stands out is that in both institutions the social status of the participants barely changed during the reform period, and yet the culture of both opera-going and politicking was gradually transformed in similar ways. The landed elite continued to dominate the membership of parliament and the opera audience after 1832. The nobility and gentry still comprised at least 71 per cent of representatives in the House of

---

[60] On the fire, see RCM, volume on the Argyll Rooms, 1807–37, newspaper clipping dated 5 Feb. 1830.

[61] Weber, *Music and the Middle Class*, 61–3.

[62] [Charles Marsh], 'The Clubs of St. James (No. 1)', *New Monthly Mag.*, 19 (1827), 129.

[63] Harling, *Waning of 'Old Corruption'*.

Commons in 1841;[64] and in 1845 21 per cent of English peers were still listed in the newspapers as attending the opera at least once, a figure that leapt to 35 per cent in 1847, the first year of the rivalry between Her Majesty's Theatre (renamed upon Victoria's accession) and the new Royal Italian Opera at Covent Garden.[65] The resilience of the aristocracy in politics in the nineteenth century extends, in this sense, to the opera audience as well.

Yet the much-abridged role of patronage in both institutions fundamentally changed their cultures. Beginning in the 1830s, parties rather than noble patrons played an increasingly important role in elections.[66] Immediately after the passing of the Reform Act, about 53 patrons still returned some 73 MPs, but that was a significant drop from the 90 peers who returned 195 MPs in 1831.[67] And the role of patrons would continue to erode thereafter. Furthermore, although ministers in subsequent decades retained the right to nominate men to various offices, these were much more likely to be administratively necessary ones that required the recipients to be hired according to merit, a marked difference from the days of 'Old Corruption'.[68] At the opera, too, noble patrons had little formal influence on the management of the opera after 1824, although some did help finance it in 1845. By the 1850s they were also much less likely to become the protectors of individual dancers, a form of artistic patronage of long-standing tradition.[69] Patronage relationships were thus much less evident in a variety of ways both in government and at the opera, a shift that ultimately changed the nature of patricians' power in both arenas.

What can we conclude from viewing the movement for electoral reform within the scope of a broader reaction against the aristocracy? At the most general level, this analysis highlights the notion of the 'aristocracy' as a cultural construct used for rhetorical (and often expressly political) purposes, much as the idea of the rising 'middle classes' played a similar role in the press during the reform era, as Dror Wahrman has persuasively demonstrated.[70] The derogatory

---

[64] This figure includes the nobility, baronetage, landed gentry, and their close relatives: W. O. Aydelotte, 'The House of Commons in the 1840's', *History*, 39 (1954), 254.

[65] These calculations are based on lists in *The Times*: in 1845, 81 of 387 peers went, compared to 138 of 390 peers in 1847. I consulted the *Royal Kalendar* to calculate the total number of peers in 1845 and 1847.

[66] John A. Phillips and Charles Wetherall, 'The Great Reform Act of 1832 and the Political Modernization of England', *Amer. Hist. Rev.*, 100 (1995), 411–36; Angus Hawkins, 'Parliamentary Government and Victorian Political Parties, *c.* 1830–*c.* 1880', *Eng. Hist. Rev.*, 104 (1989), 638–69; Norman Gash, *Politics in the Age of Peel: A Study in the Technique of Parliamentary Representation, 1830–1850* (New York, 1953), 393–427.

[67] Gash, *Politics in the Age of Peel*, 438–9; Sack, 'House of Lords', 919.

[68] J. M. Bourne, *Patronage and Society in Nineteenth-Century England* (London, 1986), 23–4, 31–2, 40; Harling, *Waning of 'Old Corruption'*, 230–40.

[69] For its history in the nineteenth century, see Ivor Guest, 'Dandies and Dancers', *Dance Perspectives*, 37 (1969), 6–49.

[70] Dror Wahrman, *Imagining the Middle Class: The Political Representation of Class in Britain, c. 1780–1840* (Cambridge, 1995).

depictions of fashionable society in the press enhanced the political attack on the peerage and probably also affected the elite's behaviour in public venues like the opera. At the same time, this perspective points to the very real connections between the opera and politics, highlighting the importance of social networks in an unreformed political culture in which patronage relationships were still important.

Perhaps most importantly, this chapter has argued that the movement for parliamentary reform cannot be fully understood without investigating elite culture, and its meanings, more broadly. Such a claim has vital implications for the historiography of the aristocracy. According to David Cannadine, the decline of the aristocracy only began in earnest in the 1880s, for 'until the 1870s, there was an exceptionally high correlation between wealth, status, and power' among Britain's elite: the richest men tended to be titled and to dominate the corridors of power.[71] Yet such figures can be misleading because authority is often such an intangible force. Surely it is significant that the snobbery, exclusivity, and extravagance so typical of the Regency period rapidly deteriorated in the 1830s. And even though one can point to a resurgence of an aristocratic style of governance among a number of Whigs in power in the 1830s and 1840s, they were a dying breed by mid-century.[72] The opera and other aspects of elite culture may thus provide a more sensitive barometer of the aristocracy's public authority than numerical calculations of their presence in arenas such as parliament and the cabinet. If that is true, then the reform movement may have been far more damaging to the legitimacy and power of the elite than the historical literature has generally acknowledged.

[71] David Cannadine, *The Decline and Fall of the British Aristocracy* (New York, 1992), 16. Some recent research suggests that the aristocracy was already becoming more open in the mid-Victorian years: see David Brown, 'Equipoise and the Myth of an Open Elite: New Men of Wealth and the Purchase of Land in the Equipoise Decades, 1850–69', in Martin Hewitt (ed.), *An Age of Equipoise?: Reassessing Mid-Victorian Britain* (Aldershot, 2000).

[72] Peter Mandler, *Aristocratic Government in the Age of Reform: Whigs and Liberals, 1830–1852* (Oxford, 1990).

10. *Reform on the London stage*

KATHERINE NEWEY

In 1832, two movements for reform coincided. In June, the first Reform Act received royal assent, while in August, a select committee of the House of Commons reported the results of its inquiry into the current state of the British theatre.[1] However, this coincidence was not accidental. Early nineteenth-century discussions of the theatre regarded it as an important cultural institution that represented particular views of the nation, while, conversely, political life in the first decades of the nineteenth century was conducted in an increasingly public and performative way.[2] In this essay I will explore a variety of views of reform to be found in the London theatre industry in and around 1832, focusing on two contrasting concepts of a reformed theatre, one emerging from the select committee, and the other from performances at two of London's popular theatres, the Surrey and the Coburg. This contrast demonstrates the limits and boundaries of parliamentary attempts at reform of the theatres, and the existence of differing views about the desirable nature of a reformed theatre. In the hectic daily clamour of attractions, novelty, and spectacle in London's commercial theatre industry in the first third of the nineteenth century, discussions about reform of the theatre were not limited to its legislative regulation. They included tub-thumping about the 'decline of the drama' and the 'national drama', discussions of the constitution and respectability of audiences, and keenly promoted demonstrations of the quality of productions at the new theatres compared with

---

[1] P.P. 1831–2, vii (679), 'Report from the Select Committee appointed to Inquire into the Laws Affecting Dramatic Literature, with the Minutes of Evidence' (hereafter 'Select Committee on Laws Affecting Dramatic Literature').

[2] For a sustained argument about the theatricality of reform politics, see Julia Swindells, *Glorious Causes: The Grand Theatre of Political Change, 1789 to 1833* (Oxford, 2001). For discussions of earlier convergences of theatre and politics, particularly on the Old Price wars, see Marc Baer, *Theatre and Disorder in Late Georgian London* (Oxford, 1992); Gillian Russell, *The Theatres of War: Performance, Politics, and Society, 1793–1815* (Oxford, 1995). For wide-ranging studies of theatricalized politics in the nineteenth century, and the specific influence of melodrama, see Elaine Hadley, *Melodramatic Tactics: Theatricalized Dissent in the English Marketplace, 1800–1885* (Stanford, 1995); Rohan McWilliam, 'Melodrama and the Historians', *Radical Hist. Rev.*, 78 (2000), 57–84.

the performances at the established Theatres Royal in Drury Lane and Covent Garden.

In examining these debates over parliamentary and popular views of theatre regulation and reform, I am also interested in identifying alternative visions, not just of the theatre, but of a reformed Britain, and challenging the long-held view that British theatre of the nineteenth century has little of interest to contribute to an account of the political life of the time.[3] The popular theatre of the reform period offers a study in miniature of a diversity of reformist opinions and practices, and a demonstration of how these differing positions constructed relationships between the theatre and the idea of the nation. Thus, the London stage during the age of reform provided a significant site for the discursive and performative construction of versions of the national culture, and particularly the delineation of 'Englishness'.

In May 1832, fired up by the 'high tide of Reform feeling' of the 1831 general election,[4] Edward Lytton Bulwer (perhaps better known as Bulwer-Lytton, the name he took when raised to the peerage in 1866) proposed a select committee 'to inquire into the state of the laws respecting dramatic literature, and the performance of the drama in this country'.[5] Bulwer's proposal was supported by petitions from the inhabitants of Westminster, St James (Clerkenwell), the city of London, and St Mary (Lambeth), 'praying for a repeal of all legislative enactments which tend to restrain the performance of dramatic entertainments in the metropolis'[6] as well as a number of extra-parliamentary meetings of interested parties calling for the abolition of the monopoly.[7] Bulwer's own intention in moving for the establishment of the committee was clear from the speech in which he proposed it: he wished to use the committee's inquiries to present a case for the deregulation of London theatres, specifically to abolish the monopoly rights of the Theatres Royal, to mitigate the censoring powers of the lord chamberlain, and to provide protection for authors through better laws of dramatic copyright. His speech gave an analysis of the existing state of theatre regulation that identified the contradictions of the system, with its tangle of legislation, royal patronage, and traditional practice claimed as legal right.

---

[3] For the standard view that there was little significant connection between the theatre and British politics in the nineteenth century, see Ernest Bradlee Watson, *Sheridan to Robertson* (New York, 1963; first pubd. 1926), who states (p. 5) that 'Of the nation's political life almost nothing is traceable in the drama'. See also Allardyce Nicoll, *A History of English Drama, 1660–1900*, 6 vols. (Cambridge, 1955), iv, 13–14, who comments that the political allusiveness of eighteenth-century drama disappeared in the nineteenth-century theatre, to be replaced by 'direct and simple exposition . . . [of] national facts unadorned save by the trappings of the patriotic imagination'; Michael Booth argues that 'the vigorous political life of the century is not reflected in the drama' in his *Prefaces to Nineteenth-Century Theatre* (Manchester, 1980), 7.

[4] Dewey Ganzel, 'Patent Wrongs and Patent Theatres: Drama and Law in the Early Nineteenth Century', *Publications Mod. Language Assoc.*, 76 (1961), 384.

[5] *Mirror of Parliament*, iii (1832), col. 2350, 31 May 1832.

[6] *Ibid.*   [7] 'A Free Stage', *Examiner*, 8 Jan. 1832, 21.

He also highlighted the deleterious effects of Drury Lane and Covent Garden's claim to a monopoly on the spoken drama – a claim they defended in large part to protect the patentees' investment. Bulwer argued that the monopoly was valid only on 'one possible ground . . . – for the preservation of the dignity of the national drama'.[8] Yet, given this, he asked the supporters of the patent monopoly, with heavy irony:

> Where are the immortal tragedies? – where are the chaste and brilliant comedies? You were to preserve the dignity of the drama from being corrupted by mountebank actors and absurd performances; you have, therefore, we trust, driven jugglers and harlequins from the national stage; you have admitted no wild beasts; you have introduced no fire-eaters and sword-swallowers; you have preserved the dignity of the national drama inviolate; you have left it such as it was when you took it from the hands of Ben Jonson or Shakespeare; for, if you have not done this, then you have not fulfilled that object for which we took from your brethren those privileges we have entrusted to you.[9]

In this speech, Bulwer highlighted the key points of the parliamentary view of theatre reform. Bulwer and his reform-minded colleagues wanted a national drama in a literary tradition, and were critical of the patent theatres' increasing use of the 'wild beasts', 'jugglers and harlequins' formerly the repertoire of the non-patent theatres. Elsewhere, Bulwer considered the theatre's contribution to the cultivation of moral improvement and respectability, asking 'Can any one who has ever, by accident, attended the smaller houses, assert that the performances and the audiences are not of the most decorous and orderly description?'[10] Significantly, Bulwer's use of the term 'by accident' here indicates a lingering anxiety about suggesting that his interlocutors would *deliberately* have attended a non-patent house, in spite of his theoretical defence of the minors' right to a livelihood throughout his parliamentary career.

Bulwer's speech, and those of other MPs who joined in support of his proposal, including Daniel O'Connell, George Lamb, John Campbell, William Brougham, and Richard Lalor Sheil, outlined the parliamentary reformers' central arguments about the state of the London theatre. Their opposition to the patent theatres' monopoly of the drama and arguments about the 'decline of the drama' restated a case that had circulated in one form or another from the mid-eighteenth century.[11] Since the establishment of the public theatres in the late sixteenth century, London theatres had been subject to complex regulatory practices which established both state censorship and the claim to monopoly rights over certain types of performance. In 1737, the Stage Licensing Act formalized the powers of the lord chamberlain to give (or refuse) a licence to all

---

[8] *Mirror of Parliament*, iii (1832), col. 2350, 31 May 1832.   [9] *Ibid.*   [10] *Ibid.*

[11] For an account of the opposition to regulation, see Watson Nicholson, *The Struggle for a Free Stage in London* (New York, 1966; first pubd. 1906).

new scripts for performance at Drury Lane and Covent Garden. Throughout this period, the lord chamberlain's powers were often invoked for purposes of political or moral censorship, as the close questioning by the select committee of George Colman, Jnr, the lord chamberlain's examiner of plays in 1832, and his deputy, John Payne Collier, revealed. While Colman prevaricated somewhat about his political censorship of plays, saying that he would 'advise' a manager for his own good to remove a reference to reform from a script,[12] Collier stated directly that Colman's instructions were to 'strike out or object to any profaneness, immorality, or anything political, likely to excite commotion'.[13]

The 1737 act also entrenched the position of the Theatres Royal at Drury Lane and Covent Garden (with the later addition of the Haymarket Theatre in the summer season) originally deriving from the letters patent awarded to Thomas Killigrew and William Davenant by Charles II in 1662. The royal patent was held to give exclusive rights to the production of the English drama in London to the Theatres Royal and to prohibit any other theatres in London from performing the 'spoken drama'. So, Drury Lane and Covent Garden claimed a monopoly on the right to present all spoken drama of the English dramatic canon, and were prepared to enforce their rights by prosecution of the non-patent theatres that trespassed on their monopoly. However, the patent theatres could not rest easy, in part because theatrical legislation tended to conflate the licensing of plays and the theatres in which they were performed. In 1755, Sadler's Wells theatre was licensed under the 'Act for regulating places of public entertainment' (25 Geo. II, c. xxxvi), and in 1787 John Palmer used this legislation to claim the legal right to produce the spoken drama at the Royalty Theatre. This threat to the patent theatres' rights was vigorously opposed by the patentees, and in 1788 the Enabling Act (28 Geo. III, c. xxx) confirmed the lord chamberlain's authority over the patent theatres in Westminster, but gave magistrates limited powers of licensing theatres and certain types of entertainment for limited periods within a twenty-mile radius of London and Westminster.[14] These convoluted legislative arrangements were further complicated by the commercial and aesthetic responses of the theatre industry to London's expansion in the early nineteenth century. By 1832, the Theatres Royal were in competition with new theatres built as commercial enterprises in areas of growing population, which produced the novelty genres of melodrama, burletta, and spectacle,

---

[12] 'Select Committee on Laws Affecting Dramatic Literature', 59.

[13] *Ibid.*, 29. For the history of censorship of the English theatre in this period, see L.W. Conolly, *The Censorship of English Drama, 1737–1824* (San Marino, 1976); John Russell Stephens, *The Censorship of English Drama, 1824–1901* (Cambridge, 1980).

[14] For a summary of the 1755 and 1788 acts as they related to the non-patent theatres, see David Thomas and Arnold Hare (eds.), *Restoration and Georgian England, 1660–1788* (Cambridge, 1989), 225–32. On the opening of the Royalty Theatre, see Jane Moody, *Illegitimate Theatre in London, 1770–1840* (Cambridge, 2000), 22–4.

designed to appeal to a growing mass market.[15] The patents no longer ensured the profit in theatrical management: their purchase prices had gone too high in a bout of speculative trading on them in the 1810s, and the income derived from exclusivity of theatrical performance, once guaranteed by the patents and by a relatively homogeneous and geographically concentrated audience, had gradually eroded. This was one version of the commonly discussed problem of the 'decline of the drama', and referred to the decline in the economic rewards of managing or investing in the Theatres Royal, and the decline in the Theatres Royal as places of fashion and influence. Another explanation of the decline, expounded by Bulwer, was the degeneration of the literary drama, as commissioned, produced, and played at those Theatres Royal – the 'immortal tragedies' and 'chaste and brilliant comedies' Bulwer asked for in the House of Commons – the dearth of which in 1832 was imputed to the desire of the patent theatre managers to make good on their investments by packing in the audiences to novelties and spectacles. The non-patent theatres talked too about the decline of the drama, largely by trumpeting their attempts to avert this decline by producing robust versions of 'legitimate' dramas in both their past and contemporary forms, always flouting the strict application of the prohibition on the spoken drama. Indeed, looked at from the minor theatres' point of view, this was not generally a period of decline, in commercial or dramatic terms, but one of regeneration and invigorating change in both the aesthetic and material practices of the London theatre profession.

As these different uses of the phrase 'the decline of the drama' demonstrate, public discussions of the state of the theatre in the 1820s and 1830s used a language that mixed legal terminology, theatrical jargon, and class-based assumptions about audience character. The terms of the debate – the 'legitimate' and 'illegitimate' drama, the national drama, the patent or 'major' and 'minor' theatres, the 'decline of the drama' – implied judgements about the relative value and authority of different genres, places of performance, and typical audiences. An analysis of these terms reveals an ideological move from the quasi-legal, but relatively definitive, category of the 'spoken drama', to a variety of ideologically inflected understandings of theatrical practice and aesthetic value. The terms 'legitimate drama' and 'legitimate theatre' offer a case in point. Through the connection of the 'legitimate' – that is, patent – theatres with a particular tradition of spoken drama (English prose and verse full-length plays from the

---

[15] For standard accounts of these economic changes and their impact on the theatre, see George Rowell, *The Victorian Theatre, 1792–1901: A Survey* (Cambridge, 1978; first pubd. 1956); Michael Booth, *Theatre in the Victorian Age* (Cambridge, 1991). For a major revisionist economic history of the theatre, see Tracy C. Davis, *The Economics of the British Stage, 1800–1914* (Cambridge, 2000), esp. pt. i, 'Competition: Theatre and Laissez Faire'. For the first detailed empirical study of the composition of theatre audiences in London, see Jim Davis and Victor Emeljanow, *Reflecting the Audience: London Theatregoing, 1840–1880* (Iowa City, 2001), esp. ix–xiv, 39–40.

Renaissance to the mid-eighteenth century), that body of writing became known as the 'legitimate' or the 'regular' drama. It was, by force of association with the legitimate theatres, the licensed, legal drama. So 'legitimacy' was used to refer to aesthetic value and respectability, as well as legal licensed status. The corpus of English dramatic writing claimed by the patent theatres to their sole use was also referred to as the 'national drama'. By then joining 'legitimate' to 'national', a broader claim was made. Not only was this category of drama licensed and respectable (legitimate), but it was also definitively English and unifying through its practitioners' and audience's patriotic identification with the great poetic heritage of the English language.[16]

However, such structures of identification could also be exclusive and coercive, and by the 1820s the national drama and the legitimate theatre were no longer to be defined simply by the performance of a certain type of play in a particular theatre, but were terms in a discursively created ideological struggle. If there were patent theatres staging the legitimate drama, there were also the 'minor' (non-patented) theatres, playing the 'illegitimate' drama, challenging the dominance of the legitimate theatre. It is here that the move from legal to cultural meaning is clearest, although at the time this shift served to confuse the relative rights and values of the patent and the minor theatres. 'Illegitimacy' did not always signify literal illegality, although the plays produced at the minor theatres were often unlicensed by the lord chamberlain, because, by an irony of past legislation, his right to censor performances outside the patent theatres was unclear (although increasingly from the late 1820s plays from the minor theatres were sent for licensing to the lord chamberlain's office). And even if the minor theatres did openly flout the 1737 act by staging performances which involved more than the 'music and dancing' to which they were theoretically limited, as George Davidge firmly asserted that he did in his evidence to the select committee,[17] these theatres were never completely closed down. In literary and aesthetic terms, 'illegitimate' was a generic catch-all for the mixed theatrical forms of farce, burletta, pantomime, and – pre-eminently – melodrama, which emerged at the end of the eighteenth and beginning of the nineteenth centuries, in part as a response to the proscription against the spoken drama enforced by the patent monopoly.[18] As Jane Moody has shown, the term 'illegitimate' referred to all those theatrical productions not regarded as 'authentic' dramatic forms, viewed with suspicion for their 'grotesque corporeality'.[19] The exclusion and illegality implied by the terms 'illegitimate' and 'minor' were

---

[16] Moody, *Illegitimate Theatre*, 65, argues that the idea of the national drama emerged during the Old Price riots at Covent Garden in 1809.

[17] 'Select Committee on Laws Affecting Dramatic Literature', 76.

[18] Joseph Donohue, 'Burletta and the Early Nineteenth-Century English Theatre', *Nineteenth-Century Theatre Research*, 1 (1973), 30.

[19] Moody, *Illegitimate Theatre*, 12.

a strong indicator of dominant cultural and aesthetic values. If the legitimate drama gained aesthetic value and cultural capital by virtue of its connection to the licensed, legal theatre, then the term 'illegitimate' implied a lawlessness which carried with it anxiety about its morality and cultural status which had to be overcome. However, claims to legitimacy and the national drama in aesthetic and cultural terms were increasingly made by the minor theatres through these mixed genres, and managers and playwrights at these theatres would claim an apparently 'illegitimate' piece as part of the national drama if it went to the heart of patriotic or national politics. By 1832 the 'illegitimate' theatre was not easily dismissed, as its energy and productivity exercised increasing influence even in the legitimizing circles of Westminster and in part drove the call for theatrical reform and deregulation. Conversely, not all the productions staged at Drury Lane and Covent Garden were self-consciously literary, poetic, or 'chastely brilliant'. In this way any clear demarcation between legitimacy and illegitimacy was difficult for all parties to maintain.

Through this thicket of legal, aesthetic, and moral justifications, the select committee endeavoured to clear a path for democratizing reform and deregulation. For most of the committee members, and certainly those identifiably active in questioning and chairing the inquiry,[20] the patents were part of a symbolic economy which circulated and controlled the expression of dramatic taste and notions of theatrical legitimacy, and embedded an idealized national identity within the idea of legitimacy. The monopoly was a check on progress, and its removal necessary for the theatre to take its proper place in a new version of the nation, based on the principles of representative democracy on the one hand, and open competition through deregulation on the other. This agenda was of a piece with moves for political reform in this period: a clearing-out of the accumulated injustices of outmoded aristocratic and corrupt practices of preferment and protectionism. Throughout the inquiry, the committee members' political and aesthetic arguments converged, as most questions and the answers of sympathetic witnesses assumed that reform on the grounds of political principle would also result in aesthetic progress of the literary drama.

---

[20] Ganzel, 'Patent Wrongs and Patent Theatres', 384, identified ten active members of the committee: Edward Bulwer (who shared most of the chairing with Thomas Duncombe), variously described as a Whig radical or reforming liberal; Henry Bulwer, Edward Bulwer's brother and an 'advanced liberal'; Frederick William Chichester, the earl of Belfast and vice lord chamberlain; Thomas Slingsby Duncombe, a Whig who later took up the Chartist cause in parliament; Colonel De Lacey Evans, a radical reformer; Galley Knight, a Whig; George Lamb, a member of the Drury Lane management committee of 1815 together with Byron, described as a 'luke-warm reformer', who stood as a Whig against the radicals; Richard Lalor Sheil, a Catholic radical whose maiden speech was in support of the second reading of the Reform Bill in 1831; John Stanley, a Whig; and Sir George Warrender. Duncombe, De Lacey Evans, and Knight all served on the 1841 Select Committee on National Monuments and Works of Art discussed by Holger Hoock in this volume.

Bulwer and Thomas Slingsby Duncombe shared the majority of the chairing, and their framing of questions was pointed and often leading. With sympathetic witnesses, such as George Davidge, manager of the Coburg (now the Old Vic) Theatre, leading questions stated the argument and required little more than agreement in answer: 'There is no doubt at the minor theatres now there are occasionally representations which, if they do not offend one's taste, offend one's judgment; do you not suppose that might be remedied, if the legitimate drama were entirely free and unrestrained . . . and the public would obtain that better representation which competition produces? – Certainly.'[21] Similarly, Edmund Kean, actor and then proprietor of the Richmond Theatre outside the centre of London, was swept along by the questioner: 'Would it not have been an injustice to the public if those houses [the minor theatres Coburg and City] had been shut up, and all the persons who thronged to them on the nights you performed there had been deprived of the pleasure of seeing you? – Yes, I think it would.'[22] Authors, such as Thomas Serle, were easily led into clear statements of their opposition to the monopoly. Serle's evidence perfectly encapsulated the spirit of democratizing reform by which the committee was motivated: 'In what manner could the monopoly be limited? – I think the principle of monopoly should, for the sake of the art, be entirely destroyed, by placing it in the power of the public to say, wherever they felt the necessity of a theatre, wherever they felt they were not adequately entertained, they might call for a new one.'[23]

Conversely, the questioning of witnesses with connections to the patent theatres was aggressively directed towards exposing the contradictory practices of the current system, and ensuring that witnesses appeared to value their financial interests above all. The standard answers of James Winston (stage manager of Drury Lane and the Haymarket), William Dunn (treasurer of Drury Lane), Charles Kemble (actor and manager of Covent Garden), John Forbes (part-owner of Covent Garden), David Morris (part-owner of the Haymarket), and William Macready (actor at Drury Lane) all expressed opposition to the 'throwing open' of the drama, on the grounds of loss of profit at the patent theatres. Morris and Forbes, for example, insisted that if the monopoly were to be broken up, the patent houses should be compensated. Forbes was categorical in his condemnation of the minor houses, opining that if the minor houses could play the legitimate drama 'you would never have a play well acted in this country again'.[24] George Bartley, stage manager and performer at Covent Garden, concurred with his employer in contending that the popularity of melodramas predominant at the minor theatres and in the provinces, such as Douglas Jerrold's *Black-Ey'd Susan* (1829) and John Baldwin Buckstone's *The Wreck Ashore* (1830), led to a decline in the drama as these plays 'do not

---

[21] 'Select Committee on Laws Affecting Dramatic Literature', 84.
[22] *Ibid.*, 88.   [23] *Ibid.*, 116.   [24] *Ibid.*, 100.

require the same talent to act them as the plays of Otway, Shakespeare, Rowe or Colman, or Sheridan, or our settled drama; hence it comes that these persons in the country have no practice in what we call the regular drama'.[25] Bartley's effort to distinguish between the legitimate and illegitimate drama by referring to particular authors and plays was indicative of the difficulties several of the witnesses revealed in defining the legitimate drama, James Winston, for example, having recourse to the circular definition that the regular drama was whatever was performed at Drury Lane.[26]

Predictably, the committee called for the abolition of the patent monopoly, and demanded a free market in some areas of the theatre industry. Its report recommended that:

> [A]s your Committee believe that the interests of the drama will be considerably advanced by the natural consequences of a fair competition in its representation, they recommend that the Lord Chamberlain should continue a licence to all the theatres licensed at present . . . Your Committee are also of the opinion . . . that the proprietors and managers of the said theatres should be allowed to exhibit . . . the legitimate drama, and all such plays as have received or shall receive the sanction of the censor . . . [A]s theatres are intended for the amusement of the public, so your Committee are of the opinion that the public should have a voice in the number of theatres to be allowed.[27]

These recommendations also pointedly included a separate and specific demand for the legislative removal of any claims by the Theatres Royal at Drury Lane and Covent Garden to the exclusive performance of the spoken word on the London stage. But the committee did not recommend complete freedom of the London stage. The principle of state control remained in the committee's recommendation that all plays produced at all theatres be subject to the censorship of the lord chamberlain's office. Ironically, this renewed commitment to censorship potentially brought the minor theatres under the purview of the lord chamberlain's office. Baulking at removing the lord chamberlain's censoring powers marks a level of tentativeness on the part of the committee that seems at odds with its largely deregulatory spirit throughout the inquiry. Yet it may, after all, be explicable in the light of the committee's enduring concern to promote aesthetic and moral legitimacy (as well as broadening the forms of institutional legitimacy) and its desire to reform the theatre so as to encourage the respectable conduct and self-improvement of the theatre's increasingly mass audience.

In spite of concerted agitation within and without parliament for reform of the theatre, Bulwer's Dramatic Performances Bill, embodying the

[25] *Ibid.*, 182.

[26] *Ibid.*, 20. See Swindells, *Glorious Causes*, 3–9, for her analysis of George Colman's prevaricating and contradictory evidence.

[27] 'Select Committee on Laws Affecting Dramatic Literature', 157.

recommendations of the 1832 select committee, was defeated in the House of Lords in 1833. The monopoly of the patent theatres over the spoken drama, although increasingly flouted and undermined, was not officially lifted until the passing of the Theatres Regulation Act in 1843, and censorship of play scripts by the lord chamberlain's office remained until 1968. Yet discussion had revealed that more was at issue than could be directly controlled by acts of parliament. The questions of the committee and the answers offered by witnesses revealed a vision of a reformed theatre that was largely still bound by elite views of what the reformed theatre should be. It was to be the theatre in which 'dramatic literature' took precedence over spectacle and novelty and the multifarious pleasures of illegitimate entertainment. The conduct of theatrical business was also to be governed by orderly expressions of democratic self-interest. A petition by local inhabitants to set up a theatre in their neighbourhood was the proposed method of developing new theatres licensed to present the English national drama. These theatres were to be 'respectable', concomitant with the general move for self-improvement of the 1820s and 1830s. They should be free to present the legitimate and national drama in forms which harked back to the generically 'pure' traditions of English tragedy and comedy – as if Shakespearean tragedy were not in actuality also the 'illegitimate' *mélange* of low comedy, song, and high tragedy about which many commentators were so anxious. The actual theatrical life that the minors were defending was of quite a different nature, and offered another model of reform on the stage and in England.

Perhaps it was Bulwer's disappointment over the defeat of his 1833 bill that led him to write later that year in *England and the English* that 'At present the English, instead of finding politics on the stage, find their stage in politics.'[28] A theatricalized politics *did* in fact have its corollary in the dramatization of politics on the stage, but such performance was to be found on the stages of the minor theatres on the south side of the Thames and in the East End. If one could have looked out to the Thames from the upper galleries of the Surrey or the Coburg in 1832, it might just have been possible to see the Houses of Parliament on the north side of the river. But although new transport links such as the opening of Waterloo Bridge in 1817 made for easier connections between Westminster on the north bank and Southwark and Lambeth on the south, in the social geography of London theatre-going the Thames still constituted a cultural as well as a physical boundary. Although managers, actors, and playwrights from the minor theatres were called as witnesses to the select committee inquiry, the minor theatres were none the less largely regarded with caution in public commentary accompanying parliamentary discussions,

---

[28] Lord Lytton [Edward Lytton Bulwer], *England and the English* (1833) repr. Knebworth edn (London, 1874), 268.

if their activities were noted at all. The emphasis of the committee on eliciting evidence from George Davidge (manager of the Coburg Theatre) and David Osbaldiston (manager of the Surrey Theatre) about the respectability and good behaviour of their audiences, and minor theatre managers' reciprocal concerns to stress their aspirations to legitimacy (in both its legal and aesthetic aspects), suggests a nervous suspicion on one side, and defensiveness on the other about the lingering illegitimacy of the minor theatres.

These were theatres catering for new, largely artisanal and lower middle-class audiences in a rapidly expanding part of London, which seems to have been largely unknown territory for the young Whigs and radicals in parliament and the progressive circles of literary and cultural London within which they moved.[29] The cultural gulf between the minor theatres and parliamentary reformers was starkly exemplified in the middle of debates over the decline of the drama in the 1820s by a reviewer's comments in the *New Monthly Magazine*:

> It would neither consist with the dignity nor the comfort of the critic to take regular cognizance of the proceedings of the minor theatres. They are the unlicensed borderers on the drama; trespassers on the wastes, who have half obtained a title by the boldness of their invasion; who are free from the control of the law . . . We think it, therefore, befitting our office to give them occasionally a judicial visit; to restrain their excesses, to encourage glimmering merit, and to detect, if possible, 'some soul of goodness' amidst their barbarities.[30]

This was the language of cultural imperialism, which consigned the minor theatres to the very margins of London as an imagined social space.

In the face of such commentary from an otherwise anti-monopoly, pro-reform journal, the minor theatres of London were fighting for visibility and legitimacy. The proscription against performing the legitimate national drama was both a material and a symbolic indication of the lack of representation of minor theatres and their audiences in the formal structures of governance. In consequence, the agitation for parliamentary reform which was represented as damaging to the business of the patent theatres[31] was taken up with some energy in the minor theatres, who connected it directly with the cause of theatrical reform, and saw both as parallel battles for access to English national culture. Osbaldiston, manager of the Surrey, started the year of 1832 with announcements in his playbills about the moves for legislative reform of the theatre and a polemic about the national drama. On his 12 January playbill he reprinted a petition, sent to him

---

[29] For a discussion of the interconnections between theatrical, literary, and parliamentary circles, see Edith Hall, 'Talfourd's Ancient Greeks in the Theatre of Reform', *Internat. Jl Classical Tradition*, 3 (1997), 283–307.

[30] 'The Drama', *New Monthly Mag.*, 18 (1826), 413.

[31] 'Select Committee on Laws Affecting Dramatic Literature', 114, 219, 221, 224–5.

by residents of Southwark, who 'respectfully request[ed] that, notwithstanding the excellence of your present performances, you will occasionally give us some portions of the National Drama . . . left by Shakespeare, Rowe, Sheridan and others, as Legacies to the English Nation'.[32] The next day, Osbaldiston announced a season of 'some highlights, part of the NATIONAL DRAMA' which included a burletta founded on *Othello*, and another on *Macbeth*, a melodrama founded on Rowe's *Jane Shore*, extracts from Otway's *Venice Preserv'd*, and a production of Sheridan's *Pizarro*.[33] On 1 February, the Surrey playbill was headed by an extract from *The Times*, quoting an article which criticized the monopoly of the legitimate drama exercised by the patent theatres and praised 'the successful efforts of the spirited Manager of the Surrey'. Following this was an announcement of 'A FREE BENEFIT for the CAUSE of the DRAMA', with performances of *William Tell! The Hero of Switzerland*, followed by a farce and a romantic melodrama.[34]

The scheduling of a patriotic drama such as *William Tell!* for a benefit night to raise money for the campaign to deregulate the theatres cannot be seen as coincidental. By presenting a play about national freedom on a night in benefit of theatrical freedom, Osbaldiston invited his audience to connect the two. Osbaldiston's strategy of connecting patriotic dramas to his own causes was evident again in the programme for his own benefit night (designed to raise a salary bonus for each member of the theatrical company). He presented 'a grand National Historical Drama', founded on 'SHAKESPEARE'S Play of KING JOHN! or, THE DAYS OF MAGNA CHARTA'.[35] This performance was to be followed by 'An entirely new COMIC SONG . . . called "Majors versus Minors!"' These bills, and the nightly entertainments they advertised, combine the power of the legitimate, national drama of Shakespeare with an explicit foregrounding of patriotic display to make their political point. Neither was the directly political eschewed by Osbaldiston, in productions or playbills, as exemplified in March 1832 by the staging of the melodrama *Blight of Ambition, or, The Life of a Member of Parliament*. Osbaldiston advertised the play as dealing directly with matters pertinent to the contemporary parliamentary political situation, and reproduced extracts of the dialogue as bait for his audience. 'Lord for Lord, say I, the people for the people, [as parliamentary representatives] and Heaven for us all! Then may we hope the rights of all classes of society will be preserved in a good, sound, glorious Constitution!'[36] Quoting such excerpts from the dialogue of the play would seem specifically designed to rouse an extra-theatrical

---

[32] Brit. Lib., 'A Collection of Playbills of the Surrey Theatre', 2 vols., playbills 311–13, playbill for the Surrey Theatre, 12 Jan. 1832.
[33] *Ibid.*   [34] *Ibid.*   [35] *Ibid.*
[36] *Ibid.* Unfortunately, there is no record of publication of this play, nor is it available in manuscript in the Brit. Lib., lord chamberlain's collection of plays.

party-political interest in the audience, encouraging it to connect the theatrical performances on stage with political performances outside the theatre.

The material practices of theatrical production at the minor theatres offer further evidence of the minor theatres' own definitions of reform politics. The Surrey production of the melodrama *Hofer, The Tell of Tyrol* provides a typical example of the way managements constructed a night's entertainment combining spectacle, sensation, and political feeling.[37] The play was first performed on Whit Monday, the traditional working people's summer holiday, and featured on the night's bill as the principal attraction in a programme of three melodramas – the other two by another Surrey regular, George Almar, *Hallowmass Eve: or, Under the Old Church Porch*, and *Attar Gull, or, The Serpent of the Valley*. All three plays were proclaimed in the playbill as 'Romantic' or 'Legendary' dramas, with *Hofer* additionally labelled as a 'Historical Patriotic and . . . National Drama'.[38] Osbaldiston played the title role of Andreas Hofer, the patriotic innkeeper of a Tyrolean village, defying the invasion of Napoleon's army. The extant play script shows that Hofer's patriotism and praise of liberty were strictly confined by religious and regal dynastic boundaries; however, knowledge of the performance energy of the melodramatic acting style suggests that Hofer's speeches were calculated to rouse the patriotic (and anti-French) sentiment of their English audience:

> this scene, so bloody, so appalling to your senses, comes but the first of many, still more bloody, if longer we forget that we are men. Are we not husbands? Are we not fathers? Have we not hearts, and brave ones, as our foes? Let us not be slaves; this country is our mother – a viper stings her bosom, let us seize and strangle it.[39]

Read in this way, *Hofer* resonates as a political play in a variety of ways: its focus on ordinary people and its linking of village and national politics suggests a radical participatory democracy, based on populist nationalism, which is simultaneously nostalgic for an idealized 'romantic' past and an actual recent past of victorious war against the French. Osbaldiston added to this effect by using the local knowledge and support of his regular audience in a meta-theatrical linkage of the fight for liberty of his fictional character with his actual fight for liberty as a theatre manager. These fictional and meta-theatrical elements of the performance of *Hofer*, together with its intertextual framings both within the evening's full programme and within the series of playbills promoting both theatrical and parliamentary reform since the beginning of the year, all contributed to a more fluid and responsive political conversation between local theatre management and its audience than the formal performances of the witnesses at the

---

[37] Edward Fitzball, *Hofer, The Tell of Tyrol* (London, n.d.); first performed 11 June 1832.

[38] Brit. Lib., 'Collection of Playbills of the Surrey Theatre', playbills 311–13, playbill for the Surrey Theatre, 11 June 1832.

[39] Fitzball, *Hofer*, 24.

select committee in Westminster might suggest. In 1832, as many commentators of the time noted, any call for liberty connected with national feeling was bound to create an excited mixture of political and patriotic response in its audience. The night's entertainment containing *Hofer* offered a view of 'the national drama' different from that represented at Westminster or in the patent theatres of the West End. The national drama at the Surrey was not a commodity to be constructed and controlled through parliamentary reform movements, but a nostalgic recall of an idealized past represented metonymically on the stage by the organic village community of the melodrama.[40]

The nostalgic recall of an idealized past might have sat oddly with some rationalist visions of reform. But the idealized worlds of popular melodrama were not necessarily so removed from popular feelings about reform. Indeed, they illuminate the imagined context in which the popular battle for reform was fought. One of the few popular plays of this period to represent parliamentary reform overtly uses just this model of a paternalist community based around the familiar fictional figure of John Bull. William Thomas Moncrieff's *Reform; or John Bull Triumphant!* was first performed at the Coburg Theatre, with the Coburg's manager, George Davidge, in the title role of John Bull.[41] The reform-minded *Spectator* used the play as an example of the 'state of public feeling on Reform', concluding that the play was 'completely successful – and so will Reform be'.[42] George Daniel's introductory 'Remarks' to Cumberland's printed edition made the same point: 'Reform was very popular at the Coburg, and . . . throughout the whole Kingdom!'[43] Later in the year, *Reform* was restaged as part of a specially advertised 'Pierce Egan Night' featuring plays adapted from popular authors' works, and Egan himself playing 'Bedford, a Reformer' in *Reform*. The programme also included the provocatively named *Guy Fawkes, or the Gunpowder Treason*, suggesting a politicized theatrical programme at once playful and intense.[44]

Like much satire and topical commentary produced under conditions of political censorship, *Reform* was superficially a simple and rather clumsy comedy, which promulgated popular patriotic and democratic sentiments. By presenting his material in a comic mode, Moncrieff was able to make pointed and pertinent comments about the current political scene and the major characters in it while escaping potential political censorship. Moncrieff constructed Britain as an estate with many tenants who had been neglected by their landlord John

---

[40] For a general theoretical discussion of this feature of melodrama, see Kurt Tetzeli von Rosador, 'Myth and Victorian Melodrama', *Essays and Studies*, 32 (1979).

[41] W. T. Moncrieff, *Reform; or, John Bull Triumphant: A Patriotic Drama in One Act* (London, n.d.); first performed 14 Mar. 1831.

[42] 'John Bull Triumphant', *Spectator*, 19 Mar. 1831, 275.   [43] Moncrieff, *Reform*, 7.

[44] Brit. Lib., 'Collections of Playbills for the Royal Coburg Theatre, 1818–72', playbills 174–5, playbill for the Coburg Theatre, 8 May 1831.

Bull, and exploited by his corrupt servants. When John Bull discovers this mismanagement, he dismisses his servants, and promises his tenants complete reform, a fair hearing in his house, and servants 'that shall lighten your burthens, not add to them'.[45] The final scene is a 'grand allegorical, loyal and appropriate tableau' with soldiers and sailors at each side, and the heroine, Albina, dressed as Britannia, singing 'Rule, Britannia!' The title and the names of the characters (Moncrieff names the tenants George Briton, Patrick Murphy, and Sandy Glaskey) suggest a broad emblematic style, capacious enough to combine broad comedy with high-sounding patriotic statements. Miles Taylor has argued that 'John Bull embodied a common and widely used critique of political power' into the early nineteenth century, and emerged as a figure who 'represented both the strengths and weaknesses of the British system, while confirming that it was qualitatively different from those of other European states'.[46] Moncrieff's use of John Bull as his central character provides further demonstration of Taylor's thesis, as this theatrical version of John Bull emblematically represented parliamentary reform as a popular movement to restore the proper social order, and justified popular action as legitimate and necessitated by John Bull's initial abdication of power in leaving his servants to run his estates so that he could enjoy his afternoon pipe, porter, and nap.

Moncrieff's *Reform* represented parliamentary reform not as revolutionary conflagration, nor as rational improvement, but as an inevitable return to the traditional English values of fairness, loyalty, and tolerance. This comic vision of a reformed and united Britain was not the corruptly aristocratic nation of the eighteenth century, but neither was it the open competition of the parliamentary radicals. It was a political and social community in which all were looked after, and each 'tenant' had justice. *Reform* and *Hofer*, together with many other nostalgic and recuperative domestic comedies and village melodramas of the 1820s and 1830s, offer examples of what E. P. Thompson identified as the battle between the new political economy of industrialism and the older 'moral economy' of the community.[47] They suggest that a different type of radical politics emerged from the minor theatres of London, which proposed a conception of the English people and nation based on strong emotion, inclusiveness, and mutual support. This popular vision of the nation and its political constitution might appear to valorize a paternalistic and pre-Reform world, but in the dynamic culture emerging from the popular theatre of the period, these elements were appropriated for the use and benefit of its largely working-class constituency

---

[45] Moncrieff, *Reform*, 27.

[46] Miles Taylor, 'John Bull and the Iconography of Public Opinion in England *c.* 1712–1929', *Past and Present*, no. 134 (Feb. 1992), 106–8.

[47] E. P. Thompson, 'The Moral Economy of the English Crowd in the Eighteenth Century', *Past and Present*, no. 50 (Feb. 1971), 79.

as ways for that community to look after itself in the face of competition and deregulation in which they were often competing at a disadvantage. In the stage productions and the management policies of theatres such as the Surrey and the Coburg, we find examples of a politicized performance culture, marginalized and suspected by Westminster, but nevertheless insisting on the right to participate in movements for reform in 1832.

11. *Reforming culture: national art institutions in the age of reform* *

HOLGER HOOCK

'Few circumstances can more fully exhibit the hitherto exclusive nature of our institutions than the fact that we have only just begun to form a NATIONAL GALLERY': P.P. 1836, ix (568), 'Report from the Select Committee on Arts and Manufactures', ix.

'In the present times of political excitement, the exacerbation of angry and unsocial feelings might be much softened by the effects which the fine arts [have] ever produced upon the minds of men': Sir Robert Peel, in *Parl. Debs.*, 3rd ser., xiv, col. 645 (23 July 1832).

The complex relationship between political discourse and institutions on the one hand, and the fine arts and their institutions on the other, is one of the most fruitful if still under-researched areas of British cultural history in the late eighteenth and early nineteenth centuries.[1] Between *c.* 1790 and the 1840s, the public status of the arts in Britain changed dramatically. The art world became intensely politicized: discussion of art and of artists' personal and institutional politics reflected, and contributed to, wider political discourses. Moreover, the arts emerged as a new policy field when increasingly ambitious artistic professions collaborated with the Napoleonic fiscal-military state to

* I would like to thank Ulrich Gotter for his very helpful comments on an earlier version of this chapter.

[1] Art institutions have become increasingly central to the study of eighteenth- and nineteenth-century British art. See Ilaria Bignamini, 'Art Institutions in London, 1689–1768: A Study of Clubs and Academies', *Walpole Soc.*, 55 (1988), 1–148; Brandon Taylor, *Art for the Nation: Exhibitions and the London Public, 1747–2001* (New Brunswick, N.J., 1999), chs. 1–2; Peter Fullerton, 'Patronage and Pedagogy: The British Institution in the Early Nineteenth Century', *Art Hist.*, 5 (1982), 59–72; David Solkin (ed.), *Art on the Line: The Royal Academy Exhibitions at Somerset House, 1780–1836* (New Haven, 2001); Marcia Pointon (ed.), *Art Apart: Art Institutions and Ideology across England and North America* (Manchester, 1994); David Solkin *et al.* (eds.), *Towards a Modern Art World: Art in Britain, c. 1715–1880* (New Haven, 1995); Andrew Hemingway and William Vaughan (eds.), *Art in Bourgeois Society, 1790–1850* (Cambridge, 1998); Paul Barlow and Colin Trodd (eds.), *Governing Cultures: Art Institutions in Victorian London* (Aldershot, 2000). See also the literature cited in nn. 2, 3, 5, 30 below.

project an image of British cultural as well as military prowess.[2] By the early nineteenth century, British artists, writers on art, and politicians for the first time engaged in coherent debates about the role of the state in relation to the social and educational functions of the arts and their organizational structures. At a time of general interest in 'reform', these debates were concerned with 'reforming culture': that is, on the one hand, with the capacity of the arts to reform popular morals and contribute to the civilizing process; and, on the other, with the reform of dysfunctional institutional structures in the art world. A history of the theory and practice of reforming national art institutions will shed light not only on such institutions but also on the wider phenomenon of 'reform'.[3]

A body of ideas about the socio-political significance of the arts was already in being by 1780. The cultivation of taste – a faculty in the spectactor by which works of art inspired the pleasures of the imagination – was considered an aspect of a morally benevolent character. According to the civic-humanist discourse dominant in the early eighteenth century, only the (male) educated few could acquire taste and concomitant moral virtue, but their aesthetic and moral refinement was seen to reflect on the polity and nation as a whole. Thus, the quality, say, of a nation's art collections and the taste of her connoisseurs helped define her state of civilization and her international prestige. After mid-century, taste was increasingly represented as generally cultivable rather than an innate capacity: whilst an intellectual understanding of the arts might be open only to the initiated few, those without much formal education were able to appreciate works of art in a sensual way.[4]

Who, though, was to provide art, whether for the few or the many? Throughout much of the eighteenth century, it was generally assumed that artists and art ought to be supported by private patronage and markets, not by the state.[5] In

---

[2] The argument for the recognition of politics and political institutions as agents and sites of cultural change in late Hanoverian Britain is more fully developed in Holger Hoock, *The King's Artists: The Royal Academy of Arts and the Politics of British Culture, 1760–1840* (Oxford, 2003).

[3] English provincial art institutions are under-explored, but see Trevor Fawcett, *The Rise of English Provincial Art: Artists, Patrons and Institutions outside London, 1800–1830* (Oxford, 1974); Giles Waterfield, 'Art Galleries and the Public: A Survey of Three Centuries', in *Art Treasures of England: The Regional Collections* (London, Royal Academy of Arts, 1998), 13–77; Hoock, *King's Artists*, 80–108. Duncan Forbes, 'Private Advantage and Public Feeling: The Struggle for Academic Legitimacy in Edinburgh in the 1820s', in Rafael Cardoso Denis and Colin Trodd (eds.), *Art and the Academy in the Nineteenth Century* (New Brunswick, N.J., 2000), 86–101, relates Scottish art institutions to political reform agendas.

[4] John Barrell, *The Political Theory of Painting from Reynolds to Hazlitt: 'The Body of the Public'* (New Haven, 1986); Stephen Copley, 'The Fine Arts in Eighteenth-Century Polite Culture', in John Barrell (ed.), *Painting and the Politics of Culture: New Essays on British Art, 1700–1850* (Oxford, 1992), 13–31, esp. 23 f.

[5] Ann Bermingham and John Brewer (eds.), *The Consumption of Culture, 1600–1800: Image, Object, Text* (London, 1995); John Brewer, *The Pleasures of the Imagination: English Culture in the Eighteenth Century* (London, 1997), 87–122, *passim*; David H. Solkin, *Painting for Money: The Visual Arts and the Public Sphere in Eighteenth-Century England* (New Haven, 1993).

contrast to many continental countries, in Britain there were no picture galleries, art academies, or exhibitions run by government or as annexes of the court, and hardly any official commissions for history painters and sculptors. The Royal Academy of Arts (1768) – the dominant fine-arts school and exhibition society in this period – enjoyed close links with George III, but it was not responsible to government or parliament. The British Museum, founded in 1753 through the purchase of the Sloane and Harleian collections for the nation at a cost of some £30,000, was initially devoid of fine-art objects of note.

After 1790, political and military conflict with France extended into cross-Channel competition in cultural display. The Royal Academy turned itself into the national adjudicator on public art and taste. The British Museum became the repository of outstanding, internationally sought-after antique sculpture, and was considered as a possible space for a national picture collection.[6] And British naval and military triumph was commemorated by three dozen national monuments erected in St Paul's cathedral. Anyone writing on art now had to take a stance on the role of the state: should art and artists be helped by state patronage and regulation, or should their development be left to private patronage and free competition between private art societies?[7] Government and parliament began to engage in new ways with the artistic professions: the state granted artists tax and customs exemptions and copyright legislation, and in turn sought the advice of Royal Academicians on coinage design and national monuments in St Paul's.[8]

As taste was defined in more inclusive ways, and as the state entered the field of art, public debate about the role of art in the nation generated pressure for change. That debate revolved to a large extent around questions of admission to cultural artefacts and institutions, and around notions of cultural transmission from the elite to the nation. It was characterized by three main themes. First, from the late eighteenth century, aristocratic cultural monopolies came under scrutiny. Second, in the context of a perceived political and moral crisis in the 1830s, some argued the need more particularly to enhance working-class access to 'rational recreation'. By then, reformers were also campaigning for the reconfiguration of national art institutions so as to enhance their efficiency, transparency, and accountability. The following three sections consider each of these themes in turn.

---

[6] P.P. 1823, iv (271), 41–56*, 'Report on the Royal Library', esp. 49 f.; Ian Jenkins, *Archaeologists and Aesthetes in the Sculpture Galleries of the British Museum, 1800–1939* (London, 1992); Brit. Museum, General Meetings, minutes, v. 1211 (26 June 1823).

[7] Compare Prince Hoare, *An Inquiry into the Requisite Cultivation and Present State of the Arts of Design in England* (London, 1806); Prince Hoare, *Epochs of the Arts Including Hints on the Use and Progress of Painting and Sculpture in Great Britain* (London, 1813); with George Foggo, 'An Investigation of the Effects of Government Patronage: Founded on Historical Evidence', *Library of the Fine Arts*, 1 (1831), 93 ff., 177 ff., 266 ff.

[8] For a full exposition, see Hoock, *King's Artists*, pt. III.

I

In the decades around 1800, the closed culture of the privileged came under increasing pressure for change, prompting both private owners of paintings and the British Museum to experiment with widening access to their collections. The collecting of old-master paintings, like the Italian opera, was a sphere dominated by the nobility and affluent gentry well into the nineteenth century. Up to the early 1800s, private aristocratic galleries in London town houses, in suburban villas, and in country houses were by and large accessible only to personal acquaintances of the owners, and to fairly select polite visitors of noble, genteel and, less commonly, professional status.[9] This enclosure of private collections was criticized as early as the 1730s; from the last third of the century artists and writers concerned with the national arts and public taste campaigned consistently to make such collections more widely accessible. It was argued that they should be held in trust as national assets so that they could function as models for native artists, display native taste to foreigners, and educate and edify a relatively inclusively defined British public. Private collections were thus seen indirectly to contribute to, and reflect the moral health of, the polity and the country's international prestige.[10] But notions of a cultural transmission from the elite to the nation were contested by critics asking for direct access for more inclusively defined publics. By the close of the century, some collectors made country house collections more accessible, with regular visiting-hours and printed catalogues. This was one attempt by a landed elite under pressure to try and present an image of greater openness and accessibility.[11]

Since this was a limited phenomenon, however, in the late 1790s artists started to campaign in earnest for a central public – or 'national' – gallery.[12] Continental developments provided the background for their campaigns. Most importantly, in 1793, the former royal Louvre was rededicated as the new French nation's museum, where every *citoyen* would view the nationalized former royal, aristocratic, and ecclesiastical collections on (theoretically) equal terms. The limited access to aristocratic collections in Britain compared unfavourably

---

[9] For metropolitan collections, see Giles Waterfield, 'The Town House as Gallery of Art', *London Jl*, 20 (1995), 47–66. For country house collections, see John Harris, 'English Country House Guides, 1740–1840', in John Summerson (ed.), *Concerning Architecture: Essays on Architectural Writers and Writing Presented to Nikolaus Pevsner* (London, 1968), 58–74; Peter Mandler, *The Fall and Rise of the Stately Home* (New Haven, 1997), prelude.

[10] For these agendas and efforts at military commemoration converging in campaigns for a national gallery, see Holger Hoock, 'Old Masters and the English School', *Jl Hist. Collections* (forthcoming, 2004).

[11] Paul Langford, *Public Life and the Propertied Englishman, 1689–1798* (Oxford, 1991), 548–50. Mandler, *Fall and Rise*, 8–10, rightly emphasizes the limits to this development.

[12] In 1777 John Wilkes had first demanded a national gallery, probably for an upper- and middling-sort public. See John Conlin, 'John Wilkes and the "Public Eye"' (University of London M.A. thesis, 1999).

with the French national collection.[13] It has been suggested that in the eyes of British patricians the very notion of a national gallery might have undermined the principle of private property; free universal access to a national collection might even prompt demands for wider political rights.[14] But the parliamentary purchase of a collection 'for the nation' would not necessarily violate the principle of private ownership, and private loans to a national collection might be presented as a way of turning private property into a publicly useful or national asset; indeed, by 1812 *Collins's Peerage* described the Stafford, Cavendish, and Grosvenor collections as 'national treasures'.[15]

Nevertheless, under the immediate impact of what they had seen in Paris during the Peace of Amiens (1802), British collectors pursued two strategies for presenting a less exclusive image, but stopped short of conceding a national gallery.[16] First, some London collections were made regularly accessible to a wider, if still confined public, including those of Thomas Hope (1804), the marquis of Stafford (1806), Earl Grosvenor (1808) and Sir John Fleming Leicester (1819).[17] Second, the British Institution for Promoting the Fine Arts in the United Kingdom was founded in 1805. It was heavily dominated by noblemen, many of whom held hereditary governorships; the Prince Regent presided from 1810. In a way that parallels opera management, it thus exemplifies aristocratic involvement in public affairs, at once a reaction to a critique of aristocratic rule and a sign of recovering aristocratic self-confidence.[18] From 1806 the British Institution ran a seasonal copying school for artists with old masters and modern British paintings on loan from private collectors, mostly its own members.

---

[13] Andrew McClellan, *Inventing the Louvre: Art, Politics and the Origins of the Modern Museum in Eighteenth-Century Paris* (Cambridge, 1994); chs. 3–4; Carol Duncan, 'From the Princely Gallery to the Public Art Museum: The Louvre Museum and the National Gallery, London', in Duncan, *Civilizing Rituals: Inside Public Art Museums* (London, 1995), 21–47.

[14] Linda Colley, *Britons: Forging the Nation, 1707–1837* (New Haven, 1992), 175; Duncan, 'Princely Gallery to the Public Art Museum', 40.

[15] Sir Egerton Brydges, *Collins's Peerage of England*, 9 vols. (London, 1812), i, x. See also Colley, *Britons*, 176; Ann Pullan, 'Public Society or Private Interests? The British Institution in the Early Nineteenth Century', in Hemingway and Vaughan (eds.), *Art in Bourgeois Society*, 27–44, at 28 f.

[16] From the 1790s, the most promising initiatives towards a national gallery were launched by the Royal Academy, for which see Hoock, 'Old Masters'. Around 1800, governments rejected several offers of private old-master collections to 'the nation'. See Count Joseph Truchsess, *Proposals for the Establishment of a National Gallery* (London, 1802); *Gentleman's Mag.*, 72 (1802), 813 f.; William Buchanan, *Memoirs of Painting: With a Chronological History of the Importation of Pictures by the Great Masters into England since the French Revolution*, 2 vols. in one (London, 1824), ii, 109 f.; Hugh Brigstocke, *William Buchanan and the Nineteenth Century Art Trade* (London, 1982), 65, 84, 474.

[17] William T. Whitley, *Art in England, 1800–1820* (London, 1928), 108 f.; Waterfield, 'Town House as Gallery of Art', 58; 'A Catalogue of Pictures, by British Artists, in the Collection of Sir John Leicester', *Annals of the Fine Arts*, 2 (1818), 104–10.

[18] *An Account of the British Institution for Promoting the Fine Arts in the United Kingdom* (London, 1805); Victoria and Albert Museum, London, R.C.V. 12, British Institution for Promoting the Fine Arts in the United Kingdom, minute books, ii, fos. 165, 170.

From 1815 it also staged the first and well-attended public-loan exhibitions of old masters in Britain, publicizing lenders' names widely.[19] These 'ephemeral museums'[20] mediated access to the closed culture of the privileged, easing pressure for direct access. A generation later, Johann David Passavant, the German artist and chronicler of Britain's art collections, acknowledged that the British Institution had 'the great merit of having been the first to unlock the concealed treasures of art belonging to the king, the nobility, and the gentry of the land, to the inspection of an enlightened and appreciating public'.[21]

At the same time that private collectors were resorting to these palliative measures, access to the British Museum's collections, which increasingly contained antique sculpture, and which were guarded by much the same social group, was also widened. The British Museum Act (1753) stated that the museum was established for 'the General Use and Benefit of the Publick'. However, the Board of Trustees, dominated by officers of state and the church, had devised admission regulations which defined the museum as an exclusive institution for recognized members of the republic of letters to use the reading room, and for the 'curious', that is those with a basic education and of genteel or middling-sort background, to enter the gardens and the collections of antiquities and natural history.[22] Admission to the collections was by prior written application and ticket during restricted opening hours, a process that filtered the audience through its sheer complexity and the requirements of literacy and leisure. Public ownership and funding were considered compatible with the exclusion of the culturally unqualified majority of the population from the premises and its contents.[23] Notions of the virtual representation of culture allowed the public and nation to benefit through the use of the British Museum collections by those who were best qualified to use them, the learned and basically educated.[24] At the turn of the century, however, restrictions were gradually being eased in response to criticism from in and outside parliament that the public ought to have easy access to collections that it funded.[25] By 1810 the ticket system had

---

[19] For detailed documentation, see Hoock, 'Old Masters'.

[20] Francis Haskell, *The Ephemeral Museum: Old Master Paintings and the Rise of the Art Exhibition* (New Haven, 2000).

[21] Johann David Passavant, *Tour of a German Artist in England with Notices of Private Galleries and Remarks on the State of Art*, 2 vols. (London, 1836), i, 59.

[22] 26 Geo. II, c. xxii; Anne Goldgar, 'The British Museum and the Virtual Representation of Culture in the Eighteenth Century', *Albion*, 32 (2000), 195–231, esp. 201–6. Standard histories include Edward Miller, *That Noble Cabinet: A History of the British Museum* (Athens, Ohio, 1974); see also D. J. Cash, 'Access to Museum Culture: The British Museum from 1753 to 1836' (University of Cambridge Ph.D. thesis, 1994).

[23] Pierre Bourdieu, *Distinction: A Social Critique of the Judgement of Taste* (London, 1984); Krysztof Pomian, *Collectors and Curiosities, Paris and Venice, 1500–1800* (Cambridge, 1990).

[24] Goldgar, 'British Museum'.

[25] *Parl. Debs.*, 1st ser., ii, cols. 933 f., 964 f. (3, 9 July 1804); iii, col. 409 f. (12 Feb. 1805); v, col. 546 f. (21 June 1805).

been abolished, and anyone 'of decent appearance' was admitted on three days per week between 10 a.m. and 4 p.m., except in August and September and on certain holidays. Visitor figures soared, from some 15,000 in the twelve months prior to the change, to over 29,000 in the following twelve months, exceeding 50,000 in 1817–18. Notions of virtual representation were thus beginning to be eroded at the (national) British Museum even more directly than at the (private) British Institution.[26]

By the 1820s the lack of a national gallery was increasingly seen as a disgrace to government, especially since, as the *Examiner* put it, one 'established by neighbouring and rival France stares us so reprehensively in the face'.[27] Sir George Beaumont unofficially offered his picture collection to the nation at the same time that parliament discussed George IV's donation of the royal library to the British Museum. MPs ranging from the radical John Hobhouse and the Whigs Lord John Russell and Sir James Mackintosh to the Tory John Croker alleged maladministration of museum collections and apathy among trustees. Moreover, it was argued that the museum's relative physical remoteness in Great Russell Street, and the fact that it did not stand 'in any public situation, inviting, by its architectural beauties, the passengers to enter', rendered it unsuitable for housing a picture collection which ought to elevate public taste.[28] Discussion of the Beaumont offer was overtaken by the death of the marine insurer John Julius Angerstein, which made available his small but outstanding collection of old masters and some British paintings. The prime minister, Lord Liverpool, and the home secretary, Sir Robert Peel, both collectors themselves, backed the purchase of Angerstein's collection for £57,000.[29] In the face of persistent opposition in the House of Commons against the British Museum as a repository, the government also bought the lease of Angerstein's house, so that the National Gallery was from the start a physically independent establishment at 100 Pall Mall, obtaining full administrative independence from the British Museum by 1828.

Thus elite culture perhaps provided a more sensitive barometer of aristocratic public authority than politics itself: the National Gallery in a sense not only pre-dated, but anticipated, political reform. Although multiple agendas converged

---

[26] P.P. 1808, vi (310), 41–50, 'Regulations Concerning the British Museum'; P.P. 1810–11, xi (168), 157–60, 'Regulations Concerning the British Museum'; P.P. 1835, vii (479), 'Report on the British Museum', 308.

[27] *Examiner*, no. 728 (6 Jan. 1822), 10.

[28] *Parl. Debs.*, 2nd ser., ix, cols. 1112–26, quotation 1121 f. (Sir James Mackintosh, 20 June 1823), cols. 1357–9 (Croker, Yorke, 1 July 1823); P.P. 1835, vii (479), 8 f., paras. 1123–6; *Quarterly Rev.*, 31 (1824), art. XII, unsigned report on John Young's 'Catalogue of the Celebrated Collection of Pictures of the late John Julius Angerstein, Esq.', 214; Felicity Owen and David B. Brown, *Collector of Genius: A Life of Sir George Beaumont* (New Haven, 1988), 210 f.

[29] For Angerstein, who rose from obscure German–Russian origins to eminence in New Lloyds, see Christopher Lloyd, 'John Julius Angerstein, 1732–1823: Founder of Lloyd's and of the National Gallery', *Hist. Today*, 16 (1966), 373–9. A useful general account in Gregory Martin, 'The Founding of the National Gallery, London', *Connoisseur*, 185–7 (1974).

in the efforts to found a National Gallery, its establishment was partly motivated by a desire to absorb pressure for wider access to private collections (and to vindicate the nation's cultural standing). The parliamentary majority for the purchase was probably orchestrated by the connoisseur-parliamentarians who were also governors of the British Institution.[30] For private collectors the purchase of a ready-made collection on the market was a convenient way of establishing a national gallery without conceding ground on the issue of private property. The new institution did not change the distribution of political power, but it removed a portion of prestigious symbolism from the exclusive control of a mainly aristocratic elite and, notionally, gave it to the nation as a whole. To be sure, at Pall Mall, the gallery was still conducted very much like a gentleman's gallery, with 24,000 visitors in May to November 1824 cramming into a space holding only two hundred at a time, and a display directed at the connoisseur, with no explanatory material or captions. When the Whig MP Agar Ellis insisted that the National Gallery must be 'situated in the very gangway of London', his public was still ambiguously defined as 'all ranks and degrees of men', 'every decently dressed person', or merchants and members of parliament, the sovereign, and men of literature and science, foreigners and 'hunters of exhibitions', 'the indolent as well as the busy'.[31] All-inclusive definitions of cultural audiences were guaranteed to remain controversial.

II

By the 1830s a perceived political, moral, and cultural crisis intensified the connections made in public discourse between reform in the worlds of politics and art. Both working-class campaigners and middle-class initiatives for diffusing useful knowledge recognized the arts and museums as means of educational advancement.[32] The post-war disturbances, turmoil over Queen Caroline's trial, and the Reform crisis – though by some considered to be diverting attention from the arts – gave renewed urgency to the neo-classical notion of art and art galleries as instruments of moral improvement. Some supported parliamentary reform in the hope that social and political stability would provide the basis for prosperity and a revival of the arts, a classical and eighteenth-century *topos*.[33]

---

[30] By 1820, a quarter of the two hundred hereditary and life governors of the British Institution were MPs: see Jordana Pomeroy, 'Creating a National Collection: The National Gallery's Origins in the British Institution', *Apollo*, 148 (1998), 46.

[31] 'Angerstein's Collection of Pictures', *Quarterly Rev.*, 31 (1824), art. XII, 213.

[32] *Penny Mag. of the Soc. for the Diffusion of Useful Knowledge*, new ser. (1841), 11, 21, 52, 68, 89, 217, 241, 265, 289, 377, 425; *Edinburgh Rev.*, 65 (1837), viii; Anthony Burton, *Vision and Accident: The Story of the V&A* (London, 1999), 14.

[33] James V. Millingen, *Some Remarks on the State of Learning and the Fine Arts in Great Britain: On the Deficiency of Public Institutions and the Necessity of a Better System for the Improvement of Knowledge and Taste* (London, 1831), 3, 5, 72.

In July 1832, with the May Days crisis fresh in everyone's memory, Peel linked the cause of the National Gallery with a political strategy, though it is perhaps ambiguous which was his primary interest: 'In the present times of political excitement, the exacerbation of angry and unsocial feelings might be much softened by the effects which the fine arts [have] ever produced upon the minds of men.' The National Gallery allowed people with little leisure the 'most refined species of pleasure', and its location near Charing Cross was well selected, where 'the great tide of human existence is fullest in its stream', as Dr Johnson had put it. The gallery, claimed Peel, 'would not only contribute to the cultivation of the arts, but also to the cementing of those bonds of union between the richer and the poorer orders of the State'.[34] Access to art for, and the spread of taste among, all classes was expected to help alleviate social tensions and the consequences of urban poverty. From the 1830s, campaigns against the vices of drinking and gambling aimed at their replacement by so-called 'rational recreation', epitomized by visits of the working classes to public parks, libraries, museums, and art galleries.[35] Reformers for the first time used crude visitor statistics to demonstrate the importance of evening, Sunday, and holiday opening of the national collections. Even conservatives like Lord Ashley believed that the industrious classes would visit the National Gallery instead of alehouses.[36] Whether expressed in some conservatives' authoritarian attempts to promote the arts as an alternative to drunkenness and crime, or in the conviction of reformers and radicals that exposure to art and its educative effect was the birthright of Englishmen, the demand for access to art as rational recreation was based on the notion that the individual could be converted from a sinful existence to develop a moral personality.[37] The line of questioning adopted by select committees suggests that the view of art as universal rational recreation (like the idea of culture moulding the working classes in the image of their social superiors) was beginning to attract cross-party support.

But the function and audiences of galleries also continued to divide cultural officials and politicians. Among British Museum officials testifying before two successive House of Commons select committees in 1835–6, a bias against the

---

[34] *Parl. Debs.*, 3rd ser., xiv, col. 645 (23 July 1832). For the complex history of Wilkins' building in what became known as Trafalgar Square, see Martin, 'Founding of the National Gallery'. On the early National Gallery, see also Taylor, *Art for the Nation*, ch. 2.

[35] Peter Bailey, *Leisure and Class in Victorian England: Rational Recreation and the Contest for Control, 1830–1885* (London, 1978); Hugh Cunningham, *Leisure in the Industrial Revolution, c. 1780–c. 1880* (London, 1980), ch. 3; Tony Bennett, *The Birth of the Museum: History, Theory, Politics* (London, 1995), 19 f. On the circus and theatre and moral reform, see Marius Kwint, 'The Legitimization of the Circus in Late Georgian England', *Past and Present*, no. 174 (Feb. 2002).

[36] *Parl. Debs.*, 3rd ser., xii, cols. 468–9 (13 Apr. 1832).

[37] For a disciplinarian reading of the National Gallery, see Colin Trodd, 'Culture, Class, City: The National Gallery, London and the Spaces of Education, 1822–57', in Pointon (ed.), *Art Apart*, 33–49.

lower orders was most in evidence at the top of the Museum's hierarchy, whereas junior staff were committed to popular instruction and amusement.[38] Some witnesses before a select committee in 1836 recommended Sunday openings as 'one of the best modes of counteracting the effect of gin palaces'. Opening on national holidays would improve the national taste and character, and, if anything, encourage better use of the collections, rather than increase the risk of physical damage.[39] The committees (amongst whose most active members the evangelical Oxford Tory MP and Museum trustee Sir Robert Inglis balanced the radical Sir Benjamin Hawes) recommended a further increase in opening hours, including on national holidays, as well as published synopses and catalogues and cheap facilities for the public to make casts from antiquities, coins, and so forth.[40]

Even the reforming camp was split. Some like William Cobbett still rejected the very notion of publicly funded galleries as long as they were seen to benefit only an aristocratic elite: 'If the aristocracy [want] the Museum as a lounging place, let them pay for it.'[41] Cobbett's critique was echoed by visual satire portraying tax money wasted on art in the face of widespread poverty and dearness of provisions, a charge levelled both at the time of the acquisition of the Parthenon or Elgin Marbles (1816) and at the exhibition of cartoons for the decoration of Westminster Palace (1843): 'The poor ask for bread, and the philanthropy of the State accords them – an exhibition.'[42] By contrast, the Christian Socialist penny paper *Politics for the People*, founded in 1848 to appeal across the divides between Whigs, Chartists, and radicals on the issues of the suffrage and industrial relations, praised the British Museum as 'almost the only place which is free to English Citizens as such . . . the poor and the rich . . . a truly equalising place, in the deepest and most spiritual sense'.[43] This echoed the rhetoric of rational recreation with which the journal described the sensual and aesthetic experience of the people in the National Gallery, 'the workman's paradise, and garden of pleasure'.[44]

But we are stepping ahead of our story. A crucial moment in the history of 'reforming culture' had been the appointment in 1841 of a select committee on all public buildings containing works of art and on 'facilities to the Public

[38] P.P. 1835, vii (479), 1–623, paras. 612, 1287–9, 1313 f., 1320–2, 1328, 2908, 3916–19.

[39] P.P. 1836, x (440), 1–931, 'Report on the British Museum', iii–v; cf. evidence paras. 2302–12 (Richardson); cf. Cunningham, *Leisure*, 91, 106 f.

[40] P.P. 1836, x (440), 1–931.

[41] *Parl. Debs.*, 3rd ser., xvi, cols.1003–4 (25 Mar. 1833); cf. xvi, col. 1341 (1 Apr. 1833), for Cobbett on the foundation of Sir John Soane's Museum.

[42] 'The Elgin Marbles! Or John Bull Buying *Stones* at the Time his Numerous Family Want Bread!!': M. D. George, *Catalogue of Political and Personal Satires in the British Museum*, 11 vols. (London, 1935–54), ix, no. 12,787 [?June 1816]. The quotation from 'Substance and Shadow, Cartoon No 1', *Punch*, 5 (1843), 22.

[43] *Politics for the People*, no. 11 (1 July 1848), 183.

[44] *Ibid.*, no. 1 (6 May 1848), 1–6, quotations 5 f.; no. 2 (13 May 1848), 38–41.

for their inspection, as a means of moral and intellectual improvement for the People'. Chaired by Joseph Hume, the Scottish radical MP for Middlesex, advocate of Catholic Emancipation, repeal of the Test and Corporation Acts, and parliamentary reform, its other active members included the radical Liverpool MP William Ewart, the moderate Whig Henry Gally Knight, and the Tories Henry Goulburn and Henry Thomas Hope.[45] It took particular care to establish that free access, especially on Sundays, to St Paul's and its three dozen mostly military monuments would benefit the population at large by spreading taste, historical understanding, and morality.[46]

Discussion of access to St Paul's evoked views from various quarters on the functions and use of the cathedral as a church and sculpture gallery. For decades, the cathedral chapter had resisted pressure from parliamentarians, ministers, and the wider public to abolish the twopence admission fee that applied outside twenty hours of weekly services. Discussion of admission fees was linked to the complex internal economic functioning of the cathedral.[47] In public the chapter insisted on self-governance, and claimed that experimental removal of barriers on the floor had converted the cathedral 'into a lobby for fashionable loungers', resembling more 'a promenade in a ball-room than a congregation in the house of God'. Free access at all times would turn St Paul's into a 'Royal Exchange for wickedness'.[48] In 1841 the evidence of some virgers, police, the cathedral surveyor, artists, antiquaries, and staff of the National Gallery and British Museum suggested that the conduct of the lower classes in public cultural spaces had in fact improved in recent times. Extended and free access appeared to make the populace more caring of the art they experienced, testified Allan Cunningham, author of *The Lives of . . . British Painters* (1829–33), with reference to mechanics, shoemakers, and joiners in the National Gallery: the mob ceased to be the mob when they acquired taste.[49] But cathedral representatives complained about two groups of visitors and two kinds of behaviour in the cathedral, which could not be policed in the same way as more confined spaces such as art galleries:

---

[45] Hume consistently championed the paying public's 'right to insist on every facility of ingress': *Parl. Debs.*, 2nd ser., xxii, cols. 1352–3, quotation 1353 (8 Mar. 1830); cf. 3rd ser., xxvii, col. 1186 (18 May 1835).

[46] P.P. 1841, vi (416), 437–635, 'Report on National Monuments', paras. 119–20, 246–50, 439–44, 1931, 2183, 2185.

[47] On compensation for loss of revenue see, for example, Edward Edwards, *A Letter to Sir Martin Arthur Shee . . . on the Reform of the Royal Academy, with Observations on the Evidence Respecting the Academy given before the Select Committee of the Commons* (London, 1839), 7.

[48] P.P. 1837–8, xxxvi (119), 447–60, 'Correspondence between the Secretary of State and the Dean and Chapter of St. Paul's', quotations 451 f. An average of some 60,000 visitors annually were registered in the 1820s and 1830s: figure calculated from P.P. 1837, xli (242), 479, 'Amount of Fees received at the Door of St. Paul's, and for Seeing the Monuments'; for criticism, see John Smith, *Nollekens and his Times*, 2 vols. (London, 1829), i, 376 f.

[49] P.P. 1841, vi (416), 437–635, 'Report on National Monuments', paras. 355, 417–18, 719–22, 1361 f., 1845, 1847, 1849, 1856, 2003, 2538, 2585–7, 2640, 2650–3, 2672–3, 2869–71.

firstly, the noise caused by idle loungers and fashionable ladies, their talking and walking, which disturbed those attending divine service; and secondly, the improper or indecent conduct of women knitting, lunch parties, and straying dogs, and of people urinating in pews, tapping monuments with their sticks, and scribbling on them.[50]

The committee report deployed the language of self-improvement and moral reform, referring to visitors as decent, orderly, and respectful. The committee adopted the position of reformist parliamentarians like the moderate Irish nationalist and education reformer Thomas Wyse, Hume, and the president of the London Art Union, George Godwin: it was satisfied with the 'general disposition of the people to appreciate exhibitions of this nature, and to avail themselves of these means of instruction and innocent recreation' without any threat to the collections, and was pleased with the large and rising visiting figures at the British Museum and National Gallery. It recommended still more liberal provisions, such as the waiving of the requirement for parties to sign the Museum visitor book, and labels and cheap classificatory catalogues. Without wanting to turn cathedrals into mere art exhibitions, it urged free admission, especially on Sundays, in order to improve public taste, spread historical understanding and, indeed, impart religious impressions; any additional staff costs ought to be defrayed from external funds.[51]

The issue of access continued to be controversial. Physical access to the indoor monuments apart, some critics demanded that modern statues be made more easily intelligible: inscriptions were often added only after some delay, and the allegorical sculptural language could be difficult to read for those without much formal education. The St Paul's chapter also resisted the political pressure crystallized in the 1841 report until admission fees were finally dropped in the context of the Great Exhibition in 1851. While the cathedral struggled to reconcile its functions as a space of worship and as the national sculpture gallery, the National Gallery, though physically and financially accessible, remained a space of social distinction dependent on the possession of cultural skills. Reformers now urged that the gallery be arranged by schools and periods. The traditional presentation of old masters of individual genius demanded learned connoisseurship on the part of the viewer. By contrast, the so-called

---

[50] *Ibid.*, paras. 11, 23–34, 43–9, 75, 78, 97, 117–18, 150–1, 331, 339, 344, 544–51, *passim*. Cf. William Wilkins, 'A Letter to Lord Viscount Goderich, on the Patronage of the Arts by the English Government', *Library of the Fine Arts*, 3 (1832), 291–307, 367–78, 472–83, esp. at 372.

[51] P.P. 1841, vi (416), 437–635, 'Report on National Monuments', iii–viii (quotation vi). The social profile of the National Gallery's early audiences, exceeding half a million by 1840, is difficult to ascertain, though the *Art Union* (2 June 1840), 90, approved of working-class visitors on Mondays. For Godwin, see Duncan Forbes, '"The Advantages of Combination": The Art Union of London and State Regulation in the 1840s', in Barlow and Trodd (eds.), *Governing Cultures*, 132.

'comprehensive' collection, which displayed the evolutionary development of art, was expected to be more widely intelligible, helped by cheap catalogues and, after 1856, simple explanatory labels.[52] Critics now moaned that poorly dressed, malodorous, working-class people visited in wet weather, often for purposes other than looking at paintings. Together with children leaving conspicuous marks on the floors, they damaged the pictures through dust, dirt, and the condensation of vapour on their surfaces.[53] Increasing visitor numbers showed the ideals of universal access and of good curatorial and preservation practices to be in conflict.

III

Parliamentary reform was a catalyst in the debate about art institutions as it was with regard to opera. As the reformed parliament encouraged further interest in cultural affairs, it shaped the debate not only on the educational and moral functions of the arts, but also on their organizational structures. Select committees probed ways of enhancing the efficiency, transparency, and accountability of art institutions, though, naturally, the extent to which aspiration translated into actual change varied. Cobbett's allegations of a scandalous 'British Museum job', with corruption and sinecures for 'aristocratic fry', could not be proven by inquiries which blamed any shortcomings on lack of funding and space rather than on trustees or staff. This allowed some museum officials to appear open to reform and to complain about inadequate collections, staffing, and accommodation. Committees urged better funding and a shift towards administration by salaried, full-time experts.[54]

Although it was the British Institution that became the guardian of the aristocratic principle in the post-1832 art world, as it reinstated hereditary governorships abolished in 1822,[55] debate about organizational reform now revolved chiefly around the Royal Academy. At issue was the discrepancy between its privileged relationships with the crown and government and a perceived lack of transparency and accountability. Britain's leading fine-arts school and

[52] Trodd, 'Culture, Class, City', 39 f.; Carmen Stonge, 'Making Private Collections Public: Gustav Friedrich Waagen and the Royal Museum in Berlin', *Jl Hist. Collections*, 10 (1998), 65.

[53] P.P. 1850, xv (612), 1–124, 'Report on the National Gallery', paras. 78, 82, 658, 682, Appendix A, 67–9.

[54] For Cobbett, *Parl. Debs.*, 3rd. ser., xvi, cols. 1003–4 (25 Mar. 1833). Cf. P.P. 1836, x (440), 1–931, 'Report on the British Museum', iii–v; P.P. 1835, vii (479), 'Report on the British Museum' (1835), 1–11; compare on the National Gallery P.P. 1836, ix (568), 1–410, 'Report on Arts and Manufactures', x. For the chequered history of reform of the Royal Society and London's wider scientific community, see D. P. Miller, 'The Royal Society of London 1800–1835: A Study in the Cultural Politics of Scientific Organization' (University of Pennsylvania Ph.D. thesis, 1981), chs. 2, 4, 5.

[55] Nicholas Tromans, 'Museum or Market?: The British Institution', in Barlow and Trodd (eds.), *Governing Cultures*, 44–55.

exhibition society had always been criticized for, *inter alia*, the marginal position of engravers, the disadvantageous exhibition of watercolours or sculpture, and inadequate study facilities; yet most critics had advocated ameliorative improvement rather than 'visionary schemes of reform'.[56] In 1769–71 the Academy was attacked in a Wilkesite critique as an example of arbitrary royal power, and, periodically, the admission fee of one shilling was criticized. From around 1820, general anti-monopolistic rhetoric was deployed against the Academy in the context of a wider critique of oligarchic structures in an aristocratic state: 'Reform in Parliament would be essentially beneficial to the Fine Arts, for then the taste and wishes respecting them would with other tastes and wishes, scientific and political, be consulted instead of those of hungry and low-thoughted holders of and strugglers for places, pensions, and sinecures.'[57] When the Royal Academy was about to move (jointly with the National Gallery) into the national building in Trafalgar Square, its constitution and activities were scrutinized by a select committee.[58] The committee sat in two sessions in 1835–6: a large 1835 committee of forty-nine MPs, and a reappointed committee of fifteen. Though the committees had a mixed party membership, both contained a sizeable radical component, especially the latter with at least nine radicals including Ewart, Hume, Dr John Bowring (a former editor of the radical *Westminster Review*), and Wyse. It was this more radical committee which heard systematic evidence – partly proffered by those marginalized by the Academy such as engravers and watercolourists – on the Royal Academy's hybrid position: it claimed to be a private society, not responsible to parliament, when under scrutiny. Its oligarchic nature was evident in the arrangement of exhibitions and in the practice of Academicians consorting exclusively with patrons over the annual dinner. But it claimed 'national' or 'public' status to secure royal patronage, diplomas, public accommodation, ex-officio appointments for the president as a trustee of the British Museum and National Gallery, and a monopoly in advising government.[59] The history painter Benjamin Robert

---

[56] For a fuller account, see Hoock, *King's Artists*, chs. 2, 3. The quotation from moderate reformer S. J. William, 'On the Condition of Architectural Students', *Annals of the Fine Arts*, 2 (1818), 22.

[57] *Examiner*, no. 687 (13 May 1821), 300 f.; no. 709 (6 Aug. 1821), 483 f.; no. 728 (6 Jan. 1822), 10; no. 736 (3 Mar. 1822), 138. Cf. *Annals of the Fine Arts*, 2 (1818), 134 f., 144, 287 f., 299 f.; *Parl. Debs.*, 3rd ser., xiv, col. 646 (J. Hume, 23 July 1832).

[58] *Parl. Debs.*, 3rd ser., xxix, cols. 553–62 (14 July 1835). The committee has been much discussed in the context of government intervention in design education. See Quentin Bell, *Schools of Design* (London, 1963); Thomas Gretton, '"Art is Cheaper and Goes Lower in France": The Language of the Parliamentary Select Committee on Arts and Principles of Design of 1835–1836', in Hemingway and Vaughan (eds.), *Art in Bourgeois Society*, 84–100; Burton, *Vision and Accident*. For a detailed analysis of the select committee's relevance in the history of the Academy, see Hoock, *King's Artists*, 300–6.

[59] P.P. 1836, ix (568), 1–410, 'Report on Arts and Manufactures', paras. 649 f., 676 f., 689, 692, 726 ff., 779, 800, 807–16, 1057, 1372, 1374, 1370.

Haydon, a self-proclaimed 'Reformer in the Art'[60] and extra-parliamentary leader of the anti-Academy campaign, summed up his political reading when asked what he disapproved of principally:

> Its exclusiveness, its total injustice . . . the academy is a House of Lords without King or Commons for appeal. The artists are at the mercy of a despotism whose unlimited power tends to destroy all feeling for right or justice . . . It is an anomaly in the history of any constitutional people the constitution of this academy. . . . It is extraordinary how men, brought up as Englishmen, could set up such a system of government. The holy inquisition was controlled by the Pope, but these men are an inquisition without a pope.[61]

Pushed by Ewart, witnesses protested that no society should be privileged, but all left to free competition.[62] The Academy's leaders mounted a spirited defence, though President Martin A. Shee also made some attempt to conciliate reformers by dismissing certain controversial regulations as not (or no longer) essential, such as the rule forbidding membership in other societies, and 'varnishing day', on which only members were allowed to touch up their paintings just before the exhibition.[63]

Although the inquiry had made hitherto obscure Royal Academy procedures transparent and the biased report lent some credibility to the view of the Academy as a monopolistic corporation, the committee stopped short of recommending constitutional reform: as long as the Academy hid behind the screen of an exclusive relation with the crown, it could not be forced to change.[64] The committee expected 'that the principle of free competition in art (as in commerce) will ultimately triumph over all artificial institutions'. In future, governments might offer prizes and commissions to different societies – thus in fact developing government's role beyond its previous scope – without privileging any particular institution.[65]

Reformers pressed for changes in other institutions as well. Royal commissions as new instruments of reform sharply rebuked British Museum trustees and officials for their blatant disregard of statutory regulations and for inefficiency, but recommendations to develop expert management at both executive and departmental level were only slowly implemented.[66] After 1850, the National

[60] Quoted Burton, *Vision and Accident*, 16.

[61] P.P. 1836, ix (568), 1–410, 'Report on Arts and Manufactures', para. 1063, also paras. 995, 1000.

[62] *Ibid.*, para. 999.   [63] *Ibid.*, paras. 1990, 2018–20.

[64] The foundation by government of the Schools of Design on the Prussian model before the end of the inquiry had drawn the teeth of the radical project. Ironically, on behalf of the Board of Trade, Academicians soon decided on the officers, inspectors, and the curriculum: *Parl. Debs.*, 3rd ser., xxxv, col. 1085 (10 Aug. 1836); Gretton, '"Art is Cheaper"', 98.

[65] P.P. 1836, ix (568), 1–410, 'Report on Arts and Manufactures', viii.

[66] *Report of the Commissioners Appointed to Inquire into the Constitution and Government of the British Museum* (London, 1850), 3–13, 35, 40 f. Cf. [T. S. Traill], 'British Museum', *Edinburgh Rev.*, 38 (1823), art. V, 396–8.

Gallery, under constant pressure from select committees and royal commissions, introduced fundamental reforms in professional collection management, archival documentation, cataloguing, cleaning, and preservation.[67]

The Royal Academy continued to be attacked as a 'stronghold of tyranny and intrigue', a 'closed borough', and a 'protectionist barricade'.[68] An 1863 royal commission considered incorporating the Academy as a state department, but eventually only recommended a charter to define its rights and responsibilities as a 'valuable permanent Council of advice and reference in all matters relating to the Fine Arts, public monuments and buildings'.[69] The proposal that the Academy should administer a national system of professional certification was part of a wider development from amateur systems to national professional norms, also entailing the professionalization of government itself. However, the Academy yet again showed itself more resistant to reform than other organizations and chose institutional independence over potentially greater influence.

IV

Between the 1790s and 1840s, public debate, both in and out of doors, about the functions of national art and adequate institutional structures helped to launch multi-faceted civilizing and restructuring reform projects.[70] The eighteenth-century closed culture of the privileged was opened up significantly: by 1850, annual visitor numbers at the British Museum and National Gallery approached three-quarters of a million each; St Paul's eventually abolished admission fees.[71]

---

[67] Taylor, *Art for the Nation*, 61–4.

[68] Morris Moore, *Revival of Vandalism at the National Gallery* (London, 1853), 17; *Westminster Rev.*, 55 (1851), 405. Cf. Martin A. Shee, *A Letter to Lord John Russell, Her Majesty's Principal Secretary of State for the Home Department, on the Alleged Claim of the Public to be Admitted Gratis to the Exhibition of the Royal Academy* (London, 1837); Colin Trodd, 'The Authority of Art: Cultural Criticism and the Idea of the Royal Academy in Mid-Victorian Britain', *Art Hist.*, 20 (1997), 3–22, esp. 12.

[69] P.P. 1863, xxvii.1 (3205), 587, 'Report of the Commissioners Appointed to Inquire into the Present Position of the Royal Academy in Relation to the Fine Arts'. Cf. Trodd, 'Authority of Art', 16–18; Edward Edwards, *The Fine Arts in England: Their State and Prospects Considered, Relatively to National Education, Part I: The Administrative Economy of the Fine Arts* (London, 1840), 178 f., 187–90, 197 f.; cf. Gordon Fyfe, 'Auditing the RA: Official Discourse and the Nineteenth-Century Royal Academy', in Denis and Trodd (eds.), *Art and the Academy*, 117–30.

[70] The cross-fertilization of parliamentary and extra-parliamentary pressure for reform requires further research. The Haydon/Ewart connection has been mentioned. The roles of Joseph Hume MP and George Foggo in the campaigns against St Paul's admission fees need studying. Edward Edwards (1812–86), the radical son of a bricklayer and a British Museum assistant in 1839–50, reacted to parliamentary inquiries with coherent reform proposals of his own. See Edward Edwards, *A Letter to Benjamin Hawes, Esq., M.P. being Strictures on the Minutes of Evidence taken before the Select Committee on the British Museum* (London, 1836); Edwards, *Letter to Sir Martin Arthur Shee*.

[71] P.P. 1846, xxv (320), 273–4, 'Return from the Trustees of the British Museum . . . ; A similar Return from the Trustees of the National Gallery'; P.P. 1846, xxv (320), 275–8 [Returns of the Number of Visitors].

Art institutions claiming national status by virtue of their funding arrangements or their statutory or self-professed mission were taken to task by reformers seeking increased transparency, accountability, and efficiency. And sites such as St Paul's were further drawn into the orbit of reform politics through the national art they acquired. Reformers had clearly established the discursive force of new practices such as 'open access', to an extent across party-political lines, and by making creative use of new instruments such as parliamentary inquiries. As the reformed concept of 'art for the nation' per se became increasingly difficult to attack, those resisting reform responded tactically, experimenting with limited access to private collections and with the British Institution. Similarly, in a failure to overcome the obstacles in the way of satisfying public demands for improving the scope and display of *British* art in the National Gallery, in the 1840s Robert Vernon's major gift of British paintings was arranged provisionally and inadequately in the basement of the National Gallery, the 'National Cupboard'.[72]

While the national argument as a key generator of reform in the art world was (potentially) inclusive, tensions over the ideological and institutional implications of 'reforming culture' persisted through to the end of the period. When the *Quarterly Review* in 1850 considered the thousands of pages of twelve reports of inquiries into the British Museum produced between 1835 and 1850, it explained the shift from men of expertise to men of rank among Museum trustees as an aristocratic reaction to the French Revolution; moreover, England's 'intellectual constitution' fostered the 'antagonism between the aristocracy of talent and the aristocracy of birth'; and the country's museological backwardness was due to laissez-faire politics and the absence of a 'meddling centralizing bureaucracy'.[73] Such complex political analogies exemplify the ways in which reform aspiration and reform in the art world related to the languages, strategies, and objectives of political, social, and moral reform. The study of national art institutions in the 'age of reform' is one way of conceptualizing the role of politics and political institutions as agents and sites of cultural change. It also asks us to consider examination of the cultural field as a sensitive detector of shifts in political tectonics.

---

[72] *Punch*, 15 (1848), 221.
[73] 'The British Museum', *Quarterly Rev.*, 88 (1850), art. VI, 138, 144, 150.

12. Irish reform between the 1798 Rebellion and the Great Famine*

JENNIFER RIDDEN

What is the place of Irish reform in the British 'age of reform', and how did the 1801 Act of Union between Britain and Ireland affect the development of reform in Ireland? The historical literature on reform has usually focused on the development of centralized interpretations of reform, their imposition on the 'periphery', and the local responses to central initiatives. These themes are particularly prominent in the Irish case since English historical interpretations of reform in Ireland usually focus on Ireland as a problem for British reformers or as a 'social laboratory', while Irish interpretations usually concentrate on responses to British policy (including reforming initiatives) as key elements in the emergence of two opposed forms of political identity in Ireland, namely Irish nationalist and Protestant Unionist identities. In contrast, this chapter considers reform movements that emerged within Ireland, which were locally led, and which represented responses to changing Irish circumstances, but which were shaped by their competitive relationship with one another, and by a changing relationship between locality and centre under the Union.

In Ireland there were two main and competing approaches to reform during the first half of the nineteenth century, which shared an emphasis on using British political structures to achieve Irish ends, and which can therefore be seen as different ways of positioning Ireland within the framework of the Union. Despite this shared framework, these approaches to reform involved different languages, different visions of what an ideal Ireland would be like, and different methods for achieving these ends. They competed with each other for both popular and middle-class support. This chapter first discusses O'Connellite ideology as a variety of Irish reform. The Catholic Emancipation campaign (aimed at allowing Catholics to become MPs) and the campaign for the repeal of the Union were aimed at renegotiating Anglo-Irish relations within the framework of a federal United Kingdom, and at renegotiating the place of Catholics within Ireland. At

* I wrote this chapter while a Research Fellow at Lucy Cavendish College, Cambridge, and revised it while a lecturer in the School of History at Keele University. I am grateful for the support of both institutions.

the same time, a cross-denominational reform movement developed in the major towns and cities in Ireland, which was led by liberal Protestant members of the elite and supported by an emerging Irish-Catholic urban bourgeoisie, and this provides the chapter's second topic. The Irish 'moderate reform' movement also sought Irish political, economic, and social reform within the political structure of the Union, but its aim was to strip religion of its divisive power in Irish society and politics. These reform movements represented an urban/rural divide in Irish politics that has not yet been fully explored. In addition, the competition between the two movements for popular and middle-class support, and for the right to define themselves as the legitimate elite, was a crucial factor in local Irish debates which complicated dualistic Roman Catholic–Protestant divisions.

I

When Ireland was incorporated into the United Kingdom by the 1801 Act of Union, it was a society fresh from attempted revolution in 1798. The emergence of mass politicization during the 1790s, which escalated during the sectarian reprisals and bloody repressions after the Rebellion, had a radicalizing effect on popular political culture in Ireland. This came to centre on a sense of Catholic political, social, and economic exclusion increasingly fused with a sense of Gaelic identity. Ireland's partial absorption into a Protestant state and nation, and the Protestant reforming zeal and millenarian fervour which reached its height in the 1820s, accentuated this growing opposition between Catholic and Protestant identities in Ireland.[1] Protestant attempts at the mass conversion of the Irish Catholic population during the so-called 'Evangelical Crusade' produced new cooperative links between evangelicals within the Church of Ireland and the dissenting churches around the common aims of mass conversion and defence of a Protestant constitution, and in the 1830s and 1840s a new conservative vision of Irish society and a defensive Protestantism emerged. Meanwhile, Catholic resentment of proselytism, of the Church of Ireland's position as an established church, and particularly of tithes during the 1820s and 1830s cut across the economic divisions among Catholics, and led to the development within pre-Famine agrarian movements of solidarity between Catholic artisans, urban and rural labourers, and farmers.[2] The combination of conflict over the Evangelical Crusade, renewed demands for Catholic Emancipation, and

---

[1] For discussions of the Evangelical Crusade in Ireland, see S. J. Brown, *The National Churches of England, Scotland and Ireland* (Oxford, 2001), ch. 2; David Hempton and Myrtle Hill, *Evangelical Protestantism in Ulster Society, 1740–1890* (London and New York, 1992); Desmond Bowen, *The Protestant Crusade in Ireland, 1800–70* (Dublin, 1978); S. J. Connolly, *Priests and People in Pre-Famine Ireland, 1780–1845* (Dublin, 1982).

[2] Tom Garvin, 'Defenders, Ribbonmen and Others: Underground Political Networks in Pre-Famine Ireland', in C. H. E. Philpin (ed.), *Nationalism and Popular Protest in Ireland* (Cambridge, 1987), 219–44, first published in *Past and Present*, no. 96 (Aug. 1982), 133–55.

Protestant defensiveness meant that religion became a major issue in political and social life.

The Protestant Ascendancy emerged from this revolutionary challenge as a weak, embattled, and isolated elite that had survived only because of British military intervention. In the fifty years after the 1798 Rebellion the Ascendancy faced the task of re-establishing itself as an effective and legitimate elite within the constitutional structure of the United Kingdom, despite challenges from below and uncertain cooperation from the British state. This reconstruction was attempted in a context of severe agricultural depression and economic change after 1815, in which seasonal food shortages and 'minor' famines became regular, culminating in the Great Famine of the late 1840s. Agrarian violence became endemic in Ireland in this period (especially in the south and west), and Ireland was under military coercion for nearly the whole of the period between 1798 and the Great Famine. In short, there were grounds for both Irish and English observers to regard Irish society as 'disturbed' and unstable.

While English observers increasingly regarded Irish problems as insoluble, Irish reformers of all varieties sought to resolve these tensions in Irish society. Their proposed solutions, and strategies for achieving those solutions, however, took a range of forms which had different implications, and which were associated with different ideologies. What they had in common was a desire to use the British state to achieve Irish ends, and in particular to use British parliamentary and governmental mechanisms to force change on local Irish oligarchies. It was the Act of Union between Great Britain and Ireland that made this possible. The creation of the United Kingdom under this act was intended to resolve the security risk which Ireland posed to Britain; but it did little to address the political demands made by the Catholics and Presbyterians which had given rise to the 1798 Rebellion because it was not accompanied by the measure of Catholic Emancipation which had been promised.

Even though it initiated a series of transformations in the way Ireland was governed for more than a century, the Act of Union did not present a practical plan for how Ireland was to be administered, or for how the various parts of the United Kingdom were to interact. Instead, these issues were resolved over the next four decades as a series of Irish administrative structures evolved which were centred on Dublin Castle, but which were imposed by a British Westminster-based government; these were similar in style to those developing in the settlement colonies. Yet these new quasi-colonial structures were superimposed on pre-existing borough corporations and grand juries in which Irish patronage structures continued to operate.[3] As a result, Irish administration was controlled by a combination of British political appointments and an

---

[3] Papers from the Royal Historical Society Conference on the 1801 British–Irish Union, in *Trans. Royal Hist. Soc.*, 6th ser., 10 (2000); Virginia Crossman, *Local Government in Nineteenth-Century Ireland* (Belfast, 1994); Neal Garnham, 'Local Elite Creation in Early Hanoverian Ireland: The Case of the County Grand Jury', *Hist. Jl*, 42 (1999), 623–42.

eighteenth-century Irish patronage system which focused on key Church of Ireland elite families, and which remained relatively unchanged from the period of the 1780s Irish parliament. Meanwhile, Irish policy formation became increasingly centralized and London-based, as the British parliament extended its sphere of activity into social and economic policy over the next half-century, in an attempt to deal with continuing 'unrest'.[4] The relationship between the Irish administration and British parliamentary and governmental policy formation was therefore complex. The government of Ireland was neither wholly British nor wholly colonial; neither wholly centralized nor wholly localized. Frustrating as this situation was for Irish reformers, it also provided opportunities for them to influence British centralized policy formation on Irish issues, and mechanisms that they could use to oppose the local Irish oligarchies.

The leaders of both reforming groups presented themselves as alternatives to the incumbent oligarchic, illegitimate, and weak Protestant Ascendancy. Their visions of Ireland's future elite, however, differed from each other, and these visions were shaped by their different approaches to the problem of attracting the bourgeois and popular support that bolstered their claims to legitimate leadership. Daniel O'Connell's ideal was a predominantly Catholic elite (although he was willing to accept the involvement of sympathetic liberal Protestants). Moderate reformers, in contrast, proposed an elite that would include both moralized Protestant and Catholic elite and professional groups, and therefore they rejected the notion of an elite (or a society) that was defined primarily in religious terms. The critique of corruption was a major feature of both the Irish reforming groups considered here, and much of this critique was expressed in terms that were recognizable in England.

II

Much of the historical analysis of Daniel O'Connell's campaigns for Catholic Emancipation and for repeal of the Act of Union has focused on the mass mobilization of Irish Catholics and the development of a popular national identity that cut across different socio-economic groups among Catholics. There is little doubt that the campaign for Catholic Emancipation reinforced the process by which Irish Catholics acquired a sense of their importance and self-esteem which was primarily connected with their religion.[5] Yet historians such as Oliver MacDonagh, Angus Macintyre, and more recently K. Theodore Hoppen and Gearóid Ó Tuathaigh have convincingly established that O'Connellite

---

[4] Joanna Innes, 'What Would a "Four Nations" Approach to the Study of Eighteenth-Century British Social Policy Entail?', in S. J. Connolly (ed.), *Kingdoms United? Great Britain and Ireland since 1500: Integration and Diversity* (Dublin, 1999), 181–99.

[5] Jacqueline R. Hill, *From Patriots to Unionists: Dublin Civic Politics and Irish Protestant Patriotism, 1660–1840* (Oxford, 1997), 347.

radicalism was a species of reform within a British constitutionalist frame.[6]
O'Connellite radicalism was a democratizing influence in Ireland because it
used the techniques of mass meetings, petitioning, and political organization. It
harnessed the Gaelic-Catholic sense of identity and exclusion that had emerged
from the Rebellion, but did not develop a programme of nationalist republicanism. Instead, O'Connellite radicals focused on changing the legislative
structure which framed Irish socio-economic and political life under the Union.
They hoped that such political change would make it possible to supplant the
Protestant Ascendancy in Ireland with a social and political elite that reflected
Ireland's majority Catholic population, so that Catholics might take a full role
in shaping their society.

The O'Connellite focus on non-violent reform within a British legal and
constitutional framework was evident as early as 1819, when O'Connell argued
that civil and religious liberty constituted one of a set of universal rights. These
rights were guaranteed by the 'ancient constitution' which was applicable in
Ireland as well as in England, and therefore the political exclusion of Irish
Catholics was unconstitutional.[7] O'Connell was consumed with the belief that
the Irish-Catholic 'nation' needed to be unshackled from the fetters imposed
by an illegitimate Protestant elite, from discrimination and prejudice, and from
tyrannical rule by the British state. His solution was to bring Irish Catholics fully
into that state so that they could reform it, and under his leadership the Catholic
Association used the language of popular sovereignty to mobilize the Catholic
40-shilling freehold vote during the 1820s. As he said at a County Clare meeting
during the 1828 election, 'If you return me to parliament, I pledge myself to
vote for every measure favourable to radical reform in the representative system,
so that the House of Commons may truly, as our Catholic ancestors intended
it should do, represent all the people.'[8] However, he did not want to open
the floodgates of revolution which would tear apart Irish society, just as the
French Revolution had torn apart France and the 1798 Rebellion had begun to
tear apart Ireland.[9] As a result, O'Connell wrote to Edward Dwyer (permanent
secretary of the Catholic Association) only hours after the successful passage
of the Catholic Relief Act through the House of Lords, saying that the act was

---

[6] Oliver MacDonagh, *O'Connell: The Life of Daniel O'Connell*, 2nd edn (London, 1991); Angus
Macintyre, *The Liberator: Daniel O'Connell and the Irish Party, 1830–1847* (London, 1965);
Angus Macintyre, 'O'Connell and British Politics', in Kevin B. Nowlan and Maurice
R. O'Connell (eds.), *Daniel O'Connell: Portrait of a Radical* (Belfast, 1984), 88–9; K. Theodore
Hoppen, 'Riding a Tiger: Daniel O'Connell, Reform, and Popular Politics in Ireland, 1800–1847',
in T. C. W. Blanning and P. Wende (eds.), *Reform in Great Britain and Germany, 1750–1850*
(Oxford, 1999), 121–43; Gearóid Ó Tuathaigh, 'Ireland under the Union: A Critique', paper
presented to the Cambridge Irish Studies Group, 13 Mar. 2001.

[7] Daniel O'Connell, 'Address to the Catholics of Ireland', *Freeman's Daily Jl*, 4 Jan. 1819.

[8] O'Connell's Address to the Electors of County Clare, June 1828, in Alan O'Day and John
Stevenson (eds.), *Irish Historical Documents since 1800* (Dublin, 1992), 34.

[9] MacDonagh, *O'Connell*, 300–1.

'one of the greatest triumphs recorded in history – a bloodless revolution more extensive in its operation than any other political change that could take place. I say *political* to contrast it with *social* changes which might break to pieces the framework of society.'[10] And as he reiterated two years later, during the campaign to repeal the Act of Union, 'I desire no social revolution, no social change. The nobility to possess lands, titles and legislative privileges as before the Union . . . The Landed Gentry to enjoy their present state, *being residents*. Every man to be considered a resident who has *an establishment* in Ireland.'[11]

There seems little doubt that O'Connell's personal experience of the French Revolution and of the Irish Rebellion predisposed him towards reform rather than revolutionary change. He consistently denounced violent methods and consequently received powerful backing from liberal Catholic clerics like Bishop James Doyle of Kildare and Leighlin. However, there may be an additional reason why O'Connellite radicalism took on reforming aims and style instead of developing into the more revolutionary form that might have been expected after the Rebellion. Political reform based on the aim of Catholic inclusion in the body politic facilitated cooperation between opposed socio-economic groups in a way that might not have been possible in a more far-reaching political movement such as the overtly revolutionary nationalist Ribbonmen.

Irish rural society had a complex socio-economic structure at the beginning of the nineteenth century. It comprised a series of interdependent groups, including large landowners (some of whom rented portions of their estates from other large landowners), minor landowners and 'big farmers', head tenants who sub-let to smaller tenants, dairymen, artisans, domestic workers and cottiers, and a large migrant labour force that spanned urban and rural society. Furthermore, the dispossessed Catholic gentry had gradually re-established some of its land tenure and wealth during the eighteenth century, by becoming either large tenant farmers or head tenants who sub-let to smaller tenant farmers and cottiers. This group of middlemen performed a wide range of brokerage functions between large Protestant landowners and small Catholic tenants, and in this role members of the 'underground Catholic gentry' were able to maintain much of their local social and cultural status in Catholic society.[12] When Ireland entered an economic boom during the French Wars sustained by the production and trade of provisions for the British army, however, a new generation of middlemen emerged which challenged the older system of Catholic middlemen and 'big farmers', and which squeezed out the Protestant middlemen as well.

---

[10] *The Correspondence of Daniel O'Connell*, ed. Maurice R. O'Connell, 8 vols. (Dublin, 1972–80), iv, 45, letter 1551: O'Connell to Edward Dwyer, 14 Apr. 1829.

[11] *Ibid.*, v, 11, letter 1957: O'Connell to P. V. Fitzpatrick, 21 Feb. 1833.

[12] Kevin Whelan, 'An Underground Gentry? Catholic Middlemen in Eighteenth-Century Ireland', in Whelan, *The Tree of Liberty: Radicalism, Catholicism and the Construction of Irish Identity, 1760–1830* (Cork, 1996), 3–58.

Between 1793 and 1815 rents increased by between 100 and 150 per cent and, as James Connery of Wexford explained in the 1820s, this 'late fatal advance in land . . . caused the hordes of semi-squires in the country who became a multitude of upstart gentry, without manners or education [and who were] oppressive to the poor' as well.[13] When the provisions trade dried up and the Irish economy entered crisis at the end of the Napoleonic Wars in 1815, the two rural Catholic middle-class groups found themselves engaged in an increasingly fierce competition for scarce resources, in which each tried to protect its position in a period of depression and economic restructuring. It seems that these new economic hardships exacerbated the sense of socio-economic and political exclusion among the old big farmers and among the smallholders and rural labourers, and that this set both groups against the new middlemen who were portrayed as 'land sharks and pirates'.[14] These new middlemen therefore became major targets for the 'midnight legislators' or agrarian protestors, who engaged in such acts as cattle-maiming and sending threatening letters to individuals who collected rents, evicted tenants, or who attempted agricultural modernization, whether they were Catholic or Protestant.[15]

What is remarkable about the O'Connellite Reform movement is that it successfully welded all these different and frequently opposed socio-economic groups, together with Catholic parish priests, into a movement of political reform, without alienating any one group.[16] As Kevin Whelan argues, the new middlemen and big farmers who had consolidated their socio-economic position in the first half of the nineteenth century assumed leadership roles within the O'Connellite movement, and were able to take on the older 'underground' gentry's mantle of cultural leadership as well.[17] Their involvement in O'Connellite reform allowed them to claim a shared Catholic and Gaelic identity with the poor, despite diverging economic interests and the growing social gulf between Catholic farmers and Catholic labourers. Yet, because the older 'underground gentry' had not been completely supplanted by the 1820s, the Catholic Association leadership necessarily involved collaboration between these new middlemen and the older group. It was from this older Catholic gentry that O'Connell

---

[13] A. P. W. Malcolmson, *The Pursuit of the Heiress: Aristocratic Marriage in Ireland, 1750–1815* (Belfast, 1982), 7, 45; James Connery, *The Reformer: or, An Infallible Remedy to Prevent Pauperism and Periodical Return of Famine* (Cork, 1828), 54.

[14] Connery, *Reformer*, 54; Louis M. Cullen, 'The Cultural Basis of Modern Irish Nationalism', in R. Mitchison (ed.), *The Roots of Nationalism: Studies in Northern Europe* (Edinburgh, 1980); Whelan, 'Underground Gentry?', 52–4.

[15] National Lib. Ireland, Drogheda (hereafter NLI), MS 9749, 'Memorandum of Occurrences' (1831); Joseph Lee, 'Patterns of Rural Unrest in Nineteenth-Century Ireland', in Louis M. Cullen and F. Furet (eds.), *Ireland and France, 17th–20th Centuries: Toward a Comparative Study of Rural History* (Paris, 1980), 223–30; Philpin (ed.), *Nationalism and Popular Protest in Ireland*; S. Clark and J. S. Donnelly Jr (eds.), *Irish Peasants: Violence and Political Unrest, 1780–1914* (Manchester, 1983).

[16] Hoppen, 'Riding a Tiger', 130–2.   [17] Whelan, 'Underground Gentry?', 54–5.

himself emerged; he was heir to an old Gaelic and Catholic family that had managed to maintain their elite status and their substantial estates in County Kerry throughout the penal period without converting to Protestantism; his personal elite status was reinforced by his Trinity College education and his subsequent legal career.[18] The emerging urban bourgeoisie of Catholic merchants and Trinity-educated professionals also played an important role in the Catholic Association leadership, as for example in the case of Sir Thomas Wyse, who emerged from a Catholic mercantile 'dynasty' in Waterford.[19] These various leadership groups were joined by the Catholic priesthood, whose roles as religious, social, and political leaders within local Catholic communities are well known. Finally, the bulk of O'Connell's popular supporters came from those groups that suffered most from economic recession and the attempted modernization in 1820s and 1830s – the rural labourers, small tenant farmers, and cottiers – and they were supplemented by a smaller group of urban labourers, artisans, and shopkeepers.

Much more research is needed on the details of how these various groups within the O'Connellite movement were related before we will be able to explain satisfactorily why it was not more fractured by socio-economic conflict. What we do know is that Gaelic-Catholic identity operated as a cultural 'glue' between the various leadership groups and between the leaders and O'Connell's supporters, and that the leadership as a whole considered itself the virtuous and legitimate elite of 'Catholic Ireland', in opposition to what it saw as a corrupt, weak, and illegitimate Protestant Ascendancy. We can also hypothesize that the O'Connellite emphasis on non-violent political reform (as opposed to the approaches which characterized the agrarian secret societies) played an important part in preventing the O'Connellite movement from dissolving into conflict between the competing socio-economic groups from which it had been forged. The movement's achievements were manifest in a series of 'monster meetings' which attracted increasing numbers of people (between 800,000 and 1,000,000 people at the Repeal meeting on the Hill of Tara in 1843), and in the emergence of an Irish Catholic vote among the 40-shilling freeholders during the 1820s which was sufficiently unified to elect O'Connell to the Westminster seat of Ennis in County Clare.[20]

While the Roman Catholic Relief Act of 1829 allowed some Catholics to participate in the Westminster parliament, it had little or no impact on Catholic

---

[18] MacDonagh, *O'Connell*, 1–29.

[19] *Ibid.*, 223. The early Catholic Association leadership also included a small group of liberal Protestant gentry, including Lord Cloncurry, whose families had typically formed part of the seventeenth-century Gaelic-Catholic elite, but had converted to Protestantism during the eighteenth century in order to maintain elite status and land. Many of this group defected when the Catholic Association became more populist after 1824.

[20] MacDonagh, *O'Connell*, 510–13; Peter Jupp, 'Irish Parliamentary Elections and the Influence of the Catholic Vote', *Hist. Jl*, 10 (1967), 183–96.

exclusion from the Irish corporations, which controlled the borough parliamentary seats and which were the main institutions of local government in the Irish cities and port towns. The Irish corporations were in general dominated by a handful of Church of Ireland elite families in each town or city. These were usually able to maintain control over the borough parliamentary seats by controlling the number and political allegiances of those admitted to the corporation as freemen, and by making sure that they outnumbered the 40-shilling freeholders.[21] Even though legal restrictions on Catholics and dissenters had been lifted in 1793, very few were admitted to the corporations as freemen in the first half of the nineteenth century, and those members of the Church of Ireland who supported Catholic Emancipation were also systematically refused admission.[22]

Consequently, as soon as Catholic Emancipation was won in 1829, the O'Connellite reformers turned their attention to breaking Protestant Ascendancy control over the corporations and the borough parliamentary seats. Using evidence gathered in a series of parliamentary inquiries into Irish political and administrative institutions over the previous thirty years, the O'Connellite reformers sought centralized British legislation that would achieve specifically Irish Catholic aims. Thus they sought the full inclusion of Catholics in Irish political life and the replacement of a corrupt Protestant Ascendancy in Ireland with a legitimate and mainly Catholic elite which reflected the population as a whole. As O'Connell put it, corporation reform would 'break a gap in the enemy's [Protestant Ascendancy's] fortifications'.[23] In a speech to the House of Commons in 1835, O'Connell argued that corporation reform would allow the Irish people access to British institutions and justice. 'This corporate monopoly . . . is the only thing remaining that prevents justice being done to the people. This and this alone, shuts the inhabitants out from participation in the advantages of British institutions; and upon this question the government are preparing to give the people of Ireland redress.'[24]

O'Connell thus attempted to persuade British politicians to take centralized action which would achieve specifically Irish aims, using language that was characteristic of British radicalism. However, a uniform civic franchise based

---

[21] Irish borough MPs were elected by a combination of 40-shilling freeholders and corporation freemen (commercial and tradesmen who had been admitted to membership of the corporation and who theoretically ran the corporation collectively).

[22] P.P. 1820, iii (209): 'Report from the Select Committee on the Limerick Election'; P.P. 1835, xxvii (23): 'First Report of the Commissioners to Inquire into the Municipal Corporations of Ireland'; J. R. Hill, 'The Politics of Privilege: The Dublin Corporation and the Catholic Question, 1792–1823', *Maynooth Rev.*, 7 (1982), 17–36; Ian d'Alton, *Protestant Society and Politics in Cork, 1812–1844* (Cork, 1980); Maura Murphy, 'Municipal Reform and the Repeal Movement in Cork, 1833–1844', *Jl Cork Hist. and Archaeol. Soc.*, 121 (1977), 1–18.

[23] *Correspondence of Daniel O'Connell*, v, 17, letter 1963: O'Connell to P. V. Fitzpatrick, 11 Mar. 1833.

[24] *Parl. Debs.*, 3rd ser., xxix, cols. 1315, 1318 (31 Jan. 1835).

on the English Municipal Corporations Act would not merely bring Catholics into the body politic; it would put nearly all of the southern boroughs under Catholic control. The Municipal Corporations of Ireland Reform Act was, in the end, a much weaker piece of legislation than that proposed by Irish reformers of all varieties, and it did not have the effect of removing Protestant Ascendancy control of the corporations in general. Dublin was a partial exception, and O'Connell was installed mayor there in the first elections in 1841 under the new legislation, though both sides gave this victory exaggerated significance.[25]

During the 1830s and 1840s, O'Connell campaigned to have the Act of Union repealed. Now that Catholic Emancipation had been won, this 'salutary restoration . . . without revolution' would give the Irish people a proper degree of control over affairs of local significance, while maintaining Ireland's place within a British constitutional framework.[26] At one point, he even suggested separate Irish and British parliaments, both subordinated to an 'Imperial' parliament which would consist of both sets of members.[27]

Repeal was a political impossibility in the first half of the century, but it was an effective bargaining tool. O'Connell used it to exert pressure on the British state in order to achieve Irish reforms, including reform of the borough corporations which were the last bastion of Protestant Ascendancy power and which defended ultra-Protestant versions of Britishness in Ireland. He was explicit about this intention in his private correspondence from as early as 1830, when he told the Catholic bishop John MacHale that,

> 'The Repeal of the Union' is good for everything. It is good as the means of terrifying the enemies of the people into every concession practicable under the present system. If I were to relax the agitation of that measure, then the men in possession of power would enjoy their state in repose and adjourn . . . all practical improvement.[28]

Overall, then, O'Connellite reformers used this period to make sense of the interaction between Irish politics and the British state, to maximize Irish influence on British policy and political decision-making, and to press for institutions that would give Irish-Catholics a greater role in the British body politic. Ultimately, the O'Connellite MPs acted as reforming Catholic representatives within the British constitutional system, not as nationalists as we understand the term today.

[25] *Freeman's Jl*, 22 July 1841; Jacqueline Hill, 'Religion, Trade and Politics in Dublin, 1798–1848', in Paul Butel and L. M. Cullen (eds.), *Cities and Merchants* (Dublin, 1986), 247–59.

[26] *Correspondence of Daniel O'Connell*, v, 11, letter 1957: O'Connell to P. V. Fitzpatrick, 21 Feb. 1833.

[27] Oliver MacDonagh, *States of Mind: A Study of Anglo-Irish Conflict* (London, 1983), 57–8.

[28] *Correspondence of Daniel O'Connell*, iv, 241–2, letter 1738: O'Connell to Bishop MacHale, 3 Dec. 1830.

III

The local basis of 'moderate' reform in Ireland has been little studied, but my own work on Limerick shows that the movement was led by liberal Protestants in the main, and that it competed with the O'Connellite reform movement for Catholic support, especially for support from middle-class Catholics.[29] Recent research suggests that urban politics elsewhere involved similar political relationships, in part because those economic and political features that produced Limerick's moderate reform movement were loosely replicated in other Irish port towns.[30] Though less than 18 per cent of the Irish population lived in towns of five hundred or more people by 1841, the urban moderate reform movement was disproportionately important in Irish politics because it provided an alternative to O'Connellite reform, and because this movement produced the majority of non-Tory Irish MPs during the whole of the period between 1801 and 1874.[31] The key elements of its political programme were Catholic Emancipation with the aim of creating a virtuous but multi-denominational elite, Unionism, and economic reform. Like the O'Connellite reformers, moderate reformers also focused on corporation reform, but for different reasons. In contrast with the O'Connellite aim of replacing the incumbent Protestant Ascendancy with a Catholic elite, moderate reformers sought to broaden the existing elite to include other Catholic and Protestant groups, and they were much more inclined to focus on economic reforms directly, because these provided a basis for coalition in urban contexts.

The inner circle of the moderate reform movement's leadership initially included Church of Ireland Whig aristocrats such as Lord Clare, the Knight of Kerry (Maurice Fitzgerald), Sir John Newport in Waterford, and Sir Henry Parnell in Wicklow. These leaders were members of families that competed with the incumbent oligarchic families (most of whom were Tory in politics after 1798) for political and economic power within the port towns. The aristocrats were largely replaced in the 1820s and early 1830s by a new generation of Church of Ireland families with 'lesser gentry' status, who were liberal in religious terms and reforming in outlook, and who were usually Liberal or Whig in

---

[29] Jennifer Ridden, *'Making Good Citizens': Irish Elite Approaches to National Identity, Citizenship and Empire, c. 1800–1850* (Cambridge, forthcoming).

[30] See, for example, Hill, *Patriots to Unionists*, 359–62; d'Alton, *Cork*; John B. O'Brien, *The Catholic Middle Classes of Pre-Famine Cork* (Cork, 1979); Thomas P. Power, 'Electoral Politics in Waterford City, 1692–1832', in William Nolan and Thomas P. Power (eds.), *Waterford History and Society* (Dublin, 1992); James Kelly, 'The Politics of the Protestant Ascendancy: County Galway, 1650–1832', in Gerard Moran and Raymond Gillespie (eds.), *Galway History and Society* (Dublin, 1996); David Dickson, 'Second City Syndrome: Reflections on Three Irish Cases', in Connolly (ed.), *Kingdoms United?*, 95–108; R. F. Foster, *Charles Stewart Parnell: The Man and his Family* (Hassocks, 1976).

[31] W. E. Vaughan and A. J. Fitzpatrick (eds.), *Irish Historical Statistics: Population, 1821–1971* (Dublin, 1978), 27.

politics. Limerick representatives of this group included Thomas Spring Rice (MP for Limerick in the 1820s, MP for Cambridge University in the 1830s and 1840s, and chancellor of the exchequer in Lord Melbourne's administration), Aubrey de Vere (poet and acerbic critic of the British Whig policy during the Famine), and Sir Richard Bourke (relative of Edmund Burke, and governor of New South Wales in the 1830s). Many were descended from families whose ancestors had converted to Protestantism during the eighteenth century, and some members of these families converted back to Catholicism or became Anglo-Catholic in the mid-nineteenth century.[32] They were connected with the Whig aristocrats in landlord–tenant, political, and often kin relationships, and these groups usually had shared economic interests. The outer circle of leaders within the moderate reform movement comprised dissenting and Catholic commercial and professional families, whose political and economic interests were similar to those of liberal Protestants. In Limerick, these included key Quaker merchants and businessmen such as Joseph Massey Harvey, and an emerging group of Protestant and Catholic urban professionals including Sir Matthew Barrington (solicitor-general for Munster) and William and David Roche (Catholic banking and commercial cousins).

When Spring Rice (an acknowledged leader of this group) itemized the moderate reform programme in 1822, his list of reforms included many of the elements that O'Connell had already popularized, including Catholic Emancipation, tithe reform, reform of the criminal code and establishment of a normal police force (to replace coercive legislation), cheap and fair legal procedures that were free of religious bias, the reduction of taxes, and a non-denominational state-funded education system. However, the tone, language, and ultimate aims were very different. Moderate reformers wanted to promote social cohesion within Ireland by stripping religion of its divisive power, and by broadening the existing elite to include wealthy and moral Catholics. As Spring Rice put it, 'a system may be devised, correcting the most grievous of the existing abuses, and tending gradually, but surely, to the improvement and happiness of the Irish people'. Notably, for Spring Rice and other moderate reformers, the 'Irish people' included all the residents of Ireland, regardless of religious affiliation or ethnic identification.

Moderate reformers promoted Catholic Emancipation strenuously, but in different terms from those used by the Catholic associations. They argued that Catholic Emancipation would also secure 'the services of men the highest in political character' for Ireland, whether they were Protestant or Catholic, and that it would therefore assist in the development of a virtuous, legitimate, and broadly Christian elite which would replace the existing corrupt and illegitimate

---

[32] David Fitzpatrick, 'Thomas Spring Rice and the Peopling of Australia', *Old Limerick Jl* 'Australian Edition' (1988), 39–49.

Protestant Ascendancy.[33] Political participation was a privilege which should be granted to Catholics as a way of demonstrating their inclusion in the British nation, and because political inclusion was one of the characteristics of free societies; it should not be granted to them as a political right based on their status as members of a Catholic nation in Ireland. As Spring Rice put it, 'I do not claim that, to them, *as Roman Catholics*, power should be granted. My claim for them is, as citizens of a free state, and not as members of a sect.'[34] The political inclusion of Catholics would promote conciliation, and it would constitute recognition that Catholics had, or were capable of acquiring through education, the political responsibility that was necessary for political participation.

By promoting an 'oblivion of religious distinctions', Catholic Emancipation would produce a more cohesive society. As Spring Rice told Lord Liverpool in an open letter, a Catholic Relief Act which gave political power to the emerging Catholic middle class would remove the main source of political and social conflict in Ireland. If, conversely, political privileges continued to be withheld from middle-class Catholics, this would prevent a 'blending of interests which might cement and consolidate the Union between the two islands', and would instead encourage political disaffection and its accompanying danger of popular revolution. As he explained: 'My Catholic countrymen are advancing in wealth; they are becoming our capitalists; they are the purchasers of lands; they are our principal merchants . . . In proportion as the Roman Catholics advance in wealth, so much the more deeply will they feel their exclusion, and more bitterly resent it.'[35]

Though the liberal and moderate reform movement was led by liberal Protestant members of the elite in the main, its most important sources of support were the urban middle-class groups which shared economic interests. Just as the boom in manufacturing and trade between 1760 and 1815 had produced a rural middle class of large farmers and land agents, it had also produced an urban bourgeoisie in the major ports, including Dublin, Cork, Limerick, Waterford, Youall, and Galway. These artisans, tradesmen, shopkeepers, merchants, and service-providing professionals (especially lawyers and bankers) were mainly Catholic, but this socio-economic group also included dissenters and Church of Ireland professionals and minor gentlemen. When the collapse in the provisions trade at the end of the Napoleonic Wars and the successive depressions of the 1820s and 1830s produced a period of economic restructuring in the ports, the urban commercial and professional class was determined to make

---

[33] [Thomas Spring Rice], *Considerations on the Present State of Ireland, and On the Best Means of Improving the Condition of Its Inhabitants: By an Irishman* (London, 1822), 38.

[34] [Thomas Spring Rice], *Catholic Emancipation, Considered on Protestant Principles: In a Letter to the Earl of Liverpool, K.G.: From an Irish Member of Parliament* (London, 1827), 11.

[35] *Ibid.*, 25.

sure that this restructuring was achieved in such a way as to ensure its own survival.[36] However, its capacity to influence economic conditions in the port towns was limited, because the corporations set and collected the port charges and market tolls, distributed fishery rights, collected rent from large amounts of corporation-owned property within the city limits, and controlled many official appointments.[37] The urban middle-class Catholics were excluded from the corporations by reason of their religion, but those Church of Ireland and dissenting commercial men, tradesmen, and urban professionals whose economic interests diverged from those of the corporation elite were also excluded. Even the local Protestant elite families who competed for local political power with the corporation elite were excluded, especially if they supported Catholic Emancipation, or if their economic interests allied them with the commercial class.[38] This created a set of shared economic and political interests among Catholic, dissenting and Church of Ireland commercial men which crossed the religious divide, and it represented a strong impetus for political action in the post-war depression.

The first strategy was to raise funds and organize legal challenges in order to fight their exclusions from the corporations, and to publicize these activities in sympathetic provincial newspapers. In Limerick and other major towns, many of these legal challenges succeeded over time, though the corporation generally succeeded in ignoring the rulings.[39] The second strategy was to set up chambers of commerce in the port towns, which organized and implemented schemes of economic reform in order to make trade more profitable, and which reinforced trade and the buoyant construction industry with other forms of economic activity. In Limerick, for example, these activities included reorganizing the butter trade, attempts to develop new manufacturing industry, re-situating economic and trade activity outside city limits, setting up new markets, and raising money by subscription to improve the economic infrastructure (including building railways, bridges, and 'Commercial Buildings', around which much of this activity revolved).[40]

Because the new chambers of commerce cut across areas of traditional corporation control, they quickly became highly politicized and by the mid-1820s

---

[36] Cormac Ó Gráda, *Ireland: A New Economic History, 1780–1939* (Oxford, 1994).

[37] Crossman, *Local Government*, 26–7.

[38] For example, Lord Pery was excluded from the corporation in Limerick as a result of his economic and political rivalry with the Vereker family, and his support for Catholic Emancipation.

[39] See P.P. 1820, iii (229), 'Report from the Select Committee on the Limerick Election', 39, 45–6, 53–5; Valentin Browne Lawless, *Personal Recollections of the Life and Times* (Dublin, 1849), 85.

[40] D. P. O'Connor, 'History and Functions of the Limerick Chamber of Commerce 1807 to 1902' (unpublished MS in Limerick Chamber of Commerce, 1948); P.P. 1835, xxvii (23), 'First Report of the Commissioners to Inquire into the Municipal Corporations of Ireland', 408; Mid-West Regional Archives, Limerick, chamber of commerce minute books.

they were performing the function of a nascent Liberal party in Ireland. By 1818 the chambers of commerce were already involved in and often financed the political campaigns of emerging Independent and Liberal coalitions, whose key focuses were Catholic Emancipation and corporation reform, and by the mid-1820s they had succeeded in achieving the election of Liberal MPs in Dublin, Cork, Limerick, Galway, Waterford, and in some of the larger market towns, like Tipperary Town.[41]

The 'chairing' parade which celebrated Spring Rice's electoral victory in Limerick's borough seat in 1820 provides a vivid symbolic representation of Irish moderate reform. It was commemorated by a large oil painting depicting the committee of Independents who had organized his campaign, supporters who carried banners from each of the guilds and trades associations, and tenants from the estates of Lord Clare and Sir Richard Bourke (his campaign manager), who drew Spring Rice's carriage.[42] The procession demonstrated a clear opposition between the reformers' broadly Christian view of virtue and liberty on the one hand, and the corruption of the corporation and the Protestant Ascendancy families which controlled that corporation on the other; marchers carried a blackboard displaying a skull and crossbones and the motto 'Sacred to the memory of Corporate Corruption', followed by a reforming 'Angel' carrying a drawn sword and the motto 'No impurity shall enter here.' The marchers also used a dramatization which is now exclusively associated with O'Connell, in which they fastened a large chain across the street and had their followers proclaim, 'See our Chain, we were Bond-slaves'; Spring Rice cut through the chain, and proclaimed, 'Behold, you are Free.' The parade concluded at the Commercial Buildings, from which a Union flag flew. This proclaimed that moderate reformers sought reform within a British constitutional setting, but that they eschewed both the exclusively Protestant overtones of the loyalism espoused by the corporation elite, and the exclusively Catholic overtones of the O'Connellite reformers.

The development of liberal theology among a minority of Church of Ireland laity was a reaction against the evangelical programme of mass conversion of Catholics during the 1820s. It provided the context within which the moderate reform movement developed the claim that Irish political groupings did not have to be defined in religious terms that, in Ireland, necessarily involved conflict. Liberal Protestants like Sir Richard Bourke insisted that the wholesale conversion of Catholics was unnecessary because Catholics were already 'fellow-Christians' and, like Protestants, Catholics acquired religious

---

[41] O'Brien, *Catholic Middle Classes*, 19; Hill, *Patriots to Unionists*, 359–62; d'Alton, *Protestant Society*; Power, 'Electoral Politics in Waterford City', 253–4; Kelly, 'Politics of Galway', 259.

[42] 'The Chairing of Thomas Spring Rice, MP', oil painting by William Turner of Oxford, commissioned by the Limerick chamber of commerce and now housed there. The following description is based on the report in the *Limerick Chronicle*, 22 July 1820.

enlightenment, Christian virtue, and political responsibility by rational means, especially through education. As Bourke concluded, 'Let us forget that Protestant and Roman Catholick are different branches; in order that we may better, and more to our benefit, remember that the tree is Christian; and that we spring from a common root.'[43]

Liberal theology formed the basis of a non-denominational political language of citizenship based on religious conceptions of the individual, improvability, and on the notion of an overarching Christian (as opposed to Protestant) state. This allowed moderate reformers in Ireland to develop a 'middle way' between the radical 'rights' language used by the Catholic Association on one hand, and the evangelical language of Protestant defence on the other. It thus provided an opportunity for urban middle-class reformers to extricate themselves from a binary model of Irish Catholics and British protestants, which worked against cooperative political activity between the various urban groups that shared economic and political interests. The sharp opposition between Irish liberal Protestants and militant evangelicalism of the kind championed by Edward Irving (a key actor in the Irish Reformation Society) distinguished the liberal stance from that of morally serious Protestants in England; the latter generally regarded militant evangelicalism as part of the 'morally serious' continuum.[44]

Moderate reforming MPs were successful in achieving a number of reforms using British parliamentary structures, for example in the areas of municipal corporation reform and education. The act which established the Irish National Schools system was introduced into parliament by Lord Edward Stanley, and so has frequently been attributed to English Whig reformers who supposedly used Ireland as a social laboratory. In fact the scheme was an Irish moderate reforming initiative that was based on the local educational experiments of such key figures as Spring Rice and Bourke, who had attempted to translate their liberal theological and religious views into practical social reforms. Bourke established non-denominational schools on his estate from as early as 1820, and gained acceptance from the Catholic parish priest for the use of secular school books instead of the Catholic catechism or the Bible, and for prayer that was '*generic* . . . containing nothing that should remind them of *specific* differences of faith; or infringe the peculiar tenets of either Church'. He argued that the development of rationality and morality was not affected by this policy, and he hoped it would 'help to nip religious prejudice and animosity in the bud'.[45]

---

[43] 'Athamik' [Richard Bourke], *Letter to the Right Hon. Charles Grant, from an Irish Layman of the Established Church, on the Subject of a Charge Lately Published, and Purporting to Have Been Delivered to his Clergy, by the Lord Bishop of Killaloe and Kilfenora* (Dublin, 1820), 38.

[44] Bowen, *Protestant Crusade*, 202. Cf. Richard Brent, *Liberal Anglican Politics: Whiggery, Religion, and Reform, 1830–1841* (Cambridge, 1987).

[45] 'Athamik', *Letter*, 54–5, 59.

In the 1820s and 1830s Spring Rice established his credibility as a reformer in the British political context through a series of influential articles in the *Edinburgh Review*, including articles on education.[46] He then used his connections with Lord John Russell and the Lansdowne circle to gain appointment as chairman of the 1828 select committee on Irish education. In this role, he was able to influence the terms of reference and selection of committee members and witnesses, and to actively shape the final recommendations. Stanley's 1830 report essentially reiterated Spring Rice's conclusions of 1828, and these recommendations formed the basis of the 1831 Irish National Schools Act, with very little adaptation. This legislative success for moderate reformers developed in an unintended way, since the National Schools quickly became state-funded Catholic schools by default when the Protestant churches withdrew. Bourke also tried to establish a non-denominational state-funded schooling system in New South Wales based on the Irish National Schools system, when he was governor of the colony during the 1830s.[47]

Irish moderate reformers were less successful in other areas during the 1830s and 1840s. They found themselves unable to prevent the extension of the British workhouse system to Ireland in 1838, despite the fact that poverty and the socio-economic relationships that produced it in Ireland were not comparable with those in England. Irish Liberals also found themselves unable to moderate British Whig policy during the Famine. As Spring Rice told Lord Bessborough during an acrimonious debate on famine relief in 1846, the Treasury 'lectures' on 'sound principle' were appalling. While Spring Rice was 'both an Economist and a Treasury man . . . [he argued that] the Government must be prepared to face much responsibility if they wish to keep society together'. The government's doctrine of self-help, in which the Irish landowners had to accept the whole burden of famine relief, was fundamentally flawed in a society like Ireland's which was economically underdeveloped, and which was experiencing a famine of such catastrophic proportions. As Spring Rice put it, the British government might 'as well to ask a child why he does not perform the functions of a man, or Hindustanis why they do not build Manchester at Benares'. Instead, he argued, Ireland should be treated as if it had suffered invasion by a foreign army; all should provide aid in resisting it.[48] The Irish Liberal failure

---

[46] See, e.g., [Valentin Browne Lawless], 'Education of the Irish Poor', *Edinburgh Rev.*, 92 (1825), 197–224.

[47] State Lib. New South Wales, Mitchell Lib. MS 403/9 (Bourke papers), Bourke to Dick Bourke Jr, 28 July 1836; see also Roger Therry, *An Explanation of the Plan of the Irish National Schools* (Sydney, 1836). Though Bourke's initiative failed as a result of virulent local opposition, the school system that eventually developed in the Australian colonies bore close resemblance to Bourke's proposal.

[48] NLI, MS 13,396/8 (Monteagle papers), Monteagle (Thomas Spring Rice) to Lord Trevelyan, 1 Oct. 1846: MS 13,396/9, Monteagle to Lord Trevelyan, 1 Oct. 1846; cf. Peter Gray, *Famine, Lane and Politics* (Dublin, 1999).

successfully to bend the Union to Irish ends and, even more catastrophically, their failure to persuade the British government to provide sufficient aid to Ireland in the extreme circumstances of the 1840s, led to widespread disillusionment among Irish moderate reformers. Some, like William Smith O'Brien, moved beyond parliamentary techniques and Unionism and instead embraced the republicanism of Young Ireland.[49]

IV

Moderate and O'Connellite reform programmes included many shared elements, but they reflected different views on the role of religion in society, on the development of national identity, and on how best to achieve reform within the Union framework. The need to attract popular and bourgeois support, in order to back up the claims made by each group's leaders that they were an alternative and more virtuous elite, produced competition rather than cooperation between these different reforming groups.

During the 1820s the O'Connellite reform movement developed awesome techniques of mass politicization and mobilization, using the Catholic associations. Yet even in this period O'Connellite reform did not entirely and permanently supplant other forms of political activity among the Catholic poor. For example, agrarian protest by such groups as the Rockites in Munster remained prevalent throughout the 1820s, as did violent tithe protests during the 1830s. Similarly, the Catholic poor participated in violent agrarian conflict organized by the oath-bound secret societies such as the Ribbon societies, whose activities were associated with an overtly revolutionary nationalist ideology. These various forms of political activity were associated with different political ideologies, focused on different programmes, and had different approaches to the use of violence. Yet there are clear indications that poor Catholics shifted their support – from agrarian protest, to the revolutionary secret societies, to O'Connell's Catholic Association, and back again – depending on particular local circumstances and events. Even so, in the brief period between the 1826 and 1829 elections, it does seem clear that O'Connell's movement was approaching hegemonic status in rural 'Catholic Ireland', and that the shifts between different forms of political activity in that period were generally towards the Catholic Association.[50] In 1829 even the Ribbonmen announced that

---

[49] Robert Sloan, *William Smith O'Brien and the Young Ireland Rebellion of 1848* (Dublin, 2000), ch. 6. In later life O'Brien returned to constitutionalism. See, for example, William Smith O'Brien, *Principles of Government; or Meditations in Exile . . . in 2 volumes* (Dublin, 1856).

[50] Garvin, 'Defenders, Ribbonmen and Others', 219–44; J. S. Donnelly Jr, 'Pastorini and Captain Rock', 136–7, in Philpin (ed.), *Nationalism and Popular Protest*; Gary Owens, '"A Moral Insurrection": Faction Fighters, Public Demonstrations and the O'Connellite Campaign, 1828', *Irish Hist. Studies*, 30 (1997), 513–41.

they would henceforth support O'Connell, and said that they were 'ready at a moment's warning to turn out if Mr O'Connell does not get justice for Ireland in parliament'.[51]

Certainly, most Protestants believed by the mid-1820s that, if successful, the O'Connellite movement would lead to the radical restructuring of Irish life and, ultimately, to Catholic supremacy. The Catholic Association's techniques of popular mobilization and the growing O'Connellite emphasis on 'rights' reinforced this fear. Only a very small number of Protestants were willing to accept the possibility of an Ireland that was entirely dominated by Catholics, and therefore O'Connellite reform was not acceptable to most Protestant reformers. On the other hand, the liberal Protestant chance of gaining parliamentary power before 1829 was largely dependent on their capacity to attract support from the Catholic 40-shilling freeholders. Before the mid-1820s, when the O'Connellite popular campaign gathered steam, Protestant reformers were able to claim the status of Catholic champions. They were the only real avenue for Catholics who wanted political reform, and for this pragmatic reason the Catholic Association supported liberal Protestant candidates in the borough seats (much to Spring Rice's chagrin, since he did not want to be associated with O'Connell's 'sectarianism' and demagoguery).[52] Most of the pro-Catholic Emancipation MPs before 1829 can be considered moderate reformers, and most distanced themselves from the Catholic Association when it became a populist organization after 1824.

Many historians have assumed that moderate reformers permanently lost their credibility in the late 1820s, in the face of the Catholic Association's popular success and the consequent passage of Catholic Emancipation, and further that the growth of popular Irish-Catholic national identity overtook the possibility of cross-denominational cooperation.[53] However, over the next four decades more Irish MPs consistently opposed both Repeal and the Conservatives than supported Repeal, even when the Repeal Association was at its height.[54] This reflects the continued importance of Protestant political families in the post-Emancipation and post-Reform electoral system, but it is also worth noting

---

[51] Quoted in Michael R. Beames, 'The Ribbon Societies: Lower-Class Nationalism in Pre-Famine Ireland', in Philpin (ed.), *Nationalism and Popular Protest*, 257.

[52] For example, *Ennis Chronicle*, 24 June 1826. For Spring Rice's reaction, see Monteagle papers in possession of Lord Monteagle, Foynes, Co. Cork, Ireland, Sir Stephen Edward de Vere to Thomas Spring Rice (second Baron Monteagle), 27 July [c. 1896].

[53] See, for example, d'Alton, *Cork*; d'Alton's conclusions have been modified by Peter Jupp and Stephen Royle, 'The Social Geography of Cork City Elections, 1801–30', *Irish Hist. Studies*, 29 (1994), 13–43.

[54] Brian Walker, *Parliamentary Election Results in Ireland, 1801–1922* (Dublin, 1978). Most British historians have overestimated the extent of unity within the Irish parliamentary party, because they have mistakenly taken O'Connell at his word when he claimed that he controlled sixty of the sixty-five non-Tory Irish MPs in 1835, even though only thirty-four of these members supported his Repeal campaign. See also MacDonagh, *O'Connell*, 401.

that this result would have been impossible without substantial and continued Catholic support for moderate reform. Far from disappearing, the competitive relationship between the moderate and O'Connellite reform movements escalated, and this produced a much greater degree of fluidity and political complexity than a simple binary conflict between O'Connellite nationalism and British–Protestant conservatism would suggest. Catholic Emancipation in 1829 did produce a seismic shift in Irish politics, but this shift was not all it seemed. O'Connell's power base had been composed of Catholic 40-shilling freeholder voters, but they were disenfranchised by an act which accompanied Catholic Emancipation, and only a very small proportion of those people regained the vote under the Irish Parliamentary Reform Act in 1832. The ensuing competition for political support between O'Connellite and moderate reformers was therefore focused upon middle-class and wealthy Catholics.

In the fifty years after the Act of Union, urban middle-class Catholics exhibited shifting patterns of allegiance and a degree of tactical voting. Many urban middle-class Catholics who had supported the moderate reform movement before 1829 briefly switched their support to O'Connell in the immediate aftermath of Catholic Emancipation, with the aim of electing Catholic representatives rather than liberal Protestants. However, when the Catholic commercial class found their wealth and social status increasingly threatened during the 1820s, and when O'Connellite reform became increasingly democratic in tone during the late 1820s and early 1830s, they realized that the hierarchical social and economic structure of Ireland within which they sought power might easily be undermined. As the English commentator Edward Wakefield explained, both the urban and rural middle-class Catholics were ambivalent, especially those that had grown wealthy in the Napoleonic boom:

> They are afraid of the populace and being uncertain which may gain the ascendancy, the government or the people, they frequently censure the government in order to ingratiate themselves with the community at large. But if the day of trial should come, self-interest would induce them to cling to the power that was successful. The truth is, these people will unite with those who are best able to secure to them the enjoyment of their property.[55]

The urban moderate reform movement provided an alternative way of demanding and achieving the reforms that the urban bourgeoisie wanted, without the potentially radical implications of O'Connellite reform which used 'rights' language, and this potentially appealed to the rural Catholic middle class as well.

Thus, despite the assumption that Catholics supported Repeal and Protestants supported the Union during the 1830s, in fact many urban Catholics responded

---

[55] Edward Wakefield, *An Account of Ireland, Statistical and Political*, 2 vols (London, 1812), ii, 545.

to O'Connell's increasingly visible radicalism during the Repeal campaign by supporting the moderates.[56] For example, Thomas Wyse (co-founder of the Catholic Association) transferred his support from O'Connell to the moderate reform group as soon as O'Connell declared the new Repeal programme in 1830; he contested the Waterford election against O'Connell in 1830, splitting the anti-Conservative vote, and then won the Tipperary seat later that year. Like other liberal Catholics, he quickly found common ground with moderate reformers in liberal religious ideas, Unionism, and in particular, education reform.[57] Similarly, in Limerick and Cork, William, David, and James Roche refused to pledge their support for Repeal despite pressure from O'Connell and the National Repeal Association, on the grounds that 'The firm cement of the union, not its repeal – the full and cordial accomplishment of its object and promise, not their violation, seemed to me the surest remedial appliance to our suffered evils – their safest corrective.'[58] By the early 1840s, the republican Young Ireland movement was challenging O'Connell's leadership within the Catholic Association; and one result was that reform-inclined members swung back to the Irish Liberal party.

On the other hand, there was growing dissatisfaction with the moderate reform movement by the late 1820s, especially among Catholic tradesmen in Cork and Dublin, and to a lesser extent in Limerick, because they felt the Liberal MPs had failed to prevent the erosion of their economic position. The artisans in Cork and Dublin became convinced that Repeal was the only way they could restore their economic security; when that failed, Cork and Dublin became fertile recruiting grounds for the Irish Confederate/Young Ireland movement in the 1840s and for the Fenians in the 1860s.[59] Furthermore, the failure of Irish Liberals to exert sufficient influence on the British state to prevent the extension of the New Poor Law to Ireland, or to produce an adequate centralized government response to the Famine, seriously undermined the credibility of Irish Liberals and moderate reformers. William Smith O'Brien provides an example of this disaffection. He had developed into a moderate reformer in the late 1820s, and had been a youthful member of the Catholic Association. However,

---

[56] Even some members of O'Connell's own family, including his brother John, were opposed to his agitation for Repeal after 1829: Public Record Office of Northern Ireland, T3075/13 (Fitzgerald papers), John O'Connell to Maurice Fitzgerald, 26 Nov. 1833.

[57] Robert Sloan, 'O'Connell's Liberal Rivals', *Irish Hist. Studies*, 30 (1996), 47–65.

[58] James Roche, *Critical and Miscellaneous Essays by an Octogenarian*, 2 vols. (Cork, 1850), ii, 124. See also [William Roche], *Ireland Vindicated; or, Reflections upon . . . the Question of a Repeal of the Act Uniting England with Ireland; and upon the Answer Returned by . . . Spring Rice . . . to the Address of the Cordwainers of Limerick . . . by A True Whig* (London, 1831). O'Connell reacted by waiving the demand for a Repeal pledge, on the grounds that Catholic MPs were preferable to Protestants.

[59] Maura Cronin, *Country, Class or Craft? The Politicisation of the Skilled Artisan in Nineteenth-Century Cork* (Cork, 1994), 102–10, 132–3; see also Tom Garvin, *Nationalist Revolutionaries in Ireland, 1858–1928* (Oxford, 1987), 7–8.

he found himself unable to support O'Connell against Vesey Fitzgerald in the 1828 election, because the O'Brien and Fitzgerald families were politically and economically linked, and because (like many other members of the local liberal Protestant elite) he was loath to support a wholesale revolt of tenants against their landlords. Even so, he became increasingly disillusioned with the Irish Liberal failure to achieve significant Irish reforms in the early 1840s. He joined the Repeal Association, then participated in the republican Irish Confederate defection from the Repeal Association, and began to write for the radical nationalist newspaper, the *Nation*. He was eventually transported to Van Diemen's Land for his part in leading the Young Ireland Rising of 1848.

Even in the sectarian atmosphere of the early 1840s there was still room for a middle path which avoided the denominational allegiances of both Repealers and Conservatives. The first elections for the reformed municipal corporations in 1841 were the scene of highly centralized and sectarian campaigns by the Conservatives and the Repeal movement in all the major towns, and as a result the sectarian tension in Cork erupted in some of the worst riots of the century. Yet Liberals who opposed repeal deliberately maintained their denominational mix and avoided sectarian electoral tactics. Though the Municipal Reform Act allowed O'Connell to become mayor of Dublin, where he established a Repeal stronghold, Liberals who opposed Repeal still won eleven seats (five were won by Catholics, six by Protestants). This result contrasted with that for those seats won by Conservatives and Repealers (led by O'Connell). In these cases, there was a close alignment between religious and political allegiance; of the thirty-six Repealers elected, all but two were Catholic, and of the thirteen Conservatives elected, all but one were Protestant.[60]

V

The long-term process of socio-economic change in Ireland which accelerated in the first half of the century had an important effect on Irish reformulations of reform language and programmes, and on the reconstitution of political groups and ideas in Ireland. However, changing economic interests cannot by themselves explain the particular reform languages that developed, nor why neither reforming group embraced republican nationalism. Neither can they fully explain the relative fluidity of political groupings in the first half of the century. If we take socio-economic change as a base factor that spanned the revolutionary period, we then need to explain how this related to the new understandings that had resulted from the 1790s experience in Ireland and, in particular, to the new circumstances of the Union. The differences between O'Connellite and moderate reforming strategies rested in part on their different assessments of

[60] Hill, *Patriots to Unionists*, 380–1.

what could be achieved within the framework of the British state, and different methods of attempting those reforms.

The Irish 'age of reform' was not a binary conflict between O'Connellite nationalism on one hand, and an alliance between the British state and the Protestant Ascendancy on the other. Instead there were competing reforming strategies that were crucial in shaping the outcome of political debate in Ireland, and that created a degree of fluidity. In addition, Irish reform involved a counterpoint on issues of centre–periphery relations which took in debates about national identity, but in which reformers shared a willingness to accept a centralized state if (and only if) this state could be used to achieve reforms that were resisted by the local Irish oligarchy. This counterpoint existed in other parts of the United Kingdom too. Even within England the expansion of the state into areas of social policy was debated between such reformers as Joshua Toulmin Smith of the 'Association of Parochial Representatives', who saw centralization as an unreasonable fetter on local reform initiatives, and Edwin Chadwick, who saw local authorities as obstacles to reform and who insisted that they should be supervised by central boards.[61] The development of a modern British state which encompassed England, Wales, Scotland, and Ireland added another dimension to these debates about centre and locality. The deliberate attempt by Irish reformers to develop centralized state legislation and social policy in order to force change on resistant local elite groups also suggests that we may need to modify the widespread belief that the various British reforming battles against corruption were necessarily aligned with attempts to dismantle the fiscal-military state in favour of a minimalist state.

The two reform movements described in this chapter represented different responses to the problem of Ireland's weak and illegitimate elite. However, the demands and needs of the various socio-economic and religious groups from which these two reform movements sought support tell us almost as much about Irish political culture and the reform movements themselves as do the ideologies and intentions of their leaders. It was the leadership's capacity to win popular support, and thus to prove their legitimacy claims, that in the end determined the relative fortunes of these two reform movements.

Differences between Irish and English circumstances were striking, and these were reflected in the different focuses of Irish and English reform. In particular, the specifically Irish circumstances made the Catholic Question and ethnic national identity a central focus of Irish radicalism and of the moderate response, while it was less pivotal in England. The framework of the Union provided problems and opportunities for Irish reformers, as it did for English reformers.

---

[61] David Eastwood, *Government and Community in the English Provinces, 1700–1870* (Basingstoke, 1997), 155–6. See also Rosemary Sweet, *The English Town, 1680–1840: Government, Society and Culture* (Harlow, 1999).

Therefore, while the Union provided opportunities for the attempted anglicization of the Irish 'periphery', it also provided opportunities for the 'periphery' to influence the 'centre'. As in other areas of 'British history', this discussion of Irish perspectives suggests that a 'British age of reform' was more marked by negotiations and competitions between different visions of reform than by a unified vision that spanned these islands. It is consequently difficult to fully appreciate British reform without also considering the relationships between the various groups of reformers within the United Kingdom and their competition for support.

13. *Empire and parliamentary reform: the 1832 Reform Act revisited*

MILES TAYLOR

The 1832 Reform Act enfranchised around half a million men in Britain and Ireland. By abolishing the small nomination boroughs, according to its critics, it disfranchised many millions more across the British empire. 'How far', asked Sir Robert Inglis, making the first opposition speech in the Commons against the Reform Bill, 'the rights of distant dependencies, of the East Indies, of the West Indies, of the Colonies . . . could find their just support in the House, I know not.' Other Tory opponents were more specific. Sir Richard Vyvyan reckoned the Reform Bill would create a 'tyrannical assembly' over 120 million in the colonial empire unless small boroughs remained open to men with imperial experience and interests. Michael Sadler thought 'scores of millions' in 'this extensive empire' would be left unrepresented. And Sir John Malcolm feared that 80 million people in India 'would not find one Representative in the British Parliament'.[1] Writing in *Blackwood's Edinburgh Magazine* in May 1831, Archibald Alison summed up the Tory case against the imperial deficiencies of the Whig reform bill: '[n]ominally professing to *extend*, this bill is really destined to *contract*, the representation, to base the legislature, not upon the *empire*, but the *island*'.[2] Without adequate representation, Tories believed that the empire – that is, the union with Ireland, the protected trade of India and Canada, and the plantation economies of the West Indies – would be lost, and, in the words of the earl of Falmouth, '[t]his great State would be divided into several small Republics, which would probably soon become the provinces of some greater Power'.[3] From first to last, inside and outside parliament, defending the empire was to

---

[1] *Parl. Debs.*, 3rd ser., ii, col. 1109 (1 Mar. 1831); cf. *ibid.*, iii, cols. 642–3 (21 Mar. 1831, Vyvyan), 1540 (Sadler); *ibid.*, iv, cols. 736–4 (Malcolm).

[2] [Archibald Alison], 'On Parliamentary Reform and the French Revolution (no. V)', *Blackwood's Edinburgh Mag.*, 29 (1831), 749. At the beginning of July, another commentator noted that 'the establishment of a constitution for England, Scotland and Ireland, on the basis of numerical representation, must have the certain effect of depriving four-fifths of the whole British empire of all representation whatever': *Observations on a Pamphlet, Falsely Attributed to a Great Person: Entitled 'Friendly Advice to the Lords on the Reform Bill'* (London, 1831), 33.

[3] *Parl. Debs.*, 3rd ser., viii, col. 107 (6 Oct. 1831).

prove a recurrent theme in Tory opposition to the reform bills of 1831 and 1832. From November 1830, when the duke of Wellington explained that he opposed parliamentary reform because it 'must occasion a total change in that society called the British Empire',[4] through to Lord Ellenborough's last-ditch attempts in April and May 1832 to salvage schedule 'B' two-member boroughs so that colonial MPs might still be elected, the imperial issue remained important. Nor was colonial representation the peculiar preoccupation of die-hard ultra-Tories. At times it transcended party. In August 1831 during the committee stage of the bill, the radical Joseph Hume tabled an amendment providing for the inclusion of nineteen colonial MPs, and in November of the same year the duke of Richmond attempted, unsuccessfully, to persuade his Whig cabinet colleagues to include a scheme of colonial representation in their revamped reform plans.

Given all this fuss it is odd that the imperial dimension of the 1832 Reform Act has been altogether ignored by historians. Preoccupied with the expansion of the franchise, historians of 1832 continue to overlook the question of the distribution of seats, and hence colonial representation itself barely merits a footnote within a large literature devoted to parliamentary reform.[5] Although there has been a recent revival of interest in the arguments of ultra-Tory opponents of parliamentary reform, the defence of the empire has not been included in analysis of the ideology of the *ancien régime*.[6] Thus historians have missed the striking proximity of parliamentary reform in the early 1830s to a series of major turning-points in the history of the British empire. The passage of parliamentary reform from 1830 through to 1833 coincided with tithe and ecclesiastical reform in Ireland, slave emancipation in the West Indies, the renewal of the East India Company's Charter, and retrenchment in colonial armed forces across the globe. Moreover, viewed in a comparative context, it is worth recalling just how many of Britain's continental neighbours were plunged into fiscal

---

[4] *Despatches, Correspondence and Memoranda of Field Marshal Arthur, Duke of Wellington KG*, ed. the duke of Wellington, 8 vols. (London, 1867–80), viii, 352–3: duke of Wellington to Maurice Fitzgerald, 6 Nov. 1830.

[5] Michael Brock, *The Great Reform Act* (London, 1973), 264. J. Milton-Smith identified the conflict over direct versus virtual representation as a 'major underlying point' of the reform debates, but did not elaborate: J. Milton-Smith, 'Earl Grey's Cabinet and the Objects of Parliamentary Reform', *Hist. Jl*, 15 (1972), 66. Arguments for colonial representation during the nineteenth century receive fuller coverage in Ged Martin, 'Empire Federalism and Imperial Parliamentary Union, 1820–70', *Hist. Jl*, 16 (1973), 65–92.

[6] J. C. D. Clark, *English Society, 1660–1832: Religion, Ideology and Politics During the Ancien Régime*, 2nd edn (Cambridge, 2000); James Sack, *From Jacobite to Conservative: Reaction and Orthodoxy in Britain, c. 1760–1832* (Cambridge, 1993); Richard Gaunt, 'The Political Activities and Opinions of the 4th Duke of Newcastle, 1785–1851' (University of Nottingham Ph.D. thesis, 2000). Catherine Hall's work is a notable exception: see Catherine Hall, 'The Rule of Difference: Gender, Class and Empire in the Making of the 1832 Reform Act', in Ida Blom *et al.* (eds.), *Gendered Nations: Nationalism and Gender Order in the Long Nineteenth Century* (Oxford, 2000), 107–35.

and constitutional upheaval in 1830, in part by the nemesis of imperial over-stretch. In France Charles X's invasion of Algeria in July 1830 was followed three weeks later by revolution in Paris, the final eclipse of the Bourbon monar-chy, and the drawing up of a new constitution. A month later, inspired by the French example, Catholic Belgium broke from the ruling House of Orange in the Netherlands. In September, some of the larger states of the German *Bund* began to rise up against the interference of Austria and Prussia, and within a year had agreed new constitutions. And two months after that the Poles turned on the imperial power in their midst, Tsarist Russia, and enjoyed six months of their own independent Diet before being crushed at Ostrolenke in the early summer of 1831. Overseas commentators certainly saw constitutional change in Britain and the empire as an integral part of this crumbling of the old imperial order. 'The "spirit of reform"', enthused one Sydney editor, 'spreads rapidly through-out Europe, and now menaces the remotest regions of the British Empire. New South Wales will not be overlooked'; while from Boston it was predicted that 'the dissolution . . . of the colonial system will probably be among the effects produced by the new principles of the constitution'.[7] The aim of this chapter is to consider parliamentary reform in the years 1830–2 within this wider imperial context. The chapter has two main themes. One is to look in more detail at the issue of colonial representation in the debates over the Reform Bill; the other is to examine the extent to which parliamentary reform at home was driven on by imperial considerations abroad: in the West Indies, India, and Ireland.

I

The issue of colonial representation raised its head early on in the reform de-bates and never really went away again. The first Reform Bill, introduced in the House of Commons by Lord John Russell on 1 March 1831, was of course far from identical to the measure that was eventually passed in the summer of 1832. The Whig government's original reform measure was different in two main respects. First, it originally provided for the representation of the whole of Great Britain and Ireland in so far as the government intended to run all three reform bills, for England and Wales, for Scotland, and for Ireland, together – *pari passu*. Only later did the government decide to put off the Scottish and Irish reform bills until the vote had been won on the English. Second, in its redistributive clauses it proposed not only the transfer of some seats from old constituencies to new, but an actual overall reduction of the number of MPs in the Commons as well. The first Reform Bill would have cut the size of the House of Commons from 658 to 596 MPs. Five extra seats each were proposed for

---

[7] *Australian*, 3 June 1831, 2; [Edward Everett], 'The Progress of Reform in England', *North American Rev.*, 34 (1832), 46–7.

Scotland and Ireland, with the net effect that English representation would have been reduced by nearly one-tenth. In other words, in attempting to devise a system for Britain's multiple union, the Whigs planned to increase the Scottish and Irish representation at the expense of the English. Although the Scottish bill was eventually managed through parliament by Francis Jeffrey, the lord advocate, its redistributive clauses were the work of Henry Cockburn, the solicitor-general for Scotland, who was determined to end the under-representation of that country, a state of affairs he compared to colonial America. To this end he drafted a measure that improved the ratio of burgh to county members, and this required additional seats.[8] The Irish schedules were the work of Lord Duncannon, who sought extra borough seats to offset the monopoly enjoyed by the existing urban corporations.[9] But the second Earl Grey was himself keen to increase Irish and Scottish representation. Although he later proved flexible on the actual final size of the Commons – 'one of the best features of the measure' – he remained committed to a greater proportionate influence for the Celtic portion of the representation.[10]

It was the scale of this discrimination against the English constituencies that provoked much of the Tory opposition to the bill during the debates in the Commons in March and early April 1831. Tory MPs and reviewers argued that the Whigs could not increase the Scottish and Irish representation without changing the terms of the Acts of Union (of 1707 and 1800 respectively).[11] They also questioned whether the Whigs could legally take away the corporate and chartered rights of small boroughs.[12] And again and again they returned to the argument that the small English boroughs were a vital part of a system of virtual representation whereby a variety of different national interests – colonial, shipping, banking, legal, and fundholding – could find support in parliament. Without small boroughs, devoid of the clamour of constituents and the intimidating cost of elections, men representing wider interests stood little chance of entering parliament. Without the small boroughs a system of purely local

---

[8] [Henry Cockburn], 'Parliamentary Representation of Scotland', *Edinburgh Rev.*, 52 (1830), 220–1; *Journal of Henry Cockburn, Being a Continuation of the Memorials of his Time, 1831–54*, 2 vols. (Edinburgh, 1874), i, 11 (entry for 23 Apr. 1831); Michael Dyer, '"Mere Detail and Machinery": The Great Reform Act and the Effects of Redistribution on Scottish Representation, 1832–68', *Scottish Hist. Rev.*, 62 (1983), 17–34; Norman Gash, *Politics in the Age of Peel: A Study in the Technique of Parliamentary Representation, 1830–1850* (London, 1953), 38–46.

[9] Gash, *Politics in the Age of Peel*, 50–64; Dorothy Howell-Thomas, *Duncannon: Reformer and Reconciler, 1781–1847* (Norwich, 1992), 153–4.

[10] *The Correspondence of Princess Lieven and Earl Grey*, ed. Guy Le Strange, 3 vols. (London, 1903), ii, 198–200, Earl Grey to Princess Lieven, 29 Mar. 1831; Sheffield Archives, Wharncliffe papers, Wh. M. 516(f), 'Note of a conversation with Earl Grey, Nov. 29, 1831'.

[11] *Parl. Debs.*, 3rd ser., iii, cols. 876–7 (24 Mar. 1831, Bankes), 883 (Wetherell); cf. Philip Pusey, *The New Constitution: Remarks* (London, 1831), 17.

[12] *Parl. Debs.*, 3rd ser., ii, cols. 1134 (1 Mar. 1831, Twiss), 1230–6 (2 Mar. 1831, Wetherell); iii, col. 774 (22 Mar. 1831, Scarlett).

representation would emerge, in which the parochial interests of voters would be uppermost.[13] The Whigs, suggested Tories in the Commons and in the Lords, were introducing a wholly new principle – that of direct representation – into the constitution. If there were to be members for Birmingham and Manchester, argued Winthrop Praed, then why should there not be members for Jamaica, Barbados, and Grenada? The logic of the bill, suggested Lord Wharncliffe, would be 'to give the colonial interests of the country some direct interest in the Representation of the House of Commons'.[14]

Such Tory alarm led to the defeat of the first Reform Bill in mid-April 1831. Concern over the diminution of the number of English seats and the marginalization of colonial interests lay behind General Isaac Gascoyne's amendment in committee for not reducing the number of English MPs and retaining the original size of the Commons. Gascoyne, MP for Liverpool and a commander of the Coldstream Guards during the 1798 Rebellion in Ireland, was especially concerned at the prospect of the over-representation of Ireland, but Michael Sadler, who seconded his amendment, saw the problem in a more imperial light: 'To diminish the number of Representatives from one part of the empire, at the same time that those in another are proposed to be increased, is to give great legislative advantage to that portion of the community which the noble Lord [Russell] thus anticipates the possibility of resisting.'[15] The Whigs were defeated on Gascoyne's motion, the first Reform Bill was shelved, parliament was dissolved, and a general election was held immediately. When parliament returned and resumed discussion of the Reform Bill in July, the Whigs had made some significant alterations. Discussion of the Scottish and Irish reform bills

---

[13] *Ibid.*, iii, col. 157 (7 Mar. 1831, North); cf. [John Fullarton], 'Reform in Parliament', *Quarterly Rev.*, 65 (1831), 295; [Sir John Taylor Coleridge], *Notes on the Reform Bill* (London, 1831), 11; 'One of the People', *An Appeal to the Common Sense of Englishmen on the Question of Reform* (London, 1831), 11; 'A Country Clergyman', *A Letter to Sir Robert Peel on the Reform Question* (London, 1831), 43. 'Why sir', declared 'Tory' in a contemporary skit, 'the members of the Cornish Boroughs, abstractedly considered, represent the interests of Manchester and Glasgow, and the Colonies, as much as Members chosen by them immediately would do': *A Dialogue on Parliamentary Reform* (London, 1831), 9.

[14] *Parl. Debs.*, 3rd ser., iii, col. 243 (8 Mar. 1831, Praed). Later in the year, as a corrective to direct representation, Praed proposed an amendment limiting voters in three-membered counties to two votes: Derek Hudson, *A Poet in Parliament: The Life of Winthrop Mackworth Praed, 1802–39* (London, 1939), 178–9; Jenifer Hart, *Proportional Representation: Critics of the Electoral System in Britain, 1820–1945* (Oxford, 1991), 10–11; *Parl. Debs.*, 3rd ser., iii, col. 1006 (28 Mar. 1831, Wharncliffe).

[15] *Parl. Debs.*, 3rd ser., iii, col. 1530 (18 Apr. 1831). One pamphleteer warned of the danger of transferring 'any portion of the remaining power of the House of Commons to persons who will use it in the dismemberment of the Empire': *Letters to a Friend, By a Liberal Supporter of Roman Catholic Emancipation and Parliamentary Reform on the Irish Reform Bill* (London, 1831), 6; [Fullarton], 'Reform of Parliament', 325–6; John Walsh, *Observations on the Ministerial Plan of Reform* (London, 1831), 61. The alarm expressed by Charles Wetherell and Lord Beresford at the disproportionate increase in the Irish representation was reported to Grey by Princess Lieven on 29 Mar. 1831: *Correspondence of Princess Lieven and Earl Grey*, ii, 98.

was put off until after the second reading of the English bill, and the case for colonial representation began to be given more serious consideration. On 5 July Sir John Malcolm, Tory MP for Launceston and former governor of Bombay, expressed his hope that direct colonial representation might be established. Malcolm had recently returned from India, mainly to defend the interests of the East India Company during the discussions of the renewal of its charter. But he also proved a doughty opponent of the Reform Bill. He saw the Whigs' measure as rushed, and too capitulating towards the fluctuating fortunes of the populous manufacturing towns.[16] Viscount Althorp, the Whig leader in the Commons, replied to Malcolm's suggestion, recognizing his concern as 'one of the most plausible objections to the measure'.[17] In the middle of August, encouraged by Althorp's admission, Joseph Hume, the radical MP for Middlesex, brought forward an amendment to the Reform Bill. Hume proposed nineteen extra MPs for the colonies: four for British India, eight for the Crown Colonies, three each for British America and the West Indies, and one for the Channel Islands. These MPs would be chosen by an electorate composed of all those eligible for jury service, and they would sit in parliament for a guaranteed three years. Hume's motion earned the support of the marquis of Chandos (chairman of the West India Proprietors) and other planters' supporters, as well as various MPs in the India interest, such as Malcolm and Charles Forbes. Malcolm later proposed a modified bill in which Indian MPs might be elected by the holders of East India stock.[18] But Althorp resisted such a large change to the bill in committee, and Henry Labouchere argued that the whole problem of colonial representation might be solved by putting colonial agents 'upon an improved footing'.

Still the call for colonial representation did not die down. Malcolm kept up his campaign in the Commons and, along with Wellington, various peers expressed their fears for imperial interests as the bill went through a second reading in the Lords during October 1831.[19] From outside parliament, a number of schemes – ranging from 'parliamentary guilds' to seats set aside specially for India and the West Indies – were put forward for ensuring that the colonies, alongside

---

[16] J. Malcolm, *Letter on the State of Public Affairs* (London, 1831); cf. Brit. Lib., Oriental and India Office Collection [hereafter OIOC], Home Misc. 735, fos. 53–6, Malcolm to Charles Cockburn, 6 Aug. 1831. Later in the year he complained that 'if the Reform Bill passes in any shape like the last we shall be beat hollow. London, the outposts & Manufacturing Towns will dictate to Ministers. Radicals in England will unite with Radicals at the Presidencies': *ibid.*, fos. 144–6, Malcolm to Thomas Williamson [Oct. 1831]; cf. J. Malcolm, *The Government of India* (London, 1833), 275.

[17] *Parl. Debs.*, 3rd ser., iv, col. 788 (5 July 1831).

[18] *Ibid.*, vi, cols. 110–43 (16 Aug. 1831); vii, cols. 183–91 (19 Sept. 1831). Malcolm was 'much embarrassed' by Hume's motion in mid-August. He felt obliged to support it, but believed the scheme was 'ridiculous'. Interestingly, Malcolm's own scheme firmly excluded female holders of East Indian stock: Brit. Lib., OIOC, Home Misc. 735, fos. 61–6, Malcolm to Sir George Murray, 19 Aug. 1831.

[19] *Parl. Debs.*, 3rd ser., cols. 1165 (4 Oct. 1831, Harrowby), 1203 (Wellington).

other non-territorial propertied interests, were adequately represented.[20] The bill was defeated in the Lords in early October, and at the end of November the cabinet discussed various modifications that they were prepared to make before the bill went to the Commons for its second reading. Among them, the duke of Richmond urged colonial representation, but again the proposal was rejected by his colleagues as being too large and too late.[21] However, the cabinet did drop the plan to reduce the size of the Commons. The number of boroughs scheduled to lose one member was cut to thirty, and when the modified third Reform Bill came back into the Commons in December, Peel for one interpreted this as a capitulation to Gascoyne's insistence on not enlarging the Scottish and Irish representation at the expense of the English.[22]

What this sequence of events shows is how the Whigs' redistribution plans were chopped and changed during 1831 in order to accommodate the criticism that English and colonial interests were being sacrificed in order to placate Scottish and especially Irish demands for more seats. By the end of 1831 there was no more talk of down-sizing the House of Commons and to some extent anxieties over the end of the system of virtual representation were calmed. The campaign for direct representation of the colonies ceased, and when the bill finally came back to the Lords in April and May 1832, Tories such as Lord Ellenborough, president of the Board of Control in the Wellington adminis- tration, concentrated their firepower on scrapping all plans for single-member seats (i.e., cut out schedules B and D), with the aim of retaining a sufficient number of small two-member boroughs so that the colonies and other 'monied' interests might be represented indirectly.[23]

How credible was the Tory charge that the small boroughs allowed virtual rep- resentation of colonial interests? Was there anything to it, or was it simply a piece of political opportunism? Critics of the unreformed parliament certainly saw the 'borough-mongering' system as propping up sinister imperial influences. In 1826 the abolitionist James Stephen claimed that the English parliament was 'enslaved' by the nominees of colonial planters. Likewise John Wade's 1831 edition of his *Extraordinary Black Book* identified the East India Company (along with the Bank of England) as one of 'the outworks, the strongholds of the borough system'. And contemporary satirical prints often lampooned Indian

[20] Francis Palgrave, *Conciliatory Reform: A Letter Addressed to the Right Hon. Thomas Spring Rice MP . . . on the Means of Reconciling Parliamentary Reform to the Interests and Opinions . . . of the Community: Together with the Draft of a Bill, Founded on the Ministerial Bill, But Adapted More Closely to the Principles and Precedents of the Constitution* (London, 1831), 14–18; *Reform, Accompanied by the Repeal of Five Millions of Taxes* (London, 1831), 26.

[21] *The Holland House Diaries, 1831–40*, ed. A. D. Kriegel (London, 1977), 86, entry for 29 Nov. 1831.

[22] *Parl. Debs.*, 3rd ser., ix, cols. 174–5 (12 Dec. 1831).

[23] *Ibid.*, xii, cols. 33 (9 Apr. 1832), 1110–11 (21 May 1832); PRO, Ellenborough papers, 30/12/24/9, 'Plan of speech' (21 May 1832).

nabobs and Jamaican slave-owners as the typical products of a corrupt electoral system.[24] But whilst it was true that in the decade or so before 1832 around one-fifth of the House of Commons was made up of East India and West Indies MPs (peaking at a total of 114 in 1820), there was little correlation between these MPs and the small English boroughs. That is to say, MPs representing colonial interests were returned by all manner of borough constituencies: large and small, open and closed. Equally, as *The Times* pointed out when discussing Gascoyne's motion, venal MPs sat wherever an opportunity arose, and were just as likely to sit for a closed Irish or Scottish borough as look after imperial interests by seeking out an English one.[25] Moreover, as the work of Cyril Philips and Barry Higman demonstrated many years ago, the East and West India interests were not monolithic blocs. Some colonial MPs supported the Reform Bill, and some were opposed.[26] The case made for the unreformed electoral system, in the shape of the small boroughs, virtually representing the empire was thus largely hypothetical. However, that does not mean that the Tory fear that a reformed parliament would sacrifice colonial interests, unless safeguards such as the small boroughs were retained, was not valid. In the Whig administration of the second Earl Grey, many Tories perceived a party being driven to the dismemberment of empire. And there were good grounds for such a view. Committed to retrenchment, reliant on the goodwill of the Irish Repeal movement led by Daniel O'Connell, and facing an electorate hungry for slave emancipation and the end of colonial trade monopolies, after 1830 the Whigs were increasingly forced to consider the imperial issues pressing on their domestic policies.

II

The first of these was retrenchment. The duke of Wellington's administration was toppled over this issue in November 1830, having since the beginning of the year withstood a series of Whig and radical calls for reductions in the estimates, public salaries, and the civil list. Although keen to trim the civil list, the duke had been unable to heed the call for retrenchment with quite the same enthusiasm as William Huskisson and Viscount Goderich. He proved particularly reluctant

---

[24] James Stephen, *England Enslaved by her own Slave Colonies: An Address to the Electors and People of the United Kingdom* (London, 1826); cf. [T. P. Thompson], 'Slavery in the West Indies', *Westminster Rev.*, 11 (1829), 277–8; John Wade, *The Extraordinary Black Book* (London, 1831), 350; M. Dorothy George (ed.), *Catalogue of Political and Personal Satires Preserved in the Department of Prints and Drawings in the British Museum*, 11 vols. (London, 1935–54), x, no. 15,421, xi, nos. 16,207, 16,610.

[25] Far from being custodians of imperial interests, nomination boroughs were 'un-national', the paper argued: 'Every close borough . . . might be considered as an extraneous power, throwing foreign goods into the magazines of the constitution': *The Times*, 13 May 1831, 2.

[26] C. H. Philips, *The East India Company, 1784–1834* (Manchester, 1940), 285; B. W. Higman, 'The West India Interest in Parliament', *Hist. Studies (Australia and New Zealand)*, 13 (1967), 1–19; Gerrit P. Judd, *Members of Parliament, 1734–1832* (New Haven, 1955), 63–9, 92–4.

to reduce the size of the army, fearing for the security of the empire and also, by 1830, wanting to keep military options open in the Mediterranean and in Europe generally as events in France, Portugal, and Belgium threatened the continental balance of power.[27] And although what proved to be the final budget of his administration in February 1830 did include further tariff revision, such as the repeal of the duty on gin, radical critics saw this as a false economy brought on by over-commitment to empire. For example, William Cobbett thought that cutting the gin duty only had the effect of helping domestic merchants at the expense of colonial rum producers, who also wanted similar special treatment. Indeed, anti-imperial rhetoric proved an important component of Cobbett's attack on 'Old Corruption'. Really meaningful tax cuts such as dropping the duty on malt, he argued, required the administration to give up its fixation with bearing the costs of overseas dominion. And as he continued his lecture tour through the rural eastern and southern counties of England during the spring of 1830, Cobbett also savaged the emigration schemes of Wellington's colonial secretary, Wilmot Horton, urging labourers to ignore state-assisted passage to the 'barren parts of empire' such as Canada, and, if they must leave, to head for America instead.[28] Criticism of the expense of empire, in other words, was an important component part of the agitation arising from rural distress on the eve of Wellington's fall.

Coming into office in 1830, the Whigs took up the stalled programme of retrenchment, with colonial retrenchment high on their list. 'There is no part of the public expenditure which admits of reformation more than that which is incurred upon the Colonies', suggested Sir Henry Parnell in his influential tract entitled *On Financial Reform* (1830).[29] Parnell, who had sat in Grattan's Irish parliament before the Union and who had been a prominent supporter of Catholic Emancipation since the days of Charles James Fox, had moved the amendment on the civil list which brought down Wellington's administration in November 1830. By 1832 his tract had gone into its fourth edition and had been the subject of various angry ripostes. What did this guru of Whig economy have to say about colonial retrenchment? Parnell proposed extensive reduction in indirect tax to the point that duties would yield revenue only rather than provide protection. Thus, he advocated a 12 per cent reduction on most

[27] *Despatches . . . of the Duke of Wellington*, iv, 106–18, Wellington to Goderich, 25 Aug. 1827; vii, 226, Wellington to Sir John Malcolm, 1 Sept. 1830; Peter Jupp, *British Politics on the Eve of Reform: The Duke of Wellington's Administration, 1828–30* (London, 1999), 20–2; Peter Jupp, 'The Foreign Policy of Wellington's Government, 1828–30', in C. M. Woolgar (ed.), *Wellington Studies*, 3 (1999), 152–83; Philip Harling, *The Waning of 'Old Corruption': The Politics of Economical Reform in Britain, 1779–1846* (Oxford, 1996), 212–16.

[28] *Cobbett's Political Register*, 13 Mar. 1830, 320–34, 339–49; 20 Mar. 1830, 352–79; 12 Mar. 1831, 659. For the importance of the call for retrenchment to rural agitation in 1829–30, see Roger Wells, 'Mr. William Cobbett, Captain Swing and William IV', *Agric. Hist. Rev.*, 45 (1997), 34–48.

[29] Henry Parnell, *On Financial Reform* (London, 1830), 231.

tariffs, complete abolition of the sugar duties, and a greater equalization of tariffs such as corn and timber, whereby the British and Canadian producer was protected against the European. Parnell also thought £4 million could be saved by reductions in colonial military expenditure – principally by making the colonies pay for their own defence – and he claimed that another £2.5 million could be saved by removing colonial preference and by reducing the charges of colonial government borne by the British taxpayer.[30] *On Financial Reform*, in other words, amounted to a radical assault on the costs of empire, as far-reaching as anything proposed by the more famous Benthamite colonial reformers after 1832, or by Richard Cobden at mid-century. What made Parnell's radicalism all the more dangerous, in Tory eyes, was that when Althorp introduced the first Whig budget in the Commons in February 1831 he declared at the outset that his views and principles were taken from Parnell's tract. Moreover, in March Parnell himself joined the cabinet as secretary of war, replacing Charles Wynn, who had resigned over the Reform Bill.[31] Among other recommendations the Whig budget proposed lowering the duties on Baltic timber, thus exposing the Canadian trade to greater competition, and also revising the sugar duties, much to the concern of East India merchants. Althorp hoped to delay most of these measures until after the second reading of the Reform Bill, but opposition pressure forced him to bring forward the Canadian Timber Duties Bill with modifications.[32] At the same time, the Lower Canadian assembly was assigned control over its revenue, but not over the civil list, which remained fixed by the imperial parliament. This uneven approach to the financial autonomy of Lower Canada fuelled resentment in the colony, especially against the English residents who dominated the legislative council and the civil establishment. An assembly by-election in Montreal in 1832 was dominated by the civil-list question, and several people were killed in subsequent riots.[33] The episode of the 1831 budget proved instructive to Tory critics such as Archibald Alison. With a reformed parliament returned by £10 householders, they concluded, colonial monopolies would be scythed at the earliest opportunity.[34] The Whigs,

---

[30] *Ibid.*, ch. 15.

[31] *Parl. Debs.*, 3rd ser., ii, col. 407 (11 Feb. 1831, Althorp); University of Southampton, Congleton MSS, MS 64/29, 'Notebook on Financial Reform', pp. 71–4, Parnell, record of conversation with Althorp (Nov. 1830); E. A. Wasson, *Whig Renaissance: Lord Althorp and the Whig Party, 1782–1845* (London, 1987), 188–9, 198. Parnell's appointment alarmed the king: *The Correspondence of the Late Earl Grey with His Majesty the King, and with Sir Herbert Taylor*, ed. Henry, Earl Grey, 2 vols. (London, 1867), i, 150–2, William IV to Earl Grey, 7 Mar. 1831.

[32] *Parl. Debs.*, 3rd ser., iii, cols. 540–9 (18 Feb. 1831).

[33] Helen Taft-Manning, *The Revolt of French Canada, 1800–35: A Chapter in the History of the British Commonwealth* (London, 1962), 340–54; Philip Goldring, 'Province and Nation: Problems of Imperial Rule in Lower Canada, 1820–1841', *Jl Imperial and Commonwealth Hist.*, 9 (1980), 38–56.

[34] [Archibald Alison], 'On Parliamentary Reform and the French Revolution: Consequences of Reform (no. IX)', *Blackwood's Edinburgh Mag.*, 30 (1831), 446–7; cf. *The Advantages of Reform, As Proposed by the Present Ministers* (London, 1831), 13–14.

too, learned a lesson from these skirmishes so early in the session. Without parliamentary reform, they were unlikely to make much progress with colonial retrenchment.

III

Ireland was a second imperial factor that the Whigs were forced to include in their equations on parliamentary reform. The Irish Reform Bill, which proposed five new seats, a £10 household suffrage in the boroughs and an extension of the franchise to certain leaseholders in the counties, is often treated as a natural extension of the English Reform Bill, framed on the same principles, but having different effects owing to the much lower value of property across the Irish Sea.[35] But what needs to be emphasized is that the Irish Reform Bill was as much an attempt to keep Ireland within the Union as a corollary of parliamentary reform on the mainland. Daniel O'Connell opened the new year of 1830 by declaring that he now advocated complete repeal of the Union. In April the Society of the Friends of Ireland of All Religious Persuasions was formed with repeal, alongside extensive tax relief, as one of its main objectives; in October, taking his cue from the summer revolt of Catholic Belgium from the protestant Dutch, O'Connell commenced an intense campaign of meetings and public breakfasts in support of repeal.[36] As agrarian distress set in across south-eastern Ireland towards the end of 1830, O'Connell advocated non-payment of tithes, as well as a run on the banks. With arrears building up quickly, the new Whig administration sent in police to enforce collection. In January 1831, O'Connell was arrested on charges of conspiracy, seditious libel, and unlawful assembly.[37] This was the backdrop against which the cabinet considered the Irish component of parliamentary reform. The support of O'Connell's party in the Commons, its numbers boosted in the 1830 general election, was required in order to carry the Reform Bill. But at the same time the cabinet were wary of giving fuel to the Repeal campaign by making extensive changes in the Irish franchise, especially the county franchise in which many of O'Connell's supporters hoped for a significant reduction, or even a restoration of the 40-shilling freehold voters who had been swept away in the Catholic Relief Act of 1829.

---

[35] K. Theodore Hoppen, *Elections, Politics and Society in Ireland, 1832–1885* (Oxford, 1984), 1–6; A. D. Kriegel, 'The Irish Policy of Lord Grey's Government', *Eng. Hist. Rev.*, 86 (1971), 22–45.

[36] Angus MacIntyre, *The Liberator: Daniel O'Connell and the Irish Party, 1830–1847* (London, 1965), 13–14; Oliver MacDonagh, *The Emancipist: Daniel O'Connell, 1830–47* (London, 1989), 34–5.

[37] MacIntyre, *Liberator*, 23; M. Tierney, 'The Tithe War in Munroe, 1831–8', *Irish Eccles. Record*, 5th ser., 103 (1965), 209–21; Stanley Palmer, *Police and Protest in England and Ireland, 1780–1850* (Cambridge, 1988), 322–31; Marquess of Anglesey, *One Leg: The Life and Letters of H. W. Paget, First Marquess of Anglesey (1768–1854)* (London, 1963), 247–8.

Throughout 1831 the Whig government therefore moved cautiously in its dealing with O'Connell in particular and with Ireland in general. Anxious to win over his party's votes for the Reform Bill, the Whigs postponed, then dropped, their prosecution of O'Connell in May, having intimated as much to him in February before the crucial vote on the second reading of the Reform Bill.[38] At the same time Lord Brougham smoothed over the concerns of both the cabinet and the king that dissolving parliament in April and holding a general election was likely to plunge Ireland into complete disorder. Despite the spread of the anti-tithe agitation through the rest of the southern counties and up into Ulster by the end of 1831, both Edward Stanley, the Irish secretary, and the marquess of Anglesey, the lord lieutenant of Ireland, resisted the introduction of more coercive public order legislation, fearful of O'Connell using it as a weapon against the Whigs.[39] In the autumn, O'Connell himself, with Henry Parnell as an enthusiastic cabinet intermediary, was considered for a peerage or even (Parnell's aspiration) a place in the administration.[40] The Whigs also made concessions over the Irish county franchise, lowering the leasehold requirement from £50 to £10 per annum, although they did resist the demand for more seats. However, whilst the schedules of English disfranchisement remained fluid, as they did until December 1831 when the cabinet finally settled on keeping the size of the Commons at 658 seats, Irish hopes (and Tory fears) of extra redistribution of MPs to Ireland remained high.[41] By the summer of 1832, with all three reform acts safely through parliament, the Whigs could remove the gloves on their Irish policy. More troops and police were sent over and the Whiteboy Act of 1797 was dusted down and enforced, resulting in a wave of arrests and prosecutions.[42] Thus, only by careful manoeuvring, and by playing a game of cat-and-mouse with O'Connell, did the Whigs prevent the Repeal agitation from undermining their plans for parliamentary reform.

IV

Two other imperial issues accompanied the contest for parliamentary reform during the early 1830s: the abolition of slavery and the renewal of the East India Company's charter. Historians have often observed that popular opinion

---

[38] *The Correspondence of Daniel O'Connell*, ed. M. R. O'Connell, 8 vols. (Dublin, 1972–80), iv, 271–2, O'Connell to Francis Blackburne, 11 Feb. 1831; MacIntyre, *Liberator*, 24; Howell-Thomas, *Duncannon*, 146–8.

[39] V. Crossman, 'Emergency Legislation and Agrarian Disorder in Ireland, 1821–41', *Irish Hist. Studies*, 27 (1991), 317–19.

[40] University of Southampton, Congleton MSS, MS 64/34/2, 'Mem. of a Conversation with Lord Anglesey' (7 Oct. 1831), Parnell to Brougham, 23 Sept. 1831 [copy].

[41] *Correspondence of the Late Earl Grey*, ii, 27–8, Earl Grey to Sir Herbert Taylor, 14 Dec. 1831.

[42] Palmer, *Police and Protest*, 322–31; P. O'Donoghue, 'Opposition to Tithe Payment, 1832–3', *Studia Hibernica*, 12 (1972), 76–108.

on parliamentary reform was fairly muted until 1831, when the resistance of the Lords and the ultra-Tories became too oppressive for the English public to bear any longer. By contrast, popular support for the abolition of slavery in the British empire reached unprecedented levels in the late 1820s and early 1830s, whilst the campaign to open up the East India Company's monopoly of the China trade was one of the initial stimuli in mobilizing manufacturing opinion in favour of parliamentary reform in the ports and especially in the cotton districts of the north-west from 1829 onwards.

In addition to being the party of reform and retrenchment the Whigs entered office at the end of 1830 as committed supporters of the abolition of slavery, especially Grey, Brougham, and the new colonial secretary, Viscount Goderich. Although it had been Lord Liverpool's government back in 1823 which had passed Orders in Council requiring West Indian legislatures to ameliorate the conditions of slave labour, subsequent Tory administrations, and even some of the new Whig ministers, were reluctant to force the issue.[43] At the general elections of 1830 and 1831 the Anti-Slavery Society, with remarkably modern electioneering tactics, targeted a number of key constituencies, grilling candidates on their antislavery credentials and helping in the return of many new MPs pledged to support the abolitionist cause in conjunction with the reform of parliament. The success of Brougham and Lord Morpeth in the West Riding of Yorkshire in the 1830 general election, and the strong showing of antislavery candidates in ports such as Bristol, were taken by some as proof of the waning electoral influence of colonial monopolies.[44] Antislavery feeling was to the fore in the most infamous example of disorder during the passage of the Reform Bill: the Bristol riots at the end of October 1831, which were sparked off by the visit of Sir Charles Wetherell, the city's Recorder and a leading ultra-Tory MP, who had played his part in the opposition to the second Reform Bill earlier in the month. Local Tories blamed the riots, in part, on the mood whipped up by antislavery lectures, and 'their choice of language': that is, 'careless use of the terms, liberty and slavery', such that the great merchants of the port stood accused of 'collecting their revenue by the whip and slave driver'. For their part,

---

[43] A. D. Kriegel, 'A Convergence of Ethics: Saints and Whigs in British Anti-Slavery', *Jl Brit. Studies*, 26 (1987), 423–50; Ian Newbould, *Whiggery and Reform, 1830–41: The Politics of Government* (London, 1990), 113–15.

[44] *Anti-Slavery Reporter*, 1 Aug. 1830, 361–8; *The Times*, 30 July 1830, 2; 7 Aug. 1830, 2; Seymour Drescher, 'Public Opinion and the Destruction of British Colonial Slavery', in James Walvin (ed.), *Slavery and British Society, 1776–1846* (London, 1982), 22–48; David Turley, *The Culture of English Anti-Slavery, 1780–1860* (London, 1991), 39–43. Yorkshire elections remained dominated by imperial issues. Invited in 1831 by the Leeds Association to contest their new borough, Thomas Babington Macaulay declared his political principles to be fourfold: opposition to colonial slavery, reform of the civil and criminal law, opposition to the monopolies suffered by the great towns (corn and the India trade), and Irish reform: *The Letters of Thomas Babington Macaulay*, ed. Thomas Pinney, 6 vols. (Cambridge, 1974), ii, 103–4: 'To the Leeds Association' (5 Oct. 1831).

local radicals retorted that the attempt of West India shipowners to assemble a bodyguard of their seamen for Wetherell fuelled local resentment of the closed colonial trade and the monopoly of the city corporation over shipping dues (the Corporation Docks were singled out for attack during the riots).[45]

As the Reform Bill debates in parliament reached their climax during the spring and summer of 1832, antislavery pressure from without continued to grow. In 1831 the Whig government took a firmer line with the West Indian assemblies, reiterating the 1823 Order and also passing a new Order in Council curbing the right of planters to inflict punishment on their slaves. In Jamaica the Whigs' new stance raised hopes of immediate emancipation, and despite the government denying this, the mood of expectation intensified, stoked up by Baptist missionaries, culminating in an insurrection of slave labourers in Jamaica in November 1831. Martial law was declared and the rising was put down with violent recrimination by the island authorities: 312 were executed.[46] The effects of the rising back in Britain were twofold. It brought fresh waves of support for the abolitionist movement, and turned parliamentary opinion further against the planter interest. In April 1832, as the Commons waited for the Lords to debate the third Reform Bill, the West India proprietors on one side and the Anti-Slavery Society on the other gathered in London and petitioned parliament over emancipation.[47] Earl Grey's government was caught in the middle, reluctant to interfere with the property rights of the Caribbean planters, but equally mindful of the need to conciliate supporters inside and outside parliament during the final throes of the struggle with the Lords. William IV made clear his sympathy lay with the planters, whilst Thomas Fowell Buxton was adamant he would not compromise over his intention to bring forward his abolition motion before the Reform Bill was passed.[48] When the Reform Bill was finally passed, the Jamaican assembly still refused to cooperate with the Orders in Council, arguing that now that they were effectively unrepresented in England, as the small boroughs had been disfranchised, they could not obey the requests of the governor, Lord Mulgrave, the crown's representative. Mulgrave dissolved the assembly, leaving the cabinet back at home fearing further insurrection.[49] It was largely in response to the lobbying of West Indies MPs, together with the possibility of further social and economic unrest in the Caribbean, that the Whigs

---

[45] [John Eagles], *The Bristol Riots, their Causes, Progress and Consequences* (Bristol, 1832), 6–7; W. H. Somerton, *A Narrative of the Bristol Riots, on the 29th, 30th and 31st of October, 1831, etc* (Bristol, 1831), 7; Susan Thomas, *The Bristol Riots* (Bristol, 1974), 17, 21.

[46] Mary Reckord, 'The Jamaica Slave Rebellion of 1831', *Past and Present*, no. 40 (July 1968), 108–25.

[47] *The Times*, 14 May 1832, 6; 26 May 1832, 4.

[48] *Correspondence of the Late Earl Grey*, ii, 243–5, William IV to Grey, 4 Mar. 1832; Charles Buxton (ed.), *Memoirs of Sir Thomas Fowell Buxton, Bt, with Selections from his Correspondence* (London, 1848), 288–92, Buxton to Althorp, 22 May 1832.

[49] W. D. Jones, 'Lord Mulgrave's Administration in Jamaica, 1832–3', *Jl Negro Hist.*, 48 (1963), 44–56.

agreed to a massive compensation of the planter interest when the emancipation and apprenticeship scheme was passed in parliament in 1833.[50]

In a similar way the campaign against the renewal of the East India Company charter in the early 1830s served to stimulate the wider cause of parliamentary reform. By the late 1820s the East India Company was suffering from both declining profits in trade, partly as a result of the commercial collapse of 1825–6, and the consequences of military overstretch in several of the principalities it had acquired since the French Wars. In 1828 Peel warned Wellington that the Company was not far from insolvency.[51] William Bentinck, appointed governor of Bengal in 1827, began the process of retrenchment in the civil and military administration, as did Sir John Malcolm, the governor of Bombay.[52] But relations between the Company and the judiciary in India remained strained, and increasing resentment was felt by British merchants and manufacturers at the monopoly enjoyed by the Company over trade with China. So when James Silk Buckingham, dubbed 'the Indian Cobbett', commenced a series of lectures in 1829, ostensibly on his travels and experiences in India, but in reality against the renewal of the Company's charter, he found considerable support in the manufacturing centres of the north-west for his call for the throwing open of the Chinese trade. In Liverpool an East India Association was set up, and in the elections of 1830 and 1831 free-trade candidates supporting the break-up of the Company monopoly and retrenchment in Indian expenditure, in conjunction with parliamentary reform, were returned by many large boroughs.[53] As with the antislavery campaign, the agitation against the East India Company threw parliamentary reform into a much sharper relief.

V

The contention of this chapter is that imperial interests were of fundamental concern to both the supporters and opponents of parliamentary reform in 1830–3. The widespread call for retrenchment, the campaign to abolish slavery, and

---

[50] Izhak Gross, 'The Abolition of Negro Slavery and British Parliamentary Politics, 1832–3', *Hist. Jl*, 23 (1980), 63–85; R. B. Sheridan, 'The West Indies Sugar Crisis and Slave Emancipation, 1830–3', *Jl Econ. Hist.*, 21 (1961), 539–51.

[51] *Despatches of the Duke of Wellington*, iv, 632, Peel to Wellington, 18 Aug. 1828; Douglas M. Peers, *Between Mars and Mammon: Colonial Armies and the Garrison State in India, 1819–35* (London, 1995), chs. 7–8.

[52] J. C. Joshi, *Lord William Bentinck: His Economic, Administrative, Social and Educational Reforms* (New Delhi, 1988), ch. 3; Rodney Pasley, *'Send Malcolm!': The Life of Major-General Sir John Malcolm, 1769–1833* (London, 1982), 138–9.

[53] Ralph E. Turner, *James Silk Buckingham, 1786–1855: A Social Biography* (London, 1934), 238–45; D. Eyles, 'The Abolition of the East India Company's Monopoly, 1833' (University of Edinburgh Ph.D. thesis, 1956), 144–8, 215. See also Miles Taylor, 'Joseph Hume and the Reformation of India, 1819–33', in G. Burgess and M. Festenstein (eds.), *Radicalism in England, 1550–1850* (Cambridge, forthcoming).

the agitation against the East India Company all helped mobilize public support for parliamentary reform. In turn, when the Whigs' parliamentary reform plans were announced, the Tory opposition voiced their concern for the Union and for the empire, a concern registered in their reluctance to reduce the number of English constituencies, and in the refrain heard throughout the early reform debates in favour of direct colonial representation as a substitute for the virtual representation of the empire which had been provided under the unreformed system. When that scheme failed, opponents of reform – most notably the 'waverers' associated with Ellenborough and Wharncliffe – attempted to reapportion the schedules of the bill so as to enfranchise non-territorial interests, including colonial interests, rather than simply concede everything to the principle of disfranchisement. The bill that finally took shape in 1832 bore the imprint of these criticisms. Historians have sometimes attributed the bill's modifications to a landed elite's desire to preserve their influence in the rural areas and cordon off the power of the towns.[54] But it is worth noting just how many features of the final Reform Act – the Chandos clause, the retention of a large number of double-member constituencies, and pegging the size of the Commons at 658 seats – were the result of pressure from the colonial lobby as much as the landed interest.

Committed to parliamentary reform for the British mainland, the Whigs had thus to steer a course between vested imperial interests abroad. In the end they won out. As the diarist Thomas Creevey observed in June 1832, 'the battle of Earl Grey and the English nation for the Reform Bill'[55] had been won, but, he might have added, at some cost to the integrity of the empire, and the unity of the Whig cabinet. No less than £20 million (half the annual UK revenue) would be paid in 1833 in compensation to the West Indies; £2 million was set aside to fund the transfer of East India Company property to the crown; £1 million was given to the holders of Irish tithes; and in addition there were incremental increases in the military and naval estimates as British forces were redirected and reconstituted to deal with unrest in the West Indies and in Ireland.[56] Within months of the Reform Bill the voices of military retrenchment in the Whig cabinet, such as John Cam Hobhouse, were silenced, and cracks appeared within the hitherto united front on Ireland, when Edward Ellice, James Graham, Lord Holland, and Lord Stanley all resigned their posts in 1833 over

---

[54] E.g., D. C. Moore, *The Politics of Deference: A Study of the Mid-Nineteenth Century English Political System* (Hassocks, 1976).

[55] *The Creevey Papers: A Selection from the Correspondence and Diaries of the Late Thomas Creevey, MP*, ed. H. Maxwell, 2 vols. (London, 1903), ii, 247, Thomas Creevey to Miss Ord, 5 June 1832.

[56] On Whig budgetary problems in the longer term, see Harling, *Waning of 'Old Corruption'*, 216–27.

the issue of further reform of the Church of Ireland.[57] And the empire itself was not bought off for long. In the longer term the reform crisis in Britain fuelled the patriot movement in Lower Canada, tripled the Irish nationalist presence at Westminster, and quickened the pace of military retrenchment in the Caribbean and in India, at the behest of penny-pinching urban voters at home. By 1837–8, with mutiny in Jamaica, rebellions in Upper and Lower Canada, war on the north-west frontier of India, and Irishmen at the head of the Chartist movement at home, it was clear that while stability might have been brought to the British mainland by the Reform Act, in the empire it was a rather different story.

[57] For difficulties over military retrenchment, see Lord Broughton, *Recollections of a Long Life*, ed. Lady Dorchester, 4 vols. (London, 1910), iv, 266–70; for the Irish church, see Richard Brent, *Liberal Anglican Politics: Whiggery, Religion and Reform, 1830–41* (Oxford, 1987), ch. 2.

14. *Reforms, movements for reform, and possibilities of reform: comparing Britain and continental Europe*

JONATHAN SPERBER

A comparison of the 'age of reform' in the British Isles with developments in continental Europe might start simply by considering what there is to compare. In the years 1780–1850, there were three broad periods of reform in different parts of the continent. First was the decade of the 1780s, the concluding phase of the reforms of Enlightened Absolutism. Following that were the reforms occurring in Napoleonic Europe at the beginning of the nineteenth century. Some were undertaken under French hegemony, as was the case among Napoleon's allies and satellites in Germany and Italy, while others were carried out in opposition to French hegemony, as in Prussia, insurgent Spain, or – more cautiously and ultimately abortively – in Russia. This reform period extended, more weakly and feebly, in the years following Napoleon's downfall until the full victory of the forces of the Restoration at the beginning of the 1820s. Finally, we can point to a period of incipient and also ultimately abortive reform in the 1840s, preceding the revolution of 1848.

Mentioning the 1848 revolution brings up the major problem of a comparison between Great Britain and the states of the European continent in this period: the question of legal and constitutional continuity. It is not just that it was frequently possible to change and ameliorate social, economic, or political conditions in the British Isles without any such break in legal continuity. Rather, the idea of amelioration through gradual change emerged as the alternative to political rupture and disjunction; reform was the – preferable – alternative to revolution. By contrast, in continental Europe even modest measures of political, social, and economic amelioration often required drastic and violent forms of political discontinuity. Reform was possible only as revolution. Thus while the main focus of this comparison will be on the three periods of reform, it is impossible not to mention the major waves of revolution in this context: particularly those of 1789–95 and 1848–51, but the 1830 revolution and its aftermath as well. The comparison will have three main focuses: the goals of reform; the agents and agencies of reform; and the conceptualization of, opposition to, and possibilities for reform. Without now getting into the details of the argument, I would suggest at the outset that overall the goals of reform movements in the British Isles and in continental Europe were more different than similar – indeed, often diametrically opposed. While there was some overlap in agents and agencies of reform, these also tended to be different in crucial ways. Finally, opposition to reform was less significant in Britain and Ireland than on the continent, and prospects for its success – especially without the intervention of violent disruptions of legal continuity through revolution or military conquest – were much greater. The differences seem greatest in the first decades under consideration, and a certain tendency towards convergence between developments in the British Isles and on the continent can be observed after about 1830. The fundamental impression nevertheless remains of two quite different political universes.

I

We begin with goals of reform. Probably the major issue of socio-economic (and, indirectly, political) amelioration in continental Europe during the years 1780–1850 was the emancipation of agriculture from the restrictions placed upon it: the liberation of the land, the people who worked it, and the results of their labour, from the many servitudes that weighed on them.[1] Not just a major issue in itself, it was also central to broader reform projects. This was very much the case with the Enlightened reformers of the 1770s and 1780s. Turgot's attempt to free the grain trade in France, and Joseph II's efforts first to regulate and to ameliorate and then finally to abolish serfdom in his realm are the two best-known instances, but Spanish reformers also freed the grain trade, and the abolition of serfdom was a crucial issue for Enlightened Absolutism in Denmark.[2] The Great Fear and the Night of 4 August were characteristic features of 1789, and the idea of abolishing feudal and seigneurial relations spread throughout the continent in the wake of the revolutionary armies. Less drastic, and generally less successful attempts to end feudal and seigneurial conditions in agriculture characterized the reign of Napoleon's allies and satellites in central and southern Europe.[3]

---

[1] Still a very useful general overview is Jerome Blum, *The End of the Old Order in Rural Europe* (Princeton, 1978).

[2] On the agrarian reforms in France, see Steven L. Kaplan, *Bread, Politics and Political Economy in the Reign of Louis XV*, 2 vols. (The Hague, 1976); Cynthia A. Bouton, *The Flour War: Gender, Class, and Community in Late Ancien Régime French Society* (University Park, Pa., 1993); for Austria, P. G. M. Dickson, 'Joseph II's Hungarian Land Survey', *Eng. Hist. Rev.*, 106 (1991), 611–34. More generally, on the reforms of Enlightened Absolutism, see H. M. Scott (ed.), *Enlightened Absolutism: Reform and Reformers in Later Eighteenth-Century Europe* (Ann Arbor, 1990), esp. essays on the Habsburg monarchy, Spain, and Denmark.

[3] John Markoff, *The Abolition of Feudalism: Peasants, Lords and Legislators in the French Revolution* (University Park, Pa., 1996); Michael Broers, *Europe under Napoleon, 1799–1815* (London, 1996), 86–95.

The emancipation of the peasantry was no less significant for anti-Napoleonic reform efforts of the period. The great Prussian reforms began with Baron Karl vom Stein's liberation of the peasantry and concluded with Karl August vom Hardenberg setting the terms of compensation for the nobility's loss of serf labour and feudal dues. The insurgent government in Spain abolished feudalism, the first of three such abolitions in the course of thirty years. An end to serfdom was a crucial issue in the proposals for reform brought forth both by the government of Alexander I in Russia, and by the revolutionary opposition to the Tsar.[4]

Particularly in the central and eastern portions of the continent, the issue retained its importance in the decades after 1820. Both the implementation of existing programmes for the liberation of rural society from its pre-capitalist restraints and the creation of new ones, however, would prove unsuccessful. (The one exception was the third and final abolition of seigneurialism in Spain, carried out in 1837 by the Mendizábal government in the midst of a civil war.) In the end, it would take the 1848 revolutions to end serfdom and seigneurialism in the Austrian empire, and in those portions of the German states where they still existed, and defeat in the Crimean War to achieve the same end in the realm of the Tsar.[5]

Agricultural servitudes were already much less prevalent in eighteenth-century Britain and Ireland, although remnants of them were eliminated by such measures as the end of price controls on grain, the division of the commons and, especially, the Highland clearances in Scotland.[6] Very much unlike circumstances in continental Europe, ending agricultural servitudes was a project of enemies of political reform: the great landlords of Highland Scotland, or the unreformed parliaments that passed enclosure acts. Supporters of more radical forms of political reform were more likely to be opponents of these sorts of measures.

Agrarian and political reform did go together in one of the lesser causes of the reform era, the abolition of tithes. After decades of both liberal and radical reformers demanding an end to tithes, they were finally commuted by a Whig

---

[4] On the Prussian agrarian reforms, the most detailed study is Hanna Schlissler, *Preußische Agrargesellschaft im Wandel* (Göttingen, 1978); a brief English-language summary in James Sheehan, *German History, 1770–1866* (Oxford, 1989), 299–301, 475–6. For Spain, see Raymond Carr, *Spain, 1808–1975*, 2nd edn (Oxford, 1975), 99–101; on reform projects in Russia, David Saunders, *Russia in the Age of Reaction and Reform, 1801–1881* (London and New York, 1992), 20, 23–5, 64, 67, 81–2, 100–1, 106, 109.

[5] A study in the unsuccessful implementation of agrarian reforms is Wolfgang Hippel, *Die Bauernbefreiung im Königreich Württemberg*, 2 vols. (Boppard, 1977). For the final abolition of seigneurialism in Spain, see Carr, *Spain*, 172, 175–6.

[6] T. M. Divine, *Clanship to Crofters' War: The Social Transformation of the Scottish Highlands* (Manchester, 1994), chs. 3–5; J. M. Neeson, *Commoners: Common Right, Enclosure and Social Change in England, 1700–1820* (Cambridge, 1993).

government in 1836.[7] Although an explicit programme of land reform became a central demand of Irish nationalists only after the mid-nineteenth century, landownership was developing as an issue of Irish politics in the 1840s. One aspect of the Irish land question, espoused primarily by English reformers, did involve a continental-style abolition of servitudes, namely the call for an end to entail and other hindrances to a free market in landed property, eventually realized in the passage of the Encumbered Estates Act by parliament in 1849. By contrast, land-reform plans of Irish nationalists calling for legal guarantees of tenants' security of tenure, or for the redistribution of landed property, implied an interference in the workings of the free land market.[8]

There was a large-scale reform initiative for the abolition of coerced agricultural labour in the British empire: the movement for the abolition of the slave-trade and of slavery. It was arguably the most massive, popular, and broadly supported of all reform measures, endorsed by many individuals who were enemies of other reforms.[9] It is difficult to see the demand for the abolition of slavery as having the same central importance to British and Irish society and to efforts at political or socio-economic reform in the British Isles as the efforts to end serfdom and seigneurialism on the continent. Serfs and peasants bearing seigneurial obligations were generally the great majority of the pre-reform society in continental Europe, but slaves had no such position, obviously not in the British Isles themselves, but not in the empire either. For all the importance of the empire or the sugar trade, the 770,000 slaves in the West Indies did not have the same place in British society as the 90 per cent of the Tsar's seventy million subjects who were serfs.

The main focus of efforts at political amelioration in continental Europe during the period under consideration was the creation of a unified and uniform governmental structure, by overriding or abolishing *ancien régime* chartered rights and privileges and by devising a system of subjects, or citizens, with equal legal rights. Once again, we can point to classic eighteenth-century reform projects such as Joseph II's attempt to create a unified code of law and system of administration, complete with the necessary territorial realignments, in the Habsburgs' chequerboard realm, the chronically futile efforts to abolish tax exemptions and fiscal privilege in the French *ancien régime*, or the Prussian General Code of 1794.[10]

---

[7] Eric J. Evans, *The Contentious Tithe: The Tithe Problem and English Agriculture, 1750–1850* (London, 1976).

[8] Peter Gray, *Famine, Land and Politics: British Government and Irish Society, 1843–1850* (Dublin, 1999), ch. 4, *passim*.

[9] See, e.g., J. R. Oldfield, *Popular Politics and British Anti-Slavery: The Mobilisation of Public Opinion against the Slave Trade, 1787–1807* (Manchester, 1995); David Turley, *The Culture of English Anti-Slavery, 1780–1860* (London, 1991).

[10] For recent studies of the question of taxation in the reform projects of French Enlightened Absolutism, see Gail Bossenga, *The Politics of Privilege: Old Regime and Revolution*
(cont. on p. 316)

Both national administrative uniformity and legal equality were central themes of the French Revolution. Efforts in the same direction, via the introduction of the Napoleonic Code and of a centralized bureaucratic administration, were characteristic features of governments in Napoleonic Europe. Although the Prussian reforms began with Stein's plans for administrative decentralization, and his neo-corporate attitudes towards legal equality, they ended up with Hardenberg, a vociferous centralizer, an enemy of corporate social or political schemes, and a statesman who kept close tabs on developments in the German states under Napoleon's influence.[11]

After 1815, political reform continued to involve the advocacy of uniformity and legal equality, although sometimes in different ways from the eighteenth century. Nationalists strove for the merger of the heterogeneous and loosely knit Italian and German states into united realms with common constitutions and legal systems. Another emerging political issue of the post-1815 period was the granting of rights to members of minority religious confessions, particularly to the Jews, but to members of minority Christian confessions as well.

In this respect, the comparison with reform aspirations in Great Britain is rather more mixed than is the case with the agrarian question. The creation of standardized suffrage qualifications in the Reform Act of 1832, and in the Municipal Reform Act, three years later, and their abolition of the many different, localized franchises and the corporate privileges that often defined them, is distinctly comparable to political aspirations on the continent. Creation of administrative uniformity was certainly an important aspect of the New Poor Law, and was part of tithe reform as well. Efforts to obtain legal equality for minority and unprivileged religious confessions also demonstrate very close parallels. Under the impact of Catholic Emancipation in Great Britain, adherents of improved status for the Jews in central Europe began talking of 'Jewish emancipation', understanding this as a removal of restrictions and discriminations. In doing so, they broke with both the older language of the 'civic improvement' (*bürgerliche Verbesserung*) of the Jews, and its practice of compelling Jews to change their religious practices and occupational structures as a precondition of an improved legal status.[12]

(*cont.*)

in *Lille* (Cambridge, 1991); Michael Kwass, 'A Kingdom of Taxpayers: State Formation, Privilege and Political Culture in Eighteenth-Century France', *Jl Mod. Hist.*, 70 (1998), 295–339; for Joseph II's reforms, cf. H. M. Scott, 'Reform in the Habsburg Monarchy,' in Scott, *Enlightened Absolutism*. The classic account of the Prussian reforms is Reinhart Koselleck, *Preußen zwischen Reform und Revolution*, 3rd edn (Stuttgart, 1981).

[11] For centralization and bureaucratization in Napoleonic Europe, see Broers, *Europe under Napoleon*, 67–70, 80–1; a very helpful comparison between the Napoleonic and the Prussian reforms is Elisabeth Fehrenbach, 'Verfassungs- und sozialpolitische Reformen und Reformprojekte in Deutschland unter dem Einfluss des napoleonischen Frankreichs', *Historische Zeitschrift*, 228 (1979), 288–316.

[12] Reinhard Rürup, *Emanzipation und Antisemitismus* (Göttingen, 1975); for a more critical account of the emancipation of the Jews, see Dagmar Herzog, *Intimacy and Exclusion: Religious Politics in Pre-Revolutionary Baden* (Princeton, 1996).

In this respect as well we can note some differences and distinctions. One of the major features of the era of reform in Great Britain was the movement to end administrative uniformity by repealing the Act of Union between Britain and Ireland. There were, of course, continental parallels. Hungarian nationalists demanded a repeal of the union of Austria and Hungary; Polish nationalists wanted a repeal of the unions created at the Congress of Vienna between the kingdom of Poland and the Tsar's empire, and between the Grand Duchy of Posen and the Prussian kingdom. The nationalist impulse behind these demands, however, whether in Ireland or on the continent, received strikingly little sympathy from English reformers.[13]

Looking at the situation more closely, the interaction between administrative unity and the agrarian question in the Habsburg monarchy of the 1840s was quite different from that of Daniel O'Connell's Ireland. It was the landlords of the Austrian empire, particularly the noble-led and dominated Hungarian and Polish nationalist movements, who strove for disunion, while the serfs, and the Slavic nationalists who tried to mobilize them, were for retaining the existence and administrative unity of the empire.[14] If we think of the pre-1850 United Kingdom and Austria as two multi-national empires, then we find the landlord class of the two realms frequently on opposite sides of the question of national autonomy and administrative unity.[15]

Starting from reform efforts in continental Europe, we can observe only a limited overlap with developments in Great Britain. By turning the comparison around, we can see that a number of central features in the British reform era lacked counterparts on the continent, or, at best, only had them to a very partial extent. There was very little to correspond to the movement for parliamentary reform. The question of reapportionment of representation never arose in continental Europe, because there were very few continuously existing legislative bodies in this period with a representation that needed to be reapportioned. Just creating a parliamentary representation in the first place, or preserving its existence once created, was the issue for early liberal (or 'constitutionalist' as they were generally known) political movements in France, the German states, Italy, Spain, and the Habsburg monarchy after 1815. Also, the pace of socio-economic change, particularly of industrialization and urbanization, was noticeably slower in continental Europe in the decades before 1850,

---

[13] Miles Taylor, *The Decline of British Radicalism, 1847–1860* (Oxford, 1995), 191–201; K. Theodore Hoppen, 'Riding a Tiger: Daniel O'Connell, Reform and Popular Politics in Ireland', in T. C. W. Blanning and Peter Wende (eds.), *Reform in Great Britain and Germany, 1750–1850* (Oxford, 1999), 121–43, at 138.

[14] This connection between the empire, different kinds of nationalism, and the emancipation of the serfs is a major feature of Roman Rosdolsky, *Die Bauernabgeordneten im konstituierenden österreichischen Reichstag, 1848–1849* (Vienna, 1976).

[15] The contrast is not a perfect one, since the German-speaking noble landlords of the Habsburg Crown Lands were generally opponents of nationalist secession and partisans of a unified empire.

so the population shifts underlying the demands for reapportionment were less evident.

Before 1830, changes in the franchise were relatively few and far between in continental Europe and typically associated with violent revolutionary discontinuities, as the history of the franchise in France between 1789 and 1799 suggests. A rare attempt to create a new franchise while preserving legal continuity was the proposal floated at the 1809/10 session of the Swedish Riksdag to transform the body from a corporate legislature, with separate representation for the nobility, the clergy, townspeople, and the peasants, into a bicameral parliament with a property franchise for elections to the lower house. The proposal was narrowly defeated and the Riksdag retained its corporate form until 1866.[16]

Developments during the early 1830s led to a convergence of efforts at suffrage reform in Great Britain and continental Europe. Following the passage of the 1832 Reform Act, calls for reform of the franchise increasingly centred on the demand for universal manhood suffrage. The revolutions of 1830 either instituted or reinforced constitutional regimes in much of western and central Europe, and generated an impetus for their creation in those states of the southern and eastern parts of the continent where they did not exist. In this context, the demand for a democratic franchise was heard ever more frequently, especially after 1840, both in constitutional monarchies with a property franchise – France, the Low Countries, the smaller German states – and in absolutist regimes, such as Austria, Prussia, and (to a lesser extent) in the Italian states. However, in the absolutist regimes, it was difficult to imagine the implementation of a democratic franchise without a revolution, so movements for reform there were more likely to be liberal at least in part, taking as a model the post-1832 British political system that democrats wished to reform. Hence the post-1830 convergence in goals of political reform was only partial.

Besides calls for a democratic franchise, and for the repeal of the Union between Ireland and Great Britain, the abolition of the Corn Laws was an important reform cause in the United Kingdom after 1832. The 'party of movement', the partisans of political change in continental Europe of the 1840s, followed the actions of the Anti-Corn-Law League with considerable interest. During Richard Cobden's triumphal tour of France and Italy in 1847, leaders of the left and centre-left consulted with him about ways to push recalcitrant governments toward reform. At the time, Cobden was surprised by how reluctant the French opposition was to engage in reform campaigns, but this reluctance may have reflected the fact that in France protectionism was often associated with support for political reform.[17]

[16] H. Arnold Barton, *Scandinavia in the Revolutionary Era, 1760–1815* (Minneapolis, 1986), 306.
[17] Simonetta Soldani, 'Approaching Europe in the Name of the Nation: The Italian Revolution, 1846/49', in Dieter Dowe, Heinz-Gerhard Haupt, Dieter Langewiesche, and Jonathan Sperber

(cont. on p. 319)

The one issue on which a post-1830 convergence might be seen at its greatest was the question of social reform. After 1830, and particularly after 1840, there developed in continental Europe a growing interest in 'socialism', the 'social question', and the possibilities of social reform. Discussions centred on the amelioration of the condition of the urban lower classes. They were characterized by a broad variety of solutions, ranging from both Protestant and Catholic plans for religious revival to a restoration of the guilds, to liberal self-help via voluntary associations, to projects for artisans' cooperatives; from legislation imposing restrictions on the labour market to legislation liberating the labour market, and to socialist schemes, often connected with ideas about the emancipation of women. In this respect, they parallel many of the discussions taking place in the British Isles at the same time. However, in a European continent still largely rural, where the majority – usually the substantial majority – of the poor followed agricultural pursuits, the issues debated only involved a relatively small proportion of the population. The debaters do not seem to have noticed this, at least until the revolutions of 1848.[18]

This brief survey of the content of reform movements in the British Isles and in continental Europe thus suggests more differences than similarities. If we think of the abolition of agricultural servitudes or of parliamentary reapportionment we see that crucial reform issues in one region were largely lacking in the other. For issues such as free trade versus protectionism, we sometimes find the adherents of reform on opposite sides of the issue in the British Isles and on the continent. Even where there were overlapping demands, as in the post-1830 calls for democratic suffrage, or nationalist opposition to multi-national empires, these demands were often raised in a quite different political context and intersected with other reform demands in quite different fashion. After 1830, the similarities between British and continental reform movements were greater than they had previously been, but strong differences remained. Similar differences characterized the agents and agencies of reform, to which we now turn.

(*cont.*)

(eds.), *Europe in 1848: Revolution and Reform*, trans. David Higgins (New York, 2001), 59–88, at 65; Willibald Steinmetz, '"Speaking is a Deed for You": Words and Action in the Revolution of 1848', in *ibid.*, 830–68, at 848; H. A. C. Collingham and R. S. Alexander, *The July Monarchy: A Political History of France, 1830–1848* (London, 1988), 352–3, 396.

[18] For just a few indications of this amorphous concern with the social question and the idea of social reform in pre-1848 continental Europe, see Jürgen Reulecke, *Sozialer Frieden durch soziale Reform* (Wuppertal, 1983); Katherine A. Lynch, *Family, Class and Ideology in Early Industrial France: Social Policy and the Working-Class Family, 1825–1848* (Madison, Wis., 1988); Jacques Rancière, *The Nights of Labor: The Workers' Dream in Nineteenth-Century France*, trans. John Drury (Philadelphia, 1989); or the older essay of F. Catalono, 'Socialismo e communismo in Italia dal 1846 al 1849', *Rassegna Storica del Risorgimento*, 38 (1951), 306–16. On the use of the phrase 'social reform' in Great Britain, see Derek Beales, 'The Idea of Reform in British Politics, 1829–1850', in Blanning and Wende, *Reform in Great Britain and Germany*, 170–1.

II

Before 1815, the primary agent of reform in continental Europe was an Enlightened state bureaucracy that attempted to implement the reform projects of Enlightened Absolutism, often against an embittered opposition on the part of the constituted bodies of the society of orders, the corporate legislatures (estates or diets), and the French sovereign courts, the *parlements*.[19] A newly reorganized state bureaucracy made up the cadre of the reform efforts in Napoleonic Europe, facing continued, if considerably weakened, opposition from the constituted bodies of the society of orders.[20] Reform projects among Napoleon's opponents, in Spain, Prussia, or Russia, were also led by a socially similar group of state officials, often with ideas that were not so dissimilar to the ones propounded by their counterparts in states supporting Napoleon. The continuation of reform efforts in the five to seven years after 1815 was generally the work of bureaucrats, although a modest degree of political participation outside the ranks of the bureaucracy gradually became apparent.[21]

Characteristic of all these bureaucratic reform efforts was their top-down and authoritarian character. While Enlightened officials might organize among themselves to increase their influence in the governmental apparatus (as with the celebrated Society of the Illuminati in the 1780s), they were strikingly unwilling to consider mobilizing popular support on behalf of their efforts. If anyone appealed to a popular audience and attempted to mobilize it politically, it was the corporate opponents of reform, as can be seen from the actions of the *parlements* and provincial estates opposing the reform projects of Turgot and Maupeou in the 1760s and 1770s, or the vehement opposition of the Hungarian Diet, along with many of the provincial diets of the Habsburg Crown Lands, to the political and socio-economic projects of Joseph II and his Enlightened officials. In many ways, one might see the origins of the French Revolution (at least until the question of 'doubling the Third' in the estates general changed the political debate) in the appeal to the 'nation' of the constituted bodies of the society of orders against bureaucratic reform projects.

Some of the anti-Napoleonic reformers, such as Stein in Prussia, or the liberals in the Spanish Juntas, did attempt to mobilize masses of the population,

---

[19] Besides the sources cited in nn. 2, 10, cf. Durand Echeverria, *The Maupeou Revolution: A Study in the History of Libertarianism: France, 1770–1774* (Baton Rouge, 1985); William Doyle, *The Parlement of Bordeaux and the End of the Old Regime, 1771–1790* (New York, 1974).

[20] Cf. Broers, *Europe under Napoleon*, 125–41, 198–201. A very good monographic study of the confrontation between Enlightened reforming bureaucracy and representatives of the society of orders in Napoleonic Europe is Elisabeth Fehrenbach, *Traditionale Gesellschaft und revolutionäres Recht: Die Einführung des Code Napoléon in den Rheinbundstaaten* (Göttingen, 1974).

[21] A particularly interesting case study, admittedly of an area that developed a political public sphere at an unusually early date, is Karl-Georg Faber, *Die Rheinlande zwischen Restauration und Revolution* (Wiesbaden, 1966).

primarily for military ends, but also, in part, in order to implement their reforms. However, this popular appeal generally ended up rebounding to the detriment of the reformers, as popular opinion, once mobilized, seemed to be more inclined to seek a return to *ancien régime* institutions (preservation of the guilds in Prussia, or the privileged position of the Catholic church in Spain) than to support initiatives for new socio-economic or political institutions. Stein's successor, Hardenberg, after some unhappy experiments with popular political mobilization, reverted to a more authoritarian, top-down approach to reform. The liberals in the insurgent Spanish government were ultimately defeated by their enemies, the 'serviles', who wished for (and largely got after 1814) a return to the *ancien régime*.[22]

There were British counterparts to the continental Enlightened, reforming bureaucrats. The Philosophic Radicals, and particularly Edwin Chadwick, 'England's "Prussian Minister"', come to mind. The New Poor Law, admittedly one of the more dubious achievements of the age of reform, has often been seen as Chadwick's work, as was the public-health legislation of the 1840s. The latest scholarship, however, has tended to downplay Chadwick's role in particular, and that of a centralized governmental bureaucracy in general, in these reforms.[23] With a little imagination, we could view the unreformed parliament as a constituted body of the society of orders, and thus identify a similar locus of opposition to reform in continental Europe and Great Britain. Recent studies of pre-reform politics have emphasized the extent of popular participation and the appeal to the unenfranchised, albeit not explicitly in defence of the existing order against reform efforts.[24] Yet such similarities once again pale before the very considerable difference in the agents and agencies of reform.

Reform movements in the British Isles were, above all, the products of voluntary associations that mobilized the population through public meetings, and impressed or intimidated the authorities through petitions and demonstrations.[25] This combination of organization and mobilization formed a nexus common

---

[22] Barbara Vogel, *Allgemeine Gewerbefreiheit: Die Reformpolitik des Preußischen Staatskanzlers von Hardenberg (1810–1820)* (Göttingen, 1983); Carr, *Spain*, 92–119.

[23] Cf. the treatment of Chadwick in Anthony Brundage, *England's 'Prussian Minister': Edwin Chadwick and the Politics of Government Growth, 1832–1854* (University Park, Pa., 1988), with that in Peter Mandler, *Aristocratic Government in the Age of Reform: Whigs and Liberals, 1830–1852* (Oxford, 1990), or the clash of opinions in Anthony Brundage, David Eastwood and Peter Mandler, 'Debate: The Making of the Poor Law *Redivivus*', *Past and Present*, no. 127 (May 1990), 183–201. Philip Harling, 'The Power of Persuasion: Central Authority, Local Bureaucracy and the New Poor Law', *Eng. Hist. Rev.*, 108 (1992), 30–54, is an attempt at synthesis.

[24] Frank O'Gorman, *Voters, Patrons and Parties: The Unreformed Electoral System of Hanoverian England, 1734–1832* (Oxford, 1989); James Vernon, *Politics and the People: A Study in English Political Culture, c. 1815–1867* (Cambridge, 1993).

[25] Charles Tilly, *Popular Contention in Great Britain, 1758–1834* (Cambridge, Mass., 1995), analyses the development of this nexus between associations and public meetings as a characteristic feature of the era.

to most reform movements, regardless of the nature of the reforms, the differences in the extent and scope of association membership, the circle of individuals addressed in public meetings or petition campaigns, or the drastic or moderate extent of proposed reforms. It runs through the entire era of reform, from Christopher Wyvill's county associations, through the Society for the Abolition of the Slave Trade to the London Corresponding Society, to the Hampden Clubs, O'Connell's Catholic Association and Repeal Association, and the Political Unions of the 1830s, to the Chartists and the Anti-Corn-Law League.[26]

It is important to realize the extent to which these movements substantially exceeded parallel developments on the European continent. The six-figure crowds present at the Spa Fields meeting in 1817, or at Peterloo two years later, might be compared with the two thousand participants in the Wartburg Festival of the German students in 1817, a cause célèbre of the central European Restoration. The tens of thousands of members in O'Connell's two associations, and the millions of Irish he addressed at his mass meetings, represented an unparalleled accomplishment, as did the millions of signatures the abolitionists or the Chartists gathered for their petitions to parliament.[27]

Here, as well, we can see some tendencies toward convergence after 1830. Except in the Tsar's empire, the centre of the reform impulse in continental Europe following the 1830 revolutions gradually moved away from the top-down planning of Enlightened state officials toward campaigns sponsored by voluntary associations.[28] The thirty thousand participants in the Hambach National Festival of 1832, or the fifty thousand members of Giuseppe Mazzini's 'secret' society Young Italy in the 1830s (both, admittedly, as much revolutionary as reform phenomena) were approaching the order of magnitude of counterpart associations or events in Great Britain. Particularly in the 1840s, a greater density and intensity of reform associations and meetings became apparent: the banquet campaign in France during 1847; the meetings of the gymnastic, sharpshooting, and choral societies in the German states; the Congress of Italian Scientists; the activities of nationalist-minded literary societies in the Habsburg monarchy; and the founding of the Association for the Welfare of the Working Classes in

[26] This contrast in agencies of reform between Great Britain and continental Europe is brought out well by Eckhart Hellmuth, 'Why Does Corruption Matter? Reforms and Reform Movements in Great Britain and Germany in the Second Half of the Eighteenth Century', in Blanning and Wende, *Reform in Great Britain and Germany*, 5–23.

[27] For two excellent recent accounts of O'Connell, see Hoppen, 'Riding a Tiger'; Gary Owens, 'Nationalism without Words: Symbolism and Ritual Behaviour in the Repeal "Monster Meetings" of 1843–5', in J. S. Donnelly, Jr and Kerby A. Miller (eds.), *Irish Popular Culture, 1650–1850* (Dublin, 1998), 242–69.

[28] On the movement from bureaucratically led to popular (and generally anti-bureaucratic) reform movements in the German states, see Koselleck, *Preußen zwischen Reform und Revolution*; Lloyd Lee, *The Politics of Harmony: Civil Service, Liberalism, and Social Reform in Baden, 1800–1850* (Newark, Del., 1980).

Prussia.[29] However, there are three qualifications that might be made about this convergence of agents and agencies of reform.

First, Great Britain and the continent together formed a gradient of organizational density, with the number of organizations, and the extent of both their membership and activity, falling off as one moves from west to east and north to south. This is largely a function of familiar processes of social and economic development, including improvement in communications and transport, urbanization, and expansion of the periodical press. Second, legal differences generally made the process of forming associations and engaging in activity considerably more difficult in continental countries than in the United Kingdom. In continental countries special police permission was generally needed either to form associations, or to form political associations, and to hold meetings, or to hold meetings open to the general public.[30] This led to the uniquely continental phenomenon of crypto-political associations: groups hiding their proposals particularly for political reform behind a façade either of moral, intellectual, or general public improvement. Examples would include the Congress of Italian Scientists, or the gymnastics, choral, and sharpshooting societies. Certainly by the 1830s, but even in relatively authoritarian periods of political repression in Great Britain, 1795–1815 for instance, reforming groups could be openly what they were, and did not have to hide as something else. (Admittedly, this point does not apply to underground revolutionary organizations, but even they seem to have been quite public by the standards of clandestine groups.)

This account of crypto-political groups leads to the third qualification. In the more authoritarian regimes of 1840s Europe, radicals sometimes denounced the whole nexus of voluntary association and public agitation for reform, in view of the strict constraints imposed by government. Mazzini vigorously condemned the adherents of 'slow progress, who believe in the regeneration of Italy via such works as infant asylums, scientific congresses, and railroads'.[31] There is a considerable contrast here to Great Britain after 1830, where even

[29] For examples of these developments, see Cornelia Forster, *Der Preß- und Vaterlandsverein von 1832/33: Sozialstruktur und Organisationsformen der bürgerlichen Bewegung in der Zeit des Hambacher Festes* (Trier, 1982); *L'Italia tra rivoluzione e riforme, 1831–1846* (Atti del LVI Congresso di storia del Risorgimento italiana, Rome, 1994); Dieter Düding, *Organisierter gesellschaftlicher Nationalismus in Deutschland (1808–1847)* (Munich, 1984); Wolfgang Kessler, *Politik, Kultur und Gesellschaft in Kroatien und Slavonien in der ersten Hälfte des 19. Jahrhunderts* (Munich, 1981); Collingham and Alexander, *July Monarchy*, 397–8; Maurice Agulhon, *The Republic in the Village: The People of the Var from the Revolution to the Second Republic*, trans. Janet Lloyd (Cambridge, 1982).

[30] Elena Mannová, 'Das Vereinswesen in Ungarn und die Revolution 1848/49 (am Beispiel von Oberungarn/Slowakei)', in Holger Fischer (ed.), *Die ungarische Revolution von 1848/49: Vergleichende Aspekte der Revolutionen in Ungarn und Deutschland* (Hamburg, 1999), 57–67, brings out both these points very effectively.

[31] Quoted in Franco della Peruta, *Mazzini e i revolutionari italiani: il 'partito d'azione', 1830–1845* (Milan, 1974), 368.

physical-force Chartists continued to support the association/public meeting nexus of reform.

It is really only during the great revolutionary waves of 1789–95 and 1848–9 that we can see in continental Europe the development of a conjunction between voluntary associations, public meetings, and pressure exerted on the government. The classic example is the organization of the 'patriots' in the French Revolution, leading eventually to the formation of the Jacobin Clubs – recognized as a model by the more militant English reformers of the early 1790s.[32] The revolutions of 1848/9 offer the greatest number and most exact kind of parallels between continental reform efforts and those of Great Britain. Mass meetings, such as the great assembly in Blaj of April 1848, when forty thousand participants gathered to hear Romanian nationalist intellectuals proclaim the abolition of serfdom in Transylvania, seem quite comparable to O'Connell's agitation in Ireland. The spread of political clubs by the hundreds and thousands in France, the German and Italian states, portions of the Habsburg empire, and even in more peaceful, peripheral countries such as Norway, testifies both to the example of the Chartists (who were greatly admired by German democrats) and to their imitation. Mass petition campaigns to the parliaments and national assemblies were a characteristic of the mid-nineteenth-century European revolutions. Of course, the creation of this nexus of association, agitation, petition, and demonstration in continental Europe was only possible after liberal governments came to power following the victories of the insurgents on the barricades in February and March 1848. The onset of reaction, particularly following the suppression of the insurgencies of the spring of 1849, would set back this form of political action in most of the continent for at least a decade.[33]

If there were thus considerable differences in the timing, scope, and legal ramifications of the association/meeting/petition reform nexus in Great Britain and continental Europe, two characteristic and significant features of British reform movements, the strong participation of women and the major role played by evangelical Protestantism, were largely lacking on the continent. The role of women in the antislavery and Chartist movements has been well documented. At first playing a supportive or auxiliary role – which might in and of itself involve

---

[32] Actually, before the Jacobin clubs became quasi-official institutions with the Jacobin seizure of power in Paris in 1793, it is unclear whether there were more Jacobins – if one will, radical reformers – in France or in England. Taking Ireland into account, there would certainly have been more in the British Isles. Cf. Michael Kennedy, *The Jacobin Clubs in the French Revolution*, 2 vols. to date (Princeton, 1982–); Albert Goodwin, *The Friends of Liberty: The English Democratic Movement in the Age of the French Revolution* (London, 1979); Nancy J. Curtin, *The United Irishmen: Popular Politics in Ulster and Dublin, 1791–1798* (Oxford, 1994).

[33] A general overview of the 1848 revolution in this sense in Jonathan Sperber, 'Eine alte Revolution in neuer Zeit: 1848/49 in europäischer Perspektive', in Thomas Mergel and Christian Jansen (eds.), *Die Revolutionen von 1848/49: Erfahrung – Verarbeitung – Deutung* (Göttingen, 1998), 14–36; a simpler, English-language account in Jonathan Sperber, *The European Revolutions, 1848–1851* (Cambridge, 1994), esp. ch. 4.

considerable activity, such as fund-raising or publicly soliciting signatures on petitions – they eventually developed separate and independent organizations, ladies' antislavery associations and female Charter associations.[34]

This kind of organized women's reform activity was not to be found in continental Europe. There was no Transylvanian Ladies' Anti-Serfdom Association. Of course, before the 1848 revolution, authoritarian Habsburg bureaucrats would not tolerate any association with overtly political purposes, opposition to serfdom was not a particularly popular cause among the urban middle class (such as it was in Transylvania), and organizations of any sort were few and far between in eastern Europe. However, the underdeveloped nature of civil society and the public sphere in pre-1850 continental Europe was not the only reason for the modest or often non-existent female participation in reform movements.[35] Rather, the few organizational initiatives in which women were involved, whether as sponsors or participants, were generally limited to charitable or religious purposes.[36]

The case for a post-1830 convergence of British and continental reform movements is, in this respect, very modest. Some women did attend the Hambach Festival of 1832, as its organizers specifically called for female participation. The early socialist movement in France – whether the bourgeois and elitist Saint-Simonians, or the much larger and more popular following of Etienne Cabet – enjoyed substantial female participation.[37] Much of the crypto-political opposition movement in central Europe of the 1840s, on the other hand, was centred in all-male choral, sharpshooting, and gymnastics societies. Admittedly, the Unitarian congregations, the 'Friends of Light' and 'German Catholics', an important part of the crypto-political opposition, had a large female following, and women were very active both in the congregations themselves and in the

---

[34] Clare Midgley, *Women Against Slavery: The British Campaigns, 1780–1870* (London, 1992); Jutta Schwarzkopf, *Women in the Chartist Movement* (New York, 1991). Similarly, Simon Morgan, 'Domestic Economy and Political Agitation: Women and the Anti-Corn Law League, 1839–46', in Kathryn Gleadle and Sarah Richardson (eds.), *Women in British Politics, 1760–1860: The Power of the Petticoat* (London, 2000), 115–33.

[35] This very contrasting position of women's public roles, between the better-developed bourgeois civil society in England and the less-developed one in continental Europe, has always seemed to me a powerful argument against the assertion of Leonore Davidoff and Catherine Hall, in their *Family Fortunes: Men and Women of the English Middle Class, 1780–1850* (Chicago and London, 1987), that the development of middle-class society drove women in England out of public life. The otherwise excellent essays in Gleadle and Richardson, *Women in British Politics*, lack this comparative dimension.

[36] See, e.g., Christine Adams, 'Constructing Mothers and Families: The Society for Maternal Charity of Bordeaux 1805–60', *French Hist. Studies*, 22 (1999), 67–86; or the 'Lemberg Women's Benevolent Association' of 1816, mentioned in Gabriella Hauch, 'Women's Spaces in the Men's Revolution of 1848', in Dowe *et al.*, *Europe in 1848*, 647.

[37] Christopher H. Johnson, *Utopian Communism in France: Cabet and the Icarians, 1839–1851* (Ithaca, 1989); Claire G. Moses, 'Saint-Simonian Men/Saint-Simonian Women: The Transformation of Feminist Thought in 1830s' France', *Jl Mod. Hist.*, 54 (1982), 240–67.

organizational networks developing from them. Yet women were always a minority of the congregation membership, while they made up a majority of the
members of the official, established churches.[38]

It is, once again, primarily in the major revolutionary waves of 1789–95 and
1848–9 that we can find women organizing, either to support men's political
activities – by arranging festivals, sewing flags and banners, gathering money
for political prisoners, and the like – or by engaging in independent political initiatives. These might include feminine pursuits such as childcare and shopping,
reformulated in 1848 as education on nationalist lines and support of national
industry, for instance, or independent discussion among women of current political events, or the open advocacy of specifically women's demands, women's
rights, and women's issues. This last and most specifically feminist example
seems to have been a predominantly Parisian concern, both in the earlier and
in the latter period.[39]

A second characteristic feature of the reform movement in Great Britain was
its close ties to various forms of Protestantism, both rationalist and Unitarian dissent on the one hand, and different versions of evangelicalism on the
other.[40] Admittedly, there were distinctly non-Protestant figures in the reform
movement – O'Connell and Benthamite Utilitarians, for instance. By no means
all, perhaps not even most, evangelicals were reformers, and evangelicals were
most influential in certain aspects of reform – movements for abolition of slavery
or for free trade, for instance – but much less prominent among those demanding parliamentary reform. Still, it would be hard to doubt the strong Protestant
tinge of the reform movement and reform culture.[41]

This prominent position of Protestantism has no continental parallel. It is not
that there were no comparable religious movements in continental Europe at the
time. Quite the opposite: Pietism among German and Scandinavian Protestants
bore striking relationships (to say nothing of personal and theological connections) to evangelicalism in Britain. However, Pietism was generally associated
with opposition to reform and strong affirmation of both the political and the
socio-economic status quo.[42]

Pietists were sometimes found on the fringes of social-reform movements,
although their notion of social reform generally involved better organization of

---

[38] Sylvia Palatschek, *Frauen und Dissens: Frauen im Deutschkatholizismus und in den freien
Gemeinden, 1841–1852* (Göttingen, 1990).

[39] For women in 1848–9, see Hauch, 'Women's Spaces'; the latest on women in 1789 and after is
Dominique Godineau, *The Women of Paris and their French Revolution*, trans. Katherine Streip
(Berkeley and Los Angeles, 1998).

[40] Cf., for instance, Harold Perkin, *The Origins of Modern English Society, 1780–1880* (London,
1969), 347–64.

[41] On the politics of evangelicals, see Boyd Hilton, *The Age of Atonement: The Influence of
Evangelicalism on Social and Economic Thought, 1785–1865* (Oxford, 1988).

[42] On Pietism, and its nineteenth-century offshoot, the 'Awakening', see Nicholas Hope, *German
and Scandinavian Protestantism, 1700–1918* (Oxford, 1995), esp. 122–46, 354–419, 457.

charity, and a more systematic effort to bring the Gospel to the poor, thus improving their morality. The classic Pietist reform cause was the founding of the Inner Mission, a joint operation of the Protestant state churches in Germany to engage in just that sort of organized charity, moral improvement, and preaching of the Gospel. Characteristically, it was formed during the revolution of 1848, and its founders saw it as an anti-socialist initiative.

Continental reform initiatives of the 1840s, and particularly the revolutionary movements of 1848/9, did show the influence of a religious rationalism, not entirely dissimilar to some varieties of eighteenth-century English dissent. The German Unitarian congregations mentioned above were one example of this, and a disproportionate number of both pre-1848 reformers and 1848 radicals came from their ranks. In the Catholic countries of Mediterranean Europe, there was a certain tendency for revolutionary and reform movements to combine anticlericalism with religious pathos, celebrating Jesus as the first socialist or the first democrat, and appealing to a better, more deist Christianity against the current practices of the Catholic church. Such movements reached their highpoint in continental Europe at a time when they had been increasingly marginalized by evangelical Protestantism in England.[43]

A comparison of agents and agencies of reform in Britain and continental Europe leads to results similar to those obtained comparing goals of reform. Before 1820/30, the difference between a movement characterized by organization and agitation and the planning of a bureaucratic elite was very strong. If anything, the popular agitation characteristic of reform movements in Great Britain was used primarily by opponents of reform on the European continent. After 1830, there was a certain convergence of means in reform movements as there was in their goals. Continental reformers took up some of the organizational and agitational forms of their British counterparts, at least in so far as authoritarian legal systems and less-developed socio-economic circumstances allowed them to.

It was above all in revolutionary situations, those of 1789–95 and, especially, of 1848–9, that the characteristic British reform nexus, between voluntary association on the one hand, and petitioning, public meetings, and demonstrations on the other, flourished on the continent. Since reform in Great Britain had emerged as the alternative to revolution, this comparison tends to show the considerable differences in projects of political and socio-economic amelioration in the British Isles and in continental Europe. Even when and where comparable reform milieux existed, cultural differences within British and continental ones, particularly pertaining to the role of women and to the place of Protestantism, were pronounced.

---

[43] See, for instance, Edward Berenson, *Populist Religion and Left-Wing Politics in France, 1830–1852* (Princeton, 1984).

III

Comparing possibilities for reform demonstrates a different development from the previous comparisons: not different starting-points followed by a later, partial convergence, but a diverging development from relatively similar beginnings. A common feature of major late eighteenth-century reform movements was the impetus of military defeat, whether suffered by the Habsburg monarchy in the War of the Austrian Succession, France in the Seven Years War, or Great Britain in the American Revolutionary War.[44] Yet the reform projects emerging from these defeats were ultimately failures. Perhaps the defeats were not disastrous enough to create a situation in which adherents of the status quo, the supporters of the constituted bodies of the society of orders (or their British equivalents), could be overcome. It was only with the truly drastic military defeats in the Napoleonic era that the blockade of opponents of reform could be broken, whether by the creation of an entirely new government, as in the Napoleonic satellite states, or by the coming to power of reform adherents in the wake of military disaster, as happened in Prussia. In contrast, reform projects in those states that were militarily victorious, or at least whose defeats were not totally catastrophic – among the Great Powers Britain, Austria, and Russia – proved abortive.[45]

In the more peaceful decades after 1815, we can see a growing divergence between Great Britain and continental Europe. At crucial moments, ruling groups in Great Britain gave up their opposition to reform in large matters, such as Catholic Emancipation, the Great Reform Act, the repeal of the Corn Laws, or the passage of the Factory Acts, and in many smaller ones. While opposition to reform in Great Britain may have brought the country to the brink of revolution, especially in 1832, on the continent existing regimes blithely went over that brink. This is most apparent in the mid- to late 1840s, at the highpoint of the abortive peaceful reform movement. In the United Diet of 1847, Friedrich Wilhelm IV of Prussia refused to make any concessions to the liberals, who were desperate to reach a peaceful accommodation with the crown (rather on the model of 1832) and to avoid a revolutionary discontinuity. Pius IX showed the same attitude toward the liberals in the Consultative Assembly he called. Even in the constitutional July Monarchy, not an absolutist regime like Prussia or the Papal States, Alexis de Tocqueville's celebrated address to the Chamber of Deputies on 15 January 1848, calling for an expansion of the suffrage as the means to prevent an imminent revolution, went unheeded.[46] In view of this

---

[44] Cf. Hellmuth, 'Why Does Corruption Matter?', 11, 21.

[45] Cf. Brendan Simms, 'Reform in Britain and Prussia, 1797–1815: (Confessional) Fiscal-Military State and Military-Agrarian Complex', in Blanning and Wende, *Reform in Great Britain and Germany*, 79–100.

[46] On these points, see Herbert Obenaus, *Anfänge des Parlamentarismus in Preußen* (Düsseldorf, 1984), 649–716; Harry Hearder, *Italy in the Age of the Risorgimento, 1790–1870* (London, 1983), 112–13; Alexander and Collingham, *July Monarchy*, 402.

stubborn resistance to reform, socio-economic or political amelioration would only be possible through disruption of legal and constitutional continuity. At the risk of sounding like a Whig historian, it is difficult to avoid the impression that the political system and the ruling elites of the British monarchy were more flexible and better able to accommodate change than their continental counterparts.

Perhaps this accommodation went along with a different understanding of the meaning of reform. As Joanna Innes has shown in her essay, 'reform' in the sense of a positive amelioration in political conditions came into common usage in Great Britain in the 1780s, and by the end of the 1820s, at the very latest, was understood as a continual and gradualist alternative to revolution. By contrast, 'reform' in eighteenth- and early nineteenth-century continental Europe retained older meanings of religious change or military innovation. The Prussian reform movement was a 'reform' movement only in retrospect. Contemporary advocates of socio-economic and political amelioration used different, albeit not less drastic language to describe their aspirations. Stein and Hardenberg explained their programme as involving 'regeneration' (*Regeneration*), 'reorganization' (*Reorganisation*), or 'a revolution in the good sense' (*eine Revolution im guten Sinn*). Napoleon explained his in terms of 'a wise and liberal administration' (*une administration sage et libérale*), or the implementation of 'liberal ideas' (*idées libérales*).[47]

It was only after the revolution of 1830 that 'reform' acquired the meaning of amelioration without a break in legal or constitutional continuity in continental Europe. This may have reflected the passing of the Reform Act in Great Britain and may also have been a discursive novelty connected with the idea of social reform. The major opposition Parisian daily during the July Monarchy to be concerned with social issues was *La Réforme*, as against the politically oriented opposition newspaper *Le National*.[48] However, as frequently noted in this chapter, such a post-1830 convergence in British and continental trends was far from complete. In German political discourse of the 1830s and 1840s all groups, from the left to the right, from revolutionaries to embittered reactionaries, endorsed the idea of reforms.[49] Finally, alternative conceptualizations of change continued, as in Mazzini's call, cited above (and by no means limited to him) to 'regenerate Italy' (*rigenerare l'Italia*).

[47] Eike Wolgast, 'Reform, Reformation', in Otto Brunner, Werner Conze, and Reinhart Koselleck (eds.), *Geschichtliche Grundbegriffe*, 8 vols. (Stuttgart, 1972–92), v, 313–60; Napoleon, cited here from Helmut Berding, *Napoleonische Herrschafts- und Gesellschaftspolitik im Königreich Westfalen, 1807–1813* (Göttingen, 1973), 116–17. Research into the discourse and concept of 'reform' in continental Europe is not well advanced, so my comments on it are very provisional.

[48] Alexander and Collingham, *July Monarchy*, 181. Cf. also Beales, 'Idea of Reform', 171.

[49] Ernst Wolfgang Becker, *Zeit der Revolution! – Revolution der Zeit? Zeiterfahrungen in Deutschland in der Ära der Revolutionen, 1789–1848/49* (Göttingen, 1999), 147–251. Something similar was probably the case in France as well, since *La Réforme*, edited by Ledru-Rollin, was openly pro-Jacobin; another paper published by an extreme leftist, Raspail, was called *Le Réformateur*: Alexander and Collingham, *July Monarchy*, 171, 181.

IV

One way to conceptualize the different forms of comparison employed in this chapter would be to suggest that Great Britain of the late eighteenth century was substantially different from most of continental Europe in that it was no longer an *ancien régime* society. This difference was central in both the movement for reform in Great Britain and the very concept of reform itself, although we might want to conceive of the early reform movement in the British Isles as the efforts of members of a post-*ancien régime* society to change a political order that still contained many aspects of the *ancien régime*. In contrast, projects of socio-economic and political amelioration in continental Europe, whether gradualist or drastic, from Enlightened Absolutism, through the French Revolution, to the Napoleonic and anti-Napoleonic changes (dubbed, retrospectively, reforms) were primarily about confronting and ending an *ancien régime* society of orders. Great Britain was tied to this socially different world by its participation in the wars and diplomacy of the Great Powers. Military defeat did have the common result of spurring on projects of amelioration, albeit quite different ones in Great Britain and on the continent.

Particularly in the central and eastern regions of continental Europe, the effort to end an *ancien régime* society ran on through the middle decades of the nineteenth century. However, following 1815, and especially after 1830, concepts of reform, movements of reform, and goals of reform similar to those in Great Britain did begin to appear on the continent. These reflected efforts to come to grips with a common post-*ancien régime* world, that might be called 'bourgeois', 'capitalist', 'industrial', or, my personal preference, a 'civil society of property-owners'. Within these common efforts, many features of Great Britain, from the strong participation of women, to the actual ability to effect ameliorations without having to resort to a break in legal and constitutional continuity, remained unique. I would not describe this difference in the linear terms of modernization theory, in the idea that Great Britain was further ahead on some path leading to the future. Rather, it might be more appropriate to say that there were a collection of paths leading to the future (or at least from the *ancien régime* to a civil society of property-owners), and the concept of reform, the movements for reform, and the successes of these movements, were a particular characteristic of the British one.

Index

Past and Present Publications

General Editors: LYNDAL ROPER, *Balliol College, Oxford.*
CHRIS WICKHAM, *University of Birmingham*

The Wild and the Sown: Botany and Agriculture in Western Europe, 1350–1850, Mauro Ambrosoli

Witchcraft Persecutions in Bavaria: Popular Magic, Religious Zealotry and Reason of State in Early Modern Europe, Wolfgang Behringer*

Understanding Popular Violence in the English Revolution: The Colchester Plunderers, John Walter

The Moral World of the Law, edited by Peter Coss

Travel and Ethnology in the Renaissance: South India through European Eyes, 1250–1625, Joan-Pau Rubiés*

Holy Rulers and Blessed Princesses: Dynastic Cults in Medieval Central Europe, Gâbor Klaniczay

Rebellion, Community and Custom in Early Modern Germany, Norbert Schindler

Gender in Early Modern German History, edited by Ulinka Rublack

Fashioning Adultery: Gender, Sex and Civility in England, 1660–1740, David M. Turner

Emperor and Priest: The Imperial Office in Byzantium, Gilbert Dagron

The Origins of the English Gentry, Peter Coss

A Contested Nation: History, Memory and Nationalism in Switzerland, 1761–1891, Oliver Zimmer

Rethinking the Age of Reform: England 1780–1850, edited by Arthur Burns and Joanna Innes

* Also published in paperback
† Co-published with the Maison des Sciences de l'Homme, Paris

Lightning Source UK Ltd.
Milton Keynes UK
08 September 2010

159620UK00001B/175/A